D0287637

THE SHORT OXFORD HISTORY
OF THE MODERN WORLD

General Editor: J. M. ROBERTS

THE SHORT OXFORD HISTORY OF THE MODERN WORLD

General Editor: J. M. ROBERTS

THE OLD
EUROPEAN ORDER

1660-1800

Second Edition

WILLIAM DOYLE

OXFORD UNIVERSITY PRESS
1992

940.25

Oxford University Press, Walton Street, Oxford OX2 6DP
Oxford New York Toronto
Delhi Bombay Calcutta Madras Karachi
Petaling Jaya Singapore Hong Kong Tokyo
Nairobi Dar es Salaam Cape Town
Melbourne Auckland
and associated companies in
Berlin Ibadan

Oxford is a trade mark of Oxford University Press

© *William Doyle, 1978, 1992*

First published 1978
Issued as paperback 1981
Reprinted in paperback 1984, 1986, 1990, 1991
Second Edition 1992

British Library Cataloguing in Publication Data
Doyle, William
The old European order, 1660–1800.—(The
short Oxford history of the modern world).
1. Europe—History—1648–1715
2. Europe—History—18th century
I. Title II. Series
940.2'5 D273 78–40250
ISBN 0–19–820386–1
ISBN 0–19–820387–X (Pbk)

Printed and bound in Great Britain by
Biddles Ltd, Guildford and King's Lynn

Human affairs . . . in which nearly
everything is paradoxical.
                    (IMMANUEL KANT, 1784)

CHRISSIE'S BOOK

GENERAL EDITOR'S PREFACE

One way in which changes in historical taste and outlook are reflected—though sometimes slowly—is in the forbidding demands of examiners and makers of syllabuses. This series is meant to be of practical value to the students and teachers who have to meet them. But such demands themselves are only reflections of deeper and more important changes in historical thinking. And that thinking must be reflected directly, as well as indirectly, in new historical books. *The Short Oxford History of the Modern World* is consciously designed to take account of the most important recent historical work. It seems worth while, therefore, to say what the developments are which have been thought important and how the principles of design of this series are related to them.

One obvious change in recent historical activity has been a geographical widening of the history we study. Parts of the world hitherto neglected, or comparatively neglected, by historians bred in the western tradition of scientific history are now for the first time attracting interest and attention. In part this is a reflection of our humanitarian and political concerns: we are coming to realize that we live in one world, and believe we ought therefore to know more about the parts of it with which we are unfamiliar. In part, too, it reflects changes in what is available as source-material. Whatever the source, the impulse is beginning to make its mark in schools and colleges. They now need books about Latin America, Africa, or Asia on the scale and at the level of those which in the past introduced them to European or English history.

This series will include such books, but also others on more familiar and traditional areas of study. There is, after all, a great need for the achievements of up-to-date scholarship to be given wide currency in English and European history. Consequently, this series is tripartite. It consists of a series of four volumes on modern European history, in which the British Isles are treated as a part of European society as a whole. The second group of four volumes is more specialized, being confined to English history. The third group will be larger and will contain introductory volumes, covering fairly long periods, on those areas and countries which are only now beginning to be studied widely. Some of these are conceived as of continental scope, the projected volume on Latin America, for example. Those on the United States and Russia, on the other hand, limit themselves to a single political entity. In each case, the books in this stream are distinguished by being about a big and important topic for which good introductory manuals are not yet easily available.

The unity which binds these books together, although they will have different levels of detail and scope, is that they all deal with the 'modern world' referred to in the title of the series. This phrase, however, is to be read in a special sense and it is this which makes the series a whole. The subject-matter of *The Short Oxford History of the Modern World* is limited in time, but the chronological limitation is not the same for each book. Conventionally, series of books on the Modern History of different countries line up all their runners at approximately the same starting-gate and get them off together, whether in 1400, 1500, 1600, or any other dramatic, convenient, or merely 'significant' moment. In this series we follow a different scheme. The latest era of world history is here defined thematically, not chronologically. It is the era in which the fundamental institutions of modern European society first take shape and then spread round the world.

Some of these institutions are so widespread that we too readily take them for granted—the national sovereign state, for example. Yet this is even in Europe only a recent innovation and in many parts of the world it did not appear until after 1945. Formally representative political systems (whether real or fictitious) are another of Europe's institutional exports to the world, and there are economic ones, too, such as capitalism, or ideological ones such as Marxist communism or Christianity. In all these instances (and many others could be cited), we have examples of a process by which European gradually became World civilization. Sometimes this has produced new examples of developed 'Western' societies; sometimes it has led to more striking disruptions of tradition and eventually to altogether new institutions and cultural forms. The process, however it ends, defines an era by the break it provides with the past. This era begins at different times in different countries: in roughly 1500 in west European history, in about 1800 in the case of Russia, and at an even later date in the history of China, for example. These are the epochs in the history of different countries and regions in which can be discerned the processes which eventually tie them into the single world in which we live.

Besides moving to different rhythms, it is another consequence of this that not all the books in *The Short Oxford History of the Modern World* will have the same pattern. Differences in presentation are needed to bring out differences of national and regional life. But they will form a coherent series in a methodological sense too. They will have in common a deliberate effort to incorporate recent research and recent thinking which has begun to change the conventional shape of historical writing. This affects both their organization and the proportions of their subject-matter. The core of a good history must be the provision of the essential basic information which is necessary to the exercise of historical imagination and judgement. But ideas about what basic information is needed have lately been changing, for example by a new emphasis on society and its structure at the expense of the traditional political narrative. Historians and their public—which includes even examiners—have begun to think that it may be more revealing to study, say, the growth of cities in nineteenth-century England, and its repercussions, than, say, the party struggle. This is only one example of the recent rapid popularizing of the old idea that history is more than past politics. This series attempts to take account of this. Many of its authors are young scholars who, because of their own research interests, are familiar with what is going on at the frontier of current historical work. They and their colleagues will seek to absorb into their accounts the flood of social, cultural, demographic, and many other sorts of monograph which has poured out since 1945 to confuse and muddle the ordinary historical student and the general reader.

The purpose of general books has, of course, always been to reduce to manageable thinking the detailed scholarship of the specialists. But another recent historical tendency has made it all the more important that this should be done. This is the problem, facing teachers of history at all levels, of the crumbling of boundaries which delimited and landmarks which directed their studies. The conventional separation of English and European history is now often an encumbrance to understanding the many processes in which this country was as much involved as any continental state: industrialization is an example. Another would be our changing views of the importance of certain dates. 1917, for example, or 1941, can be defended as much more significant breaks in the continuity of European history than 1914 or 1939. In some places, old guidelines seem almost to have disappeared altogether.

In part these changes arise because much new evidence is becoming available; in part it is because research has addressed itself to old evidence in a new way; in part it is a matter of changing perspective. More fundamentally, it reflects a basic truism about history: that it is theoretically boundless, a continuing debate, and that historians in each generation re-map and re-divide its subject-matter in accordance with their interests and the demands of society.

This series tries to provide a new map. It is bound to be provisional; that is of the nature of general history. But general history can be scholarly in its standards and imaginative in its presentation. Only by combining both qualities can it provide the authoritative guidance which each generation of readers needs if it is to pick its way through the flood of specialized studies now pouring from what has become one of our major cultural industries.

J. M. R.

PREFACE

Nobody who attempts to write a survey of an immense period of history can expect to emerge unscathed; and if what follows fails to stand on its own merits, no amount of preliminary justification will save it. Nevertheless, one aspect perhaps needs some explanation, and this is the absence of any section on literature and the arts. No account of this period could be truly comprehensive without some treatment of its brilliant aesthetic achievements; but to include an adequate account of them would add enormously to a text that is already too long. Nor could I be sure of my own competence in the various fields I should need to cover. Without this, and without illustrations, any survey of the arts would be only too likely to become a meaningless list of names and titles which would tell the reader very little worth knowing. Rather than overburden him so pointlessly, I have preferred to concentrate on matters I feel happier with. The most I can hope is that some readers will be spurred by what they read here to explore the aesthetic side of the period with other authors whose expertise I could never emulate.

I am enormously indebted to the researches of countless scholars on whom I have relied for information and ideas. I hope that most of them would not be too horrified by the use I have made of their work. I am particularly grateful to John Roberts for offering me the chance to write the book, for his helpful and indulgent editing, and for his patience in waiting for me to finish. Utrick Casebourne, who first began criticizing my work when we were undergraduates together, has kindly read through the whole text and made many valuable suggestions for its improvement.

This is a York book. It has occupied most of my vacations and research terms since I arrived here, it was written in the wonderfully congenial surroundings of the J.B. Morrell library, and most of its ideas were formulated in the stimulating atmosphere of the History Department, where my historical education really began. I have also been writing it as long as I have been married. My wife has typed it, read it, criticized it, cursed it, and sometimes even praised it. This, and so much else, makes it her book too.

York, August 1977   W. D.

PREFACE TO THE SECOND EDITION

So much new material has appeared on this period over the fourteen years since my original text was completed that nothing short of a brand new book could do full justice to all the ways in which our knowledge has progressed and our views have changed. The modest aim of this second edition, however, is merely to rectify what have been shown to be factual errors, to remove ideas that no longer seem tenable, to adjust a number of emphases previously misplaced, and above all to revise the bibliography. The result is that although the broad shape and length remain the same, there are changes or adjustments to half the pages, some of them substantial. I am particularly grateful to Don Bailey and Dan Stone for devoting more time than I had any right to expect to suggesting ways in which a second edition could improve on the first. My other debts are the same as before, and the last ten years have shown how profound they are.

W. D.

Bristol
December 1991

CONTENTS

INTRODUCTORY

In 1660 Europe was emerging from half a century of violent convulsions. It was, many contemporaries thought, a 'time of shaking', an 'age of iron'. Yet until fairly recently historians tended to ignore the Jeremiahs of the seventeenth century. Was this not the 'grand', the 'golden', the 'splendid' century? The solemn magnificence of classical literature, of Baroque architecture and music, spoke for themselves. The heavy pomp of Versailles seemed to epitomize the aspirations of a whole century. Such glories diverted attention from over forty years of savage warfare which had left no part of the continent untouched, and from the bitter rebellions and civil wars which had convulsed every major state at some time during that same period. And the intellectual life of the time was seen as an inexorable progress towards enlightenment, rather than a desperate search for certainty where all former authorities had been called into doubt.

But since the Second World War a more sombre and tragic view of the period has emerged, thanks largely to the statistical researches of economic and social historians. They have been able to show that the mid-seventeenth century was a period when the population growth of the sixteenth was slowed down and in some areas even reversed by famines and epidemics. They have demonstrated that the economy of Europe lost its sixteenth-century buoyancy, that the great price-rise of that century came jerking to an end, and that by 1660 a continent-wide agrarian depression was setting in. These findings, taken together with the wars, rebellions, and intellectual ferment that were already familiar, have changed our view of the mid-seventeenth century, and have convinced most historians that this was an age of crisis.

Beyond that, there is little agreement. The exact nature of the crisis, its chronology, and its general significance are all subjects of continuing dispute. What seems clear, however, is that in 1660 in several fields the worst was over. By the end of that year the whole continent was at peace for the first time within most people's memory. The last of the great rebellions had come to an end with the restoration of Charles II in England. Descartes had produced a method of inquiry which seemed capable of resolving every intellectual doubt. It is true that demographic stagnation and economic torpor would persist until the end of the century, and in many cases beyond; but that actually helped to promote a return to social and political stability. It would be more than a century before Europe was to undergo so general a crisis again.

ECONOMY

1. Fundamentals: Population, Prices, and Agriculture

In basic economic terms, the lives of most people were not much different in 1800 from what they had been 140 years before. The European economy remained overwhelmingly agricultural and the pattern of agriculture in most areas had hardly changed. Agricultural inertia was perhaps the basic economic fact of the period. Yet important changes had taken place, with wide ramifications. Certain areas *had* revolutionized their agriculture. The population of Europe was much larger in 1800 than in 1660. The cost of living had soared. Such changes made the details of people's lives very different from those of their ancestors—even if individuals were scarcely aware of them.

Demographic Recovery

Population is power. Political thinkers agreed that this was self-evident and most believed that, in comparison with ancient times, the world was underpopulated. One of the major problems of politics seemed to be how to stimulate population growth. 'Europe', wrote Montesquieu in 1748, 'is still today in need of laws which favour the propagation of the human race.'[1] This orthodoxy did not go completely unchallenged. Hume, the most perceptive mind of the age, denied in 1752 that the ancient world was more populous than the modern. Several decades of controversy followed, in the course of which emerged the doctrine later to be named after its most lucid expositor, Malthus, that population presses constantly upon the limit of resources. But how well founded was the belief in Europe's depopulation?

In general terms it was groundless. Between 1660 and 1800 the population of Europe almost doubled, rising from around 100 million to 187 million. The greatest increase took place in the second half of the period. The average annual rate of increase between 1650 and 1750 was 2·4 per thousand, whereas between 1750 and 1800 it was 4 per thousand. The late seventeenth century and the early decades of the eighteenth was a period, if not of depopulation, at least of relative stability. But by the time the question became controversial, the population had begun to soar.

The general trend concealed important regional differences. Some areas saw a very modest rise, such as the Dutch republic with its 10 per cent. Even France, with over 42 per cent, was unremarkable for the age, although entirely typical in that most of this growth came after 1740. In any case, with over 21 million inhabitants in 1700, France had a head start on the rest of

---

[1] *Esprit des lois*, Bk. XXIII, ch. XXVI.

Europe. Only Russia came near to the 29·1 millions she had by 1800. But other regions made far faster progress, especially those that had been most stagnant in the seventeenth century. Italy went from 13 millions to 18 millions. Spain from 7·5 millions to 10·5 millions. The British Isles, saw the population of England go from just over 5 millions in 1660 to 8·6 millions in 1801, while Ireland went from 3 millions in 1725 to around 5 millions in 1800. In Germany it took until the 1730s to recover the population levels of before the Thirty Years War, but after that some eastern regions saw increases of 100 per cent or more. The most spectacular advances came in the east, where the Russian population rose by 70 per cent (to around 30 millions), and that of Hungary trebled.

The greatest advances resulted from immigration and colonization. German settlers flooded into Hungary and southern Russia as the Turkish power shrank and frontier regions became more stable. Brandenburg–Prussia was repeopled after the Seven Years War with immigrants from southern Germany. Empty areas attractive to colonists tended to have high birth-rates, since the easy availability of land made early marriage and consequently longer periods of fertility possible. Yet population also soared in areas such as Ireland or Spain, from which many immigrants originated; so clearly other forces were also at work. Most historical demographers believe that the general increase was caused not so much by a rising birth-rate, as a declining death-rate. But what was responsible for this?

Most dramatic was the disappearance of plague. In 1660 it was still one of Europe's greatest scourges: by 1760 it had disappeared from the west and was obviously waning in the east. The great London plague of 1665, in which 100,000 people died, was the last major outbreak in the British Isles. The murderous outbreak in Provence in 1720, when nearly half the 90,000 inhabitants of Marseilles perished, was the last in France. In Spain the last major epidemic ended in 1685, in Austria in 1713, in Italy in 1743. Improvements in quarantine were one reason for the decline; although it is impossible to say how far such organized counter-measures were responsible for the crucial disappearance of the black rat, with its infection-bearing fleas. Plague persisted longest in eastern Europe, where quarantine was less well organized and wars and civil disruption more frequent and far-reaching. In such conditions both rats and human carriers moved about freely. During the great Northern War the epidemic of 1708–13 ravaged the whole theatre and far beyond; Danzig and Copenhagen lost a third or more of their inhabitants and less spectacular effects were felt in south Germany and even Italy. There were heavy losses in Russia during the massive upheavals of the 1770s. Besides, other diseases persisted; there were no appreciable medical or hygienic improvements, except for certain of the very rich, who benefited slowly from such crude preventives as smallpox inoculation. Smallpox, though perhaps in long-term decline, is the disease by which literature remembers the eighteenth century, yet typhoid, dysentery, typhus, and syphilis continued to be endemic and sometimes epidemic.

The growth of population coincided with a decline in the scale and intensity of warfare. The years from 1672 to 1721 saw massive operations and huge armies sweeping across most of Europe, but between 1721 and 1792 the scale, frequency, and length of wars were more restricted and armies in the field were smaller and better disciplined. The eighteenth century consequently saw a decline in the civil disruption, requisitioning, looting, destruction of crops, spread of infections, and other problems which war always entailed.

The fundamental question remained that of the food supply. European agriculture undoubtedly had the spare capacity to sustain a growth in population, as it had done in the sixteenth century; and there was less land under cultivation in the late seventeenth century than a hundred years before. Yet the populace remained perilously at the mercy of harvest failures and famine. The early 1660s were lean years throughout Europe. The 1690s were disastrous, with high rates of mortality everywhere. The famine in Finland, in 1696–7, carrying off as many as a third of the population, was the worst in modern European history. The winter of 1709, when people died in the streets of Paris from cold and hunger, was remembered in France for decades. But this great crisis was the last. Eighteenth-century famines no longer brought massive mortality, either in France or in other parts of western and northern Europe. This development was revolutionary, heralding a new pattern of population growth without periodic severe and devastating crises. The reason for this must have been partly that plague no longer aggravated food crises and partly that the parochial economy of so many areas was breaking down, with more supplies arriving from further afield. The spread of new high-yield staples, such as maize or potatoes, also played a part. The Netherlands, Catalonia, and England benefited from agricultural revolutions which transformed their food-producing capacity. But though most of Europe remained untouched by such developments, the population still rose. This suggests that more basic forces may have been at work, such as a change in the climate. In the late sixteenth century, a shift from a 'continental' type of climate to a more 'maritime' pattern, cooler and damper in spring and summer, was not favourable to cereal production. A slow return of warmer, drier summers as the eighteenth century progressed may have improved the yield of cereals. In addition there is some evidence that better cereals, such as wheat, were spreading at the expense of others, perhaps again as the result of climatic improvement.

The causes of the demographic recovery of the eighteenth century were complex, and remain controversial. What is certain is that it was one of the most momentous developments of the century, whose consequences affected all aspects of life. The demand for food created by a larger population helped to stimulate agricultural improvements and land clearance. In heavily populated areas it also led to land hunger and an increase in vagabondage. Growing markets accelerated the development of trade and the exploitation of colonial supplies. Towns, after a century or more of relative stagnation, began to expand again. Armies, so long constrained in their tactics by shortages of manpower, were able by the 1790s to fight on a new and more aggressive scale. Manufacturers were able to draw on cheap and plentiful labour for large-scale production. The list is endless; and although in none of these cases was population growth the only force at work, its fundamental importance cannot be doubted. The only development of comparable general significance was the rise in prices.

Price Movements

The later seventeenth century may have been dismal and tragic, but for those who survived its wars, famines, and epidemics, it was at least a time of cheap living. The great price-rise, beginning in the sixteenth century, had come to and end by 1660, to be followed by three generations of price stability. Foodstuffs were relatively cheap and stable until the late 1680s. The early 1690s and the late 1700s saw catastrophic harvests combined with warfare and epidemics, which led to a rise in average prices until about 1720. Then followed another twenty or thirty years of cheap food, as war and epidemics receded and harvests, despite occasional general failures like that of 1740, tended to improve. From around 1750 prices for most commodities began to rise again throughout Europe and continued to do so, at an accelerating rate, into the next century.

The movement of prices was closely linked with that of population. The years from 1660 to around 1750, when population was static or moved only sluggishly, saw the general index of prices behaving in a similar way. Relative price stability reflected the limited demands of a static population. Then, from the mid-eighteenth century, as population began to rise, so did prices. In England a population rise of three-fifths over the whole century was accompanied by almost a threefold rise in the price of cereals. In Spain population rose over the century by 43 per cent, but most prices almost doubled. Between the 1730s and the 1780s the French population rose by about 25 per cent, whereas prices went up by 62 per cent. It is striking that the price-rise, once begun, outstripped that of population. It suggests that, although the two were obviously linked, population was not the only factor affecting prices.

The supply of precious metals, for example, may also have played some part. In the early seventeenth century a considerable fall in the supply of silver from Spanish Peru led to a boom in copper. But the rush into copper coins solved few problems; copper merely tended to drive out the silver left in circulation. In Sweden, Europe's main copper producer, the introduction of a copper standard produced a currency of unmanageable size, then led to a disastrous experiment with paper money, and finally reduced the country to a natural economy. In Poland the issue of copper coins between 1659 and 1666 produced a 50 per cent fall in the real value of the *grosz* before the experiment was discontinued. In Russia the depreciation of the currency following a similar innovation ended only after riots of protest rocked Moscow in 1662 and forced its abandonment. In Spain the overissue of copper coins produced wild inflation, which successive recalls, revaluations, and debasements did nothing to check. By 1680 copper accounted for 95 per cent of the specie circulating in Spain. A devaluation of certain coins in 1664 had produced only a temporary respite from inflation, and by 1680 the silver premium on copper coinage had reached 275 per cent. In these desperate circumstances the government devalued copper coinage to one quarter of its 1660 value, with the result that wholesale prices crashed by 45 per cent. Although copper inflation affected all countries, most avoided the extreme fate of Sweden or Spain by limiting new mintings before the situation got out of control. But without this element of inflation prices might well have fallen more than they did over Europe as a whole between 1660 and 1680.

Such was the true influence of metal supply on prices—it restrained or emphasized movement already under way. Few people now believe that Spanish silver was the decisive factor in the price-rise of the sixteenth century, although most agree that it did play some part. Until recently it was believed that price stability after 1660 was connected in some way with a fall in silver shipments in the seventeenth century. We now know, however, that these shipments recovered strikingly after 1660, at the very time when prices had stopped rising.[2] From the 1690s Mexican silver mines began a production which maintained itself steadily throughout the subsequent century. Between then and the 1760s fabulous gold deposits found in the Minas Gerais, in Brazil, swelled the flow, so that by 1703 more gold had been produced there than had been mined throughout the world for two centuries. Yet all this time prices in Europe remained steady. When eventually they did begin to rise, these vastly extended supplies of bullion must have sustained the trend, especially in Spain and Portugal. Price inflation in the later eighteenth century was steeper in the Iberian peninsula than over most other parts of Europe. Much of the gold flowing into Portugal flowed out again through trade with England, where it probably influenced prices and certainly facilitated the establishment of a gold standard. The eighteenth century saw a more general trend towards stabilizing the value of coinage. Portugal also acquired a gold standard, Spain had stabilized her volatile currency by 1725, and in 1726 the French currency was given the value it retained until the Revolution. Spain and Portugal were not able to maintain stability for long, and inflation of the coinage returned in the last three decades of the century; but at least they had enjoyed half a century of unaccustomed monetary calm. Spain's later problems were aggravated by paper money, which failed to retain its value. Wherever such currency was introduced in the later eighteenth century, the effect was the same and the rise in prices was only accelerated. The notorious and catastrophic paper inflations of the American and French revolutions are only the two most extreme examples of what usually resulted when governments succumbed too precipitately to the temptations of a paper currency. Even so, these paper inflations came on top of a price level which was already rising. Increases in bullion supply or other such monetary developments could only sustain the rise. It is unlikely that they caused it.

---

[2] See M. Morineau, 'D'Amsterdam à Séville: de quelle réalité l'histoire des prix est-elle le miroir?', *Annales E.S.C.* (1968).

The most convincing explanation of why prices rose faster than population lies in the state of harvests, which caused the price of cereals to fluctuate wildly from year to year. A few bad years, such as 1693−4, 1708−9, or 1740−1 could push up the average price for several years. So the average level of the 1690s and the 1700s was higher than that of decades either side, and the 1740s saw the beginning of the general rise of the later eighteenth century. In the absence of any long, abnormal run of good harvests, such as those of the 1670s and 1680s, or the 1720s and 1730s, the average price after a rise tended not to fall as low as it had been before. In a time of population growth, alternating short periods of good and bad harvests, such as characterized the later eighteenth century, steadily pushed up the general price level. Grain set the level of most other agricultural commodities; and eventually other prices, though far less temperamental, tended to follow the trend.

Not everybody was directly affected by price movements, because not everybody used money. Most transactions in Europe were probably still conducted by barter, no money passing at all. Nor were such procedures altogether primitive and inconvenient. When currency collapsed, as it did in Sweden in the 1660s, the state survived by collecting taxes and rents in kind. In the 1690s the French economist Vauban recommended Louis XIV to levy a tax in kind of one-tenth, to ease accurate assessment; and between 1725 and 1726 there was a short-lived attempt to introduce a levy in kind of one-fiftieth. After prices began to rise later in the century, the attractions of taxation in kind increased; it seemed an easier way to tax rising agricultural profits than by costly reassessment in the teeth of the taxpayer's hostility. Property owners were not deceived; they knew from experience that if they were owed rents or dues in kind they would reap the full benefit of the rise and only their tenants would suffer. In this way even the millions who continued to live under a largely natural economy were not immune from the indirect effects of price fluctuations. The fate of the peasantry in eastern Europe was also intimately connected with the price that lords could obtain for their produce. Peasants had owed their decline into a new serfdom largely to the sixteenth-century price-rise. The relative scarcity, and therefore costliness, of labour in the later seventeenth century ensured that there would be no return to gentler conditions.

Labour was the one commodity whose price did not follow the general trend. Demographic stagnation in the later seventeenth century ensured that labour was relatively scarce and relatively dear. Real wages were high. But when the population began to grow, so did the supply of labour. Consequently wages failed to keep pace with rising prices and there was a fall in the standard of living of wage-earners. Not everybody was a wage-earner. An important proportion of peasants fell outside this category. But the less secure sections of rural society, those who did not enjoy enough land to assure self-sufficiency or those with none at all, depended at least partially on wages. So did the inhabitants of towns. These groups lived relatively well in the seventeenth and early eighteenth centuries, although short-term rises in food prices following harvest failures could rapidly eliminate the gains of years. Then, from around 1750, a general deterioration set in. Some areas escaped it. The labour-intensive agriculture of Catalonia was never over-supplied, so wages, which in the early eighteenth century had been uncharacteristically low, kept up with prices in the long run. The expanding industries of northern England also needed all the labour they could get, and paid for it. Nevertheless between 1760 and 1795 the cost of living in England as a whole rose by at least 30 per cent, whereas wages rose only by 25 per cent. In rural regions untouched by industrialization and in older, well-populated areas like London the position was less favourable. In France the disparities were far worse: wages rose very slowly over the century, on average about 26 per cent from the 1730s; yet the cost of living rose by 62 per cent. In Spain between 1750 and 1800, with the exception of Catalonia, cereal prices doubled but wages rose only some 20 per cent. Even as far away as the Urals prices rose rapidly from the 1770s, and the government-regulated wages paid to factory workers failed to keep pace.

So the economic position of labour deteriorated in the later eighteenth century. But the preceding age of cheaper living was hardly more favourable to the working population in other ways. Scarcity of labour had induced political authorities to restrict its mobility wherever they could. The English Settlement Law of 1662 tended to keep unemployed labour where it was, and so to keep wages down. In Scotland between 1641 and 1672 coalminers were reduced to serfdom and the 1690s saw abortive attempts to extend this status to other workers. In Sweden the Hiring Act of 1686 restricted the number of workers that commoners might employ, to the benefit of aristocratic employers, and for a time in the eighteenth century peasants were forbidden to keep more than a certain number of children at home. But it was the east-European serf who suffered most, as lords in Russia, Poland, and the Habsburg lands sought to extend forced labour services while at the same time curbing the serf's means of resistance. When population began once more to grow, lords still found reasons for continuing the process, because free labour seemed the cheapest of all and apparently maximized rising agricultural profits. Thus in many places the price-rise had the paradoxical effect of accelerating or intensifying developments which originated in completely opposite conditions.

A Backward Agriculture

Just as price changes might accelerate trends in employment which they did not cause, so higher profits might retard agricultural change as much as promote it. If the old methods were more profitable as demand grew, why change them? And for most of our period, agriculture lacked the stimulus of growing demand to encourage improvement. It is little wonder that in 1800 most of European agriculture was as technologically primitive as it had been, not just in 1660, but for centuries beforehand.

In the far north and east of the continent, in the forests of Finland, Russia, and parts of Poland, many communities lived simply by burning a section of forest, growing crops for several years on ash-enriched soil, and then repeating the process elsewhere when the land was exhausted. In more densely settled areas, agriculture required more regular organization, and found it in the system of open fields which dominated grain-growing areas throughout the continent. Open fields were usually common fields; every family in a community had a stake in them. They were usually cultivated in strips, each strip being assigned to one man. In this way labour was evenly divided and all parts of a field assured of attention. The system was directed to the production of large yields, all strips in the same field growing the same crop at the same time. Yet there were obvious disadvantages. Every cultivator was forced to move at the pace of the slowest and most primitive; individuals could not make innovations or experiments without the concurrence of their neighbours; common rights, such as gleaning after harvest or free-range grazing by cattle, also diminished the autonomy of individual strip cultivators. In addition, lords usually enjoyed certain pre-eminent rights detrimental to agriculture, such as freedom to hunt over common fields, to keep doves or rabbits, and increasingly they tried to consolidate and enclose their demesnes. In the west such enclosures had long existed. In Poland and the Habsburg lands the process of demesne enclosure was one of the characteristic trends of the eighteenth century; while in Russia even in 1800 the demesne of many lords was still made up of strips scattered among those of their serfs so that they themselves had no opportunity for innovation and their land suffered from the same depredations as that of the serfs. The yield of such consensus agriculture depended largely upon the methods favoured by the consensus.

Unfortunately, methods were not progressive. Grain cannot be fruitfully grown on the same land for several consecutive years. It must therefore be rotated. In Mediterranean Europe, and in the cold far north where winter corn could not be sown, a two-field, two-year rotation was generally practised—one year grain, one year fallow. Northern and central Europe mostly followed a three-year system of winter corn, spring corn, and then fallow. A field lying fallow was not all waste. Cattle might be pastured on it and manure it at the same time. But the quality of the pasture was poor, and consequently so were the cattle and their manure. The system of rotation required crops which restored the soil yet sustained cattle more fruitfully than the usual combination of common pasture and fallow. In most of Europe, even by 1800, there was little sign of this.

Livestock was as much the key to the situation as crop-rotation. Its poor quality required improvement. Yet selective breeding, except of horses, was practically unknown and certainly unpractised. Artificial water meadows with their lush grass for fattening cattle, were complex to manage and unsuited to common cultivation. Rare in the west, they were practically non-existent in the east. There was a general shortage of manure. The largest source of animal manure in Europe, the vast flocks of the Mesta, the Spanish wool monopoly, was completely wasted on the flocks' own exclusive sheep-walks. But there was also a shortage of livestock itself, the main source of motive power. Weak and under-developed animals pulled ploughs badly and could manage only small loads, to the detriment of both production and transport. Yet more livestock could be reared only at the expense of crops designed for human consumption. Since there was rarely enough food to sustain many cattle in winter, most had to be killed off each autumn, with consequent loss of meat and manure. Finally, cattle were subject to diseases. Preventive measures were crude; humans died in their thousands and even tens of thousands, but cattle plagues carried off hundreds of thousands of beasts. Governments might order the closure of markets, preventive slaughter, and burying of infected carcasses, but disease spread most rapidly in wartime, when the civil authority of governments was often weakest and great peripatetic herds followed armies around to keep them supplied. Serious epidemics swept the whole of Europe in the war years between 1711 and 1714, and 1744 and 1745.

Structural weaknesses were aggravated by primitive techniques. Grain was still sown broadcast, the most haphazard of methods. Ploughs merely scratched the surface of the soil, hardly turning it over,[3] and three, four, or even more ploughings were normal before land was ready to be sown. In southern and south-eastern areas, ploughs were often drawn by oxen, a slower and less economical means of propulsion than horses (in the 1780s there were still almost twice as many oxen in Europe as horses). The more effective the plough, the heavier it would be and the larger the team required to pull it. The best ploughs required more animals than most peasants could muster, not to mention extra hands beside the ploughman to tend them. Then at harvest time most work was still done by the sickle, rather than the more economical scythe; Peter I of Russia was unable to promote a general changeover to the scythe and as far west as France attempts by large landowners to promote its use encountered the conservative hostility of smaller cultivators.

Poor communications helped to perpetuate all these circumstances. Away from coasts, navigable rivers, and the great highways of exceptional areas such as eighteenth-century France, communications were atrocious. Roads were often little more than muddy and treacherous tracks; even quite short distances made the costs of transport prohibitive to all but the largest conveyors. This put production for distant markets beyond the resources of most small men, encouraging self-sufficiency as the highest ideal, rather than providing incentives to produce a marketable surplus. Small producers tended to sell any surpluses to larger neighbours, often their own lords, who could pay low monopoly prices—an uninviting market. Although these goods swelled a lord's own marketable surplus, he was not always able to reach the most favourable market owing to restrictions laid by governments on grain exports in the interests of avoiding local famines and civil disturbances. Throughout the eighteenth century reforming economists repeatedly denounced restrictions on inter-provincial and international trade in grain, as prejudicial to the general level of productivity. 'The progress of commerce and agriculture', wrote the physiocrat Quesnay in 1757, 'go together; export only ever carries off a superfluity which would not exist without

---

[3] On stony and shallow soils, on the other hand, this was perhaps for the best, a fact dogmatic agronomes sometimes failed to realize.

it.[4] But governmental moves to implement the logic of such ideas were hesitant, even late in the century, and often coincided with famines on a scale to tax the best-regulated system—as in France in 1775 or the late 1780s, or in Spain in the 1790s. Only areas which exported their best grain and existed on staples made from inferior strains—Poland for instance—allowed an unrestricted trade.

Finally agriculture was retarded by social factors—attitudes to profits, systems of inheritance, the distribution of landownership, the form of leases. In most of Europe these conditions, though varied, were more or less prejudicial to improvement. The largest properties were invariably owned by noblemen, and the prejudice among them against working their own lands was almost universal. This resulted in a reluctance to plough agricultural profits back into the land and a preference for spending them in conspicuous consumption. There was thus little money for financing improvements. 'Whenever you stumble on a Grand Seigneur,' wrote Arthur Young, the English agronome, 'even one that was worth millions, you are sure to find his property a desert.'[5] This was an exaggeration; but certainly very little revenue was earmarked for improvement on most great estates.

Smaller landowners too were often plagued by the laws of inheritance. In most countries the law stipulated some sort of division between heirs. It was often possible to favour one heir above others, but seldom to avoid any division at all. Entails to keep estates together were obtainable in Spain, Italy, and much of Germany, but although their legal status grew stronger as time went on, only those who could afford expensive lawyers could draw them up, and they were often used to build up vast neglected *latifundia*. Those who could have benefited most from the stability of property which resulted from entails—smaller or middling proprietors—either could not afford them or were unwilling to disinherit their dependents. Nor did agrarian reformers, who often criticized entails on the grounds that they immobilized the land market, see their potential value to small proprietors. The French revolutionaries abolished them. Reforming Spanish ministers would have liked to. Yet the stability born of primogeniture underlay the advanced agriculture of Catalonia and of England.

Conditions of tenure were important too. 'Give a man the secure possession of a bleak rock, and he will turn it into a garden; give him a nine year lease of a garden, and he will convert it into a desert'—thus Young, exaggerating again,[6] but rightly claiming that modes of tenure had crucial ramifications. In tenurial terms, Europe could be broadly divided into lands where serfdom existed and lands where it did not.

Agricultural Inertia : Serf Europe[7]

Serfdom, like slavery, looked cheap and profitable. A captive labour force

[4] *Encyclopédie*, art. *Grains*.
[5] *Travels in France during the years 1787, 1788, and 1789.* 29 Aug. 1787.
[6] Ibid., 30 July 1787.
[7] See also below, p. 96–102.

worked without pay, and since serfs paid their lord dues as well as working for him, their condition seemed a positive improvement on slavery. The difference between the two was not easy to see, but Adam Smith summed it up succinctly:

In the ancient state of Europe [he wrote in 1776[8]] the occupiers of land were all tenants at will. They were all or almost all slaves; but. . .they were supposed to belong more directly to the land than to their master. They could, therefore, be sold with it, but not separately. . .This species of slavery still subsists in Russia, Poland, Hungary, Bohemia, Moravia, and other parts of Germany.

Serfdom, then, was bondage to the land—although in Russia by Smith's time even this essential link had fallen into decay. But whether peasants were bound to the land or to their master, the difference in economic terms was minimal. From the Elbe to the Urals agriculture was conducted on broadly the same principles, which only accentuated the technological backwardness of this vast area. In reality serf agriculture was neither cheap, nor efficient, nor (by western standards at least) particularly profitable.

The heart of the problem was that the serf had no incentives to increase production, either for himself or his lord. His tenure was often uncertain. In Russia he was liable to be moved wherever his master thought fit, and even when this did not occur, frequent redistributions of holdings for taxation purposes (from which there was no appeal) had similar consequences. In the more settled areas of Hungary, away from the Turkish frontier, lords might force their serfs to exchange their strips for inferior ones of the lord's choice. In eastern parts of Germany a lord might deprive a serf, or prevent land from passing to his heirs, whenever he liked. Such practices meant that many peasants never acquired a sustained interest in any particular piece of land. Nor was it of much consequence to most lords that they should. Throughout eastern Europe during this period there was a constant movement towards the enlargement of estates and their exploitation as single units (*Gutsherrschaft*). In Russia, Poland, Hungary, and Bohemia absentee magnates owned vast stretches of territory, while the obligation of Russian nobles to serve the state (until 1762) made absenteeism in effect official policy. Such lords cared for little but their regular revenues. They had no interest in promoting, encouraging, or even acquiescing in improvements. Men who owned so much saw increasing yields here or there as marginal and took no steps to favour them.

The most important disincentive, however, was the burden of services serfs owed to their lords in return for the plots they held. Services could take the form of dues in cash or in kind, or forced labour. Generally speaking the relative scarcity of labour in the seventeenth century intensified the demand for forced labour. At the same time the stabilization of prices led lords to consolidate and extend their demesnes at the expense of better serf holdings in order to maintain their profits. This too swelled the demand for labour: by 1700 three days of forced labour a week seems to have been usual throughout

---

[8] *Wealth of Nations*, Bk. III, ch. 2. Serfdom had in fact only been abolished in Smith's native Scotland the year before!

eastern Europe and everywhere lords might exact more on special occasions, such as harvest time. On the large estates of central Russia, Poland, or Bohemia, yet more time might be taken up in travelling to and from work. The inevitable result was that the serf's own land received inadequate attention and was often neglected at the most crucial times, when the lord's work took priority but there was the same urgency for everybody. Nor did lords themselves escape the consequences of unrewarded labour. It would be a sin, reported the Russian agrarian reformer Alexander Radischev in the 1780s, for a serf to work the same way for a master as for himself. 'No matter how hard you work for the master, no one will thank you for it.'[9]

Some lords, who saw this clearly enough, attempted to diminish labour services while increasing dues. In Russia the early eighteenth century witnessed a steady expansion of the number of peasants subjected to dues. In the Habsburg lands, lords exacted a regular one-sixth of a peasant's produce, plus a host of incidental and occasional fees and dues. In times of stable prices, the tendency was to commute as many dues as possible into cash payments, with the implication that a peasant must produce for the market to raise the cash. This ought to have been a spur to improvement, but since, thanks to poor communications most peasants were unable to reach the market except through the lord himself, the process was self-defeating. Alternatively peasants took other work in order to earn wages, and neglected their land all the more. Besides, the price-rise of the later eighteenth century diminished the attraction of dues in cash, and in Russia there was a reversion to dues in kind and indeed a revival of forced labour, hitherto in full decline.

To all this must be added the unreliability of the serf labour force. A serf's life, especially in Russia, was harsh, and if it proved too much he might always take the risk of running away. To the Pole or the Hungarian the wild but free frontier regions, though menaced by the Turks, were temptingly close. Southern Hungary was an area of free communities, at least until the later eighteenth century, to which the Habsburg government was prepared to welcome colonists without too much inquiry into their origin. Frederick II of Prussia annoyed his neighbours after 1763 by his vigorous policy of attracting immigrants on favourable terms. The Cossack regions of south-eastern Russia and empty Siberia beyond the Urals also welcomed a steady stream of refugees from bondage. The astonishing numbers of peasants absconding had obvious damaging effects on the stability of the labour force. So did the conscription imposed in Russia by Peter I upon the most ablebodied. Perhaps worst of all, in terms of the disruption they caused, were the constant rebellions that were almost part of the system itself.[10] Huge risings such as that of Stenka Razin or Pugachev, whose driving forces included peasant hatred for landlords, immobilized the economic life of whole provinces. So did the petty local revolts which were almost an everyday

---

[9]   Quoted in R. and E. Forster, *European Society in the Eighteenth Century* (1969), 138.

[10]   See below, pp. 117–25.

occurrence. They were at least as destructive as the visitations of international warfare which periodically devastated these eastern lands.

The result of all these adverse circumstances was a lamentably low level of productivity, and indeed a declining one. The average yield of crops sown in eastern Europe between 1550 and 1700 fell by 17 per cent. In western Europe between 1500 and 1800 grain could be expected in a good year to yield six or sevenfold for every seed sown, and in advanced areas the ratio had reached well over 10:1 by the later eighteenth century. In the east it remained constant at just over 4:1. In Poland it had reached 5:1 in the sixteenth century, but 200 years later it had fallen to between 3 and 4:1. All classes, landlords and serfs alike, lost by this, but inevitably the peasant suffered most. In Hungary where seignorial dues ate up nearly 16 per cent of an average peasant's income, the loss of income during periods of forced labour must have been equivalent to far more. In those parts of Germany in which lords enjoyed the benefits of *Gutsherrschaft*, but where forced labour had been commuted for cash payments, dues took between 30 and 40 per cent of a peasant's income. Such payments came before royal taxes, which also took a substantial share, further depressing any surplus. Thus, on the vast domains of the archbishop of Gniezno, in Poland, production in the eighteenth century was still 6 per cent less than in the sixteenth century on the lord's demesne, but the production of the serfs on their own lands was 37 per cent less. For all the technical backwardness and other drawbacks that hindered agricultural advance, the institution of serfdom itself, with its burdens, was the greatest obstacle of all.

By the mid-eighteenth century this realization was spreading, if only as a by-product of controversies about colonial slavery. 'The experience of all ages and nations', Adam Smith believed, '. . .demonstrates that work done by slaves, though it appears to cost only their maintenance, is in the end the dearest of any. . .The planting of sugar and tobacco can afford the expense of slave cultivation. The raising of corn, it seems, in the present times, cannot.'[11] But such arguments made no impression east of the Elbe, where serf owners could imagine no other form of economic organization and where the only debate turned upon how they could screw most out of the peasants. Where criticism occurred, it was based upon more abstract humanitarian grounds, often invoked by governments when (as they increasingly did) they began to attack or undermine serfdom. Humanitarianism was not their most important reason in practice: what they wanted was a higher tax-yield from the peasantry, unlikely to be obtained so long as lords monopolized their serfs' productive energies. The demands of lords were therefore diminished only to increase those of the state. The idea of improving agriculture by such means was hardly considered.

Agricultural Inertia: Peasant Europe

All serfs were peasants, but not all peasants were serfs. In south and west

[11] *Wealth of Nations*, loc. cit.

Germany, Sweden, France, Spain, and Italy the bulk of the peasantry were free men in that they were not legally bound to someone else's soil. Some islands of bondage did persist—for instance in Franche Comté—but they were dwindling. Yet the absence of legal bondage seldom diminished economic bondage to large proprietors, nor did it mean that services to lords did not exist. The main difference was that in the west lordship did not always imply ownership. Dues, and sometimes labour services, could be exacted by lords who did not own land and from proprietors who did. In Germany this complex of rights was known as *Grundherrschaft*, in France as *directe*.

The organization of land was therefore more complex and diverse in the west than in the east. In Sweden in 1700 the peasants owned about one-third of the land, whereas 150 years earlier they had owned a half. Their small plots had been easy to absorb into the larger units owned by the nobility. By 1700 crown and nobility held about equal amounts, around one-third each. Many (but not all) noble estates tended to be consolidated into large manors producing for the market, but crown lands were usually leased out piecemeal; so over two-thirds of Sweden was cultivated on a small scale, while the rest was worked by landless labourers. Fiscal laws discouraged the division of inheritances, but property was nevertheless supposed to be divided between heirs and tiny units were increasingly common as the eighteenth century progressed—not the most propitious situation for agricultural progress.

In Spain the majority of the rural population was landless, neither owning nor renting property. Yet this majority was concentrated in central and southern districts, areas of noble *latifundia* managed for their absentee owners by profiteering stewards. In northern districts only a quarter of the population had no land to work for themselves, and small peasant properties were common. Renting in small plots was even more usual, with renters out-numbering peasant proprietors by nearly a half. Their leases were invariably long, but with the rise in agricultural prices in the later eighteenth century holders tended to sublet for short periods of a few years and then to renew the sublease at an increased rate. Often several levels of subletting developed, with disastrous results, since any profit from the land was rapidly eaten up in rents and the property itself exhausted for short-term gains.

Perhaps the most glaring example of short-term exploitation was to be found in Sicily, whose inhabitants lived by the export of wheat, most of it grown on large estates in the hands of the nobility. The recession of population of the seventeenth century, with its attendant shortages of labour and stagnation of grain prices, induced landlords to offer long or perpetual leases of small parcels of their estates for fixed rents. In the eighteenth century the recovery of the market and the price-rise made such arrangements less attractive; new leases were no longer offered, and old ones were unilaterally terminated. To replace them lords introduced a short lease of three to six years comprising a whole estate. The lessee was required to pay rent in advance, in return for which he was given a free hand to exploit an estate until the lease fell in. This led to overcropping and exhaustion of the cornfields, neglect of even the most elementary principles of rotation, deafforestation, and slaughter of stock on a grand scale, not to mention the screwing of the maximum out of the unfortunate peasants who actually worked the land, normally under very unfavourable sharecropping contracts.

France was a country of sufficient size and climatic and geographical variety that most types of tenure and cultivation were represented there, from the serfdom of Franche Comté to scattered allodial islands of free tenure, from the sophisticated rotations of Walloon Flanders to the forest-burning dirt-farming of the Mayenne. French trunk roads were the best in Europe by the eighteenth century, but when it came to reaching distant markets this advantage was outweighed by internal tolls and government restrictions designed to promote provincial self-sufficiency. Seignorial rights were still strong. In 1660 perhaps just less than half the land belonged to the peasantry, a third to the nobility, a tenth to the church. The last two categories owned most of the seignorial rights. By 1789 the peasants' share had probably fallen somewhat, to the benefit of bourgeois initially, but the nobility ultimately, since the bourgeois normally used their land as a basis for social climbing. The number of the landless had increased. The largest holdings were always in noble, rather than peasant, hands; they tended to be larger and easier to keep together in the north than in the south. The small plots of peasant proprietors suffered from endless subdivision under all the various laws of inheritance coexisting in France. This alone was enough to prevent much progress. When peasants innovated, it was in desperation, because other crops failed, rather than with the intention of maximizing profits—potatoes for example were introduced only after harvest failures. By contrast few of the larger landowners worked their own domains, even though true *latifundia* were rare. The great absentee magnates of Versailles and even the greater regional nobles acted like their counterparts in Spain or Sicily and leased out whole estates on relatively short contracts. The results were similar, though perhaps not quite so drastic. Some French scholars believe that these short leaseholders were responsible for the only innovations that occurred in French agriculture before the Revolution; even so, most of them exploited their charges for a quick profit with little regard for long-term improvement. Medium-sized holdings, at least south of the Loire and in Brittany, were mostly exploited by sharecropping. Under this system the lessor provided the land, the seed, the stock, and the implements, in return for a proportion of the crop. The lessee took all the risks, with little freedom to experiment and less incentive. As a result, France saw no agricultural revolution in the eighteenth century. Comparison between yields of the early eighteenth century and those of 1840 reveals next to no difference. The only 'revolutionized' agriculture in France, that of the north-east, was already achieving its high yields by 1750.

France, Spain, and Italy produced specialized crops apart from the staples which took up most of the land. Olives formed the most important and lucrative crop of the maritime provinces of the kingdom of Naples. A steady rise in olive-oil exports from Naples over the eighteenth century testifies to its value. It was also important along the Mediterranean coast of Spain, in southern Portugal, and in Provence. Olives had the advantage over grain of a high yield per acre and their yield was not affected by small plots. These circumstances, combined with the importance of oil in Mediterranean food and the eighteenth-century growth in population, led to a rapid expansion of olive groves at the expense of arable which alarmed some economic thinkers. On an altogether larger scale the same was true of wine, which more and more peasants took to growing as a cash crop on odd patches of ground to eke out their livings. In some areas, such as the Bordelais and parts of Catalonia, vines became the dominant crop. In France by the early eighteenth century the government was attempting to prohibit new plantings on the grounds that they diminished arable; and certainly the planting of vines diverted energy and attention from the need for improvements. Vines themselves required no improvement except for progressive refinements of immemorial techniques; they encouraged agrarian conservatism. At the same time they were even more vulnerable than cereals to climatic variations; in 1709 and 1777 the crop of most of France and much of the rest of southern Europe was completely lost. Worse, the 1777 disaster came at a time when the mania for vines had overreached itself into a general overproduction. So the 1770s and 1780s saw wild and spectacular price fluctuations on the wine market, far worse than was by then common in cereals, but affecting the lives of almost as many people in southern Europe.

Finally, peasant Europe was burdened with the weight of seignorial dues. In contrast with eastern European practice, forced labour was rare, and where it existed—as in western parts of Germany—it entailed only a few days a year. In France forced labour for the building of state roads, universal by the 1730s, was more common than that owed to lords. But seignorial monopolies of essential services such as milling and wine-pressing were common everywhere, and so were dues in cash or kind. Quite bewildering in their variety, they ranged from small token payments to proportions of a crop, mutation fees, entry fines, and so on. They could usually be enforced in the lord's own courts. Then everywhere, those with land owed tithes to the church—even in England and Ireland, where the rest of the seignorial apparatus had largely disappeared by 1660. It is true that tithes seldom reached the notional tenth, but they still robbed producers of an important part of their crop. When they were added to other obligations, it seems unlikely that most cultivators escaped with less than a tenth of their product to pay to various authorities, and some must have owed a good deal more. In Germany and eastern France lords took advantage of the chaos and destruction following the Thirty Years War to revise and increase the dues owed to them, a movement of 'seignorial reaction' parallel to the increase of burdens on the serfs at the same time further east. And when prices rose in the eighteenth century the burden of dues in kind increased everywhere, even if those previously commuted into cash payments were eroded in value. Whatever their form, however, it seems indisputable that such payments impeded agricultural progress. They diminished net yields, net profits, incentives to improve, and indeed the capital to permit this. Peasants were the main losers, especially in Spain and southern Italy; but in areas like France and Germany, where the social structure of property was more complex, large landowners often owed dues to others, as well as being owed dues themselves. So a very diverse spectrum of cultivators had their production burdened and inhibited by what lawyers called the 'feudal complex'. On the other hand, many a small noble proprietor, especially in poor areas, survived only through the addition to his revenues represented by dues. There was little reason to improve his own lands when he could supplement his revenues by preying on those of others.

Some contemporaries realized this. In the 1760s the king of Sardinia authorized the buying out of seignorial rights. The French lawyer Boncerf, protected by the minister Turgot, contended in his *Inconveniences of Feudal Rights* (1776) that these rights were more trouble than they were worth to levy, encouraged legal obscurantism, and impeded agricultural progress. But his work was condemned as subversive, and the contention that these rights were not profitable was in many cases plainly wrong. Even the revolutionaries of 1789 only attacked 'feudalism' under the pressure of peasant insurrection. It was ironic therefore that the French Revolution proved the main spur to the attack elsewhere.

Signs of a Breakthrough

Was there a way out of the agricultural impasse? The seventeenth century hardly even saw the problem: agricultural inefficiency seemed part of the natural order of things, to be taken for granted. The business of economic thought was to devise ways of increasing the state's reserves of precious metals, which could be done through manufactures and trade, but not through agriculture. Suggestions for improvement were mostly confined to manuals for the individual cultivator, and even the number of these diminished as prices stabilized in the latter half of the century. It was the manifest failure of aggressive mercantilist policies that directed public attention to the neglect of agriculture they entailed. In the 1680s and 1690s, as the burden of incessant warfare increased the misery of a series of naturally lean years, critics of Louis XIV advocated peaceful encouragement of agriculture as an alternative to ruthless international competition. Yet this 'Christian agrarianism'[12] amounted to little more than a call for a natural economy, and implied no theory of improvement. The contemporary Austrian Becher, on the other hand, retained the protectionism and manufactures of the mercantilist state, while insisting that the peasant and the land he worked must lie at the base of all sound economic order. He and his cameralist colleagues opened the way to the idea that agriculture was after all an elastic source of taxable wealth, and it was on this assumption that successive Habsburg monarchs set about alleviating the seignorial burden on the peasantry. The appeal of the physiocrats to French governments from the late 1750s onwards was similar. In the atmosphere of military failure during the Seven Years War, physiocrats pointed

[12] Term of L. Rothkrug, *Opposition to Louis XIV* (1965), 234 ff. See too below, p. 67.

out that the extra money that Louis XV needed for success could only come from an increase in his subjects' taxable wealth. Trade and manufactures, they believed, could not provide this increase. Since land was the source of all expandable wealth, agriculture should be encouraged by freeing the market of all restrictions in the form of tolls, privileges, and export controls. By the end of the century such *laissez-faire* policies—the term was a physiocratic one—had become the orthodox prescription of advanced economists in most countries. This did not mean that governments were always heedful. The French government promoted clearings, gave timid encouragement to enclosure, endlessly considered abolition of internal customs barriers, and nervously by turns freed, restricted, and then freed again the export of grain. The Spanish government encouraged colonization and made noises threatening common fields and *latifundia*. But the results in both cases amounted to very little. Policies were too often assumed to result from the preachings of theorists, when all they had done was to win their praise.

In practical terms, agronomes had more influence than political philosophers, but even that was relatively slight. Few important new works on practical agriculture appeared between 1650 and 1750, although many older ones were reprinted. Most of the new works were on limited technical aspects of such pursuits as market gardening. Large, general theories, such as the seed-drilling advocated in Jethro Tull's *Horse Hoeing Husbandry* (1733) took many decades to be generally implemented even in advanced England. Elsewhere, enthusiasts like Duhamel de Monceau in France, advocating the introduction of English methods, were lonely voices, although their numbers grew over the later eighteenth century. Most cultivators remained uninterested in theory and hostile to innovation. Historians have attributed too much in this to the influence of the written word. What signs there were of a breakthrough in the old agricultural pattern came from practical necessities rather than the heads of propagandists, however loud and insistent.

Even if the theorists had won a more appreciative audience, it is unlikely that the fullest implementation of their views would have produced spectacular advance, since they put forward only a few of the many varied requirements for an all-round breakthrough. There was no single panacea. Enclosure, or scientific rotation, or new crops, or seed-drilling, would take improvement so far, but their impact would be limited without other factors such as growing demand, changes in land tenure, redeployment of labour, improved communications, and so on. Agricultural advance was a complex process in which several interdependent trends needed to operate together. Areas in which only some changes occurred did not go the whole way because not enough other favourable conditions were present. Good communications with an accessible export market, for example, had brought about increased cereal yields in the hinterland of Danzig. This had been achieved by the abandonment of serfdom itself and cultivation by a workforce of landless labourers. But the rest of Poland could not benefit from such immediate stimuli. The introduction of maize produced dramatically increased yields of consumable food (up to 40:1) in certain areas such as northern Italy or south-west France, where it became established in the 1690s as an alternative to more traditional cereals whose yields were so low in that decade. By the mid-eighteenth century maize was the staple diet in Venetia. Yet in the absence of more manure, which it required in huge quantities, maize exhausted the soil in the same way as other grains, and fallow was not eliminated. Another potential revolution was the spread of potatoes, notably in Germany and Ireland. It, too, was accelerated by harvest failures, like that of 1740 in Ireland, or that of 1770 in Germany. By 1800 potatoes rather than cereals were the staple diet in many parts of Germany and nearly all of Ireland. Like maize, the potato yields large crops per acre and can sustain a much higher population because its nutritional value is also higher. It helped to promote early marriage by facilitating existence on smaller plots more cheaply and speedily acquired. A revolutionary crop, then; yet it too exhausted the soil in time without plentiful manure; its cultivation positively encouraged subdivision of holdings by making subsistence on small plots realistic. Its bulk and tendency to rot did not make it easily transportable to distant markets. In the long run therefore potatoes reinforced subsistence agriculture among the peasantry and induced a dependence whose dangers were tragically shown in the great Irish famine of 1845. Only when other changes had also occurred did potatoes contribute to a balanced advance.

A true revolution in agriculture depended upon simultaneous progress on a wide range of fronts. By the eighteenth century this had only occurred in three major areas—the Netherlands, Catalonia, and England. In the Netherlands, most of the work had been done well before 1660. The area was small and well served by a network of canals, so communications were excellent. Capital from commercially rich cities financed constant improvements. In addition the western and southern provinces, where progress was most dramatic, were areas of small, independent tenures; landlords had limited power and owners worked for themselves. The United Provinces were fortunate in avoiding the scourge of foreign invaders to disrupt agriculture. Louis XIV's invasion of 1672 was the only major incursion of this type until the 1780s, and the flooding of the polders which immobilized him did far less harm to agriculture than most other forms of warfare. These were important prerequisites. Yet basically the advance in the Netherlands resulted from a very special set of circumstances—high food demand from the most densely populated cities of Europe, combined with ease of access to the abundant granary of the Baltic, so that local agriculture was not overwhelmed with the demand for cereals. The inhabitants could therefore concentrate on market gardening, intensive cattle-rearing, and the production of industrial raw materials like flax, hemp, and dyestuffs rather than staples. Dutch and Flemish agriculture·was remarkably specialized even in the sixteenth century and the techniques it evolved were those ultimately to revolutionize agriculture elsewhere. Here such techniques as deep ploughing, row planting, and regular weeding first appeared. These in their turn placed heavy demands on labour which only an abundant population could supply. At the same time small plots, being more easily worked at such an intense level, proved no disadvantage. The intensive manuring which such cultures required made cattle-rearing profitable, while the low-lying, often alluvial soil of the area made excellent water meadows to provide cattle with high-quality fodder. The sixteenth century saw widespread reclamation from the sea, in the course of which sophisticated drainage techniques were evolved. This new land, being rich but unsuitable for arable, was mostly employed in dairying and cattle-rearing. By these means, and by the use of night soil from the cities, the 'manure barrier' to advance was broken down. At the same time fallow was eliminated on most of the remaining arable, by systems of rotation employing crops first grown as commercial propositions (e.g. flax, madder, or woad) or as cattle feed (e.g. clover, coleseed, or turnips). These crops had the advantage of resting or reconstituting soil tired by cereal cultivation, and therefore could be rotated with cereals. In Flanders long rotations with infrequent fallows were known as early as the fourteenth century. By the seventeenth century in most parts of the Netherlands fallow had disappeared, fodder crops being grown either on land that would be fallow elsewhere, or immediately following the harvest on lands growing cereals. In Flanders too, convertible husbandry, in which there was no permanent pasture and no permanent arable, the two alternating at intervals of between three and six years, had been practised since the later middle ages, resulting in better pasture and more abundant crops. In all these ways high yields were obtained from lands that were not naturally rich. The recession in agricultural prices after the mid-seventeenth century gave Netherlands agriculture the final push in the direction of specialization, since horticultural cash crops maintained their prices better than cereals. Cereal cultivation expanded once more in the later eighteenth century, when it had the full benefit of well-tried improvements. Indeed, such was the satisfaction of Dutch cultivators with progress, that they resisted the refinements and further improvements by then coming out of England. The average yield of crops in the later eighteenth century had already been attained in good years by the later sixteenth. Yet at between 15 and 20:1 for wheat, even better for barley, and not much worse for oats and other crops, these results left those of most other areas far behind.

The breakthrough in Catalonia was essentially the work of the eighteenth century, deriving its initial stimulus from the need to reconstruct a countryside more devastated than the rest of Spain by the Succession war. As in the Netherlands, much depended on the proximity of a large local urban market—in this case Barcelona. And to an even greater extent progress resulted from irrigation.

To a person, from the north of Europe, [marvelled Young[13]] there can hardly be a more striking spectacle than the effect of watering in these southern climates; it converts an arid stony waste, which would yield nothing but vines and olives, and on which every sort of grain would hardly return the seed, at once into fields, pregnant with the richest harvest; on such soils, it gives almost the whole value of the land; and on the richest, it raises it,

---

[13] *Travels during the Years 1787, 1788, and 1789* (1794), II. 327.

at the least, double; and, in some instances, five times. It enables the cultivator to have a succession of crops, more important than anything we know
in the north.

Fallow, eliminated in the irrigated lowlands, soon disappeared on higher,
drier, land, where forage crops increasingly alternated with cereals to support
more manure-producing animals. Around Barcelona and other smaller towns
the immediate area, as in the Netherlands, was given over to market gardens.
Much of their grain came from abroad and the city merchants positively
obstructed plans to irrigate inland grain lands and so increase cheaper local
supplies. Owing to the abundance of the valleys, the hillsides above them
could be devoted entirely to uninterrupted stretches of olives and vines, and
Catalonia became the main supplier of European wine and brandy to Spanish
America. All this progress was facilitated by Catalonia being a land of compact, enclosed holdings around family farmsteads which passed from generation
to generation by a system close to primogeniture. In contrast, by 1800 the
productivity of agriculture around Valencia, comparable in its technical level,
was being impaired by excessive fragmentation due to a divisive law of
inheritance. Catalan tenures were indeed subject to lordship, but it was distant in authority and power, and its financial burden was light. Finally, a
population growing more rapidly than in many other parts of Europe played
an important role. Landless labourers in search of easy money took leases
to plant vines on waste land above the valleys and so provided the driving
force of vineyard expansion. Abundant labour was also required to
work the complexities of irrigation and elaborate and intensive courses of
rotation. To do so profitably it had to be cheap, and the wages of Catalan
agricultural workers hardly rose at all in the first seventy years of the eighteenth century, although they more than doubled in the last thirty. Their
wages thus lagged far behind prices and profits of cultivation for much of
the century—increasing their misery, but bringing sizeable profits for their
employers to reinvest. When, after 1770, this advantage disappeared, the
essential progress had already been made.

Most significant for the future, in the sense that it laid the basis for the
first industrial revolution, was the breakthrough in England. It began in the
late sixteenth and early seventeenth centuries when tenants, faced with rents
rising more rapidly than profits, sought to increase their marketable yields
through new crops and new techniques. The proximity of a major city,
London, once more proved of crucial importance in stimulating intensive
production in the south and east, and its steady growth throughout the seventeenth and eighteenth centuries was simultaneously a tribute to the efficacy of
these innovations and a constant spur to further progress. England was small
and water communication, even before the canal and road improvements
of the eighteenth century, was relatively good.

A basic element in increased production was simply the extension of the
cultivated area, which was going on long before 1660 and was mostly complete
by 1720. But more scientific cultivation of all land, new or old, was the
revolutionary feature. By 1660 much of England, like Flanders, was culti-

vated by convertible or 'up and down' husbandry, with pasture and arable alternating at intervals of between five and twenty years. By 1750 it was universal, resulting in better grass for livestock feeding when land was in pasture; whilst on arable, cereal yields were often tripled. The late sixteenth and early seventeenth centuries also saw the introduction of artificial water meadows—which again improved the fodder and therefore the manure of livestock—and the same industrial and winter-feed crops that had already eliminated fallow and allowed cattle to be kept alive over the winter in the Netherlands—woad, flax, coleseed, sainfoin, lucerne, clover, and turnips. Marl, lime, seaweed, and other artificial manures such as the Dutch used were also employed. In the early seventeenth century many agricultural writers visited the Netherlands and returned full of enthusiasm for the introduction in England of what they had seen; but parallel developments were often well established independently, so the true extent of their influence is difficult to gauge. By 1660 however, it is clear that English agriculture was already partly revolutionized, with crop yields, though not so high as in the Netherlands, better than those of most of Europe.

Subsequent developments emphasized these trends. In 1660 the abolition of the crown's feudal revenues freed landlords from the financial burden of a lucrative racket. Tithes were progressively commuted into fixed cash payments and the law became increasingly hostile to prescriptive tenures by peasants, a trend which facilitated enclosure. An important minority of English land had already been enclosed by 1660, but early-seventeenth-century governments had sporadically opposed further enclosure. Now they disclaimed all interest; landlords were free to promote it by all means, including the ultimate instrument of sovereign power, the act of parliament, essentially the work of an assembly of large landowners. Enclosed land was more easily rotated, worked, and experimented with; selective breeding of cattle was facilitated, even though we should not underestimate the degree of innovation which the English open fields had hitherto witnessed. So from 1660 the flow of enclosures, either by stature or private agreement, increased, reaching its peak between 1760 and 1780 and again during the French wars of the end of the century. By 1800 most cultivated land in England was enclosed and in 1802 came the first general Inclosure Act. Enclosure was costly, easier for the large owner than the small, and it further encouraged the concentration of larger estates in fewer hands which the low profits of agriculture up to the 1750s had produced. Primogeniture, reinforced by the rigid entail known as the strict settlement, maintained estates in the same hands for generations and so facilitated sustained, long-term improvements in large-scale cultivation. So did leases, which, though often not long, were regularly renewed in the same hands. In the eighteenth century England became a land of large proprietors, tenant farmers, and landless labourers—the latter a depressed but relatively flexible labour force.

In these circumstances the famous 'Norfolk' system of crop rotation was evolved—alternation of wheat and barley with clover and turnips. It was on enclosed land that English breeders such as Bakewell and Coke improved and fattened their stock. But even before the height of enclosing, agricultural productivity as a whole had soared. From 1673 there was a bounty on exported grain and the disruption of the Baltic lands by war enabled English exporters to capture an important slice of the Dutch cereal market. Meanwhile Englishmen ate growing quantities of meat and only the best white bread, grown from seed which by 1800 yielded ten or twelve-fold on average. All this reflected a formidable growth in agricultural productivity of between 10 and 15 per cent between 1650 and 1750. By the late 1760s, as population growth accelerated, England had ceased to export grain, but not until the later nineteenth century was she forced to import most of her needs. Much of this progress had been achieved by specialization. It was still an agriculturally diverse country and not all areas were suitable for great improvements. Accordingly some, like the south and south-east, prospered exceedingly, while less fertile northern areas may actually have declined. Yet in some ways it was crucial for future economic development that both should occur. For advanced intensive agriculture was already essential to sustain London and the swollen industrial cities of the near future; and northern industry derived much of its stimulus from the inhabitants of depressed agricultural areas seeking to make a living by other means elsewhere.

2. Motors of Progress:
Towns, Money, and Manufactures

All economic progress depends in the last analysis on a breakthrough in agriculture. Not until agriculture is able to feed and sustain large towns can economic life diversify, specialize, and bring forth productive innovations. Not until towns are substantial does capital tend to accumulate fast enough to finance these expensive but ultimately beneficial changes. Not until population is concentrated in large towns is a work-force not tied to agriculture available in sufficient numbers to diversify production. Without an agricultural revolution, in fact, there could have been no industrial revolution.

This is not to say that agricultural improvements always led to an industrial breakthrough. In the Netherlands, where the age-old cycle of subsistence farming was first broken, and where urbanization advanced most rapidly, little further economic progress was made after 1700. Whether the Dutch economy merely stood still or positively declined is still the subject of much debate, but it is indisputable that in the eighteenth century other states overhauled the Dutch republic and soon pulled far ahead. An agricultural revolution, then, is an essential enabling factor in economic progress. But many other obstacles also need to be removed if economic life is to be revolutionized on other fronts and is to expand in new ways at unprecedented rates. The removal of these obstacles in certain favoured areas was perhaps the most momentous development of the eighteenth century.

Urban Stagnation and Recovery

For most towns, as for the countryside, the years between the mid-seventeenth and mid-eighteenth centuries were relatively stagnant. Only the last half-century witnessed anything like a general recovery of growth. With the exception of the Netherlands, only a small proportion of the population lived in towns at any time. In general, the proportion grew smaller towards the east, as did the average size and geographical density of towns. The urban population was greatest in the west of the continent, where towns were thickest on the ground. The Netherlands, Italy, France, and Western Germany were rich in well-established urban life, even if most of their towns were small by modern standards. East of the Elbe, settlements deserving the name were far fewer, often separated from each other by hundreds of miles of trackless forest, the great majority of town-dwellers were concentrated in capitals (or former capitals)—Moscow, St. Petersburg, Warsaw, or Budapest.

Although capitals were important everywhere, in small territories their predominance was overwhelming. In 1650 Amsterdam accounted for 8 per cent of Dutch population; in 1700 Naples housed around 5 per cent of the population of the Two Sicilies; and by 1750 London had no less than 11 per cent of that of England. In such states no province was far enough from the metropolis to sustain major rivals. Paris, on the other hand, Europe's largest city in 1660 with the exception of Constantinople, and still second largest in 1800, never accounted for more than $2\frac{1}{2}$ per cent of the inhabitants of France (or 10 per cent of its urban population). Madrid and Vienna accommodated comparably small proportions. Moreover, unlike most other towns, capitals grew steadily in population throughout this period. London progressed from 400,000 in 1650 to 900,000 in 1800, Paris from about 450,000 to around 650,000 in 1790. Further east, Berlin grew from 8,000 in 1648 to 150,000 in 1790, almost rivalling by then the 220,000 of Vienna. Warsaw, numbering around 30,000 in 1750, had reached almost 120,000 by 1794. St. Petersburg, which did not even exist in 1700, had a population of 218,000 by 1789.

The reasons for the growth of capitals were complex. London, Amsterdam, Copenhagen, Lisbon, and Naples were ports which would have been important in any case; Paris, Madrid, Vienna, and Berlin had little intrinsic commercial importance. Capitals chiefly prospered because they *were* capitals—centres of political, legal, and social life in an age when all these spheres were growing more centralized. As the pretensions and preoccupations of governments expanded, so did the numbers of government servants, especially at the centre. In states building up their prestige through war, such as Prussia or Russia, huge military establishments swelled the population of their capitals; in 1789 for example over 55,000 (or one quarter) of the population of St. Petersburg were military personnel or their families. Where justice was centralized, as in London or Naples, the population was swelled by the teeming personnel of numerous courts of law and a steady procession of litigants; a French traveller reported (perhaps somewhat over-credulously) in the 1780s that the legal population of Naples was as much as 30,000. Similarly, those states governed wholly or partly by estates or parliaments saw their capitals receive 'great influxes of wealth and employment whenever these bodies met. The fury of Dubliners at the abolition of the Irish parliament in 1800 sprang from the prospect of losing this regular stimulus. Besides, all capitals were also social centres, where the rich and fashionable came to be near the sources of power and to meet each other. They brought with them huge numbers of servants and expensive habits of conspicuous consumption which sustained a whole range of industries such as building, the manufacture of luxury goods, and the provision of services. In this way capitals were self-sustaining. When they were also great international ports, the growth was doubly spectacular.

How far these developments were of general benefit was debatable. In one sense capitals were enormous parasites. Unless they were also ports, their wealth was derived almost totally from the country, only a small proportion of it returning in the form of payment for foodstuffs, raw materials, and manufactures. French physiocrats despaired at such a pattern, for the key to their programme was to promote reinvestment in agriculture. Paris, for them, was a 'bottomless pit' in which absentee landlords squandered their revenues. 'In those towns', Adam Smith noted, 'which are principally supported by the constant or occasional residence of a court, and in which the inferior ranks of people are chiefly maintained by the spending of revenue, they are in general idle, dissolute, and poor; as at Rome, Versailles, Compiègne and Fontainebleau.'[1] Such great centres of 'luxury' seemed to hinder rather than to promote the expansion or wider circulation of wealth. Yet perhaps these condemnations were somewhat one-sided. Large conurbations had economic tentacles stretching often hundreds of miles into the countryside and could serve as a stimulus to agricultural innovations. Arguably the scale of their demand for other basic commodities such as clothing or fuel stimulated the development of new techniques which were to revolutionize economic life. Without London the Durham coalfield would have gone unexploited and Manchester might have found a less buoyant market for its cheap, mass-produced cottons.

Some provincial cities shared the characteristics of the capitals; especially in territorially large states, where neither government nor society could be too tightly centralized. The seats of French provincial *parlements*, for instance, were major legal and administrative centres. Many French towns petitioned for the establishment of such higher courts during judicial reforms in 1771 or 1788; they knew that litigation is only undertaken by the rich, who spend money while they are about it. Similarly, the meeting places of estates, in those provinces that had them, enjoyed booms whenever they met. But the vast majority of provincial towns could not depend on such stimuli. Those that were not ports derived most of their importance—not strictly localized—from their function as market towns. The fair at Beaucaire, in southern France, for example, was a market of international reputation. Inevitably such places were few, and the influence of most market towns, unlike that of provincial capitals, was confined to their immediate localities. There, indeed, it could be important enough. Town dwellers tended almost everywhere to own the best and largest units of rural property in their districts, which they often improved with capital accumulated in an urban context. Many peasant proprietors, not to mention nobles, were in debt to urban creditors in their local market towns. But none of this promoted widespread economic change in the way that the growth of capitals did.

Few provincial towns experienced sustained growth throughout this period. If their population did grow, it was largely to recover old levels after decimation by plague or warfare in the mid-seventeenth century, notably in the case of the cities of Germany, badly damaged by the Thirty Years War, or of Italy, ravaged by plagues. Nor did major French cities such as Rouen or Toulouse, or Spanish cities such as Barcelona, Valencia, or Seville make much progress, reflecting the over-all deceleration in population growth before 1730, uncompensated by any of the advantages enjoyed by national capitals. As centres of pestilence where deaths constantly exceeded births, cities required constant new injections of rural immigrants to sustain their populations, let alone to grow. But after 1660 the attraction of provincial towns was limited. Country life was relatively cheaper than it had been and certainly healthier than in the

[1] *Wealth of Nations* Bk. II, ch. 3.

towns, as the exodus of townsmen at the onset of plague showed. Nor were provincial towns able to offer expanding opportunities for employment. The evolution and spread of the 'domestic' system in textile manufacture brought new employment to the countryside but benefited only those few townsmen who organized and managed the system. Besides, the organization of economic life in towns was constrained in the strait-jacket of guild organization.

Most trades in well-established towns were organized into monopolistic guilds, which existed in theory to protect their members and maintain high standards of production. In the United Provinces and England the importance of trade and therefore of large merchants in the economy had undermined their position, but elsewhere the middleman was less important. Accordingly, far from declining, guilds were actually spreading in the mid-seventeenth century and continued to do so up to about 1750 in France, Spain, Sweden, the Austrian Netherlands, and throughout Germany. Shrinking markets suggested that success would come from improving standards—a dubious proposition, but superficially logical; a stagnant labour market also fostered institutions that controlled and rationed the work-force more closely. Governments were sympathetic, well aware that such organizations were convenient to tax. So Colbert reinforced old laws in 1673 by decreeing that all French trades should be organized into guilds. Similarly the Spanish government in 1679 established a Board of Trade and Currency to supervise guilds and their taxation, and encouraged the expansion of the Five Greater Guilds of Madrid, an association of merchants which by the early eighteenth century controlled most of the economic life of the city. But when the economic pace began to quicken once more, in the later eighteenth century, the grip of the guilds no longer seemed so beneficial. They now appeared restrictive, hostile to change, impeding commerce with endless demarcation disputes, and burdening their members with debts. For the physiocrats they were artificial restrictions on the free play of commerce. For a brief moment in 1776 Turgot managed to abolish them in France, but it took the revolutionaries in 1789 to destroy them totally and finally. In the southern Netherlands, where guilds were even more strongly entrenched, the government of Maria Theresa refused to allow them to acquire new privileges, preparing the ground for Joseph II to decree their virtual abolition in 1787, after several years of attrition. But these reforms were forgotten in the uprising which followed. It took a twenty-year campaign among Spanish economists to bring about some loosening of the monopoly of Spanish guilds over various occupations in the 1790s. As usual, the reformers probably blackened the picture. The guild of Lyons silk-weavers, for instance, comprised one quarter of the city's work-force, and its co-ordinating role was a major factor in the boom which silk weaving underwent in Lyons between the 1730s and 1770s. Similarly, the Five Greater Guilds of Madrid channelled much of governmental paternalism which was important in stimulating Spanish eighteenth-century economic progress, buying up and reinvigorating enterprises throughout the country and in the colonial empire. Even so, it is scarcely open to doubt that the guild system, strengthened in the seventeenth century, did little to promote the economic recovery of the eighteenth, and that those towns in which guilds remained strong were not usually those that led the urban revival.

For the resumption of urban growth, when it came, was not universal. Inland towns and older centres of economic activity, such as Toulouse, Norwich, and a number of Rhineland towns, continued to mark time throughout the eighteenth century, scarcely expanding their population and not branching out into significant new economic fields. So did ports such as Seville and Venice, which were ill placed to exploit new and expanding areas of trade. On the other hand, those trading with Europe's overseas colonies had begun to gather momentum by the 1690s and within half a century some of them were experiencing spectacular booms. Cadiz had already in the later seventeenth century overtaken Seville as Spain's main colonial entrepôt. Seville, weakened by crises in the American trade in the 1620s and 1630s, and then by the loss of 60,000 inhabitants from plague in 1649, was finally vanquished by the introduction of ships too large for its shallow river. In 1717 the controlling organ of colonial commerce, the House of Trade, was transferred to Cadiz, which by 1787 had attained a population of 66,000. Barcelona, itself exporting large supplies of food and especially wines to the Indies, saw a dramatic recovery. So did Marseilles, France's link between Asia and America, whose population rose from just over 20,000 on the morrow of its notorious plague in 1720, to almost 100,000 in 1800. Bordeaux, less handicapped to start with, climbed to a similar total from around 40,000; on the eve of the French Revolution the volume of its trade was exceeded in Europe only by that of London. The population of Bristol rose from 20,000 around 1700 to 64,000 in 1801, and Glasgow went from around 13,000 in 1708 to nearly 84,000 in 1801. Most spectacular of all perhaps was Liverpool, which was little more than a village in the mid-seventeenth century but by the later eighteenth was a town of 78,000 and England's second seaport. There was little room in such places for the sedate organization of the guilds. Where they existed, they were simply by-passed, their trades dwarfed by the massive expansion of shipbuilding, refining, and other activities associated with colonial products. More traditional trades, such as building to house the soaring population, also flourished, but the scale of the demand was beyond guild control or capacity to supply. The unruly mobs of construction workers who roamed the streets of cities such as Bordeaux and fought inter-union battles, were a dangerous witness to the failure of the old agencies of organization and the triumph of the 'free trades'.

The colonial boom did not survive into the nineteenth century, by which time Bordeaux and Cadiz had joined Venice in the economic backwaters, and Bristol was standing still. Liverpool and Glasgow continued to flourish because they, unlike the others, had industrial hinterlands. Most industry was conducted in the countryside. Only in rare areas was it concentrated within towns, like the silk-weaving in Lyons. But in the course of the eighteenth century there was striking expansion of completely new towns in areas where new industries were set up. Between 1725 and 1800, 298 new communities in Russia acquired the status of town, most of them in such areas as the southern Urals, where industry was expanding. Most spectacular of all, again, were the new towns of England. Birmingham, a centre of metal manufacture, grew eightfold between 1675 and 1800, with a great acceleration after 1760. The cotton town of Manchester more than trebled its population between 1773 and 1801, when it reached 84,000. Around it and its port, Liverpool, grew up a series of satellite towns, populous in their own right by older standards, so that by 1801 one quarter of the population of England was living in urbanized south Lancashire.

The population explosion of the later eighteenth century, therefore, coincided with and fed an urban explosion in capital cities, ports, and certain industrial communities. It also boosted the relative importance of smaller towns, with less than 5,000 inhabitants, which had borne the brunt of urban decline during the preceding generations. The economic consequences were far reaching. Urban expansion, for instance, would have been quite impossible without massive immigration from the countryside to compensate for the cities' continuing excess of deaths over births. Thus towns, which had always drained the countryside of its wealth, now drew increasingly on its manpower. Perhaps this was an additional spur to the evolution of labour-saving rural technology. The investment of urban capital in agriculture certainly was. It is no coincidence that the breakthrough in agriculture came in the hinterlands of cities rich in accumulated capital—around the Dutch cities, London, and Barcelona. Through trade towns had always been the main centres of capital accumulation. What marked the urban expansion of the later eighteenth century was the unprecedented scale of this accumulation. It meant that, even when capital had been invested in all the traditional ways, there was still plenty to spare to finance newer, and more productive, activities.

Wealth and its Investment

Most of the wealth produced under the old order was simply squandered— it was not reinvested in productive enterprises. Rather than finance innovations and expansion in trade or manufactures, most men of means preferred to invest their resources in ostentation, high consumption, or social climbing. Only the prospect of enormous returns, or the closing of more traditional fields of investment could persuade them to abandon these time-honoured and wasteful ways.

Among noblemen conspicuous consumption was a duty. They spent their money on fine clothes, coaches, lavish houses, and gambling. It is true that their expenditures helped to sustain armies of servants, tailors, wigmakers, grooms, masons, and decorators, but urban luxury industries were the main beneficiaries, while the areas in which estates were situated were drained of their resources. In the 1720s between a quarter and one-sixth of rents paid in Ireland went to absentee landlords, many of whom spent them on high living in Dublin, London, or Bath. On the eve of the French Revolution, the duc de Saulx-Tavanes expected an annual income of over 95,000 *livres* from his Burgundian estates; but he spent it all in Versailles and Paris, reinvesting only a little over 4 per cent annually in the lands that had produced these revenues. In England, by contrast, the reinvestment rate was between 7 and 11 per cent in the eighteenth century; but England boasted no spend-thrift court to draw magnates to the capital; they had local duties as justices to keep them at home. And agricultural improvement had already impressively demonstrated the value of high reinvestment rates.

The waste of agricultural potential from under-investment was all the more glaring in that plenty of new capital was always being poured into the purchase of land. Land was not particularly profitable in most areas: in France in the 1780s it yielded no more than between 2 and 4 per cent of capital value per year, although rents had risen substantially since the 1760s. Land was not bought for profit, but for social prestige. It was the pre-eminently aristocratic form of wealth, enabling a man to live off his revenues without manual work, as all noblemen aspired to do. Those bourgeois with social ambitions hastened to immobilize their profits, as soon as they could, in landed estates, abandoning the commercial ladder by which they had so far climbed. It is true that when they first took possession of estates, they often introduced the harsher and more rigorous values of business into their administration. But they seldom introduced agricultural innovations, any more than the nobles whom they were aping. If profit and enrichment had been their aim, they would never have bought land in the first place.

In France the ambitious bourgeois had the further option of buying offices. At the moment of its abandonment, in 1790, the venal structure of offices may have represented a capital investment of as much as 1,000,000,000 *livres* and most prices had been moving strongly upwards since mid-century. Yet here again the yield on investment was in most cases very low, compar-able to that on land. 'This multitude of offices' lamented Necker in 1784,[2] '... keeps up a spirit of vanity, which makes men renounce the establishment of trade and manufacture, at the moment when by the accumulation of their fortunes, they might give them the greatest extension ... I do not hesitate to say that these dispositions prevent ... the full development of the strength and initiative of trade.'

Men of wealth preferred not to take the risk. They preferred low, steady returns in money and high returns in status and prestige, to all but the most alluring of gains made speculatively. Unfortunately speculative investment was usually the most productive. The only low-yield, prestigious investment with a productive side was lending to governments, who used some at least of the money they borrowed to finance productive enterprises, even if the latter were mainly industries supplying their military machines. But most lenders preferred to buy annuities which saddled governments with regular payments long after the capital advanced had been exhausted. Almost half the annuities paid out by the city of Paris on the government's behalf in 1789, for instance, dated from the Regency or beyond. The capital tied up in buying annuities could have been put to work far more productively if it had been directly invested in trade and industry rather than lent to governments for low, steady returns.

[2] *De l'administration des finances*, iii. 148–9.

Powerful forces were at work to perpetuate this cautious, status-seeking mentality. Throughout the period land, which remained the source of most wealth, was largely owned by the nobility, with their anti-commercial outlook. In an age of ever fiercer and more comprehensive international competition, trade remained extremely hazardous. It was only in western areas that trade was far-ranging, highly developed, and profitable enough to produce substantial surplus capital. It is true that the collapse of Law's 'system' in 1720, or the debt renunciations in 1770 and 1771, shook the faith of French lenders in government stock, but the government needed their money so badly that it was prepared to offer terms and interest rates so favourable that they could not be resisted. Even the cautious investors of Holland, who held half the British public debt by the later eighteenth century, were induced by the favourable terms offered by French loans in the 1780s to buy French stock in preference. So the annuities market received reinforcement at the very moment when it seemed about to crumble.

Yet the reorientation of Dutch investment in foreign public debts is perhaps more significant as a sign of change in the age-old pattern of values and investment. The Dutch were becoming uneasy about investment in the British national debt because it had been too successful. The utter reliability of British government stock, guaranteed by the Bank of England and yielding interest rates as low as 3 or 4 per cent, had enabled successive governments to raise the level of debt with excessive ease. By 1784 the funded debt stood at £227,240,597 and worries were being voiced that no state, however healthy, could carry a burden of this size for long. Hume, Adam Smith, and many other writers predicted bankruptcy if its increase went on; sinking funds were instituted to help to bring the level down. To secure a full subscription of the loans of the last years of the American Independence war, North's government had to offer more attractive terms than ever before, the equivalent of between 6 and 7 per cent. This suggested that capital formerly invested in government stock was now going elsewhere. Nor, probably, was it going into land, for booming agricultural revenues were prompting landowners to hold on to their property, and in any case the mechanism of the strict settlement kept many estates off the market that might otherwise have been sold. In other words, the traditional safe investments for surplus capital, the 'funds' and landed property, were either no longer as attractive as they had once been, or were simply no longer available. Even the East India Company, whose stock had yielded a steady 7 or 8 per cent between 1722 and 1755, ran into difficulties in the course of the 1760s, and in 1772 it had to be rescued from bankruptcy by the government. Yet all this came at a time when the rapid expansion of British overseas trade was creating unprecedented accumulations of capital. Those who owned it had little alternative but to plough it back into their own enterprises or risk it in financing innovations—roads, canals, new technologies—which would in their turn help to produce greater wealth. Here at least, the old pattern of unproductive investment had been broken.

This is not to say that Europe had seen no private investment on any scale in productive enterprises before. But it had been largely confined to a few people, most of whom were so rich that even when they had invested heavily in ostentation, land, office, and all the other traditional fields, they still had money to spare. And most of the industry financed in this way was in mining and metallurgy, which were really only alternative ways to agriculture of exploiting landed property. Industrialists tended to be not the bourgeois we might expect, but noblemen. Thus in France, over half the forges operating in the 1780s were noble-owned; in some provinces the proportion rose to well over 80 per cent. Similarly, the greatest coalmines of France were owned by dukes and peers who used their influence at court to protect the industries and to secure new concessions for their expansion. It is true that in many cases these facilities were leased to bourgeois businessmen who took most of the risks while noble proprietors simply lived off steady revenues. Equally, however, some nobles organized joint-stock companies to increase their working capital. The mines of Anzin, opened in 1734, were financed from 1757 by a joint-stock company most of whose shareholders were nobles. By 1789 they were employing a work-force of 4,000 and using twelve steam engines. The metallurgical complex of Le Creusot was similarly financed from 1782 by a noble-dominated joint-stock company. Nobles took the initiative here, as did the duke of Bridgewater in 1759, when he mortgaged his estates in order to finance a canal from his coalmines at Worsley to Manchester—a major breakthrough in the transport revolution without which the industrial expansion of the later eighteenth century in England could not have occurred.

The transport revolution was perhaps the first fruit of the expansion in ready capital that characterized the eighteenth century in England. It was enormously expensive, yet with the exception of military roads driven through the Scottish Highlands, it was entirely the work of private initiative and the concentration of private capital. The first 'turnpike trusts', to improve specific sections of road were set up in the first years of the eighteenth century, and an average of eight a year were authorized by parliament from then on until mid-century. Between 1750 and 1770 the rate was nearer forty a year, and after a lull of twenty years, reached over fifty-five a year from 1791 onwards. The canal boom was even more spectacular. In 1760 there were only two short canals, in Lancashire, but the obvious benefits they brought in cheapening transport costs, led to the authorization of no less than 165 new canals between 1758 and 1802, by which time there were between 600 and 700 miles of artificial waterways in Great Britain, most of them linking areas of great economic importance that had been impossibly separated hitherto. In addition, many rivers had been improved over the preceding century to make them more easily navigable. We should not, certainly, underestimate what had been done during the same period to improve communications on the continent. Under Peter I the Vyshevolotsk canal system was built to link the Caspian and the Baltic. France by 1789 had a network of first-class roads, the best in Europe, which had been practically non-existent before the 1730s. She also had about the same length of canals as England, linking arterial rivers, many of them (like the canal du Midi linking the Garonne with the Mediterranean) conceived and largely built as early as the later seventeenth century. But very few of these French works were financed by private capital. It was the central government, or the Estates in provinces such as Languedoc or Burgundy, that planned and carried through these projects. Similarly in Prussia, where six new canals were built between 1746 and 1775; or in Spain, where the government of Charles III began construction of a system of modern arterial roads radiating from Madrid. Between 1753 and 1808 about 200 miles of canals were also dug. These works were ambitiously planned and lavishly constructed at enormous expense; but, even in the minority of cases when they were actually finished, unlike the canals of France or Prussia they often linked areas of no economic importance and consequently were under-used. Private capital could never have been induced to finance works of such uncertain value.

Banking and Credit

The productive investment of capital in Great Britain was much facilitated by the expansion of banking. In 1660 banks were not well developed. A few municipal institutions existed, such as the Bank of Amsterdam or that of Hamburg, and these continued to flourish. In 1775 the Bank of Amsterdam had 2,000 tons of bullion in its vaults and over 2,000 depositors; between 1712 and 1780 its business grew by 125 per cent. Most banking in 1660 however was in the hands of private individuals or small companies, most of whom were never wholly bankers. Sometimes they were goldsmiths, such as those who dominated London banking until the 1690s; sometimes they were public officials, who speculated in moneys they had collected in taxes before the dates on which they had to hand them over to governments; most often they were merchants, who conducted most of their business in promissory notes. By 1700 governments, already the biggest spenders in economic life, were finding these structures inadequate for marshalling the capital they needed to borrow, and state banks began to appear. The first was founded in Sweden in 1656. In 1661, to avoid the inconvenience of Sweden's cumbersome copper currency, it began to issue notes—the first true banknotes in European history. But they soon suffered the fate of most early experiments with paper money: they were overproduced, and lost their value in a dramatic crash. The first successful state bank was the Bank of England, established in 1694—a private company, but totally dependent on the British state's financial needs for its existence. Other state banks followed—in Austria in 1705, in Prussia in 1765, in Spain in 1782. Only in France was no form of state bank successfully established. There, the financiers who handled the state's long- and short-term credits consistently opposed any attempt to concentrate credit for the state's benefit. Law's 'Royal Bank' of 1720 would have done this, and so emancipated the French financial system from the grip of profiteering financiers who dominated it at every stage, taking large rake-offs and even sometimes lending the government its own money! But by linking his bank with the dubious commercial venture of the Louisiana Company,

Law ensured that it would disappear in the general collapse of confidence in that company's prospects. By the mid-1720s the financiers were once more in control of the government's finances—a control retained until 1789.[3] Their survival in itself did a good deal to channel French capital in the direction of annuities in preference to productive investment.

State banks or their equivalents, once well established, did much to promote easier conditions of credit. It is not surprising therefore to find that private banking also developed most rapidly in the country of the first and most successful of the state banks, Great Britain. By 1700, the London goldsmiths had already been largely superseded as the main bankers of the capital by a number of private firms, many of them catering for specific trades or economic groups. By 1725 there were twenty-five banking houses in London, rising to fifty-two by 1786. Their expansion benefited directly from the proximity of the Bank of England and the credit which it fostered. More striking, since Bank of England notes rarely penetrated deep into the provinces, was the establishment of 'country banks'. The first was set up in the thriving port of Bristol in 1716; and from 1760 onwards the movement accelerated rapidly. In 1755 there were still only twelve important country banks: in 1793 there were 400, often closely interlinked, and most of them having dealings with London too. The effect was to facilitate and accelerate the circulation of wealth in the country and to enable British merchants and manufacturers to draw on capital which their continental counterparts were quite unable to tap. By the issue of notes, often in smaller denominations than those of the Bank of England, these country banks immensely expanded the money supply at a moment when the British economy needed to absorb far more capital than ever before.

It was a crucial advantage, because shortage of specie was one of the basic problems of the European economy. However much the mines of America increased the supply of bullion, it was never enough to keep pace with European demand; if only because the trade with the East, which required very few goods that Europe could supply, had to be balanced up in silver. With the exception of Great Britain, which through its trading links with Portugal and Brazil, was effectively on a gold standard by the later eighteenth century, silver was the basic measure of value everywhere. But as a result of the demands of the eastern trade, it tended constantly to disappear. No amount of recoining (such as in England in 1696—8, or in Prussia in 1763), prosecution of coin clipping, or avoidance of cheap expedients such as debasement, was able to keep abundant silver supplies in circulation. The development of banking and the spread of banknotes was the eighteenth century's response to this situation. But it also saw the full development of an older form of negotiable paper, the bill of exchange. Ever since the sixteenth century merchants had been conducting much of their business in this form rather than in specie. The stock exchanges of Amsterdam and London, as well as several smaller institutions in other major ports, had been established largely

---

[3] For a full analysis of this system, see J. F. Bosher, *French Finances 1770–1795: From Business to Bureaucracy* (1970).

to handle the traffic in them, and they continued to do so. But with the ever-growing problem of marshalling credit for governments, the character of the metropolitan exchanges ceased to be wholly commercial, for government stocks were offered there. The exchanges founded at Hamburg (1720), Paris (1724), and Vienna (1771) were none of them primarily commercial in purpose. At the same time the very existence of a huge market in government stocks on these exchanges attracted other business, notably that of joint-stock companies, which also reached their full development during this period.

Undoubtedly the expansion of credit had an economically stimulating effect. Nowhere did banking develop to the extent it did in Great Britain, but by the early eighteenth century the exchanges of the continent were dominated by the activities of a few Protestant banking houses based in Geneva and Amsterdam. The Catholic French government, with no state bank, could not have maintained its credit without the help of Protestant bankers, and in Necker it eventually appointed one of them to manage its finances between 1777 and 1781. The greater industrial enterprises of France in the later eighteenth century were largely financed by capital raised on the Paris *bourse*, too. At the same time the development of the exchanges laid economic life more open than before to the activities of speculators who were interested only in manipulating stocks for a quick profit. The crash of 1719−20 which brought down Law's 'system' vividly illustrated these dangers: it was in fact Europe-wide. It began with a wave of post-war speculation on the exchanges of Amsterdam and London as well as in Paris. Carried away by grossly exaggerated estimates of the profits to be had from the colonial trade, governments sponsored great companies—the Louisiana Company in France, the South Sea Company in England—which were soon wildly oversubscribed. Many private companies were also launched to benefit from the public mania for investment. When the bottom fell out of the market, thousands of investors were ruined, credit shaken everywhere, and trade disrupted. The Bank of England itself only just survived the crisis, but Law's French equivalent did not, and the scars left by this experience had still not healed in France by 1789. When a public discount bank was at last set up in 1776, the public refused to invest in it, and it became the plaything of speculators. The appearance of its stock on the Paris *bourse*, together with the massive loans contracted by Necker, had produced, by the 1780s, a new boom in the stockmarket; but by 1786 it was seen to be based on prospects no more solid than those of 1720. The market began to waver, credit grew difficult, and this did much to bring on the final financial crisis of the French monarchy.

But significantly the crash of 1720 had not destroyed the new circumstances which had produced it. By the mid-eighteenth century in western Europe, the worlds of trade, industry, and public finance were more closely interlinked than they had ever been before. All depended for their healthy functioning on a complex system of credit; and credit was grounded in the last analysis in the shifting sands of public confidence. When anything shook that confidence, such as a series of bad harvests in the late 1760s and early

1770s, credit became tight, there were waves of bankruptcy in both the commercial and financial worlds, and the very stability of governments themselves came into question.[4] The late 1780s showed the same symptoms. So did the years following the disastrous winter of 1795. Yet in the eyes of merchants, manufacturers, financiers, and government alike, this vulnerability seemed a small price to pay for the emancipation from the constraints of an economy limited by always scarce supplies of precious metals.

Manufactures: The Pre-industrial Pattern

Even in 1800 the economy of Europe, with the exception of isolated corners such as northern England, Catalonia, or the Urals, remained largely pre-industrial. This is not to say that there were no industries; merely that they were organized in different ways, and used different techniques, from those that were to emerge in the nineteenth century. The characteristic unit of production was the small workshop, not the factory; and these small workshops supplied a far more limited range of human wants, for the peasants who made up the overwhelming mass of pre-industrial society were largely self-sufficient. Manufactures for more than very local markets were largely confined to three areas of production—luxury goods, military supplies, and textiles.

Luxury goods covered a far wider range than they now do. One industry which expanded very steadily throughout the period, for example, was printing and book production, fed in its turn by paper manufacturing. But since literacy, without which this expansion could not have occurred, was still the privilege of a minority even in 1800, books were a luxury. As to more conventional luxuries, most governments, convinced that they were a potent means of enriching the state, fostered and subsidized them. The pattern for such policies was set by Colbert under Louis XIV. He believed that if luxury goods of the finest quality were produced in France, they would both discourage the purchase of foreign products and capture foreign markets at the same time. So he sponsored and protected companies that made fine lace, carpets, mirrors, and tapestries. Other governments followed the French example, particularly the small states of Germany. The fine porcelain produced at Meissen in Saxony from 1710 onwards is perhaps the best-known example, although it was untypical in its success. Most such enterprises did not last long, or were kept afloat by constant subsidies from the governments that had founded them. Frederick II of Prussia, successive electors of Bavaria, and the prince bishop of Osnabrück all poured away money on unsuccessful porcelain manufacture. The market for such luxuries was far too limited, and although it undoubtedly expanded towards the end of the eighteenth century, both the rate and the scale of this expansion remained modest. The consumers of expensive luxuries remained a small minority of the population. Once they had acquired prestigious items of high quality, they were unlikely to replace them with more—unless there was a change in fashion,

---

[4] See J. F. Bosher, 'The French Crisis of 1770', *History* (1972), 17–30, for analysis of a crisis in France which also affected other countries.

which normally led them to buy from new sources. Thus from the 1770s Meissen porcelain was thrown into difficulties by the competition of French Sèvres. Throughout this period, starting in the 1660s, the most conspicuous luxury item, worn by all men in the upper ranks of society, was the wig. When, abruptly in the 1790s, wigs went out of fashion, the livelihood of thousands of artisans collapsed spectacularly.

Labour-intensive though they were, even the greatest luxury industries were not major employers. In a fairly typical small state such as Bavaria in 1770 only 0·12 per cent of the labour force was absorbed by manufactures. Far more important in providing industrial employment were activities designed to meet military needs. Perhaps the greatest industrial complexes of the age were naval dockyards, concentrating in one place shipbuilding, ship-repairing and maintenance, ropemaking, cannon-founding, and a whole range of service industries for naval personnel. The Royal Navy was the largest single employer and one of the most influential economic units in the British economy. In Prussia the same could be said for the army. Between 1754 and 1784 Frederick II's government established no fewer than six new ironworks in the newly acquired province of Silesia; in 1768 it set up a special Department of Mines and Ironworks to prospect for mineral deposits and oversee their exploitation. The purpose was almost exclusively military, as was that of Peter I's government in Russia, in fostering and protecting the industries of the Urals. A thousand miles from any significant centres of population or consumption, served by atrociously bad roads by which pig-iron could take up to two years to reach the Baltic for export, the Urals by 1760 were nevertheless probably the greatest industrial area in Europe. By 1800 over 300,000 were employed in their mines and forges, and the annual output of pig-iron exceeded 160,000 tons. The achievement was all the more remarkable in that in 1700 there had been hardly any industries there. Sweden had dominated the international market for pig-iron, with only France among major states supplying all her own needs. In the late eighteenth century Sweden, still producing 50,000 tons of high-grade pig-iron, was Prussia's main supplier. But England, the other major buyer, now imported most of her pig-iron from Russia; 80 per cent of the products of the Demidov factories, the largest Russian industrial chain, went to England. By this time the state patronage under which Peter I had launched the Urals' fortunes was diminishing in importance; a growing proportion of the Urals' industries were privately owned and managed. But this growth in the private sector coincided with the end of expansion. The Urals were soon to be left behind in stagnation by more efficient and technically sophisticated industrial areas elsewhere—most notably in that very England which for the moment still absorbed so many of their exports.

Military requirements not only stimulated mining and metallurgy. Armies had to be clothed, and the generalization of uniforms between 1660 and 1700 led states to assume responsibility for this. Large contracts were placed for woollen cloth, and where private enterprises were unable to supply the state's needs, it established factories of its own, such as the Berlin wool warehouse, or the Moscow woollens factory, which already around 1720 employed 593 skilled workers. Governments sometimes established factories for producing woollen cloth for non-military markets, such as that set up at Guadalajara in Spain with the help of fifty Dutch weavers in 1718. But without a guaranteed market it was difficult to dispose of the high quality and expensive products of this institution, which lurched from crisis to crisis for the rest of the century, only kept afloat by repeated lavish subsidies from the state. Factories were the productive instruments of the future, but not this sort. Pre-industrial factories were merely collective workshops, concentrations of many individual items of manually operated plant under a single roof. Nineteenth-century factories housed huge machines driven by external sources of power and tended by, rather than worked by, human hands. Until this crucial change was made, so far from profiting from the open market, factory products seemed to survive only when they were protected from it.

Most textile production, however, was not concentrated under one roof. The whole trend of the age, at least until the 1770s or 1780s, was in the opposite direction. This was the heyday of the 'putting out', or 'domestic' system of industry, in which manufacture, financed, organized and marketed from towns, was actually carried on in innumerable small households in the country. It had not always been so, and quality textiles, such as silk, continued to be largely produced under tight guild regulations in urban workshops like those of Lyons or Valencia, throughout the eighteenth century. But when the labour shortages of the later seventeenth century, which pushed up the wages of skilled urban artisans, led the organizers of ordinary textile production to seek means of reducing their costs, the most effective proved to be the transfer of spinning and weaving to the countryside. Under this system, the urban entrepreneur, or 'putter-out' bought the raw materials, whether wool, cotton, or flax, and distributed or sold it for manufacture to innumerable rural households in the region around. He then either collected or bought back the finished product and marketed it. Peasant labour, often part-time, was cheap, and in many areas it was not organized into guilds. Rural spinners and weavers provided their own wheels and looms, minimizing the organizer's capital investment. It is true that this rural work-force was seldom as skilled as that of the urban trade guilds and its products were of far lower quality. But they were mainly produced for the lower end of the market, where high quality was not at a premium.

This system first developed in the woollen and linen industries. By 1700 it was well established around centres such as Amiens or Abbeville in France, Leeds, Halifax, or Exeter in England, Aachen in Germany, or Leyden and Haarlem in the Netherlands. In Sedan, in eastern France, twenty-five urban businessmen gave employment to 15,000 peasants in manufacturing woollen cloth. A Warrington sailmaker claimed before 1750 that he had given employment to 5,000 people. And when cotton, imported from warmer regions overseas, came to be spun and woven in Europe (rather than imported) at the end of the seventeenth century, it was organized along the same lines around centres such as Barcelona, Manchester, or Rouen. 'There are all sorts of cotton manufacture made up at Rouen and in the area 15 leagues (about 40 miles) around it,' wrote an aristocratic French traveller in the 1780s,[5]

One must admire the activity of the Normans. This activity does not interfere at all with. . .daily work. . .The farmer works on the land during the day and it is in the evening by the light of the lamp that he starts his other task. His workers and his family have to help. When they have worked all week they come into the town with horses and carts piled up with the material. . . Among those who do the buying there are many agents who buy for merchants and then the goods pass to America, Italy and Spain.

The manufacture of cotton goods was the most important new European industry in the eighteenth century. It began as an attempt to imitate luxury goods from the east, but European yarns were poor and had to be reinforced by linen, which limited their appeal. Cotton manufacture was often inhibited by prohibitions aimed (ironically) at imported eastern goods which were thought to offer harmful competition to European woollens. But from around the middle of the century, when French, Spanish, and British manufacturers began to export cotton goods of less fine quality to the growing European establishments of the tropics and sub-tropics, the industry began to boom. French cotton cloth production doubled between 1732 and 1766. In 1760 the Catalan cotton industry employed 10,000 workers; in 1800 this number had risen to 100,000, two-thirds of them women, working in over 3,000 workshops. Initially English production expanded far less rapidly, for English labour was dearer and the buoyant European market for English woollens absorbed much of it. In the 1750s and 1760s there seemed a real danger that British cotton production would not be able to meet the rapidly expanding demands of areas such as the north American colonies. It could never have done so without a series of radical technical innovations which appeared during these years and enabled the industry to meet and overcome French, and to a lesser extent Spanish, competition. They also transformed it into the first modern industry, the pattern for the industrial revolution which was to change the European economy beyond recognition over the next century.

Manufactures: Technical Innovation

Why technology advances is a subject of constant debate among economic historians. But they are mostly agreed that the eighteenth century witnessed a major technological breakthrough in Europe, which opened the way to the methods of production of the world we live in, and which first occurred in Great Britain. England by 1700 was already the richest nation in Europe. Its agriculture was being transformed, its overseas trade was expanding, its financial system was already more sophisticated and flexible than that of most other countries, and the wages of its workers were higher than those earned on the continent. But these advantages also posed problems. Expand-

[5] Quoted in S. Pollard and C. Holmes, *Documents of European Economic History* (1968), i. 91.

ing trade and expanding markets increased demand, to place a growing strain on the productive power of a country with a relatively small yet highly paid work-force. Unless production could be increased without at the same time massively increasing costs, expansion could not continue. At the time nobody saw the problem in such broad terms; they did not have the information to formulate such an analysis. But most sectors of economic activity—agriculture, mining, metallurgy, and textiles—were affected and individuals could see clearly enough the problem of meeting growing demand without incurring prohibitive costs. Technological innovation, aided by the investment of the greater capital resources of a rich society, was the means by which it was solved.

Chronologically, the first step was the introduction for industrial purposes of the steam-engine. Steam-engines were invented by Savery (1698) and Newcomen (1705) and were rapidly adopted first for pumping water out of mines and then for winding. By 1733 there were fifty-one in existence, over forty of them in Great Britain. By the time the patent on these machines expired in 1781, at least another 300 steam-engines had been produced. In 1769 meanwhile James Watt patented a more sophisticated machine which cut down by 75 per cent the energy required to make it work—a major break-through in cutting the costs of steam power. It took seven years before Watt's system emerged as commercially viable, but then its success was rapid: by the end of the century perhaps 500 Watt engines were in use in Great Britain, adapted not only to pumping and winding, but to driving machinery. In 1784 a Watt steam-engine was first employed to drive the plant of a cotton mill—the essential formula in British industrial expansion of the early nine-teenth century. Nevertheless in the eighteenth century the main benefits of steam power were felt in the mining industries, above all in coal. Even in 1700, there was a serious shortage of wood for burning. Coal filled the vacuum, and the improvement of mining, thanks to steam pumps, was important in allowing it to do so.

In their turn, steam pumps depended on increasing technical sophistication in the metal industries. Watt's engine could never have been commercially constructed without the precision cylinder boring techniques evolved by his Birmingham partner Matthew Boulton in founding cannon under a military contract of 1774. But long before then important innovations had also been made in metallurgy. Until the eighteenth century iron and steel were smelted with charcoal, heat being maintained by bellows driven, in sophisticated production, by water power. Since production was therefore scattered in wooded areas increasingly remote from normal trade-routes, costs were increased. One reason why England imported so much Baltic iron was that it was cheaper to bring it from Sweden or Russia by sea than overland from native centres of production. But the wood famine brought change here too. In the first decade of the eighteenth century, Abraham Darby succeeded in smelting marketable quantities of iron from coke. By the 1740s the superior quality of coke smelting was generally established both for iron and steel, and in 1760 steam power was first employed to provide the blast for a coke furnace. This process however was still incapable of producing the easily worked wrought iron of charcoal smelting until Henry Cort's 'puddling and rolling' process, patented in 1784, both simplified production and eliminated impurities. The last recorded charcoal furnace had been built in 1775; by the end of the century the charcoal industry was dead. The geography of iron production had also been revolutionized; furnaces were no longer scattered, but concentrated on or near coalfields well served by canals and navigable rivers such as those of south Wales, south Yorkshire, or the west midlands. So transport costs fell as the scale and versatility of production rose. Imports of Baltic iron by 1800 had levelled off. Great Britain had become a major iron exporter.

This important change in the pattern of British exports was far from the most important. In 1700 the largest item in British exports was, as it had been ever since the Middle Ages, woollens. They accounted for 70 per cent of total value. By 1800 the absolute value of woollen exports had almost doubled, but their proportion of total British exports had fallen to 24 per cent. The major export, accounting for 39 per cent of the total, was now an item whose percentage had been too small to calculate in 1700—cottons. This was spectacular enough, but when we realize that most of this phenomenal growth had taken place since 1780, it is even more striking. Such an industrial explosion was unprecedented and could not have occurred without a series of major innovations which, from the middle of the century onwards, transformed the techniques of cotton production. The first, John Kay's flying shuttle of 1733, doubled a weaver's output and was widely adopted in cotton weaving from the 1750s onwards. The immediate effect of more productive weaving was an increased demand for yarn, with a search for devices to improve the productivity of spinning. The first response to the challenge was Hargreaves's 'spinning Jenny' patented in 1768, which enabled a single operator to work up to 100 spindles. The next year Arkwright produced the 'water frame', which spun yarn by water rather than by manual power. In 1779 Crompton produced the 'mule' which worked several hundred spindles and within a few years had been adapted to steam power. There was now a danger that supplies of spun yarn would outstrip the ability of weaving to absorb it. Frantic experiments to produce a power loom culminated in 1787 in Cartwright's invention. Technical innovation had now become a self-generating process, whose rewards were vividly demonstrated in the booming market for whatever cottons Lancashire could produce.

Technical innovation led to massive economies in production. More could be produced in far less time with far less labour. But organizational innovation could also produce significant economies. By the mid-eighteenth century the domestic system of production may have been stretched to its economic limit: goods were being produced further and further from their marketing centres so that transport costs were beginning to outbalance the putter-out's savings on plant and wages. The logic of mechanization, by contrast, was concentration; so that production by the new machines was essentially production in factories. The first textile factories were not in the cotton industry, but in silk spinning. A mechanical process for spinning silk thread or 'throwing' had been invented in Italy in the sixteenth century. It was introduced to England in 1717, by the Lombe brothers, who built a large water-powered factory to house it in Derby two years later. It was 500 feet long, several storeys high, and employed 300 operatives. Other 'throwing mills' of this sort were founded over the next half-century. And with the advent of the water-frame, by which many machines could be driven from a single power-source, factory production came to cotton manufacture. In 1771 Arkwright built a spinning factory which employed 300 at Cromford. By 1781 it employed 900. By 1790 there were 150 large, water-powered factories throughout the English north and midlands; even wool spinning was beginning to be affected. Steam-powered mills had also made their appearance, and, freed of the necessity for siting near swift-flowing water which made the earliest textile mills rural institutions, they began to be concentrated in towns. By 1800 the domestic system of industry was far from dead, except perhaps in cotton manufacture. But the factories that were to replace it were spreading rapidly. Around them the towns—Manchester, Birmingham, Leeds—that were to become the great industrial conurbations of the next century were already mushrooming.

No comparable set of developments had yet occurred on the continent. People came to England from all over Europe to view the steam-engines, advanced forges, foundries, and cotton mills which were transforming industry. Sometimes they copied or imported these devices; but the continent's superior reserves of cheap manpower lessened the attraction of installing innovations that were initially very expensive. Nor was it before the 1780s that Great Britain attained levels of productivity which dwarfed anything ever seen before and so demonstrated beyond dispute that her technical innovations were more than just expensive toys. It took the removal of tariff protection against English goods by the treaty of 1786, following which France was flooded with cottons both cheaper yet higher in quality than native products, to demonstrate to the French just how far Manchester had moved ahead of Rouen in cotton production. Then there was a scramble to install jennies, water-frames, mules, and other English inventions as they appeared. The cotton manufacturers of Barcelona did the same. Governments everywhere tried to attract skilled British craftsmen. But no sooner had Europe become aware of the British example, than contact with it was abruptly shut off by the wars of the French Revolution. During a decade of more rapid technological advance than ever the continent, dominated by a France which regarded Britain as an enemy, was largely cut off from the latest developments. So Great Britain surged yet further ahead in production; the war also allowed her, by sweeping her continental competitors from the seas, to capture larger overseas markets to absorb this growing productive capacity. This was as crucial as the overseas demand had been in calling forth the British industrial breakthrough in the first place. The industrial revolution could not have occurred had it not been preceded and then fuelled by a commercial revolution which transformed Europe's relationship with the rest of the world.

3. Wider Horizons: Trade and Empire

No event [wrote the Abbé Raynal in 1770][1] has been so interesting to mankind in general, and to the inhabitants of Europe in particular, as the discovery of the New World, and the passage to India by the Cape of Good Hope. It gave rise to a revolution in the commerce, and in the power of nations; as well as in the manners, industry, and government of the whole world. At this period, new connexions were formed by the inhabitants of the most distant regions, for the supply of wants they had never before experienced. The production of climates situated under the equator, were consumed in countries bordering on the pole; the industry of the north was transplanted to the south; and the inhabitants of the west were clothed with the manufactures of the east.

By 1660 the first phase of this European expansion was over. The Spaniards had established in Central and South America the largest territorial empire the world had ever seen, but the flood of precious metals with which it had engulfed Europe for the best part of a century had lost its momentum and the future role of the empire seemed uncertain. The Portuguese had begun to exploit the sugar-growing potential of Brazil, but their great east-Indian spice-trading empire was in ruins, the bulk of it captured in the early seventeenth century by the interloping Dutch. Europe was now dependent on overseas sources for fundamental goods which it could not produce for itself, or only at great cost—spices, tobacco, sugar, cottons, dyestuffs, and tropical hardwoods. It was not yet able, however, to send the regions of supply anything like the same volume of European goods in exchange, for heavy woollens and European hardware had little market in the tropics. The balance was made up in silver, mined in America and sent to Europe, only to be shipped from there in enormous quantities straight to the east. The arrival of the Europeans in America and Asia had certainly contributed towards the evolution of a world economy, but the role of Europe itself, apart from that of the indispensable middleman, was primarily that of a consumer. The most important development of the next phase of European expansion, which lasted up to 1800 and beyond, was the transformation of Europe into a major supplier of goods to the rest of the world. Only then did the great bulk of Europe's inhabitants begin to benefit more than marginally from their continent's world domination.

Colonies

In 1660 the only substantial numbers of Europeans overseas were in Spanish

[1] G. T. Raynal, *A Philosophical and Political History of the Settlements and Trade of the Europeans in the East and West Indies* (trans. W. J. O. Justamond, 1813) i. 1–2.

America, where they had risen from 120,000 to 650,000 over the preceding century. Even there, the enormous size of the empire meant that white settlers were very sparse. The other empires, the Dutch and the Portuguese, were by contrast trading empires, whose territories (with the exception of Brazil) were largely confined to commercial enclaves where Europeans came to make their fortunes, but rarely settled and even more rarely reproduced themselves, for there were no European women.

But even in 1660 there were signs of change. A growing European demand for sugar had already led to an intensive colonization of certain West Indian islands and more accessible parts of Brazil, first by white settlers and then, increasingly, by black slaves brought from Africa. Even more important, European colonies had begun to establish themselves all along the North American seaboard, after several generations of fruitless experiments. By 1660 there were between 60,000 and 70,000 British and Dutch colonists in North America, perhaps two-thirds of whom had been born in Europe,—which shows how new this development was. In 1667 the Dutch colonies became English under the treaty that ended the second Anglo-Dutch war, and by 1700 the population of British North America had risen to a quarter of a million, most of them now American born. The colonial population, with abundant land and natural resources, was soon more than reproducing itself; and constant immigration, now increasing from non-British parts of Europe, added further impetus to its growth. By 1776 the population of the thirteen British colonies had risen to 2,600,000. Nothing comparable to this phenomenal growth occurred in the empires of other powers. The number of French settlers in Canada in the 1660s scarcely exceeded 4,000, had not reached 20,000 by 1700, and was still less than 70,000 when Canada became a British possession in 1763. Not more than 200,000 Portuguese emigrated to Brazil between 1700 and 1760, only a fifth of the number of negro slaves who were transported there from Africa in the same period. The population of Spain's American colonies, after a catastrophic collapse down to the mid-seventeenth century, rose by 50 per cent before 1800, reaching 14,600,000. But most of this rise was accounted for by an element which was numerically unimportant in the north, the native Indians. In 1800 the white population of these vast territories had still reached only about 2 million, by which time the former British colonies, the United States, were approaching $5\frac{1}{2}$ million.

There was, then, an enormous increase in the number of Europeans (by birth or descent) living overseas, the greatest part of it accounted for by settlement in areas barely touched in the mid-seventeenth century. The problem is to explain it, for Europe was far from overpopulated when this movement really got under way. Some European colonization resulted from state planning, notably the French settlements in Canada or 'New France'. French traders were established in Canada before the time of Colbert, but he organized them and subjected the colony to close control. They were, in his view, important potential markets for home-produced goods, as well as a source of commodities unavailable in Europe. But the harsh winters and inhospitable forests of Canada made it unattractive to settlers, and the regulation to which they were subjected once there did nothing to increase its appeal. Nor were the French any more successful in colonizing Louisiana, at the mouth of the Mississippi, where they founded a fort in 1699. Despite the inflated hopes raised by Law's plan of 1719 to make its trade the keystone of an economic miracle, it was peopled mainly by transported criminals rather than by voluntary settlers; and after the collapse of Law's 'system' Louisiana stagnated. Much more potent as a spur to emigration was the hope of making a fortune—of which, again, Canada and Louisiana offered few prospects. The first Europeans had gone to America in search of gold, and it was the discovery of large gold deposits in Brazil in the 1690s that promoted most Portuguese emigration in the subsequent sixty or seventy years. By 1709 the Minas Gerais region, a wilderness twenty years before, had a population of about 30,000; and by 1720 the home government was so alarmed by the exodus from certain Portuguese provinces that it forbade emigration without a royal licence. But neither government encouragement nor hope of gain peopled the most spectacular region of European colonization, the British colonies of the North American seaboard. From the start most of the immigrants to British North America had been refugees, from either religious or political oppression, or from economic hardship. Pennsylvania, for example, was founded in 1682 as a haven for Quakers. After 1685 hundreds of Huguenots expelled from France also found their way to America. With the passage of the Toleration Act in 1689, however, the stream of religious refugees from the British Isles dried up, their place being taken by transported criminals (for which the last colony, Georgia, was largely founded in 1733) or inhabitants of areas struck by economic adversity, such as Ulster or northwest Scotland. The religious element now came largely from the immigration of Germans, who accounted for 250,000 new arrivals between 1700 and 1770. Successive British governments, afraid that emigration would diminish home manpower, paid premiums for transporting Germans to America right down to 1776. By that time (if black slaves are also included) over a third of the colonial population was of non-English origin, with the newcomers concentrated in the frontier areas that were expanding most rapidly.

A further attraction of the British colonies was that they were self-governing and largely free from the interference or regulation of the home government. This was exceptional, for most European states with colonies regarded them merely as provinces of the mother country beyond the seas and therefore subject to a central direction as close, if not closer, than that of the homeland. The pattern had been set by the Spaniards, who governed the whole of their empire from a council of the Indies sitting in Madrid. The colonial regional viceroyalties had little freedom of action, serving merely as channels for the transmission of orders from Spain to the *corregidores* who represented the king at local level. Yet in practice this system was slow, cumbersome, corrupt, and vitiated by venality of offices at all levels. This was one reason why the reforming ministers of Charles III began to introduce, as in Spain itself, a system of intendants modelled on that of France. Starting in Cuba in 1764, by 1790 the system had been introduced everywhere. Administration now became more efficient, but, staffed by appointees of Spanish birth, it only increased the long-standing hostility of the American-born 'creole' aristocracy, who had monopolized local office under the old system, towards the peninsular Spaniards who transmitted the king's orders to them. In Brazil, similarly, government grew more autocratic. When civil war broke out in Minas Gerais in 1708−9 between the backwoodsmen who had first found gold and the *emboabas* or newcomers from coastal regions and from Portugal who were pouring in to exploit the find, the viceroy used the opportunity to clamp a tight semi-military system of government on the region. In 1740 the diamond-producing district was effectively sealed off from the outside world by troops. The arrival in power of Pombal (1755) who was determined to mobilize the total resources of the Portuguese empire, marked a new stage in the extension of central control. The resistance of the Jesuits to his attempts to impose secular control on their Indian protectorate in Paraguay was only the most spectacular sign of resentment at the growing pretensions of the Lisbon government to control and regulate every aspect of life in South America. Such resentment was largely absent in Canada, but close control from France had been a feature there from the start. When Canada became British in 1763, the new rulers proclaimed their intention ultimately to establish representative government; but the Quebec Act in 1774 recognized that, quite apart from the fact that the population was made up of Catholics who enjoyed civil rights in no other British dominion, the French colonists had no tradition of self-government and would be content to be ruled more directly.

This act, however, scandalized the English-speaking colonists of North America, who were by then on the point of severing their links with Great Britain. To them it seemed added proof that the home government was bent on destroying all colonial independence. Most British colonies had been endowed, from their foundation, with representative institutions. They varied from colony to colony in their structure and in the number of colonists entitled to vote, from the relative democracy of certain New England colonies such as Massachussetts or Rhode Island to the aristocratic oligarchies of Virginia and the Carolinas. Each colony had a governor, appointed from England by the crown, or the colony's proprietor, depending on its constitution. But these governors commanded no troops except colonial militias, and above all they were paid by the colonial assemblies. The seventeenth century saw an attempt to reverse this democratic drift. James duke of York refused to grant New York a representative assembly between its capture, in 1664, and 1683. Then as King James II he began to reorganize the northern colonies into a centralized 'Dominion of New England' which, while not unrepresentative in some of its features, was clearly designed to subject the colonies to closer control through the agency of a single supreme governor. With James's overthrow in 1689 the scheme collapsed and the colonies entered a period of 'salutary neglect' during which they each developed along their own lines, making their own laws with the minimum of interference from Europe, except in wartime. Even then such interference was increasingly resented. The most distinctive of all their diverse privileges was freedom from taxation, a right not enjoyed by the overseas colonies of any other European state. Taxes were raised in the thirteen colonies by the authority of their own legislatures, not by parliament in London. And, thirty years before the Stamp Act sparked off an ultimately fatal quarrel over taxing America, Walpole's Molasses Act of 1733 was denounced as detrimental to colonial rights. It was, protested Rhode Island's agent in London 'divesting them of their rights and privileges as the King's natural-born subjects and Englishmen, in levying subsidies upon them against their consent, when they are annexed to no county in Great Britain, have no representative in Parliament, nor have any part of the legislature of this kingdom'.[2]

The home government held that this act was not a measure of taxation at all, but rather one of trade regulation. As such it fell into a sphere in which only the central government of the empire was competent to make policy. This was axiomatic among all the European powers with colonies. However varied the motives of those who emigrated, and however unconcerned they and their descendants became about the affairs of Europe, all governments viewed colonies as primarily designed to enrich the mother country. If they had no economic value, they had no value at all. Their trade must therefore be controlled and regulated so as to promote the home country's interests. Here again Spain set the example. Theoretically all trade with her American colonies had always been channelled through the agency of the 'House of Trade' in Seville, transferred in 1717 to Cadiz. From here a small syndicate of merchants shipped goods to and from selected ports in America. As far as possible American exports were concentrated in two great annual convoys sailing for Spain. But by the end of the seventeenth century this system was falling apart. Convoys sailed irregularly, and in many years not at all; the number of ships was also much diminished. Interlopers from Holland, France, and England traded directly with most Spanish American ports in relative freedom, and smuggling accounted for perhaps two-thirds of the total trade of Spanish America by 1700. At the Peace of Utrecht, Spain attempted to fob off foreign interlopers by allowing the British and the Dutch to send a ship a year each of goods to Central America. The British also gained the *asiento*—the right to import slaves into South America.[3] At the same time however the new Bourbon authorities in Spain made strenuous efforts to refurbish the remains of the exclusive system. A body of semi-independent coastguards was organized and the annual convoy system worked sporadically on until the end of the century. The Portuguese system was also tightened up in the eighteenth century. In principle trade to and from Brazil was confined to Portuguese nationals, most of it concentrated in annual fleets. In 1755 Pombal set up a council of commerce to control this trade, placing the commerce of the two most underdeveloped Brazilian regions in the hands

---

[2] Quoted in I. R. Christie, *Crisis of Empire, Great Britain and the American Colonies 1754–1783* (1966), 14.

[3] The *asiento* had been largely in Dutch hands until 1694. After that the Portuguese held it, and the French won it in 1701.

of monopolistic companies. Such companies were nothing new: they were the most popular means of organizing colonization in the seventeenth century. The French settlements in Canada and Louisiana under Louis XIV, for example, were dominated by a succession of government-organized companies. Their basic aim was to concentrate the trade and wealth of a colony in the hands of nationals of the state to which the colony belonged. Right down to 1763 non-French traders were rigorously excluded from Canada—an easier task, admittedly, than keeping them out of the French West Indies.

Much English colonization had also been conducted in the early seventeenth century by chartered monopoly companies, but by 1700 their help was not needed. This did not leave the trade of British colonies open to all comers. Between 1660 and 1696 a series of measures, collectively known as the Navigation Acts or the Acts of Trade, effectively confined the trade of British colonies with the outside world to ships that were British owned, built, or manned. In addition, all the most important articles of colonial production, such as sugar, cotton, tobacco, or naval stores were 'enumerated', which meant that they could only be exported directly to British territory. It is true that some regulations were framed to protect the colonies' European markets—for example tobacco would grow in England but was prohibited in order to benefit Virginia. But on the whole the mother country was far more concerned to restrict than to promote any colonial production that might rival her own. In the seventeenth century there was little sign of this, but as the colonies grew they began to produce many goods previously imported from Great Britain. Home producers saw this as a threat, and by 1750 they had persuaded parliament to restrict colonial production of woollens, hats, and hardware. The Molasses Act of 1733 tried to force the thirteen colonies to buy British West Indian sugar, even though it was dearer than French. In practice these measures were widely evaded owing to the inadequacy of the colonial bureaucracy, but their very existence rankled with the colonists. Attempts after 1763 to enforce economic controls on the empire more rigorously did much to provoke thoughts of independence.

Plantations

When the English and French first began to colonize the Americas, they had more success in the islands of the West Indies than on the mainland. In 1660 there were probably as many Englishmen in the West Indies as on the whole of the northern continent, and many more Frenchmen than in Canada. By 1700 this situation had completely changed. Mainland colonists now far outnumbered those of the Caribbean. The population of the Caribbean colonies of Europe had indeed continued to grow, but most of the increase was made up by the dramatic expansion in the number of black slaves that accompanied the triumph of sugar production.

In the early seventeenth century most of Europe's sugar had come from Brazil, where the techniques and organization of production that were to flourish in the next century were developed. The Portuguese found that sugar was most economically produced on large plantations with a well-regimented work-force of slaves. Many native Indians were enslaved at first, but their falling population made them difficult and expensive to find, so from early in the sixteenth century the Brazilian plantations were mostly being worked by blacks brought from Africa. Fifty thousand had been imported by 1600 and over half a million arrived over the next century. By their labours Brazilian sugar experienced a boom down to the 1670s. So lucrative did this trade seem that the English and French began to introduce sugar commercially to their West Indian islands from the 1630s onwards. Here, since the problem of labour was even more difficult, the Brazilian model of large plantations and an imported slave-labour force was rapidly adopted. Barbados, the first island to commit itself to sugar, had already reached its peak by 1660. An island notable a generation earlier for the number of its small proprietors, it had by then been largely consolidated into a few hundred big estates; by 1673 it was producing a quarter of the output of all Brazil. Between 1643 and 1680 its population of black slaves rose from 6,000 to 35,000, with so much of its surface area devoted to sugar that three-quarters of the food supply had to be imported. By 1680, too, Barbados was paying the price of monoculture in terms of soil exhaustion and rising costs; but the pattern it had set was to be repeated in most of the other Caribbean islands over the next century and a half.

The success of Barbados led other islands to introduce large-scale sugar production. But by now the demand in Europe was levelling off, with the result that by 1670 the market was oversupplied. Prices slumped and did not begin to recover until after 1690. Not until this recovery did the economy of sugar and slaves resume its spread across the Caribbean, but from then on expansion was almost constant. By 1730 Guadeloupe, Saint-Domingue (the western half of Hispaniola, won by France from Spain in 1697), and Jamaica had become major producers, the last two on such a scale that in the early 1730s prices briefly slumped again owing to oversupply. By 1740, however, demand had once more recovered, and continued to grow, interrupted only by colonial wars, until the 1790s. By 1780 Jamaica was almost totally given over to sugar and in Saint-Domingue coffee and indigo were also booming. From the 1760s even the Spaniards (who had never shown much interest in it before) began to plant sugar on a large scale in Cuba, the largest island, and by 1800 Cuban production was expanding faster than any other. So lucrative had the market become that plantations were being established in Mauritius and the Philippines, at the other side of the world. The figures for West Indian sugar production show the scale of the boom: in 1655 it stood at not much more than 7,000 tons per year. By 1767, excluding Cuba, this total had risen to 144,000 tons, and it went on rising until the 1790s. Small wonder that the European nations considered the sugar islands their richest assets and devoted much of their naval efforts in the mid-eighteenth-century wars to isolating or capturing those of their enemies. When the elder Pitt in 1763 denounced the return of Guadeloupe to France after the Seven Years War, he had many sympathizers. They would have preferred to return Canada, a much vaster but infinitely poorer territory.

The sugar islands were governed and managed according to the same principles as the mainland colonies. British islands had representative assemblies to manage their internal affairs; French islands were governed more autocratically by intendants. But they also had sovereign councils, the equivalent of French *parlements*, which served as supreme lawcourts and in effect represented the richest residents. Sugar colonies were subject to the whole range of commercial restrictions borne by others. They were forbidden to export their products directly to foreign territories or to import supplies from them. Such a system initially gave the British islands a clear advantage, in that they could import their supplies from North America, whereas the French had to supply themselves from distant Europe at far greater cost. By the early eighteenth century, however, the British islands were absorbing fewer supplies than the rapidly expanding economy of New England could produce, and thanks to soil exhaustion their sugar was more expensive and lower in quality than that of the still-expanding French islands. Increasingly, therefore, the New Englanders turned to supplying the French islands. Since their goods were cheaper than those brought from France, the colonists welcomed them. Both home governments tried to prevent these developments, but restrictions were widely evaded, especially in wartime when the French islands survived the severance of their links with France by the British fleet only through the supplies of interloping British colonists! When hostilities ended, it never proved possible to return to the pre-war pattern. Whilst the British government, in 1764, attempted to reinforce the laws restricting colonial trade with the French islands, the French experimented with limited access for interlopers. When the rebellious British colonists became their allies in 1778, they felt obliged to allow them free access. Amid loud protests from the western ports of France, the trade of the French West Indies was officially declared open in 1784.

These protests illustrate a further important feature of the economic network based on sugar—the bitter divisions between groups involved in it. Metropolitan merchants antagonized planters by their support for exclusive trade regulations. Planters antagonized merchants by evading the regulations, as well as by incurring large debts to the homeland which a shortage of coinage in the colonies made it impossible for them ever to clear. But even the colonists themselves were deeply divided. The richest West Indies proprietors were almost always absentees, spending their lavish revenues in Europe and neglecting the plantations which were their source, despised and often cheated by the white managers they left in the isles, who along with smaller resident proprietors felt they alone represented the islands' true interests. Yet these claims in their turn were contested by the growing numbers of mulattos. When, in 1787, the French West Indies received representative assemblies, the whites insisted on monopolizing them despite mulatto protests—especially in Saint-Domingue, where mulattos were almost as numerous as whites. Agitation over this issue, fanned by the political ferment that overtook France in the next few years, did much in its turn to arouse the unrest among black slaves which broke out in the great rebellion of 1791.

Black slavery was the basis of the West Indian economy; without it, sugar could not have been commercially produced and without its expansion the sugar boom could not have occurred. Around 1680 the slave population of the British West Indies was between 60,000 and 70,000; that of the French, about 21,000. A century later the British total had risen to around 400,000, and twice that number if we add the slaves in the new United States; that of the French was now well over half a million; that of the Spanish Caribbean was around 100,000; while that of Brazil had reached between 800,000 and 900,000. And since (with the exception of slaves in North America) this black population never succeeded in replacing itself naturally, much less expanding, it was maintained and increased only by a flourishing slave trade operating from the ports of Europe and North America. Naturally this trade expanded too. In the later seventeenth century 968,000 slaves were taken forcibly by Europeans from Africa and landed in the Americas. In the eighteenth century the number rose to 6,000,000, the greatest increase occurring between 1760 and 1790.

The oldest slaving nation, and still in the later eighteenth century second only to the British, were the Portuguese. They had pioneered the 'triangular trade', in which they sailed to the coasts of Africa and there exchanged fire-arms, drink, or tobacco for slaves. They then transported their human cargo to America (the notorious 'middle passage') and returned to Europe laden with tropical produce. When the Dutch, English, and French entered the slave trade in the seventeenth century they did so at first through monopoly companies—the Dutch West India Company, the English Royal African Company, the French Senegal Company. But company operations were largely ruined by the endless credit they were forced to extend to planters during the depression in sugar prices between 1670 and 1690, and by the early eighteenth century they had mostly disappeared, leaving the slave trade largely in private hands. Merchants dealing primarily in slaves were never very numerous, even in the most important slaving ports, such as Nantes, Liverpool, or Providence, Rhode Island. Nor did their profits ever constitute a large proportion of the total yield of the Atlantic colonial trade. Yet extravagant claims have often been made about the eighteenth-century slave trade. It has been alleged that it was fantastically profitable, and that these profits played a fundamental part in financing the British industrial revolution.[4] Abolitionist stories of the inhumanity and mortality of the middle passage have also been endlessly repeated, with enough concrete examples (like that of the 143 slaves jettisoned from the British slaver *Zong*, to save water, in 1781) to make them credible. But the profits realized by the British slave trade did not exceed 10 per cent in the later eighteenth century, and those of French and Dutch slavers were far less. Even if the total profits of British slaving had been invested in industrialization, they would not have amounted to more than 1·59 per cent of total industrial

---

[4] Eric Williams, *Capitalism and Slavery* (1944).

investment; and even the pioneering cotton industry, situated close to the main British slaving port of Liverpool, is unlikely to have derived more than 3·5 per cent of its capital investment from slaving profits. As to the middle passage, it is true that in the seventeenth century almost a quarter of slaves transported often died before arrival in America, but by the later eighteenth century the death-rate had fallen to between 8 and 10 per cent—a lower rate of mortality than among the crews transporting them. It was not in the slavers' interests to lose a large proportion of their valuable cargo. None of this is to minimize the immense human and economic consequences of the trade. Even if few slaves were actually captured by Europeans in Africa, most being bought from African warrior chiefs, the very presence of slavers and their permanent outposts along the coast sent severe shock waves deep into Africa. The transplantation of millions of blacks from one continent to another permanently changed the character of all the various societies established in America. And without the slave trade the whole sugar economy which boomed so spectacularly in the eighteenth century, and the prosperity that this boom brought to western European ports from Glasgow to Lisbon, could never have occurred. To this extent Europe's growing taste for tropical luxuries was gratified only at the expense of the black races of Africa.

The rapid growth of the slave population in the Americas left whites increasingly uneasy. Fears of slave uprisings haunted both the resident creoles (fearful for their lives) and absentee owners (worried about their revenues). Already by the 1730s the expansion of plantations in the larger islands was being hampered by the raids of 'maroons', or slaves who had escaped to the mountains. In Jamaica it took several years of full-scale war to put them down. Clashes between planters and maroons continued throughout the century, but not until the 1790s did the long-dreaded rebellion occur, and then it was in a French territory already torn by four years of conflict between whites and mulattos over who was to benefit most from the Revolution in Europe. But Saint-Domingue was the largest, richest, and most varied of Europe's sugar colonies and, apart from Cuba, the only one which had not yet reached the limits of expansion. Slaves outnumbered whites by ten to one, yet they were probably more harshly treated there than in many other islands. So that when, in response to a decree giving freeborn mulattos full civil rights, the whites began to arm and talk of independence, the slaves saw an opportunity to revenge themselves on a group who could no longer rely on support from Europe. In August 1791 an enormous and bloody uprising broke out, in which over 1,400 properties were ravaged and more than 1,000 whites massacred. At a blow the prosperity of Saint-Domingue was destroyed. The example, spreading to other islands, threatened to ruin them too. In 1795 there was another serious maroon rising in Jamaica. Nothing the French could do, not even a conditional emancipation of slaves proclaimed in 1792, nor a total, unconditional abolition of slavery in 1794, was able to restore the situation. Nor was an Anglo-Spanish invasion after the outbreak of war with France in 1793 any more effective. By 1800 some semblance of order had been restored by the former slave Toussaint L'Ouverture, who had defeated the British and announced his loyalty to revolutionary France, while at the same time proclaiming himself governor-general of life of a virtually independent black-ruled Saint Domingue. But the old prosperity was gone. Martinique was still in French hands, but cut off by British fleets from contact with Europe. The British had captured the other French islands, although at a cost of nearly 70,000 men, most of whom perished through disease. But they had cornerd the market for re-exporting sugar to the European mainland, which they had lost to the French in the 1730s. The British sugar islands looked set in the mid-1780s for a rapid decline in the face of French competition and the loss of North American markets; the collapse of the French Caribbean empire gave them a new lease of life, so that in 1800 the West Indies trade accounted for a larger sector of British commerce than ever before. As a result, despite a growing chorus of criticism from abolitionists, the slave trade continued to flourish. The awful example of Saint-Domingue, far from strengthening the abolitionists' case, convinced much uncommitted opinion that it was folly to allow any freedom to black savages. As in so many other fields, the events of the French Revolution postponed liberal reforms for at least a generation.

Counters and Factories

Not all European expansion overseas took the form of founding colonies or establishing plantations. Only if there was no alternative did Europeans set out to conquer and rule overseas territories. Otherwise, as in the case of the slave coasts of west Africa, they were content merely to set up forti- fied trading posts, usually known as 'counters' or 'factories'. The classic region of trading posts was east of the Cape of Good Hope. Here, in 1660, the European presence was largely a trading presence. The Portuguese, who had first opened the Cape route to India, held a coastal principality stretching for 100 miles north of Goa; the Spaniards claimed the Philippines, the French held Mauritius and Reunion,[5] and the Dutch were laying claim to large stretches of western Java. Yet most of the Dutch domination of the East Indies, the tightest commercial monopoly east of the Cape, was achieved through a mere string of trading posts stretching from the Bay of Bengal to the Moluccas. The English, who earlier in the century had tried to dispute this control, were left only with toeholds on the Indian subcontinent at Madras and (from 1662) at Bombay. Nobody dreamed of colonizing or sub- jecting these eastern shores. Even as late as 1767, the secretary of the British East India Company could declare that: 'We don't want conquest and power; it is commercial interest only we look for.'[6] By then, however, the difficulties of this doctrine were already overwhelming. There was no way in which trade and power could long be kept apart.

Originally Europeans had gone to the east in search of pepper and spices—

---

[5] Then called, respectively, the Île de France and the Île Bourbon.
[6] Quoted in P. J. Marshall, *Problems of Empire: Britain and India 1757–1813* (1968), 17.

goods which remained the mainstay of Dutch eastern trade until, late in the eighteenth century, coffee planting was established in Java. The Dutch periodically made attempts to establish a complete monopoly in spices, but their competitors (European or local) always managed to find sources beyond Dutch control. In any case, by 1700 spices had been ousted from first place among Asian exports to Europe by cotton and cloth, mostly made on the Indian subcontinent. India was the most important region of European expansion in the east in the eighteenth century, not only on account of its cottons, but also for its saltpetre (an essential ingredient of gunpowder) and silks. To tap these commodities new European factories were established —by the French at Pondicherry in 1674, and by the English at Calcutta in 1686. But it was not only through the exports of India that these outposts flourished and grew rich over the next century. Originally established for the 'Europe trade', they rapidly became involved in the 'country trade' of local traffic. So Europeans also became Asian traders, plying between Asian ports, and only their profits reached Europe. Finally, a growing proportion of the trade of factories around the Indian Ocean consisted in re-exporting to Europe goods bought further east, in Japan and China. Ever since 1640 Japanese trade had been officially closed to Europeans, except for a small Dutch post which dispatched only two cargoes a year. In 1660 China was not open, except to the Portuguese established at Macao. But in 1684 foreign traders were allowed to establish themselves in a compound outside Canton, which during the next few decades became a flourishing entrepôt for all European trade with China. The basic commodity was tea, most of which went to England and British North America. Between 1730 and 1785 tea exports from Canton rose by over 600 per cent; beside them silk and porcelain, the other principal Chinese exports, were of very limited value. Much of this trade reached Europe only via factories further west; when the Dutch attempted to corner the Canton tea trade in the 1730s by direct trading, they soon found the cost prohibitive.

Except for the country trade, activity in the eastern seas was nowhere in private hands. The trade of Portugal operated under the same system as that of Brazil—concentrated into two or three annual, state-organized shipments. The Spaniards sent an annual galleon across the Pacific between Manila and Mexico, again under government supervision. But Dutch, English, and French activity (and that of lesser powers with eastern interests, such as Denmark) was organized by chartered monopoly trading companies—bodies which seldom flourished in the Atlantic trade but were only too successful further east. The Dutch East India Company, formed in 1602 from an amalgam of smaller bodies, was a national institution, in which each of the United Provinces provided capital and shared dividends. Its directors (the 'XVII Heeren') were elected by nominees of the various provincial governments, but shares in the company were open to all; its fortunes were a barometer of the whole commercial life of the Republic. The English company, founded in 1600, was by contrast mainly the affair of a handful of London merchants. Few objected to this in the company's early years, during which it fought a losing battle against the Dutch for a share in the spice trade. But when, after 1660, trade with India began to show worthwhile profits, the company's monopoly came under attack. In 1698 a rival company was chartered and a decade of enervating competition followed until the two joined forces in 1709 to monopolize eastern trade once more. By the 1720s the company was the country's largest trading organization and perhaps its greatest single employer outside the armed forces. It also enjoyed extensive influence in politics. Such assured power contrasted vividly with the French company, established in 1664 with royal support, but undercapitalized and over-regulated from the start. It founded Pondicherry, but was constantly being urged into non-commercial ventures, such as the fruitless colonization of Madagascar. By 1706 it had ceased to send ships to the east and was licensing private traders, and in 1720 it was almost destroyed in the collapse of Law's 'system', into which it had been incorporated. Not until after 1730 did the French company, freer now of government interference, begin to show a profit, and its port at Lorient to prosper.

The main problem facing the European East India companies, as their business grew and their trading networks became ever more complex and extensive, was how to control their own agents at two or three times the distance of the Americas, when it took months or even years to make contact with them. From the start the ambitions of the companies and their servants diverged. The companies sought reliable dividends for their shareholders; their servants went east to make their own fortunes. They were paid so little that the temptation to make money at the expense of both the natives and their employers was irresistible. The British company allowed its servants to invest in country trade, well aware that in addition to satisfying their desire to enrich themselves, the country trade brought to the company's factories local goods that could be used to pay for Indian and Chinese exports instead of silver. The Dutch company tried to monopolize country trade in its own hands, with the result that it was cheated and ignored by its own employees on a vast scale. Even more seriously, company employees in the east often took unilateral decisions to intervene in local politics without first consulting their European masters. Between 1619 and 1677 the Dutch company gradually came to be the only effective political authority in Java, mainly thanks to a ruthless acceptance by Dutch governors on the spot of every opportunity to acquire influence by exploiting the power struggle between native princes—and each time in express defiance of the 'XVII Heeren'. In the 1690s Job Charnock, founder of Calcutta, declared war in the English company's name on the Mughal emperor himself; and when this emperor, the ferocious Aurangzeb, died in 1707, an era of chaos began in Indian politics in which the agents of the European companies could not fail to become involved. Central authority collapsed and in 1729 a Persian army sacked Delhi. Throughout the sub-continent local princes fell to feuding between themselves, and some turned to the Europeans for allies.

Until the 1740s the Europeans in India had tried not to become involved in the conflicts of their mother-states; but when Great Britain and France

went to war in 1744 the British refused a non-aggression agreement offered
by Dupleix, the governor of Pondicherry. In the fighting that followed
Indian princes were impressed by the qualities of the troops of the rival
European companies; and in subsequent years Dupleix exploited their interest
by offering French troops as mercenaries. In payment, Dupleix began to
accept gifts of territory and revenues—a policy his superiors in Paris encouraged
until, in 1752, he began to be defeated by British forces playing a similar
role. So that when the Seven Years War broke out officially in 1756, the
European trading rivals in India were already in conflict, each backed by a
network of Indian allies. The most formidable friend of the French was
Suraj-ud-Dowlah, nawab of Bengal, who captured the British base of Calcutta
and exterminated most of his prisoners in the notorious 'black hole'. The
Company sent Robert Clive from Madras to recover Calcutta, and in 1757
he was able to rout Suraj-ud-Dowlah at Plassey. A determined effort by the
French to regain the military initiative with reinforcements from Europe was
held off, and one by one all the French factories fell. They received them
back at the peace in 1763, but were not allowed to fortify them. From
now on India was a British sphere of influence, into which other European
powers were allowed only on suffrance. A spectacular naval campaign fought
in the Indian Ocean by the French in the subsequent war (1778—83), though
it coincided with a burst of Indian resistance to ever-growing British power,
proved unable to restore the French position.

In times of open war the efforts that had brought the British to supremacy
were supported by the government's naval strength. The fact remains, however, that most of the fighting had been done by servants of the East India
Company, against the Company's known policy, and often in defiance of its
express instructions. After Plassey Clive deposed Suraj-ud-Dowlah and established a puppet regime; the Company found itself the controlling power in
Bengal. Then in 1765 Clive undertook, on the Company's behalf, to collect
diwani, or imperial revenues, in Bengal, thus assuming direct civil authority in
India's richest province. Meanwhile public attention had been drawn to
Indian questions by the increasing number of 'nabobs' returning from India
fabulously enriched, who used their wealth to buy influence, often in the
controlling circles of the Company itself. By demanding the payment of
exorbitant dividends, they had forced it into financial difficulties by the late
1760s, difficulties aggravated by governmental demands for a share in the
very uncertain *diwani* profits. Since the Company could meet its obligations
only by borrowing, by the time of the Europe-wide credit crisis of the early
1770s it was facing bankruptcy. No government could willingly allow so
important a body to collapse. A subsidy was arranged—but at a price. A
Regulating Act of 1772 made the supreme authorities in British India the
nominees of government rather than of the Company, and a further Act of
1784 placed the direction of Indian affairs from London in the hands of a
board of control which was in effect a committee of the Privy Council.
By the end of the century the British government had assumed political
responsibility for substantial tracts of the Indian sub-continent, and the

Company, after a brief and unhappy spell of temporal power, was once more left a primarily commercial concern—although it continued to supply most of the personnel by whom British India was to be governed.

The British government did not willingly assume territorial power in India. By the time the 1784 Act took effect, Great Britain had just lost most of its empire in North America, and was reluctant to risk repeating such a humiliation. Shelburne's declaration in 1782, 'We prefer trade to dominion',[7] remained the keynote of most European activity east of the Cape. Most of the exploration of the Pacific which marked the latter half of the eighteenth century was sponsored by the governments of rival states with a view to finding new trading outlets or establishing outposts that would strengthen existing trade-routes. The achievement of a navigator such as Cook was remarkable— between 1764 and 1779 he explored several groups of Pacific islands, circum-navigated New Zealand, mapped the east coast of Australia for the first time, proved that there was no lost continent between these lands and Cape Horn, and explored the coasts of Alaska in a fruitless search for a northern passage to the Atlantic. But none of this brought the immediate commercial benefits that were hoped for. Australia was poor and empty; the only use the British could find for it was as a depository, from 1788 onwards, for trans-ported convicts. For years to come the Pacific islands would remain little more than staging posts for whaling expeditions. The China trade was the great success story of the century's last decades; by the 1790s it had become the main commercial concern of the East India Company, while India proper became largely a staging post. But when, in 1792 and 1794, the British and Dutch respectively sent missions to China with instructions to negotiate an opening of the trade of that great empire beyond the narrow confines of Canton, they were rebuffed. So the greatest European activity in eastern seas in the later eighteenth century took place in areas where it was already well established before the attempts to find new outlets. And it was at its most spectacular in those regions—India and Java—in which dominion as well as trade characterized the European presence.

Patterns of Trade

Overseas expansion was not new in European history in 1660, but that date marked the end of one phase and the beginning of another. The old overseas empires had been created by Spain and Portugal, their commercial value founded on a few commodities that Europe was unable to supply for her-self—bullion and spices. The new empires arising after 1660 were the creation of the maritime nations of the north—the Dutch republic, England, and France—and were founded on the supply of a far more varied range of goods; on sugar, coffee, and tea, on cottons and silks, on saltpetre, tobacco, dye-stuffs, and tropical woods, as well as on new sources for spices and bullion. The new empires had a far broader economic base than the old and the range

[7] Quoted in V. T. Harlow, *The Founding of the Second British Empire 1763–93* (1952), i. 6.

of their products revolutionized European trade, to lift it out of the stagnation into which it had fallen in the mid-seventeenth century. Over-all figures for European trade do not yet exist, but those of the individual states make the general drift more than clear.

In 1660 the dominant trading nation in Europe was the Dutch republic. During the first half of the century the cheap and capacious *fluits* of the Dutch sailors had made them Europe's carriers, and by 1670 they had more merchant ships than all their main rivals combined. Already, however, the original foundation of Dutch commercial prosperity, the Baltic trade, had gone into a recession; and when in the eighteenth century it recovered, stronger rivals prevented the maintenance of the near-monopoly the Dutch had enjoyed in earlier days. The years between 1650 and 1670 also brought signs of determination by England and France to diminish the Dutch share of their own trade, in the form of the Navigation Acts and Colbert's tariffs against Dutch imports. Finally, from 1672 until 1713 the Dutch were involved in three enormously expensive wars against France, whose cost was crushing taxation and commercial disruption. As a result, by 1720 Dutch trade had ceased to expand, accounting from then on for a shrinking proportion of European commerce as a whole. With her East Indies spice and coffee empire, her West Indies bases in St. Eustatius and Guiana, and her important role in the slave trade, the Republic remained in the first rank of Europe's overseas trade, far outstripping the puny efforts of Austria, Prussia, or the Scandinavian states. She remained the important local carrier she had been a century before: in 1785 over two-thirds of her trade was still European. Nevertheless by then she had been left far behind by France and Great Britain.

French trade undoubtedly benefited from the aggressive attitude of Louis XIV's government towards Dutch competition. By 1690, with the exception of Baltic traffic, most French commerce was being carried in French, not Dutch, ships—including that of the colonial sector, which leaped forward in the thirty years after 1660. The quarter-century of wars from 1689 onwards brought expansion to an end, but it resumed spectacularly with the Regency. Between then and the Revolution, French trade as a whole grew fivefold, the European sector fourfold, and the colonial sector tenfold— a rate of expansion not matched by any other country. Exports of native products trebled, playing a far greater role in French trade than in Dutch. French agriculture sent considerable supplies to the West Indies and French wines supplied the whole of Europe, with the notable exception of England. French manufactures meanwhile dominated Mediterranean markets and, through re-export from Spain, much of Latin America. Nevertheless the most striking sector of both Dutch and French trade was colonial re-exports. In 1783 it was estimated that over three-quarters of Dutch imports from Asia were re-exported directly to other European countries. And at Bordeaux, a port which in 1782 handled a quarter of all French overseas trade, three-quarters of sugar imports and four-fifths of coffee imports were re-exported. French colonial re-exports increased eightfold over the eighteenth century; by 1730 the French had driven the British out of the European market for many such commodities by undercutting their prices.

This was ominous; for British trade, too, had been revolutionized by the colonial link in the latter half of the seventeenth century. Earlier, the major element in English trade had been the export of woollens, much of it handled by the Dutch. By 1700 the Navigation Acts had driven the Dutch out of English harbours, not to mention those of English colonies; and the woollen trade, although it had expanded, had been overtaken by other sectors. By this time, one-third of all goods sent out of England consisted of re-exported West Indies sugar, Virginian tobacco, and Indian cottons. Thus far English development ran parallel to that of France, although even now the volume of English trade was much higher. The next thirty years saw the French win the battle for the European re-export markets, with their cheaper sugar and coffee; while tariff walls went up against Indian cottons at the demand of woollen producers in most countries. As a result, British re-exports, already a third of all exports in 1700, had only risen to 40 per cent by 1750, and to 55 per cent by 1790. Yet British overseas trade as a whole continued to expand: between 1716 and 1788 it grew almost two and a half times. This was made possible by yet another change in the character of British trade, which by the later eighteenth century had made it quite different from that of any other country—the growth of colonial markets for British manufactures.

One such market was the Portuguese empire, first opened to the British by the Methuen treaty of 1703, at the very moment when the first Brazilian gold discoveries were beginning to reach Europe. Port wine now supplanted claret on British tables, and much of the gold pouring out of Brazil over the next half-century found its way to the British Isles. In return, British-produced foodstuffs and textiles dominated the Portuguese market, and from there that of Brazil. 'The trade of the English at Lisbon', noted a French merchant in 1730, 'is the most important of all; according to many people, it is as great as that of all the other nations put together.'[8] Between 1700 and 1760 Portugal took between 9 and 12 per cent of British exports, and between 1731 and 1745, 18 per cent of British exported manufactures went there. This trade played an important role in helping Britain to readjust its commerce in the face of French competition, and by the time it began to decline, after 1760, an even larger market had appeared in the form of the thirteen North American colonies. This was the result of the colonies' phenomenal population growth within a system which kept out foreign competitors; by 1776 the colonies had a third as many inhabitants as England itself and the high wages paid there gave the colonists impressive purchasing power. By mid-century they were beginning to develop some of their own industries, but it was to be several generations more before they ceased to depend on imports of cloth and metal goods. Meanwhile their expansion brought fundamental changes to the pattern of British trade. Whereas the proportion of British exports to Europe fell from 71 per cent to 51 per cent between 1701 and

[8]   Quoted in C. R. Boxer, *The Portuguese Seaborne Empire, 1415–1825* (1969), 169.

1790, exports to America rose from just over 6 per cent to 30 per cent. And cheap North American supplies of rice and indigo had, by the 1770s, begun once more to boost the level of colonial re-exports to Europe. Nor were the British unaware of the increasing commercial importance of their North American colonies; this knowledge underlay their conviction that if the colonies succeeded in the struggle for independence in the 1770s, British prosperity would be ruined. The period of the war brought severe difficulties for British trade, but once peace was made, against all orthodox expectations, North American trade rapidly recovered. With the establishment of large-scale cotton growing in the southern states the link became even closer, because it was from here that the factories of Lancashire drew their raw material. In 1800 this was still largely in the future, but already British trade had embarked on the steep and spectacular rise that accompanied the emergence of modern industry. In the twenty years following the American war it almost doubled in value, while that of France, decelerating since 1770, was devastated by the commercial disaster of the Revolution. In laying the foundations for these developments, colonies had played a crucial part. They had enormously expanded the scale, expertise, and capacity of European trade, an essential precondition for the marketing of industrial products. And they had begun at last to be markets for European goods as well as providing raw materials, which helped to boost Europe (or parts of it) into the role of producer to the world as well as consumer.

None of these developments proceeded as smoothly as a long-term view seems to suggest. At crucial points trade was disrupted or redirected brutally by extraneous factors, notably by war and changes in the tariff policy of various states. Usually in imposing tariffs, embargoes, blockades, or even declaring war, governments had clear economic aims. They were hoping to strengthen their own economies at the expense of their rivals. This was entirely in the logic of the economic orthodoxies of the day, which historians loosely label Mercantilism.

Mercantilism, Empire, and their Enemies

Neither the term 'mercantilism', nor any like it, was known to contemporaries before French economists, and later Adam Smith, began to attack what they called the 'mercantile system' in the later eighteenth century. But from that time onwards the term was adopted by historians to describe the principles that appeared to guide the economic policies of states in the seventeenth and eighteenth centuries. Agreement on using the term has not prevented disagreement about its precise significance, yet mercantilism remains the most convenient label for the habits, principles, and outlook according to which early modern states sought to manage their economies.

Mercantilism meant the taking of positive steps by states to increase the wealth of their subjects. Economic matters were too serious to be left to take their natural course; governments felt obliged to intervene in order to maximize their own state's share of available wealth. But what was wealth? To men of the time, the answer was obvious. Wealth was 'treasure', gold and silver bullion. The aim of economic policy was to augment a state's stock of precious metals by promoting their inflow and limiting their outflow. 'The ordinary means', wrote Thomas Mun, in the classic English mercantilist tract, printed in 1664,[9] '... to encrease our wealth and treasure is by *Forraign Trade*, wherein wee must ever observe this rule; to sell more to strangers than wee consume of theirs in value.' It was this emphasis on attaining a favourable balance of trade that made later critics label the system 'mercantile'. There were several important corollaries; the most obvious was that exports should be encouraged by all means—exports of finished goods rather than of raw materials, so that foreigners should derive no profit from them that did not accrue to the original producer. Consequently mercantilists took little interest in agriculture. Few people foresaw in the seventeenth century how dramatically agricultural productivity might be improved in the right circumstances; even if they had, they would have declared agricultural produce part of a country's natural stock, to be devoted to feeding and augmenting its population, rather than that of other countries. The true energies of the state, meanwhile, should be devoted to encouraging manufactures. The aim was to supply all domestic needs while at the same time exporting as much as possible to other countries. Foreign imports were discouraged by high protective tariffs and attempts were even made to exclude foreigners from transporting and marketing exported manufactures. This was the spirit of English and French measures against the Dutch between 1660 and 1700. As Colbert put it: 'Inasmuch as we can diminish the gains which the Dutch make from the king's subjects and consumption of the goods which they bring us, by that much will we increase the money which should flow into the kingdom by means of our necessary commodities, and by that much will we increase the power, the greatness and the abundance of the state.'[10] Mercantilism, then, was an intensely competitive outlook. One state's gain was another state's loss. War was merely economic policy pursued by other means, a natural and often positively desirable instrument for promoting a state's prosperity and diminishing that of rivals.

An ideal mercantilist state would be totally self-sufficient, needing nothing it could not itself supply. Accordingly, statesmen were always looking for new sources of wealth in which they could establish a monopoly or at least a share. Once, therefore, colonization and trans-oceanic trade had revealed their potential, governments became concerned to control and regulate them in the state's best interests—to establish a foothold in all the varying fields of overseas operation and to confine the benefits of their own colonies, plantations, and trading posts to their own nationals. This was the logic behind the British Acts of Trade which constricted the economic freedom of the American colonies, behind the Dutch East Indies spice monopoly, and behind the 'exclusive' principle which confined the trade of the French

[9] *England's Treasure by Forraign Trade, or, the Ballance of our Forraign Trade is the Rule of our Treasure* (repr. 1928), 5. The work was originally written in the 1620s.
[10] Quoted in P. Deyon, *Le Mercantilisme* (1969), 100.

West Indies to French ports. There was no conception of colonies as entities in their own right; they existed solely for the benefit of the mother country. They should be peopled as far as possible not by the state's able-bodied subjects, but by criminals, beggars, slaves, religious dissenters, or foreigners. The benefits that colonists derived from the imperial connection, such as guaranteed European markets for their raw materials and protection of their trade by the powerful navies which were another consequence of overseas competition, were purely incidental.

These principles and assumptions, first elaborated into a system by England and France in their envy of Dutch commercial predominance, were being adopted by most states by 1700. In Germany and eastern Europe measures that can be called mercantilist were still being introduced by rulers such as Frederick II or Joseph II long after the thinking on which they were based had come under attack in the west. Indeed, the failures of German mercantilism were often pointed to by critics as proof of their case. The trading companies and manufacturing industries founded by German governments either rapidly collapsed or were only sustained by high protective tariffs or lavish subsidies, diverting resources which might have been more fruitfully invested elsewhere. Yet most historians now believe that the eighteenth-century critics of mercantilism, and the nineteenth-century historians who accepted their case, overstated it. On occasion, protective policies did foster permanent economic growth. The commerce of France and England was permanently stimulated by the protective measures of the later seventeenth century. French textile production and metallurgy certainly benefited from Colbert's paternalism and protection. British economic growth in the eighteenth century derived enormous stimulus from exclusive guaranteed markets in Ireland and the thirteen colonies. When the time came for industrial 'take-off', mercantilist restrictions might well have been a hindrance rather than a help; but in establishing the preconditions, protective state policy had played an essential part.

Mercantilism was never without its critics. Colbert was scarcely dead when a group of French writers began to denounce his policies as the source of the ruin and misery that coincided with Louis XIV's last two great wars. Merchants lamented that they were not free to buy in the cheapest markets; clerics denounced the warlike implications of Colbert's policies and the immorality of the taste for luxury fostered by his emphasis on manufactures; while discontented noblemen pointed out the rural misery brought about by the neglect of agriculture. By interfering with the natural course of economic life, they all implied, the state had brought disaster upon itself. 'Nature alone', wrote Boisguilbert, the most distinguished of these critics,[11] '. . .can keep order and maintain peace; all other authority spoils everything when it mixes in affairs, however well-intentioned it may be. . .[Nature's] first intention is for all men to live comfortably by their labour, or by the labour of their ancestors. . .' In England meanwhile writers such as Child, North, and Davenant

[11] *Dissertation sur la nature des richesses*, quoted in Rothkrug, *Opposition to Louis XIV*, 362.

denounced retaliatory tariffs against foreign competitors as misconceived attempts to maintain a favourable balance of trade. They did not yet go so far as to claim that a balance was not essential; but to procure it, there was no need for a favourable balance with every other state. This argument pointed away from protectionism towards free exchange.

But it was not until half a century later that full-scale alternatives to mercantilism began to be suggested. Just as mercantilism was the product of the depressed conditions of the seventeenth century, when resources seemed limited and economic life sluggish, so when expansion resumed, more optimistic, liberal doctrines began to appear. As in so many fields, Hume took the lead in exposing the hollowness of the orthodoxies of his time. Among his *Essays* (1741–2) were discussions of trade which demolished the intellectual foundations of mercantilism. The true wealth of a country, he pointed out, lay in its people and in its industry, not in its stock of precious metals; besides, the recent expansion of credit had made precious metals less necessary. Tariff wars and protectionism benefited nobody, for all trade was beneficial in stimulating economic activity; therefore all restrictions were harmful. Meanwhile, in France, the physiocrats sought to stand mercantilism on its head. According to them, the true basis of all wealth was not precious metals, not manufactures, but land and agriculture. The sure way to enrich a country was to stimulate its agricultural productivity by eliminating as many as possible of the obstacles to what they (following their predecessors under Louis XIV) called the natural economic order. In a word this meant free trade. Free trade would raise the price of goods, higher prices would stimulate productivity, and so in the long run produce abundance. Accordingly, physiocrats advocated the abolition of controls on the grain trade and of internal customs barriers, the end of all economic monopolies and privileges, and the diminution of burdens on agriculture. Next to agriculture, trade and manufactures were secondary activities, incapable of increasing wealth if agriculture did not provide a basis; to attempt to stimulate either in isolation, therefore, was a waste of time. The physiocrats—Gournay, Quesnay, Mirabeau, Turgot, Mercier de la Rivière, Dupont de Nemours—were a tightly organized group of propagandists. Between about 1750 and the mid-1770s they used all the techniques of publicity to spread their views. They wrote articles, published a journal, the *Citizen's Ephemerides*, and substantial volumes such as Quesnay's *Theory of Taxation* (1761), Mirabeau's *Friend of Mankind* (1756), or Dupont de Nemours' *Physiocracy* (1768). For a brief period (1774–6) Turgot was actually in charge of the French finances. Consequently the physiocrats had some success in getting their views implemented. But they also provoked considerable opposition, so that changes of ministry often brought the abandonment of physiocratic measures before they had time to take effect. Besides, it was hardly enough simply to reverse the priorities of mercantilism. To decry the importance of commerce and manufactures was in fact to turn away from the road to future economic advances. It was one of the merits of Adam Smith to see this.

Smith, a Glasgow professor, was already a well-known philosopher when his *Inquiry into the Nature and Causes of the Wealth of Nations* was published in 1776. In the early 1760s he had visited France and met the physiocrats at the height of their influence. He shared many of their beliefs, although the basic principle of his thinking was quite different. The true basis of wealth, for Smith, was labour, and the way to increase it was through the division of labour. From the outset he ignored the question of money and the debate over the respective value of manufactures or agriculture. Everything depended not on the type of activity, but on the labour expended in it. The aim of economic policy should be to deploy labour where it was most productive— and like Hume and the physiocrats Smith believed that nature herself would bring this about, provided that her processes were not interfered with. The 'mercantile system', in his view, was just such an interference, pressed upon governments by the greed of merchants, who sought the profits of monopoly at the expense of their countrymen. Smith argued that, far from promoting the wealth of nations that had adopted them, the restrictions of the 'mercantile system' had positively damaged it. To arguments that British prosperity had been founded upon such measures as the Navigation Acts, Smith countered that it had come about in spite of them, and would have been even greater without them.

Even the regulations by which each nation endeavours to secure to itself the exclusive trade of its own colonies are frequently more hurtful to the countries in favour of which they are established, than to those against which they are established. The unjust oppression of the industry of other countries falls back, if I may say so, upon the heads of the oppressors, and crushes their industry more than it does those of other countries. [12]

In these terms Smith condemned the whole principle and apparatus of overseas empires; nor was he unaware that he did so at a time when the authority of Great Britain over her North American colonies was in dispute. In his view the mother country derived nothing but loss from these colonies as they were then managed. The ideal solution would be an amicable separation. This separation came in the very year of Smith's publication, and although it was far from amicable, it put his arguments at once to the test. Peace was made in 1783 in a bitter spirit, with the new nation excluded from the British market by a tariff wall. Yet despite this, Anglo-American trade soon resumed and then began to grow rapidly. By the time he died in 1790, Smith appeared to have been proved right.

The *Wealth of Nations* stood at the crossroads of European thought on overseas expansion, but it was by no means the first work to question the whole principle. In England the scattered pamphlets of Josiah Tucker had been proclaiming many of the same ideas since before the Seven Years War. Colonies were a useless drain, mercantilism a misconceived system. A separation between Great Britain and her colonies would benefit both sides. Tucker lived to see this separation and the vindication of his arguments. So did the leading French anti-colonialist, the abbé Raynal, whose *History of the Two Indies*,[13] first published in 1770 and constantly revised in the light

---

[12] *Wealth of Nations*, Bk. IV, ch. 7, part III.
[13] Its familiar title. See above, p. 47, n.1.

of events down to 1789, was one of the most widely read and influential books of the century. Many hands besides Raynal's co-operated in its writing, including that of Diderot. The range of its information on the overseas activities of Europeans made it an essential work of reference. But at the same time it was an open and sustained attack on everything the Europeans had done. The merchants of Europe had enriched themselves at the expense of the rest of the world; the European impact had been catastrophic, bringing disease, enslavement, and oppression. The supreme proof of Chinese wisdom was their resolute exclusion of Europeans. As to colonies, independence was their destiny, and Raynal urged the European states to renounce them before they themselves were renounced.

On this question, events were on the critics' side. Other aspects of overseas activity, however, showed no signs of breaking down. The British grip on India grew steadily tighter. Loud denunciations of the cruel and ruthless methods by which the servants of the East India Company enriched themselves, a chorus which went on from around 1760 until the impeachment of the governor-general Warren Hastings between 1788 and 1795, led to less rapacious government; but only through a strengthening of direct state control. Slavery continued to expand unchecked, despite a swelling volume of condemnation from all sides. Almost every major figure of the Enlightenment (with the curious exception of Hume) condemned slavery as the very negation of natural justice. To this principled objection Raynal added a prudential one—that sooner or later there would be massive and bloody slave uprisings. More weighty still, Smith denied that slavery was profitable. The most powerful anti-slavery impulse, however, came from the evangelical convictions of a number of devout Christians who believed in the equality of all men in the sight of God. Such a man was Granville Sharp, who in 1772 brought an action in the British courts against a master who had recaptured a runaway slave called Somerset in England. Somerset was freed; and although, contrary to a widespread belief, this decision did not automatically free all slaves residing in England,[14] it did lead to a prolonged debate on the ethics of slavery, culminating in the formation in 1787 of the London Abolition Committee, whose aim was to campaign for the abolition of the British slave trade. The next year the Society of the Friends of the Blacks was founded in France to pursue similar aims. Both societies encountered bitter opposition from West Indian planter interests, yet in England at least by the early 1790s the prospects for abolishing the slave trade began to look promising. But news of the slave rising in Saint-Domingue dashed these hopes for another fifteen years.

Despite a growing volume of criticism directed at all aspects of European activity overseas and the economic outlook that lay behind it, they were far from discredited by 1800. Some statesmen were now pondering doubts over the wisdom of colonization, but no sooner had these ideas taken root than Malthus's gloomy forecasts of overpopulation, published in

[14] See J. Walvin, *Black and White; the Negro in English Society, 1555–1945* (1973), 121–9.

1798,[15] began to point to a new use for colonies. Everybody had by now read Adam Smith, but many remained unconvinced that free trade and peace would bring universal blessings. Indeed, the wars of the French Revolution were to bring economic warfare of a scale and intensity that made previous outbreaks seem mild; and they brought worldwide gains and rewards to Great Britain which seemed to vindicate all that the fiercest mercantilists had ever advocated.

[15] T. R. Malthus, *Essay on the Principles of Population as it affects the future Improvement of Society.*

SOCIETY

4. Ruling Orders

European society was largely dominated by rich, hereditary, landed oligarchies. Most of the members of these groups also enjoyed nobility. Human society has never existed without élites, but those of the post-industrial world are numerous, diverse, and difficult to assess in their relative importance. Before 1800 matters were much simpler. Most wealth, most power, most privilege, and most prestige tended nearly everywhere to be concentrated in the hands of a single social group, universally recognizable. Like all social categories, it was considerably blurred at the edges, with an infinite number of local variations. No one term used by historians—aristocracy, landed interest, privileged order, feudal class—captures its full character. Yet the reality was concrete enough. It was the basic feature of social organization throughout Europe.

Nobility

Every state in Europe except certain Swiss cantons recognized the existence of a nobility, a social group enjoying some form of legally established hereditary superiority. The French revolutionaries subsequently attacked this principle. Consequently the doomed nobility of France may be taken as a classic example.

The French state was held to comprise three orders or estates:—the clergy, the nobility, and the third estate. This division originated in the medieval organization of society into those who prayed, those who fought, and those who worked. The nobility had done the fighting—noblemen still regarded the military career as peculiarly their own. Nevertheless in practice the nobility seldom invoked any justification other than the fact that it existed and always had. When the estates-general, representing all the king's subjects, met, the nobility and clergy elected their own representatives and sat in separate houses. The nobility had a complex internal hierarchy of titles. At the top came the princes of the blood royal and (in 1775) forty-seven dukes and peers; together they made up the peerage, the élite among the élite. Below them came ever more numerous categories of marquises, counts, viscounts, barons, knights, and esquires without further distinctive title. All nobles enjoyed a number of privileges. They took special precedence on public occasions, carried swords, boasted distinctive coats of arms, received special treatment in the courts, and above all benefited from certain fiscal advantages. They were personally exempt from the *taille*, the basic tax, although in certain areas they often paid it on the basis of their landed possessions. They contributed to a number of other taxes at special rates. They were indeed subjected to various new taxes introduced from 1695 onwards, but *taille* exemption remained an essential touchstone of noble status. Equally essential was a certain lifestyle—'living nobly' without manual work (which included retail trade). Those who broke the rule underwent derogation, or loss of nobility, which might entail the degradation of the offender's whole family, since noble status was transmitted through the male line to all children.

Organization of the nobility into an order was common throughout Europe. In Sweden, much of Germany and most of the Habsburg domains the nobility was represented in a separate house of the diet or estates of the realm. In Hungary and Poland they alone were represented. In Spain the nobility was an order with clearly defined limits and prerogatives; while in the Italian mercantile republics of Venice and Genoa noble families had their names entered in special public 'Golden Books'. Equally common was the principle of hierarchy within the order. Scales of titles were universal, except in Poland. In Hungary the diet was divided between an upper house of magnates sitting in person and a lower consisting of representatives of the lesser nobility. The Emperor Charles V had organized the Spanish nobility into a small élite of grandees (of whom there were 113 in 1707), a larger body of titled nobles, and an enormous army of proud but untitled gentlemen—the notorious *hidalgos*, a category drawn so widely as to include every male inhabitant of certain Basque provinces.

The privileges enjoyed by noblemen varied immensely, although social precedence, sword-bearing, coats of arms, and special standing at law were universal. In Poland and Hungary the nobles regarded themselves (with greater justification in Hungary) as descendants of a conquering race. In most countries there were special schools for the sons of noblemen to be educated apart, such as the Spanish *colegios mayores*, or the state-service training colleges established by Peter I in Russia. Even where these did not exist, in practice nobles were predominant in such prestigious institutions as the Collège Louis le Grand in Paris, or English public schools such as Westminster and Eton. Common burdens, like billeting of troops or forced labour services did not fall upon nobles. Nor, above all, did the full weight of taxes. The Hungarian nobility prided themselves on their complete exemption from all direct taxes—although some of the lower reaches of the order did pay certain local levies. Until 1775, when a universal chimney tax was introduced, the Polish nobility too were largely exempt. So were various German nobilities, including that of Brandenburg. Elsewhere nobles paid taxes at reduced, privileged rates and in so far as dominated tax-granting assemblies, they could influence the over-all size of the burden. The French nobility by the later eighteenth century, was probably subject to a higher tax-burden than most of its continental counterparts.[1]

The prohibition of manual or degrading work was in most areas even stronger than in France, and it was reinforced by the prejudices of nobles themselves. The pride of poverty-stricken Spanish *hidalgos*, disdaining gainful

---

[1] See Betty Behrens, 'Nobles, privileges and taxes in France at the end of the Ancien Regime', *Economic History Review* (1962–3). Whether it actually paid as much as was expected is another matter. See articles by G. J. Cavanaugh in *French Historical Studies* (1974–5).

work, was the despair of economic thinkers. In Spain living nobly meant living in idleness. The same applied in Spain's satellite, Naples, but equally in Poland, where the repeal in 1775 of the rule against trading had no noticeable effect. In Sweden, Prussia, and certain other German states the formula was stated in more functional terms. Nobles denied common outlets for their energies were expected, more or less explicitly, to serve the state in the army or the administration. The great and surprising continental exception to this rule was Hungary, where the nobility thought of itself as a nation of free men not to be bound by artificial restrictions. If there was prejudice here, it emanated from the domesticated, absentee magnates of Vienna, not the local petty nobility who were so often its mainstay elsewhere.

Two nobilities were so idiosyncratic that they deserve special treatment. In Great Britain there was no noble order. Only the peers of the three kingdoms enjoyed any corporate status: technically they alone were noble. But their privileges were minimal and they certainly enjoyed no fiscal exemptions of any kind. It was obvious to contemporaries however that the gentry were for all practical purposes the equivalent of continental nobles, with their social pre-eminence, knighthoods, armorial bearings, and leisured lifestyle. 'I think proper', wrote James Boswell, son of a Scottish judge without hereditary title, 'to take the title of Baron in Germany, as I have just the same right to it as the good gentry whom I see around me.'[2] The gentry dominated the lower house of parliament, and behaved like an order, even if legally not one. In this respect Hungary was the closest continental parallel. Perhaps the crucial British difference was that status was not inherited by all members of a family. Eldest sons alone inherited titles and patrimonies, under the law of primogeniture. Younger sons had to make their way. This, and the absence of any law of derogation, made the frontiers of social distinction extremely fluid. Prejudice against trade did exist among British gentlemen, but it had no legal backing and was by no means universal. Younger sons, thrust into the world without a patrimony, were seldom restrained by Hispanic pride from seeking a living in trade. They knew that it was the quickest way to achieve parity with their elder brothers. But this tendency can be exaggerated. Few sons of peers or greater gentry became merchants. For them, like their continental counterparts, the army and the church were considered more appropriate.

The other exception was Russia, whose nobility underwent bewildering changes in status. In 1660 nothing resembling a western-style nobility existed. There were great magnates or *boyars*, who owed their prominence entirely to the reigning monarch's favour; and there were knights or *dvoriane*, who held estates peopled with serfs in return for military service. The law-code of 1649 had completed the evolution of the *dvoriane* into a hereditary class by recognizing their sole right to own serf-exploited land. Their military obligations remained, but were not really burdensome until the reign of Peter I. That monarch, however, was almost always at war, his demands for

[2] F. A. Pottle (ed.), *Boswell on the Grand Tour: Germany and Switzerland 1764* (1953), 116. Wittenberg, 1 Oct. 1764.

officers were constant, and he expected the *dvoriane* to serve the state, either as administrators or as soldiers and sailors, throughout their lives. In 1711 he decreed the establishment of a national register of *dvoriane* and their children in order to enforce universal service. Then in 1722 he promulgated a 'Table of Ranks', which created a western-style hierarchy of titled nobility. Yet the resemblance was superficial. Rank derived from service alone, and only the higher ranks were hereditary. They were open to all who served the state, whether *dvoriane* or not. The reigns of relatively weak mid-century monarchs brought the gradual whittling away of the obligation to serve, however, until in 1762 it was lifted completely. From then on service, as in Prussia, was expected but not exacted. Finally in 1785 Catherine II issued a Charter of Nobility which marked the full development of the westernized institution, by recognizing the nobility, whether Petrine or *dvoriane*, as one constituted order. Its privileges included freedom from obligatory service, personal tax exemption, freedom from billeting and corporal punishment, the exclusive right to own land and serfs, and the inviolability of noble status without judgement by peers. The corollary of this last provision was that in Russia trade and manufacture could not degrade. Peter, fearful that such activities would distract energies from state service, had insisted that they should. In 1785, however, Catherine recognized them as a noble privilege, in this at least ignoring most western precedents.

Nobles were always a small proportion of the population, although it varied immensely from area to area. In Poland nobles may have numbered 725,000 by the eighteenth century, in a very sparsely populated land. In Hungary in 1786 they numbered 306,528 or 4 to 5 per cent of the population, a similar proportion to that in Spain, where swarms of *hidalgos* swelled the nobility to 480,000 in 1787. An estimate of half a million *dvoriane* in Russia in 1737 was, proportionately, quite modest, perhaps 14,000 peerage and gentry families in England constituted around 1½ per cent of the population. The French nobility, recent estimates of which vary between 110,000 and 350,000, was under 1 per cent by any calculation. Sweden's 8,910 nobles (in 1760) accounted for only ½ per cent, and the 1,300 names in the Venetian Golden Book in 1775 were hardly a measurable proportion at all of the republic's 2·2 million inhabitants. But small proportions seldom indicated insignificance. They tended rather to emphasize the gulf between privileged nobility and the rest of society. In Hungary, Poland, or Spain huge numbers of the technically noble were on the contrary hardly distinguishable in material terms from the population at large. Nobility meant very little unless buttressed by wealth, and specific sorts of wealth at that. 'Without money,' noted the physiocrat Mirabeau in 1756, 'honour is nothing but sickness.'[3]

Land

'Fortune', Montesquieu advised his heir, 'means a status, not goods.'[4] Nowhere was this more apparent than in the possession of land, which in

---

[3] *L'Ami des hommes* (1762 ed.) i. 123.
[4] Quoted in R. Shackleton, *Montesquieu: a critical biography* (1960), 203.

pre-industrial society was not only the most abundant source of wealth but also the most prestigious, most respectable, most honourable and socially desirable. Nobles had come to think of land as an essential part of their dignity. The commercial nobles of Venice, Machiavelli[5] had noted, were 'gentlemen more in name than reality' because their wealth was not derived from landed estates. But by 1660 the Venetian nobility had begun to cut free of its mercantile origins to invest in estates on the mainland. The commercial nobles of Genoa found the barren hills of the Ligurian hinterland less inviting, but had compensated themselves with estates in the kingdom of Naples. By this time admittedly the trade of these famous commercial republics was in decline, but commercial profits remained in most circumstances greater and more accessible than anything land could offer. In other words, profit was seldom the main motive for acquiring land. Much more important were pride and prestige. Consequently in 1660 the United Provinces were the only important remaining state not ruled by a landed oligarchy. There alone the old landed nobility, concentrated in the eastern provinces, were eclipsed by the mercantile burgher magistrates of Holland. And in the century that followed even they, conscious of their own 'aristocracy', came increasingly to adopt titles and noble lifestyles, in which land was a basic component. And families once landed were reluctant to backtrack. Travelling in Ireland in the 1770s, Arthur Young noticed, 'the contempt in which trade is held by those who call themselves gentlemen ... I have remarked the houses of country gentlemen being full of brothers, cousins, etc. idlers whose best employment is to follow the hare or fox; *why are they not brought up to trade or manu-facture? Trade!* (the answer has been), *they are gentlemen.*'[6]

Accordingly nobles were Europe's most significant landowners. The Russian *dvoriane* had the exclusive right to hold all serf-cultivated lands. Peers and gentry between them owned between 70 and 85 per cent of England around 1790. Around 1780 85 per cent of Denmark was noble property. In Spain around 1800 roughly 52 per cent of the land was in noble hands; in Venetia in 1740 50·9 per cent of private property was noble owned; in France in 1789 nobles owned between a quarter and a third. Even after Charles XI of Sweden had resumed many of the royal lands alienated to them during his minority and earlier, the Swedish nobility in 1700 was still left in possession of a third of the kingdom's territory. Even where the nobility as a whole did not own most of the land, invariably individual nobles owned the largest estates. A quarter of England was owned by 400 families; a third of the vast Habsburg empire was held by a comparable number. British peers, such as the dukes of Bedford or Devonshire, might own over 50,000 acres and bring in as many pounds per annum. Such landlords rivalled independent German princelings, but they in their turn were outshone by the magnates of eastern Europe. The estates of the Radziwills in Poland were half as large as Ireland and those of the Czartoryskis or Potockis were similar. The richest

---

[5] *Discourses*, i. 55.
[6] Quoted in *A Tour in Ireland*, ed. C. Maxwell (1925), 207.

Hungarian magnate, Prince Esterhazy, owned about 10,000,000 acres and enjoyed revenues of 700,000 florins annually. Eleven others brought in more than 150,000. By comparison the greatest French fortunes, even those of princes of the blood royal, were mediocre. French noble estates also tended to be scattered, and less easy to exploit as units.

The source of such differences again lay in the law of inheritance. Primogeniture kept estates together down the generations, but it was not practised outside the British Isles and certain idiosyncratic regions such as Catalonia. Elsewhere some degree of division of inheritance was normal and widely felt to be most just. Peter I's attempt to keep noble tenures in realistic units by allowing them to be entailed upon a single heir (1714) was resisted by the *dvoriane* and abandoned in 1731. Repeated attempts by Frederick II to introduce entail to his domains, though intended to buttress noble wealth, were also resisted. Entails in France were still relatively rare in 1789; the most that could be done was to favour a particular heir with a larger portion and hope to recoup losses with dowries. Meanwhile division meant dispersion. Uneconomic portions came onto the market, available for purchase by would-be nobles. Frederick constantly lamented the steady acquisition of former noble estates by aspiring bourgeois. For similar reasons it was easier to attain a noble lifestyle in France than elsewhere, and the land market remained buoyant. By contrast entails restricted social mobility. The 'strict settlement', which reinforced primogeniture in England, made it practically impossible for an owner to alienate his family estates. By the late eighteenth century it had severely restricted the land market. Even more rigid was the unbreakable Spanish *mayorazgo*, which maintained intact the vast neglected *latifundia* of southern Spain. Spaniards had also popularized this institution in Italy and south Germany in the form of the *fideicommissum*, which now kept the mainland domains of Venetian nobles and the enormous estates of the Habsburg magnates together.

Most nobles were by no means magnates, but their domination of the land did not end with ownership. The tenth of France owned by the church, for instance, belonged to ecclesiastical corporations whose controlling members were usually noble. Above all, nobles often enjoyed rights over lands far more extensive than those they actually owned, in the form of overlordship. East of the Elbe, where lordship and ownership usually coincided, seignorial dues and services were the equivalent of rent. In Russia a noble's wealth was usually calculated in terms of the due-paying serfs he owned, rather than in land. In Great Britain on the contrary dues had disappeared and freeholders owed the local lord nothing but the deference demanded by wealth and power. In France, northern Spain, western Germany, and Italy, lordship was a valuable and coveted commodity. Lordship meant jurisdiction, enforcing its claims with private courts. In 1797 seventeen cities and a third of the villages of Spain were part of so-called 'lay seignories', to whose noble proprietors their inhabitants paid dues in kind. They were also forced to use the lord's monopoly services, such as milling and baking, and subject to the depredations of his exclusive hunting and fishing rights. In Naples, at around the same time, about 600 'baronial' families controlled some 2,200 fiefs drawing dues and revenues from two-thirds of the kingdom's inhabitants. Until 1789 almost the whole of France was subject to burdens of this sort, bewildering in their variety and relative value. There was nothing to prevent non-nobles in France from acquiring such rights, even though they had originated as institutions of noble-landholding. By the eighteenth century more 'feudal' rights were in non-noble hands than ever before. Nevertheless, the vast majority still belonged to the nobility. Perhaps three-quarters of the land of France had noble overlords, and even more if the lordships of the church are included. In southern districts (as in Sweden and much of Germany) there was the added complication of lands as well as persons enjoying noble or non-noble status. Owners of the 'noble' land enjoyed special privileges irrespective of their personal status, while nobles who owned non-noble land did not. This illustrates an important but frequently overlooked point about 'feudalism'. Nobles were its main beneficiaries, but they also frequently bore a share of its burdens. In Brandenburg for instance, they could not sell or mortgage their holdings without permission of their royal overlord. Many could therefore see some appeal in the attacks directed at these burdens later in the eighteenth century and they were by no means united in defence of 'feudal' obligations.

The link between landownership and laws of derogation was clear. Landed revenues were the obvious means to 'living nobly' without manual work or trade. In Poland landownership was actually prohibited to non-nobles, and Frederick II of Prussia tried to maintain the same principle. But such rigidity was rare, and in France and England especially the fact that landed income was distinctively noble did not always mean that noble income was exclusively landed. In 1701 Louis XIV opened wholesale trade to the nobility, although recently ennobled merchants were the main beneficiaries. In Brittany local custom allowed 'sleeping' nobility, whereby impoverished families might suspend their status for a generation to profit from trade, but later resume it, refurbished. And most French heavy industry was noble-owned. Government stocks and offices also claimed an important segment of noble capital. In England, nobles with lands on coalfields—like the duke of Bridgewater in Lancashire or the marquess of Rockingham in Yorkshire—seldom failed to exploit their good fortune; younger sons (in contrast to Ireland) had fewer scruples about going into trade, at least among the petty gentry; and investment in 'the funds' was by the eighteenth century attracting considerable sums from the landed. In Russia or Hungary, equally without a law of derogation, activities deemed ignoble elsewhere were open to nobles, but in eastern Europe, where trade was much less important and profitable and government stocks rare and unreliable, opportunities to diversify income seldom arose. The great exception was the coalfields and manufactories of the Urals, worked by serfs who in their turn were owned by nobles such as those great entrepreneurs, the Demidovs. But these industrialists had attained noble status as a result of their activities, and until 1762 at least the *dvoriane* had little time to spare from state service. The industrial activities of nobles everywhere, in fact, were usually mere extensions of landownership, incidental rather than central to their fortunes. Investment in stocks, too, was almost always peripheral. Since land was the source of such an overwhelming proportion of all wealth, the nobility, by dominating it, gave its pretensions to social superiority the most reliable of economic foundations.

Power

Land was power, and ought to be power. These were assumptions so obvious that they hardly needed to be stated. But they clearly underlay such policies as that of the English in Ireland, who, after the defeat of Catholic forces in 1691, deliberately set out to dispossess Catholic landowners and replace them with loyal and reliable Protestants. By 1703 only 14 per cent of Irish land was still in Catholic hands and a deliberate suspension of primogeniture in their case was designed to reduce that proportion still further. The 5,000 or so landlords of the 'Ascendancy' constituted a sort of Protestant nobility controlling, in England's interest, the mainsprings of power in eighteenth-century Ireland.

It was a natural response, for everywhere these mainsprings were in the hands of noble landowners. Justice at the lowest level was almost invariably dispensed by them, whether directly on behalf of the state as justices of the peace in Great Britain or Russia, or indirectly in their own right as feudal overlords with private jurisdiction in the rest of the continent. Polish landlords retained the power of life and death over their serfs until 1768. Courts were not simply tribunals of justice, but bodies of administrators with a degree of executive power. Few appellate jurisdictions were in private hands, but again such higher courts were staffed by nobles or their equivalents. The most famous examples were the French *parlements*, regional supreme courts whose offices ennobled their holders but which were recruited increasingly from the nobility.

Administrators and civil servants, a category of officers which first acquired a distinct character during this period (the term 'civil service' was first used in Russia in 1714) also tended at the higher levels to be nobles. After the Table of Ranks took effect, higher administrators in Russia were noble by definition. The French intendants, and the members of the privy council from whose ranks they were recruited, were almost all nobles of legal family background. Frederick William I of Prussia by contrast attempted, between 1713 and 1740, to exclude nobles from administrative office and elevate in their place commoners without independent estate. But his success was limited in a country where educated bourgeois with a sense of public responsibility were rare, and Frederick II reversed the policy.

I cannot help adding [he wrote in 1768] some words in favour of the nobility. I have always spoken of them with distinction and consideration, because this body provides officers for the army and subjects for all the great positions of the State. I have maintained it in possession of its lands and I have placed obstacles in the way of commoners to make the purchase of noble lands difficult for them. These are my reasons: if commoners possess lands, they open their way to all employments. Most of them think meanly and make bad officers; one cannot send them anywhere.[7]

It was universally felt that nobles made good officers. An order which derived many of its privileges, such as sword-bearing or tax-exemption, from its presumed warrior origins regarded a military career as natural, if not indeed as a birthright. This situation hardened in the eighteenth century. After Peter I not all Russian nobles were officers but all officers were nobles. Frederick William I's preference for non-nobles in government did not extend to the army, and in 1739 only eleven out of 250 Prussian general and field officers were commoners. Frederick II elevated this preference to a principle of policy, and by 1786 of 689 officers above the rank of major only twenty-two enjoyed no nobility. French edicts of 1718, 1727, and 1781 excluded non-nobles from most commissions. Navies, it is true, recruited their officers more widely, but most Russian naval officers were noble, and there were élite groups elsewhere like the French 'grand corps'. In maritime England however, the ideal career for a second son was, curiously enough, felt to lie in the army.

If there was a third son, his obvious place was the church. Here noble dominance was not as universal, but bishops tended to be recruited from the ruling orders whose position the church upheld. Nine-tenths of French bishops under Louis XIV were noble, and even more by Louis XVI's time. Nobles also dominated all the richest abbacies and monopolized the best-endowed chapters. The prince-prelates of Germany, such as the archbishops of Mainz, Trier, or Salzburg, were elected by exclusive noble chapters; most popes were scions of the closed Roman nobility. Even in Spain, where the higher nobility was not attracted by holy orders, the greater prelates, like the immensely rich archbishop of Toledo, tended to be at least of *hidalgo* rank. In England and Ireland the gentry penetrated the parish clergy and the 'squarson' became a stock character of literature. This was possible because elder brothers owned not only land but advowsons. In Catholic countries with the existence of noble monasteries and chapters there was less need than in Protestant countries to set indigent nobles to the actual cure of souls.

In all these spheres nobles wielded power. They staffed the institutions through which it was exercised. Perhaps more surprising, in a period traditionally described as one of 'absolutism' and of the curbing of noble pretensions, is the extent to which nobles decided how power should be deployed. They did this by dominating estates and diets, both at local and national level. The powers wielded by these bodies varied enormously, but they existed in some form almost everywhere. In France the estates-general did not meet until 1789, but provincial estates convened regularly in certain provinces; in Brittany every nobleman had a right to sit there in person. There were no estates in Naples, yet the Sicilian parliament continued to meet. Neither the Habsburg nor the Hohenzollern domains had any central representative body, but local bodies proliferated And both in these

[7] Quoted in H. Brunschwig, *La Crise de l'état prussien à la fin du XVIIIe siècle et la genèse de la mentalité romantique* (1947), 60.

realms and in those such as Sweden, Great Britain, or Poland, where the representative assemblies largely ruled the state, the nobility dominated the representation. Swedish nobles sat in a separate house, overshadowing the three others. In Hungary and Great Britain magnates sat in their own chamber, but the lower houses were also largely made up of landowners. A significant proportion of British MPs (one fifth in 1760) were in any case sons of peers or holders of Irish or Scottish titles, and an Act of 1710 imposed a minimum landed qualification for membership. Only in Russia (where there were no representative institutions of any kind until after 1775), Spain, and the United Provinces, among major states, were representative bodies not a vehicle of noble power. In the Dutch republic, as in certain small German states such as Württemberg, the estates were the voice of towns, usually the weakest point in the authority of landed oligarchies, and the main source of hostility to their dominance in the later eighteenth century.

Finally, nobles dominated policy-making itself. When monarchs so largely chose their own ministers, it was always possible for non-noble adventurers to rise high—men like Squillace in Spain, Law or Necker in France, or Struensee in Denmark. Most significant however was their rarity. Monarchs largely chose to be advised by nobles. In Sweden nobles enjoyed a monopoly of high public office. Even Louis XIV's chosen collaborators, 'vile bourgeoisie' to the jaundiced eyes of hypersensitive dukes, all enjoyed prior nobility, which Louis felt only right to decorate with titles. Iron-fisted ministers with anti-noble reputations, such as Pombal in Portugal, Tanucci in Naples, or Haugwitz in Austria, were nobles themselves. And however much the policies of Joseph II or Gustavus III seemed to threaten noble political interests, their details were largely worked out with the help of noble ministers. 'With us', wrote Gustavus in 1778, '... democracy seeks to gain the upper hand and all my efforts are aimed at re-establishing the old high nobility.'[8] It was normal for kings to be surrounded by courts, where socially they met only noblemen. In these circumstances noble influence was inescapable, and no monarch ever made and only one (Joseph II) even considered a serious attempt to destroy the fabric of their power. Some tinkered with the machine, but Joseph alone (with characteristic rashness) dreamed of dismantling it, to his mother's scandalized horror.

Recruitment

Nobility, so its holders liked to think, was of the blood and acquired only through inheritance. A Hungarian was either of conquering Magyar stock, or he was not, and on that depended his status. In the early eighteenth century the count de Boulainvilliers similarly attempted to trace the French nobility back to the Franks. Commoners, in his view, were descendants of conquered Gauls. Few took him seriously; but many nobles spent an inordinate time trying to prove the length of their pedigree and plenty of shady genealogists

---

[8] Quoted in H. A. Barton, 'Gustavus III of Sweden and the Enlightenment', *Eighteenth Century Studies* (1972), 13.

were prepared to make a living by helping them. Nobody was anxious to admit that he or his ancestors had ever been anything but noble.

In reality closed nobilities were extremely rare. Many distinctions, such as membership of the order of Malta in Catholic countries or 'presentation' at court, were barred to those without distinguished noble extraction. But only in places such as Venice or Genoa, with their Golden Books, or Rome, where Pope Benedict XIV formally declared the ranks closed in 1758, was noble status itself confined to an exclusive caste. When this happened, as the spectacular decline of the Venetian nobility showed, inbreeding produced a serious decline in numbers and ultimately loosened the noble grip on power itself.[9] Even in Hungary and Poland lack of demand from suitably qualified outsiders was at least as important as lack of warrior forebears in minimizing ennoblements. The same was true in the Dutch republic, where noble prestige was eclipsed by that of the urban regents. Elsewhere nobility remained to varying degrees within the reach of socially aspiring outsiders.

The essence of being noble was to be recognized as such, and there were always some social climbers who sought this recognition without any formal right to it. Nowhere was this easier than in England, where anybody who owned land might see his family recognized socially as gentry within three generations at the most. Nor, in a state where most privileges were purely honorific, did this much matter. Where nobles enjoyed tax-exemptions, however, legitimacy was much more important, and in the 1660s Colbert launched inquiries in France to uncover false nobles and reduce the number of those claiming tax exemption. Only authentic titles in writing were accepted, and those without them (whether genuinely noble or not) lost their exemption. But such inquiries did not recur after 1680; a hundred years later false nobles, among them such unexpected figures as Brissot, Danton, and Robespierre, were as common (in every sense) as ever.

Apart from noble ancestry, the essential difference between a legitimate and a false nobleman lay in royal appointment. Ennoblement was a distinction that only kings could properly confer. Even in Great Britain knighthoods and baronetcies, like peerages, emanated from the king alone. This seldom meant that a king made a personal decision in each case; more usually people in state service were ennobled by their office. The extreme example of this was in post-Petrine Russia, where before 1762 there was no nobility, personal or hereditary, without state service; but equally, in the upper ranks, no service without nobility. Similarly, in France the upper judiciary consisted (in 1789) of some 4,000 ennobling offices. But here the system was more subtle and complex. Offices were originally marketed by the state, but once bought they became pieces of real property which their owners might sell or (on payment of a small regular tax) bequeath at will. This system was important because most offices ennobled only gradually, over three generations. It brought the state revenue, in the form of the initial purchasing price, and mutation fees at each subsequent change of owner. At the same time it

---

[9] See J. C. Davis, *The Decline of the Venetian Nobility as a Ruling Class* (1962).

channelled the energies of the socially ambitious rich into state service for minimal remuneration, and left the state as the final arbiter of social mobility. It was a brilliant system. The main disadvantages were that venality diverted commercial and industrial wealth which might otherwise have been reinvested more productively; and it encouraged the most successful producers of wealth in the community to abandon their activities at the height of their success in order to achieve nobility.

The first disadvantage applied equally to the wealth of the numerous nobles who always bought a substantial proportion of available ennobling officers because those that did not ennoble were considered below their dignity. The second resulted from the existence of nobility itself rather than from the specific conditions of France. British, German, or Swedish merchants were no less eager than their French counterparts to abandon trade once their fortune was made, and to invest it in symbols of social prestige and ambition. For wealth was the universal key to ennoblement. However diverse the systems and rules in various states, the exclusive beneficiaries everywhere were the rich. To become a noble was expensive, whether by purchasing land, lordships, ennobling office, or one of the notorious titles which Louis XIV periodically put on the market at times of grave financial need. In France it became axiomatic that while not every nobleman was rich, every rich man was noble. In 1726, for example, well over half the farmers-general of taxes, proverbial for their wealth, were noble, a proportion which had risen to over two-thirds by 1786. True nobility, wrote the Hanoverian official Ramdohr in 1791,[10] 'is usually derived from birth into a "superior family" whose aristocratic origin goes back into the remote past; it may, however, also be due to the specific conferment of a patent of nobility by a specific sovereign prince at a specific time. It must be accompanied in either case by wealth.' From 1758 large sums were demanded of Spaniards aspiring to *hidalgo* rank, with the result that over the next half-century the numbers of the Spanish nobility may have dropped by as much as a third.

Thus the most common reason for apparent noble exclusivism was the lack of demand from qualified outsiders for entry into the charmed circle. Throughout eastern Europe and much of Germany, Italy, and Spain, a moneyed middle class, with or without social pretensions, hardly existed. In the Dutch republic it did, but there the burgher oligarchy was the object of social ambition. In Ireland mercantile wealth, substantial by the later eighteenth century, was mainly in the hands of Catholics who preferred their religion to joining the Anglican ascendancy. But even if rich men ambitious to become nobles had been more common, the barriers would have been formidable. Ennoblement through venal office was largely confined to France; elsewhere the emphasis lay far more strongly on land. But throughout Germany and Scandinavia purchase of 'noble' land by non-nobles was more or less stringently forbidden; besides, there and in Spain and Italy entails kept the best and most extensive estates off the market. Even in England,

---

[10]   Quoted in K. Epstein, *The Genesis of German Conservatism* (1966), 184.

where there were no legal restrictions on land purchase, strict settlements ensured that by the later eighteenth century, when landed profits were improving rapidly, relatively little was being sold. Accordingly Europe's richest and most enterprising middle class found its avenue to social ascent progressively narrowing. This may, paradoxically, have done a good deal to promote reinvestment of its wealth in more productive spheres at a crucial time in England's economic development.

From this point of view social ascent may have been too easy in France for her economic good. There is little evidence there that opportunities for ennoblement decreased as time went on. The absence of strong entails, or primogeniture, or restrictions on non-noble land purchase, kept the market buoyant. It is true that there was a tendency for access to the most prestigious ennobling offices, those of the *parlements*, to be limited to nobles; but other ennobling offices meanwhile proved more popular than ever, especially with the merchants of western seaports. By 1789 the 900 offices of king's secretary, complete sinecures which exempted their holders from all the normal rules of derogation but conferred full hereditary nobility, were the most expensive and sought after in France. On the eve of the Revolution, the French nobility was probably more open than its English counterpart and therefore the least exclusive in Europe. On the other hand, in France all the members of a family inherited nobility, whereas English younger sons returned to the common pool. This alone left the English gentleman far less remote from his social inferiors, in psychological terms, than any French *gentilhomme*.

Exclusivism is not only measurable in terms of access to nobility. Equally important is the question of marriage. To become genuine, declared Ramdohr,[11] technical nobility 'must be followed by intermarriage with families of acknowledged aristocratic status.' Yet again, traditions against marrying outside the nobility tended to be strongest where the opportunities were rare in any case—where non-noble wealth was uncommon, or where entails made fortunes less dependent on fat dowries to maintain them. In France neither of these circumstances obtained, and 'regilding the arms', or less politely 'restoring the fields with muck' were literary clichés describing the well-established practice among nobles of marrying daughters of rich commoners. Thus much of the wealth of the duc de Choiseul, peer and minister, was derived from his wife, granddaughter of 'Crozat the rich', most opulent financier of the early eighteenth century. No less than 62 per cent of the traceable daughters of the farmers-general of the taxes in the eighteenth century married noblemen, 28·3 per cent of them great nobles of the court.[12] In England the story was similar; landowners seldom scrupled to marry 'into the city' in order to refurbish or improve their fortunes, and the chosen fathers-in-law were usually only too flattered at the alliance. In Sweden noble

[11] Loc. cit.

[12] Y. Durand, *Les Fermiers généraux au XVIIIe siècle* (1971), 342. Many farmers-general were themselves noble, but in most cases their ennoblement was relatively recent.

marriages to commoners rose over the eighteenth century from one- to two-thirds. In high society, whether in Paris, London, or Stockholm, wealth dissolved all barriers of birth, privilege, or prestige in a way that it did not in less advanced capitals—where riches were virtually a noble monopoly anyway. In these circumstances the suspicious, envious, lesser nobility of the provinces became the true custodians of older noble values and ideals.

The Aristocratic Life

So far the term 'aristocracy' has been avoided with some care. It is a political term, dangerously vague for analysing social categories. Yet most nobilities saw themselves as aristocracies; made up, quite literally, of the best elements of society, most suitable in every way to govern it. 'If there are races among animals there are races among men,' wrote Margrave Karl Friedrich of Baden, a celebrated model of an enlightened monarch.[13] 'For that reason the most superior must put themselves ahead of others, marry among themselves and· produce a pure race: that is the nobility.' Sycophantic commoners reassured them in such views. 'Nobility', wrote Edmund Burke, for long the pensioner of the marquess of Rockingham, 'is a graceful ornament to the civil order. It is the Corinthian capital of polished society. . .It is indeed one sign of a liberal and benevolent mind to incline to it with some sort of partial propensity. He feels no ennobling principle in his own heart, who wishes to level all the artificial institutions which have been adopted for giving a body to opinion, and permanence to fugitive esteem.'[14]

The nobility's view of itself involved a number of activities deemed peculiarly appropriate. Basic was 'living nobly' on landed revenues. Here prejudice and general opinion reinforced the letter of the law. Yet to live off the land was not necessarily to till the soil. In parts of France a noble was allowed to work only a certain proportion of his lands in person, on pain of derogation. The richer a noble was, in general, the less likely he was to reside on his estates. The allurements of town life or, in the case of the greatest nobles of all, of court and capital, were irresistible. Great nobles therefore tended to be absentees, seeing their lands in terms mainly of rentals or regular income. This was inevitable when great estates were concentrated in the hands of a few magnates—they could not regularly visit, much less reside on, all the properties they owned. Even so, estates at any distance from the centre of the fashionable world held little appeal. 'To say the truth', wrote Viscount Palmerston in 1761 of the Irish county from which he derived over half his income,[15] 'I think Sligo and the adjacent counties the most dreary waste I ever yet beheld.' It took political disgrace to make the duc de Choiseul take an interest in Chanteloup, or Viscount Townshend experiment with turnips in Norfolk.

Yet absenteeism should not be exaggerated. Most nobles were never absentees. Relatively prosperous though they might be, they simply could

---

[13] Quoted in Epstein, *Origins of German Conservatism,* 189.
[14] *Reflexions on the Revolution in France* (1910 edn.), 135.
[15] Quoted in B. Connell, *Portrait of a Whig Peer* (1957), 352.

not afford it. Few historical legends are more persistent, yet more misleading, than that Louis XIV denuded the French provinces of nobility and concentrated them at Versailles. In reality only a small proportion of great magnates flocked to court; most of the nobility remained in their provinces, lived at least part of the year on their estates, and reinvested income in them. Many were shrewd and careful managers, a world away from the profligate spendthrifts of Versailles. Similar contrasts existed throughout much of the continent. On the other hand, in Spain, southern Italy, and parts of Germany, the provincial nobility notoriously immured itself almost perpetually in towns; and in Russia and Prussia, where the state demanded constant service, the lesser nobility were quite as inclined to neglect their estates as great magnates proverbially did.

One reason for the costliness of metropolitan life was the need for display. Social importance was emphasized by an ostentatious lifestyle. In Spain and southern Italy hordes of retainers were kept in constant attendance. A Spanish duke in the 1780s might have a household of 300 or more; while forty years earlier Lady Mary Wortley Montagu had complained that in Naples 'Two coaches, two running footmen, four other footmen, a gentleman usher, and two pages are as necessary here as the attendance of a single servant is at London.'[16] But England had its own forms of extravagance, such as the immense country houses erected between about 1690 and 1740, at a time when returns on land, and therefore the temptation to invest in agriculture, were low. Marlborough's Blenheim, Devonshire's Chatsworth, and Carlisle's Castle Howard all date substantially from that period. These palaces were crammed with treasures amassed during the Grand Tour, a continental journey of several years which rounded off every young English gentleman's education. The great cities of the continent swarmed with English *milords,* spending liberally and collecting indiscriminately. In France, where residence in the royal palace was the ultimate privilege, two establishments had to be maintained, one in Paris and one at court—with the additional expense of moving with the king from one to another of several palaces. Most ostentatious of all were the magnates of the Habsburg empire, who not only resided at court and kept impressive urban palaces in Vienna, but also, in the later eighteenth century, adopted the English fashion of country seats. Well over 200 were built in Hungary alone between 1740 and 1780, of which the most famous was Esterhaz, the 'Hungarian Versailles', built after 1762 by Prince Miklos Esterhazy. Here the prince spent part of every year in royal state, entertained by a resident orchestra of twenty to thirty, playing a constant stream of new pieces by their resident conductor, Haydn. Display on this scale was quite beyond the resources of the average nobleman. Nevertheless it represented an ideal, and accordingly modest country seats were modestly 'improved', provincial towns had their social 'seasons', and noble life was dominated by an endless round of visits, entertainments, and that universal pastime of a bored leisured class, cards.

[16] R. Halsband (ed.), *The Complete Letters of Lady Mary Wortley Montagu* (1965– 7), ii. 214. Naples, 6 Dec. 1740.

The inevitable result of ostentation was debts. Those incurred through high living at court or in the metropolis were the most spectacular, although few accumulated them at the speed of the comte de Genlis, who at twenty lost 50000 livres at 'play' in a single night. Besides, if courtiers habitually overspent the revenue of their properties, monarchs were often willing to rescue them with handsome pensions or well-paid sinecures from public funds. Nor was this always the generous gesture it seemed; subjects dependent on royal largesse were more easily controlled than those who were financially self-supporting. No less than a third of the duc de Saulx-Tavanes's income in the 1780s came from royal grants of this sort; and a great lord was defined in 1721 as 'a man who sees the king, speaks to ministers, has ancestors, debts, and pensions'.[17] Yet debts arose more often from prudence than from its opposite. If most nobles, particularly heads of families, had debts far in excess of their incomes, they usually resulted from loans and mortgages incurred to pay bequests and marriage portions. Such commitments were part of the very structure of a property-owner's family life and alarmed nobody.

Never before had the qualities expected of noblemen been so universally agreed on. Europe was dominated by an international aristocracy, whose passports were connections and good breeding. Travellers went armed with sheaves of letters of recommendation which opened up society along their route by introducing them to acquaintances of their acquaintances. The Bohemian nobility residing in Prague, wrote an early-eighteenth-century traveller, 'are polite and civil to Strangers, whom they know to be Persons of Quality'.[18] And a person of 'quality' normally marked himself out, quite apart from the letters he carried, by certain standards of accepted conduct. 'You may possibly ask me,' wrote the earl of Chesterfield, 'whether a man has it always in his power to get into the best company? and how? I say, Yes, he has, by deserving it; provided he is but in circumstances which enable him to appear upon the footing of a gentleman. . .good breeding will endear him to the best companies.'[19] Again, however, the criterion was a metropolitan one.

There should be in the least, as well as in the greatest parts of a gentleman, *les manières nobles*. . .attend carefully to the manners, the diction, the motions of people of the first fashion. . .the language, the air, the dress, and the manners of the Court, are the only true standard. . .for a man of parts, who has been bred at Courts, and used to keep the best company, will distinguish himself, and is to be known from the vulgar, by every word, attitude, gesture, and even look.[20]

Most noblemen, however, believed that their position required more than ancestors, an extravagant style of life, and the polish of good breeding. Even more important were less tangible qualities, most of which were bound up in the concept of honour. Honour meant obligation—how a man was

[17] Montesquieu, *Persian Letters*, LXXXVIII.
[18] Quoted by R. and E. Forster, *European Society in the Eighteenth Century* (1969), 87, from the memoirs of baron de Pollnitz (1757).
[19] *Letters of Lord Chesterfield to his Son*, 9 Oct. O.S. 1747.
[20] Ibid., 12 Nov.O.S. 1750.

expected to behave and how he expected others to behave towards him. Its mainspring was pride. According to Montesquieu, himself a provincial noble of distinguished lineage, honour in the last analysis was mere prejudice. It was nevertheless the motivating principle of all true monarchical states (which meant states with nobilities), and was no mean impulse which could 'oblige men to perform all difficult deeds, requiring strength, with no other reward than the fame of these deeds'.[21] Like most prejudices, honour allowed no compromise; those whose honour was impugned felt obliged to restore it, whatever the cost. Social life was scarred with spectacular and very often disruptive disputes over precedence, deference, and the tiniest points of protocol. In earlier times disputes of this sort between individuals had been resolved by duelling, but the mid-seventeenth century witnessed a determined drive by governments to stamp this practice out. In 1679 Louis XIV reinforced earlier, and largely unenforced, prohibitions, and directed all disputes normally resoved by duels to a special tribunal of honour. Even so, they never died out completely; and in England, where there was no ban, duels may even have grown more common.

The most obvious quality tested in a duel was courage. A cowardly nobleman was held to be a contradiction in terms, a betrayal of the order's warrior origins. This attitude underpinned noble predominance among army officers and the hereditary bravery of nobles was often invoked, as a fact as much as an ideal, in defence of the institution of nobility. Military virtues were closely linked to the ideal of service. The obligation to serve the state or the monarch was seldom as clearly defined as it was in Russia or Prussia, but most nobilities saw themselves to some degree as service nobilities. Honour bound all noblemen to serve their king in war, even if opinions differed as to whether other forms of service might be equally honourable. But service had its corollory: the monarch must treat his faithful nobility as they deserved, in accordance with their rights and their dignity. This meant, reflected the duc de Montausier in Louis XIV's early years, granting them 'all the advantages of utility, of goods, offices, employments, honours, advancement, protection, &c, that shall be possible'.[22] It was a demanding list, but monarchs ignored it at their peril. When nobles were disaffected, it was normally because kings seemed not to be allowing them the rewards to which they felt entitled. Unfortunately such matters were seldom entirely within a monarch's control.

Inner Tensions

From the outside, as the propaganda of French revolutionaries in 1789 shows, the nobility appeared a monolithic institution, powerful and united in defence of its interests. In reality, noblemen were often bitterly divided among themselves. Internal division was perhaps the most important characteristic of nobilities, and it goes far towards explaining why they were so easily upset during the revolutionary decade.

[21] *Esprit des lois*, Bk. III, chs. VI and VII.
[22] Quoted in J.-P. Labatut, *Les Ducs et pairs de France au XVIIIe siècle* (1972), 375.

The most obvious division was between old nobles and new. Most nobles grudgingly acquiesced in the replenishment of their order by outsiders, but very few would openly commend it. They knew that most new nobles owed their elevation to money, which rich nobles despised and poor ones envied. Molière's play *The Bourgeois Gentleman*, ridiculing the aspirations of a social climber for the amusement of Louis XIV and his courtiers, vividly exemplifies these attitudes. The classic example of division between new and old was the famous French distinction between nobles of the sword and nobles of the robe; the former being the traditional warrior nobility, the latter, newcomers ennobled by the purchase of high judicial office. Distinct traditions of this sort existed right down to the Revolution, and in the pre-revolutionary crisis there were plenty of signs of hostility to the *parlements* and their political pretensions among the rest of the nobility. Utopian purists such as the duc de Saint-Simon insisted that holders of ennobling offices in the magistracy were not nobles at all; more realistic writers—for example Archbishop Fénelon— equally concerned about the adulteration of the nobility, conceded that the robe was noble but advocated the restriction of ennoblement through restriction of venality. Yet in social terms even as early as 1660 the division was practically meaningless. Only a minority of office-holders in most *parlements* had been ennobled by the offices they held, and were therefore in no sense new nobles. Most of them were sons of other office-holders, but some, and a growing proportion, came from so-called 'sword' families. Inter-marriage between robe families and those of other nobles was also well established and their lifestyles were identical. In Paris at least, all that remained of the old social distinction was a literary tradition. What strength it retained lay in the provinces; for although intermarriage and interpenetration occurred there too, it took place only at a minimal level of prosperity, far above that of most provincial nobles. The latter envied the self-styled 'senators' of the provincial *parlements* their wealth, and the institutional power it had bought them in the judiciary and administration. Such power, they believed, should be the prerogative of all nobles according to their talents, and not a pluto- cracy among them, where money appeared to confound all other distinctions of rank, ancestry, and honour.

The fact was, however, that most nobilities *were* plutocracies; the most fundamental antagonism between nobles, transcending all others, was between rich and poor. In an order characterized by honours and distinctions, there were countless reasons for one noble to consider himself better than another; nobility was, in a famous phrase, 'a cascade of disdain', most of it traceable to an economic or financial source. Pride in ancestry was never stronger than in the Spanish *hidalgos* or the Hungarian 'sandalled' nobility, who had little else to distinguish them. A long lineage could also confer distinct material advan- tages at royal courts, where, in order to cope with the pressure of the numbers wishing to live there and enjoy the offices and perquisites, monarchs confined access to those who could prove a distinguished ancestry to the satisfaction of royal genealogists. Even genuine proofs cost money, but the rewards could be substantial. The hierarchy of titles also roughly reflected the hierarchy of fortunes—an indigent prince or duke was a sensational rarity; equally, a rich noble without a title would sooner or later acquire one. Wealth largely determined where a nobleman could live. The expense of life in court or capital was such that, while not all provincial nobles were poor, most poor nobles were provincial. All these circumstances produced divisions within nobilities far more significant than the superficial professional rivalries of 'robe' and 'sword'.

Poverty and provincialism left petty noblemen constantly afraid that their more fortunate fellows would try to cut themselves off from the rest of their order. Thus they vigorously—and successfully—resisted repeated attempts by the peers of France to constitute themselves into a body with a status and prerogatives distinct from the rest of the nobility. In England a peerage bill, designed to limit the numbers of the House of Lords, was rejected by the Commons in 1719. 'How can the Lords expect the Commons', asked Robert Walpole in the crucial debate, 'to give their concurrence to a bill by which they and their posterity are to be for ever excluded from the peerage? How would they themselves receive a bill which should prevent a baron from being made a viscount, a viscount an earl, an earl a marquis, and a marquis a duke?'[23] Similarly in Spain the new Bourbon authorities after 1700 found little difficulty in eliminating the grandees from the controlling councils of government, because they were divided among themselves and were, as the French ambassador wrote to Louis XIV in 1711, 'odious to the lower nobility'.[24]

Above all, the small nobility envied the great their opportunities. Public life was a constant competition among nobles for the limited patronage at the disposal of the state, where the rich and the metropolitan (in a long French literary tradition 'les Grands') enjoyed all the advantages. Living at the centre of things, knowing those who dispensed the patronage, they naturally held most of the higher appointive offices of state and also exercised wide influence, or 'interest', so as to secure the best military commissions and corner the most remunerative ecclesiastical benefices for their relatives. They took the most prestigious and lucrative provincial offices from under the noses of local aspirants, spending the revenues in the capital and confiding their duties to underpaid deputies. It was notorious that courtiers enjoyed all the best and largest pensions, while provincials, where they secured anything at all, received only the most petty appointments, and perhaps token military pensions. All this came at a time when governments seemed steadily intent on whittling down nobles' fiscal privileges and taxing them ever more heavily. The absenteeism of the great was the final insult. It demonstrated their contempt for the provinces that sustained them, and nowhere more vividly than in the Habsburg empire, where the magnates of Vienna even abandoned their native Czech or Magyar for the German and French of the imperial court. Few provincials would have disagreed with a late-eighteenth-

---

[23] Quoted in J. F. Naylor, *The British Aristocracy and the Peerage Bill of 1719* (1968), 269.
[24] Quoted in H. Kamen, *The War of Succession in Spain* (1969), 107.

century Breton magistrate when he declared that 'the court nobility has, at all times, been the most pronounced and the most dangerous enemy of other nobles.'[25]

Such antagonisms were at their sharpest in regions that were virtually sub-states rather than provinces. The resentments of the numerous petty gentry of Hungary, many of whom were also alienated from the prevailing order by their Protestantism, played an important part in the great rebellion of 1703–11. Agitation in Ireland, which culminated in the granting of legislative independence in 1782, owed much to the resentment of the Ascendancy against the use of Irish patronage for English political purposes; and a bill to tax absentees was only narrowly defeated in 1773. Yet the nationalistic element in these cases only added spice to antagonisms clearly visible even without it. British politics largely operated for much of this period in terms of a conflict between 'court' and 'country' parties. The court party was made up of those members of parliament who tended to support the government in return for, or in the hope of, a share of its patronage. This entailed living in London, dancing attendance on parliamentary divisions. 'Country' members suspected London; they agonized at its expense and begrudged every day spent away from their estates. In political terms they condemned the power and extent of patronage; they opposed waste, corruption, higher taxes, expensive continental wars, tinkering with the church, and central government interference in the localities. And although they were normally disunited, numerically they were a parliamentary majority and could block any legislation they unanimously disliked, such as the peerage bill. The provincial nobles of France, equally opposed to wasteful court patronage, high taxes, and centralization, enjoyed no such representation at the centre, much less power; accordingly their frustrations were greater. The remonstrances of provincial *parlements*, especially against tax increases, gave some voice to their views. In them the waste and extravagance of the court were repeatedly blamed for the state's financial difficulties. But remonstrances were occasional documents, often ignored by the government. Nor did the *parlements* command the full confidence of most provincial nobles. The petty nobility of France, marooned within the narrow horizons of its provinces, excluded by its poverty from most worthwhile employments, yet unable to assemble to voice its grievances and aspirations, was recognized throughout this period as one of the most intractable of social problems.

Two possible solutions were often canvassed: either remove the poverty or ensure that it entailed no disadvantages. Removing the poverty entailed removing both the laws and the prejudices against nobles entering trade: in 1701, when trade was depressed, the government confirmed a half-forgotten rule that nobles might engage in wholesale trade without loss of status. The effect, however, was more to induce recently ennobled merchants to continue trading, than to encourage nobles to abandon their prejudices. The trade wars of the mid-eighteenth century brought renewed discussion of the

[25] Quoted in J. Meyer, *La Noblesse bretonne au XVIIIe siècle* (1972), p. 249.

question, and in 1756 the abbé Coyer advocated wholesale ennoblement of merchants (and, by implication, an end to the law of derogation) in his *Trading Nobility*.[26] When, in 1767, the provisions of 1701 were eventually confirmed, it was declared that thenceforth two merchant families a year would be ennobled; but retail trade was never opened to nobles. In any case there was no sign of any general change in their attitude, so clearly expressed by Montesquieu[27] in 1748: 'Some. . .think that there should be laws in France to encourage the nobility to trade; this would be the means to destroy nobility there, without any use to trade.' The Spanish experience was similar. In 1675 nobles were authorized to engage in commerce; in the 1760s, amid repeated requests from economic societies, the government reissued this law in various seaports, and in 1783 throughout the country. But on no occasion did it elicit the least response on the part of the nobility.

Poor nobles preferred to have their poverty cancelled out by privileges. It was they who defended tax-exemptions or preferences most vigorously and who, being resident on their estates, exacted their 'feudal' rights most minutely. Above all, they believed that the state owed them a livelihood in the profession for which they were most fitted—arms. Until 1762 Russian nobles, were guaranteed military employment whether they liked it or not. In Prussia the officer corps was deliberately reserved almost entirely for nobles, but there were still too many candidates for available commissions. It took until the late eighteenth century to persuade them that an administrative career was equally honorable—a case of 'sword' prejudice against 'robe' far more serious than in France. At least in Prussia both influential magnates and rich, socially ambitious bourgeois were relatively rare, so that there was not the aggravation of competition from the wealthy. In Great Britain and France, however, commissions were purchasable on the open market, with the result that the superior wealth of great nobles on the one hand, and that of ambitious commoners or recently ennobled newcomers on the other tended either to push the price of commissions beyond the petty nobility or to maroon them permanently in the cheapest and most junior ranks. This was far more serious in France than in Britain, where the army was relatively small and the navy of mediocre social prestige. In 1683 Louis XIV expressed a wish to confine the recruitment of naval officer cadets to noblemen; his motive, like that of the rules of 1718 and 1727 which restricted the recruitment of most army officers to nobles, was to favour the petty nobility. Yet so long as purchase existed, they remained at a disadvantage. There was uproar when the government decreed, in 1750, that in future service as an officer should ennoble commoners. It seemed a positive incentive to purchase. The same year did indeed bring the establishment of a military cadet school in Paris reserved for noblemen, but this ignored the root of the problem. In 1756, incensed by Coyer's idea of a trading nobility, the chevalier d'Arc, grandson of Louis XIV on the sinister side, published his *Military*

---

[26] *La Noblesse commerçante.*
[27] *Esprit des lois*, Bk. XX, ch. XXII.

Nobility or the French Patriot. A sustained attack on the corrosive effect of wealth, it called for an officer corps open to nobles alone and an end to purchase. But d'Arc also prescribed compulsory service, with default punishable by derogation, and such Russian-sounding ideas won little support. Under the ministry of Saint-Germain (1775–7), who wished to professionalize the army, the gradual phasing out of purchase was at last begun. At the same time the Military School, which had rapidly been taken over by the inevitable rich bourgeois and influential courtiers, was supplemented by twelve provincial schools for officer cadets of poor noble stock. In 1775 the navy excluded non-nobles from officer cadet schools, and by 1780 a number of ecclesiastical benefices were being reserved for poor nobles. The most famous development came in 1781, when non-nobles and even those ennobled in recent generations were excluded from most commissions in the army. There was not, however, enough time before 1789 for petty nobles to derive much benefit from such measures; in retrospect they became famous (or infamous) as examples of noble disdain for commoners.

The problem of the poor nobility was an important element in a wider debate on luxury. Fénelon, disgusted by the contrast between the conspicuous consumption of metropolitan high society and the misery of the provinces in the last twenty-five years of Louis XIV's reign, partially blamed the king's policy of gathering his most eminent subjects around him at court. Court life, and its metropolitan extension, set ruinous standards of ostentatious living which drained the provinces of wealth and corrupted the nobility. D'Arc made a similar point half a century later, and although several of the *philosophes* (such as Montesquieu) remained unconvinced of luxury's tendency to corrupt, the physiocrats had no doubts. Luxury encouraged manufactures (that economic dead end) and concentrated absentee landlords in the capital, away from the true source of wealth. This was the warning given by Mirabeau in *The Friend of Mankind* (1756). He believed that the nobility, as landowners, were the key to the state's prosperity. Their social pre-eminence could be more easily justified in economic terms than on the more traditional military lines. They must, however, prove themselves worthy of this role by residing on their estates, living frugally, and reinvesting their revenues in agriculture rather than luxury. 'The words *countryman* and *provincial* have become ridiculous,' he complained. '. . .everybody has wanted to be a man of the court or of the town, and farewell to the fields.'[28] Mirabeau's book was a eulogy of all the rustic qualities the jaded sophisticates of Paris reviled; for him the true friend of mankind was the provincial noble.

Mirabeau was well aware that something more than the modest prosperity of sound agriculture and the consciousness of serving humanity was needed to make provincial life attractive to nobles who would otherwise avoid it. So he proposed to give them political power too, in the form of provincial estates. He was not alone in proposing this, nor was the idea found only in

[28] *L'Ami des hommes*, i. 133.

France. The emancipation of Russian nobles from service in 1762 did not produce the return to the land and agriculture that the government hoped to see; and when in 1775 local government was reorganized, a further inducement was offered by the establishment of local assemblies of nobles with extensive administrative power. These bodies were reinforced and elevated in 1785; they now became organs of provincial noble autonomy. Yet there was no tradition of corporate action among Russian nobles and no tradition of autonomy either, so that the new assemblies remained totally subordinate to the officers of the central government.

This was not at all what Mirabeau's followers, in the forty years that followed his proposals, had in mind. When they proposed the revival of lapsed provincial estates, their object was to give noblemen an active, independent hand in provincial government, such as they enjoyed in those provinces in which estates had survived. Estates, unlike *parlements*, were bodies of representatives and, again unlike *parlements*, they had the theoretical power to refuse tax increases. By the 1770s a revenue-hungry government had come to see the value of associating the governed with government, and in 1778 two experimental provincial assemblies were actually set up. But they were quite unlike estates; they were bodies of appointees, nor did nobles enjoy an advantageous position in them. Similar objections applied when Calonne proposed, in 1787, to extend this system to the whole country. It was not until the chaotic conditions following the collapse of central authority in the summer of 1788 that the idea of estates gained any practical momentum, and then the initiative came from provincial nobles themselves. Most of the projects then proliferating insisted that absentee landlords, or anybody enjoying any sort of court office or pension, should be ineligible. Beyond that, however, there was little agreement on the form, the powers, or the composition of the proposed estates. Only in Dauphiné did the estates actually convene; elsewhere, bickering was still going on when the elections to the estates-general diverted public attention, and the opportunity was lost.

This was the story all too often when nobles tried to improve their position by concerted action. They were paralysed by their own internal divisions, and seemed able to work together only for negative ends, defending their existing interests against governments. The Bible of the nobility, after 1748, was Montesquieu's *Spirit of the Laws*. By the end of the century it had been translated into every major European language. Its appeal was obvious: Montesquieu professed to show that, by its very nature, a monarchy was a government of laws, that these laws were protected, and the monarchy prevented from toppling into despotism, by the existence of an 'intermediary' power, the nobility. Nobility seemed built into the nature of things. What nobles often failed to see was that the exalted role assigned to them by Montesquieu remained essentially defensive; that they too could unbalance a monarchy by claiming the political initiative. Fortunately for kings, the basic inability of jealous noblemen to unite behind any such initiative also seemed built into the nature of things.

5. The Ruled: the Country

Noble supremacy was rooted in the countryside. The rural population—
scattered, unprotected, unsophisticated, and totally absorbed in producing
the means of subsistence—offered far less resistance to control than townsmen. And in 1660 this control was tightening, as the deceleration in over-all
population growth brought diminishing agricultural profits and landlords
sought to compensate by harder pressure upon those beneath them. The
whole of Europe found itself in the grip of an agrarian reaction, in the course
of which the peasantry found its rights, independence, and standards of living
curbed by the appetite of its lords. When agricultural profits recovered, in the
eighteenth century, the peasantry regained none of the lost ground. The
power of large landlords continued to grow, only to be curbed eventually
by governmental intervention which itself was undertaken in an attempt to
redistribute the peasant's burden in the state's favour, rather than to diminish
its total weight. Most peasants suffered to some extent from these circumstances. But as usual, serfs suffered most of all.

Serfdom

Perhaps half the peasants in Europe were serfs in 1660, as a result of a massive
expansion of serfdom in the east at a time when it was rapidly declining in
the west. East of the Elbe, that great social and economic frontier, serfdom
was now the rule; west of it, the exception, although it still survived in many
areas of western and southern Germany, northern Italy, and eastern France.

The strict meaning of serfdom is still the subject of academic controversy.
The most generally accepted definition is 'hereditary bondage to the land';
a true serf was part of the stock of an estate, but distinguished from a slave
by the fact that he could not be sold separately from the land to which he
was bound. Such bondage had several important corollaries. It meant that
the serf was not free to move his domicile and not free to marry or take a
trade without his lord's consent; that he was subject to his lord's private
jurisdiction; and above all that he owed various services, in cash, kind, labour
or all three, to the lord. In practice there were endless variations on these
basic themes. When Joseph II abolished personal serfdom (*Leibeigenschaft*)
in his hereditary domains in 1781, certain provinces were able to claim that
this institution did not exist and therefore could not be abolished. But the
bulk of its most notorious characteristics undoubtedly did exist, and the
point was a legal quibble.

As a general rule, serfdom grew harsher and more arbitrary the further
east it was found. In Russia bondage to the land, with the minimal security
it entailed, had almost disappeared by 1660. Serfs were sold without land,
like cattle, often at public auctions. It is true that a sizeable and growing

minority of Russian peasants were not serfs—almost 40 per cent in 1762. These were the 'state peasants', holding their land directly from the tsar, but not bondsmen on his private estates. Even they could be arbitrarily transferred into private ownership and servile status by the monarch's whim; as between 300,000 and 400,000 non-Russian peasants found when the territories where they lived were annexed between 1772 and 1795.

Conditions were perhaps least oppressive in the Austrian lands, where a fee secured a lord's permission to move, marry, inherit land, or take a trade. It is true that the árbiter in cases of dispute was the lord's court, but appeal to royal jurisdiction was possible; the sole practical restraint was the cost. Appeals were also possible in Hungary and Poland, but to bodies of local landowners, who were much less likely to be sympathetic. Permission to move or to marry was also more than a salable formality in these kingdoms. Hungarian lords enjoyed the right to force peasants to exchange their plots and could also, through their courts, impose corporal punishment. In Poland until 1768 they could inflict capital penalties. Yet even Polish and Hungarian serfs enjoyed minimal rights—to a plot and the means to cultivate it. The Russian serf enjoyed none. He only had obligations. There was no appeal from the Russian lord's decision. A lord's powers were so extensive that he scarcely needed the authority of a court to reinforce them. They were strengthened when Peter I made lords responsible for collecting their peasants' taxes and furnishing a regular number of military recruits. When in 1767 a group of serfs dared to complain to Catherine II of ill treatment, she promptly made any such attempt to invoke higher authority punishable by lords themselves. Russian serfs had no right to move, but could themselves be moved, sold, or separated from their families. The murder of a serf carried light penalties, and all other punishments were completely at a lord's discretion. Serfs could also be hired out, and the factories of the Urals were largely operated by serf labour. A law of 1734 offered batches of state serfs to anybody proposing to establish a factory or reaching a certain level of production in one. The only escape from subjection lay in flight; in Hungary and Poland there were elaborate regulations to prevent peasants from absconding and to recover them if they did. But, in the earlier part of the period at least, when labour was scarce, lords were often willing to poach serfs from one another and to protect runaways. The runaway's salvation was that rights of pursuit lasted only a limited time, except in Russia, where the law-code of 1649 had abolished time-limits for recovery and strictly forbidden other lords to harbour runaways. Flight was therefore very hazardous; the fact that it remained a major problem emphasizes how many peasants considered these risks preferable to continued subjection.

Still more oppressive than personal restrictions were the services and dues exacted by lords, theoretically in return for the tenure of a plot of land. The most universal of these was forced labour (*barschina* in Russia, *robot* in Habsburg lands). The great estates of Austria, Bohemia, Hungary, and Poland were divided into domain ('dominical' land in Austria, 'allodial' in Hungary) and peasant holdings ('rustical' land in Austria, 'urbarial' in Hungary). Domain work, done by serf forced labour, was increasingly in demand. By 1700 forced labour averaged perhaps three days a week, a day of twelve to fourteen hours, in most areas of serfdom. In Hungary and Poland, however, four days was not uncommon; the exact amount depended upon the size of a serf's holdings, and of his family. The obligations of Russian serfs, not being related to the land, were not so well defined; everything depended upon the whim of the master, but even so three days of *barschina* were perhaps normal under Peter I. By the 1780s as much as six days was not unknown, with peasants attending to their own land on Sundays or at night. This increasing demand resulted from rising prices, which made the dues in cash or kind (*obrok*), into which many labour services had been commuted before mid-century, less attractive.

In theory *obrok* and *barschina* were alternative obligations. In practice the uneven pace of commutation between 1650 and 1750, along with the arbitrary powers enjoyed by Russian lords, left most serfs subject to both. Elsewhere dues in both cash and kind had always been required as well as *robot*. Price inflation was a further influence. Dues in kind were cumbersome to collect, and so long as prices were stable lords preferred to compound them for cash payments. When prices began to rise, however, fixed sums were clearly less attractive, and dues in kind came back into favour. Throughout the Austrian lands dues absorbed on average at least one-sixth of a peasant's gross product; in Hungary it was more like a fifth. An additional burden was the use of expensive manorial monopolies and endless occasional fees and dues. Substantial losses, as great in value as many dues, might also result from damage caused when lords exercised their right to hunt over the peasants' land. It is true that, outside Russia, serfs received various rights in return for all these obligations. In addition to their plots, they had access to common lands and to seignorial charity in times of economic disaster; lords often supported important local amenities, such as schools and orphanages; and even the hated seignorial courts were a form of public service. Nevertheless there can be no serious doubt on whose side the balance of advantage lay.

Until the mid-eighteenth century, serfdom went unchallenged as one of the foundations of society. The only serious criticism came from the inarticulate complaints of the serfs themselves, when periodic revolts gave them the fleeting hope of some alleviation in their burdens. Revolts invariably failed, but did not always fail to produce improvement. Governments had no interest in a social order so harsh and rigid that it was in perpetual danger from rebellion. As Maria Theresa wrote in 1775, 'People who have no hope have nothing to fear, and are dangerous.'[1] As a result of a Bohemian rebellion of 1679, in which the increasing weight of lords' demands had been a major grievance, Leopold I in 1680 restricted *robot* in that kingdom to three days and forbade excessive or unusual tasks. He also forbade innovations in seignorial demands and confirmed the peasants' right of appeal to the crown

[1] Quoted in C. A. Macartney, *The Habsburg and Hohenzollern Dynasties in the seventeenth and eighteenth centuries* (1970), 173.

through its local officials. Yet these measures remained isolated, the product of temporary crises, and the fact that they had to be renewed by Charles VI in 1717 and again in 1730 shows how rapidly they were forgotten. Besides, they merely regulated serfdom, leaving its basic principles untouched. The whole of eastern Europe was horrified when, in 1742, Emperor Charles VII offered emancipation to the serf population of Bohemia in return for their support against the Habsburgs. Such rash promises threatened the whole fabric of society itself. Nevertheless, within a few years the government in Vienna was seriously considering far-reaching reforms which would change the institution of serfdom beyond recognition.

The heart of the issue was the peasant as taxpayer. Serfs overwhelmed by payments and services to their lords had nothing left for their kings. The sole restriction on a Russian master's treatment of his serfs had traditionally been that he should not ruin them, so that they were unable to pay their taxes. Peter I was able to insure himself against even this by making lords responsible for their peasants' tax returns; and so no real conflict arose between the respective claims on the peasant of lord and tsar. The essence of Austrian plans for financial reform, however, begun in the late 1740s, was to diminish rather than to increase the role of nobles in tax-collection and to limit the obligations of serfs to their lords. The first step was to give clear definition to these obligations. Thus in 1767, after years of obstruction by a suspicious diet, Maria Theresa unilaterally promulgated an 'urbarial patent' for Hungary, which standardized such matters as the size of peasant holdings upon which all obligations, private and public, were assessed. From here it was only a short step to defining the obligations themselves, and in 1771 *robot* was restricted in the fragmentary province of Austrian Silesia. In lower Austria in 1772 it was confined to two twelve-hour days; and a series of disastrous harvests in subsequent years, followed by widespread peasant unrest and a full-scale rebellion in Bohemia in 1775, lent added urgency to the problem. In 1775 *robot* in Bohemia was once more limited (as in 1680) to three days; in 1778 a similar regulation was issued for Carniola.

By this time not only imperial tax-collectors were interested in limiting serfdom. Objections to the institution itself, both practical and philosophical, were increasingly heard. Even in the seventeenth century defenders of serfdom, such as the Austrian cameralist Becher, had bitterly attacked the habits of lords, and like later cameralists he had emphasized that the well-being of the peasant underpinned that of society as a whole. The physiocrats took such arguments a stage further, for they believed that the key to prosperity was property unencumbered by short leases, insecure tenure, or the burdens of forced labour or seignorial dues. By all these standards serfdom stood condemned as economically retrogressive. 'As long as peasants do not have complete property rights,' wrote the cameralist Justi, a notable influence on Joseph II, in 1760, 'they lack the most noble motive, the most effective incentive to cultivate their lands to the best of their ability, for they must always fear that they or their children will be evicted. . .States where one estate or one class of people is subjected to another, have as monstrous a constitution as those which existed in the most barbarian times.'[2] So the objection was humanitarian, too. Hereditary bondage to the land, much less to a master alone, as in Russia, seemed irreconcilable with the natural liberty into which all men were born. Consequently from around 1760 arguments of political expediency, economic benefit, and philosophic benevolence began to flow together in condemnation of serfdom. As Sonnenfels, another of Joseph II's mentors, put it in 1777, 'Humanity and the public welfare demand that the lot of the peasant be a bearable one.'[3]

It is a problem to decide whether all the talk had any practical results. Catherine II throughout the 1760s preached the improvement of serf conditions, sponsored an essay competition on the advantage of peasant property, and thereby stimulated a good deal of discussion about agrarian problems in such bodies as the "Free Economic Society' of St. Petersburg. But most of this discussion turned on whether *obrok* or *barschina* screwed most out of the serf, while the empress resisted all practical suggestions for reform, especially after the great rising of 1773–4. When Alexander Radischev, a minor civil servant, defied the censors and published an impassioned attack on serfdom in his *Journey from St. Petersburg to Moscow* (1790), he was exiled to Siberia. But even when legislation was issued, there was no guarantee of its enforcement. Frederick II formally abolished serfdom in Pomerania in 1763, and after 1772 extended the abolition to newly annexed west Prussia. But since nothing was done to enforce these laws, landlords ignored them. The only practical reform came on crown lands, where Frederick by abandoning the right to resume serf holdings at the death of each tenant, guaranteed them hereditary rights. In 1779 Louis XVI emancipated serfs on French royal domains but refrained from attacking the property rights of private owners: thus in 1789 there were still about 140,000 serfs in France. In Denmark under the meteoric ministry of Struensee (1770–2) forced labour was restricted and royal lands were sold to peasants, but these reforms were reversed when he fell. Nothing further was done until a Grand Agrarian Commission, beginning twenty years of activity in 1786, inaugurated a long series of piecemeal reforms which ultimately succeeded because public opinion had time to appreciate the accumulating economic benefits of an emancipated peasantry.

It was essential to win over the serf-owners themselves, all powerful in their localities, if measures of improvement were to stand any chance of success. The first effective reforms came from private individuals. In the 1730s, at the very moment when the hold of Danish landlords over their serfs was being increased by making them responsible for military recruitment (1733), the first minister Bernstorff began to convert his own serfs into leasehold tenants free of dues and services. In 1784 Archdeacon Coxe, that indefatigable traveller and observer noted that since 1760 'a few nobles of benevolent hearts and enlightened principles' in Poland had begun to emancipate numbers of their serfs, with dramatic results in terms of population

[2] Quoted in E. M. Link, *The Emancipation of the Austrian Peasant 1740–1798* (1949), 103.
[3] Quoted ibid. 105.

increase and the wealth of the peasants concerned. King Stanislas Poniatowski and his chancellor Zamoiski, who both had emancipated serfs of their own, also gave energetic support to writers advocating agrarian reform. Yet as Coxe also noted, 'The generality. . .of the Polish nobles are not inclined either to establish or give efficacy to any regulations in favour of the peasants, whom they scarcely consider as entitled to the common rights of humanity.'[4] The diet in 1780 rejected a law code proposed by Zamoiski, which included improvements in serf conditions. Polish peasants who became Austrian or Prussian subjects under the partitions sometimes benefited unexpectedly from reforms in those states. But most became Russians, and for them conditions grew positively worse.

Nothing illustrates the intricacies and frustrations of the serf problem better than the experience of Joseph II. When he became sole ruler of the Habsburg domains in 1780 he had already been fuming for years over the slow progress of agrarian reforms. Regulations forced through in the preceding twenty years had been largely ineffective owing to the intransigence of serf-owners. Nor had lords been impressed by the so-called 'Raab system', introduced on crown lands in Bohemia after the rebellion there, under which dominical land was divided up between peasants in return for cash rents and no forced labour. Joseph extended this system to most crown lands after 1780, as a gesture of confidence in its benefits; but still only a few nobles followed his example. Joseph never showed much confidence in the power of example alone, and from the start he was resolved to legislate. There was no question of abolishing the whole apparatus of serfdom at a stroke. Even Joseph II could recognize a political impossibility on that scale. However he did feel that piecemeal measures over a period could achieve much the same result.

The first step was to abolish the personal restrictions of servile status. In 1781 *Leibeigenschaft*, personal serfdom, was abolished in Bohemia, Moravia, and Silesia. The next year similar measures followed in various Austrian provinces and in 1785 they were extended to Hungary. From then on peasants were free to marry, move about, or embrace a trade without their lord's permission. In 1781 too a *Strafpatent* limited the penalties which a lord's court could impose, and an *Untertanspatent* improved appeal facilities by granting peasants official advocates. In subsequent years manorial monopolies were also restricted, and the rights of lords to interfere in peasant inheritances were whittled down almost to nothing; thus security of tenure, that universally agreed fundamental of peasant prosperity, was virtually established. Although all these measures provoked impassioned protests from the estates and diets of the emperor's various domains, not to mention his own principal advisors, Joseph overrode all opposition. Yet the heart of the problem, the lord's right to forced labour, remained untouched. In 1783 Joseph established a scale upon which lords might commute *robot*

[4] W. Coxe, *Travels into Poland, Russia, Sweden and Denmark* (4th edn. 1792), i. 146.

into cash payments, but it was essentially voluntary and few chose to take advantage of it. He was soon convinced once again that legislation was the answer, and in 1789 the so-called 'physiocratic urbarium' was issued. Its main purpose (and hence its nickname) was to institute a single tax on land like that advocated by the French economists. In order to facilitate the taxation of peasants, however, forced labour services were abolished; peasants were now to retain 70 per cent of their gross income free of dues and taxes; the remaining 30 per cent was to be divided between the lords and the state on a basis of $17\frac{7}{9}$ per cent for the former and $12\frac{2}{9}$ per cent for the latter. This was breathtakingly radical. Peasants, who before had been lucky to retain 30 per cent of their product, now stood to benefit enormously. But it was also too simple by half. Even if lords had been content to see labour services and dues commuted into cash rents, a flat rate of $17\frac{7}{9}$ per cent seldom accurately reflected their value, nor would the sums involved have enabled them to hire the labour force they had lost at market rates. The compensation, both arbitrary and inadequate, would rapidly have compelled lords to split up domains no longer economically viable into small peasant tenures. This was precisely that Joseph wanted, having dreamed for years of attacking the magnates of his realms. It would have been a social and economic revolution of the first magnitude. The unprecedented ferocity of protest forced Joseph to postpone the end of *robot* by a year. This did little to improve matters and chaos was avoided only by Joseph's death in the spring of 1790 when the new law had been in operation only a matter of months. By then most of Joseph's other reforms had already been abandoned in the face of noble hostility. His successor Leopold II now withdrew the 'physiocratic urbarium' and *robot* continued after all as the basis of the empire's economy.

Yet Joseph had achieved something. Leopold refused to withdraw any of the reforms introduced before 1785, even in Hungary. Personal serfdom had gone forever, and the state continued to guarantee the peasant a minimum of judicial protection. These measures also inspired other German states, such as Baden in 1783, or Mainz in 1787, to abolish serfdom. The debate on Joseph's policies forced even the most intransigent opponents of reform to re-examine their position. The result was that the 1790s saw, as well as widespread reaction, an actual increase in the (admittedly small) number of voluntary commutations of *robot*. The most eloquent tribute came from the way the peasants themselves revered Joseph's memory for years afterwards. 'We stand by all the regulations of our Emperor and King, Joseph II', declared a Hungarian peasant petition of 1790, 'we shall not let one jot of them be abolished, for all of them are as sacred, just and beneficient as if God Himself had suggested them to him...Let us then honour him by raising a marble column in each of the fifty-two counties of the country for the well-earned glory of his memory.'[5]

[5] 'The Peasant's Declaration', in B. K. Kiraly, *Hungary in the late Eighteenth Century* (1969), 248–9.

Peasant Tenures in the West

The work of reformers such as Joseph II was popular among serfs, not least because it confirmed their widespread and deeply held belief that they were the true owners of the land. At law however, serfs *held* land, but never owned it. So true peasant proprietors were usually found only in the west. Even there, the proportion of land in peasant hands was seldom impressive; and the small size of peasant plots meant that they wielded far less economic power than their numbers might seem to warrant.

Peasant property was at its most extensive in France, where it probably declined over our period from something approaching 40 per cent to something nearer 30 per cent. Swedish peasants owned 31·5 per cent in 1700, but by contrast had increased their share to 52·6 per cent in 1815. In Spain the proportion was much less—about 22 per cent in 1797—and that was concentrated in the northern provinces. Around the same time small owner occupiers accounted for about 20 per cent of the cultivated acreage of England, a slight rise on preceding decades, but almost certainly less than a century earlier. In Ireland the confiscations of the 1690s completed the destruction of the Catholic landowning peasantry, peasant proprietors were as scarce there as east of the Elbe, and the brutality and arbitrariness of the confiscations had created similar traditions of peasant ownership. 'Families were so numerous, and so united in clans', Young noted in 1778, 'that the heir of an estate was always known; and it is a fact that in most parts of the kingdom the descendants of the old landowners regularly transmit by testamentary deed the memorial of their rights to those estates which once belonged to their families.'[6]

The basic fact about peasant property was its almost universal decline, which every circumstance, whether general or local, seemed to promote. Peasant property, small by definition, was unable to produce as economically as the larger units of the nobility or the church. In times of rising food prices, such as the later eighteenth century, peasant proprietors might indeed hold their own; but between 1660 and about 1750 agricultural profits were low or stagnant. Many English peasant proprietors were forced to sell out. The slight (and temporary) revival in their numbers towards 1800 reflected the farming boom which accompanied the French wars. Outside the British Isles and Catalonia, moreover, the disadvantages of small properties were accentuated by the division of inheritances. Entails, which enabled nobles to circumvent normal laws of inheritance, were far too complex and expensive for most peasants; and so each generation saw plots, already small, subdivided yet further into even less economic units. The exceptional case of Sweden, where the proportion of land in peasant hands grew, is explained by a deliberate royal policy of converting due-paying tenants into tax-paying freeholders, and by the absence of entails.

A further pressure on the peasant proprietor was the weight of seignorial

---

[6] *A Tour in Ireland*, 193–4.

dues and obligations, the relics of an otherwise vanished serfdom. By 1660 'feudal' tenures had largely disappeared in the British Isles, and the Swedish proprietor was free of them by definition. In Italy, Spain, and France, on the other hand, overlords still enjoyed a great diversity of rights. The forced labour basic to serfdom had largely died out, although some French and west-German overlords could still exact several days a year; but dues in cash or kind were common, and so were manorial monopolies, private jurisdictions, and hunting rights. Such things are, as Joseph II found, hard to quantify, and even calculable dues differed so widely from place to place that any generalization can only be approximate. In France, however, dues can seldom have amounted to less than a tenth of a peasant's gross revenues, a proportion which, in years of bad harvests, might increase to as much as a quarter. For this outlay the peasant, unlike a serf, received nothing in return.

Since it was generally easier for a peasant to lease land than to own it, many small proprietors supplemented holdings they owned by leasing further plots. Still more rented all they had, and so long as prices were relatively stagnant, long leases on very favourable terms were common. In return for dues in kind, rather than cash rents, Swedish tenants enjoyed almost perpetual rights to their holdings: it was in recognition of this that the crown in the early eighteenth century began to allow its tenants to redeem their dues. In southern Italy and Sicily long, and even perpetual, leases of small plots were often granted to peasants at fixed cash rents; and when in the 1690s a Protestant Irish parliament prohibited Catholics from taking leases longer than thirty-one years, its intention was penal, which shows how long a normal lease was expected to be. When prices began to rise, however, long agreements at fixed rentals appeared increasingly uneconomic. Between 1770 and 1789 redemption of dues in kind was suspended in Sweden and only resumed for political reasons. In Sicily in 1752 landlords were allowed to cancel perpetual leases unilaterally and profited from this to dispossess small tenants, consolidate their plots into larger holdings, and lease them over short periods of three to six years to profiteering stewards.[7] Even in Ireland thirty-one years began to seem generous, and landlords sought both to shorten the term of new leases and to grant them to outsiders who could outbid local peasants. Sicilian peasants often reacted to dispossession by becoming brigands and bandits; and in Ireland, where the peasantry acknowledged no moral right in the landlords in any case, agrarian terrorists persecuted new tenants. In Ulster competition for leases was exacerbated by religious differences, and by the early 1790s land hunger among the peasantry and rapacity among landlords had reduced much of rural Ulster to a state of civil war between Protestant and Catholic peasants banded into rival secret societies.

The economic pressures affecting conditions of tenure were similar everywhere, but the results were as diverse as local circumstances. The rise in prices from the mid-eighteenth century led Spanish landlords to press for a

---

[7] For the consequences of this, see above, pp. 18–19.

freedom with leaseholders similar to that their Sicilian counterparts had received in 1752; but in 1763 the council of Castile, dominated by ministers who believed in peasant property, refused to allow unilateral cancellation. Holders of long leases in Galicia and part of Asturias, however, responded to this victory by subletting their tenures for higher rents than they themselves paid, and this, combined with partible inheritance, led to an intensive subdivision of the soil and a top-heavy rent-structure which made agriculture totally uneconomic and confounded well-intentioned theorists. By contrast, the perpetual leases of Catalonia were protected by a form of primogeniture, but, obsessed by the evil of the great entailed estates of Castile and Estremadura, reforming Spanish ministers often failed to realize that security of tenure benefited peasant agriculture little without integrity of inheritance.

The commonest form of lease in France, as well as in northern Italy and parts of Spain, was share-cropping. In principle, the lessor provided the land, the equipment, stock, and seed, and the lessee the labour; both profits and losses were shared. In practice there were endless variations, almost all unfavourable to the tenant. In many places the lord took more than a half of the product; in others he did not provide most of the stock or seed; sometimes the sharecropper bore all the cost of seignorial dues, and in northern France he always paid his landlord's taxes. Contracts were usually informal or verbal, which left the precise terms of a lease uncomfortably vague. The object of sharecropping was clear—to maximize returns from a peasantry too poor to afford cash rents, for a minimum initial outlay. Despite its inefficiency, this system was fostered by rising prices, because its returns came in kind which a lessor could then sell for a market price. And in good years the share-cropper might subsist adequately too. In bad years however his obligations overwhelmed him, and in the later seventeenth century as many as 60 per cent of sharecropping leases fell in before their term in some provinces. Then the unfortunate tenant would forfeit whatever stock and equipment he might own to the lessor. It is true that a quarter of all leased land in France was let out for a simple cash sum, but it was often sublet in its turn to sharecroppers. French leases seldom exceeded nine years and rents were almost always reviewed on expiry. The turnover rate of tenants was, therefore, staggering, and the lives of peasants who hoped to live by renting were insecure in the extreme.

In the late eighteenth century population growth increased the land-hunger of peasants, which placed landlords in a very favourable position. Demand for leases was also swelled by the growing number of unviable plots of peasant property resulting from larger surviving families. The inevitable result was to swell the ranks of the most numerous peasant group, the landless labourers. The *latifundia* of central and southern Spain had long been worked by miserable day labourers, and the spread of such estates in southern Italy created its own landless work force. In England the proportion of landless labourers almost doubled between 1690 and 1830. This was once thought to result from enclosures and the overwhelming costs which they imposed upon small proprietors. Undoubtedly some of the latter did disappear for this reason; but England was already a land of large estates and substantial leasehold farms, as well as primogeniture which penalized younger sons before the population acceleration began. Enclosure not only did not create the problem; it positively helped to alleviate it by boosting the demand for day labour on enclosed farms when the supply was growing fastest.

To contemporary economists, however, a profusion of landless labourers seemed the worst of evils. The object of economic policy was to increase tax-revenue. To do this, taxable wealth had to increase, and the only easily taxed source of wealth, as well as the most extensive, was land. Over-large estates tended, they believed, to be neglected, their productive potential not fully realized. The ideal was a land of peasant proprietors or at least secure tenants. 'Enforced poverty', wrote Quesnay, the most prominent of the physiocrats, 'is not the way to render the peasant industrious: it is only a guarantee of the ownership and enjoyment of their gains which can put heart into them and make them diligent. . .It is the wealth of the inhabitants of the countryside which gives birth to the wealth of the nation. . .POOR PEASANTS, POOR KINGDOM.'[8] 'The whole secret', wrote Olavide, a Spanish administrator and convert to French ideas, in 1768, 'consists in giving them, thanks to a long lease, or by alienation, the property of a small morsel of land on which to live with their family and their cattle. They will then be happy proprietors and their great number will ensure the abundance, the prosperity, and the wealth of the state.'[9] Much the same arguments that condemned serfdom in the east condemned large estates and 'feudal' dues in the west.

Yet despite the talk of physiocrats, of Neapolitan intellectuals, and of the members of the Spanish economic societies known as the 'Friends of the Countryside', no serious steps were taken anywhere to break up *latifundia*. When Boncerf attacked 'feudal' dues in 1776, his book was burned by order of the French courts and his arguments fell on deaf ears. Only in Savoy was the buying out of seignorial rights authorized (1771). In the preceding decade indeed, reformers had gained a commanding voice in the Spanish government, but many of their policies had ambiguous results. The colonization of the Sierra Morena with German smallholders, begun in 1767 and enthusiastically supported while Olavide, its originator, was governor, languished after he was indicted by the Inquisition in 1773. An English traveller noted that in the mid-1780s 'these new settlements swarm with half-naked beggars.[10] The only area in which any states operated a sustained agrarian policy was that of common lands and rights.

Attacks on common rights by overlords and large proprietors were a permanent feature of village life and a constant source of litigation. There

---

[8] 'General Maxims', quoted in R. L. Meek, *The Economics of Physiocracy* (1962), 259.

[9] Quoted in M. Defourneaux, *Pablo de Olavide ou l'Afrancesado (1725–1803)* (1959), 149.

[10] J. Townsend, *A Journey through Spain in the Years 1787 and 1788* (2nd edn., 1792) ii. 292.

was a tendency among lawyers to uphold the encroachers, but the widespread survival of common rights showed that this tendency had by no means triumphed. But from the mid-eighteenth century governments, paradoxically in the hope of increasing peasant properties, lent the attack open support. Between 1766 and 1768 a series of Spanish laws decreed the division of all municipal 'wastes' and commons into plots for needy peasants, and in the 1780s the rights of the Mesta to keep huge stretches of central Spain as open grazing were restricted. In 1789 the division of village commons in order to redistribute them to the poor was also authorized in Sicily. But both there and in Spain the beneficiaries of these measures lacked the capital to manage their allotments successfully, and although the number of peasant proprietors undoubtedly increased, most of the new private property was ultimately sold to larger landowners. Throughout the 1760s in France the secretary of state Bertin sponsored a whole series of local measures abolishing common rights, such as gleaning and collective grazing, and issued another series permitting enclosure and division of common lands. Bounties offered to clearers of 'waste' land also encouraged infringement and contesting of common rights. These reforms were piecemeal, however, and the opposition aroused from village communities deterred the government from issuing any general laws.[11] When bad harvests in the early 1770s left subsequent governments more aware of the dangers of over-hasty innovations, the impetus to reform died down. Thus by 1789 there had still been no spectacular decline in French commons. This contrasted with England, where eighteenth-century enclosures brought a massive extension of cultivated area, mainly at the expense of commons and heaths. Between 1760 and the end of the century well over two million acres of commons or waste were enclosed, and all without any interference at all from the government, which until 1793 professed no overt interest in agrarian questions. In a land dominated by large proprietors the English village community had nothing like the corporate strength of the French, so resistance was relatively weak. In any case most English peasants enjoyed no common rights, although many usurped them. Only those who could prove rights received plots in compensation, but most of them could no more find the capital to fence and stock their allotments than Spaniards or Sicilians. Consequently they sold out to richer neighbours; and the elimination of commons, in the one country where it succeeded, helped concentrate land in fewer hands rather than spread it out among more.

Public Burdens

The difficulties of peasant life were compounded by obligations to the state, many of which became more onerous, at least in money terms, between 1660 and 1800. They fell into three broad categories: tithes, taxes, and military service.

Tithes were destined for the upkeep of parish clergy and were levied everywhere except in Russia. In principle they amounted to a tenth of the

[11] See H. L. Root, *Peasants and King in Burgundy: Agrarian Foundations of French Absolutism* (1987).

fruits of the soil, payable in kind. In practice perhaps a majority of tithes had by this time been commuted into cash payments, which meant that as a burden they began to diminish after about 1750. Equally, however, those still levied in kind became more burdensome. It is true that the amount actually levied seldom amounted to a tenth; in France, for instance, it averaged about 8 per cent, in Italy far less. Nevertheless it still often represented a substantial proportion of a peasant's product, and few public burdens moved him to more resentment, evasion, and litigation. Most resented of all were abuses by which many tithes failed to reach parish priests at all. In England many went to lay impropriators, who employed vicars at stipends of only a fraction of tithe yield. In Catholic countries monasteries followed similar practices. The absentee Anglican parsons of Ireland employed profiteering 'proctors' to levy their tithes from a Catholic population which was already maintaining its own clandestine clergy. It was against the rapacity of these proctors that the Whiteboys, the nocturnal terrorists of the 1760s, largely directed their attacks.

Similar inequalities pervaded taxation. Great Britain was the only state in which there were no privileged groups enjoying a lighter tax burden or partial or even total tax exemption. The land tax, introduced in 1693 and the basic British tax for almost a century, exempted the landless and those whose property was worth less than £20 a year. Taxation affected most English peasants only when landlords passed on their own burden in the form of higher rents or through the price of goods subject to excise. In Sweden only freeholders paid direct taxes; but tenants of either crown or nobility paid equivalent sums in dues. Elsewhere, the peasant alone bore the full weight of taxes; he alone was not entitled to any alleviations or exemptions. Every new privilege indirectly increased his burden, since most taxes, assessed by governments according to their own needs rather than the taxpayers' capacities, gave rise to fixed quotas. Towns, always more complex to tax than the countryside, could often 'buy off' governments with lump sums, throwing more of the burden of local quotas onto the countryside. Individual townsmen often used their privileged status to protect their rural properties, with a consequent increase in the burden on the other inhabitants. But even without the complications of privilege, the arbitrary assessment of quotas, which communities or parishes were left to make up as best they could, led to endless friction between peasants over their relative obligations. Russian communities could redistribute the holdings of their inhabitants in order to preserve the principle of viable tax units, but in the west where private property was so well established, poor owners had to manage as best they could. Nor did revenue officers normally take account of hardship in times of natural disaster. 'For a long time,' complained a south-western French village in 1789,[12] 'the tax assessment on men has always fallen independently of the yield of the land. *Pay and Die*! says the collector to the people who

[12] Quoted in P. Goubert and S. Denis, *1789: Les Français ont la parole* (1964), 138–9.

have seen their vines frozen or their harvest hailed upon.' Without powerful friends, peasants found it almost impossible to appeal successfully against their assessments. In eastern Europe, where lords bore the responsibility of collecting and transmitting their serfs' tax revenue to the government, it was out of the question, and lords had a free hand. In Austria they were known to charge their peasants interest on tax arrears, which they themselves pocketed. On the other hand, lords who levied taxes had an interest in keeping their general level low in order to protect their own dues. Western officials and tax-farmers had no such incentives; their interest lay in pushing collection to the utmost limits of rigour so as to increase their own fees and profits. Consequently whereas peasant unrest in the east tended to be directed mainly against seignorial dues, in the west the grievance was equally often taxation.

Most hated of all, perhaps because it was the most difficult to evade, was indirect taxation. Most of the revenue of Spain and Naples came from sales taxes. The relative depopulation of Castile was often blamed upon the tendency of peasants to migrate to Spain's less heavily taxed peripheral provinces. But even there they could not escape the high prices of the state monopolies, such as tobacco and salt. France and Prussia also had tobacco monopolies, and salt was a state monopoly almost everywhere. Even in England, where the market was free, it bore a high level of duty. The notorious French *gabelle* was at once the most efficient and the most hated salt tax of all, for under it each subject was compelled to buy a fixed annual minimum irrespective of his needs. The exemption of most of the rich and the lighter load borne by certain western provinces only increased the bitter resentment felt by those subjected to its full weight.

There is no doubt that in most countries the nominal tax burden rose over this period. The difficulty is to decide how far, if at all, the true burden on the peasant increased. Unfortunately it is seldom possible accurately to assess the weight of taxation at a given moment, let alone over a long period. Joseph II's 'physiocratic urbarium' fixed $12\frac{2}{9}$ per cent as a reasonable proportion of a peasant's income for the state to take in 1789; but around the same time a Hungarian economist estimated that the average peasant in his country was paying between 16 and 17 per cent. In mid-eighteenth century Spain basic sales taxes alone took 14 per cent of the value of each transaction. With the addition of other charges such as duties on basic food stuffs like meat, wine, and sugar, the total loss to the peasant's gross income can hardly have been less than 10 per cent. Taxes in France around 1700 may have taken anything between 5 and 10 per cent, with the two-twentieths imposed between 1749 and 1756 doubling the demand; though in subsequent decades, when assessments were not revised, rising prices made this less steep than it appeared. Peter I's reform of Russian tax assessments in 1724, by which a tax on amorphous 'households' was replaced by a universal poll-tax on all non-nobles, entailed perhaps the most massive increase in tax-demand witnessed anywhere during this period. Between 1724 and 1769 the tax burden of the average male Russian taxpayer rose by 181 per cent. In short, although the real rise in taxation was not as great, thanks to inflation, as the nominal one, areas in which peasants paid less in 1800 than in 1660 were extremely rare.

Not all public burdens were payable in cash or kind. States, like lords, also exacted labour services for public works—notably roadbuilding. Throughout Europe the parishes or communities through which roads passed were responsible for their maintenance; this normally involved labour by the parishioners themselves—one more burden escaped by townsmen. All English householders were obliged to spend six days a year, providing their own equipment, on road repairs. This did not necessarily guarantee good roads. 'Teams and labourers coming out for statute work', noted the *Gentleman's Magazine* in 1767, 'are generally idle, careless, and under no commands . . . They make holiday of it, lounge about, and trifle away their time . . . in short, statute work will never mend the roads effectually.'[13] In northern Ireland an attempt in the 1760s to introduce forced labour on the roads was successfully opposed by terror gangs calling themselves 'Hearts of Oak'. To judge from the atrocious state of continental roads, the difficulties were universal. The great exception was France, where a network of first-class roads was largely maintained by forced labour, the famous *corvée*. Practically unknown under Louis XIV, the system spread rapidly under his successor, and was regularized nationally by a set of rules issued in 1738. Even then, its weight varied between twelve and thirty days a year, and some provinces never adopted it. The sole common feature in all provinces was the exemption enjoyed by nobles, ecclesiastics, and practically everybody of wealth or influence. The relative efficiency of the *corvée* sprang from its supervision by the local officers of a royal Board of Bridges and Roads; but still complaints about the quality of work were constant, and in the 1760s several intendants began to commute services into money payments. In 1776 Turgot attempted to abolish the *corvée* and replace it with a tax. But when he fell this law was reversed, only to be renewed in 1786 after another decade of progressive local commutation. During all this time the issue was the subject of a fierce public debate. To the contention that *corvée* made inferior roads with twice the effort of contract labour, physiocrats and their sympathizers added the argument that days lost in forced labour were days lost to agriculture. Opponents of these views were often more against replacing the *corvée* with a new tax, than positively for the existing system. But neither side consulted the peasants who actually bore the burden. Reformers took it for granted that they opposed it, but if the choice lay between a few days' desultory annual labour and payment of yet another levy on top of dues, tithes, and taxes, many peasants preferred to labour and save their money.

The most onerous labour service of all was perhaps conscription into the armed forces. And if, with the exception of France, forced-labour services showed no sign of becoming more rigorous, conscription certainly did. In Prussia, the military state *par excellence*, everybody was theoretically liable to military service from 1713. In 1732–3 the country was divided into cantons, each of which had to make up the numbers of a given military unit

[13] Quoted in S. and B. Webb, *English Local Government. Vol. 5, The Story of the King's Highway* (1913), 30.

where volunteers were lacking. In peacetime conscription involved only two months' spring training a year, but since townsmen and workers in most industries were exempt, the burden was borne almost entirely by the peasantry. The Russian system was even more harsh and arbitrary. Recruits served for life and might never return home. From the 1700s every able-bodied male between twenty and thirty-five was liable to conscription whenever the government needed troops. There were ninety-four such occasions between 1724 and 1830, on each of which every village was called upon to provide between 1 and 3 per cent of its eligible population. And although it was possible to buy and equip substitutes, the cost still fell on the village community. From 1724 Russian nobles were responsible for enforcing this system on their serfs, giving added force to their already huge powers. In 1733 Danish nobles were endowed with similar powers in recruiting, which they used to tie their peasants to the soil in a form of serfdom. Compared to this, the burden of military service in the west seemed light; conscription was confined to the recruitment of militias, essentially part-time forces for emergencies. Only the French militia, created in 1688, was a full-scale reserve army recruited by lot among able-bodied unmarried men between sixteen and forty. Those chosen served for six years. In peacetime this might only mean a few weeks' training a year, but in war it could lead to active service far from home. As usual, the rich, including richer peasants, enjoyed exemption, and the burden fell on those least capable of bearing it. Peasants went to extravagant lengths to avoid the draw, including flight and even self-mutilation. When conscription for a militia was introduced in Ireland in 1793, eight weeks of rioting claimed 230 lives. For this capricious, uncertain, and arbitrary obligation came on top of burdens that were already, in bad times, near to overwhelming. The most eloquent expression of the peasant plight remains perhaps the much quoted complaint of the French peasant woman who told Young in 1789 that:

Her husband had a morsel of land, one cow, and a poor little horse, yet they had 42 lbs of wheat and three chickens to pay as a quit rent to one seigneur, and 168 lbs of oats, one chicken and one sou, to pay to another, besides very heavy tailles and other taxes. She had 7 children, and the cow's milk helped to make the soup. It was to be hoped, she said, that there would be some alleviation soon, for taxes and dues are crushing us.'[14]

Peasant Life

Among the peasantry, far more than among town dwellers, the family was a basic economic unit. All its members, even young children, were expected to contribute to the common upkeep by their labour, even if only by gleaning, gathering berries, watching livestock, or begging in the streets. Wives were accustomed to the heaviest manual work, which inevitably took its toll; the peasant woman who complained so eloquently to Young in 1789, though she had had seven children and looked sixty or seventy, was only twenty-eight. Children might increase a family's difficulties. 'Landless labourers', wrote a

---

[14] Young, *Travels*, 173.

Norman parish priest in 1774, 'get married, bring up a first child, have a great deal of difficulty in bringing up a second, and if there is a third, their work is no longer enough to pay for food and other expenses.'[15] Landed peasants, on the other hand, often had large families in the hope of strong sons to help cultivate their plots; in some areas killing or abandonment of female children was a well-established practice. Yet large families usually created more problems than they solved in terms of maintenance—particularly when the head of the family died and the property was shared out. The larger the family, the smaller and less economic the inheritances. It seems clear that the fall in infant mortality that began in the eighteenth century was accompanied by increasing attempts at contraception in order to keep families down. But the methods used were sporadic, crude, and, on the general level, largely ineffective. This is why the problem of the poor grew so much more acute and visible towards the end of this period; more peasant children were not being born, but more survived, despite the unhygienic conditions under which most peasant families lived: in winter they took their animals into their houses for warmth, with all living creatures huddled together around the common fire or stove in horrifying squalor. 'The house of an Irish peasant', observed the philosopher Berkeley,[16] 'is the cave of poverty; within, you see a pot and a little straw; without, a heap of children tumbling on a dung hill.' The same could have been said of much peasant housing throughout Europe.

Not all peasants lived in squalor on the borders of subsistence, however. There was a well-established economic hierarchy within each community, in which two basic divisions eclipsed all others: one was between those with land (either owned or leased) and those without; the other, and arguably the more important, was between those who had enough land to survive natural calamities, and those who had not. By far the smallest group consisted of those with enough land, a highly favoured minority. In the area around Beauvais in northern France, for example, 80 per cent of the land-owning peasantry in the 1670s owned less than 25 acres, when in contemporary conditions 65 acres was essential to assure economic survival in a bad year, and 30 in a good one. Less than 10 per cent of the peasantry—a comfortable élite— had over 65 acres. They intermarried among themselves, mingled with the local nobility, and lent money to their less fortunate fellows. The same general pattern seems to have been widespread. As far away as Hungary, half a serf's lot was theoretically enough to sustain a family, being between 24 and 54 acres according to area. But by the end of the eighteenth century only a minority of peasants held much more than quarter lots and only they avoided a regular agricultural deficit estimated at an average of 25 per cent. In other words, the great majority of peasants with land did not have

---

[15] Quoted in A. Davies, 'The origins of the French peasant revolution of 1789', *History* (1964), 28.

[16] *A Word to the Wise, or an exhortation to the Roman Catholic Clergy of Ireland* (1749) in *The Works of George Berkeley*, vi. (1953, ed. T. E. Jessop), 236.

enough to assure self-sufficiency. It was an ideal towards which most aspired, but few attained. Meanwhile peasant plots lay at the complete mercy of the weather; rents, dues, tithes, and taxes imposed a steady burden on an agricultural yield which was unsteady in the extreme. The basic fact about peasant life was therefore its precariousness; the majority were unable to subsist on agriculture alone.

Still, there were many ways of supplementing earnings. The most obvious was to take another job, or to let wives or children do so. The vast majority of peasants had some such supplementary source of income. Most industry was organized on a 'domestic' basis, by urban contractors who farmed out work among the peasants of the surrounding countryside. Most lace was made in the home by peasants' wives. Most carding, spinning, and weaving was done in villages surrounding textile towns. The low prices and high labour costs of the later seventeenth century reinforced this pattern at the expense of urban manufacture, for peasants, with other sources of income and no guild organization, could be paid less than full-time urban artisans. Thus the deep hostility of the town dweller towards the countryman was aggravated, to burst out in unsettled times. Even more important, dependence (however partial) on income from manufacture placed the peasant at the mercy of trade cycles and fluctuations in demand, as capricious in their way as the harvests. In fact harvest failure and recession in demand for textiles were linked, and usually struck together, limiting the insurance value of part-time weaving. By 1800, moreover, the mechanization of spinning and weaving had reversed previous trends. The most extensive of manufacturing industries began to concentrate once more in towns, pricing peasant work out of the market. So, at the very moment when land-hunger was at its height, a major supplementary source of income was offering less and less relief.

Another possibility was to borrow. The countryside was full of lords, lawyers, and even richer peasants who were prepared to lend cash or seed to less fortunate neighbours, always on the security of property or anticipated future revenues. Alternatively, apparently indulgent creditors allowed arrears of rents, tithes, dues, or taxes. Yet if it continued over several years, this process was usually fatal because peasants were never able to make enough profit to pay off their mounting debts. A bad harvest spelled certain disaster, for it left the peasant with no alternative but to default. His creditors would then foreclose, seize his goods, and even confiscate his lands. Extending credit to peasants who had no hope of repaying was an accepted way of estate-building on the cheap, each run of bad harvests bringing a clear increase in the holdings of large proprietors at the expense of their poorer neighbours and debtors. The victims, if they were lucky, might simply find themselves transmuted into tenants. But if they were already tenants, they joined the ranks of the landless. When, in the unrest of the spring and early summer of 1789, French peasants burned down lords' houses, it was to destroy their records—not only of seignorial dues, but also of debts outstanding.

Many peasants saw a way out of their difficulties in temporary or permanent migration. When seasonal demand for agricultural labour was slack

at home it was common to migrate to other areas where it was high. Mountainous regions such as the Alps, the Pyrenees, or Wales, where agriculture
was poor and mainly pastoral, and winter work impossible, were famous for
the seasonal migrant labour they provided. So were areas where the land was
intensely subdivided and therefore particularly uneconomic, such as Galicia
or Ireland. Seasonal labourers often walked hundreds of miles in search of
work. In the poor villages of the Auvergne, one government official noted in
the 1770s, 'The land does not return to the cultivator the fruits of his labour;
the subsistence of half the inhabitants depends on the emigration of the other
half.'[17] Accordingly they migrated in their hundreds for the vintage in
Catalonia, and even paid their taxes in Spanish money. Every summer the
building sites of Paris were flooded with masons from the Limousin; the hay
and cornfields of south-eastern England were harvested by seasonal workers
from Ireland or Wales. Or families might send away certain of their members
for years on end, in the hope of receiving regular extra income from their
remittances. These migrants made chiefly for the towns, where most of them
became unskilled labourers or domestic servants. Galician waiters and water-
carriers were stock characters in Spanish literature, while in Paris 'Savoyard'
became a synonym for an uncouth servant, and 'Swiss' for a porter. The
immense growth of towns like London, Bordeaux, or Lyons in the later
eighteenth century is mainly accounted for by peasant immigration rather
than natural increase. Finally, an able-bodied peasant might enlist, returning
home after many years with the colours. The Swedish, Dutch, French, and
Spanish armies all had regiments of Scotsmen or Irishmen, or both; the pope
and the king of France had regiments of Swiss bodyguards. On the other
hand flight from militia service may have accounted for quite as many depar-
tures as enlistment.

Sometimes whole families would migrate. Huge stretches of virtually
empty territory offered a tempting prospect, either in America or in eastern
Europe. Between 90,000 and 110,000 peasants left Ulster for America
between 1720 and 1775, driven out by rising rents, uncertain harvests, and
wild fluctuations in the linen market. Frederick II offered elaborate privileges, exemptions, and premiums to immigrants, particularly after 1763, and
between 300,000 and 350,000 arrived during his reign. The most numerous
influxes, like the 40,000 or so who arrived from Saxony and Bohemia in the
early 1770s, represented peasant refugees from harvest failures and rural
upheavals. Others went to Russia, where under Catherine II about 75,000
colonists, mostly Germans, were settled in unoccupied territory.

There were other expedients short of total emigration. Crime offered
many opportunities when policing was sporadic, and when many crimes at
law were not popularly recognized. Tax-evasion was a major industry, in
which peasants would go to elaborate lengths to appear poorer than they

---

[17] Quoted in J.-P. Poussou, 'Les Mouvements migratoires en France et à partir de la
France de la fin du XVe siècle au début du XIXe siècle: approches pour une synthèse',
Annales de démographie historique (1970), 68.

were in order to be under-assessed. Smuggling, very profitable in an age of heavy excises, was another, not only in frontier regions and along coasts, but also between provinces and in and out of towns. In the highlands of Scotland before 1745, where cattle were of more value than money, clan chiefs locked in bitter local rivalries actively encouraged rustling from other clans by their peasants; but such solidarity between landlord and tenant was exceptional. More typical was the situation in England and Ireland, where peasants risked the savage penalties of game laws which confined hunting, trapping, and shooting to those who owned or leased substantial estates, in order to exercise what they regarded as their natural right to poach. In mountainous regions banditry was a way of life, with peasants giving tacit support to outlaws who preyed on landlords or their agents. It was a point of honour never to betray them. Their exploits were celebrated in songs and folk-tales, for they sprang from the peasantry themselves and, unfettered by the obligations of family and property, seemed enviably free of the pressures which constrained most rural life.

When all expedients failed, however, and the harvest was poor or creditors foreclosed, the peasant joined the ranks of the rural landless. Their lot was either to find paid daily work or to become beggars. The proportion of the landless varied greatly. In England in 1690 they outnumbered the landed by two to one, a proportion which grew somewhat over the subsequent century. Nowhere else, except perhaps in southern Italy and in southern Spain, were the landless in so clear a majority. In France in 1789 perhaps 40 per cent of the peasantry, some 11,000,000, had no land, or none beyond a mere cottage. Between a quarter and a third of the rural population of Sweden in 1760 was in a similar position. In Spain numbers were fairly evenly balanced, but the distribution was extremely uneven; northern provinces had as few as 25 per cent without land whereas in the south and in the centre the proportion approached or even surpassed English levels. East of the Elbe, by contrast, the landless labourer was seldom in a majority. In Hungary in 1767 landed serfs outnumbered cottagers and the landless by over two to one. In Russia, most striking of all, the practice of periodic redistribution of land by each community for taxation purposes meant that totally landless peasants were very rare indeed.

However precarious the lives of most landed peasants, those of the landless were worse. They had nothing but their own labour to depend upon, and no way of diversifying their resources. Those with a skill, like vineyard workers, at least had some work of some regularity, for all the best vines were worked by day labour. But such skilled labourers were always a minority. It is true that in the earlier part of this period there was a relative shortage even of unskilled labour, so that wages sustained a high real level. From the 1730s however, the rise in prices and the acceleration of population growth began inexorably to depress the position of wage earners; naturally peasants who were totally dependent on wages were hardest hit. By the 1770s the market for agricultural day labour was over-supplied, with real wages generally on the decline. The effect was to promote migration into towns and areas of high labour demand, but even they could not absorb the whole surplus. The result was a steady and spectacular expansion in the number of paupers and the level of rural unemployment. In the social hierarchy of the countryside, the line which divided landless labourers from beggars, vagrants, and vagabonds became increasingly hard to draw.

All these categories expanded enormously. In 1790 the indigent population of the French countryside was estimated at between 5 and 10 per cent, but modern estimates place it at over 30. In 1787 nearly 5 per cent of the population of the Palatinate were described as beggars. Almost a century before that over 10 per cent of the English population were receiving poor relief, and if the trebling of the poor rates between 1680 and 1780 is any guide, the number must have grown considerably. In Catholic countries, where begging friars were an everyday sight, there was no shame attached to mendicancy, and ecclesiastical almsgiving was a major if dwindling source of poor relief. In most Protestant countries this tradition had died, but in some, parishes were empowered to levy rates on all their landed inhabitants for the relief of the poor. Apart from Denmark, however, poor relief was not centrally co-ordinated. Its workings were capricious; its whole spirit seemed calculated to keep available help down to a minimum. In Brandenburg and England, for example, the basic principle of the system was that each parish should be required to care only for its own poor. Consequently, the notorious English Settlements Act of 1662 stipulated that anybody arriving in a parish who seemed likely to become a charge on its poor rates, might be transported back to the parish of his or her origin at that parish's expense. A Prussian law of 1696 enacting similar principles and a Spanish one of 1778 both had little effect. In England repatriating pauper immigrants became a major parish activity and a source of endless quarrels and litigation between village communities. From 1697 no English pauper was legally entitled to travel without a pass from his native parish stating his destination, on pain of being whipped as a vagrant. The effect, if not the aim, was to prevent the poor from moving to where there was work, and for this reason the settlement laws were increasingly condemned. That such laws fell far short of solving the problem of the wandering poor is shown by the massive rural immigration which sustained the growth of towns, and the constant fear of vagrants, vagabonds, 'sturdy beggars', and 'brigands' which haunted the lives of more sedentary peasants.

For vagrants, the 'floating population' of the countryside, had nothing to lose, no roots, and no loyalties. The bandit heroes who passed into folklore shared the same enemies as the peasantry from which they sprang, operated within a clearly defined territory, and observed certain crude rules. Vagrants observed none. They were notorious for the careless way in which they started fires, especially in northern Europe where most rural buildings were made of wood. They were also feared, with good reason, as carriers of disease; and the eagerness of parish officers to push infected beggars on, often with bribes, to other parishes, only enhanced this reputation. Above all they were feared as criminals, who robbed and terrorized without compunction. 'One cannot help oneself in the country as in the town,' complained a Pomeranian magistrate whose house had been sacked by vagabonds in 1786.[18] 'There are no prisons here and the peasants allow travellers (whom they ought to keep watch on) to pass through out of fear.' And this well-founded suspicion and fear in its turn bred a limitless credulity. Rumours about bands of brigands or marauders spread rapidly, especially at times of great psychological tension, such as the weeks before harvests. Wherever they penetrated they caused panic. The most famous of such panics was the 'great fear' which swept through much of rural France in July 1789, which led to chateau-burning, intimidation of strangers, and even the lynching of unpopular landlords.

What made this panic more intense and more wide-spread than usual was the way peasants' hopes of reform had been raised during the electioneering of the previous spring. High hopes were to be expected after peasants had been invited to state their grievances, for normally there were no such opportunities for complaint. In Ireland, Bohemia, Catalonia, and parts of Russia and Poland lords often did not even speak the same language as their peasants. The separate house of the legislature representing the peasants in Sweden was quite exceptional. The rulers of society usually only took notice of the harsh conditions of peasant life when open revolt forced them to do so.

Rural Unrest

Peasants did derive some protection from their communities. A basic institution of peasant life, the community was both a focus of loyalty and a source of authority. It had legal obligations, such as the upkeep of the parish church, public order, poor relief, and the apportionment of taxes. Equally, however, the community enjoyed certain rights, notably over common lands. In northern Spain and France these rights were so well established and documented that communities did not hesitate to sue usurpers of them, even encroaching landlords. These communities were better placed to defend themselves than those of the British Isles, where large proprietors could secure the enclosure of both private and common land, with no possibility of appeal, by act of parliament. British landlords were known to transplant whole villages in order to have uninterrupted views over their landscaped parks. Similarly in Russia, despite powerful community traditions lords might encroach on common rights without fear of complaint from inhabitants —who were after all their property too. The effective power of communities was everywhere strictly limited. They had no right to appoint their priests, apportion their tithes, or assess their taxes. If they elected officers, the latter had no way of imposing their authority and yet were answerable to higher authorities for neglect of their duties. Election to such posts was universally regarded as a personal calamity. Communities were at their most effective in focusing loyalty and in organization not so much in normal times, as when frustrated peasants took the law into their own hands.

The reluctance of most peasants to do this is striking. For all the weight

---

[18] Quoted in H. Brunschwig, *La crise de l'état prussien*, 130.

and injustice of the burdens under which they laboured, by far the most frequent cause of peasant unrest was the price of food. Since most of them had insufficient land to sustain themselves, they sold all they grew and bought their bread, so that they were no better off than the urban wage-earners who suspected them so profoundly of hoarding and profiteering; in bad years bread could absorb well over half the income of both. Peasants on the other hand, as primary producers, could see the middleman's profit; consequently they were extremely sensitive to the fairness and justice of prices, not to mention frauds or adulterations. Most rural disturbances were protests against excessive prices or the poor quality of bread or flour. It is no coincidence that they usually broke out in market places, on market days, where peasants gathered in force, often excited with social drinking, united by common interests and purposes, and able to exchange information. Thus fortified, they could abuse, threaten, or attack millers or bakers for overcharging or adulterating their wares. If they resisted, the crowd often took over their stock and sold it at a 'fairer' price. Arguments about general price-levels failed to impress them, for such rioters were uninterested in the world outside their own neighbourhood, beyond preventing scarce supplies from going there. From intimidation it was a short step to ransacking the houses and barns of suspected hoarders and attacking, unloading, and selling any consignments of grain found on local roads and bound elsewhere. In an excited atmosphere rioters were always more than ready to believe the wildest rumours and always assumed that shortages were artificially created; either the work of selfish profiteers or of wicked ministers whom the king (pathetically believed to be benevolent) would dismiss if only he knew what they were doing.

The 'wicked ministers' argument was lent strength after about 1760 by the triumph of doctrines of free trade in grain. The physiocrats and their counterparts in Italy, Spain, and Great Britain, were united in arguing that the market would be self-regulating and self-rationing if it were freed of restrictions. A free market would mean high prices, but these in turn would stimulate production and therefore in the long run increase supplies. Many administrations were convinced; accordingly, export restrictions were removed in France in 1764 and in Tuscany in 1765; internal controls were also removed in France in 1763 and in Spain in 1765. The last remaining marketing regulations in England, where export had been free since 1670, were repealed in 1772. These changes were not always final: in France, for instance, policy fluctuated spectacularly with changing ministries. Unfortunately however, the relaxation of controls often coincided with lean years, and advance rumours promoted speculative hoarding. French rioters believed in a ministerial plot or 'famine pact' to starve the poor by refusing to control excessive prices. Similar charges were heard in Spain in 1766. Yet most high prices owed little enough to government policies; those of 1709, 1740, 1756–7, 1772–3, and 1782 in England, or of 1660–3, 1693–4, 1709, 1725, 1740, 1770, or 1775 in France, were the direct result of deficient harvests. They produced general waves of rioting; and localized rioting, resulting from local shortages, was even more frequent. In England alone 235 outbreaks have been noted between 1735 and 1800.[19] But what characterized them all was their transience. Food rioters seldom sought more than cheaper food, and when they got it they were satisfied. If concessions were slow in coming, more ominous talk was heard, but it was more often in terms of stringing up local authorities rather than of overthrowing the whole social or political order. And popular price-fixers were remarkably scrupulous in paying merchants the proceeds of their forced sales; outright looting or plunder were exceptional. Food riots, in short, offer no evidence of profound peasant dissatisfaction with the established order—merely with those who were presumed to be perverting it for their own selfish ends.

Evidence of deeper discontent is offered by rural terrorism. Less frequent than food rioting, it tended to be more persistent where it did occur. The classic case was Ireland, where in the 1760s the Whiteboys began to resist enclosure of commons by destroying fences and maiming cattle. Subsequently they extended their activities to terrorizing tithe proctors, middlemen in general, and takers of dear leases. The example spread, and for over ten years much of rural Ireland was in the grip of elusive, nocturnal terrorists. Only an emergency act, allowing landlords to take brutal and sweeping countermeasures, restrained the epidemic, and it resurfaced in the 1780s and 90s, this time exacerbated by sectarian antagonisms. The so-called 'Levellers' revolt' in south-west Scotland in 1724 was really an outbreak of nocturnal marauding of this type, designed to deter landlords from evicting tenants in order to enclose their arable plots for pasture. But as soon as landlords began to temper their zeal for agricultural 'improvement', unrest rapidly died out. This suggests that agrarian terrorism was occasioned by very specific grievances and often grievances of abuse. Catholic though they were, the Whiteboys did not oppose Anglican tithes as such—merely excessive rigour in levying them. Here too there was little thought of bringing about fundamental social changes. Broader objectives, hostile to the whole social order, only seemed to emerge in the course of disturbances which caught the authorities off guard, and so demonstrated that their control was far less firm than it normally appeared.

Full-scale peasant wars or revolts, unlike mere riots or terrorism, tended to be the product of a whole range of grievances, triggered off by crises which added unbearable aggravations. The *Germania* in Valencia, for instance, the only substantial Spanish revolt of this period, began as a refusal of seignorial dues after years of concerted litigation and appeals to the crown had failed to alleviate the burden. But what precipitated the revolt and sent 2,000 men marching on Valencia before troops dispersed them, was the continent-wide harvest failure of 1693. When Louis XIV introduced a whole series of new indirect taxes in 1674, there were riots in the major cities of western France from Bordeaux to Rennes, which inspired the peasantry of Brittany to rise in revolt, for they had also heard rumours of an imposition of the hated

[19] G. Rudé, *The Crowd in History: a study of popular disturbances in France and England 1730—1848* (1964), 35.

gabelle, from which the province was exempt. For almost two months in 1675, bands of peasants, often hundreds strong, roamed southern Brittany sacking tax-offices, intimidating officials, but also attacking unpopular land-lords and burning their castles. 6,000 troops were called in to contain the outbreak, but before they reached full strength the rising had disintegrated for lack of a concerted plan. Its aims, however, went well beyond the with-drawal of the stamped-paper duty. The peasants were as much against seig-norial dues as against new taxes; they wanted a general alleviation of their financial burdens. This aspiration reflected a particularly exacting local seignorial regime, which had grown harsher in the 1670s as lords found themselves pressed by falling rents and profits. At the same time Dutch naval activity had damaged the cloth trade upon which many peasants depended for supplementing their incomes; no less than twelve new taxes had been imposed on them since 1664. The duty on stamped paper, and the rumours of more, were simply the last straw.

The war of the Camisards in Languedoc between 1702 and 1705, un-doubtedly ignited by persecution of the Protestant peasantry of the Cévennes, was rooted in the grievance (shared with the Irish) of paying tithes to support a clergy that was not their own. It also occurred at a time of profound economic crisis, after a decade of disastrous harvests, falling agricultural revenues, and rising taxation. The part played by such circumstances has perhaps been underestimated: 'Their capitation is as important as their religion in their seditious enterprises,' noted a local bishop in 1702.[20] Religious fervour, however, gave the rebels a strength and courage out of all propor-tion to their 2,000 men. The rebellion took three years and an army of 30,000 troops to break, and a further six years of vigorous persecution to mop up. Even then, despite the obliteration of hundreds of villages, Pro-testantism was not extirpated among the Languedoc peasantry.

This was the last major peasant revolt in the west until the 1780s. Echoes of the *Germania* re-emerged in Valencia during the Spanish Succession war, but finally disappeared with the defeat of the Habsburgs, whom the peasants supported against the Bourbons, favoured by their lords. The last English peasant revolt was also triggered by political coincidence, when the rural weavers of the west country, impoverished by a depression in the wool trade and harassed by the intolerant policies of the established church, rallied in 1686 to the ill-fated attempt of the duke of Monmouth to supplant James II. There was nothing comparable for another 144 years in England, and in France the next true uprising of peasants after the Camisards was in the chaos of July 1789. The reasons for the disappearance of rebellion lay in rising agricultural prosperity over the eighteenth century and the increasing rarity of crisis years in which famine, plague, war, and heavier taxation struck simultaneously, leaving the peasant with nothing to lose but his life. East of the Elbe there was no such general improvement in conditions. Revolts there were always more common than in the west and showed no sign of becoming

[20] Quoted in E. Le Roy Ladurie, *Les Paysans de Languedoc* (1966), i. 627.

less so. Some areas did escape major troubles, such as the Hohenzollern domains; but over most of eastern Europe peasant revolts were endemic, and on a bigger scale than in the west.

Bohemia, for example, saw a major rebellion in 1679 and an even larger one in 1775. The former was led, in a year of plague, by richer peasants complaining that lords were increasing their *robot* and imposing new fees and dues at the same time. Taking refuge in Bohemia from the Viennese plague, the emperor was able to observe the situation at first hand, and in 1680 he imposed limits on *robot*. Yet ninety years later, despite two intervening renewals, these restrictions remained largely inoperative. Meanwhile since 1748 there had been massive tax increases throughout the Habsburg empire, of which Bohemia and Moravia bore a disproportionate 35 per cent; and three successive harvest failures between 1769 and 1771 plunged the kingdom into a chronic famine. Joseph II was so horrified by a visit in 1771 that he began to press Bohemian lords to relieve the pressure on their peasants by reducing *robot* demands. A patent on this subject was issued in 1774, which aroused intense peasant expectations of improvements—a 'great hope' comparable to that which swept France in the spring of 1789. But the patent, permissive rather than mandatory, was ignored and it was presumed (not without some justice) that lords and their agents were obstructing the imperial will. Garbled rumours reaching Bohemia from the distant Steppes, where Pugachev had rebelled two years before,[21] encouraged direct action; consequently the early months of 1775 brought revolts. By the spring much of the kingdom was in the hands of peasant bands who burned castles, intimidated stewards, and declared the abolition of *robot*. As in 1679, better-off peasants, with most to lose from heavy burdens, seem to have been most active, and late in March 15,000 insurgents, ill armed and ill organized, marched on Prague, only to be dispersed by troops. The kingdom remained restless for the remainder of the year. The experience scared landlords so much that the government was able, in the years that followed, to limit *robot* far more effectively and generally than had seemed possible only a few years before.

Hungary saw even more uprisings. The mainstays of the rebel armies of Thököli (1678–81) and Rakoczi (1703–11) were peasants hoping to throw off the control of landlords whom they identified with Habsburg rule. Rakoczi's rebellion was a national movement involving all classes, but he was remembered by the peasants in later years as their own Messiah, who would one day return to lead them to greater success. There were further regional disturbances in 1735, 1751, 1753, 1755, 1763–4, 1765–6, and 1784, mostly provoked by sudden rises in dues or *robot* obligations, often on particular estates. These revolts spread rapidly, the rebels extending their complaints to taxes and tithes. Twenty thousand peasants were involved in the Croatian revolt of 1755; in the Transylvanian rising of 1784, the fiercest and most bloody since 1711, 30,000 rebels butchered hundreds of nobles and their families in a hitherto remote and untamed region which had seen a

---

[21] See below, p. 123–5.

rise of between 400 and 1,000 per cent in seignorial burdens over the century. Most of these risings, like those in Bohemia, were fairly short-lived and easily put down by troops; but they were a warning which governments, if not lords, realized it was dangerous to ignore. So the disturbances in Transdanubia in 1765–7, less an armed uprising than a boycott of *robot*, tithes, and taxes affecting several whole counties, had finally pushed Maria Theresa into promulgating the urbarial patent of 1767 without further parleying with the diet; and the Transylvanian explosions of 1784 led to Joseph II's final abolition of Hungarian serfdom in 1785.

Timid these reforms may have been; but at least they demonstrated some recognition on the part of Habsburg rulers that peasants did have legitimate grievances. There was never any such recognition in Russia, although peasant conditions were the worst in Europe, and rebellions larger, more frequent, and more savage than anywhere else. The instinct of the Russian serf was not to rebel but to flee. Even after the abolition of time-limits for the recovery of runaways in 1649, flight remained the central problem for serf-owners, and more laws were issued on this problem than on any one other. Between 1719 and 1727 alone, at least 200,000 serfs were reported missing. One of the most popular destinations for fugitives was the south-east, along the Don, the Volga, and the Yaik rivers—the land of the Cossacks. Cossack freedom was legendary: they never handed back fugitives, they paid no taxes, and they governed themselves by elected representatives. Agriculture, for them, was the gateway to subjection, and so it was forbidden. Instead, the Cossacks lived by herding and above all by marauding along the wild frontier, for the policing of which they were paid a government subsidy. It was among them that the most massive peasant revolts of both the seventeenth and the eighteenth centuries in Europe originated.

The seventeenth-century outbreak, led by Stenka Razin, arose from the sort of combination of adverse circumstances that provoked western risings. By 1660 the constant influx of fugitives across the Don had created severe problems of overpopulation and underemployment. Nor were matters eased by governmental attempts to conciliate southern neighbours by restricting Cossack piracy in the Black Sea and the Caspian. War with Poland also disrupted grain supplies and pushed up the price for the Cossacks who grew none of their own. In 1666, 500 Cossacks marched on Moscow to demand employment in the war. As soon as they left Cossack territory disaffected serfs began to swell their numbers and the march became a revolt. Eventually the rebels numbered 2,000, and although they were dispersed by the threat of troops long before reaching Moscow, they left the country disturbed all along their line of march. The next year troops clashed with a private marauding expedition bound for the Caspian under Stenka Razin. Razin spent two years terrorizing this great lake, and returned to the Volga in 1669 loaded with plunder, a popular hero whom hundreds flocked to join. When the government tried to disband this private army, Razin proclaimed open revolt. The tsar, he declared, was being misled by crafty and malignant *boyars*, a class of parasites who must be destroyed. This was a call for the overthrow of the whole social hierarchy. The reputation for invincibility which Razin's long run of successes had won him made many believe that he could achieve it. In 1670 he took Tsarytsin and Astrakhan with much slaughter, and then marched up the Volga towards Moscow with an army which grew over three months from 6,000 to 20,000 men. By the end of the year 800 miles of the river was completely out of control, as well as large stretches of the Don and western Siberia. All classes of the subject population, townsmen as well as peasants, rallied to Stenka Razin's horse-tail standard.

Yet in the end Razin's army was no match for the seasoned troops that his foray to Astrakhan had allowed the government time to assemble. In October 1670 he was defeated before Simbirsk, and, his invincible reputation in ruins, he retreated southwards. The following spring he was handed over by the official Cossack authorities, to whom he was as great a threat as to the central government itself. He was executed in Moscow in 1671. But the south remained disturbed until the end of that year; tens of thousands of rebels and mere suspects were killed in the course of the rising's suppression. What could not be suppressed was the memory. Immortalized in hundreds of folksongs, Stenka Razin, who loved the poor and hated their lords, became, like Rakoczi, the legendary protector who would one day return and this time triumph. In troubled times, this legend was an inspiration to further revolt.

It played a part, for instance, in the rising of Bulavin, another Cossack, in 1707. This revolt began in opposition to governmental attempts to pursue fugitives into Cossack territory, but it rapidly recruited a diverse collection of opponents of the growing power and reforming zeal of Peter I. Notably it was supported by large numbers of Old Believers,[22] who regarded the foreigner-loving tsar as Antichrist. The year 1708 witnessed forty-three separate outbreaks of peasant unrest in Russia, but Bulavin's was the largest, recruiting 30,000 adherents with manifestos echoing Razin in their call for the overthrow of not only Peter's rule, but the power of landlords in general. It was doubly dangerous in that it coincided with a rising of the Bashkirs, a semi-independent frontier tribe, and also with war against Sweden. Yet although Bulavin at one point took the Cossack capital of Cherkassk and had himself elected their leader, unlike Razin's his movement never spread beyond Cossack territory. He too, however, alienated the ruling oligarchy, who were only too willing to abet the imperial troops besieging Cherkassk. Bulavin killed himself rather than be taken; the rebellion was soon overcome and the whole Don basin garrisoned with imperial troops.

But not all Cossacks lived on the Don, and when their heartland was tamed, those who preferred the old freedom moved further east to the Yaik. Here, almost sixty years later, the greatest rising of all broke out—that of Pugachev. Pugachev was an adventurer, a Cossack and former soldier, who late in 1772 proclaimed to the Yaik Cossacks that he was Peter III, the Empress Catherine's husband, murdered in 1762. Pretenders were traditional

[22] See below, p. 161–3.

among Russian rebels—Razin had set one up—for it lent legitimacy to their cause. Peter III, who in emancipating the nobles from compulsory service had raised hopes of serf emancipation, and who had then been disposed of by a foreign wife with no legitimate claim to the throne, was particularly popular. Pugachev was preceded by at least ten other false Peters. His rising was also preceded by fifty-three serious disturbances in southern Russia over a decade. This unrest sprang from the frustration of hopes raised first by Peter III's policies, and then by talk of reform surrounding the fruitless legislative reform commission of 1767. The Yaik Cossacks, allowed to fish in their abundant river only with governmental permission and subjected during the Turkish war of 1768−74 to ruthless recruiting in defiance of their traditional liberties, had their own reasons for discontent. So did the near-by Bashkirs, who had risen twice (in 1735 and 1755) since Bulavin's time against ever tightening control, and had both times been bloodily suppressed. So too the serf labourers, hired out by their masters to work under extremely harsh conditions in the factories of the Urals, further north. To all these groups Pugachev appealed when he promised, as tsar, to restore their lost liberties. 'This is a revolt', noted General Bibikov, who did most to put it down, 'of the poor against the rich, of the slaves against their masters.'[23] Pugachev's aim was to destroy both the state and the nobility which sustained it, as his numerous manifestos made clear. By the end of 1773 his army of perhaps 15,000 men had captured or beseiged most of the important governmental centres of the south east and the southern Urals.

The government was slow to appreciate the gravity of the situation, but once it did its well-trained and well equipped troops mounted a successful counter-offensive. By early 1774, after much bloodshed, the besieged centres had been relieved and order seemed to be returning. Pugachev's name, however, was by now already legendary, and he was soon able to reconstruct an army of 8,000 men which, in a change of tactics, paralysed the newly reconquered regions with ferocious lightning raids. In June 1774 he marched into the settled, agricultural heartland of serfdom itself. This was the most dangerous moment of all. Kazan was sacked and although Pugachev was subsequently driven off by troops, his progress back south touched off serf uprisings along the whole length of the Volga. Perhaps 3,000,000 peasants were involved and over 3,000 nobles and officials murdered. The decade since their emancipation from compulsory service had seen the return of many petty nobility to their estates, where they enforced their powers with unprecedented determination; Pugachev inspired the serfs to take their revenge. 'Those who hitherto were gentry', declared his most famous manifesto, '. . .those opponents of our rule and disturbers of the empire and ruiners of the peasants—seize them, punish them, hang them, treat them in the same way as they, having no Christian feeling, oppressed you, the peasants.'[24] For five weeks of the summer of 1774 it was feared that the whole empire might erupt into one huge serf uprising. In fact, however, the rising

[23] Quoted in P. Avrich, *Russian Rebels 1600–1800* (1972), 211–12.
[24] Quoted ibid. 227.

was almost over. The Don Cossacks, whom Pugachev expected to raise, were unsympathetic. The peasantry of the Volga, through the disorders they had perpetrated over the summer, had brought a famine on themselves, and were ready as winter drew on for a return to normality. Above all, the conclusion of peace with the Turks in July released a seasoned army for use against the rebels. In August Pugachev failed to take Tsarytsin, and his army was defeated. The next month his few surviving followers turned him over to the authorities and in January 1775 he was executed.

Pugachev's execution did not end the disturbances. Not until early 1775 was peace generally restored to the Volga, and that only after savage punitive reprisals. But in the long run these proved brutally effective, for the rest of Catherine's reign witnessed only seven further significant outbreaks of peasant unrest, all of them localized, and none in areas touched by the Pugachev episode. The weight of serfdom did not diminish as a result of the revolt; indeed, the empress's reaction was only to identify her interests the more closely with those of the serf-owning nobility, scared out of their wits by what had happened, and convinced that only intransigence could prevent it from happening again.

Pugachev's rising was more than just a peasant revolt; it was almost a revolution, which came nearer to overthrowing a whole social order than any other movement in Europe before 1789. Yet peasants neither began it nor provided its driving force, which came rather from Cossacks and Bashkirs resentful of the relentless extension of government control into their hitherto untamed frontier homelands. Only when these rebels achieved successes did peasants rise in their support, and only then when they passed close by. Pugachev was already in retreat from Kazan when he electrified the peasantry of the Volga. They rose only when somebody else exposed the weakness of the authorities; and they used this opportunity to wreak vengeance on their oppressors and claim a return to good old days rather than seek to establish some newer, more just order. Even in full-scale revolt, peasants remained profoundly conservative. They sought to prevent or reverse change rather than promote it. It took political imagination to see more radical possibilities, and this was much more likely to be found among the inhabitants of towns.

6. The Ruled: the Town

The social structure of the countryside, diverse and varied though it was, was simple compared with that of the towns. Yet, with the exception of the Netherlands, towns housed only a minority of the population. By the later eighteenth century the proportion of Englishmen living in towns was still only about a third. In France it was around 23 per cent in 1800. Elsewhere the proportion was even less, especially towards the east. In Sweden in 1760 it was 6·7 per cent. In Russia, although it nearly doubled over our period, it was still only 4 per cent in 1796. Yet this urban minority provided the most dynamic and the most vital sections of the population.

The difference between rural and urban life was less clear than it is today. Most towns were very small, hardly more than villages. Even in highly urbanized France until late in the eighteenth century there were not more than sixty or seventy towns of over 10,000 inhabitants, and only eight of 50,000 or more. In Poland, at the other extreme, out of about 1,500 officially recognized towns, 90 per cent had fewer than 1,000 inhabitants. Like villages, towns swarmed with livestock, pastured often on extensive open spaces in the very heart of the community. Even the largest and most crowded cities contained odd patches which could sustain draught animals, pigs, and poultry. Many towns also owned common lands; the most extensive of all, the municipal lands of Spain, were larger than the holdings of the crown, the church, and the nobility. The central event in the calendar of most small communities was market day, once or twice a week, when peasants came in from the surrounding countryside to sell their produce. On such occasions towns seemed little more than extensions of rural society and the rural economy. Peasants were subject to the same fears and anxieties about the price of food and its supply as townsmen: the popular price-fixing and grain-rioting which swept Paris in April and May 1775 originated miles from the capital, deep in the country-side. The example spread so rapidly because it was a common response to a shortage felt in town and country alike.

But perhaps the most striking link with the countryside was that urban numbers were maintained only by rural immigration. The death-rate in towns was consistently higher throughout this period than the birth-rate. Yet most towns maintained their populations, and after about 1750 many grew spectacularly—an achievement due to the constant inflow from the country-side. Immigration was the most basic feature of urban society. Not only did it make the very survival of towns economically possible; not only did it put expatriate peasants and townsmen into daily social contact; it also gave urban society an altogether more transient, less settled character than that of the countryside and provided a constant inflow of new experience to be absorbed into the town-dwellers' outlook. In this way it cut the town off from the country quite as much as it helped to link them.

Immigration involved the abandonment of rural life for something more promising or in any event different. And it was the differences between town and country which, in the last analysis, counted for most. Town-dwellers were more concentrated, their occupations more specialized, their experience of affairs more diverse, their submissiveness to authority less certain. They were not tied down by the inflexible rhythms of agricultural life. Indeed, there were few things a townsman despised more than a peasant. Dependent in the last resort on the peasantry for their food supplies, they nevertheless simply closed their gates in the faces of the hungry rustics who streamed in towards urban markets in times of famine. Such gestures made clear how little the townsman felt he had in common with the peasant. Economically, mentally, and socially, they lived in different worlds.

Urban Life

Urban life was more crowded. Most well-established towns had walls. In Great Britain, safe from invasion beyond the Channel, defences were allowed to crumble and be demolished; growing communities such as Birmingham, Liverpool, and Manchester never acquired them. Throughout much of France, where the power of Louis XIV largely banished the fear both of foreign invasion and of domestic upheavals, ramparts also fell into decay. Elsewhere, however, walls were maintained; it was useful to close city gates each night to protect public order or to keep out undesirables in the event of famine, plague, or rebellion. Trade entering or leaving by a limited number of gates was also easier to tax, and between 1783 and 1789 French tax-farmers spent immense sums actually building a brand new wall around Paris solely to prevent the evasion of entry tolls. Walls ensured that the chief direction for expansion was upwards; and accordingly most major cities were filled with tenement blocks of five, six, or more storeys: 71 per cent of the houses in Lyons in 1791, for example, had four or more storeys. People lived literally one on top of another; and in general the higher the storey, the poorer the occupants. Separate houses were a luxury reserved only for the extremely rich. There was eventually a limit to the height to which buildings could be safely constructed and no alternative to expansion beyond the walls. Even then the desire to remain as close to the defences as possible kept suburban housing tall and crowded. The most populous cities remained compact, with social distinctions seldom becoming geographical too. Sprawling London by contrast had distinct artisan areas and leisured suburbs, at least by the eighteenth century, and the development of the planned New Town to the north of old Edinburgh began, after 1760, to divide the classes there. German and east-European cities segregated their extensive Jewish populations into ghettos, and Moscow pushed its numerous foreigners into a so-called 'German suburb' beyond the walls. But all these were exceptions to the rule that most city-dwellers lived in far closer contact with social groups other than their own, than did peasants. The result can only have been to emphasize the importance of common experience and to promote greater social harmony than was usual in the countryside.

Other consequences were less desirable. Overcrowding made most towns extremely insanitary, the natural breeding grounds for infectious diseases. Edinburgh, with its lofty tenements and narrow alleys, was typical. 'Every street', wrote a traveller in 1705, 'shows the nastiness of the inhabitants: the excrements lie in heaps...In a morning the scent was so offensive that we were forc'd to hold our noses as we past the streets and take care where we trod for fear of disobliging our shoes, and to walk in the middle at night for fear of an accident to our heads.'[1] Berlin, it was said, could be smelt from 6 miles away. The result was an extremely high death-rate, 4 to 5 per cent per year. When plague, or any other sort of epidemic, struck, it always did most damage in towns. The great plague of 1665 carried off 28 per cent of the population of London; that of 1656 may have accounted for almost half the population of Naples and Genoa. In the great east-European epidemics of 1709–13 Danzig lost half its population and Copenhagen a third. Marseilles lost 40 per cent of its inhabitants in the epidemic of 1720 and Messina lost over 60 per cent in 1743. As late as 1771 plague carried off over 56,000 inhabitants of Moscow, or a quarter of its population. The onset of epidemics was marked by the flight of richer townsmen into the healthier countryside, leaving the poorer classes behind to suffer; and often, incidentally, helping to spread infection beyond the towns by carrying it with them. So it was the poorest inhabitants of towns who were most seriously affected by disease, and they who had to be most steadily replaced by peasant immigration.

Another consequence of overcrowding was the constant danger of fire. A year after the great plague of 1665, London was struck by the great fire, which destroyed over 13,000 houses in the city. A fire in Brussels in 1695 destroyed 3,830 houses; a tenth of Moscow was burned down in the summer of 1773, while three-quarters of the city of Rennes was swept away by flames in 1720. Comparatively few people perished in these fires, and the destruction of dangerous and insanitary dwellings was positively beneficial. The buildings which replaced them were usually planned more solidly and spaciously, with opportunities for creating better sanitary arrangements. Meanwhile, however, thousands had lost their homes, and pressure on the already overcrowded accommodation that remained was intensified.

So city life was hazardous and vulnerable. But it was also privileged. Urban wages tended to be higher than rural ones. In times of disorder, walls afforded protection not available to peasants, and most larger towns had garrisons to man them too. In times of famine, supplies had to be brought into towns to be marketed, and most rural producers simply could not afford to hoard their produce in the way townsmen feared. In Catholic Europe, where towns were crowded with monasteries and convents, poor relief through almsgiving was far more abundant and regular than in the countryside. Townsmen were free from forced labour on the roads; and

[1] Quoted in T. C. Smout, *A History of the Scottish People, 1560–1830* (1970), 367.

though press-gangs were more active in the teeming cities than in the country-side, towns were not generally obliged to furnish regular quotas of conscripts. Townsmen also paid fewer tithes to the church: most owned no land on which they might be levied, and those who did had often managed to com-mute them into fixed money payments, which dwindled to nothing in real value when prices rose. Above all, towns bore a relatively light burden of taxation. Accurate direct taxes were almost impossible to levy on those, like most townsmen, whose assets were invisible. Consequently few were levied. Prussian towns paid no direct taxes at all. The inhabitants of certain major French cities, such as Paris, Bordeaux, Rouen, and a number of others which between them accounted for most of the urban population, were exempt from the *taille*, the main direct tax.

It is undoubtedly true, on the other hand, that towns were easy to tax indirectly. Excise duties on basic commodities, levied at their gates, were a major source of state revenue in France and particularly in Prussia, where the efficiency of the *régie* in raising their yield and suppressing smuggling after 1766 did much to blight the economic recovery of towns after the Seven Years War. The impact of excise-gathering is reflected in the popular hatred it aroused. The first symbols of the old order attacked by the Parisians in July 1789 were the toll-gates in the new customs-wall; and it is hardly a coincidence that the middle-class townsmen who dominated the various revolutionary assemblies of the 1790s sought to restructure French taxation by the complete elimination of indirect taxes. The fact remains, however, that in his relative freedom from direct burdens the townsman was far better off than the peasant; and when this advantage was added to the numerous small exemptions, privileges, reductions, and special rights that the cor-porations of most towns had secured for their inhabitants over the years and enshrined in their hallowed books of customs, there seemed no comparison at all.

It was these advantages, rather than the hazards of over-crowding and ill health, that impressed discontented peasants, and made them head for the cities. Besides, town life seemed freer. Russian towns, admittedly, were full of serfs employed as domestic servants or hired out by their masters to urban manufacturers; but elsewhere there was no serfdom in towns, no seignorial dues or jurisdiction of any importance, and no restrictions on movement like the English laws of settlement. So the power and social control exercised by lords and nobles appeared weaker than in the country.

Whether it was actually weaker is another question. The groups who dominated the countryside were also very prominent in the towns. No town of any consequence was without its noble residents for part at least of each year. Capitals and regional centres had their social 'season' when most pro-minent families were in residence and spending freely. Their expenditure sustained luxury trades and their domestic arrangements called for an endless supply of servants. In all except the most flourishing centres of trade or manufacture, therefore, the ruling orders were the direct or indirect source of most employment. In Moscow the nobility owned over half of all accommodation. What they lacked by comparison with the countryside in legal power to dominate the lives of the lower orders, they more than made up in economic power. However much the lives of townsmen and country-men differed, they largely obeyed the same masters. And the economic pattern in which they were involved, based on revenue rather than on capital, did not enrich the community. Rather it kept its poor majority wretched, idle, and abject. All but a few lucky peasant immigrants found that, in becoming town-dwellers, they had merely exchanged one form of poverty for another.

Urban Poverty

The most striking and spectacular feature of towns was the poverty of most of their inhabitants. Being more concentrated than in the country, it was more noticeable, although not necessarily easier to measure. The really poor, without regular employment or other visible means of support, paying no taxes and having no fixed address, often did not appear in official records. But their share of the urban population was always substantial. In Paris, a great capital, or Mainz, an average German cathedral city, the proportion was about one-quarter. In Berlin or Cologne it was nearer one-third. In commercially more active cities the proportion tended to be lower, but it was still striking enough. In Lyons in 1791 it was about one-sixth, in London six years later, about one-eighth. And over the preceding century these proportions had grown more rapidly than the growth in over-all urban population. The popu-lation of Berlin doubled between 1750 and 1801; but the number of its poor grew tenfold. The 1780s saw the foundation, all over the continent, of Philanthropic Societies, voluntary associations of the rich devoted to organiz-ing more effective means of poor relief. These were essentially urban bodies, and were a sure sign that the problem of the urban poor was forcing itself upon public attention with increasing urgency.

Who were the urban poor? They were the least well-adapted, least skilled, least well-rooted elements in the towns; most of them were not townsmen by origin but those rural immigrants who were the main feature of urban popu-lations. They were poor because few towns provided enough employment to absorb all the labour that flowed in from the countryside. Opportunities fluctuated, so that many of the unemployed and indigent at any time were only temporarily in that state. Even so, a large proportion never found any work, and this proportion grew over the eighteenth century. A graphic illustration of the scale of urban poverty is the number of abandoned children, offspring whom parents could not afford to keep. In Paris in the late seven-teenth century around 3,000 foundlings a year were taken into charitable institutions. A century later this number had doubled, and in 1772 the 7,676 foundlings represented 40 per cent of children baptized in the city. In Brussels, in 1783, 2,050 foundlings represented one-eleventh of newborn children; in Madrid in 1786 the proportion was 16 per cent, in Venice over the century it averaged 9 per cent.

Not all, not even most foundlings were the product of pauper marriages.

But most were the product of poverty all the same. Many must have been illegitimate precisely because fathers wished to avoid burdening their marriage. Large numbers must have been the direct result of prostitution, a major industry of larger towns and the most obvious way for a poor or underpaid woman to earn badly needed money. There were said to be over 50,000 prostitutes in London in the 1790s, and between 20,000 and 25,000 in Paris a decade earlier. In the poorest quarter of Mainz, no less than 31 per cent of the female population earned money in this way. Admittedly, those who provide the figures tended to include a very wide range of women; young widows, for instance, were often stigmatized as whores on suspicions hardly justified by the evidence. Yet the pressures driving poor women into prostitution were obvious, and the scale of the problem not to be denied. Nor were foundlings the only obvious result; venereal diseases ravaged European cities in the later eighteenth century as never before.

Closely linked to prostitution was crime. There were organized gangs of criminals such as that of Cartouche, whose 200 followers kept rich Parisians panic-stricken between 1717 and 1721. Like rural brigands, such figures often became heroes of popular folklore. But they remained exceptional. The characteristic urban crime was petty theft, the typical criminal a pauper without other apparent means of support. Most crime was directed against property rather than against persons; violence was incidental. People stole because they were too poor to survive in any other way. Their thefts were occasional, unsystematic, opportunistic, not evidence of a professional life of crime.

If poverty spawned any profession, it was begging—the obvious resort for the poor. Some threw themselves into it with singleminded efficiency.

Great numbers of sturdy Beggars [wrote an English observer in 1729][2] loose and vagrant Persons, infest the Nation, but no place more than the City of London and parts adjacent. If any person is born with any defect or Deformity, or maimed by Fire or other Casualty, or any inveterate Distemper, which renders them miserable Objects, their way is open to London, where they have free liberty of showing their nauseous sights to terrify People, and force them to give money to get rid of them.

Faked ailments or hideous sores could attract the compassion of the rich, or simply scare them into almsgiving by the fear of infection. Some parents were not above deliberately maiming their children in order to draw attention to their plight—although the hazards of birth and infancy among the poor normally and naturally assured a fair proportion of grisly afflictions. Beggars set their children to the work almost from the moment they could walk and talk; they operated in family units because children, by their number and their readier impact on the consciences of passers-by, were often the most effective earners. But the intended victims were mostly well aware of how easily they could be hoodwinked, and their reaction was often to withold alms rather than give them to cases that might not be truly deserving. Alms,

---

[2] Quoted in Dorothy Marshall, *The English Poor in the Eighteenth Century* (1926), 232.

whether private or corporate, were after all limited, and should, so it was thought, be reserved only for those really unable to work, rather than for 'sturdy beggars' who refused to do so. This attitude, logically so clear, completely overlooked the fact that the root cause of poverty was that enough work was simply not available. Begging was merely its symptom.

The urban poor enjoyed one major advantage over their rural counterparts: towns were usually better endowed with charitable institutions. In Catholic Europe the church regarded poor relief as one of its major functions. In 1787 an English observer[3] noted of the archbishop of Granada that:

Beside private pensions to families and occasional relief in seasons of distress, he provides nurses in the country for 440 orphans and deserted children; he sends poor patients to the hot baths. . .where he actually maintains fourscore; and he daily distributes bread to all the poor, who assemble at his doors. Once. . .he had himself the curiosity to count the number of these miserable creatures, and found the men two thousand, the women on that day three thousand and twenty-four; but at another time the women were four thousand. In this bounty he is imitated by forty convents, at which are distributed bread and broth, without discrimination, to all who present themselves. The Carthusians alone give annually sixty thousand reals.

Most monasteries and convents, everywhere concentrated overwhelmingly in towns, distributed some alms. In addition there were 'general hospitals' intended to house foundlings, the sick, and the aged. Originating in France in the early seventeenth century, they were staffed by the Sisters of Charity. A law of 1662 authorized the establishment of hospitals throughout France, and by 1789 there were 2,185. By that date they were to be found, though less extensively, throughout Catholic Europe. Though publicly authorized, they were not publicly supported, depending on the private donations, legacies, and endowments of the pious rich for most of their funds—a fluctuating and uncertain source. Nor were they concerned with the technically 'able-bodied' poor, by far the majority. In short, although charity was more easily available in towns than in the country, its scale was still not commensurate with the problem, aggravated by the rise in population.

The anti-clerical thinkers of the Enlightenment did not fail to notice these inadequacies. They were the fruit, they concluded, of indiscriminate distribution of relief. Though a cleric and certainly not a leader of opinion, the English traveller Joseph Townsend was moved to some not untypical reflections by his observation of poverty in Spain. 'Filth and nastiness, immorality and vice, wretchedness and poverty,' he declared, were 'the inevitable consequences of undistinguishing benevolence . . . How evident it is . . . that he, who finds employment for the poor, is their greatest friend; whilst he, who indiscriminately feeds them, should be ranked among their enemies.'[4] He admitted that without indiscriminate relief, the poor must perish. But 'with it, they propagate the race. Without it they would have no existence. With it they increase and multiply the objects of distress. Surely then charity ceases to deserve that name when it extends the bounds of human misery.' The implication was that the poor must work or die; but since the very lack of work was the heart of

---

[3]   J. Townsend, *Journey through Spain*, iii. 57–8.   [4]   Ibid. 17.

the problem, the whole argument was misconceived. Nor was it altogether fair to condemn ecclesiastical almsgiving as indiscriminate. Wealthy Spanish bishops might be able to afford charity for all comers. But most benevolent institutions, painfully aware of their inadequate funds, were constantly devising rough and ready distinctions, inevitably unjust, between those entitled to relief and those who were not. The beneficiaries tended to be those known by long residence within a district, or those whose moral characters were deemed good—the 'deserving' poor in fact. The homeless, rootless, floating population who often most needed relief were usually the last to get it. When the need was most pressing, for instance during famines, urban authorities would simply drive the undomiciled population out into the countryside.

The absence of large, well-endowed ecclesiastical corporations highlighted the problems of poverty in Protestant countries and served to evoke a more imaginative response, such as that of Denmark. In 1683, the Danish law accorded all paupers a legal right to relief in the form of employment on public works, organized by the state and financed out of indirect taxation. Throughout most of Protestant Europe, however, poor relief was not centrally co-ordinated, but in the hands of parish officers who received little or no renumeration. In Brandenburg a law of 1696 authorized parishes to provide work for the deserving poor and punishment for the undeserving, but all relief was to be financed out of voluntary contributions. Consequently with the exception of Berlin, where the government subsidized a Directory of Poor Relief to which any pauper might apply, relief in Prussian towns was mostly dependent upon the vicissitudes of private initiative, and very inefficient. Mostly it became a matter of periodic campaigns to drive beggars out into the countryside. Not until after 1740 were poor houses established in most major Prussian towns, and then only after local authorities had been empowered to levy compulsory poor-rates. In Scotland the elders of the kirk had to finance relief entirely out of voluntary donations. In Holland church elders, and in England overseers of the poor did levy compulsory poor-rates in each parish. Yet a fair and accurate collection of such rates was, as in the case of taxes, far more difficult to achieve in towns than in the country. In both the main concern of the authorities was to keep the rates low rather than adequate. Dutch towns were particularly well provided with privately endowed almshouses; and in the early decades of the eighteenth century the parishes of larger English towns, led by Bristol, began to unite to set up common 'workhouses' where the able-bodied poor could be employed. In 1722 parliament encouraged this expedient, and the next year overseers were empowered to withold relief from those refusing to enter a workhouse, able-bodied or not. By the 1780s most English urban poor relief was probably 'indoor' rather than 'outdoor', but workhouse conditions were generally so squalid (and sometimes deliberately kept that way) that all but the most abject strove to keep out of them. The remedies devised for poverty, in fact, were often more cruel than the condition itself, and were persistently based on the mistaken belief that many paupers were idle from preference rather than necessity. Yet perhaps anything was better than the situation in Russia, where each order in society was responsible, in towns, for the relief of its own poor. This meant that the poor should relieve themselves and expect nothing from others. How they were to do this was never made clear.

Varieties of Employment

The unemployed poor never made up the majority of urban populations. No town or city could have survived if they had. The great majority of town-dwellers earned their living, even if for many employment was never more than temporary, at the mercy of economic fluctuations.

In garrison towns and capitals of militarily ambitious states such as eighteenth-century Russia or Prussia, soldiers formed the largest single occupational group. Such towns remained exceptional: more usually the largest group was that of domestic servants. No less than 16 per cent of the population of Paris were servants in the 1780s. In 1789 there were 20,000 servants in Vienna, or 9 per cent of the city's inhabitants; in 1798 in Berlin there were 15,000 of them, or 11 per cent. These were capitals, where rich employers were concentrated, but provincial centres had similar proportions—11 per cent of Toulouse, for example in 1695, 7 per cent in 1789. Only in manufacturing centres such as Lyons, was the proportion as low as 4–6 per cent (1791). Among domestics there was always an elaborate hierarchy. At the top came skilled servants—stewards, butlers, or cooks, who might spend a lifetime with a single master or family. But most were unskilled lackeys or chambermaids, who often moved rapidly from job to job in conditions of poor pay and extreme insecurity. John Macdonald, a Scottish footman and one of the few servants who left memoirs,[5] was not the lowest type of servant. He was experienced in travel and an accomplished cook. Yet between 1746 and 1779 he served no fewer than twenty-seven masters. He had begun his career typically enough: born in the countryside, orphaned young, after a year of intermittent begging and odd jobs in and around Edinburgh he became a postilion, though still a child. Most unskilled domestics were rural immigrants—in Paris in the 1780s, for example, 87 per cent were. Even in Moscow or St. Petersburg, where probably the bulk of domestics were serfs, they were brought in from the countryside. Unlike most of their fellow-immigrants, servants enjoyed a minimum of comfort and security. Their wages might be low and irregularly paid, but most received free board, lodging, and sometimes clothing—items which took up the bulk of most wage-earners' income. On the other hand they had no defence against instant dismissal (or worse, if they were serfs), and they needed a former employer's reference to get another job. A Parisian regulation of 1720 required all domestics to obtain a leaving certificate, without which they might be arrested as vagabonds, whom employers were forbidden to take on. It was estimated in 1796 that at any moment there were 10,000 servants out of work in London. Isolated from one another in the garrets of their masters' houses, servants could have

---

[5] *Travels in various parts of Europe, Asia, and Africa* (1790), republished as *Memoirs of an eighteenth-century Footman* (1927).

little sense of common interest and no opportunity to combine in self-defence. It was even difficult to marry and set up a family unless the master was prepared to support them all, which was a rare event. Domestics were also isolated from other employees by the distinct pattern of life, their frequent participation in their employers' privileges, and their obvious dependence as signified by the wearing of liveries. No doubt many took pride in the glory reflected upon them from their masters, but the French Revolution was to show, through innumerable denunciations, that a nobleman's most dangerous enemy might be his former servant. Domestics knew that despite the relative comfort of their lives, they were despised by other workers. Employers were known to recruit servants from naive and malleable rustics rather than from the more self-assured natives of towns. In Lyons the wealth of domestics tended to be greater than that of the silk-weavers who were the mainstay of the city's economy, but this hardly ever induced the children of weavers, let alone their parents when temporarily unemployed, to go into 'service' for a living.

The distinction between town-born and immigrant, in fact, persisted long after the immigrants' absorbtion into urban life, through the types of occupation they found. Most immigrants who did not slide into beggary or become servants ended up as casual or day labourers. Thirteen per cent of the population of Paris in the 1780s fell into this category, which included dockers, porters, chairmen, waiters, shop assistants, and a whole range of manual workers. These groups had, if anything, even less organization than servants. They drifted in and out of employment, begged or stole when there was none, and married fellow immigrants. They lived in overcrowded cellars or garrets among their own kind, largely cut off both from servants and more skilled artisans. It was among them primarily that gin-drinking was rife in London between the 1690s and the 1750s, a cheap and effective way of forgetting the miseries of life. Admittedly not all immigrants were unskilled. The seasonal labourers in the building and construction industries provide an example. Unlike unskilled immigrants, they were extremely well organized, extremely tough, and often united by their origin from quite small geographical areas, like the Limousins who were the mainstay of Parisian building trades. But these features isolated them just as completely from the sedentary world of the urban artisan.

The only place where townsmen and immigrants might frequently be found working side by side was in factories. Unknown at the beginning of the period, these large concentrations of workers producing under one roof were still rarities at the end. However, it was estimated by 1779 (somewhat fancifully perhaps) that in Barcelona 30,000 workers were employed in cotton and calico factories with work-forces running into hundreds. In 1771, 12,681 people worked in 113 factories in Moscow, thirty-one of which employed over 100 workers, and two, over 1,000. A calico factory founded in Berlin in 1756 was soon employing 700 workers, and not long afterwards similar establishments were being set up in various north French towns. Yet major cities like London or Paris saw little activity of this sort. The wallpaper factory of Reveillon, with its 350 employees, is famous as the first major institution to be sacked by the Paris mob in April 1789; but it also deserves to be remembered because there was nothing comparable in the rest of Paris. Most Russian factories, the largest and most numerous in Europe, were not situated in towns at all. Most of the spinning mills built in northern England in the later eighteenth century were set up on mountain rivers away from towns; although of course towns often mushroomed around them.

The characteristic unit of production was the small workshop under an individual master, employing only a handful of artisans. The average number of workers per workshop in Paris was probably not more than three, a scale also found in Stockholm. They tended not to be immigrants, but native-born townsmen and their children, often living in well-defined areas of towns, where their particular trades had been long established, like the silk-weavers of Spitalfields in London, or those of Lyons, who tended to avoid the southern parishes of the town and its suburbs. Such circumstances gave them a greater sense of common identity and common interests than most immigrants could ever have. So did the intimate family atmosphere of the workshop and the traditional professional solidarity of each trade. A skilled trade was amost invariably an organized one—in most towns by means of guilds. Their purpose was to protect the interests of all those following a trade and to maintain the standard of its products. They formalized and gave legal standing to their members' common interests. All this meant that skilled workers were used to acting and responding together to changing economic circumstances. And so they, and not the rootless, shifting, and miserable immigrants, were the dangerous classes in times of uncertainty. They had more to lose when times changed and were more used to acting together to preserve established ways.[6]

Not all was harmony in the community of skilled workers. As among servants, there were well-established hierarchies, which were a source of much tension. Apprentices, at the lowest level, were often hard to differentiate from servants. They lived with their masters and waited upon them in return for instruction in a trade rather than wages. Like servants, they were usually completely within their master's power. Nor were they entirely emancipated from it on becoming qualified craftsmen. Good references were essential when changing masters, and a French law of 1781 compelled all workers to carry a work record, which all employers had to endorse. The same law reiterated the banning of all combinations of workers to secure higher wages or better conditions. In England combinations were prohibited in certain trades in 1726 and 1749, and were generally proscribed in 1799. Throughout Europe such organizations were viewed by governments, and naturally by employers, with the deepest suspicion. Yet they certainly existed, as action against them shows. Building workers had long been notorious for their secret societies. On the continent other trades had also formed brotherhoods, with three major ones in France, not confined to particular trades and

6 G. Rudé, 'The growth of cities and popular revolt 1750–1850' in J. F. Bosher (ed.), *French Government and Society 1500–1850* (1973), 166–90.

especially active outside Paris. They had links and imitators in Germany, the Netherlands, Italy, and Spain. Their avowed purpose was mutual aid to fellow workers and defence against victimization. Yet rival brotherhoods often spent much time in mutual recrimination, and, although they could occasionally organize strikes or boycotts in particular places, they were not very effective in consistently furthering their members' interests. Most craftsmen had no clear or steady idea of themselves as a working group with interests fundamentally opposed to those of their employers.

The whole idea of guilds[7] took no account of such a possibility. In principle each one enshrined a ladder of attainment by which every workman might climb to be an employer. 'The motive of a man', wrote the Lyons master-weavers in 1761, 'who chooses a craft is to work in it, not as an artisan all his life, but as a master.'[8] Guilds controlled admission to masterships by demanding a 'masterpiece' as a proof of competence and by levying admission fees which rose dramatically both in France and the Austrian Netherlands. Those of most Brussels guilds almost doubled between 1650 and 1710. But it was not difficult to become a master, as their numbers show. In Spain by the late 1780s they outnumbered journeymen in the silk, wool, blacksmith's, carpenter's, and tailor's trades. Throughout the century the journeyman silk-workers of Lyons were always outnumbered by masters. Workshop production, in fact, depended on the existence of large numbers of small masters specializing in particular aspects of each trade, and subcontracting to one another. Their payrolls expanded or contracted according to the job in hand, and few journeymen worked permanently for one master. Thus at every level solidarities outweighed antagonisms. In Lyons the true antagonism was not so much between masters and journeymen, as between the whole body of silk producers, whatever their status, and the handful of great merchants who controlled the product's outlets and dictated the pattern of production. When, in 1744, a new law confirmed the dominance of the merchants, there was a week of riots and strikes, led by masters, which the local authorities were quite unable to control until the law was (temporarily) abrogated.

Nor were conditions of work a source of many confrontations between employers and employed, despite the fact that these conditions were uniformly poor. Most urban artisans worked in cramped, insanitary, badly lit, and badly ventilated workshops—but so did their masters. The working day normally began before dawn and ended after dusk. Working days of fourteen or sixteen hours were normal, and even when all breaks were taken into account, the effective working day was still between ten and thirteen hours, six days a week. The bookbinders of Paris were unsuccessful when in 1776 they struck for a reduction of their working day from sixteen hours to fourteen. In Catholic Europe the proliferation of official Saints' days provided some leisure. Even after the abolition of seventeen religious holidays in 1666,

[7] Understanding of this question has recently been transformed by M. Sonenscher, *Work and Wages: Natural Law, Politics, and the Eighteenth Century French Trades* (1989).
[8] Quoted in M. Garden, *Lyons et les lyonnais au XVIIIe siècle* (1970), 285.

there still remained twenty-four in the year when work was forbidden in the Paris area, and there were far more in Spain and Italy. In Protestant England, by contrast, there were only three religious holidays; but London workers were free on the eight days a year when there were public hangings, and a well-rooted tradition, persisting far back into the eighteenth century, allowed English workmen to extend their Sunday leisure into Monday. The advent of factories, well designed and purpose-built, often brought an improvement in the working environment. But any gains were offset by the regularity and monotony required to tend machines not operated by manual power, and the loss of the intimate, patriarchal family atmosphere of the small workshop.

When masters and their craftsmen did clash, the issue was most often wages. The prime concern of masters was to keep wages as low as possible. 'To assure and maintain the prosperity of our manufactures', wrote the director of manufactures to the king of Prussia in 1786, 'it is necessary that the worker should never get rich, that he should never have more than what he needs to feed and clothe himself well. In a certain class of people, too much ease weakens industry, engenders idleness and all the vices which follow from it. To the extent that the worker grows rich, he becomes difficult about the choice and wages of his work.'[9] He need not have worried; very few workers earned more than the bare minimum he considered desirable, and many earned a good deal less. Inventories of artisans' goods made after their deaths show that there was seldom enough money for extra comforts. Few families left more than a table, chairs, a bed, a cupboard, and a few cooking pots. It is true that urban wages tended to be higher than rural ones, but most townsmen had no land, not even a garden, to supplement their subsistence, and no extra seasonal work like harvesting. Worse still, when prices began to rise wages generally lagged behind them. Only in areas of rapidly expanding demand for labour, such as Catalonia and northern England, did wages keep up. In most towns, the real wages of artisans probably declined, in a labour market which was over-supplied. Few workers were in a position to compare their lot with that of their ancestors, and such long-term trends bothered them little. What really mattered were short-term economic fluctuations. In Paris, London, and the growing cities of northern England in the later eighteenth century family men spent half or more of their weekly income on bread, and most of what was left on other foodstuffs. Any increase in the price of these commodities or any reduction in wages imperilled their whole existence. Wage reductions could at least be met by strikes, such as those of the Parisian stocking-weavers in 1724, or stonemasons in 1785; or by wrecking workshops, as the Spitalfields silk weavers did in London in 1765. But wage-earners were helpless in the face of rises in the price of bread caused by deficient harvests. Then, they saw their wages quite literally eaten away. Higher food prices of course reduced demand for other goods and induced employers to reduce wages or lay off workers—and so misfortunes

---

[9] Quoted in P. Léon, *Economies et Sociétés préindustrielles*, ii, *1650–1780* (1970), 395–6.

tended to coincide. It was at these moments that the urban populace became really dangerous.

Urban Unrest

The authorities in towns drew little distinction between strikes and riots; they were all forms of subversion—the one easily sliding into the other. Peaceful strikes stayed peaceful only if they achieved their ends quickly; but the very readiness of the authorities to arrest leaders and break strikes by force, rather than yield to strikers' demands, meant that peaceful settlements were extremely rare. Some strikes, especially in the later eighteenth century, were occasioned by the introduction of labour-saving machinery, but most were about wages—resistance to cuts, or more often demands for rises. They usually coincided with acute short-term economic crises, when the cost of living suddenly rose beyond artisans' pockets. In France there was a clear correlation between the frequency of industrial disputes and times of economic difficulty, the most disturbed periods being the 1660s, 1685–1724, and 1770–89. The post-war problems of the British economy in the early 1720s and then again in the 1760s were the background to years of bitter industrial disputes in London. Most strikes by far were among textile workers—the biggest and most highly organized complex of trades in Europe. The first organized strike in eighteenth-century Spain was at a Guadalajara cloth factory in 1730. Declining government orders following the end of wars caused most of the difficulties which led to strikes in the biggest woollen factory in Moscow in 1722, 1736, 1742, 1749, and 1762—despite the fact that most of the labour force was made up of serfs.

The natural corollary of the strike was the petition. Strikers knew that since the civil authorities' sympathies were all on the side of their employers, it was important to convince them that their case was reasonable. In England there were frequent petitions to local justices who had the power to fix wage rates as well as control of the forces of public order. In London petitions to the king and parliament were a well-established form of protest. Crowds of many thousands would accompany petitions to Westminster, in open defiance of the act of 1662 which forbade 'tumultuous petitioning'. French workers in Paris and other judicial centres looked to the *parlements* to protect their interests, as they frequently did when guilds or confraternities brought lawsuits in demarcation disputes. So they regularly petitioned them to intervene in industrial disputes. Marches to petition the king and his ministers at Versailles were not unknown. Such intimidating demonstrations always gained verbal satisfaction, which was usually enough to disperse them, but most achieved little beyond that. The lesson was that only violence made much impact; accordingly most strikes rapidly led to intimidation of obstinate employers, sacking of their property, and wrecking of workshops—activities which in their turn only confirmed the authorities in their suspicions, their prejudices, and their determination to smash the movements by force. Even when action was successful 'ringleaders' were invariably singled out and punished as a warning against further disorder.

Industrial disputes could touch off more general disturbances. When a London employer dismissed his English labour force and took on cheaper Irish workers in 1736, a week of disturbances followed in which mobs of up to 4,000 roamed east and south London attacking Irish immigrants and their property. But such generalized unrest occurred most often after sudden rises in the price of bread, exactly as they did in the countryside. In Paris there were bread riots in 1709, 1725, 1740, 1752, and in 1775 the famous 'flour war' created panic which spread into the capital from the countryside and led to intimidation of bakers and grain merchants and popular price-fixing. The situation, resulting from a poor harvest, had been aggravated by the government's lifting of all previous restrictions on the grain trade. A similar unfortunate coincidence of poor harvest and abolition of controls occurred in Spain in 1765; the result was hoarding and widespread panic in the spring of 1766 in which bread prices rose in many towns by a half or more. Mobs 10,000 strong rampaged through Madrid, their example encouraging almost seventy outbreaks in provincial towns in the ensuing months. In 1773 there were extensive bread riots in Palermo, and 1789 witnessed them in Barcelona and Paris. Reveillon's factory was sacked that spring, not in an industrial dispute, but because he had publicly approved wage-rates that were inadequate in famine conditions. This was a horrible misunderstanding; he had been speaking of rates that ought to be adequate rather than ones that actually were. The hungry populace did not appreciate such fine distinctions, mistaking his sympathy for indifference. Yet behind the stern and repressive face they presented against all disorder, local authorities were often sympathetic to the grievances of bread rioters and pressed strongly for subsidized prices.

The people are not wrong to complain [wrote a Bordeaux magistrate after bread riots in the city in 1773] they are in no state to pay for their bread. . . their normal remark is to say we prefer to die on a gibbet rather than die of hunger, it's shorter. Think how impossible it is to calm the progress of sedition, above all when it has a cause as general and imperative as feelings of hunger or only the fear of famine. It is wisest to end it all by ways of gentleness and charity. . .Why insist on keeping up the price of bread?. . .As for me, I confess, it seems to me that in a country where taxes are carried to excess, the king is bound to assure his subjects the only thing they have left: their lives.[10]

Though not as frequent as industrial disputes or bread riots, tax riots were often bigger and more spectacular. Sometimes grievances over rising taxes brought whole cities out in open rebellion, such as Rennes and Bordeaux in 1675, when Louis XIV crowned a decade of increases with a stamp duty on all public paper. The populace was led, or at least not discouraged, in its protests by the magistrates of the local *parlements*, who were later exiled for long periods to smaller and less inflammable towns. In 1733 parliament was

[10] Quoted in W. Doyle, *The Parlement of Bordeaux and the End of the Old Regime 1771–90* (1974), 205.

so intimidated by London riots against proposals to extend excise duties that Walpole's government dropped the idea for fear of losing its parliamentary support. Another explosive issue was religion. Mobs in London in 1708 and 1715, and in Birmingham in 1791, attacked the chapels and houses of Protestant dissenters in the name of 'Church and King'. In the 1670s Catholics had been the object of attack, as they were in the Gordon riots of 1780. On this occasion parliament's rejection of a petition against recently granted concessions to Catholics triggered off a week of disorder in which the main prisons and the houses of public figures were attacked and burned. The outbreak, the worst and most extensive disorder in any European city in the century before 1789, was only put down by troops at the cost of 285 killed, 173 wounded, 25 hanged, and 12 imprisoned.

Yet few urban riots were a matter of only a single issue. Anti-Catholic demonstrations such as those of 1780 were directed as much against foreigners, the Irish, and the rich, as against Catholics as such. The Porteous riots in Edinburgh in 1736 began (in their support for convicted smugglers) as a protest again taxation, but when troops fired on the crowd they were transformed into a demonstration against the authorities and the alien English government they represented. The Madrid riots of 1766 blamed the alien minister Squillace not just for higher bread prices, but for the renewal of abandoned regulations against wearing the traditional Spanish clothing of cloaks and wide-brimmed hats. The only clear common feature of riots is that they were against change. Mobs were conservative. However oppressive and constricting the established order, at least it represented accepted, tried, and agreed ways of doing things. Riots were usually directed at those who seemed to threaten these ways, whether tax-collectors or ministers who sought to abandon price controls, or suspicious foreigners, or cheaper immigrant workers, or even those who rejected the established religion. The reason for the mobs' conservatism is evident from their composition, where it can be reconstructed from police records. Observers usually blamed the dregs of society—beggars, vagrants, the unemployed, criminals, and immigrants without roots. In fact, these groups seem to have played relatively little part in urban disturbances. Having nothing, they were largely unaffected by taxes, bread prices, wage rates, foreign competitors, or any of the other causes of riots. Indeed, major upheavals disrupted the flow of charity upon which they relied. Mobs were essentially made up of people with something to lose—skilled workers, petty tradesmen, small masters, and journeymen—people with incomes which were just adequate, and an established position and function in society which marked them out from the lowest of the low. They rioted to defend an order which guaranteed their position, and against innovations which seemed to threaten it.

The motives of rioters were seldom political, but the issues that roused them often were. Powerful men did not scruple to manipulate mob violence for political ends, especially in capital cities—nowhere more easily than in London. The anti-Catholic mobs of the 1670s were encouraged by those who wished to exclude James duke of York from succession to the throne, in order to intimidate parliament and the king. The riots against dissenters in 1708 were incited by inflammatory sermons against the Whigs. The excise riots of 1733 were encouraged by Walpole's opponents in parliament and in the city in the hope of bringing him down. Riots in Moscow in 1662, caused by inflation attendant on an excess of copper coinage, were used to force the tsar to dismiss his chief advisers. The panic caused by the French invasion of the Dutch republic in 1672 led to riots in The Hague which culminated in the lynching of the de Witt brothers, who had dominated the state for over twenty years. The populace was encouraged by the Orange party, whom the de Witts had consistently attempted during that time to exclude from power. Similarly, the Madrid riots of 1766 were deliberately encouraged by some grandees and clerics in order to terrify Charles III into dismissing not just Squillace (in which they succeeded) but all his reforming 'enlightened' minsters such as Jovellanos and Campomanes (in which they did not).

Mobs were therefore an important political tool. Their largely non-political grievances tended to be manipulated by the powerful for their own political ends. If in the process the rioters gained what they wanted for themselves, that was incidental. Only in the later eighteenth century did mobs begin to riot for their own political purposes. The clearest case was the riots in the city state of Geneva in 1770 and 1781, part of a long-developing movement on the part of the ordinary native-born inhabitants of the city for a degree of participation in its oligarchic government. More ominous for the future were the disturbances over John Wilkes in London in 1768, 1769, 1770, and 1771. Wilkes was an adventurer patronized by the city of London and various opposition groups in parliament. Parliament's refusal to allow his election for Middlesex, after repeated majorities, coincided with industrial unrest following a series of bad harvests, and there were riots to the cry of 'Wilkes and Liberty'. Whether the rioters wanted anything very specific, beyond the election of Wilkes, is doubtful. Wilkes himself cared about little but his own interests. Yet willy-nilly he symbolized resistance to government and a parliament which represented only a narrow oligarchy. Middlesex had one of the largest and most broadly based electorates in England. The mobs who rioted in Wilkes's favour were implicitly supporting claims to a say in power for people more like themselves.

These stirrings proved ephemeral. There was no echo of them in the far more dangerous Gordon riots a decade later. It was the populace of French cities, rather than of English ones, that first intervened in politics in its own right, and with its own political aims. Even then it took the unprecedented experience of the Revolution to stir them into action. But the example was contagious, and the tradition of popular agitation going back to Wilkes ensured that England in the 1790s also rapidly acquired a popular movement with its own political programme.

The Urban Rich: the Bourgeoisie

In striking contrast to peasant revolts, urban riots caused few deaths. Most of the casualties were caused by the forces of suppression. But urban riots often brought widespread and spectacular destruction of property. Riots were seldom caused by hatred of the rich, but they provided an irresistible excuse for venting this hatred. The most obvious targets for looting and pillaging were the sumptuous town houses of noblemen, the visible symbols of the ruling orders and their power. Almost as obvious, however, were the houses and installations of other prominent citizens such as merchants, bankers, and lawyers–the bourgeoisie. They were even more vulnerable. The noble could discreetly withdraw to his estates, secure in the knowledge that both he and his property were beyond the mob's reach. Most bourgeois had no such refuge. As the very name implied, bourgeois fortunes were fundamentally urban. The bourgeoisie profited and prospered from urban pursuits and urban needs. They constituted each town's non-noble élite, dominating the town as the nobles dominated the countryside.

Yet the bourgeoisie are notoriously hard to define and pin down. The very name is a subject of endless controversy, for it had, and has, a variety of different meanings. Nor does the most convenient and usual English equivalent –'middle class'–do justice to its subtleties. A bourgeois was a town-dweller, but quite evidently not all town-dwellers were middle class. Many continental towns had a legally defined group of burghers (*bourgeois*), usually a narrow group of notables enjoying various privileges and qualifying for the status mainly through heredity or great wealth. Very few members of urban middle classes penetrated these exclusive ranks, whereas often local noblemen did. Yet a true bourgeois was by definition not a nobleman. Nor, equally, was he an artisan, an employee working with his hands. This leaves a broad social range, from the richest merchant down to the modest master craftsmen, a group which might at first sight seem to have almost nothing to bind it together at all. In fact, however, two crucial features were common to all bourgeois. The first was wealth. Vast though the range might be, and concentrated though the greatest fortunes might be in very few hands, no bourgeois was really poor by comparison with most of the population, and even the humblest among them could afford more than the barest necessities of life. Secondly, the bourgeoisie were rising. Attempts are frequently made to explain historical phenomena in terms of a rising bourgeoisie or middle class. Such attempts ignore the fact that the bourgeoisie, by its very character, is always rising. The bourgeoisie is social mobility in action; the wealth of its members gives them social pretensions beyond their origins, but also the means of fulfilling these pretensions. It is the most dynamic element in society.

Another common idea is that in certain periods the bourgeoisie was a new social group. It did indeed always contain a fair number of new men and their families, but so long as there have been towns, and so long as there have been, for example, merchants or lawyers, there has been a bourgeoisie. So it is not the appearance of a bourgeoisie, or its 'rise' that the historian needs to look for. The significant movements are its expansion in numbers or in wealth; the inclusion of unprecedented elements in its ranks; and above all the emergence of a collective class-consciousness to make the bourgeoisie see itself no longer as a group of travellers between one social situation and another, but as a class in its own right, with its own permanent interests. None of this happened in Europe between 1660 and 1800, but the beginnings of all three processes were apparent by the later eighteenth century.

Because they are so hard to define, the bourgeoisie are equally hard to enumerate. One fact is clear: like the towns which spawned them, they were far more numerous in the west than in the east. In the west they outnumbered the nobility and the ruling orders in the population as a whole. In England, where the nobility or its equivalent accounted for about 1½ per cent, the non-agricultural middle ranks of society made up just under 9 per cent in 1688, rising to around 15 per cent in 1803. In France in 1789 at least 1,700,000 bourgeois made up 6 per cent of the population, while in Spain the proportion may have been 10 or 11 per cent. In contrast, the Russian bourgeoisie accounted for only $2\frac{1}{2}$ per cent in 1762, or half the size of the nobility. In Hungary it probably did not reach 2 per cent. Where bourgeois were concentrated, in the towns themselves, their proportion of the entire population was inevitably higher; in France, for instance, it could be anything between 15 and 40 per cent. Finally, it seems clear that the numbers and wealth of the bourgeoisie expanded. The English middle class, as we have seen, grew over the eighteenth century by more than a half. Its share of the national income grew from around 20 per cent in 1688 to over 40 per cent in 1803.[11] Comparable statistics are not available for other countries, but French historians believe that the bourgeoisie of their country more than doubled in size between 1660 and 1789.[12] Its wealth undoubtedly increased too, owing primarily to the growth of trade with the rest of the world in the later eighteenth century.

For trade was the motor of the bourgeoisie. Every bourgeois family made its initial fortune in trade, the only way to accumulate capital rapidly. The archetypal bourgeois was a merchant, and the colonial boom of the eighteenth century saw a rapid growth of the mercantile communities in such cities as Barcelona, Cadiz, Bordeaux, Marseilles, Nantes, Bristol, Glasgow, Cork, and Hamburg. Economic expansion also brought the appearance of new bourgeois groups. Manufacturers for instance, were a category not recognized by the demographer Gregory King when he surveyed the English population in 1688; yet by the end of the next century they accounted for at least 4 per cent of the English bourgeoisie and 23 per cent of its wealth. The calico manufacturers of Barcelona, classed as 'idlers' by tax officials at a loss for a definition, were numerous enough to form a professional association in 1772, and cotton manufacturers followed their example in 1799. Even in France, where noble capital predominated in mining and metallurgy, most large-scale enterprises in the paper and textile industries were under bourgeois

[11] These and other figures for England are calculated from the estimates in H. Perkin, *The Origins of Modern English Society 1780–1880* (1969), 20–1.

[12] The latest calculation scales down earlier estimates suggesting a tripling of numbers. See J. Dupâquier *et al.*, *Histoire de la Population française, II De la Renaissance à 1789* (1988), 72.

control. In the greater seaports and capital cities, financiers and bankers were also of growing importance. There was certainly nothing new about bourgeois lending money to governments; but as the cost and scale of government activities mounted, and fiscal systems were subjected to increasing strains, they became dependent on credit as never before. As early as the mid-seventeenth century financiers were an important section of the Dutch bourgeoisie, the only rivals in Europe of the local nobility in wealth and power. In the eighteenth century, while Dutch trade stagnated and then declined, Dutch financiers continued to flourish and invest in foreign governments. The wars of Louis XIV created unparalleled opportunities in France for lending to the government and provisioning its forces, making bourgeois capital an essential part of the machinery of government. From the 1690s England took on similar burdens; a substantial 'funded interest' grew up, centred on the Bank of England and deriving its revenues from government stock and contracting.

The wealth of all these groups was mainly liquid, fundamentally different from the largely proprietary fortunes of the ruling orders. This is not to say that it was much more easily realizable. Apart from those of manufacturers or shipowners, with their extensive and costly equipment, assets tended to be largely invisible, tied up in stocks, credits, and negotiable paper. Nor was affluence evenly spread. The bulk of bourgeois wealth, like that of the nobility, was concentrated in very few hands. Each town had one or two fabulously rich notables—such as Georges Roux of Marseilles, François Bonnaffé of Bordeaux, or John Glassford of Glasgow—standing above the merely comfortably off ranks of their fellow bourgeois. Except in capital cities, where there were abnormal concentrations of very wealthy financiers and bankers, only such rare individuals had fortunes comparable to those of greater nobles. But almost everywhere there were many nobles poorer than the poorest bourgeois—often indebted to bourgeois too. In these circumstances the latter could be forgiven for thinking their own way of life and outlook superior to that of society's self-styled leaders.

The differences were clear. Nobles extolled idleness, despising trade and productive activity. The bourgeois by contrast worked for his money. Nobles were expected to live spectacularly and spend generously; the bourgeois virtues were sobriety, discretion, and thrift. How else could they have amassed their fortunes? Some historians argue that changes in artistic fashion in the eighteenth century reflected the increasing importance of more earnest and sober bourgeois values. The subtle and reflective novel supplanted the heroic epic; the moralizing domestic drama challenged classical tragedies and amoral comedies; everyday subjects began to rival the historical and mythological themes for painting favoured by noble patrons. The Enlightenment itself, some claim, was largely the elaboration of a bourgeois world view which demanded that everything should be justifiable in practical terms: most *philosophes*, like most writers and painters, were unambiguously middle-class. But they always had been: and if all this represented a counter-culture, there is little evidence that the nobility regarded it as a threat to its own values, and nobles willingly promoted the new movements with their patronage. Nor did writers and artists themselves reject or even attempt to avoid the notice of the ruling orders. A much clearer sign of cultural class-consciousness among the bourgeoisie was in religion, where large numbers dissented from established creeds. Many British merchants and manufacturers were Baptists, Congregationalists, or Quakers, and nearly all the trading community of Ireland were either Presbyterians or Roman Catholics. The bourgeoisie of certain southern French cities, such as Montauban, Nîmes, or Montpellier was dominated by Protestants, while French government finances were increasingly dependent upon Protestant bankers based in Switzerland. In Germany and eastern Europe, much of the trade and finance of major cities such as Hamburg, Berlin, or Frankfurt was in the hands of Jews, who were also important in western commercial and financial centres like Amsterdam. Often the religion dictated the occupation. Jews and other religious dissidents were usually debarred from all positions of public power and responsibility, so that only trade and finance were left. But if these policies were intended to bring dissidents into conformity, they largely failed; indeed they helped to awaken the dissidents before other groups to the social and political injustices of established regimes. It was hardly a coincidence that some of the most vocal leaders of bourgeois political aspirations in both England and France in the 1780s and 1790s were members of religious minority groups.

Yet when all is said, the evidence for the evolution of a distinct bourgeois class-consciousness before the 1789s is scanty, and often speculative. Nor does it compare in weight or clarity with evidence the other way—the obvious desire of most bourgeois to abandon their status and enter the nobility.

To be a merchant, wrote a merchant of Dunkirk in 1701, is to be looked on with contempt. . .So the merchant leaves his trade to withdraw to the countryside or buys himself an office to get out of this slavery. And if he does not, children who have seen the treatment their fathers have received get out themselves, spending on offices or land the money which would have remained in commerce, if they had found there the necessary protection and some marks of distinction which would have shielded them from the contempt which they meet with.[13]

Almost everywhere the social élite despised trade as base and degrading. The principle was under constant attack, whether in books such as Savary's *Perfect Trader* (1675) or Coyer's *Trading Nobility* (1756) or through innumerable attempts by governments to repeal or amend laws against derogation. But the impact was minimal. The ruling orders continued to impose their prejudices on society as a whole, and most of the bourgeoisie, as their behaviour shows, accepted them. No sooner had they made their fortune in trade, than they rushed to invest it, not in expanding their business, but in social climbing.

Not all bourgeois were merchants or financiers. A very important sector of the bourgeoisie were what we now term 'professional men'—some teachers,

---

[13] Quoted in P. Sagnac, *La Formation de la société française moderne* (1945–6), i. 162.

some doctors, many government servants, and innumerable lawyers. The very cost of training for these professions meant that their members were usually already at least second-generation bourgeois—sons of trader fathers who chose to place their families on the ladder of respectability as soon as even the lowest rung was within reach. The opportunities were abundant enough, for these groups too were expanding. The growth in governmental power and ambitions led to an expansion in the number of civil servants. The growth of trade itself expanded the 'professional' bourgeoisie to handle its growing legal and administrative needs. Even in commercial cities the trading element often found itself outnumbered and usually forced to share the responsibility of municipal government with lawyers. The 'professional' element predominated in inland capitals such as Berlin, Vienna, or Madrid, or provincial judicial centres such as Toulouse and Dijon. Nowhere was the 'professional' bourgeoisie better established than in France, where the proliferation of offices marketed by a loan-hungry government constantly siphoned off most new bourgeois wealth and talent from trade. Over 51,000 venal offices remained the classic vehicle of social mobility down to 1789. Their rising price in the latter half of the century bore witness to the unchanging priorities of France's expanding bourgoisie.

To abandon trade for an office or profession meant reinvesting capital in something more respectable, something that moved the bourgeois towards the noble ideal of living off unearned revenues. Annuities or government stock were a first step: in France, England, and especially in the Dutch republic thousands of bourgeois derived the bulk of their revenue from *rentes* or 'the funds', at low but reliable rates of interest. In this they were already half way to 'living nobly', since many nobles had money invested in this way. But since nobody could convincingly live nobly without owning land, eventually socially ambitious bourgeois would turn their thoughts in this direction. Often they began by buying up urban properties, and the typical bourgeois usually owned more town houses than the one he lived in. Then came the great step of purchasing estates in the countryside, the final renunciation of origins, the ultimate acceptance of noble values. Nobles were often far from flattered, seeing the invasion of the land market by moneyed townsmen as a threat to their own position. Yet they could not stem the flow; indeed, they were often prepared to marry the well-endowed daughters of the newcomers in order to maintain a hold on their own properties. The failure of the burghers of Holland to develop into or supplant the local nobility, even though they outshone them, is largely explained by the lack of available land around their cities. Elsewhere, the immediate surroundings of prosperous cities were largely bought up by bourgeois aspiring to become nobles or gentry. In France in 1789 the bourgeoisie owned around 25 per cent of all land. This by itself was not enough to ennoble them, as it almost was in England where three generations of possession conventionally made a gentleman. But it was an essential prerequisite for total acceptance into a status which could then easily be acquired at law simply by purchasing an ennobling office.

Inevitably, the bourgeoisie were not popular with other groups. They outbade both peasants and poor nobles in land sales; they lent money and then ruthlessly foreclosed if debtors fell into arrears; they paid their workers low wages and used violence to break strikes. In short their dynamism was a socially disruptive force. Yet, paradoxically, nothing was further from the minds of most bourgeois than disturbing the established order of things. Bourgeois, as their wealth, comfort, or freedom of action showed, were doing well out of society. They largely accepted its values and had no interest in changing it. They were insulated by their wealth from the fears, anxieties, and pressures that animated the mob, which they feared and despised with all the vehemence of the ruling orders themselves. For both groups, the highest political virtues were order and stability.

Yet bourgeois had their dissatisfactions. To accept (as their eagerness to escape showed they did) the inferiority of their own position meant accepting a good deal of gratuitous snobbery and unpleasantness from nobles. And this could only be borne so long as every good bourgeois had the expectation that he or his family would continue to rise. But as the eighteenth century progressed there were signs that this was becoming harder. In Great Britain, the Dutch republic, and Switzerland the new rich found themselves excluded from urban government by closed oligarchies of better-established families. The strength of entails and improving agricultural profits restricted the amount of land available to promote social mobility. The rising price of French venal offices was a symptom of increasing competition for status, and moves to restrict entry to better positions in the army and clergy to poor nobles were interpreted as anti-bourgeois. All these developments disturbed the rich commoner's confidence that his industry would receive its ultimate reward in social promotion and raised questions about the justice of the existing order. Yet at least he *had* got rich. Many of the middling and lesser 'professional' bourgeois did not even have that to console them. Often their families had abandoned trade without sufficient capital to ensure continued social promotion once the initial transfer to a more respectable livelihood was made. They found themselves marooned in relatively unprofitable positions, too poor to rise yet too proud to go back. Such circumstances produced intense frustration, not to mention envy of those fellow bourgeois who had stayed in trade and could now buy themselves the ultimate respectability—noble status—without trouble or effort. Like lesser nobles, 'professional' bourgeois hated and mistrusted the power of naked wealth to undermine and dissolve all the certainties and values they respected and lived by. And like the very mob they despised, they were opposed to the forces of change. Yet such conservatism bred change in itself—in this case the first emergence of a coherent political class-consciousness during the crisis of 1788–9. The anti-aristocratic creed of equal political rights and careers open to the talents did not originate among merchants, financiers, or capitalists. It arose from the anxiety-ridden, uncommercial bourgeoisie, the overabundant, overeducated petty lawyers and office-holders, whose aspirations the old order had fostered but had been unable to gratify.

ENLIGHTENMENT

7. Religion and the Churches

The lines dividing western Europe into Catholic and Protestant in 1660 had not changed significantly in 1800. France, Spain, Italy, the Habsburg dominions, Poland, and southern Germany were Catholic. Great Britain, the United Provinces, northern Germany, and Scandinavia were Protestant in one form or another. Russia and certain neighbouring territories observed their own variant on Greek Orthodoxy. In 1660, however, France harboured an important Protestant minority, Poland an Orthodox one, Protestant Holland was in fact half Catholic, and in Ireland Protestant England ruled an overwhelmingly Catholic population. Such dissident communities were profoundly mistrusted by governments, associated as they were with civil wars and attempts for over a century to change the established order. Only in the United Provinces, where a Protestant government ruled a fairly evenly divided population, was toleration implemented with any goodwill and even there formal laws forbade Roman practices.

The religious division of Europe was fundamental. It represented not only different interpretations of Christian doctrine and practice; by 1660 these differences had hardened into historical traditions with a power of their own. The most vivid contrasts of all appeared in everyday matters—between the Latin liturgy and elaborate ceremonial of the Roman rite and the vernacular sobriety of Protestant worship, between celibate Roman priests and the married ministers of Protestantism and Orthodoxy, with their clerical dynasties; and between the monasticism of Catholic and Orthodox Europe and its conspicuous absence elsewhere. In France in the eighteenth century there were 125,000 clergy, in Spain 170,000; in Sweden by contrast there were 14,000, and England may have had a similar number. The difference was accounted for by regular orders. Protestantism was further distinguished by its very diversity. The Lutheranism of Germany and Scandinavia, for all that it had in common with the Church of England, entertained no formal links with it. The Calvinist Presbyterians of Scotland, Holland, and Geneva were unsure whether Catholics or their own less extreme Protestant brethren were the more in error; while in Holland, parts of Germany, and England there was a multiplicity of minor sects, sharing with the Jews scattered throughout Europe the burden of the hostilities and suspicions of the majority.

The common basis of these very diverse groups lay in practising, believing congregations. Most people believed in a supernatural world with which the idea of God could be identified. Whether they knew clearly what this implied is more doubtful. 'Enlightened' thinkers called religion superstition, a charge unfair to saints, scholars, and mystics. Yet it described the religion of most Christians with much justice.

Popular Religion

The Reformation, by dividing Europe into various alternative creeds, made all religious authorities more determined to control the faithful. Their efforts were supported by secular political authorities, well aware that firm religious establishments consolidated their own power. The key to control was the parish; in Protestant and Catholic Europe alike the sixteenth and seventeenth centuries brought a renewed emphasis upon parochial observances such as regular attendance at the sacraments, Sunday churchgoing, and catechizing children by resident clergy. Yet whether all this resulted in greater understanding and spiritual awareness on the part of ordinary parishioners remains problematical. In the countryside at least the period after 1660 was certainly an age of observance. But was it an age of faith?

The question is notoriously difficult, especially for Catholic Europe. Protestant churches, with their vernacular liturgy, emphasis on Bible-reading, and greater degree of lay participation in services, were able to soak their members in the language and ideas of religion, so that even if official observances fell into relative neglect, revival movements aroused an immediate and understanding response. Catholicism depended for its impact upon deeds rather than words. The impact on the popular mind of the veneration of saints, images, and relics, of processions and pilgrimages to holy places, might be even stronger than that of Bible-reading; but it was far less distinct from magic, and doctrinal ignorance was the despair of evangelizing clergy. 'In respect of religion, articles of faith,' wrote a Flemish priest of his late seventeenth century flock, 'there is not one of them able to contradict the preaching they hear; but some still keep old errors in their hearts, which they could only defend on the grounds that their fathers told them so, but which they defend tooth and nail'.[1] The most deep-rooted popular faith in 1660 was in what the educated were already beginning to regard as superstitions—magic, omens, and witches.

The clergy encouraged this tendency by equating natural phenomena with the action of God. Omens, like the comet of 1680, were interpreted as signs of impending disaster throughout Europe. Natural calamities, such as the Marseilles plague of 1720, the Lisbon earthquake of 1755, or local floods or harvest failures, were all seen as divine retribution on the sinful. Sin was the work of the Devil. All this emphasized that the supernatural powers intervened in worldly affairs. In Catholic and Orthodox countries the faithful were encouraged not only to seek but to expect such intervention in their everyday lives in the form of miracles effected by the protective or curative powers of relics, images, pilgrimages, or saintly intercession. The touch of an English or French king was supposed miraculously to cure scrofula, 'the King's Evil'—though hygienic British monarchs abandoned the practice after 1714. Frequent resort by priests to exorcism emphasized that there were evil as well as good supernatural forces. It was hardly surprising then that when church magic failed them, the credulous should turn to the rival services

[1] Quoted in J. Delumeau, *Le Catholicisme entre Luther et Voltaire* (1971), 206.

of the Devil. Nor had the Reformation necessarily freed Protestantism of these tendencies, but it did preach the virtues and rewards of self-help, whereas recourse to magic resulted from a sense of human powerlessness. By 1660 belief in magic and the Devil were probably less powerful in Protestant parts than elsewhere, but there was a fairly continuous and continent-wide decline in the prestige of all occult forces throughout the period. Intellectuals grew more sceptical of supernatural interventions in the natural world. Some of this scepticism filtered down; expanding technology brought the environment more obviously under human control, making recourse to the supernatural seem less necessary. By 1660 belief in witches was on the point of decline throughout western Europe, which, unlike the east, had been swept by a 'witch craze' over the previous two centuries. The causes of this decline were complex and are still a matter of debate. The strengthening of parochial control was undoubtedly important, for with heresy and witchcraft linked in people's minds, when the one was excluded, so was the other. The spread of toleration over the eighteenth century taught people that dissident beliefs or practices were not to be feared. Alleged witches were often poor beggars who had been refused alms by better-off people who in their turn subsequently suffered misfortune. Their accusations were the product of superstitious guilt. But with the growth in public poor relief the obligation of private charity shrank, and accordingly the occasions for accusation diminished. Significantly, the witch craze had never secured a firm hold in Spain or Italy, where monastic charity was extensive and the Inquisition had kept heresy under iron control. Above all perhaps, judges grew increasingly sceptical of evidence in witchcraft trials, and reluctant to convict. A French edict of 1682 defined magic and witchcraft as crimes, but crimes of deception. In 1736 the crime itself was abolished in Great Britain, and by 1750 trials had become universally very rare. Such developments did not of themselves change popular mentalities, nor was the jurisprudence of all countries so advanced. Numerous alleged witches were executed in Scotland in the early 1660s, in Sweden and south Germany in the 1670s, and there were occasional executions in Poland and Switzerland as late as the 1780s. Even in England a 'witch' could be lynched by a mob in 1751. But when witchcraft ceased to be a crime the motive of retribution behind most accusations could not be satisfied. Judicial scepticism was increasingly shared by all educated men, and as powerful men who did not believe in witches refused their support to those who did, such attitudes spread. 'In this part of the country', wrote a traveller in the Scottish Highlands in 1769, 'the notion of witchcraft is quite lost; it was observed to cease almost immediately on the repeal of the witch act; a proof what a dangerous instrument it was in the hands of the vindictive, or of the credulous.'[2] Even if popular superstition and talk of witches remained widespread in 1800, its horrific manifestation in torture, violence, and burning had been curbed. Besides, the political intensity of the previous decade had turned popular hostility and suspicion in new directions.

[2] Quoted in A. J. Youngson (ed.), *Beyond the Highland Line* (1974), 135.

One of the strengths of religion was its power to impart a sense of group or political identity. Mobs which cared nothing for theological differences ran wild with sectarian frenzy against members of dissenting creeds. The Jews, who had suffered from such sentiments long before the Reformation, continued to do so. The Inquisition enjoyed popular support in Spain and Portugal in its attempts at a systematic elimination of Jews from the peninsula, and the influx of Iberian refugees to France and England fanned old gentile hostility. In 1753 the British government was forced by mob action to withdraw a bill giving Jews civil rights. But since the Reformation rival groups of Christians attracted the most hostility. The anti-Catholicism of the London populace was notorious. Fear of it paralysed Charles II's government for much of the 1670s, when rumours of a 'Popish Plot' to overturn the Protestant state held too strong a popular grip to be safely scorned. In 1780 proposals to relax the penal laws against Catholics provoked the Gordon riots. In Languedoc, where Protestantism remained strong even after the revocation of the Edict of Nantes, the Catholic population was often seized with hysteria against the dissident minority, especially in times of natural calamity or war against the Protestant powers. It was in such conditions that the most famous judicial martyr of the eighteenth century, the Protestant Jean Calas, was executed at Toulouse in 1762; while the political emancipation of the Protestants of Nîmes and Montauban in 1789 sowed the seeds of Catholic counter-revolution. Religion was an even closer binding element for persecuted minorities. When Louis XIV's attacks on the Languedoc Protestants threatened their whole cultural and psychological life at a time of economic recession, their reaction was violent. Imbued with the certainty of the coming Apocalypse by inflammatory sermons and convulsing prophets, they broke into a fanatical rebellion which tied down a full-scale army between 1702 and 1705, and did much to perpetuate and intensify the fears of their Catholic neighbours. Even more spectacular was the grip of Old Belief in Russia. The attempts made in the 1650s and 1660s by the church hierarchy, with state support, to revise liturgical practice along Greek lines provoked a schism which spread beyond the ranks of the clergy.[3] Old Believers regarded strict adherence to every detail of the old practices as an essential sign of their Russian identity, and of the special place occupied by Russia and its church in God's design. They resisted with fanaticism all attempts to impose conformity, their ideas playing an important part in popular opposition to authority throughout the eighteenth century and beyond.

Everywhere the educated men who ruled society scorned such 'Enthusiasm', but they feared it too. It drew on reserves of energy that governments were seldom able to tap. Yet these same educated men did much to make enthusiasm uncontrollable, especially in Protestant countries, when they insisted through the official voice of the established churches that God did not regularly intervene to work miracles in individual lives like some benevolent magician. The 'natural religion' so fashionable in the eighteenth century[4] elevated God

---

[3] See below, p. 161–3.
[4] See below, p. 196–9.

to a higher but infinitely remote plane, as the creator and the ultimate rewarder of the faithful and the virtuous, but not as a personal force. The disappearance of the divine magician left an emotional void which natural religion could not fill. Enthusiasm did. Not only, therefore, did it occur among religious minorities under pressure, but also among popular masses for whom established religious practices had lost much of their meaning. German Pietism, for instance, began in the 1670s as a closely disciplined and academic revival of the Lutheran spiritual life. Intensive preaching and Bible study led individuals through traumas of spiritual doubt to the acceptance of Christ as their personal Saviour. Through courts and universities these doctrines evangelized nobles and clergy. Zinzendorf, founder of the Moravians, was a product of Pietist education, but he led them beyond its limits. Acceptance of personal salvation led to a blind reliance on divine providence; Moravian communities took their decisions by lot or by opening the Bible at random, yet the number of religious renewals made by the Moravian example throughout Protestant Europe and in North America testifies to the emotional appeal of a religion of the heart. Most famous among those influenced by the Moravians was the indefatigable John Wesley, who founded Methodism in England in a long lifetime of preaching salvation through the personal love of Christ. Methodists believed that God constantly intervened in individual affairs, if not by miracles, then by providence. It was God's work, reflected Wesley, that the guns of Newcastle trained to repel the Scotch rebels in 1745 were aimed to miss the suburban house where he was staying, yet so directed too 'that none could come near our house . . . without being torn in pieces'.[5] Wesley also preached belief in the Devil, demons, and a medicine hardly distinguishable from ancient magic. Thousands heard him, and his meetings often witnessed scenes of mass religious hysteria which characterized enthusiasm at its most alarming. By the second half of the eighteenth century Methodism had been organized by Wesley into the most vigorous and well-managed religious group in England; the 356 chapels built by 1784 in areas scarcely served by the established church bore witness to its popular appeal. Catholic Europe was far less fertile ground for enthusiasm. Even the anti-intellectual Moravians and Methodists needed a basis of biblical literacy for their growth. Nevertheless spectacular outbreaks did occur. When in the early 1730s the French Government began for the first time in fifteen years resolutely to persecute Jansenist clergy, they responded by predicting the Apocalypse; and the people of Paris were profoundly impressed in 1731 by reputed miracles, prophesyings, convulsions, and holy rollings at the tomb of a Jansenist deacon in the cemetery of Saint-Médard. A worried government ended the popular sensation by closing the cemetery, but 'convulsionism' remained fashionable behind closed doors.

Educated men were disgusted. The scenes at Saint-Médard convinced Diderot of the absurdity and indignity of religious fanaticism. Orthodox Lutheran clergy drove Zinzendorf from several German courts before he

---

[5] *Journal of John Wesley*, Sunday 22 Aug. 1745.

set up a separate Moravian community. Anglican clergy closed their churches to Wesley (incidentally assuring him larger audiences in the open air). In this way popular religious sentiments, strong yet uprooted, were denied an established place in society, to become a force for spectacular disruption in unsettled times.

Established Religion

The failure to harness enthusiasm was ironic, for established churches were nothing if not instruments of control. 'What could exist without a dominant religion?' asked Empress Maria Theresa.[6] 'Toleration and indifference are exactly the surest ways of destroying the established order. What else is there to harness bad instincts?...Nothing is so necessary and beneficial as religion...If there were no state religion and submission to the church, where would we be?' In 1660 Europe looked back on a century and a half of bitter religious warfare, a melancholy legacy which suggested two possible and diverse conclusions. Either religious divisions should be tolerated, or they should be eliminated. Attempts at this second solution had been responsible for much of the carnage in earlier years, yet it died hard. Not until the later eighteenth century did toleration, rather than discrimination against dissenting minorities, begin to appear more likely to promote religious harmony.

Every state had an established church, most enjoying a legal monopoly of public worship. Citizens were by definition its members, whatever other sect they individually professed to subscribe to. The religious wars had determined what churches should be established, and even in those areas in which the outcome was still unsettled in 1660, within thirty years the situation had clarified. In 1685 France's Protestant minority was shorn of its privileged constitutional position and legally obliterated; while the downfall of James II and VII in 1689 resulted in the final consolidation of Anglicanism (shakily restored in 1660) in England and Ireland, and its abandonment in Scotland. Not until the French republic officially renounced religious responsibilities in September 1794 were there any further changes in the religious affiliation of states.

The function of an established church was to uphold the established order. Established churches monopolized civil ceremonies such as baptism, marriage, and burial. They enumerated people for taxation. Notices promulgated at Sunday services were the main means by which governments notified the illiterate governed of their intentions or requirements. The clergy also played the predominant role in pursuing and repressing subversive ideas. In 1660 the only state without an official and active apparatus of censorship was the Dutch republic, where the central power was weak, with true authority in the hands of innumerable local authorities of very diverse persuasions. The lapse of the English Licensing Act in 1694 signified the end of most censorship in Great Britain, but elsewhere the grip of authority remained strong. In France censorship was shared between the government, the courts, and the Sorbonne

---

[6] Quoted in A. Latreille, *L'Église catholique et la révolution française* (1946) i. 45.

(the Paris Faculty of Theology), none of which was noted for religious liberalism; but conflicts between them allowed more free expression than under more monolithic regimes. But in Austria the Jesuits dominated successive institutions of censorship until 1759, and from 1752 an official *Catalogue of Prohibited Books* was issued. In Italy the papal inquisition regularly issued an *Index* of prohibited works theoretically binding on all Catholics. Yet the *Index* was also a convenient guide to subversive literature, and the inquisition was not allowed to operate in France or the Austrian empire. Even in Italy its efficiency was uncertain. 'Freedom of thought on religious matters', wrote a French traveller in 1739, 'and sometimes even freedom of speech is at least as great in Rome. . .as in any town I know.'[7] The same could not be said of Spain, Portugal, or their empires, where native inquisitions wielded semi-autonomous secret police powers and issued their own, more stringent *Index*. Almost any conceivable unorthodoxy could be given a religious twist in order to interest the inquisition. Indeed, with the final extinction in Spain of the persecuted Jewish community, completed by about 1730, the inquisition found itself increasingly committed against the spread of foreign ideas of a completely secular nature. This, rather than an increasingly tolerant spirit, explains the decline in its more spectacular activities, such as heretic burning, over the eighteenth century.

Above all, the established churches controlled public education. At the popular level, often the only education available was the rudimentary catechizing of the local priest or pastor. The public schools at which the rich and powerful were educated were managed by the clergy. Until the 1760s the ruling orders of Catholic Europe were largely educated by the Jesuits or by rival but less extensive teaching orders such as the Piarists or Oratorians. Since one of the main functions of universities was to train prospective clergy, they were bastions of orthodoxy. It was no coincidence that the ideas that did most to undermine accepted values flourished and were disseminated where the clerical grip on public education was weak, as in the Dutch republic, or in private institutions with no public standing. The English Tories, styling themselves the 'church party', saw such dangers clearly enough when they attempted in the Schism Act of 1713 to subject private dissenting academies, a mushroom growth since the Toleration Act of 1689 and already the most vigorous force in English education, to episcopal control. Only a change of government forestalled them. 'Everybody', wrote a French cleric in 1753, 'who keeps particular masters at home can have his family taught the most dangerous opinions with impunity. . .make them imbibe their poison to the dregs, and instead of leaving Christian children to religion and submissive subjects to the crown, they will merely leave behind them rebels in heart and soul, atheists in conduct and belief.'[8] How far the radical frame of mind of young revolutionaries in the 1790s was created by the educational chaos which followed the expulsion and dissolution of the Jesuits from Catholic Europe in the 1760s and 1770s remains to be measured. But the effect was surely substantial.

[7] Y. Florenne (ed.), *Le Président de Brosses* (1964), 132.
[8] Quoted in J. Lough, *The Encyclopédie* (1971), 269.

If the churches educated and supported the ruling orders, the latter in turn supported and encouraged the church in preaching to the populace the injunction of St. Paul: 'Obey them that have the rule over you, and submit yourselves.'[9] In the last analysis the men of property who ruled society determined which creed should prevail, as James II and VII found when he attempted to impose his own Catholicism on England and Scotland. The Calvinist monarchs of Brandenburg in contrast carefully refrained from disturbing the Lutheran practices of their nobility and peasants. So did the Catholic electors of Saxony. But the involvement of the ruling orders in the established churches was more than ideological. They often owned ecclesiastical patronage, especially in Protestant countries, inherited from dissolved monasteries. They used it to provide for their relatives and clients. In Catholic Europe monasteries retained numerous impropriated livings, but here too aristocratic control was complete, since the inmates of the richest monasteries, nunneries, and chapters were usually nobles. In France the nobility practically monopolized the bench of bishops: in the 1780s a quarter of the episcopate was in the hands of thirteen families. The established churches were in a sense a gigantic system of support for noble families, although in a clerically over-populated country such as Spain (2 per cent of the population) there was plenty of room for other classes too. In Russia, where the clergy married and benefices passed by inheritance, the clergy had few aristocratic links. In Protestant countries, where clerics were often also the sons of clerics, lay control of patronage ensured that the church remained at the disposal of needy nobles whenever necessary.

Church and nobility derived their wealth from the same source—land. The church owned about one-tenth of the land in France (mainly concentrated in much higher proportions in the north and east), and about three-eighths in Austria. In Russia it owned almost 1,000,000 serfs. The greatest proprietors were monasteries, their disappearance in Protestant countries bringing a drastic fall in church landownership. Some Protestant prelates, like the bishop of Durham with his booming coal revenues, were still extremely rich, but the churches in general were not, and accordingly enjoyed even less independence of secular power. Thus paradoxically Protestant churches with little to give enjoyed no special fiscal exemptions (the Church of England gave up its right of self-taxation in 1664), while the immensely rich Catholic church enjoyed advantages and exemptions almost everywhere. Once in the undying grip of the church, however, property enjoyed these benefits for ever. Governments grew increasingly hostile to the extension of mortmain; it was prohibited in France in 1749 and in Austria in 1767, although in Spain such measures never got beyond the stage of impassioned discussion. In Russia bequeathing land to the church was forbidden, a rule powerfully reinforced by Peter I. In 1701 Peter also took over the management of monastic revenues, and although after his death they recovered financial autonomy, in 1764 all ecclesiastical revenues were secularized, so that the church became totally dependent on

---

[9]　Hebrews 13: 17.

the state for its income. If Joseph II had lived long enough, he might have forced through a similar comprehensive reduction of the church's independence in Austria. Ruling orders, however, realized that any attack on property, no matter whose, was an attack on the sanctity of the principle itself, and were reluctant to approve such a dangerous example.

It is true that the churches provided services as well as controls. The standard justification for monasteries increasingly under attack was their charitable work. Even the most rabid anti-clericals excluded from condemnation the charitable orders which kept hospitals and poor houses. Orders not founded for such specific purposes confined themselves to the distribution of alms, a worthy enough pursuit, but one which failed to impress advanced thinkers. Charity, they thought, promoted idleness. In any case the greater part of monastic wealth was not spent on such activities, but rather on grandiose building projects and additional comfort for the lives of inmates. Hardly any of the church's great wealth went on a still more essential service —the cure of souls. Parish clergy (except in Orthodox Europe) were separately endowed with tithes, which though seldom amounting to a tenth of produce, were levied more rigorously and precisely by 1660 than ever before. The value of those taken in kind could only improve as prices rose. Yet often monasteries or other ecclesiastical corporations had impropriated them, and priests received only a proportion of their value in a fixed sum of cash, which was far less favourable when prices rose. In France this sum (*portion congrue*) remained unaltered between 1686 and 1768, although by 1786 it had been belatedly raised by 150 per cent. To the payer the impropriation of tithes by bodies already rich enough seemed scandalous, with tithes already a constant irritant between priest and parishioners. In Ireland, where the vast majority of the population repudiated the established church and paid to maintain their own priesthood, they were particularly resented. Their collection on behalf of absentee incumbents by professional agents compounded the grievance, which was the source of much agrarian terrorism throughout the eighteenth century. But tithes were property and, although they did not gladly pay their own share, the landed classes seldom questioned their legitimacy.

Established churches taught political as well as social obedience. Kings were appointed by God and answerable only to Him. On no account should they be resisted. The experience of the turbulent mid-seventeenth century reinforced this lesson, and in the years following 1660 political passivity was elevated into the highest of goods. 'Does one not fight for legitimate authority in suffering everything from it without protest?', argued Bossuet, the most eloquent spokesman of the French church, in 1681, '. . . No pretext and no reason allows us to revolt, we must revere the Heavenly order and the character of the Almighty in princes, whatever they do. . .their crown is untouchable; . . .there lies the most assured foundation of public tranquility.'[10] The church of England made non-resistance its central doctrine until James II's

[10]   Quoted in A. G. Martimont, *Le Gallicanisme de Bossuet* (1953), 406.

attempts to undermine its own established position in favour of Catholicism made such an extreme standpoint untenable. When the revolution of 1688−9 showed that the doctrine only meant non-resistance to an Anglican Stuart, the term was abandoned. In Russia in 1660 the subservience of the church was in some doubt. The patriarch Nikon, taking advantage of his personal hold over an impressionable young tsar, had asserted the equality of the civil and ecclesiastical powers, and sometimes the superiority of the latter, in his own person. And although the tsar had taken advantage of a withdrawal by Nikon from public life in 1658 to reject his pretensions, the struggle continued until 1667, when a council at last deposed the patriarch. From then on the civil power steadily asserted its supremacy, and with the abolition by Peter I of the patriarchate itself in 1721 the subordination of the church became complete, controlled from then on by a 'Holy Synod', an assembly totally under the control of the civil power, and chaired by a layman. 'The fatherland', declared the *Ecclesiastical Regulation* which set up this new regime, 'need not fear from an administrative council the sedition and disorders that proceed from the personal rule of a single church ruler. . . when the people see that this administrative council has been established by decree of the Monarch. . .they will remain meek, and put away any hope of receiving aid in their rebellions from the ecclesiastical order.'[11]

Why were the churches so willing to preach obedience? Because they were controlled by governmental nominees. Everywhere bishoprics, deaneries, and abbacies were in the gift of the state. In Catholic countries papal confirmation was required, and the pope could create embarrassment by refusing it, as he did in the case of Louis XIV's appointments between 1680 and 1693, after they had quarrelled over regalian rights. But in general the pope did not demur. In Orthodox Russia the patriarch confirmed the tsar's appointments until the abolition of his office. In Protestant countries there was none to dispute the monarch's choice, while the votes of bishops in bodies such as the English and Irish Houses of Lords endowed the choice of reliable candidates with special importance. In Presbyterian states, where congregations chose their own ministers, the clergy had more independence, especially since their churches governed themselves by assemblies. The General Assembly of the Church of Scotland inherited some of the national representative character of the Scottish parliament when that body disappeared in 1707. Yet such well-established clerical bodies did little to disrupt the political order. Assemblies which did, like the English convocations, torn from 1689 to 1717 by recriminations between bishops and lower clergy, rapidly brought about their own suspension, all the easier to impose after the clergy had abandoned separate self-taxation. The French clergy never made that mistake, and accordingly their assemblies continued to meet every five years until 1789. Their credit, which enabled the king to raise cheaper loans than he could obtain unaided, was an additional inducement to him to uphold their right; especially when carefully rigged elections ensured that bishops and

[11] Quoted in J. Cracraft, *The Church Reform of Peter the Great* (1971), 154−5.

other government nominees dominated all business.

States had little to fear from clerical assemblies, properly managed, and often much to gain. If the life of the Anglican church atrophied in the eighteenth century, it was partly because no convocation was allowed to meet and provide for changing circumstances. It took the authority of a council formally to depose Nikon in 1667. Clerical assemblies were of particular use to Catholic monarchs who found themselves at loggerheads with the pope; the classic case was Louis XIV's quarrel over regalian rights in vacant sees, which culminated in his convocation of an extraordinary clerical assembly in 1682. This body promulgated the famous four Gallican articles, taught in France until the Revolution and invoked in most eighteenth-century quarrels over papal jurisdiction throughout Catholic Europe. They affirmed the supremacy of the secular power, the limitation of papal authority by the customs and privileges of the French church, and the ultimate superiority of a general council of the church over the pope. Papal power remained a serious flaw in state control over the church—one of which monarchs grew increasingly conscious. In the century after 1682 the pope found his power slowly whittled away. Concordats were renegotiated with Sardinia (1741), Naples (1741), and Spain (1737 and 1753), with the effect of diminishing yet further the already limited patronage the pope exercised. From 1758 to 1777 Portugal, under the ministry of Pombal, ostentatiously ignored the papacy's existence. Perhaps the most serious blow of all was the expulsion of the Jesuits, those papal shock troops, from Portugal (1759), France (1764), Spain (1766), Naples and Parma (1767). The way monarchs combined together to force the pope to dissolve the order completely in 1773 seemed the final humiliation. Yet by 1789 Habsburg princes had subjected the Holy See to further indignities. Joseph II dissolved monasteries, redrew ecclesiastical boundaries, imposed clerical oaths to the state, introduced religious toleration, and permitted anti-clerical pamphleteering, all without any reference to the pope. An unprecedented visit by Pius VI in 1782 to Vienna failed to dissuade the emperor from his violently erastian policies. Meanwhile in Tuscany Joseph's brother Leopold renounced papal jurisdiction and taxation, while a third brother, as archbishop-elector of Cologne, joined other German arch-bishops in issuing the so-called 'Punctuation of Ems' (1786) which denounced most forms of papal authority over bishops. In 1789 the papacy was at bay, apparently on the verge of collapse. Nobody could foresee the dramatic revival in its fortunes which the next two decades were to bring.

Religious Disputes: Orthodox Europe

In 1660 the established churches, having in general defeated their rivals, were none the less still menaced by internal schism. Nowhere was this problem more acute than in Russia, whose whole history in this period may be written in terms of the impact of rival foreign influences upon native conservatism. Mid-century wars with Poland brought contact with the anoma-lous Uniate church, Orthodox in practices but acknowledging papal authority, and inspired a horror of unpatriotic compromise. Russians believed that since the Great Schism and then the fall of Constantinople, only one true and independent centre of Christianity remained—Moscow, the 'third Rome'. The practices of Russian Orthodoxy were sacrosanct in their purity.

As the seventeenth century progressed, however, foreign comparisons convinced some clergy that purity was what the Russian church lacked. The priesthood was as ignorant as the laity, with little understanding of its own rites. The rites themselves, diverging in certain particulars from those of the Greek Orthodox church, seemed also to require reform. With the elevation of Nikon to the patriarchate in 1653 the reformers triumphed. Within months of his accession, Nikon had introduced a new psalter and a new missal, in which changes were prescribed to bring Russian practices more into line with Greek Orthodoxy. These changes seem trivial enough—making the sign of the cross with three fingers rather than two, altering the number of prostrations and cries of alleluia at various points in the service, and so on. But to many they were a betrayal of the true church. In subsequent years Nikon proceeded to rewrite much doctrinal literature and to replace objects of veneration such as icons. To effect these reforms he worked through councils attended by Greek prelates, a final insult. Nor did the decline of Nikon's position after 1658 and his eventual fall in 1667 affect official policy. His own abrasive style may have aggravated opposition, but his reforms were those of a party, not of a single man, and they had the complete support of the state in the person of Tsar Alexei.

Nikon's reforms provoked a schism. Under the leadership of certain forceful individuals such as the Archpriest Avvakum and institutions such as the Solovetsky island monastery in the White Sea, opponents of the reform coalesced under the name of Old Believers. Nikon's reforms were introduced at a time of particular religious and visionary fervour in Moscow, a receptive atmosphere for the apocalyptic predictions of his opponents. A visitation of plague in 1654 was seen as a judgement of God. The reforms were portrayed as the work of Antichrist, and since the number of the Beast was 666, his reign could be expected to begin in 1666. The government scorned such expectations. Avvakum was exiled and then imprisoned, and a determined drive began to extirpate all opposition with the excommunication of Old Believers by the same council that deposed Nikon. So religious dissent became equated with political dissent, Old Belief in its turn becoming a rallying cause for a wide range of discontents. It took ten years and a full-scale siege to subdue the Solovetsky monastery in 1676. Violent persecutions in Moscow in the early 1670s failed to stamp out Old Belief there, as its re-emergence during the succession crisis of 1682 shows. But it was at its strongest in areas remote from central authority, or in frontier regions, where isolated yet elusive recalcitrant priests found it easy to evangelize—areas colonized by Old Believers fleeing from persecution. When pursuit of them led inevitably to an extension of governmental authority, revolts often ensued. More spectacularly still, other groups went out to meet Apocalypse half way by burning themselves to death. As many as 20,000 may have perished in this way in the 1670s and 1680s.

Tsar Alexei died in 1676, but the persecution did not end. Avvakum was burned at the stake in the early 1680s. In 1682 a disputed succession offered Old Belief the hope of better times, its adherents among the Moscow garrison contributing to the success of the winning side. But the demands of Old Believer leaders for the complete abandonment of thirty-five years of increasing secular control were so arrogantly put that the new regime was alienated and persecution redoubled: heresy and schism became capital crimes. Old Believer communities withdrew into even greater isolation in the silent northern forests, and in their turn divided into sub-sects. Some believed, as priests consecrated before the reforms died off, that subsequent consecrations by established bishops were irredeemably tainted, and therefore that they must do without priests. This meant doing without marriage too. Others accepted apostate clergy. But 'priestly' and 'priestless' alike were united in hostility to a government of Antichrist and many refused to pray for the tsar. Peter I (for once) abandoned violence, but not unnaturally he still regarded Old Believers as disruptives, subjecting them to double taxation and to fines. He also authorized a missionary effort to reconvert them, but with little success. In 1718 there were estimated to be more than 200,000 Old Believers in the towns of the diocese of Novgorod alone, and in Russia as a whole perhaps 20 per cent of the population rejected the established church. Most were ordinary peasants or Cossacks, but some, debarred by their nonconformity from the public duties which Peter imposed on the whole population, prospered as merchants—like Huguenots, Jews, or English non-conformists further west.

Slowly, after several predicted dates had passed uneventfully by, the Old Believers ceased to expect the Apocalypse, and mass suicides by fire died away. The accession of Peter III in 1762 marked the beginning of a new era of toleration. Double taxation and other penalties remained for the moment, but Peter and his successor Catherine recognized the benefits the state could reap from the economic vigour of Old Believers. In 1771 a group of them were even allowed officially to establish themselves in Moscow. In 1784 the pejorative term 'schismatic', along with many disabilities including the double tax, was abandoned. The involvement of the more turbulent Old Believers of the Cossack lower Volga in Pugachev's rebellion provoked no change in this general policy, which brought the rewards Catherine expected. Old Believers were among the most prominent capitalists behind Russian industrial expansion in the early nineteenth century.

Religious Disputes: Protestant Europe
No part of western Europe saw a schism as spectacular as that in Russia, but splits did occur in Protestant areas. Catholics too were often bitterly divided, but never to the point of schism.

England in 1660 was a byword for religious upheaval. The Anglican church had been overthrown in 1645, but the confusion thus engendered had spawned a whole host of minor extremist sects, and it was partly to combat such dangerous confusion that a Presbyterian parliament was willing to restore

Charles II. Charles returned promising toleration, but, believing with his grandfather that 'no bishop' equalled 'no king', he restored the Anglican establishment. Negotiations with the Presbyterians about 'comprehension' or re-amalgamation into one church failed: the restored bishops were not really interested, nor were the landowners represented in parliament, in whose eyes religious radicalism led to other sorts. By 1662 Anglicanism had been totally restored, its organization, doctrines and practices largely unchanged. Those who could not conform were ejected—1,909 clerics and academics in all, or about one-fifth of the clergy. They and their congregations were excluded from all public offices and even forbidden to worship together. Yet they resisted James II's attempts to win their support and after his fall there were further attempts to achieve comprehension with the established church. These too failed, and the Toleration Act of 1689 officially recognized the separate existence of the dissenters by granting them freedom of worship. 1689 also brought another schism, when between 300 and 400 Anglican clergy believing in Divine Right refused to swear allegiance to the new regime. These non-jurors lingered on in separation until the late eighteenth century, but, unlike the Old Believers, they attracted little lay following.

The dissenters were different. A concerned laity was essential for sects which chose their own ministers. In the early eighteenth century they numbered in all perhaps 300,000, divided between the three main sects of Presbyterians, Congregationalists, and Baptists and minor groups such as the Quakers. These numbers declined as the century progressed, yet their importance if anything increased, owing largely to their continued exclusion from all posts of public responsibility and power. Exclusion from public life made them champions of private enterprise and new ideas. They dominated the mercantile community of many ports. They pioneered the teaching of more practical and technical subjects in their academies. Prosperity brought property and respectability; gradually Anglican fears subsided. From 1727 the government allowed dissenters to take municipal office on a year-to-year basis. Parliament however, remained closed to them, and from the 1760s they provided a driving force behind the movement for reform of representation and the franchise. Ironically, this renewed their reputation for political disruption, and may even have postponed the willingness of the Anglican squires to grant them full civil equality. At any rate they did not achieve it until 1828.

Two issues divided dissenters from Anglicans. In church government, dissenters rejected bishops; although they differed among themselves as to where authority should lie instead. In doctrine, most dissenters were Calvinists, believing that God predestines men to be saved or damned and that they are powerless to change their fate. Anglicans, by contrast, were Arminians, believing that Christ died for all men, that none is predestined to salvation or damnation, but that salvation is open to all those who sincerely aspire to it. Arminianism was a broadminded doctrine, emphasizing spiritual endeavour rather than doctrinal purity. Profoundly Protestant in that it took the Bible alone as the source of all authority, it nevertheless recognized ambiguities and inconsistencies and discouraged dogmatizing on such an uncertain basis. 'I have ever thought', wrote Bishop Burnet, a leading spokesman for Anglican Arminianism, 'that the true interest of the Christian religion was best consulted, when nice disputing about mysteries was laid aside and forgotten'.[12] Such views were congenial to state churches, where opinions permitted by the government counted for more than those deemed righteous by the godly. They were also compatible with religious toleration, for Arminians believed that a certain latitude was permissible to fallible humans sincerely seeking the truth. By the 1690s they had come to be known as latitudinarians; their leaders were among the most prominent bishops. The flexible, pragmatical common sense of latitudinarianism shone out. Yet it had its dangers. To minimize differences promoted a complacent acceptance of things as they were. Problems did not go away for being ignored, and there was a limit to how far latitude could go before becoming meaningless. By 1717 Bishop Hoadly of Bangor could suggest without any sense of incongruity, that there was no scriptural basis for an organized church at all, that the church was nothing more than the whole body of sincere believers. And ever since the Restoration, some Cambridge divines had been treating the Trinity with scepticism, affirming that Christ, as the son of God, could neither be divine himself nor the same person as His Father in any way. Between the 1690s and the 1720s learned Anglican circles were rocked by controversy on this question, but the debate was even more important to the Presbyterians, who in 1719 divided into opposed Trinitarian and Unitarian camps. Beginning as a dissident minority, the Unitarians appealed more readily to the rational and deistic temper of the times, and by the end of the century were more numerous than their parent body.

The Trinitarian controversy made many Anglicans draw back from the bland complacencies of the extreme latitudinarians. The 1690s witnessed the birth of new evangelizing fervour which resulted in the founding of various missionary societies for propagating the Gospel. But it took John Wesley to give Arminianism a new force and direction when he began to evangelize on his return from America in 1738. Wesley believed firmly in the virtues of individual effort and the availability of salvation to all. He taught that the Bible was the only source of spiritual authority and he preached submission to the established church. But he was firm on the Trinity: if Christ was not God, how could He have taken away men's sins by sacrificing Himself? Indeed this was the centre of Wesley's message, that Christ will take away the sins of any man who sincerely seeks His help. And those who had been saved in this way knew in their hearts—unlike true Calvinists—that this was so. Emotional certainty, scornful of reason, was the new element in Methodism; and it was this, not any doctrinal unorthodoxy, that the Anglican hierarchy suspected. Nothing could have been further from Wesley's mind than secession from the established church, even though by 1750 the Methodists had their own national organization. It was the intransigence of the

---

[12] G. Burnet, *The History of My Own Times* (1823 edn.), vi. 114.

Anglican hierarchy that promoted the eventual schism in 1784. Wesley, finding the bishops unwilling to ordain priests in the United States and to purge the Prayer Book of its political content, began to ordain his own preachers. He also produced a new book of *Sunday Service*. In 1773 many clergy had petitioned parliament for prayer-book reform, with no success, and had relapsed into silence. The Methodists preferred nonconformity. By Wesley's death in 1791 they numbered 72,000 in England and 64,000 overseas, more numerous already than any other dissenter sect, and rapidly to outnumber them all together.

So England remained the home of religious schism and controversy. The other major Protestant movement of the period, German Pietism, represented an attitude to religion rather than a sect, but it probably affected more people than any other comparable development. Its roots were similar to those of Methodism in that it sprang from the inevitable spiritual inadequacies of state churches forbidden to be too controversial. The Lutheran churches of north Germany veiled their subserviency after 1648 by a retreat into arid theological disputation, but they failed to catch the imagination of the laity. In his *Pia Desideria or True Evangelical Church* of 1675 Philip Jakob Spener called for a sustained attempt to touch the hearts of the faithful. Like any Arminian, Spener held that spiritual devotion was more important than doctrinal orthodoxy. But inspiration was required: Spener advocated a new style of preaching, vigorous efforts to evangelize and propagate knowledge of the Bible, and the organization of conventicles in which the faithful might encourage each other's devotions. Above all he emphasized practical Christianity—sober habits and good works. Even more than by his books, Spener was influential through his preaching. When in 1691 he became court preacher in Berlin, the success of Pietism (initially like so many proud names a term of abuse) was assured. As early as 1679 he had done much to promote poor relief in Frankfurt. Now he and his disciples helped to launch similar reforms in Brandenburg. In 1694 the elector allowed them to found a Pietist university at Halle, where clergy of an appropriately evangelical stamp might be trained. Halle rapidly became more than just a university. Under the inspiration of Pietism's great organizer Francke, schools and a model orphanage were founded. Halle became a centre for the printing of Bibles and devotional literature, as well as the headquarters for the first overseas missions that Lutheranism had ever promoted. Most Prussian officials in the eighteenth century were educated in this atmosphere at Halle, alongside many from other German principalities. Here they imbibed and in their turn fostered the values of Pietism—sobriety, diligence, practicality, benevolence, an indifference to dogmatic disputes, and a propensity for toleration. Arguably these aspects of the movement were even more influential in German life than the 3,000,000 Bibles distributed before 1800 by the Canstein Bible Institute.

Scorn for dogmatic differences did not necessarily remove Pietism from controversy. Orthodox Lutheran theologians distrusted the latitude of Spener's views, and in 1695 the university of Wittenburg, that Holy Office of

Lutheranism, accused him of 263 doctrinal errors. Spener refused to be drawn into debate, but attacks continued. As time went by even the Pietists themselves began to persecute error: in 1723 the mathematician and philosopher Wolff was expelled from his Halle chair on account of the breadth of his views, only to be restored by Frederick II on his accession in 1740. But both the strength and weakness of Pietism was that it had no strong-willed, long-lived Wesley to unify and hold it together. This meant that it had few orthodoxies to violate and little authority to punish such violations. What was heresy in Halle passed unnoticed in Tübingen, the academic centre of south-German Pietism. On the other hand there was nothing to restrict the growth of such luxuriant strains as Zinzendorf's Moravianism, a religion of the heart pressed to extremes. Pietists, not to mention more orthodox Lutherans, viewed the enthusiastic excesses of the Moravians with disquiet; yet there was no authority to expel them and they never expressed any desire to separate themselves from the Lutheran confession.

The appeal of Pietism or Methodism was personal, yet the development of both was essentially conditioned by politics. Wesley's political views and the dilemma posed by American independence were basic determinants of Methodism's character. Much of Pietism's initial growth depended on the favour of Frederick of Brandenburg. The same applied in the case of most religious divisions. All English Whigs were not dissenters but most dissenters were Whigs, for they were the party of toleration. The strength of Latitudinarianism sprang from the appointment by the Whigs of so many of its leaders to bishoprics; the bitterness of the controversies it aroused reflected the fact that most of their subordinate clergy were Jacobites or Tories. Similarly, in the United Provinces before the 1690s the Arminians were, in the words of an English observer 'rather. . .a party in the State, than a sect in the Church', supporting the authority of the estates-general and its diffused local constituencies; as opposed to the Calvinists, looking for support and protection to the Stadtholder, and 'passionate friends to the house of Orange'.[13] The spread of toleration did not necessarily do anything to weaken the link between religion and politics. Toleration itself was often a more explosive issue than sectarian dissensions had been. Nor was the political problem unique to the erastian churches of Protestant Europe. The Orthodox schism was about much more than liturgical innovation, while in Catholic Europe there was the added complication of papal authority.

Religious Disputes: Catholic Europe

The Catholic Church of 1660 had been largely fashioned by the Counter-Reformation launched at the Council of Trent a century before. The purpose at Trent had been to meet the challenge of Protestantism by redefining or reasserting the fundamental character of the one true church, with the result that certain tendencies and traditions triumphed at the expense of others. Yet many of the discredited ideas and practices continued to thrive in the

[13] Sir William Temple, 'Observations upon the United Provinces of the Netherlands' in *Works* (1751), iv. 179–80.

teeth of authority. Some were easily stigmatized as heresy, such as the 'Quietism' preached in influential circles in the 1670s and 1680s, a mystical doctrine of complete contemplative passivity and submission to God's will, denying the value of all human effort. Not surprisingly its proponents were condemned as heretics. No church dedicated to the reconquest of lost souls could tolerate doctrines of indifference to the temporal world. But other traditions, judged heterodox since Trent, were less easy to pin down. Authority tended to lump them together under the general name of Jansenism.

Jansenism was created by the Jesuits, in the sense that they used Jansen's name to stigmatize those who opposed them. A Jansenist, observed the Cistercian Cardinal Bona, was little more than a Catholic who disliked the Jesuits. But to oppose the Society of Jesus was to oppose the most characteristic product of the counter-Reformation. The Jesuits who existed to win back souls to the church—an end which justified a certain flexibility of means—preached latitude in liturgical practices and observances. So flexible were they in their eagerness to convert the pagan Chinese, that they stretched Catholic liturgical practice almost out of recognition to accommodate local customs. Their European enemies seized on this news when it penetrated back, and between 1693 and 1704 the 'Chinese Rites' controversy shook the Church. Their eventual condemnation by the pope was the Jesuits' first major defeat. Even so, they remained formidable, both intellectually and politically; they had evolved casuistry, a whole science of moral alternatives derived from the ambiguities of the Bible, the fathers, and later authorities; and had won the support of secular authorities. Educators of the élite of Catholic Europe, they confessed kings and evangelized on the farthest frontiers of overseas empires. They had also gained the tacit support of ecclesiastical authority for their theology of free will. Men were free to accept or reject God's saving Grace.

Jansenism originated as a protest against this position. But quite apart from the suspicious similarity of certain doctrines in Jansen's book *Augustinus* (1640) to Calvinism, any doctrine that men were for ever predestined to salvation or damnation was totally subversive of all that the Jesuits stood for. There was little point in attempting to convert those whose fate was already decreed. Inevitably they attacked the *Augustinus*. The book, however, found defenders in France among the disciples of Saint-Cyran, a fashionable rigorist confessor and friend of Jansen. Saint-Cyran's influence was not wide, but it touched important people, and he spent four of the five years before his death in 1643 in prison as a subversive. To his followers, concentrated around the lawyer family of the Arnaulds, defence of Jansen was a duty. In a series of brilliant vernacular polemics Antoine Arnauld defended the reputation of both Saint-Cyran and Jansen throughout the 1640s and 1650s. His major point about the *Augustinus* was that five predestinarian propositions on Grace singled out by its enemies as heretical were indeed so, but that they were not in the book.

What made the controversy so dangerous was that it also involved the very principle of papal authority. Enemies of Jansenism naturally looked to Rome to condemn it. Jansen's defenders did not presume to question the pope's right to define heresy, but they did dispute any pretension to infallibility on matters of fact—whether the five propositions were in the book or not. Moreover once the pope intervened (as he did in three bulls between 1642 and 1657) the traditional enemies of papal jurisdiction in France—the law-courts, the Sorbonne, and some secular clergy—were quick to allege infringement of the traditional liberties of the Gallican church and the prerogatives of the French king. That the government, suspicious of all dissidents, was willing to support the pope's condemnations only increased the anxiety of these bodies. They in their turn became identified with those they defended. Jansenism thus came to mean not only moral rigorism, predestinarian theology, and hostility to the Jesuits, but also opposition to papal pretensions and to regimes that upheld them.

In the 1660s it seemed possible that a confrontation might be avoided. Louis XIV succeeded in making all clerics subscribe to a formulary resolving the dispute over the five propositions by obfuscating the issues. Under the Peace of the Church (1668) even the fastidious nuns of Port Royal, a convent dominated by the Arnaulds and the spiritual headquarters of Jansenism, came to terms. A decade of peace followed and Jansenist writers stressed their orthodoxy by launching polemics against Calvinism. They even defended papal rights. Unfortunately the issue they chose was Louis XIV's annexation of the revenues of vacant sees. The king's hostility was rekindled and persecution resumed. In 1679 Arnauld fled to the Spanish Netherlands, never to return. Port Royal was forbidden to take new novices and eventually, in 1709, destroyed. It was not so easy, however, to destroy the issues that Jansenism brought into focus, and the persecution inaugurated a new and more disruptive phase.

In 1684 Arnauld was joined in exile by Quesnel, the Oratorian author of a *New Testament in French, with Moral Reflexions*. A popular work of piety, it contained not only a watered-down predestinarianism, but also subversive ideas about the position of bishops. Quesnel suggested that priesthood was more important than rank, and that authority should lie not so much in the hierarchy as in the whole body of clergy, who would elect their bishops. These ideas were derived from Edmond Richer, an early seventeenth-century Sorbonne theologian prominent in his day but neglected until Quesnel, coupling his views with so many others officially suspect, gave them new relevance. If the state persecuted Jansenism through the bishops, then Jansenists became equivocal about bishops. Parish clergy everywhere who felt any grievance against the hierarchy became sympathizers. The logic of this 'Richerist' strain was that the church should be governed at all levels by councils rather than by individuals—almost the presbyterianism the doctors of Trent had striven so hard to avoid.

All these trends coalesced in the controversy over the bull *Unigenitus* of 1713, which condemned 101 of Quesnel's propositions. Noailles, archbishop of Paris, had once recommended the *Moral Reflexions* to his clergy, yet he subsequently condemned other works which, some asserted, propounded the same opinions. Jesuit enemies of Noailles saw the chance to embarrass him, and between 1695 and 1711 controversy raged over Quesnel's position on the long-dormant question of Grace. In 1703 moreover, the Bourbon authorities of Spain seized his papers in Brussels, discovering evidence of a Europe-wide correspondence with sympathizers which horrified Louis XIV. He determined to eliminate what looked like an international conspiracy once and for all. At his request the pope issued *Unigenitus*. Yet the bull intensified rather than eliminated controversy, for it revived the issue of the pope's jurisdiction within France, so recently challenged by Louis himself in the four Gallican articles of 1682. The *parlement* of Paris registered the bull only as a law of the state subject to safeguards for the 'liberties of the Gallican Church', and Louis XIV died before he could override this setback. The Regency government wavered, but in 1717 four bishops irreconcilably opposed to the bull forced the issue by appealing against it to a future council of the church. They were joined by about 3,000 parish clergy and hundreds of doctors from various theological faculties. The government attempted to impose silence, but with such numbers now involved controversy continued unabated throughout the 1720s. 'Only bishops and courtier priests seeking preferment', wrote one observer in 1727, 'have joined the Jesuit party; all the ecclesiastical second order, most of the Paris middle class, the law, the third estate, and even. . .women and the populace, all are aroused against the Jesuits and oppose what is happening'.[14] Most of Paris was Jansenist, he noted, and in 1728 a clandestine news sheet, the *Ecclesiastical News*, began weekly publication to gratify the public appetite for information. The culmination of Jansenism as a mass movement came at the Saint-Médard cemetery between 1730 and 1732, when reverent thousands watched the spectacle of God manifesting His favour to the opponents of *Unigenitus* through miracles and convulsionary hysteria.

Cardinal Fleury, first minister and a prince of the church, was determined to stamp out Jansenism. Having bluntly declared in 1730 that *Unigenitus* was a law of the state, he closed the Saint-Médard cemetery; and by a careful policy of appointing only the most orthodox bishops, purging the Sorbonne of recalcitrant doctors, and evoking contentious cases of ecclesiastical law to the royal council, he slowly smothered controversy. Matters remained quiet until 1749, when certain Parisian priests acting on their archbishop's orders began to refuse the last rites to those who could not produce a note from their confessor to say they accepted *Unigenitus*. The object was to unmask Jansenist confessors, but the effect was to allow people to die without the sacraments. Controversy exploded when one victim of this policy recovered and complained to the *parlement*. Four years of acute crisis followed and in 1753 the *parlement* launched a massive remonstrance against clerical power in the secular state. As a result it spent sixteen months in exile. It returned under a law of silence, but when in 1756 the government asked the pope to discourage refusal of sacraments by encyclical there was further

---

[14]   E. J. F. Barbier, *Journal historique et anecdotique du règne de Louis XV* (1847–56), i. 264.

trouble at this recourse once more to the very outside authority that was at issue in *Unigenitus*.

By 1760 Jansenism had acquired an astonishing variety of meanings. The original issue of Grace was largely forgotten, but the term was still used to describe many types of moral asceticism. Quesnel's *New Testament* had been in the vernacular, and Bible reading by the laity also seemed suspect. Few members of the *parlements* took much interest in theological questions, and many of those who did were Jesuit educated; nevertheless their obdurate Gallicanism in the face of *Unigenitus* earned them the name of Jansenists. Parish clergy critical of their bishops and of inequitable diocesan administration; secular clergy hostile to regulars; these too were included. Until the 1770s French politics polarized under religious labels, with Jansenism a general term of condemnation applied by those in power to those who disagreed with them, 'the antithesis', as one despairing historian put it, 'of anti-Jansenism'.[15] Yet all these diverse strains united in their opposition to papal pretensions; an attitude pushed to such extremes that some Anglicans even entertained serious hopes that one day the churches of England and France might form an episcopalian, but popeless, union. Finally there was the most constant factor in Jansenism—hostility to the Jesuits. There were Jansenists in this sense throughout Catholic Christendom.

Jansenism had begun in the Netherlands, and only there did it retain anything of its early purity of meaning. When the church of Utrecht, a Catholic enclave in an officially Protestant country, refused to accept the condemnation of Jansen contained in *Unigenitus*, the pope accordingly refused to invest its bishops and proclaimed it schismatical. The republic of Venice and the kingdom of Sardinia remained true to well-entrenched anti-papal traditions in refusing to accept the bull; while in the Austrian Netherlands it took a law of silence, a purge of the Louvain theological faculty, and the exile of the erastian canon jurist Van Espen, to impose it in 1730. In Spain neither the original controversies nor that over *Unigenitus* made much impact, but when the Jesuits and the Inquisition combined in 1747 to place various works emanating from the Augustinian order on the Spanish *Index* as Jansenistic, there was an outcry not only from the affronted order but also from the growing body of lay opinion hostile to the powers of Inquisition, Jesuits, and pope alike. So Spanish Jansenism was born, and it was much encouraged in 1759 by the accession of Charles III, who in his twenty-five years as king of Naples had completely renegotiated the kingdom's relations with the pope. In Germany, later Jansenism took the name of Febronianism, after Febronius, who had studied under Van Espen. In his *Of the Present State of the Church and the legitimate power of the Roman Pontiff* (1763) Febronius sought to eliminate doctrinal differences between Catholic and Protestant mainly at the expense of papal authority. Against it he exalted the rights of secular princes. Neither prompt inclusion on the *Index* (1764) nor subsequent recantations by the author prevented enormous sales of this book and

---

[15] L. Ceyssens, cited in *English Historical Review* (1956), 159.

translation into most of the languages of Catholic Europe. It had particular success in Austria, where a small group of influential Jansenists had already succeeded in prising the Jesuits out of such powerful bodies as the imperial censorship commission. They now looked forward to the eventual succession to sole power of the Emperor Joseph to push anti-papal policies much further. Febronius provided convenient justification for many of their beliefs.

The way forward had already been demonstrated in 1759, when the expulsion of the Jesuits from Portugal changed the whole outlook of Jansenists. From patient sniping at the enemy they moved to all-out attack, for Pombal had demonstrated what could be achieved by a determined government. Friends to Jansenism in the French *parlements* seized the opportunity of a Jesuit lawsuit to drive them out of France, and by 1767 they had been banished from Spain and the Bourbon states of Italy. By 1769 Austria was the only major state left harbouring them, but when his mother died Joseph seemed certain to follow his fellow monarchs' example. In these unpromising circumstances Clement XIV had little alternative but to dissolve the Society of Jesus completely (1773).

This, the most important event in eighteenth-century Catholic history, was a major turning-point for Jansenism. The accusation largely disappeared with the accusers, and after 1773 its decline was rapid. The anti-papal policies of governments in Austria, Spain, and Naples largely took over the Jansenists' programme and only in two states did distinctive strains survive. One was Tuscany, where the Grand Duke Leopold authorized Ricci, bishop of Pistoia and Prato, to implement widespread reforms in his diocese. These included promotion of vernacular Bible reading, printing new editions of Quesnel and other Jansenist tracts, and hostility to regular orders. In 1786 a diocesan synod approved a new scheme of administration based upon an elected synod of clergy. It also adopted the four Gallican articles of 1682 in overt hostility to the pope. But there was popular opposition to Ricci's attempts to purify liturgical practice, not to mention strong disapproval of his organizational proposals from most of his fellow bishops and the pope. A council of Tuscan bishops in 1787 proved lukewarm in its support, and in 1791, after Leopold's departure for Austria, Ricci resigned. His reforms were abandoned and in 1794 most of the work of the Pistoia synod was condemned by a papal bull.

In France, however, Jansenism enjoyed some late triumphs. The *Ecclesiastical News* continued its clandestine publication, only finally disappearing in the 1790s. Jansenist rhetoric also deeply influenced the language and categories of political debate of the pre-revolutionary years. Above all, Richerism flourished, and Richer's works, republished in the 1750s, stimulated a series of new works exalting the rights of parish clergy. They proved an inspiration to those agitating for revision of the parish priests' *portion congrue* in the 1760s and again in the 1780s. Around 1780 itself there was a minor revolt of parish priests against 'episcopal despotism' and the monopolization of administrative offices in the church by bishops' well-connected nominees. This outburst was rapidly quelled with promises, soon abandoned. But the priests had their revenge in the elections to the clerical estate in 1789, which unlike those for the assemblies of the clergy, the bishops were unable to rig. Only forty-seven bishops out of 135 secured election, and the clerical delegates arrived in Versailles determined on radical church reform. The Civil Constitution of the Clergy of 1790, with its elective bishops and in-difference to the pope, was profoundly influenced by Jansenist ideas evolved over the previous century, and when the 'constitutional' church it set up shrivelled in the anti-clerical atmosphere of the Terror, it was former Jansenists who did most to keep it alive. But the Revolution gave the Church of Rome more important enemies than those within its own bosom, and by the time the Jesuits were recreated to fight these new battles (1814), the opponents who had brought them down were largely dead and forgotten.

8. The Progress of Doubt

This was the age of Enlightenment; and Enlightenment meant an attack on the church. Of course, anti-clericalism in Europe was almost as old and deep-rooted as Christianity itself. Medieval monarchs had exploited it to promote their own secular authority; the Protestant reformers proclaimed the priesthood of all believers in conscious rejection of clerical pretensions; the Counter-Reformation's reaffirmation of the church's priestly character provoked new friction with the laity.

But none of this hostility went beyond certain clear bounds. Kings wished to extend their control over the church rather than to diminish its influence. Protestant reformers wished to purify the church rather than to undermine it. Nobody questioned that there should be a church, that it should play a major part in the functioning of society, or that the core of ideas which lay at the centre of all the various Christian creeds represented at least some aspect of eternal truth. Nor did most men challenge these assumptions between 1660 and 1800. But a growing minority did, and their views circulated widely.

This was a novel situation. By 1800 hardly any aspect of the church, religion, or the values they upheld remained unchallenged. And since the church took a standpoint on practically every aspect of human existence, the challenge was comprehensive. The lengths to which it would be carried could hardly be foreseen in 1660. Yet its basis had already been firmly laid in the intellectual upheavals of the preceding decades. The scientists and mathematicians of the early seventeenth century had already confirmed the doubts expressed by sceptics in the late sixteenth century. The structure of knowledge long maintained by ecclesiastical authority was already in ruins. The problem now was how to replace the fallen edifice. Beyond that loomed another problem—whether it could be replaced so long as the church retained any authority at all.

Rationalism Rampant

To some it seemed that Cartesianism had brought an end to half a century's intellectual uncertainty. Descartes, in his *Discourse on Method* (1652), had provided a sure key to knowledge after pushing doubt itself to extremes. By 1660 Cartesianism had already captured the minds of most of Europe's advanced thinkers. By 1700 it had become general orthodoxy. Half a century later it was penetrating those last bastions of Aristotelianism, the universities, although by then advanced thinkers had moved far beyond it.

Cartesianism in the late seventeenth century comprised a method of reasoning from self-evident propositions on principles analogous to those of a geometrical proof. It was also a philosophy which accepted the existence of God as the ordainer of a mechanistic, ordered universe; and defined man as a blend of mechanical body and immortal soul, implanted at birth with certain basic notions. Finally, it was a system of physics based upon matter's primary qualities of motion, weight, and extension, accepting Copernican cosmology, but explaining celestial mechanics in terms of a complex series of vortices in the fabric of matter. Since none of these aspects lent support to traditional Christian dogmas, Descartes was on the *Index*. Provincial theologians continued to anathematize his name for decades. But more subtle minds saw that a system of ideas with which God could in some way be reconciled was better than complete scepticism.

By 1670 this point had been well observed and the ensuing decades saw important attempts to blend Cartesianism with more traditional orthodoxies. In *Of the Search for Truth* (1674) Malebranche, a French priest of the Oratory, began a long lifetime of tireless dedication to this cause. 'Monsieur Descartes', he believed, 'discovered in thirty years more truths than all other philosophers.'[1] He had enabled men to consign Aristotle and the scholastics to the rubbish heap and opened the way to a simple, clear, and immediate perception of divine truth. Malebranche's synthesis was however neither simple nor clear. Accepting Descartes's method and physics, he attempted to resolve the problem of the dualism of mind and matter on Christian principles. The doctrine he adopted was occasionalism. Apparent causes of physical events, he argued, were merely the *occasions* of God's causal activity; for God's will is the only true cause of everything. How the mind caused the body to move no longer required explanation; the dualism of the two entities was an illusion.

But many remained unimpressed, dismissing Malebranche's system as a mere play on words. More orthodox Christians found his occasionalism, with its implication of God in everything, too redolent of pagan pantheism. This danger seemed particularly acute in the 1670s, when the system of the Dutch Jewish philosopher Spinoza first attracted notice, for it was even more overtly pantheistic. Spinoza's faith in God and His existence was every bit as profound as that of Descartes or Malebranche. So was his belief in a rigorous, mathematical reason. But like Malebranche he felt impelled to resolve the problem of dualism, which he did by postulating an infinite God, the only true substance, of whom all finite phenomena—mind, matter, everything—are merely partial attributes. 'God is one, that is. . .only one substance can be granted in the universe, and that substance is absolutely infinite. . .Whatsoever is, is in God, and without God nothing can be, or be conceived.'[2] This was pantheism indeed. It was also cosmic determinism. God, Spinoza believed, created everything to fulfil a function, and by its very nature it could only fulfil that function in the preordained way. So everything was preordained; and since God was good, everything worked in the long run for the best. The idea of evil therefore was merely the product of defective understanding. The true philosopher would stoically accept

[1] *De la recherche de la vérité* (1962 edn.), I. iii, §II, p. 18.
[2] *Ethics*, i, propositions XIV and XV.

misfortunes in the knowledge that, in the view of eternity, it was all part of a beneficent divine design.

None of this was remotely acceptable to Christians. Malebranche was indignant when critics compared him to Spinoza, but more orthodox thinkers were in no danger of running the risk. Even Augustinians, who could accept the determinism, could not stomach a system that excluded sin, while purist disciples of Descartes could not accept that mind and matter were not separate substances. So the *Ethics*, published in 1677 after Spinoza's death, was greeted with universal hostility. The furore was all the greater in that the author was known also to be responsible for the *Theologico-Political Treatise* of 1670, a work devoted mainly to destroying the credibility of the Old Testament. Prophecy and miracles were subjected to the rigorous test of reason and found to be the products of mere human superstition and credulity. 'Men think it pious to trust nothing to reason and their own judgment, and impious to doubt the faith of those who have transmitted to us the sacred books. Such conduct is not piety, but mere folly.'[3] The point of theology, politically justifiable in itself, was obedience rather than truth; and it should be accepted as such, for obedience was necessary to political tranquillity. This explosive work was translated into French in 1678, by which time others too were subjecting the sacred texts to minute and rational scrutiny. Most notable was the French Oratorian, Simon, who published his *Critical History of the Old Testament* in 1678. This work, renewing Spinoza's doubts, was on the *Index* within five years, and Simon, despite repeated professions of orthodoxy, expelled from the Oratory. Undaunted, he turned in subsequent decades to the New Testament, creating an equal sensation and handing much subversive ammunition to religious sceptics. Yet, like Malebranche, he always denied affinities with Spinoza, whose reduction of divine revelation to a mere historical phenomenon useful mainly as a political expedient placed him in the same category as Hobbes. Hobbes and Spinoza, the arch-blasphemers, embodied all the opinions that orthodox men of the late seventeenth century hated most. By 1680 they were both dead. Neither left a school of disciples, yet their uncompromising solutions to the central problems of philosophy and politics were a major stimulus to further discussion for decades.

Unlike Hobbes, however, at least Spinoza was no pessimist. This alone was enough to ensure that his views were considered for more than the purposes of refutation. Among those whose ideas owed most to Spinoza was the German Leibniz, who met him in 1676. Leibniz, like Descartes, was a mathematician, who disputed with Newton the honour of having invented the infinitesimal calculus. His logic, as subtle as that process, was applied to evolving a system which would reduce the baffling variety of things into one harmonious whole. A man of encyclopedic knowledge, Leibniz sought to reconcile extremes by blending their common factors, whether it was Protestants and Catholics, or Christians and Cartesians; but no single great work published in his lifetime[4] embodied the

---

[3] *Tractatus Theologico-Politicus*, ch. V, in *Works* (1917), i. 192.
[4] His *New Essays on the Human Understanding* were not published until 1765.

sum of his opinions, which were constantly evolving and which (an added complication) he often bowdlerized almost out of recognition in order to promote his own renown. Like all the great rationalists, Leibniz believed in God, and his work drew on all the classic 'proofs' of His existence. His God was not Spinoza's universal substance, bound by the necessity of His own nature; rather He was much more like the traditional creator, a free agent able to create several possible worlds. Being good, however, God naturally chose to create the best world possible. The existence of evil, the obvious objection to such an explanation, Leibniz explained as merely intended to demonstrate, through contrast, creation's predominant goodness. Thus in this best of all possible worlds, even evil promotes good. As to substance, divided by Descartes into God, mind, and matter, and totally fused by Spinoza into God, Leibniz held that in fact there were innumerable substances, all unique, and all containing within themselves the pattern of their own development. He called them *monads*. Physically independent of one another, if monads act together (as the working of the world proves they do) then it is because God has ordained for each one independently that they should. Thus, although his system marks a major advance in admitting the principle of development and evolution, Leibniz remains in his way as great a determinist as Spinoza.

Unlike Spinoza, Leibniz left a following. By the time he died in 1716, a number of German academics had found inspiration in his works, the greatest among whom was Christian Wolff, the leading German rationalist and determinist of the early eighteenth century. Leibniz's name had become widely known outside learned circles only in the last years of his life. Wolff, by schematizing a system from his scattered writings, brought real fame to his master, but left him with a reputation completely different from that of the rigorous, subtle, and in many ways highly advanced thinker for his time, which he now enjoys. Even in the work published while he lived, there were hints of these qualities. But Wolff expunged them, presenting the Germans with a Leibniz cold, dry, formal, rational, and schematic to a fault; an optimist whose bland confidence that all was for the best revolted men of the next generation. Yet before the 1750s, many had been content to share it, in England as well as Germany. Mandeville's *Fable of the Bees* claimed in 1705 that the sum of private vice was public virtue, while Pope declared two decades later, in famous lines, that:

> All nature is but Art, unknown to thee;
> All Chance, Direction, which thou canst not see:
> All Discord, Harmony not understood;
> All partial Evil, universal Good.[5]

It was comforting to those who were happy, if comfort they needed; it was solace to established powers and authorities, for it meant their position was divinely ordained: 'One truth is clear, Whatever is, is right,' Pope concluded. But it was ironic that Descartes's universal doubt, so alarming to his contemporaries, should ultimately flatter the complacency of their grandchildren.

---

[5] *Essay on Man* (1733).

Leibniz knew France, and many of his most illustrious French contemporaries, well. Yet his thought made little impression on the insular world of the French intellect, except to the extent that he disagreed with Descartes. French thought was dominated between 1660 and the 1720s by a quarrel between Ancients and Moderns. The terms derive from a literary controversy which reached its height in the 1680s and 1690s. Poets and epigrammatists exchanged polemics concerning the authority of ancient literary models and the superiority of modern writers to the ancients whose rules so many of them had adopted. But more was at stake than literary reputation. To be modern was to throw off authority, to proclaim with Descartes that no received knowledge was acceptable unless it conformed to reason. To be modern was to write in French, not Latin; to reason with Descartes, not Aristotle; to accept the cosmology of Copernicus, not Ptolemy. The danger was that modernity also involved rejection of traditional Christianity, although to a man the moderns disclaimed any such thought. Even those who admired Malebranche's audacity in attempting to construct an outright 'modern' theology remained sceptical of his success. Both sides simply attacked him, as they did Leibniz.

The most significant contributor to these controversies was the polished, though mediocre, Fontenelle, important as the first of that characteristic breed of the Enlightenment, the *philosophe*. 'A long dispute on philosophic matters', he once declared, 'can contain little philosophy.'[6] For a *philosophe* was essentially not an expert but a popularizer. Fontenelle established himself in this role following the success of his *Talks on the Plurality of Inhabited Worlds* in 1686. This work expounded, in a light, urbane form the main principles of Copernican cosmology and the Cartesian explanation of it. It marked the final triumph in France of Copernicanism, and was also an important step towards the victory of the Moderns. Fontenelle was a resolute, if discreet, Modern. All his life he remained a committed Cartesian. As perpetual secretary and historian of the Academy of Sciences he did much to propagate general awareness of scientific progress. His eulogies of great men when they died consolidated their importance. He lived until 1757, but his last major work (published when he was ninety-five), a defence of Cartesian vorticist physics, was largely ignored. By the middle of the eighteenth century Cartesianism had been eclipsed by a set of ideas less schematic, less pretentious in their claims, but certainly more congenial to the common sense of humanity.

Descartes Dethroned: Newton

Descartes had set out to restore certainty to a world deprived of it by the discoveries of the previous two generations. But hardly had his system begun to win acceptance when further advances undermined it too.

Throughout the whole field of what was known as 'natural philosophy' the middle decades of the seventeenth century saw a series of advances which

---

[6] *Eloge du P. Malebranche* in H. Poetz (ed.), *Pages choisies des grands écrivains: Fontenelle* (1909), 200.

confirmed the implications of previous work and filled in many unexplained gaps. The microscope (invented by Galileo around 1615) brought the most spectacular discoveries. With it the Italian Malpighi confirmed Harvey's earlier hypotheses on blood circulation by discovering the capillaries (1661); the Dutchman Swammerdam chronicled the reproduction of insects; and his compatriot Leeuwenhoek revealed human spermatozoa and a whole world of bacteria invisible to the naked eye. At the same time the experiments of the Englishman Boyle were demonstrating that neither Aristotle's earth, air, fire, and water, nor the sulphur, mercury, and salt of contemporary alchemists sufficiently explained the variety of chemical phenomena. Experiments by Torricelli and Pascal with barometers, and by Boyle with an air pump, were able for the first time to create and demonstrate vacuums. Aristotle had held that vacuums were impossible; Descartes agreed. Both held that the universe is filled with substance and that physics was explained by movements within it. The effect of the new developments was to complete for ever the ruin of Aristotle, but also to spread scepticism about Descartes.

Cartesians took comfort from the fact that no alternative to their explanation of the universe existed. And since theirs was logical and self-consistent, the experiments which yielded the disruptive new information must either be wrong or misunderstood. Certainly sceptics could provide no credible alternative; until the work of Isaac Newton.

> Nature, and Nature's Laws lay hid in Night.
> God said, *Let Newton be*!, and all was *Light.* [7]

Thus Pope summed up the eighteenth-century view of Newton's achievement, for in him all the diverse streams of activity which had made the scientific revolution flowed together. Like Galileo, Descartes, and Boyle he was a polymath—astronomer, physicist, and chemist all at once. Like all the great rationalist thinkers he was a mathematician of genius. But unlike them he was also a prolific and resourceful experimenter. Too often mathematicians had constructed supremely logical systems which were beautifully self-consistent but devoid of empirical basis—Descartes's *Principles of Philosophy*, expounding his physical system, was the outstanding example. Equally, however, much sevententh-century experiment had been random, slipshod, unsystematic, and designed to produce spectacular effects for the amusement of the fashionable rather than solid information. Newton combined careful, thoughtful, disciplined experiments with a formidable mathematical imagination and expertise, to produce a new synthesis which explained everything the Cartesian system comprehended, and much it did not.

Newton's major discovery was the principle of gravitation. Kepler had already demonstrated that the planetary orbits were not perfect circles, but ellipses, a piece of information so awkward that both Galileo and Descartes chose to ignore it. Newton's theory made sense of such discordant facts. He showed that it was a universal principle in nature that bodies tend to attract each other, and that this principle explained all aspects of their motion. In

---

[7] *Epitaph. Intended for Sir Isaac Newton, in Westminster Abbey* (1730).

his *Mathematical Principles of Natural Philosophy*, published in Latin in 1687 as the *Principia Mathematica*, he propounded a series of clear laws of motion according to which the gravitational principle invariably worked. Newton's universe was, like that of Descartes, simple, uniform, and law-abiding. It differed profoundly in that it could be mathematically described and was largely empty. Unable to dispute the mathematics, critics of Newton such as Leibniz and the other great scientific polymath of the age, Christian Huygens, concentrated on the emptiness. They found it hard to accept that bodies which had no physical contact with each other could nevertheless influence each other's movements. It was as though Newton was reintroducing some occult and mysterious force, redolent of Aristotle, into a universe reduced by Descartes to pure and obvious mechanics. It is true that Newton's mind was littered with hocus-pocus. He devoted many of his later years to squandering his mathematical talents on biblical chronology. He infuriated his critics by refusing always to say what gravity was. The fact remained that mathematically it worked, and explained more than any rival system. Inexorably this led, in the fifty years following the publication of the *Principia*, to its general acceptance as the true cosmology.

Newton also made fundamental discoveries in the study of light, which he separated into its primary colours by the use of a prism. He was able to calculate the maximum efficiency of refracting telescopes and to improve upon them by inventing an instrument which worked by reflection. He seemed to clarify and synthesize all that he touched. He became president of the Royal Society, Master of the Mint, and in 1705 was knighted. Such honours were a clear sign of the prestige his work had brought to science, and indeed to the reputation of England for natural philosophy.

Newton's system took longer to gain acceptance on the continent, where Cartesian orthodoxy was far more firmly entrenched than it ever had been in England. When, after his death in 1727, Fontenelle delivered a public eulogy of Newton in Paris, he carefully refrained from endorsing his system, much to the disgust of London society. Not until the 1730s was his triumph so secure among the learned that his system could penetrate to the public at large. Voltaire's *Philosophical Letters* of 1734 introduced him to French readers as the 'destroyer of the system of Descartes',[8] and by 1737 awareness of his work had become such an essential of polite knowledge that Algarotti's *Newtonianism for Ladies* and other such works of popularization became best-sellers. No learned society in the later eighteenth century was without its plaster bust of Newton; the *Encyclopedia* of Diderot declared the *Principia* an 'Immortal work, and one of the finest that the human mind has ever produced'.[9]

The lessons of Newtonianism were fundamental to eighteenth-century thought. Newton had shown that 'nature is exceedingly simple and conformable to herself.'[10] Nature worked by clear and inexorable rules. How the

---

[8] *Lettres philosophiques*, xiv, 'sur Descartes et Newton'.
[9] Art. *Newtonianisme*.
[10] Conclusion to the *Principia* : Quoted in M.B. Hall, *Nature and Nature's Laws* (1970), 324.

universe began Newton could not explain, without the postulate of God. He remained a fervent believer, even to the extent of suggesting that God occasionally interfered to adjust the celestial mechanism. Yet strictly speaking the logic of his own laws inferred that this was never necessary. The Newtonian universe, like the Cartesian, had no place for God except as the remotest of first causes. So although he destroyed the system of Descartes, Newton did nothing to give God a more active role in his own. His sallies into biblical scholarship convinced nobody, and his disciples, embarrassed, did their best to consign them to obscurity.

Even Descartes's method did not survive undamaged. The Cartesian universe had crumbled because it bore no relation to ascertained reality; at the first empirical test it collapsed. But Newtonianism was born of experiment; it was a true picture of reality. Thus eighteenth-century men came to mistrust logical 'systems'. The 'spirit of system' became a term of abuse, because it was felt that all systems distort reality. Doubt remained essential; reason remained essential; but the bases for resolving doubts, for exercising reason, must be empirical.

Descartes Dethroned: Locke

Newton worked in an England where empiricism had always been strong, the homeland of Bacon. So it is not surprising that the philosopher of the empirical principle which Newton so brilliantly exemplified should also be an Englishman. John Locke was no speculator, but a man of the world, a physician, and a fellow of the Royal Society. He characterized himself as 'an under-labourer in clearing ground a little, and removing some of the rubbish that lies in the way of knowledge'. He derived his inspiration, he said, from contemporary 'master-builders'—Boyle, Huygens, Newton.[11] Nevertheless he had travelled in France and Holland, and read Descartes. He even agreed with Descartes that God's existence could be logically proved, that human existence was proved by thought, that reason was the indispensable guide to thinking, and that the body was a machine. But he did not agree that men had any innate ideas, even of God.

This denial was the starting-point of his *Essay Concerning Human Understanding* of 1690, the product of two decades of meditation. For Locke, all knowledge consisted of ideas imprinted on the mind by sensation. The human mind at birth was empty: 'White paper void of all characters, without any *ideas*. How comes it to be furnished? Whence comes it by that vast store which the busy and boundless fancy of man has painted on it with an almost endless variety? Whence has it all the materials of reason and knowledge? To this I answer, in one word, from *experience*.'[12]

Such a doctrine would inevitably offend many churchmen. It was outrageous to suggest that souls were born without the idea of God. Besides, Locke followed the execrated Hobbes in declaring that the origin of the ideas of good and bad lay in the sensations of pleasure or pain rather than in

---

[11] *Essay Concerning Human Understanding* : 'Epistle to the Reader'.
[12] Ibid., Bk. II, ch. I, § 2.

some innate moral sense. Nor did his (initially anonymous) pamphlet of 1695 on *The Reasonableness of Christianity* help his reputation as a Christian, for it denied original sin, the literalness of the scriptures, and the credibility of the Trinity. Few took his professed Anglicanism seriously.

Locke's views were equally opposed to Cartesian orthodoxy. To reject innate ideas was flatly to contradict Descartes. To make experience the touchstone of knowledge was implicitly to diminish the role of pure reason. And the concept of *ideas* totally undermined the whole basis of Descartes's system, which was the proposition that everything clearly and distinctly perceived is true. Locke implied that nothing is clearly and distinctly perceived as it truly is, but only in the form of an idea. He seldom pushed his arguments to logical conclusions. Like a true scientist, he distinguished between the secondary qualities of matter, such as colour, taste, or smell, which were messages of the senses purely relative to the observer; and the primary qualities such as weight and extension, which had an independent existence, however imperfect an idea the observer had of them. To this extent he retained some implicit vestiges of Cartesian dualism. But within twenty years the Irishman George Berkeley, destined to become an Anglican bishop, had pushed Locke's logic forward to suggest that the observer has no more proof of the independent existence of primary qualities than of secondary ones. Indeed, there was no proof that matter itself existed beyond the idea of it in the mind. Most post-Cartesians resolved the problem of dualism by eliminating mind, becoming materialists. Berkeley resolved it by eliminating matter. Matter has existence only through being perceived; our guarantee of the physical world therefore lies only in the eternal, omnipresent perception of God.

Berkeley's doctrines puzzled and confused his contemporaries, who laughed at them. Dr. Johnson believed that he was refuted simply by the act of kicking a stone. Locke himself might have agreed, for it was a commonsensical reaction. Such qualities made his own philosophy by contrast an instant and continuous success. Like a true Modern, Locke wrote in the vernacular, and this had the paradoxical effect of retarding his impact outside England at first. But once Voltaire discovered him, simplified him, and presented him to the French-speaking world hand in hand with Newton in the *Philosophical Letters*, his success was assured.

The sensationalist psychology took Europe by storm. Its implications were in their way as fundamental as those of Newtonian science. It meant that men were born equal, with minds equally blank, that, since circumstances were infinitely diverse, and men were moulded by those circumstances, there were no general rules to which they could be expected to conform. Accordingly differences of custom and opinion were to be tolerated. This was the gist of Locke's own *Letter concerning Toleration* of 1688. But equally most circumstances were themselves man-made and could therefore be changed when it appeared appropriate and justifiable. Thus Locke taught that those who wish to mould men, mould their circumstances; and it was entirely appropriate that he was also the author of *Some Thoughts Concerning Education* (1693). Education was nothing less than the key to human behaviour.

This view was hardly novel. Not for nothing was education everywhere in the hands of the clergy. What *was* dynamically new was the logical integration of the principle into a system of thought which also tended to undermine all that the church stood for. Its implication was that education and enlightenment stood or fell together; and that to banish the superstition and nonsense still put out by the church, its hold over education must be broken. In this way the spreading of enlightenment became a political problem. By this chain of reasoning religious doubt ultimately led to political action.

Sources of Criticism

Newton's cosmology and Locke's psychology made criticism of prevailing orthodoxies—Christian or Cartesian—positive. They offered alternatives to systems whose obvious defects had not brought them down before for lack of convincing replacements. They gave criticism added point, so that by 1700 something like a sustained critical movement was beginning to emerge, assailing authority on a remarkably uniform set of premisses. Most criticism was grounded in the conviction that there existed alternative ways of life and thought to those prevailing in Europe.

The intellectual alternatives appeared in a Europe already increasingly aware of cultural differences. By 1660 Europe was beginning to organize and consolidate the knowledge of the world overseas which it had acquired during the previous century and a half. It was becoming clear that no amount of ingenuity could force it into the traditional biblical world picture. Other civilizations existed, whose values appeared to be in no such state of crisis as those of Europe. China for instance, was large, peaceful, prosperous, and meritocratic. Its legislators appeared to be philosophers. Yet it had never enjoyed the blessings of Christianity, and indeed claimed to have been in existence long before 4004 B.C., the date accepted by most Christian authorities as that of the creation of the world. Such was the picture sent back to France by the writings and translations of Jesuit missionaries anxious to prove how susceptible their chosen province was to evangelization. These immensely popular works were soon translated into English and German in response to a seemingly inexhaustible demand for travel literature. The contrast between Europe and China seemed vivid, nor was there much doubt to whose credit: 'Our circumstances seem to me to have sunk to such a level,' declared Leibniz in 1697, 'particularly with regard to the monstrous and increasing breakdown of morality, that one could almost think it necessary for the Chinese to send missionaries to us.'[13] Wolff lost his chair at Halle in 1721 for comparing Confucianism with Christianity; and in the hands of Voltaire the cult of Chinese superiority approached worship.

China was only the most spectacular and best reported of distant lands. Siam, India, Ceylon, Persia, Egypt, and Turkey were all visited and minutely described before 1700. Even those unwilling to weigh the relative moral worth of civilizations found such accounts invaluable as a stimulus to new

---

[13] Quoted in W. Franke, *China and the West* (1967), 62.

thought: Locke's works are full of arguments derived from foreign examples. It was soon apparent too that inhabitants of these exotic countries might find Europe strange; and although few had the opportunity to testify to this, words were rapidly put into their mouths by satirists. Incredulous literary foreigners, such as the *Turkish Spy* who exposed to the French their own foibles from time to time after 1684, were created to comment on the absurdities of European manners and institutions.

Nobody used foreign examples to more effect than Montesquieu. As a young man he brought the genre of satirical comment by bemused orientals to its highest point with his *Persian Letters* of 1721. Holding the attention of less steadfast readers with periodic snippets of sexual innuendo, this supposed correspondence of a Persian visitor to Paris subjected European customs to hostile comment at a time when the uncertainties created by Louis XIV's death had not yet been resolved. The dominant themes were scorn for the volatile character of French public life, and ridicule of the church, the papacy, and all the pretensions of religious authorities. Twenty-seven years later the mature Montesquieu elaborated in detail many of the half-formulated ideas of 1721 in the *Spirit of the Laws* (1748). This was not a work of satire or even, ostensibly, of criticism; but rather an analysis of how various types of society order their politics. Accepting completely the assumptions of Lockean psychology, Montesquieu set out to examine how societies and their laws are moulded by circumstances; laws for him were not abstract rules, but rather 'the necessary relationships which derive from the nature of things'.[14] So the *Spirit of the Laws* was a work—the founding work—of political sociology. And it argued from copious examples, drawn from all over the known world. With Montesquieu the explosion of travel literature which had marked the second half of the seventeenth century began to do more than simply support criticism of established customs. It served to promote the first serious investigation of how customs come to be established in the first place.

Scarcely less striking in the *Spirit of the Laws* was the wealth of allusion to the classical societies of Greece and Rome. Classical values were another potent source of cultural relativism, more familiar because the church taught them in the schools it controlled, yet more insidious because they made up so large a part of every literate man's education. The awkward fact about antiquity was that it was pagan. Educational tradition had circumvented this problem by stressing that all antiquity's worthwhile features had been borrowed from the Jews, the chosen people, and only its defects had been original. The last great exposition of this doctrine was in Bossuet's *Discourse on Universal History* of 1681: 'Scripture', he baldly declared, '. . .by its antiquity. . .would deserve to be preferred to all the Greek histories, even were we not to know that it was dictated by the Holy Spirit.'[15] The researches of Spinoza and Simon, however, had already placed such statements beyond credulity when they were made. Ever since the Renaissance interest in classical

---

[14] *Esprit des Lois*, Bk. I, ch. 1.
[15] *Discours sur l'histoire universelle* (1825) i. p. 57.

civilization for its own sake, rather than as the mere catalyst of primitive Christianity, had been growing. The lesson of Greece and Rome, like that of China, was that societies could be peaceful and well ordered, and that public and private virtue could flourish, and toleration prevail, in a world unaware of Christianity. The message of Gibbon's *Decline and Fall of the Roman Empire* (1776–87) was that Christianity was responsible for destroying 'the mild indifference of Antiquity'[16] and most of its other virtues too. Nor had the quarrel of the Ancients and the Moderns undermined Antiquity's cultural prestige; for the most part it was about whether the Moderns observed classical rules as well as or better than classical authors themselves. The actual rules remained above dispute. Classical society and history were better chronicled, better known, and better understood than anything in the Christian Middle Ages. The superiority of the written evidence itself showed greater accomplishment. Montesquieu might demonstrate that the history of Merovingian France could be reconstructed in some detail and made to yield important conclusions about the character of French society.[17] But this pioneer work merely puzzled when it did not bore most of his readers. In 1748 interest in, let alone praise for, the gothic 'dark' ages was viewed as perverse or eccentric; but everybody pillaged the classics for examples, arguments, models, and inspiration. 'There is not a philosopher in antiquity', wrote Voltaire, 'who failed to set men an example of virtue and to give lessons in moral truth.'[18] This was, he implied, more than could be said for most theologians since then.

The most pressing incentive to consider alternative ways of thinking and acting came from political opposition. People persecuted or excluded on account of their religious nonconformity were often perfectly orthodox in most of their attitudes. But the shock of rejection could provoke passionate ideological reactions, with sweeping and radical criticism of the order by which they had been spurned and the attitudes which motivated it. In this sense Louis XIV was a major progenitor of new ideas and the critical spirit. His costly, aggressive foreign policies, the economic assumptions behind them, and the centralizing, fiscally exacting, domestic policies they necessitated provoked a thoughtful aristocratic opposition which hoped to reverse many of them when he died. Archbishop Fénelon, the most eloquent spokesman of this group, became an advocate of international peace which he believed would result from encouraging agriculture and decentralizing the state. Such views prefigured the economic analyses of the physiocrats half a century later. The king's religious policy was even more crucial. The revocation of the Edict of Nantes, that last great manifestation of Counter-Reformation intolerance, was an intellectual turning-point of European importance. It scattered throughout Europe a leaven of French Protestants profoundly hostile to religious intolerance and absolute monarchy. Among them was Pierre Jurieu, who prophesied Louis's apocalyptic ruin, but in the process

[16] *Decline and Fall of the Roman Empire*, ch. XVI.
[17] *Esprit des lois*, Bks. XXX and XXXI.
[18] *Dictionnaire philosophique*, art. 'Philosophe'.

subjected the whole organization of state and society in France to scornful and withering criticism. His depiction of the plight of his co-religionists did much to suggest the virtues of a toleration that he himself would certainly not have practised, given power. At the same time the Huguenots who fled to the Protestant refuges of England and Holland did much to propagate, for the first time in French, the liberal ideas they found there.

The most famous of these refugee publicists was Pierre Bayle, acknowledged by the foremost thinkers of the Enlightenment as one of their founding fathers. He was seen as the model sceptic, unconvinced by accepted explanations of anything; the foe of superstition who, in his *Divers Thoughts on the Comet* poured scorn on those who believed that the comet of 1680 was a portent of divine wrath. The summit of his achievement was, however, the *Historical and Critical Dictionary*, first published in 1697 and much supplemented thereafter. Here Bayle extended his criticism to a huge range of knowledge, much of it biblical, demonstrating the follies, crimes, delusions, and inconsistencies of both sacred and profane history. For evidence he drew freely on both contemporary travel literature and the classics, pointing out repeatedly that non-Christians were often moral and virtuous, whereas Christians and the Old Testament heroes whom they revered, such as David, had frequently been neither. The great moral, constantly reiterated, was that in an imperfect world nobody had a monopoly of truth or virtue, and that therefore toleration was the most basic of public necessities. All shades of religious opinion, and not least his own Huguenot co-religionists led by Jurieu himself, were offended. Bayle also attacked modern system-builders, such as Descartes, Spinoza, and Leibniz, unerringly exposing the weak points of their arguments. His claim to have remained a Christian has led some commentators to see his prime purpose as not so much to expose superstitious error, as to demonstrate the limitations of human reason, its inability to resolve anything satisfactorily. 'Our Reason serves only to confound every thing and make us doubt of every thing. . .Thus, the best use that can be made out of the Study of Philosophy is to know, that it is a Path which leads astray, and that we ought to seek another Guide, which is the light of Revelation.'[19] Whether this was a sincere profession of blind faith, in the absence of any rational certainty, or merely an empty gesture towards the orthodox, cannot be known. More clear is the fact that Bayle, from the intellectual security of his Dutch exile, set an example of systematic doubt, and pungent expression of it, which inspired many a young sceptic of the next generation and continued to infuriate dogmatists of all persuasions. The *Dictionary* remained a steady seller throughout the eighteenth century—a sure tribute to the importance of the multifarious questions it raised.

Spreading Enlightenment

There had been critical ages before. What distinguished the Age of Enlightenment was the universality of its criticism and the size of the audience to

---

[19] *Historical and Critical Dictionary*, art. 'Bunel'. (English edn. of 1735).

which it appealed. 'Enlightened' writers set out consciously to marshal public opinion in support of their programme. They courted it by avoiding the narrow specialisms and rarified habits of academic thinking. They flattered it by couching their language in terms of an appeal to good sense. The term 'philosopher' came to mean almost anybody who thought about matters—a lofty title open to all. It was one thing to aspire to such influence. It was quite another to attain it. Enlightenment spread, not only on account of the intrinsic appeal of its doctrines, but also because of a number of favourable historical circumstances.

Printing was an obvious prerequisite; the polemical battles of the Reformation and especially the biblical emphasis of Protestantism had produced the first works of mass circulation, in small and easily handled form. In this way religion helped to sharpen the weapons subsequently used against it. Equally important was the freedom to print and publish without restriction, which in 1660 existed only in the Dutch republic and a few city states. Conditions in the United Provinces were indeed crucial in the propagation of new ideas. Not only was the republic a haven for persecuted thinkers such as Descartes, Locke, or Bayle, not to mention natives like Spinoza, who would never have enjoyed toleration elsewhere. It was also the seat of an enterprising and vigorous publishing industry which benefited from unrivalled means of distributing its products through the continent-wide activities of Dutch merchants. Dutch publishers served the whole of Europe in all of Europe's languages; they printed works which would never have been allowed to appear in their native lands. Even when censorship became relatively slack or sporadic, timid authors could still print 'Amsterdam' on their title-pages to deflect suspicion. With the lapse of the Licensing Act in 1694 England too became an open market for printers and publishers, while remarkably low costs in eighteenth-century Scotland did much to facilitate the publication of the astonishing range of original work which made up the Scottish Enlightenment. The rest of Europe lagged far behind. In the east both printing presses and a literate public were thinly scattered. In Spain and Italy the Inquisition spent more and more of its time acting against subversive literature, although in Naples a traditionally anti-papal government allowed the publication of works such as Giannone's *Civil History of the Kingdom of Naples* (1723), which undermined the authority of the church on legalistic grounds, and the city republic of Lucca became an important centre of unsupervised printing and publishing. In France printers were licensed and rigidly controlled by the state, but much depended on the character of the Director of Bookselling, the chief censor. The relative ease with which the *Encyclopedia* was published owed much to the fact that the Director between 1751 and 1763 was the tolerant Malesherbes. Clashes of jurisdiction between crown, courts, and church, all with powers of censorship, also favoured dangerous works; but in any case the first half of the eighteenth century saw a flourishing market in clandestine works, often in manuscript, which the various authorities were unable to catch up with. And for those determined to appear in print the independent Protestant republic of Geneva offered French-language printing and publishing beyond French jurisdiction yet within easy reach. Montesquieu's *Spirit of the Laws* and many other major works likely to be offensive to Catholic orthodoxy were first published there. Important too as centres of French book-production abroad were Bouillon, just across the north-east frontier; Neuchâtel, an enclave of Prussian jurisdiction in Switzerland; and, most surprisingly of all, the papal enclave of Avignon.

The role of Protestantism in spreading Enlightenment was not confined to stimulating large-scale and cheap book production; it also promoted the use of the vernacular. By 1660 Latin, that Romish language, had been on the decline for some time in Germany, England, and the Netherlands in all fields except the most strictly academic. Vernacular Bibles had bred vernacular theology and after that no subject was sacred. The newer the idea, the more likely was it to be framed in a language any literate man could understand, giving innovators a distinct advantage. Nor could Catholic Europe remain immune from the trend. Descartes's *Discourse* was in French, and the appearance in French of Arnauld's *Of Frequent Communion* in 1644 marked the invasion of theology itself. Jansenists consistently favoured vernacular Bibles and works of devotion in order to make the truths of religion more immediate; but they also, as the Jesuits realized, made them easier to dispute. Initially at least the decline of Latin as the international written language, if it democratized learning, may also actually have impeded the international circulation of new ideas. Hobbes and Locke were well aware that their works were unlikely to be read on the continent in English, and this is why both *Leviathan* and the *Letter Concerning Toleration* appeared in Latin versions too. By the 1680s, however, French, purified and refined by the labours of the French Academy and exalted by the cultural prestige of Louis XIV, was rapidly becoming the new international language. By 1700 its triumph in polite circles was complete. 'The boundaries of the empire of Latin are visibly receding,' declared the Berlin Academy in 1745, 'while the French language now occupies the place that Greek occupied at the time of Cicero—everyone learns it.'[20] In Germany it even supplanted German as a first language among princes and aristocrats, much to the disgust of later patriots such as Herder, or Goethe, who nevertheless admitted that in his youth in mid-century Frankfurt: 'I had become acquainted with the [French] language through a bustling life and with a bustling life through the language. It had become my own, like a second mother-tongue, without grammar and instruction—by mere intercourse and practice.'[21] The result was that the works of French publicists and philosophers were read far beyond the frontiers of France; even the English founding fathers of Enlightenment came to most people's acquaintance through French accounts and translations. The eighteenth-century intellectual world was, through French, cosmopolitan; but it was also socially exclusive, because the language was only available outside

[20] Quoted in D. Maland, *Culture and Society in 17th century France* (1970), 100.
[21] *The Autobiography of Johann Wolfgang Von Goethe*, trans. J. Oxenford (1971), ii. 96.

France to those who could afford an expensive education. Later 'enlightened' ideas therefore tended to have most currency precisely among those whose privileges and vested interests they were, in time, to do so much to undermine.

Exclusive though it was, the French-speaking cultural élite was nevertheless very different from the oligarchy of Latinized knowledge represented by the universities. Bastions of traditional learning, the universities found themselves increasingly isolated in outmoded systems of thought. Those (not by any means all) that deigned to take notice even of Cartesianism began to do so only when it had already been abandoned by most educated opinion. Most contributed nothing at all to the Enlightenment. Oxford and Cambridge, where Boyle, Wren, Locke, and Newton had taught or studied in the seventeenth century, fell asleep in the eighteenth. They were, Gibbon noted, from bitter experience:

founded in a dark age of false and barbarous science; and they are still tainted with the vices of their origin. Their primitive discipline was adapted to the education of priests and monks; and the government still remains in the hands of the Clergy, an order of men, whose manners are remote from the present World, and whose eyes are dazzled by the light of Philosophy. The legal incorporation of these societies. . .had given them a monopoly of the public instruction: and the spirit of monopolists is narrow, lazy and oppressive: their work is more costly and less productive than that of independent artists; and the new improvements so eagerly grasped by the competition of freedom, are admitted with slow and sullen reluctance in those proud corporations, above the fear of a rival, and below the confession of an error.[22]

There were exceptions. The Dutch universities of Utrecht and Leyden drew over half their students from foreign countries through the renown of their lawyers or doctors like Boerhaave, the most famous physician of the century, who taught at Leyden. Some north-Italian universities also remained vigorous. The universities of Scotland, notably Glasgow and Edinburgh, were at the very centre of the fertile intellectual life of their country in the later eighteenth century. Scottish professors, paid for their teaching rather than the positions they held, remained active. In contrast to the previous century, Wolff stood almost alone in continental Europe as a university professor of major intellectual importance.[23] But Scotland's universities boasted Hutcheson in philosophy, Ferguson and Robertson in history and sociology, Adam Smith in economics, and might even have had Hume if he had not made his sceptical views plain before aspiring to the chair of philosophy at Edinburgh.

Enlightened learning was spread primarily through Academies, self-recruiting societies whose purpose was to promote and exchange ideas on topics of mutual interest. They were normally incorporated under some form of official patronage. Many, like the Jeux Floraux of Toulouse, boasted roots deep in the middle ages, but the first recognizably modern academies sprang up in sixteenth-century Italy. The most famous was the Tuscan Accademia

[22] *Memoirs of My Life*, ed. G. A. Bonnard (1966), 49.
[23] If we exclude Giambattista Vico, professor at Naples. But in his own time Vico was an isolated figure, and influenced contemporary thought little—in contrast to Wolff. Vico's real influence came in the nineteenth century.

della Crusca, a literary society dating from 1582, but no less than four others of comparable vintage were flourishing in Tuscany in 1700. Tuscany had also produced the first major scientific academy, the Florentine Accademia del Cimento, a body of scientists acknowledging the inspiration of Galileo which flourished between 1657 and 1667. The year 1660 saw the formation of the Royal Society of London, while six years later Louis XIV endowed the Paris Academy of Sciences. The role of such bodies was crucial in the progress of the scientific revolution. Newton, Boyle, and all the major figures in English science reported their experiments to the Royal Society, while its *Philosophical Transactions* passed them on to the world. Huygens announced his discovery of the pendulum clock under the auspices of the Academy of Sciences. The societies corresponded with one another, making the progress of science a matter of international concern. Quick communication of results did much to accelerate progress and eliminate needless duplication of work. Leibniz spent much of his life trying to persuade various German princes to set up academies, constituent parts, as he saw them, of an international republic of learning held together by mutual correspondence. Apart from the establishment of a rather artificial academy in Berlin in 1700, his efforts met with much interest but little success; nevertheless, his appreciation of the potential role of academies was sound enough. In the next generation of the techniques of correspondence and co-operation pioneered by the scientific societies of Paris and London were to be widely employed by less specialized bodies for the exchange of less technical information. The most prestigious by far of the non-scientific academies was the French Academy, founded in 1634. Its forty members, like the Cruscans of Florence, were formally dedicated to producing a dictionary of their native language, but they regarded the whole range of literary culture as their sphere. A 'chair' in the Academy was the ambition of most French writers, and although a number were always held by princes and generals of no intellectual distinction, many of the major figures of the French Enlightenment, such as Fontenelle, Montesquieu, Voltaire, and d'Alembert, achieved membership. By the 1760s the 'philosophic party' had captured the Academy and used its prestige to enhance that of their own ideas. Neither London nor Vienna offered equivalents to the French Academy, but imitations were set up in Madrid (1713), St. Petersburg (1724), Stockholm (1735), and Dresden (1768). The accession of Frederick II of Prussia in 1740 revitalized the drooping Berlin Academy, even if that meant importing French luminaries. Perhaps even more important than metropolitan foundations were provincial academies, such as the Edinburgh Select Society, founded in 1754 to promote good English, but rapidly becoming the main forum of the city's intellectual life. Similar societies mushroomed in the small cities of Tuscany in the early eighteenth century, while in France the century between 1670 and 1770 saw local academies founded in most major provincial towns. They may have aped Paris; but they also made a quite distinctive contribution to the spread of Enlightenment by sponsoring public literary competitions. It was through his entries to competitions held by the Academy of Dijon, for instance, that Rousseau first became widely known for his views on the corruption of civilization and the origins of inequality. Such bodies also corresponded with their equivalents abroad, subscribed to the major periodicals of the day, and elected famous men into honorary or corresponding member-ship. By these means they brought the local élites from whom they recruited themselves into contact with the most advanced thought of their day.

Academies did not enjoy a monopoly. Informed but regular gatherings in coffee-houses, clubs, and salons were equally important in spreading En-lightenment. One example was the Entresol Club, where some of the sharpest minds of Paris in the 1720s met over tea to discuss public affairs. Its disso-lution by the government in 1731 shows the extent of its influence. More persistent were the salons, usually run by formidably intellectual hostesses of social consequence. The first salons, in the mid-seventeenth century, were mainly literary in their interests, but a hundred years later the gatherings of such ladies as Mme Geoffrin, Mme d'Epinay, and Mme Necker witnessed discussions on every conceivable topic. In such polished surroundings the leaders of society mingled with the leaders of opinion, encountering their ideas in the most congenial circumstances.

Never before had so much ingenuity been deployed on the attractive presentation of new ideas. The eighteenth century saw a proliferation of literary gazettes and periodicals in which the latest books and ideas were reported, analysed, and criticized. The most important prototype was Bayle's *News of the Republic of Letters*, appearing between 1684 and 1687. Since academies and learned societies subscribed to such journals. it became possible to be well informed about the intellectual scene without having read any major works. 'Philosophy' made great progress through such smatterings, conveyed in unpromising-sounding journals such as the Milanese *Coffee* which began publication in 1763. Enlightenment came late to Spain, through the almost single-handed efforts of the Benedictine monk Feijóo, who between 1726 and 1759 produced fourteen volumes of literary mis-cellany, the *Universal Critical Theatre*, in which he watered down and simpli-fied for Spanish consumption ideas long current further north but new to Spain. There were few copies of Bacon, Descartes, or Newton for Spaniards to read, but from Feijóo they could glean the essentials of their thought.

Dictionaries served a similar purpose; they standardized and popularized knowledge at the same time. The 1690s saw, in addition to the first edition of the French Academy's great dictionary of the French language, at least three more broadly conceived works of reference claiming the name, not to mention Bayle's great work. 1704 saw the first edition of the *Dictionary of Trévoux*, a Jesuit compendium of knowledge; 1728 brought Chambers's *Cyclopaedia or an Universal Dictionary of Arts and Sciences*; while between 1732 and 1750 the German publisher Zedler produced a sixty-four-volume *Great Complete Universal Lexicon of All Sciences and Arts*. Of these works, only Bayle's was openly critical and polemical in its purposes. The rest set out to inform, and the distinction was clear. But the great *Encyclopedia or Reasoned Dictionary of Sciences, Arts and Crafts*, launched in France in 1751 by Diderot and d'Alembert, boldly set out to do both at once. Originating in a project merely to translate Chambers's *Cyclopedia* into French, this enterprise rapidly grew into an attempt, seventeen folio volumes long, to summarize the current state of knowledge:

to gather together the knowledge scattered over the surface of the earth, to explain its general system to the men with whom we live, and to transmit it to the men who shall come after us, so that the works of past centuries should not have been works useless for the centuries that shall follow, so that our descendants, becoming better informed, shall become at the same time more virtuous and happier, and so that we do not die without having deserved well of the human race.[24]

To this end the editors assembled an unprecedented range of technical information contributed by a very broad spectrum of experts, many of them craftsmen. Its ten volumes of plates magnificently illustrated this side of its achievement. But the *Encyclopedia* was more than an attempt to summarize. It was also an attempt to persuade, to convince a cultivated public of the value and importance of certain ideas. 'It is', wrote d'Alembert,[25] 'principally by the philosophic spirit that we shall attempt to distinguish this dictionary. That above all is the way it will win the support which we most appreciate.' *The Encyclopedia* epitomized the sum of 'Enlightened' opinion in the mid-eighteenth century. A collective enterprise to propagate a distinctively modern view of the world, it stood at the crossroads of the Enlightenment.

The New Synthesis

What then was the new consensus of 'enlightened' opinion symbolized by the *Encyclopedia*?

It was anti-Cartesian. Descartes had, noted d'Alembert in the *Preliminary Discourse* 'dared to show intelligent minds how to throw off the yoke of scholasticism, of opinion, of authority—in a word, of prejudices and barbarism.'[26] This was his eternal glory, but, d'Alembert declared, neither his psychology, his philosophy, nor his physics was any longer acceptable. With the progress of knowledge, his authority had been supplanted by that of Locke and Newton.

The credit for this lay mostly (though d'Alembert did not flatter his contemporary by saying so) with Voltaire, and it was appropriate that it was his name that subsequent generations seized upon when they sought an epitome of what the Enlightenment was all about. Voltaire was in no sense a scholar; his 'ruling passion [was] for the cultivation of the Belles-lettres.'[27] He built his early reputation, which carried him into the Academy, on poetry and plays. Nor, however appealing some find it to imagine him so, was he a revolutionary. He loved high society and the money his brilliant financial speculations brought him far too much to desire major upheavals. Yet he completely redirected French thought in 1734 with the introduction of the literate public to Locke and Newton through his *Philosophical Letters*. As

---

[24] *Encyclopédie*, art. *Encyclopédie*, by Diderot.
[25] *Advertissement* to vol. iii.
[26] R.N. Schwab (ed.), *Preliminary Discourse to the Encyclopedia of Diderot*, 80.
[27] 'Autobiography' in T. Besterman, *Voltaire* (1969), 549.

early as 1700 Locke had been translated into French, but few had read him. Even fewer had struggled with the technicalities of Newton's *Principia*, in its academic Latin, although Maupertuis proclaimed his acceptance of them in his *Discourse on the Face of the Stars* (1732). Voltaire simplified and explained them in witty, clear, and concise French, and if this alone was hardly enough to sell the *Letters*, their malicious anti-clericalism and pointed contrasts brought them in for judicial condemnation. From then on their success was assured, and so was that of the pioneers they praised. In 1746 Condillac, the 'French Locke', produced an *Essay on the Origins of Human Understanding* which treated the problem with more logical rigour than Locke himself had ever aspired to, suggesting that language was the vital link between sensation and reflection, those twin pillars of the Lockean understanding. D'Alembert made the principles the *Encyclopedia*'s dogma in his *Preliminary Discourse*, and Condillac elaborated them further in his *Treatise of Sensations* of 1754. By then the sensationalist psychology had become an orthodoxy. Similarly, Voltaire elaborated his popularization of Newtonianism with the *Elements of the Philosophy of Newton* of 1738, and the *Encyclopedia* announced that the Englishman had 'lifted the veil which hid the greatest mysteries of nature.'[28] *Philosophes* maintained close touch with advances in the scientific world, and performed experiments themselves, acknowledging Newton as their guide and inspiration. He had shown that nature was an organic whole, self-consistent and working by simple, clearly ascertainable rules; and that the key to these rules was experiment. These conclusions too had attained, by the 1750s, the status of philosophic dogma.

The implications of such basic assumptions were far-reaching. The foundation of morality, Locke had taught, was the pursuit of pleasure and the avoidance of pain. There was therefore no absolute moral law beyond that inherent in the logic of nature itself. Diderot in his letters *On the Blind* (1749) and the *Deaf and Mute* (1751) went so far as to suggest that morality differed according to the endowment of senses; a blind or deaf man would have different values from one who was not. Similarly, Montesquieu showed in 1748 that human customs and institutions differ according to geography and climate. Morality was, in fact, a product of physical circumstances; morality was relative.

It followed that nobody had a monopoly of truth or rectitude. There must therefore be toleration. Even before he had observed it in practice in England, Voltaire had been convinced by reading Bayle of the blessings of toleration. The *Henriade* (1723), his great epic poem about Henry IV and the wars of religion, was dominated by this theme. And the *Encyclopedia* reserved its most extravagant language for this subject. An intolerant man, wrote Diderot, was 'an evil man, a bad Christian, a dangerous subject, a bad politician and a bad citizen'; in an intolerant state 'the prince would be nothing more than an executioner in the pay of the priest', for 'men who are wrong in good faith are a subject for complaint, but never for punishment.'[29] Such

---

[28] *Encyclopédie*, art. *Wolstrope.*
[29] *Encyclopédie*, art. *Intolérance.*

sentiments echoed Locke, but they were also deeply felt by men writing under the constant shadow of a capricious censorship liable at any time to succumb to priestly pressure. The age between Locke and Rousseau was not notable for its political theory. Even Montesquieu's teachings about political obligations were incidental, for his intention was to analyse rather than to prescribe. But among the random, pragmatic, and inconsistent political ideas arising within this period, toleration was a theme which recurred constantly. It was the supreme political virtue acknowledged by all.

Toleration meant respect for human opinion; it reflected uncertainty about ultimate truth. *Philosophes* did not overestimate the human capacity for progress. Voltaire, d'Alembert, and Rousseau were all inclined to believe that they lived in an age of decline and decay. Nevertheless they believed that human capacities were the only means men had of discovering the truth. And although they often declared that human inadequacy proved the need for revealed religion, they did so to protect themselves from the authorities. 'Time will show the distinction between what we have thought and what we have said,' wrote D'Alembert to Voltaire in 1757.[30] Nothing, they thought, demonstrated the authenticity of any religion claimed by other men to be revealed. Even revelation had to be reasonable. 'The first principle of a true religion'—D'Alembert again—'is not to propose any belief that conflicts with reason.'

Religion was not excluded as such. In both the Cartesian and the Newtonian universe there was plenty of room for God. The machine needed a designer, the clock a winder. Deism therefore seemed perfectly acceptable to most *philosophes*, who, as in so much else, had earlier English examples before them. From around 1690 there was a renewed outburst of the deistic thought already well established in England. Locke's *Reasonableness of Christianity* (1695) came close; while Toland's *Christianity not Mysterious* of 1696 frankly condemned both the ideas of revealed religion and God's intervention in the system of nature through miracles. Shaftesbury, in his *Inquiry Concerning Virtue or Merit* (1699) argued for the existence of a good God, but, convinced by Spinoza's ciriticism, derived nothing from scripture; he declared himself the enemy of all sectarian 'enthusiasm'. Eagerly absorbed by the *philosophes*, he was translated by Diderot. Collins's *Discourse of Free-thinking* (1713) also won their praise, while the title of Tindal's *Christianity as old as the Creation, or the Gospel a Republication of the Religion of Nature* (1730) spoke for itself. The message of all these tracts was that religion must be reasonable, or it was mere superstition. But to be reasonable it also had to be simple, clear, logical, and obvious. Tindal's 'Christianity' was so purged and rarefied as to be unrecognizable to most practising Christians. It was in fact deism, the only religion acceptable to most *philosophes*. D'Alembert aroused a tremendous controversy, which led ultimately to his resignation from the *Encyclopedia*, when, in an idealized article on Geneva, he suggested with obvious approval that most of the ministers of religion in that Calvinist

[30] Quoted in J. Lough, *The Encyclopédie*, 208.

state were 'perfect Socinians'.[31] A few went further. By the 1750s Diderot had passed through deism to atheism. So had the most important other contributor to the later volumes of the *Encyclopedia*, the baron d'Holbach. To them the distant, non-interfering, first-cause God of the Deists was so remote as to have no relevance to human life; he was dispensable; the universe might just as well have come together by chance. This possibility contained, as Diderot clearly saw to his intense anguish, the seeds of a profound cosmic pessimism. Deism stopped short at that; it assumed that the Great Designer was benevolent and had endowed men with goodness and a capacity to control their fate. Deists were cautious optimists.

We should beware of attributing too much intellectual symmetry to the thought of a very numerous and diverse set of individuals, but this complex of opinions did have a certain logical self-consistency. One supreme fact drew them together more tightly than any logical links: all seemed to contradict in one way or another the dogmas and practices of established religion. Atheists and deists alike could unite on this. If no ideas were innate, where did that leave men's immortal souls? If morality was relative, what about the unique rectitude of Christian ethics? If nature invariably worked by fixed rules, how were miracles possible? If all knowledge was to be subject to free inquiry, what scope was left for the church's authority and the revelation of which it was the custodian? If toleration obtained, could the church *have* any authority? Everywhere the entrenched clergy and its supporters stood resolved to avoid these problems; *philosophes* were equally determined to raise them. So the Enlightenment was not anti-religious, but it certainly was anti-clerical, carrying matters beyond the domain of the intellect. The clergy enjoyed temporal power. If Enlightenment were to progress further, sooner or later 'philosophy' would have to turn its attention to practical politics.

[31] i.e. deists, *Encyclopédie*, art. *Genève*.

9. A Doubtful Progress

The greatest problem about the Enlightenment is to estimate its influence. *Philosophes*, most of them brilliant publicists, ostentatiously applauded measures of which they approved. It was easy to infer that they had brought them about. 'Opinion governs the world,' Voltaire proudly declared in 1766, 'and in the end the *philosophes* govern men's opinions.'[1] But the events claimed as successes by the Enlightenment were usually the product of complex circumstances in which the state of advanced opinion was only one strand. Not surprisingly, the results often fell far short of expectations. By the 1780s the philosophic tide had left few European intellectuals untouched, but the concrete achievements remained fragmentary. As Kant declared in 1784, it was the Age of Enlightenment, but not an enlightened age.[2]

It was not only the strength of 'prejudice', or 'superstition', or even (as Kant thought) laziness or cowardice, that made progress so uncertain. It was also the fragmentation of the forces of Enlightenment themselves. The first decade of the *Encyclopedia* was a time when all these forces seemed to approach consensus. D'Alembert believed, rightly, that the middle of the century, when the great dictionary began to appear, was a turning-point. Surprisingly however, it was not a turn towards ultimate unity, but rather to diversity of a new sort. Doubting voices raised earlier now found their lonely persistence attracting attention, while the new orthodox found themselves under criticism from others who felt that their logic could be carried much further. The *Encyclopedia* sowed seed as well as bearing fruit. By the time its text was complete, in 1765, the consensus of the 1750s had dissolved. The advantages of Enlightenment were as clear as they were ever to be, but the question now was how to implement them. In the face of practicalities the clear prescriptions of the 1750s dissolved into complexity. The movement lost its unity. No wonder then that its final achievement proved so uneven.

Natural Religion and Beyond

The case of 'Natural Religion' clearly illustrates the ambiguity of the Enlightenment's success. The term came from England, but it described something found all over Europe—the apparent compromise of Christianity with the spirit of the age. Natural religion conformed to d'Alembert's criterion of what was acceptable, because its touchstone was reason. It did not base its claims on revelation or on such supernatural evidence as miracles; rather it pointed to the harmony of nature, the relative sociability of men, and their recognition of moral obligations, to prove the existence of a benevolent

[1] Quoted in T. Besterman, *Voltaire*, 427.
[2] 'Answer to the question "What is Enlightenment?" ' in H. Reiss (ed.), *Kant's Political Writings* (1970), 58.

divine purpose. This was the famous 'argument from design'. Its advocates believed that Christianity could be reduced to a few simple and clear precepts. Obscurities in the Bible were obviously mere misunderstandings. Such principles seemed designed to outflank hostile criticism by abandoning more vulnerable doctrines. 'Do not fear that you will lose the religion of your fathers,' declared a German preacher in 1788. 'Reason does not undermine religion, but only its excrescences. You will lose prejudices but retain the essence of religion. The latter will, indeed, stand all the more firm in the future the more closely it approaches the light of reason. When harmonized with reason, it will no longer have to fear the latter's attack.'[3]

But in 1788 this was to argue after the event. The assumption that Natural Religion was a response to philosophic attack was only partly correct. In the seventeenth century both Catholic Jesuits and Protestant Arminians had argued that reason alone can clarify the ambiguities of revelation. English Latitudinarians and some German Pietists had come a long way towards renouncing theological 'excrescences' before any serious philosophic criticism had begun to be levelled at Christianity. The deism of Locke, Toland, Collins, and Tindal flourished in a latitudinarian atmosphere; and in so far as it served to inspire the *philosophes* (as it undoubtedly did), enlightened hostility to Christianity was as much a result as a cause of the development of natural religion. Nevertheless criticism, when it came, could only accelerate its development. The trend was particularly marked in Germany, where radical theologians systematically sheared Christianity of most of its central doctrines, leaving a pale creed of good feelings and universal benevolence. The most typical German work was Reimarus's *The Principal Truths of Natural Religion* (1754), which propounded a deistic creed and was defended in the 1770s by the playwright Lessing against the attacks of the principal champion of Lutheran orthodoxy, Pastor Goeze of Hamburg.

Goeze's main contention was that neither Lessing nor Reimarus was a Christian, an accusation which Lessing never answered directly. English protagonists of Natural Religion, however, had been at pains to stress that it was not synonymous with deism. In his *Discourse Concerning the Unchangeable Obligations of Natural Religion, and the Truth and Certainty of the Christian Revelation* (1706), Samuel Clarke attempted to show that, although reason alone could not guide men to all the truths of the Christian revelation, revelation itself contained nothing against reason, so that deists were wrong to reject it. Thirty years later Bishop Butler produced *The Analogy of Religion, Natural and Revealed, to the Constitution and Course of Nature* (1736), which argued from the uncertainty of human knowledge to the likelihood of the basic propositions of the Christian revelation. Gone, however, were traditional certainties; Butler's most frequent assertion goes no further than that a thing is probable.

The attempt to distinguish between natural religion and deism was in fact a losing battle. God could be reconciled with reason in a way that Christ and

---

[3] Quoted in K. Epstein, *The Genesis of German Conservatism*, 116–17.

the multifarious doctrines surrounding His worship never could. Nor did talk about 'true Christianity', a religion shorn of these doctrines, prove in any way satisfactory. The most notable effect of the writings of Clarke, paradoxically, was to persuade the century's most influential advocate of natural religion, Rousseau, of the truth of deism. Rousseau was as anti-clerical as any *philosophe*, scorning miracles and all the other evidences of revelation. But he believed that the human heart needs religion and that the harmony of nature and the essential primitive goodness of men were ample evidence of a benevolent God. These views were elaborated in the *Profession of Faith of the Savoyard Curate*, a discourse embedded in the didactic novel *Emile, or Education* (1762). Basically Rousseau's argument for God was the Argument from Design, but he added a subjective element not susceptible of rational examination and indeed derived from ideas directly opposed to the orthodoxies of the age. This was the conscience, 'an innate principle of justice and virtue'[4] in the depths of men's souls which only God could have put there and which was in itself sufficient evidence of His existence. To resurrect the possibility of innate ideas was revolutionary, but Rousseau went further: he partially rejected the sovereignty of reason itself. 'Too often reason deceives us, we have only too many grounds for dissenting from it; but conscience never deceives; it is man's true guide; it is to the soul what instinct is to the body; whoever follows it obeys nature.'[5] God existed for those who *felt* He existed. This was a convenient argument, and one that Christians could use. The Methodists used it. But it had no objective validity, and those reared on rationalism preferred more traditional proofs. Typical was Thomas Paine, who had an autodidact's capacity for announcing what others considered old-fashioned or obvious with unusual clarity. Reason proved, he proclaimed in *The Age of Reason* (1794), that 'the only religion that has not been invented, and that has in it every evidence of divine originality, is pure and simple Deism.'[6] But he and all other later deists except English Unitarians (who persisted in believing that they could reject Christ's divinity yet remain Christians) shared with Rousseau the conviction that natural religion and Christianity had nothing in common. 'Of all the systems of religion that ever were invented,' Paine asserted,[7] 'there is none more derogatory to the Almighty, more unedifying to man, more repugnant to reason, and more contradictory in itself, than this thing called Christianity.'

One thing however all believers in a God, Christian or otherwise, did agree on: society needed religion to keep it together. Rousseau was certain that it was a natural and necessary corollary of civil society. His most notorious disciple, Robespierre, horrified by the chaos which seemed to accompany

---

[4] 'Profession de foi' in R. Grimsley (ed.), *Rousseau's Religious Writings* (1970), 157.
[5] Ibid. 153–4.
[6] *The Age of Reason*, in P. S. Foner (ed.), *The Life and Major Writings of Thomas Paine* (1945), 600.
[7] Ibid.

the 'dechristianization' of 1793, sought to buttress the return of order with his 'cult of the Supreme Being'. No well-ordered or virtuous society, he believed, could be made up of atheists. Yet this proposition had been open to doubt at least since the time of Bayle, who delighted in extolling atheism's paradoxical potential for virtue. Atheists among Bayle's contemporaries kept quiet, but they did exist. The most notorious (though not until after his death in 1729) was the French country priest Jean Meslier. Outwardly orthodox while he lived, he left a voluminous manuscript which bitterly denounced the whole apparatus of religion, which he saw as nothing more than a device by which some men are able to dominate others. He saw no proof that God existed, and too much evil in the world to believe that He ever could. This so-called *Testament* was prominent among the clandestine literature circulating in manuscript in France in the first half of the century. In the 1760s Voltaire published extracts from it, after his own faith in a benevolent God had been shattered by the Lisbon earthquake of 1755.

This natural calamity was a turning-point in eighteenth century thought. On 1 November an earthquake and a series of tidal waves destroyed Lisbon, and as a result perhaps 15,000 people died. It was difficult to go on believing that a world in which such events were possible was one in which all was for the best. The earthquake was the final death blow to the cosmic optimism propounded by Leibniz and Pope. To Voltaire it demonstrated God's callous indifference. To others it suggested that He did not exist at all, confirming the suggestions of a growing band of bold thinkers, such as the physician La Mettrie, whose *Man a Machine* (1747) and *Man a Plant* (1748) outraged even *philosophes* by their open materialism. God might exist, La Mettrie said, but since there is no way of knowing, He is irrelevant to human affairs. Men are machines, sensation is their motive power, they have no immortal souls. By the 1750s Diderot too had progressed to the ultimate conclusion that God positively did not exist, though he rejected the blind and deterministic materialism of La Mettrie. And Diderot converted the most notorious atheist of all, d'Holbach, to the views he spent much of his later life propagating. D'Holbach conducted a Paris salon throughout the last thirty years of the old regime, which was the nerve-centre of French atheism. He also produced a stream of books and pamphlets, unceremoniously pillaging Meslier, against Christianity, deism, and indeed all religion. His best-known work, the *System of Nature* (1770) proclaimed that only matter and motion existed, that both were eternal and therefore had no need of a creator.

So a small but growing number of thinkers, increasingly openly, were rejecting not only Christianity but also any religion as the century went on. They carried doctrines of natural religion, evolved from Locke's psychology, to what opponents of 'philosophy' justifiably saw as their logical conclusion. Rousseau, who did not accept Locke's psychology, disclaimed any part in this. By the time he wrote *Emile* Locke had been refuted, although more conventional men preferred not to admit it. Rousseau proposed alternatives to Locke, but he had not demolished him. That privilege fell to David Hume.

The Foundations Destroyed: Hume

Hume constructed no system; he simply showed that the accepted system of his day led nowhere. He had the most penetrating critical intelligence of the century, yet with complete orthodoxy he accepted that reason and experience were the only keys to knowledge. His achievement was to demonstrate that even they produced no certainty, that the assumptions upon which the Enlightenment based its thinking led to a dead end.

His fundamental work, the *Treatise of Human Nature*, later revamped as the *Inquiry concerning Human Understanding*, was first published in 1738. It carried the psychological principles of Locke to their logical conclusions. Berkeley had argued that, on Lockean principles, matter could not be shown to exist; only mind was self-evident. Hume contended that not even the existence of mind itself could be convincingly demonstrated; the only sure reality was an unending stream of *impressions*, whose true nature was beyond comprehension, but without which the idea of mind had no meaning. Nor was there any logical proof, in a world in which only impressions certainly existed, that any thing was the cause of anything else. Causality was a mere inference from phenomena repeatedly occurring together. Hume pointed out that this proved nothing. The principles of knowledge used by all advanced thinkers until Rousseau were thus shown to be fundamentally unsound.

Needless to say, the demonstration of the inadequacies of reason and experience was also fatal to any idea of reasonable religion. Hume spent much of his later life elaborating criticisms of religion, which all stemmed from his original arguments. If there was no proof that mind existed, how much less was there of any such thing as an immortal soul? If causality was nothing more than conjunction, the Argument from Design, which assumed that all things require a cause, collapsed. Besides, it was ultimately based on the analogy of the temporal world, which bore no necessary resemblance to any sphere in which an omniscient, almighty, Supreme Being might move. These were the lines clearly advanced in Hume's *Dialogues Concerning Natural Religion*, written in the 1750s but not published until 1779, when he had been dead and safe from attack for three years. They exposed the weakness of arguing, like Butler, from analogy and more generally showed up natural religion for the vague and inconsistent compromise that it was. Hume could hardly, then, be expected to defend revealed religion, and in his essay *Of Miracles* he disposed of the strongest evidence for that, too. The notion of a miracle was repugnant to reason—'no testimony for any kind of miracle ever amounted to a probability, much less to a proof.'[8] Yet Christianity could not be reasonably believed without miracles. This did not make Hume an atheist. He once told an indignant d'Holbach that he did not believe there was any such thing. Rather he was a profound sceptic. Religion was 'a riddle, an aenigma, an inexplicable mystery. Doubt, uncertainty, suspense of judgment appear the only result of our most accurate scrutiny, concerning this subject.'[9]

---

[8] *Essays* (1903 edn.), 540.
[9] *The Natural History of Religion*, ed. H. E. Root (1965), 76.

But suspense of judgement still meant suspense of belief, whether in Nature's God or the more specific mysteries of Christianity.

Not surprisingly Hume's contemporaries found it hard to accept that he had demolished the whole intellectual foundation of their age yet offered nothing concrete to replace it. Since he embarrassed them, they ignored him. His *Treatise*, he recalled in famous words, 'fell *dead-born from the press*'[10] and his other philosophical works fared only slightly better. Presbyterian divines warned Scottish congregations against him, and he only became widely known in England when he took to writing the *History of England*. Even this work proved controversial for its sympathy to the Stuarts. By the 1760s he was celebrated in France as a foe of religion, but Condillac retained authority on the subject of human understanding. In Spain he was chiefly known for his economic essays, while in Germany he remained almost unknown until discovered and elevated by Kant into an opponent deserving demolition in his turn. Kant and Rousseau were Hume's true successors; not because either carried his ideas forward but because they both set out in directions which avoided the dead end to which he had brought philosophy. Both did so, in their very different ways, by rejecting what Hume had accepted from Locke— the impossibility of innate ideas. For Rousseau, conscience was innate; for Kant, rejecting Hume in his *Critique of Pure Reason* (1780), the mind had an innate capacity for imposing intelligibility upon the messages it received through the senses. Yet the immediate influence of both was limited. Kant was no *philosophe*; he was a dry academic writing for his own kind. Rousseau fell out with every major thinker he met and remained more talked about than understood. Meanwhile the conventional Enlightenment ground on, with enough apparent worldly success to prevent it from seriously facing the awkward questions about its own outlook that these lonely figures had raised.

Toleration

Even religious toleration, that unanimous aspiration of enlightened thinkers, did not always owe its progress to them. Between 1660 and 1685 it was positively in retreat. The English parliament restored Anglican uniformity, persecuted dissenters, and baulked attempts by Charles II to abrogate intolerant laws. Louis XIV systematically undermined the legal safeguards enjoyed by the French Huguenots, culminating in 1685 with the revocation of their guarantee of toleration, the Edict of Nantes. In Russia a government wedded to the Nikonian reforms ruthlessly persecuted recalcitrant Old Believers. Only in the Dutch republic, with its decentralized constitution and evenly divided confessional groups, did toleration persist; but when Spinoza dared to praise his native land for this,[11] most contemporaries saw in such praise only one more reason to condemn him.

Yet 1685 was a turning-point. The persecution of the Huguenots outraged Protestant opinion and even many Catholics were unenthusiastic. Bayle had already fled to Rotterdam, from where he was to preach ceaselessly the

---

[10] 'My Own Life', in *Essays*, 608.

[11] *Tractatus Theologico-Politicus*, ch. XX.

virtues of toleration; and at the height of the crisis, Locke in his Dutch exile produced the influential *Letter Concerning Toleration*. The effect of the revocation in England did much to unite Protestants in the face of James II's attempts to divide them, and the regime which succeeded his publicly abandoned religious intolerance in the Toleration Act of 1689. In fact the concession was limited to freedom of worship for Protestant dissenters. All non-Anglicans remained excluded from positions of power or influence, and until 1714 persistent efforts were made to circumscribe their position still further. Laws against Catholics, meanwhile, were reinforced, with a savage penal code in Ireland, which attempted to deprive the huge Catholic majority of all access to wealth or influence. Nevertheless there was now more toleration under the British crown than under most others, a fact which, underlined by the prestige of Locke, impressed contemporaries. From 1727 the remaining civil disabilities of Protestant dissenters were suspended from year to year. 'If there were only one religion in England,' observed Voltaire,[12] 'despotism would be to be feared; if there were two, they would cut each other's throats; but there are thirty, and they live together in peace and happiness.'

The revocation of the Edict of Nantes affected every Protestant state in which Huguenot exiles settled, above all the Dutch republic and Brandenburg. They witnessed not only the pathetic prospect of refugees from a brutal persecution, but also, in time, some striking economic results. The Huguenots were skilled and industrious; 200,000 of them left France as a result of Louis's policies, carrying their skills with them, setting up prosperous communities wherever they went, and often importing techniques hitherto unknown. Governments were impressed, as much by France's apparent loss as by their own gain. In reality the impact of the persecution on the French economy was not as serious as many contemporaries or subsequent historians believed.[13] But the belief was what counted. The lesson was clear: toleration was good for an economy. When Voltaire sought a scene to epitomize the blessings of toleration in England, he chose the Stock Exchange.

Practical arguments of this sort did far more than abstract moralizing to promote toleration. Only church-dominated states, such as Salzburg whose prince archbishop expelled 17,000 Protestants in 1732, remained immune to their appeal. Frederick II certainly did not; indeed he had an extra practical incentive from 1742, when half a million Catholics had become his subjects with the conquest of Silesia. But Frederick was genuinely indifferent to confessional divisions and had the example of industrious Huguenot settlers to underline the economic benefits. So in its turn Prussia became an example of toleration, followed by the Austrian empire in 1781. Joseph II had already done much to curb the persecution that his mother would cheerfully have authorized during their co-regency, and now granted freedom of worship to all denominations except those who, he claimed, did not know what they believed—deists, of all people. Even Catherine of Russia urged her

---

[12] *Lettres philosophiques*, Letter VII.
[13] See W. C. Scoville, *The Persecution of the Huguenots and French Economic Development 1680–1720* (1960).

ill-fated law-reform commission of 1767 to institute 'a *prudent Toleration* of other Religions, not repugnant to our orthodox Religion and Polity',[14] and although nothing came of that, the empress ceased to persecute the Old Believers.

In France the remaining Huguenots went relatively unmolested after the bitter war of the Languedoc Camisards. But periodic outbursts of anti-Protestant feeling did occur, during one of which, in 1761, a Toulouse Protestant called Calas was accused of murdering his son to prevent his conversion to Rome. When, on plausible enough evidence, Calas was executed, Voltaire, convinced that it was an example of the worst religious intolerance and bigotry, launched a spectacular propaganda campaign to rehabilitate his name by securing the reversal of the verdict. After twelve pamphlets and one full-scale *Treatise on Toleration* (1764), he finally succeeded in 1765. The Sirven case (1762–75), another alleged murder by Protestants to prevent apostasy, and that of La Barre (1766), when a reader of his own *Philosophical Dictionary* was executed for blasphemy, involved Voltaire in further energetic campaigns. Although these contributed to the spread of opinion favourable to toleration in France, the government still trod with extreme caution. Not until 1787 did it propose to grant civil status to Protestants. Even then the clergy and much of the populace were hostile.

The most forceful argument then advanced was that the Protestants had proved, by a century of tranquillity, that they were good citizens and loyal subjects. Similar arguments were proposed in favour of Catholic relief in England and Ireland in the 1770s and 1780s. They were impressive, but hardly logical. One reason for submissiveness had undoubtedly been the very comprehensive severity of the penal laws. They demonstrated that intolerance could be very effective in dispelling the political threat originally presented by nonconformity. Now, when the laws were relaxed, as in France or Ireland during the early 1790s, the result was to draw the dissidents back into politics in an attempt to progress beyond toleration to equality. This in turn rekindled deep-rooted popular sectarian hostility among the dominant groups and helped to promote a new intolerance.

So toleration triumphed slowly, partially, and ambiguously. In 1789 it had still to extend its blessings to much of Italy and the Iberian peninsula. Even where governments were convinced, their subjects were frequently less malleable; popular prejudices were not changed by laws. Besides, hardly anybody advocated a toleration without limits. Professed atheists remained rare and profoundly suspect; Joseph II still punished deists; and even the most illustrious *philosophes* such as Diderot, d'Holbach, and Voltaire, were unable to rise above the universal popular hatred of the Jews. Judaism was an exclusive religious sect; it seemed no better, and possibly worse, than Christianity itself in its 'fanaticism' and 'superstition'. Germany produced more enlightenment in this respect. The single example of Moses Mendelssohn, a believing Jew yet a disciple of Leibniz who sat at the very centre of the Enlightenment

[14] 'Instruction to the Commissioners,' no. 495, in W. F. Reddaway (ed.), *Documents of Catherine the Great* (1931), 289.

in Berlin, inspired Lessing to celebrate Jewish wisdom in *Nathan the Wise* (1779), and the Prussian diplomat Dohm to advocate full civil equality for Jews in *On the Civic Improvement of the Jews* (1781). But the criticism aroused by such works was intense and Joseph II's emancipation of Jews in his territories was an example not followed elsewhere in Germany until some time later. Even then it is hard to see whether emancipation did not promote rather than diminish popular anti-semitism.

Education

To legalize toleration was of little benefit if children were still taught at school that intolerance was a virtue. Enlightenment could hardly progress far if education continued to inculcate the principles of 'prejudice', 'superstition', and 'fanaticism' to which it was most opposed.

Philosophes, though aware of this, were also aware that it was an extremely dangerous subject. 'The art of forming men', wrote the financier and amateur philosopher Helvétius, 'is in all countries so closely linked to the form of government, that it is perhaps not possible to make any considerable change in public education without making one in the very constitution of states.'[15] This was so true that for many years few were prepared to join Helvétius in advocating general educational reform and in being prepared to face the consequences. Locke's brief *Some Thoughts Concerning Education* (1693) and Condillac's heavy and cumbersome *Course of Studies* (1775) were both based on the idea, utopian for all but a few, of individual tuition. Their own experience as teachers was confined to this. D'Alembert in the *Encyclopedia* explicitly declared that individual and private tuition was superior to any public system.[16] The most influential work on education of the century, Rousseau's *Emile* (1762) was rooted in the assumption that man, born innocent, is corrupted by the unnatural ways of society and that therefore the best education must take place in isolation. Thousands among the literate and privileged had their lives warped in subsequent years by attempts to bring them up, like Emile, according to nature; but happily only they could afford it. Most of those (still a minority) who received any formal education did so collectively, in public institutions. About these the *philosophes* had much less to say: they deplored their domination by the clergy, but generally agreed that it was impossible to eliminate clerics or theology entirely. They did however suggest that religious subjects should be approached late, when the judgement was fully formed. There was also general agreement that schools should lay more emphasis on learning by experience rather than by rote, and on more practical subjects like mathematics and the sciences.

Piecemeal changes along similar lines were made in the early eighteenth century, with little debt to philosophic thought. Often those who introduced them were extremely hostile to change, seeking to produce more, not fewer, religious minds. In England, while the traditional grammar and public schools and the two universities remained Anglican and hide-bound in the classics and

---

[15] *De l'esprit* (1758), Discours 4, ch. XVII.
[16] Art. *Collège*.

theology, private dissenting academies offered an education that was non-conformist but strong in mathematics, geography, and elementary science. In north Germany the Pietist university of Halle, with its attendant schools, inspired many other institutions to adopt its vernacular learning and diminish the role of theology. In Catholic south Germany, the Habsburg dominions, and Poland, the late seventeenth century saw the spread of the Piarists, a teaching order which laid special emphasis on mathematical skills. Admittedly the leader of Piarist education in Poland, Stanislas Konarski, had read and absorbed Locke and Montesquieu, but neither his intention nor that of his order was to undermine faith. The syllabus of Konarski's Warsaw College for Young Gentlemen, founded in 1740, was largely vernacular and strongly scientific. By the 1760s even the Piarists' most formidable rivals, the Jesuits, had adopted many features of the teaching pioneered in this school. In France the Oratorians catered to a growing minority of the rich who sought more than the old Jesuit prescription of classical languages and theology. They offered classical literature rather than language, more history, more mathematics, and although their theology tended to be rigorist and sometimes Jansenistic, there was less of it. Both Montesquieu and d'Alembert were products of Oratorian colleges.

On the other hand Voltaire, Diderot, Helvétius, and most of the other French *philosophes* who (unlike Rousseau) had received a formal education, had received it from the Jesuits. They were a living warning to those who (like Helvetius himself) believed in the limitless power of education to mould minds; for in them the Jesuits had clearly failed. Or had they? In so far as the Jesuits were the self-appointed champions of orthodoxy and of ecclesiastical involvement in politics they were certainly their enemies. The persistent attacks of the Jesuit *Journal de Trévoux* on the *Encyclopedia* showed that the feeling was reciprocated. Yet *philosophes* also recognized from personal experience that the Jesuits, emphasizing the importance of human reason, had a certain breadth of approach. They were, said d'Alembert, 'accommodating people as long as you do not show that you are their enemies, [who] give you some freedom of thought. The Jansenists, without consideration or enlightenment, want you to think like them; if they were the masters, they would exercise the most violent inquisition over work, mind, speech and morals.'[17] *Philosophes* attacked the church, but as d'Alembert implied, the Jesuits had far more to fear from Jansenists.

Yet neither, alone, brought about the collapse of the Jesuits between 1759 and 1773. They fell, not through attacks on their involvement in politics, but through that involvement itself. Pombal expelled them from Portuguese territories after they had resisted his attempts to impose royal authority on their theocratic sub-state in Paraguay. His example came at a moment when the French Jesuits were about to appeal to the *parlement* of Paris in a case arising from the bankruptcy of their trading house in Martinique. The magistrates, long-standing enemies of Jesuit ultramontanism, took the

[17] *On the Destruction of the Jesuits in France*, quoted in R. Grimsley, *Jean d'Alembert (1717–1783)* (1963), 187.

opportunity to investigate the whole constitution of the order and found it subversive. Subsequently they persuaded the government to ban the society from France entirely (1764). Spain, Naples, and Parma rapidly followed the example; Clement XIV was elected in 1769 on the clear understanding that, as soon as circumstances were favourable, he would dissolve it.

The fall of the Jesuits in 1773 was the most important educational event of the century. Around 1750 they had numbered 22,000, of whom 15,000 taught the children of the ruling orders in 669 colleges and 163 seminaries throughout Catholic Europe and South America.[18] These bodies were now dissolved, their assets confiscated, their staffs either scattered or deported. How were they to be replaced? Faced with this practical opportunity, *philosophes* suddenly became deeply interested in education. La Chalotais, procurator-general of the *parlement* of Rennes and author of perhaps the most eloquent judicial report against the Jesuits, produced in 1763 an *Essay on National Education*. The title suggested the theme—that the gap left by the Jesuits should be filled by a uniform, nationally organized system of secondary education, staffed by nationally qualified teachers using officially approved textbooks. Ecclesiastics were to be largely excluded from teaching and religion was to be a matter of instruction outside school only. Meanwhile Helvétius was inspired to follow up the scandalous success of his *Of Mind* (1758) which contained the seeds of his educational ideas, with a sequel, *Of Man, his intellectual faculties and his education*, published posthumously in 1772. Lockean principles, he believed, logically implied that men were born equal, and that their subsequent inequality was largely the result of differing circumstances, the most important being the type of education they received. By control of this, inequality itself might be controlled; indeed, Helvétius believed that 'Education can do anything.' Religion should be rigorously excluded from education, and only laymen should be licensed teachers. Diderot was predictably less optimistic. In his *Plan of a University* (1773) he advocated a secondary education based almost entirely on the sciences until its last stages, but reluctantly conceded that some consideration of religion could not be eliminated. National co-ordination and organization were essential. Rousseau too stressed this in his *Considerations on the Government of Poland* (1772), in which the utopianism of *Emile* was set aside. He suggested that Poland needed to assert and define her national character, and that a national educational system under a central board of guardians was the best means.

When this actually happened in Poland, however, it owed little to Rousseau's advice. By 1773 the Jesuits had already modernized their teaching under Konarski's influence. Upon their disappearance their extensive estates were confiscated and put at the disposal of a Commission of Education entrusted with the organization of a national system implementing the reformed principles more fully, exactly as Rousseau had advocated. The 'national'

[18] Figures derived from E. Préclin and E. Jarry, *Les Luttes politiques et doctrinales aux XVIIe et XVIIIe siècles*, Vol. 19 (ii) of A. Fliche and V. Martin, *Histoire de l'Église* (1956), 683–4.

character of the instruction given by these schools was vividly reflected in the 'patriotic' revolts of the 1790s.

It was ironic that France, the home of so many educational plans, never profited from the opportunity presented by the fall of the Jesuits. Seven of their eighty-six colleges were taken over by their old rivals, the Oratorians. Others were put under municipal control, or grafted on to other failing institutions. But there was no plan of any sort. In 1766 the university of Paris introduced a competitive qualifying examination, the *agrégation*, designed to produce better teachers, but no other steps were taken. The opportunity was missed. French education remained chaotic and unco-ordinated until beyond the Revolution; and it is interesting that the generation which made and guided that Revolution grew to maturity in such conditions.

Even in Spain more was done. Charles III's government replaced the Jesuit domination of schools and universities with close supervision of its own. It banned Jesuit works and doctrines and prescribed the teaching of anti-papal views, with much talk of education being a public service. This was far from shaking the clerical grip on Spanish education, but at least enough controversy was created to prompt thought. The most spectacular results occurred in the Habsburg dominions where, thanks to the protection of Maria Theresa, the declining power of the Jesuits did not disappear until their general dissolution in 1773. By then widespread educational reforms were already under consideration and only the total impossibility of replacing the thousands of clerics who still dominated education at all levels prevented a bold secularization of the whole system. Laymen of anti-clerical views were introduced into key university chairs, while syllabus reform diminished the role of theological and classical studies in favour of what was useful to the future bureaucrats whom the government believed the universities were there to educate— German and other modern languages, law, political science. Mathematics, history, and geography were introduced into school curricula and the first steps taken towards setting up a universal system of compulsory education. Released from the brake of his mother's prejudices, after 1780 Joseph II pushed such reforms much further. All teaching orders except the Piarists were now dissolved. By 1790 a greater proportion of children were at primary school in the Austrian domains than in any other part of continental Europe. But Joseph's watchword was utility; and although children would be better subjects if provided with the elementary skills of reading and writing, over-education should be avoided. Accordingly the teaching of non-practical subjects declined dramatically and so did the number of secondary schools and universities. Fees were pitched prohibitively high so as to discourage any aspirants to education for its own sake. Religious precepts were still taught, although now their precise content was determined by the state, with a view to confirming the subject's submissiveness. None of the small clique of fervent anti-clericals around Joseph questioned the utility of this: religious education clearly had some use, after all.

To non-Catholic rulers this was a truism. Frederick II, personally indifferent, believed that children must be instructed in religion if in nothing else. Under him Bible-based elementary education spread in Prussia, but higher education enjoyed a status as ambiguous as it did under Joseph, supported by the state almost exclusively as a nursery for bureaucrats. In Russia education in the western sense simply did not exist—despite Peter I's grandiose plans for universal elementary instruction—outside a few metropolitan institutions catering for the nobility. In 1786 Catherine decreed the establishment of a new elementary system, and in the next fifteen years the number of schools in Russia doubled. Even so, in 1795 they still hardly numbered over 1,000, a derisory number for a population so huge, and although the more advanced taught modern subjects, they also reserved a sizeable amount of syllabus time for 'a reasonable understanding of the Creator and His holy law'.[19] The same could be said, curiously, of the most thorough, universal, and efficient educational system in Europe, that of Scotland. Its object was to produce a Christian nation, with the church, in the form of local presbyteries, exercising a final veto on all teachers and subject-matter. Later in the century the foundation of independent private academies was to demonstrate a certain dissatisfaction with this state of affairs. Yet neither free discussion nor enlightenment were seriously hampered by ecclesiastical involvement in the educational system, as the scale and quality of the Scottish Enlightenment amply showed. *Philosophes* tended to forget that education in religion gave alert minds something taxing to argue against.

Towards Utility

Of all the church's ways, none incensed *philosophes* more than monasticism. Monks and nuns were idle and unproductive; they hoarded wealth, and, being sworn to celibacy, they did nothing to increase the population. Their uselessness was continuously laboured throughout the *Encyclopedia*. 'The prodigious number of *monasteries*', wrote Jaucourt, author of a quarter of the whole work and therefore typifying its general view, 'which has continued to subsist in the Catholic church, has become a charge on the public, oppressive and manifestly promoting depopulation; it is enough to glance at Protestant and Catholic countries to be convinced of it. Commerce enlivens the one, and monasteries bring death to the other.'[20] Diderot shared this view; but in his novel *The Nun* (1768, but unpublished in his lifetime) he went beyond his philosophic colleagues to attack the pernicious effect of monastic life on the individual character. It was true that few regular orders were totally contemplative. Many were involved in education and most dispensed some form of charity. But neither religious education nor charity impressed their enemies, in whose eyes the one promoted superstition, the other idleness. Only those orders that ran hospitals and asylums sometimes found themselves exempted from general criticisms; but equally often ardent critics overlooked their special contribution.

Hostility to monasticism was far older than the Enlightenment. Nor did

[19] Quoted in P. Dukes, *Catherine the Great and the Russian Nobility* (1967), 242.
[20] Art. *Monastère*.

it take philosophic propaganda to alert governments to the pernicious effects of too many religious. Colbert grimly noted that there were no monks in Holland and England; in 1666 he forbade the founding of new communities without royal permission and suppressed all those founded in the previous three decades. In fact, the great Counter-Reformation expansion in religious orders was already losing its momentum in France, although in Germany, torn by warfare earlier in the century, it continued in full vigour until the end of the century. After 1700 the monastic population ceased to expand—in France by 1750 it was positively on the decline. Such trends had the paradoxical effect of highlighting the abuses of the system: huge accumulations of landed wealth in the hands of underpopulated spiritual corporations, especially when they were exempt from taxation, seemed increasingly intolerable. Everywhere governments moved against mortmain, and the ease with which the Jesuits were dissolved suggested even more radical policies. The French church, thoroughly alarmed, established a 'Commission of Regulars' to put its own house in order; between 1766 and 1784 it dissolved 426 religious houses, made access to vows more difficult and abandonment easier, and even wound up certain minor orders. The main victims were contemplatives: preaching, teaching, and charitable foundations, all performing useful functions, survived a policy which derived more ideological inspiration from the Jansenistic self-esteem of the secular clergy than from the criticisms of pagan philosophers. But elsewhere governments took direct action without consulting the church. In Russia in 1764 Catherine confiscated all ecclesiastical property; thenceforth its revenues were administered by a 'College of Economy' which paid stipends to the clergy. At the same time many monasteries were completely dissolved by the monarch who proclaimed to Voltaire that her motto was 'Utility'.[21] The archbishop-elector of Mainz dissolved monasteries in the 1780s in order to increase the endowments of his city's university. Above all, Joseph II shared his chancellor Kaunitz's belief that 'the many thousands of monks could be replaced by a few hundred secular clergy and priests actively concerned with the cure of souls.'[22] Kaunitz had already hedged the monasteries about with restrictive regulations before Joseph attained sole power, but after 1780 a frontal attack was mounted. In the space of a few years, with the dissolution of 700 houses belonging to contemplative orders in the Habsburg domains, the monastic population fell by nearly two-thirds. Only orders performing a public service, such as the Piarists, remained. Abandoned monastic buildings were turned to public use, sales of monastic property helped to finance the emperor's educational reforms and institutions of public charity. Undoubtedly one motive was a Colbertian desire to remove a dead weight from the economy; the influence of German and Flemish Jansenists also played its part. But if anything was owed to the writings of *philosophes*, they were Italian rather than French, their influence penetrating through Lombardy.

[21] 11–22 Aug. 1765. Quoted in Reddaway, *Documents of Catherine the Great*, 4.
[22] 21 June 1770. Quoted in T. C. W. Blanning, *Joseph II and Enlightened Despotism* (1970), 128.

Most notable was that of the historian Muratori, himself a priest, who preached moral rebirth through a Christianity that wasted nothing on display, but was economical, practical, benevolent, and utilitarian.

Whether or not the decline of the cloister was their doing, *philosophes* could only applaud it. Monasticism derived its justification ultimately from the doctrine of original sin—that men are born irremediably evil, with the implication that since little can be done to improve human society, the holiest withdraw from it. The Enlightenment rejected such a view; no qualities, let alone inherited evil, were innate. Thus men and society were capable of infinite improvement. The touchstone of morality ceased to be what was least offensive to God; it became what was most useful to Man. On this criterion monasticism lacked any justification. Yet the view was not necessarily unchristian. A renewed emphasis on practical religion, benevolence, and good works had characterized all Christian sects since the Reformation. Few of the regular Catholic orders founded during the Counter-Reformation had been primarily contemplative. So the utilitarianism of the Enlightenment grew up in an atmosphere already sympathetic.

Implicit in Enlightenment thought from the start, the principle of utility was slow to develop into a conscious criterion for judging everything. Its progress can be vividly seen, for example, in the evolution of prize-essay subjects announced by academies. Literary and theoretical subjects which had dominated earlier in the eighteenth century were completely outnumbered in the 1780s by practical subjects concerning agriculture, technology, and social problems. The *Encyclopedia*, with its philosophical essays side by side with expositions of technical matters, stood in this as in so much else at the crossroads. The shattering of Leibnizian optimism by mid-century natural calamities upset any idea that a benevolent nature had ordained a world where all was for the best; it was as good, and only as good, as men could make it. Not only the Lisbon earthquake played its part here. A catastrophic famine in southern Italy in 1764, for instance, turned the attention of Neapolitan radical thinkers away from the traditional sniping at the church towards the urgent practicalities controlling food supplies. At the same time the ever-growing pressure of taxation, and the social problems it gave rise to, promoted renewed speculation on questions of economics and the expansion of wealth. Attacks on monastic wealth and privileges were only the first stage. By the late 1750s the whole science of modern economics was being born in the writings of the physiocrats, who adopted the propagandizing methods of the *philosophes* in the firm conviction that their science would be useful to their fellow men.

The theory of utility, when at last it came to be formulated explicitly, was derived inevitably from Locke, from his contention that the mainsprings of human action are the pursuit of pleasure and avoidance of pain. With God non-existent or at best non-interfering, these principles clearly implied that good equalled nothing more than pleasure, and evil no more than pain. Morality was a matter of results rather than motives. What was good was merely what men found useful, that is to say pleasurable. The first to expand at length on this theme was Helvétius, that believer in the formative power of circumstances, who declared in 1758 that 'Customs. . .have always found their source in the real or at least apparent utility of the public.'[23] Absurd customs were merely those that had lost their original justification. In 1764 the Milanese Beccaria based a whole theory of criminal law on even more explicit utilitarian principles. Laws, he declared, in *Of Crimes and Punishments,* ought to be formulated by 'a cool examiner of human nature, who knew how to collect in one point, the actions of a multitude, and had this only end in view, *the greatest happiness of the greatest number*'.[24] Jeremy Bentham, still a student when Beccaria wrote, had already been inspired by Helvétius. In subsequent years, he made this principle the keystone of his philosophy of utility, which won the adherence of a whole school of English thinkers in the next century.[25]

Utilitarian morality was purely social. The main problem was how to reconcile individual with general happiness, pleasure, or utility. However it was to be done, there was at least general agreement on the means. It was to be through legislation. 'Morality', declared Helvétius, 'is a frivolous science if it is not compounded with politics and legislation.'[26] The most powerful circumstances moulding human character, and promoting an unnatural inequality, were the laws and institutions under which men lived. This was Montesquieu's contention too, but he had held that laws are in their turn conditioned by factors beyond human control, such as geography and climate. Helvétius rejected this: laws, though they conditioned human beings, were the product of men alone and could be changed by men according to their utility. The general good was best promoted by laws that penalized the excessive pursuit of individual good. The law was to be an instrument of social engineering. Rousseau, no utilitarian, devised a closely similar theory of political obligation. Setting out in his *Social Contract* (1762) to explain the paradox that 'Man was born free, and everwhere he is in chains',[27] he assigned to legislation the key task of achieving a balance between the body politic's infallible general will towards its own good and the shortsighted particular will of individuals, which blinded them to their deeper common interests. To Rousseau, obedience to a self-imposed law, in the form of the general will of political society, was true freedom; there was no anomaly in forcing people to be free.[28] There was no room in Rousseau's Utopia, any more than in Helvétius's, for social deviants. For him the state was perfectly justified in executing those who refused to conform to its laws and even—so far had principles evolved in a circle—to the religion established by law.

True utilitarians were not so sure. Pain being evil, its infliction by the law had few redeeming features, above all when it took the form of torture.

---

[23] *De l'esprit*, Discours 2, ch. XIII.

[24] *An Essay on Crimes and Punishments* (1767), Introduction, 2. The first formulation of the 'greatest happiness principle' in fact appeared in Hutcheson's *Enquiry Concerning Moral Good and Evil* (1725) § VIII.

[25] See the opening passages of *Introduction to the Principles of Morals and Legislation* (1789).

[26] *De l'esprit*, Discours 2, ch. XV.

[27] *Social Contract*, Bk. I, ch. 1.

[28] Ibid., Bk. I. ch. VII.

'It is', wrote Beccaria,[29] 'confounding all relations, to expect that...pain should be the test of truth, as if truth resided in the muscles and fibres of a wretch in torture.' All shades of enlightened opinion shared this hostility to torture. Bayle and the *Encyclopedia* condemned it; Voltaire campaigned ceaselessly against it. Its use in fact declined significantly as the century went on. In England (but not Scotland) it had largely disappeared some time before 1660; in Holland it had gone by 1700, though not formally abolished. It was abolished in Sweden in 1734, in Prussia in 1740, in Baden in 1767, in Saxony in 1770, in Denmark in 1771, and in Austria in 1776. France had to wait until 1788 for its final abolition, although it was restricted in 1781; but only Spain and Russia (notwithstanding Catherine's loud declarations of intent) among major states postponed abolition. Undoubtedly the endless preaching of *philosophes* played its part in this progress, especially the later stages. Yet the trend was already established long before the full flowering of the Enlightenment, owing most, it seems (like the decline in witchcraft prosecutions), to the dissatisfaction of legal authorities with its practical use in establishing reliable evidence. In the case of capital punishment, however, judiciaries were more cautious. Beccaria roundly denounced it, but found much less progress to applaud; far fewer were prepared to go with him beyond condemning simply the abuse of the death penalty. Only in Tuscany was the experiment of total abolition made, but within a few years it was felt necessary to reintroduce it. Elsewhere, there was some progress in reducing the number of capital crimes. Even where, as in England, the number grew, there was an even greater rise in the number of convicts reprieved.

Opponents and Nonconformists

By the 1760s the Enlightenment was becoming respectable. *Philosophes* may not have brought about most of the events they applauded, but could almost be excused for thinking that they had. Statesmen praised them, monarchs sought their advice. Catherine of Russia corresponded with Voltaire and Diderot—the latter visiting St. Petersburg at her invitation. Voltaire spent several years (1750–3) as Frederick's guest in Berlin and corresponded with him throughout their lives. D'Alembert advised Frederick on academic matters (though from the civilized distance of Paris). Academies throughout Europe were taken over by the adherents of Enlightenment. Even Pope Benedict XIV, a civilized and courteous man, was known to correspond with *philosophes*. In his later years Voltaire established himself on a lavish estate at Ferney near Geneva, where he played host to hundreds of curious travellers who made a point of passing through, some to talk with him, but most merely to listen and to stare at this modern Socrates. His last trip to Paris in 1778 was one long festival of triumph, the exhaustion of which probably did a good deal to bring about his death.

Yet to conquer kings, academies, capital cities, was not to conquer opinion. And public opinion remained hostile to much of what the *philosophes*

[29] *Essay on Crimes*, ch. XVI, 58.

stood for. For every bold new work to struggle to the light through the net of censorship, there were tens, sometimes hundreds, of refutations. Most, inevitably, emanated from the clergy. In France until the 1760s the Jesuit *Journal de Trévoux* was a monthly forum for criticism of all new ideas, subjecting the *Encyclopedia* in particular to minute scrutiny. The Jansenist *Ecclesiastical News* was also predictably hostile. For the less sophisticated, weekly sermons in their parish churches warned of the dangers of incredulity. In Protestant countries the sermons of such eloquent clerics as the Hamburg Pastor Goeze or Wesley did much to stiffen resistance to unbelief. To the learned still other clerics addressed massive works reaffirming the truths of religion, such as the *Notice to the Clergy on the Dangers of Incredulity* (1770) of Lefranc de Pompignan, archbishop of Le Puy; or the *Certainty of the Proofs of Religion* (1767) of Bergier, canon of Notre Dame, who from 1770 enjoyed an annual pension to encourage further writing in defence of the faith. In England William Warburton, bishop of Gloucester, defended revealed religion in *The Divine Legation of Moses* (1737–41) and later made celebrated attacks on the philosophy of Hume.

Clerics were not the only defenders of faith. Fréron's *Literary Year*, appearing from 1754 onwards, attacked Voltaire and the Encyclopedists with a vigour and ridicule matching their own. In 1757 Moreau gave the *philosophes* a scornful nickname, which stuck, in his *New Memoir to serve for the history of the Cacouacs*; and in 1760 they were characterized as little more than a noisy mutual admiration society in Palissot's satirical play *The Philosophers*. What scandalized the lawyer Linguet, who between 1777 and 1792 ran a journal of comments called *Political Civil and Literary Annals*, was the fanaticism and intolerance of the philosophic sect, which he considered worse than the religious varieties they denounced. The result of such persistent attacks was to attribute to the *philosophes* a conscious unity which in reality they had never had. Thus was born the legend of a philosophic plot to subvert the morals of European society. It was already implicit in the two volumes of *The Helviennes, or Philosophic Provincial Letters* (1781–88) of the Abbé Barruel, a contributor to Fréron's *Literary Year*, and was elaborated in 1797 in his *Memoirs to serve for the history of Jacobinism*, in which the whole of the French Revolution was attributed to a conspiracy of philosophers and freemasons. The most eloquent version of this legend came in Edmund Burke's *Reflexions on the Revolution in France* (1790). Burke spoke of a 'literary cabal', which 'had some years ago formed something like a regular plan for the destruction of the Christian religion', pursued 'by endeavouring to confine the reputation of sense, learning, and taste to themselves or their followers'.[30] In 1790 their critics had more concrete reasons for blaming them than before the French Revolution. Intellectual conservatism in the pre-revolutionary age is perhaps best exemplified by Samuel Johnson, critic, lexicographer, and aggressive conversationalist, a devout Christian constantly assailed by black doubts and ungrateful to those who fostered them: 'Rousseau, Sir, is a very

[30] *Everyman*, ed. 107–8.

bad man. I would sooner sign a sentence for his transportation, than that of any felon who has gone from the Old Bailey these many years... Sir, do you think him as bad a man as Voltaire?—Why, Sir, it is difficult to settle the proportion of iniquity between them.'[31]

But not all critics of the Enlightenment were conservatives. As time went on growing numbers began to conclude either that it had not gone far enough, or that, in pushing forward, it had taken false directions. The most celebrated was Rousseau himself. Although he began as a *philosophe*, befriended Diderot, and wrote articles for the *Encyclopedia*, his first major work, the prize discourse of 1753 on the question of whether the restoration of the arts and sciences had purified or corrupted morals, revealed his profound unorthodoxy. Rousseau proclaimed his faith in man's innate goodness or at least innocence —in itself a rejection of Lockean premisses. Far from being significant only in society, men were corrupted by society. No wonder that, believing this, Rousseau increasingly distrusted the worldly, sophisticated circles in which more and more *philosophes* moved. In the *Letter to d'Alembert* (1758) he made explicit his break with them by defending the right of his native republic of Geneva to prohibit theatres, a policy d'Alembert had criticized in his *Encyclopedia* article on the city. Theatres, for d'Alembert an essential sign of civilization, signified for Rousseau decadence and corruption. He spent the last twenty years of his life in rural retreats, his isolation increased by a pathological obsession that the world was conspiring against him. This was partly true: *philosophes* naturally felt injured by his attacks. Voltaire considered his writings books against the human race. Constituted authorities in 1762 believed that both *Emile* and the *Social Contract* were subversive of good order and public morals; they were condemned and Rousseau fled into exile. Johnson spoke not only for himself when he declared that such an avowed enemy of society deserved all that society did to him. Rousseau's mind was full of obvious contradictions, which his own repulsive self-righteousness often concealed from him. Yet there was no limit to the startling implications of his thought. In him, the conviction that nature was basically good survived the Lisbon earthquake; he dismissed Voltaire's disillusion by pointing out that but for society there would have been no Lisbon to destroy in the first place. Society perverted nature. Those who sought virtue should therefore attempt so far as was possible to reject social artificialities and conform to nature's dictates. Nor was reason required to ascertain what these were; natural instincts, embodied in conscience, were far more reliable guides. Such thinking was revolutionary in every sense of the term. It offered radical new criteria for the reformation of human institutions and, more dangerously, it offered seductive justifications for action: feeling and the emotions. No need henceforth to offer reasons for acting. Willing was apparently enough, and men were, presumably, entitled to what their infallible consciences told them they ought to have. This was far closer to Hobbes's version of the rights of man in the state of nature[32] than Rousseau would have cared to admit.

[31] J. Boswell, *The Life of Samuel Johnson LL.D.* (1791), 15 Feb. 1766.
[32] See below, p. 231–2.

If individual feelings, rather than universal reason, were the true main-springs of human activity, then the individual rather than society was what mattered. This was the central assumption of the outlook that was to take shape towards the end of the century as Romanticism. Rousseau did not create it, but more than anybody he appealed to the generation among whom it was to flower. Nowhere was his influence more profound than in Germany, where the aridity with which both rationalism and empiricism were taught recalled the Lutheran theology of the previous century and invited a similar emotional reaction. To those dissatisfied with German intellectual life Rousseau came as a prophet. 'Rousseau', Goethe recalled of his student days in Stras-bourg, 'had really touched our sympathies.'[33] Herder showed by constant, though critical, references, how formative Rousseau's influence had been; and Kant, already a mature scholar of high reputation, was completely bowled over when he first read *Emile*. Apart from his stress on the emotions, Rous-seau's emphasis on wild nature appealed to Germans absorbed in creating a poetry of 'storm and stress' under the influence of Herder's *Of German Race and Art* (1773). Above all, Rousseau symbolized opposition to the main-stream of the French Enlightenment, which to Germans meant quite simply French literature, in its turn symbolizing the French culture of Germany's ruling orders. If German culture was ever to assert itself, this French domina-tion must be overthrown. One way to do this was to decry the *philosophes* as the embodiment of the French spirit. For Herder no abuse seemed too extreme. 'Its age of literature is finished. . .', he wrote of France in 1769, 'the nation is living on the ruins. . .The taste for encyclopedias, dictionaries, extracts and spirits of the writing shows the lack of original writings. So does the taste for foreign writings.'[34] Nor was he entirely wrong. By 1770 the great names were ageing, their most important work behind them. Nobody comparable was emerging to take their place. By the mid-1780s Kant, in distant Königsberg, was the only indisputable literary and intellectual giant left in Europe; those who came closest to him were fellow Germans like Herder, Goethe, and Schiller. The French literary world, symbolized by the Academies, was by then under the domination of talents essentially mediocre and derivative, if they deigned to write at all. In their hands the ideas of the Enlightenment became stale with sterile repetition, yet they suppressed attempts to develop new directions by their control of learned societies and the world of publishing. *Philosophes* in power, especially the second-rate, had become as Linguet had predicted, quite as intolerant as the priests they felt so proud to have overthrown.

Flights of Fancy

The scientific revolution of the seventeenth century had been crucial to the origins of the Enlightenment, yet much of the eighteenth century saw nothing comparable in terms of scientific advance. It was in general a period of

---

[33] *Autobiography*, ii. 105.
[34] *Journal of my voyage in the year 1769*, in F. M. Barnard (ed.), *J. G. Herder on Social and Political Culture* (1969), 101.

consolidation and detailed correction rather than of dramatic breaks. Its triumphs were cumulative—for example, Buffon's *Natural History*, a massive work of biological classification which began to appear from 1749 and continued for forty years, which time and time again approached the threshold of evolutionary theory. In areas where the seventeenth century had seen no decisive reorientation, such as chemistry, the wildest speculation continued; controversy raged for decades about phlogiston, a supposed universal substance released by burning. The breakthrough came in the 1770s and 1780s with the French amateur Lavoisier, who, building on and synthesizing the work of British experimenters such as Black, Cavendish, and Priestley, discovered oxygen and laid the foundations of chemical classification of the elements. In 1783 he launched a general attack on phlogistical theories which established him as the Newton of chemistry. Yet the overthrow of phlogiston still took decades, because, as a universal yet invisible principle, it had impeccably Newtonian credentials. It was like the electricity revealed by the experiments of Volta and channelled by Franklin's lightning conductor; or like the universal fluid which, in the theories of the Austrian doctor Mesmer, conducted the world's life-force—magnetism. In Mesmer's view, obstructions in the flow of 'animal magnetism' were the source of most illnesses. They could be removed, and afflictions cured, by therapeutic sessions around tubs filled with iron filings and bottles of 'magnetized' water, to which patients attached themselves by grasping iron rods. So far was new science but old magic writ large, that such doctrines seemed perfectly credible. Mesmerism swept the fashionable world of France in the 1780s, claiming many 'cures'. Scarcely less successful was the self-styled Count Cagliostro, who between 1770 and 1789 made a comfortable living in the capitals of Europe by selling miraculous spells, potions, and philtres to credulous members of high society. There was no clear frontier between science and pseudo-science. Matters which, a century before, had fostered unbelief and scepticism, were by 1780 appealing equally to the growing romantic taste for the mysterious, the awe-inspiring, and the indefinable.

These symptoms of revolt from reason disturbed established authorities, both political and intellectual. Hitherto the church had monopolized mystery with its steadying hand, but the new fashions were harder to control. Cagliostro meddled in everything, was expelled from France in 1786, and died in a papal prison. An official commission of the Academy of Sciences (including Lavoisier and Franklin) investigated Mesmerism and pronounced it a hoax. But too many aspiring publicists and established public figures were committed to Animal Magnetism, and controversy continued until politics diverted everybody's attention in 1787. Even then it played its part: future revolutionary leaders (of one brand or another), such as Lafayette, d'Eprémesnil, Duport, Carra, Bergasse, and Brissot, had first met in defence of Mesmerism, and the hostility of established authorities pushed them into attitudes critical of the authorities themselves. Those struggling to make a living by writing and seeking fame by espousing new ideas, to whom official condemnation was a mortal blow, hated those bodies that propounded it. The disciples of Voltaire and Diderot who now peopled the academies and enjoyed comfortable perquisites seemed deliberately bent on excluding new talent and condemning new ideas deemed by their anxious propagators to be potentially of universal benefit to mankind. In this situation lay the origins of the hatred many poor writers bore the institutions of the old regime.

Most disturbing about Mesmerism was its tendency to organize itself into secret cells of initiates, the Societies of Harmony. Yet secret societies became highly fashionable in the course of the eighteenth century, as was shown by the success of Freemasonry, which first emerged from obscure English origins in the early part of the century. The masons who formed the Grand Lodge in London in 1717 and whose rules were codified in 1723, were a body dedicated to mutual self-help, philanthropy, and toleration, under the banner of deism but behind the veil of a secret set of rules and initiation rites. Masonic lodges were self-recruiting clubs, non-political, moderately Enlightened, but spiced with an element of mystery. Their most regular activites were purely convivial, however, and Masonry spread rapidly. 'By 1740 it was an accepted and well known feature of English life',[35] and had begun to spread elsewhere. By 1730 there were lodges in Paris and by 1789 there may have been as many as 50,000 French Freemasons, with lodges in every significant town. The 1730s also saw the start of particularly rapid progress in Germany and Italy. The movement was joined by leaders of society— monarchs such as the Emperor Francis I, Frederick of Prussia, and possibly even Louis XV, statesmen, innumerable noblemen, public officials, and even *philosophes* including Montesquieu, Voltaire, Helvétius, and d'Alembert. Masonry was not a popular movement but a fashion among the established, the comfortable, the respectable, 'people of quality'. It vaunted equality, but only for equals. However there is no doubt that (despite the doctrinal bickerings which created deep divisions for much of the century), it promoted benevolence and sociability and facilitated inter-provincial and international contacts. The cosmopolitanism of eighteenth-century culture owed it a distinct debt.

Nobody believed in mid-century that Freemasonry seriously threatened established institutions. It was true that the pope had condemned it in two separate bulls (1738 and 1751). Rome saw it as a spearhead of deism, and the masonic God, acknowledged by masons of all religions, certainly sounded like a lowest common denominator. But the bulls had no effect; not only Catholic laymen but also many priests continued to join lodges. Any society professing itself secret arouses suspicions, but Masonry was familiar enough to those in power to dispel most qualms. 'Everybody is in it,' wrote Queen Marie Antoinette in 1781; 'so everything that happens there is known: where then is the danger?'[36] More disturbing however was the rise of a number of quasi-masonic organizations, adopting the masonic form and its secrecy, but not

---

[35] J. M. Roberts, *The Mythology of the Secret Societies* (1972), 22, upon which the following account is almost exclusively based.
[36] Quoted in Roberts, op. cit. 168.

necessarily masonic ideals. The most notorious of these were the Bavarian Illuminati.

The Illuminati were founded in 1776 by Adam Weishaupt, a professor of law. Their object, though secret, was clear: to penetrate the institutions of the Bavarian state (perhaps the most orthodox in Catholic Europe) and bring about enlightened reform on a basis of social equality and anti-clericalism. Weishaupt's Bibles were the works of materialistic French pagans such as Helvétius and d'Holbach; he aimed at a direct involvement in politics which Freemasons had always avoided. The society prospered, however, and by 1780 its members had begun to penetrate Freemasonry itself, to become a sect within the sect; its influence had also spread beyond Bavaria's frontiers, notably to the Austrian domains. But by 1784 many of the secrets of the Illuminati had leaked out and the electoral government began to suspect that this secret order was simply a vehicle of Joseph II's ambition to annex Bavaria. It certainly professed aims for Bavaria that he was already implementing in his dominions. Consequently the government decided to ban all secret societies, and in 1785 Freemasons and Illuminati specifically. In 1787 a whole series of confiscated documents were published illustrating the extent of the 'plot' that had been thwarted.

A tremendous controversy ensued and was still going on when the French Revolution broke out. Its effect was to throw deep (and generally undeserved) political suspicion onto all Freemasons. In Germany the conspiracy served to confirm the growing romantic hostility to Enlightenment and all it stood for. Everywhere those who regretted the disappearance of the Jesuits asked themselves whether it had been the result of some more successful masonic plot. Suspicion bred credulity. In these circumstances when the French Revolution erupted, its opponents naturally rushed to conclude that it too was the result of a conspiracy of Freemasons. No doubt the accusation held a grain of truth, for no movement as widespread as Freemasonry in the France of the 1780s could be totally without significance. There certainly was a tendency for Freemasonry to involve itself in public issues, such as judicial crusades, slave emancipation, and the opposition of the *parlements* to the government. But none of this amounted to anything resembling an Enlightenment conspiracy. Indeed, the Freemasonry of the 1780s was as much touched by the flight from reason as its romantic critics. The mystical, ritualistic, and emotional impact of its rites grew more significant, and works such as Mozart's *Magic Flute* or his *Masonic Funeral Music* demonstrated the religious response it could evoke. Freemasons may have had little enough directly to do with the end of the old regime but, like Mesmerism, Gothick novels, 'storm and stress', and the religious revival which was to sweep intelligent circles in the 1790s, its mysteries were heralds of the end of the Enlightenment.

PUBLIC AFFAIRS

10. States and their Business

Before 1789 the idea of the state, as we understand it now, was only half-formulated. If, for instance, we define a state as an autonomous political unit recognizing no sovereign power over itself outside itself, then Europe had few indeed. Only non-Catholic countries were free of the jurisdictional claims of the pope. There were over 300 autonomous territories in Germany, far more than in the rest of Europe put together, but all technically subordinate parts of the Holy Roman Empire. Yet that shadowy structure in itself was not a state at all, since it had no real control over its hundreds of constituent parts. How, too, should we classify Hungary, Scotland before 1707, or Lorraine before 1768, where dynastic accidents had reduced their nominal independence to almost nothing? Rigorous modern definitions are seldom flexible enough to comprehend the diversity and complexity of old-regime political institutions.

Most states were geographically very small, the greatest number being concentrated in Germany, Switzerland, and to a lesser extent Italy. German and Italian states of greater size and importance, such as Naples, the papal dominions, Bavaria, Saxony, or Brandenburg–Prussia stood out among innumerable tiny principalities such as Parma, Baden, or Hesse, ecclesiastical lordships such as Cologne, Mainz, or Salzburg, and city republics such as Venice, Genoa, Lucca, Geneva, or Berne. East and west of this central strip of Europe small states had once existed, but by 1660 were largely absorbed into bigger and stronger political units. With the exception of Russia, most major states were still recognizably amalgams of smaller ones absorbed by military conquest, dynastic logic, or even mutual agreement. Their former independence was often recalled by the continued existence of peculiar institutions in provinces such as Catalonia, Scotland, Sicily, Brittany, or Bohemia. And the piecemeal way in which most large states had been built up was also reflected in some very untidy geography. The southern Netherlands, for example, ruled before 1713 by the king of Spain and afterwards by the emperor of Austria, were hundreds of miles from any of the other territories of either monarch. Until 1772 Prussia and Brandenburg were separated by a wide corridor of Polish territory, while their common ruler also had territories in Cleves and Mark on the Rhine, at the other end of Germany, and even at Neuchâtel, in Switzerland. The Dutch stadtholder was prince of Orange, an enclave in southern France. The pope ruled another enclave at Avignon. After 1714 the king of Great Britain was also elector of Hanover. Few European states had any obvious geographical, ethnic, or linguistic unity, nor was it widely felt that they should have. The power of states, however, did not depend on their size, or even on their wealth. The Dutch remained among the richest nations in Europe in the eighteenth century, but their international power shrank spectacularly; while Prussia became a great power on the most meagre of resources. The important thing was the use they made of their size and their resources—a matter of politics and constitutions.

No state had a 'constitution' in the modern sense of a single document containing all the fundamental rules for the state's functioning. The first such instrument was that dictated to the Swedish diet by Gustavus III in 1772. The first to be adopted by agreement was that of the United States, formulated in 1787, and that promulgated in 1791 by the French National Assembly. Before that time a constitution comprised not one document, but a collection of customs. 'By constitution,' wrote Bolingbroke in 1738, 'we mean, whenever we speak with propriety and exactness, that assemblage of laws, institutions and customs. . .directed to certain fix'd objects of public good, that compose the general system, according to which the community hath agreed to be govern'd.'[1] Yet most constitutions of the old regime suffered from the disadvantage that the 'objects of public good' were often not agreed. The fundamental character of the state, which modern constitutions are supposed to define, was always open to debate; it was never entirely clear which customs were fundamental and truly 'constitutional', and which could be changed. The modern notion of a constitution slowly emerged over the eighteenth century as a way to overcome these ambiguities. The 'written' constitutions of the United States and revolutionary France were designed to limit the power of governments to change the form of the state to suit their own convenience.

Forms of Government

Montesquieu, the most influential political writer of the eighteenth century, divided forms of government into three species: republics, monarchies, and despotisms.[2] Of these he clearly regarded republics as the most admirable but the least viable. They could only flourish, he thought, while they were small in area; and most of them in his time were little more than city states. Their systems of government were bafflingly diverse. Most of them took the form of councils or hierarchies of councils, with executive power always in the hands of more than one officer. This, it was believed, was the best way to ensure that a city's customs were not subverted by magistrates with monarchical ambitions. The respective roles and powers of the various councils, however, still gave rise to disagreement; conflicts on this issue tore Geneva apart in the 1730s, the 1760s, and the 1780s; the built-in weakness of the executive meant that since no party was able to carry a solution, outside powers were finally called in to impose one. Checks and balances were also the essence of the constitution in the two great mercantile republics of Venice and Genoa, both headed by a single elected executive officer, a doge. In both he was merely a figurehead with no freedom of action; real power in Venice lay with the senate, a body of 300, elected in turn by the great council of all nobles whose families were in the Golden Book; executive authority

---

[1] *A dissertation upon parties* (8th edn., 1754), 141.
[2] *Esprit des lois* (1748), Bk. II, ch. I.

belonged to officers nominated by the great council. The system was de-liberately designed to prevent any one of them from engrossing too much power. The results were impressive. Venice witnessed none of those inter-necine struggles that lacerated Geneva and sometimes Genoa. But the real political problem for Venice and Genoa was not so much the distribution of power within the city, as the relationship between the city and its exten-sive territories. Neither the Venetian *terraferma* stretching from the Adriatic up into the Alps, nor the Genoese island of Corsica had any say in the way they were ruled. As the eighteenth century went on the burghers of pros-perous *terraferma* towns such as Bergamo came increasingly to resent their powerlessness, while in Corsica a revolt broke out in 1729. Genoese control was never fully restored and a further revolt in the 1760s culminated in the island's annexation by France in 1768.

Republics were generally too small and their governments too weak to resist the designs of great powers. Those that had survived had done so largely as diplomatic pawns, with the exception of the Dutch republic, Europe's largest, wealthiest, and (in 1660) the only great power among them. The United Provinces were what Montesquieu called a 'confederate republic'[3] of nine territories. Eight were governed by estates, bodies of representatives nominated largely by the burgher oligarchies of the major towns. Executive power in the civil sphere was in the hands of an elected pensionary, while each province's military forces were commanded by a hereditary stadtholder who was, in five provinces, the prince of Orange. The government of the Republic as a whole was in the hands of the states-general—a body of deputies nominated by the estates of seven provinces—and a twelve-man council of state. There was no chief magistrate, but in practice the grand pensionary of Holland, by far the richest and most power-ful province, was the dominant influence in policy-making, at least in peace-time. In time of war the dominant voice was that of the captain general, commander of the republic's armed forces and that same prince of Orange who was stadtholder of five provinces. The prince, the only official in the Republic with a power base wider than a single province, emerged as one of those figures so feared in other republics—a potential monarch. Between 1672 and 1701 William III was king in all but name, with far more power than he wielded as king of England, as he often complained. On the other hand long minorities, such as his own, that between 1711 and 1747, and that after 1750, prevented the establishment of a strong dynasty, and were used by republicans to sap the bases of Orange power. These antagonisms overshadowed the whole of Dutch politics. Broadly speaking, republicans preferred peace, neutrality, religious toleration, and all that favoured trade. Their headquarters was Amsterdam. Orangists stood for foreign adventures, an English alliance, the rights of the poorer, land-locked provinces, and intolerant Calvinism. Usually they had on their side the popular masses, resentful of the urban oligarchs who were the mainstay of republicanism. The ambiguities were

---

[3] *Esprit des lois,* Bk. IX, ch. III.

never finally resolved before French revolutionary armies destroyed the old republic and its politics for ever.

It is striking that in talking of monarchies Montesquieu nowhere used the term 'absolutism'. No description is more frequently applied to the period 1660–1789 than that of an age of absolutism, yet the term was unknown to contemporaries. The concepts of absolute power or of an absolute monarch were familiar enough, but it was the nineteenth century that codified them into a general theory of 'absolutism'—a system and philosophy of government by unlimited power. Absolute kings were not restrained by parliamentary assemblies. But on this definition very few monarchs in the period 1660–1789 could be truly described as absolute. According to Montesquieu an unrestrained king was a contradiction in terms:

'Intermediary powers, subordinate and dependent, constitute the nature of monarchical government, that is to say, of that where one person governs by fundamental laws. . .These fundamental laws necessarily presuppose middling channels through which power flows: for, if there is only in the State the momentary and capricious will of a single person, there can be nothing fixed, and consequently no fundamental law.'[4]

Montesquieu saw that in most contemporary monarchies the king was restrained by the nobility—'no monarch, no nobility; no nobility, no monarch.' Nobles exercised restraining power in practice mostly through estates or parliamentary assemblies. In Great Britain, Sweden, Poland, and certain German states such as Württemberg these bodies were deemed to represent the whole of the ruler's dominions, but more often they represented regions, provinces, or corporate groups such as the clergy, the very forces obstructing the national unification which most nineteenth century historians saw as the ultimate political good. These historians therefore tended to understate, overlook, or deprecate the very real limitations which such bodies placed on centralizing monarchs. They often failed to appreciate, too, the way that the rights of towns, lawcourts, guilds, or other corporate bodies set limits to kingly power. And they minimized the extent to which kings themselves were prepared to recognize laws which they should not infringe. Yet the very fact that estates and assemblies continued to be convoked, or that corporate bodies retained their rights and privileges, was a sign that monarchs did feel bound to accept restraints. This is not to say that they never sought to evade them, but few rulers singlemindedly set out to overthrow the laws, customs, and privileges of their subjects if their ends could be achieved otherwise; and the normal state of relations between kings and their intermediary bodies was one of unspectacular harmony. This too confirmed the impression of 'absolutism'; it was easy for historians to assume that if there was calm, authority must have imposed it. But before 1789 political calm more often reflected a lack of strong central authority. It was attempts to extend the power of central government that caused trouble.

There was, then, no self-conscious 'absolutism'; but certain monarchs were more absolute than others. The weakest king in Europe, the king of

---

[4] *Esprit des lois*, Bk. II, ch. IV.

Poland, was elected to his office by the nobility but only after agreeing to a whole series of limiting conditions collectively known as the *pacta conventa*. In the event of a disputed election, the candidate who agreed to the most concessions—and in effect bound himself to be the weakest king—would be chosen; unless the Russians intervened to impose a candidate. The king could not choose his own ministers (officers were irremovable), had no bureaucracy at his disposal and no power to tax. Most powers were vested in the two-chamber diet, consisting of a senate of great magnates and bishops, and a house of deputies elected by dietines, representative assemblies of the nobility of each county. The diet convened every two years, its power limited by the rule that all decisions had to be unanimous; the veto of a single deputy could block any measure. Nobles also had the right of 'confederation', or legalized rebellion. The result of such a constitution was that Poland had no real government at all above the level of the dietines. Since a weak Poland was Russia's bridge to the west, it was in the Russian interest to pose as the defender and protector of Polish 'liberties'. However, when the experience of the first partition (1772) awoke many Poles to the dangers of a weak government, a movement for national regeneration arose which culminated in 1791 in the promulgation of a new constitution. Election to the throne was abolished and the king endowed for the first time with real powers. But its only result was to provoke a confederation, which the Russians intervened to support. The crisis was only resolved by further partitions, culminating in 1795 in Poland's total disappearance.

In 1649 the English monarchy had been abolished and King Charles I executed. Europe was shocked by the prospect of subjects rising up to execute their ruler; but anxious kings could take solace over the next eleven years that the new republic could find no stable government. In 1660, therefore, the monarchy was restored. The limits of royal power were not clarified, but Charles II was too anxious to avoid another exile to persist in the few attempts he made to explore them. James II, however, in his determination to return his kingdom to Catholicism, pushed his powers to the limit. He built up a large standing army and packed his administration with low-born Catholics. By remodelling the franchise he hoped to be able to pack parliament with servile nominees. But such policies seemed to threaten the whole social as well as political order, and in 1688 a group of notables invited William of Orange to intervene. When James fled, William was made king by parliament. His main objective was to bring his new realm into a European war against Louis XIV: it proved to be the most expensive yet known and was financed by parliamentary taxes and loans raised on parliament's credit. The effect was to establish parliament decisively as the dominant element in government. By 1714 when yet another parliamentary nominee succeeded to the throne, authority in Great Britain was agreed to lie with the king *in* parliament. By that time, too, Scotland's separate parliament had been absorbed (1707), and in 1720 Ireland's was placed in a subordinate position to that of Westminster. Yet parliament's triumph did not reduce British government to the impotence of Poland's. The king retained control of foreign policy, and had enough influence, direct or indirect, on parliamentary elections to ensure favourable majorities for most of his policies. He was obliged by custom to choose his ministers in parliament, but this meant in practice that he chose men who could manage it and get his business done. The government's opponents constantly complained that the 'influence of the crown' deprived parliament of all true independence; but such charges were little heeded until the 1760s and 1770s showed what disasters a stubborn royal policy could bring about without effective parliamentary opposition.

The key to the British parliament's triumph was its control of finance. Elsewhere, too, the estates or parliaments that remained most vigorous were those that retained the right to consent to taxation. There were the estates of Württemberg, a single chamber representing towns and the clergy but no nobles. Often compared to the British parliament, they used their financial power to block attempts by successive dukes to create an independent standing army. Even so, they were easily browbeaten and often triumphed, like Dutch republicans, through dynastic accidents such as the death of ambitious dukes, rather than by their own inherent strength. Sweden was a similar case. The premature deaths of Charles X (1660) and Charles XII (1718) resulted in long regencies during which the four-chamber diet (nobles, towns, clergy, and peasants) consolidated its authority. During the 'age of freedom' from 1720 to 1772 royal power was reduced to nothing and the state was managed by a council and committees of the diet nominated by nobles. Politics was dominated by party conflict between 'hats' and 'caps' with no royal power to restrain factional excesses. But the king was only partly dependent on the diet for his revenues; a large proportion came from royal estates, and the lower houses of the diet were positively enthusiastic about Charles XI's policies of resuming estates alienated to the nobility. So it was relatively easy for him (after 1680) and for Charles XII to shake off parliamentary restraints. In 1772 Gustavus III ended the 'age of freedom' by promulgating a new constitution which restored his power to dissolve the diet, veto legislation, and appoint his own ministers. Popular disgust with the drifting and increasingly violent factionalism of the 1760s won this *coup* widespread support. Sure of his underlying strength, Gustavus showed no sign at first of wishing to dispense with the diet altogether. 'I had absolute power in my hands,' he wrote soon after the event, '. . .but I considered it nobler, grander. . .and certainly surer for my future government, myself to limit the royal authority, leaving to the nation the essential rights of liberty and keeping for myself only what is necessary to prevent licence.'[5] But his warlike and expensive policies of the 1780s created renewed opposition, culminating in the noble plot by which he was assassinated in 1792.

No monarchy in Europe was more complex than that of the Habsburgs. With the exception of a brief interlude between 1740 and 1745, they mono-polized the office of Holy Roman Emperor, even if access to the office strictly depended on election as King of the Romans by the archbishops of

---

[5]   Quoted in Barton, 'Gustavus III' in *Eighteenth Century Studies* (1972), 12.

Mainz, Trier, and Cologne, the king of Bohemia, and the princes of Branden-burg, Saxony, Bavaria, the Palatinate, and (after 1708) Hanover. But the emperor had no real power over those parts of the empire of which he was not already hereditary ruler. There was an imperial diet which, lacking any coercive power, was little more than an occasional conference of diplomats. The Aulic Council, a sort of high court of appeal, over which the emperor presided, gave him some role as arbitrator between German states and indeed between contending parties within them. The estates of Württemberg, for example, repeatedly appealed to the Aulic Council in their disputes with their prince. But here again the emperor wielded only moral authority. The true power of the Habsburgs lay in their hereditary lands, less a state than a collection of states, each separately administered and each having its own institutions. The Habsburgs, from their original base in the Tyrol, had gone on to become archdukes of Austria, Styria, Carinthia, and Carniola, and kings of Bohemia and of Hungary. They also ruled Lombardy and after 1660 acquired the southern Netherlands (1713) and Tuscany (1737). Most of these territories had their own estates or diets with the power to grant taxation and recruit troops. Monarchs had to deal with them piecemeal, so that new legislation often took years to be implemented. The various provinces were often able to extort confirmations or extensions of their privileges during periods of international weakness. In Hungary the diet surrendered its right to elect the king and resist him by rebellion in 1687 only in exchange for the confirmation of all its other powers. Similar promises were extorted in 1723 in return for an agreement to the Pragmatic Sanction allowing Maria Theresa to succeed to the throne, and again in 1740 when she did succeed. When eventually the empress began to move against the autonomy of the estates, however, it proved so easy that laws were increasingly pushed through (as she put it) *iure regio*, without consultation. Even in Hungary she summoned no diet after the mid-1760s, issuing laws of the first importance on her own authority. Joseph II went even further: he ignored the estates, called no Hungarian diets, and abolished the separate administration of Hungary. Ignoring the historic units of his empire, he divided it into thirteen identical 'governments' and made German the official language in all of them. This overriding of constitutional traditions did not by itself create the near-chaos into which the Austrian empire was collapsing by the time Joseph died. But the absence of restraint did facilitate his more controversial policies.

In 1698, alarmed at threats to the Irish parliament's independence, the Dublin scientist William Molyneux wrote: 'The *Rights of Parliament* should be preserved *Sacred and Inviolable*, wherever they are found. This kind of Government, once so *Universal* all over *Europe*, is now almost *Vanished* from amongst the Nations thereof.'[6] Our survey so far shows how wrong he was. Yet in his lifetime many parliaments did disappear and the most spectacular achievements were those of states where they apparently had.

---

[6] *The Case of Ireland's being bound by Acts of Parliament in England Stated* (1698), 174.

The obvious example was Louis XIV's France.

The French estates-general had not met since 1614. Their consent was officially required for all new permanent direct taxes, but by a thorough exploitation of the sale of offices, indirect taxes, and direct levies of limited duration, the government had eliminated the need to assemble them. The tradition of the estates as the highest council of the nation did not die, and at times of political crisis calls were heard for them to be convoked. But it took a crisis of unprecedented dimensions to force the government into this fatal step in 1788–9. Meanwhile, some French provincial estates continued to meet, notably those of Brittany and Languedoc. They raised their own taxes and paid for their own administration, though they had no real freedom to resist royal policies. The source of their continued existence, as of that of the assembly of the clergy, was the confidence they commanded in the financial community. They could raise loans for the government at cheap rates, and so on balance seemed more of a help to the king than a hindrance. Most of France, however, was without estates, protected from excesses of royal power only by the king's own willingness to observe the law. The king of France, the mid-eighteenth-century chancellor Lamoignon once observed, was a monarch to whom everything was possible, but not everything was permitted. He was bound by the law, though not legally answerable if he broke it. In fact French kings hardly abused this position. Nothing illustrates their respect for legal forms better than the powers of the *parlements*, the supreme courts of appeal of Paris and a number of outlying provinces. New laws took effect only when they were 'registered' by the *parlements*, which had the right to send remonstrances to the king on defects in the laws before registering them. Remonstrances were supposed to be secret, but by their publication and by delaying registration of laws pending royal replies, the *parlements* could rally public opinion and make themselves vehicles of opposition. Yet no king removed these rights. In 1673 Louis XIV merely restricted them, and in 1715, in return for the quashing of Louis's will by the *parlement* of Paris, the regent reversed this restriction. The courts' powers were not questioned again before 1789, even in the years of increasingly vocal opposition from the *parlements* up to 1771. The remodelling of the *parlements* which brought this phase to an end, left their powers intact.[7] Yet the relative ease with which this remodelling was carried through, even against loud public outcry, showed how easily changes could be made in France if a government were determined, ruthless, and sure of what it wanted. The law could have been overridden. But few French administrations saw any need to do so. It was no coincidence that Montesquieu, who defined monarchy as a government of one man according to law, tempered by intermediary bodies, was a magistrate in the *parlement* of Bordeaux.

Spain was another country in which apparently limitless royal power was tempered by respect for traditional legal forms. It had no national parliament but the various kingdoms of which it was made up each had their own assemblies

[7] See below, p. 315–16.

or *cortes*. After 1662 the *cortes* of Castile had ceased to meet except on ceremonial occasions: the moneys they were supposed to grant were secured increasingly by direct negotiations with each of the towns represented in them. But the *cortes* of the various kingdoms of the crown of Aragon, covering over a quarter of the country, continued vigorously until the Succession war. These kingdoms—Aragon, Navarre, Catalonia, and Valencia—had been protected by *fueros*, or charters, assuring their separate status, but after the war, in 1707, Philip V revoked the *fueros* by right of conquest. Yet the former Aragonese kingdoms still retained many of their separate legal, administrative, and fiscal institutions, even if the continued existence of these rights and privileges now depended, as in France, upon the king's seeing no disadvantages in them.

To the extent that Spain had nothing like the *parlements*, the king was more absolute than the king of France. So was the king of Portugal, whose booming private revenues from gold mining in Brazil enabled him in 1697 to dispense with his own *cortes*. So was the ruler of Naples, for although the Sicilian parliament never ceased to meet, it always granted whatever supplies were demanded practically without question. The nobles who dominated it were well aware that they and their kind would pay very little of the taxes they were voting for. The most absolute ruler in a small state, however, was the king of Denmark. Having persuaded the majority of the estates, against noble opposition, to proclaim the monarchy hereditary in 1660, Frederick III dissolved them and they were not reconvened. The meteoric career of Struensee in 1770−2 showed that the most far-reaching reforms could be introduced in Denmark on the sole basis of royal confidence. Only a violent *coup d'état* could remove such a minister.

In 1660 the scattered territories of the elector of Brandenburg all had their local estates, just like the Austrian empire. The Great Elector Frederick William in his early years had gone out of his way to establish co-operation with them. However, his struggle in 1653 to persuade those of Brandenburg to finance a permanent standing army convinced him that they must be subdued. They were never to meet again in full session; with the introduction in 1667 of the excise tax, an indirect levy on towns and not subject to the estates' consent, there was no more reason for their meeting. In 1663 the Prussian estates also agreed to a standing army and an excise, after some bullying, and although they continued to meet throughout the elector's reign, they did not survive into the eighteenth century. This was in contrast to the Rhineland duchies of Cleves and Mark, where they went on playing an important part in local administration; but these small detached territories were never crucial to the functioning of the Prussian state. With an increasingly centralized and efficient bureaucracy Prussian rulers after 1688 could say, with King Frederick William I, 'We remain King and Lord and can do as we will.'[8] Yet they still continued to observe certain restraints.

---

[8] Quoted in R. A. Dorwart, *The Administrative Reforms of Frederick William I of Prussia* (1953), 33.

They never attempted to infringe the Brandenburger nobles' right of tax-exemption or their control over the lives of their serfs. Administration and justice at the lowest level remained largely untouched in noble hands. And when Frederick II authorized judicial reforms it was on the principle that 'the laws must speak and the ruler must remain silent'.[9] Prussia's exemplary bureaucracy worked by elaborate rules, observed even by the king. So the 'first servants of the state', as Frederick II described Prussian rulers, still fitted Montesquieu's definition of a monarch.

This could not be said of Russian tsars. In Montesquieu's terms Russia was not a monarchy, but a despotism, ruled by will, not by law. The obvious case Montesquieu had in mind was the Turkish empire, ruled, it seemed, by the sultan's caprice. The very word 'Constantinople' evoked shudders of disgust as a byword for tyranny and arbitrary power. Yet Russia was just as obvious an example. There was not even that most fundamental of all laws, a clear line of succession to the crown. Louis XIV's legitimization of two bastard sons was regarded as one of the most outrageous acts of his reign, so basic and inviolate was the law of succession. Charles VI's empire was left weak for a generation by his anxious efforts to gain approval for the Pragmatic Sanction allowing his daughter to succeed him. But in Russia there was no need for such elaborate manoeuvres. The only sure title to the throne was the support of the armed forces. Peter I owed his throne to the preferences of the palace guard, and Catherine II could not have deposed her husband in 1762 without the support of guards regiments. Peter even had his own son executed in 1718, with no law to stop him. Nor were there any Russian intermediary bodies to restrain the ruler. A national representative assembly, the *zemsky sobor*, had met periodically in the early seventeenth century, but it was never convoked after 1649. No nobility of the western type existed either, enjoying political rights and corporate organization. Legislation in Russia was a matter of the ruler's will alone, the only limit being the difficulty of enforcing it universally in so vast a country. The thousands of new laws promulgated by Peter I at once showed the ease with which he could legislate and the difficulty of making new legislation effective; many institutions were created and then remodelled several times in the space of a few years. Yet Peter imposed a bureaucratic hierarchy on Russia comparable to that of Prussia, which in itself began to circumscribe the ruler's freedom of action exactly as it did in Prussia. One reason why Peter III was overthrown was that by a policy of governing through favourites he was undermining the position of the supreme administrative body, the senate, whose members helped to promote Catherine's *coup*.[10] Indeed, Catherine seemed determined to circumscribe her own power still further. In her instructions to the legislative commission which she convened in 1767, she frequently plagiarized Montesquieu with approval; the very notion of a law code, which the commission was convoked to establish, seemed to imply a

[9]   Quoted in D. B. Horn, *Frederick the Great and the Rise of Prussia* (1964), 67.

[10]   See M. Raeff, 'The domestic policies of Peter III and his overthrow' *American Historical Review* (1970), 1289–1310.

certain renunciation of personal power. The establishment of local assemblies of nobles in 1775 and finally the charter of nobility a decade later even seemed designed to establish a Montesquieuan intermediary body in the Russian state. Yet we should not be deceived. The legislative commission produced much interesting information, but not a lawcode, for Catherine took no action on its suggestions. The assemblies of 1775 were advisory, simply grafted on to the bureaucratic hierarchy; the charter of 1785 largely confirmed the nobility in rights they already enjoyed and in no way extended their political role. Catherine might not in practice enjoy, or even claim, Peter's freedom of action, but she did nothing to limit what power she did enjoy. As Diderot observed when, in 1774, he read the instructions of 1767:

The empress of Russia is certainly a despot. Is it her intention to keep despotism and transmit it to her successors or to abdicate it? If she is keeping despotism. . .let her make her code as she pleases. . .If she abdicates it, let this abdication be formal; if this abdication is sincere, let her consider jointly with her nation the safest ways to prevent despotism from being reborn.[11]

She did no such thing, and Diderot concluded: 'I see in Her Imperial Majesty's instruction a project for an excellent code; but not a word on the means of assuring the stability of this code. I see there the name of despot abdicated; but the thing preserved, but despotism called monarchy.'[12] No wonder Catherine was infuriated when, eleven years later, she read these remarks.

Theories of Government

Despotism was the central political problem of the age. The word itself did not become fashionable until the time of Montesquieu, but most political thinkers felt bound sooner or later to grapple with the problem as it was raised by Thomas Hobbes in 1651.

In his *Leviathan* Hobbes set out to vindicate strong government. Appalled by the chaos of the English civil wars, he argued that to question or flout established authority was never legitimate. Men were naturally equal, their natural rights limited only by their strength. In the state of nature each man had a right to keep anything he could; inevitably this was a state of mutual warfare between each individual. Political society was established by mutual consent to avoid the horrible consequences of such a situation. It took the form of setting up a sovereign power, thenceforth the only source of all authority, law, and morality: 'The sovereign power. . .is as great, as possibly men can be imagined to make it. And though of so unlimited a power, men may fancy many evil consequences, yet the consequences of the want of it, which is perpetual war of every man against his neighbour, are much worse.'[13] The power of Hobbes's sovereign was unlimited, and as the source of justice the sovereign could do no wrong. The subject had no right to object to any of the sovereign's actions, nor could he change the sovereign or call him to

---

[11] 'Observations sur l'instruction de l'impératrice de Russie aux députés pour la confection des lois' in P. Vernière (ed.), *Diderot: oeuvres politiques* (1963), 345.

[12] Ibid. 457.

[13] *Leviathan*, Part II, ch. 20.

account. The sovereign was the sole arbiter of his own succession and law was nothing more than the sovereign's will. Since, in Hobbes's view, the sovereign was the only legitimate representative of his subjects, there was no place for restraining powers: 'That king whose power is limited, is not superior to him, or them, that have the power to limit it; and he that is not superior, is not supreme; that is to say, not sovereign.'[14] There was, said Hobbes, no difference between a king and a tyrant; tyranny was only a pejorative term for monarchy.

Ten years later Louis XIV assumed personal power in France and began to lay claim to an unprecedented degree of authority. He probably never read Hobbes, but his theoretical spokesmen, like bishop Bossuet, certainly had. Bossuet's account of the origins of society in his *Politics drawn from the very words of Holy Scripture,*[15] written for the heir to the throne, was the same as that of Hobbes. Fallen mankind was so miserable and insecure in a state of nature that a sovereign was set up by mutual consent to provide government and authority. Once the sovereign was established, it was never legitimate to disobey or resist him. But Bossuet's reason for obedience was not Hobbes's. Along with the Anglican divines who under Charles II elaborated the doctrine of non-resistance, Bossuet argued that since royal authority came from God, to resist the king was to resist God Himself. It followed that kings were responsible at least to God for the exercise of their power. This responsibility imposed certain restraints: kings were morally bound to serve their people, govern justly, behave reasonably, protect the weak, and observe certain fundamental laws which could not be changed. The king was 'absolute with respect to constraint; there being no power capable of forcing the sovereign, who in this sense is independent of all human authority. But it does not follow from that that the government should be arbitrary.'[16] Under arbitrary government, subjects were slaves with no property to call their own, not even their lives. There was no law but the prince's will; a 'barbarous and odious' principle.

Despite these differences, Hobbes and Bossuet were at one in asserting that royal power could not and should not be limited by any earthly machinery. Although this was in direct contrast to the political realities of most states, few writers of any importance disagreed with them before the 1680s. The memories of mid-century disorders, and the lack of clear authority which had supposedly engendered them, were too fresh. In Germany Pufendorf, though disagreeing with Hobbes over whether men were naturally unsociable, and whether the contract of association in society was also a contract to set up a government, concurred that once set up the sovereign was not to be resisted. In his pseudonymous *On the state of the German Empire* (1667) he deplored the decline of the Empire and blamed it on the alienation of the emperor's monarchical power. Unlike Hobbes, he admitted the possibility of limited monarchy, but in *On the Law of Nature and of Peoples* (1673) he argued

[14] Ibid., ch. 19.
[15] First published 1709 but written thirty years earlier.
[16] *Politique tirée des propres paroles de l'Ecriture Sainte* (1818 edn.), 404.

that rather than rebel, opponents of the sovereign should leave the country. In England 1680 saw the publication of *Patriarcha* by Sir Robert Filmer. Filmer had died in 1653; his tract had been written in his last years but never published. It was now unearthed to bolster the claims of 'divine right' monarchy. According to Filmer, kings enjoyed paternal power granted them by God; their subjects were a family owing them filial obedience, and it was against nature to challenge their authority. The argument was neither memorable nor particularly competent, but it was important for the replies which it provoked, the first serious replies to the authoritarian drift of the previous thirty years.

The *Discourses concerning Government* of Algernon Sidney were not published until 1698, fifteen years after Filmer's death. Sidney's version of the origins of society hardly differed from that of Hobbes, but he believed that nobody ever irrevocably alienated all his natural rights to a sovereign. If sovereigns abused their power, subjects were fully justified in rebelling. A better way of protecting their liberties, however, was to set up a limited government with provisions for regularly changing the magistrates. Sidney believed that monarchy was no more natural than any other form of government, but that it embodied more dangers than most others. These views, and his execution for alleged complicity in a plot to assassinate Charles II, led later generations such as the French revolutionaries of 1793 to revere Sidney as a republican martyr.

A far more influential reaction to Filmer, however, was that of Locke. Though not published until 1690, when they seemed designed to vindicate the 'glorious revolution' of the previous two years, the *Two Treatises of Civil Government* were largely written almost a decade earlier to refute Filmer. It was the second treatise that achieved lasting importance, for there Locke argued that absolute monarchy was not just inconvenient and dangerous, but against the law of nature. 'Government', Locke declared, 'has no other end but the preservation of property.'[17] The state of nature was not a state of war; property, which Locke defined as whatever a man had mixed his labour with, could exist in it. But disputes were inevitable, and where there was no higher authority, war was the only solution. Government was instituted to avoid such war. It was essentially an arbitrator. This followed from the principle that no man should be judge in his own cause; but it also followed that the subject did not alienate all his rights to the government when he agreed in setting it up, because then it too could be judge in its own cause. 'And hence it is evident that absolute monarchy, which by some men is counted for the only government in the world, is indeed inconsistent with civil society, and so can be no form of civil government at all.'[18] The only legitimate forms of government were those in which no power was absolute, but all were restrained by other powers. The powers of government should be separated, so that they balanced one another: 'The first and fundamental positive law of all commonwealths', said Locke, 'is the establishing of the

---

[17] *Second Treatise*, § 94.
[18] Ibid., § 90.

legislative power',[19] for the power to make law was the supreme power in the state. But the power to make laws was and should be separate from the power to execute them, and from the power (called 'federative' by Locke) to conduct relations with other states. All these powers were merely delegated by the majority in the community, which was the ultimate constituting authority and had the right to revoke the mandate of all who exercised them. If the executive were to use its power to upset the balance and attack the legislative, this would be a breach of the fundamental principles by which the state worked and the end of the contract on which it was based. In these circumstances the community had every natural right to remove the offending executive. The implication was that rebellion against a monarch who broke the law was both legitimate and necessary. 'In all states and conditions the true remedy of force without authority is to oppose force to it. The use of force without authority always puts him that uses it into a state of war as the aggressor, and renders him liable to be treated accordingly.'[20] It was obvious why these arguments were so well received in England in the 1690s. The idea of a balanced constitution and a separation of powers seemed to describe the situation that had emerged after the recent revolution; the arguments about rebellion seemed to justify the means by which it had been effected. Locke's ideas rapidly embedded themselves into the stock defences and explanations of their constitution employed by Englishmen. They did not foresee that American colonists, imbued with the same constitutional tradition, would eventually find in Locke justifications for their own revolution.

The controversy surrounding the excesses of the Stuart kings produced these doctrines in England, while the disasters of Louis XIV's later years gave rise to condemnations of absolute power in France. The most virulent denunciations came from expelled Huguenots such as Jurieu, author of the anonymous pamphlet series *The Sighs of Enslaved France aspiring to Liberty* (1689–90). Here the word 'despotic' was first used in the sense in which the subsequent century was to understand it—to describe arbitrary power under which life and property depended upon the caprices of a single man. Jurieu, though welcoming the English revolution, seems to have held the traditional view that there was a distinction between legitimate, absolute monarchy, and the despotism into which Louis XIV's rule had so plainly now degenerated; but Bayle, as always, was sceptical. Since even the sultan observed some laws, Bayle concluded with characteristic ambiguity, he was an absolute monarch too and despotism was merely a derogatory term for monarchy. To accept this however was too painful for most Frenchmen, for it implied that France was a state without laws and that Louis XIV could not be criticized or restrained, whatever he did. Most kept, therefore, to the traditional distinction: 'It is a matter', wrote Fénelon, Louis's most formidable Catholic critic in 1710, 'of recalling the true form of the kingdom, and of tempering despotism, the cause of all our woes.'[21]

[19] Ibid., § 134.

[20] Ibid., § 155.

[21] Quoted by R. Derathé, 'Les philosophes et le despotisme', in P. Francastel (ed.), *Utopie et institutions au XVIIIᵉ siècle* (1963), 61.

None of these criticisms of Louis's rule was elaborated into an alternative theory like Locke's reply to Filmer. In fact, the period between Locke's *Second Treatise* and the publication in 1748 of *The Spirit of the Laws*, a period that saw the flowering and maturity of the Enlightenment, produced no notable developments in political theory. Men's minds were elsewhere, and most were content to say, with Pope:

> For Forms of Government let fools contest;
> Whate'er is best administer'd is best.[22]

The writings of the German cameralists exemplify this attitude very well. Writers such as Seckendorff, Becher, Hornigk, Schröder, or Justi were more interested in what states should do than in the authority by which they did it. Their writings were strewn with references to the quality of various forms of government, but there was no unanimity among them and often little consistency in the works of individual writers. None set out to construct a coherent theory of political obligation; a government justified itself in cameralist eyes if it used its power wisely. Their aim was to suggest the ends governments should pursue and to prescribe the best administrative arrangements for doing so. Cameralism was bureaucratic, rather than political, theory. The writings of its exponents derived more from the well-established German university tradition of administrative studies than from the advanced thought of the day, even if they were increasingly overlaid with appropriately 'enlightened' sentiments. But the leaders of Enlightenment itself often had a similar attitude. So long as the power of the church was curbed, toleration promoted, and laws rationalized, the authority by which such things were done was of secondary importance. And if constitutional restraints on power obstructed the achievement of these laudable ends, these restraints were to be condemned. The whole career of Voltaire illustrates his willingness to support and praise any government, whatever its form, so long as it pursued policies of which he approved.

Montesquieu's *Spirit of the Laws* was at first sight neutral. He did not set out to say how things ought to be, but rather how they were, and why. His purpose was analytical; he avoided theorizing on original contracts, states of nature, or the origins of political authority. Certain types of state existed—a fact to be explained rather than condemned or justified. Yet the very way Montesquieu chose to classify states clearly revealed his own prejudices. All three forms of government were animated by a basic spirit. In republics it was virtue, which Montesquieu defined as love of country; in monarchies it was honour; in despotisms it was fear. Obviously the first two spirits were different in kind from the third; their effect was to moderate the government, and for Montesquieu moderation was the essence of all acceptable constitutions. Ruling out republics, which Montesquieu did not consider really viable in modern times, the only governments he found acceptable were monarchies (moderated by intermediary powers) and that of Great Britain. The latter fitted none of his three categories exactly, but it preserved political liberty by the separation of the three powers of executive, legislative,

---

[22] *Essay on Man*, Ep. III, 303–4.

and judiciary. A refinement on Locke, this famous analysis was influential even in Great Britain and certainly moved the framers of the United States constitution forty years later. It betrayed a fundamental misunderstanding of how the British constitution actually worked, but it made Montesquieu's own preferences clear. No good government could be immoderate. Despotism, however, was exactly that, the worst of all possible governments: 'One cannot speak of these monstrous governments without shuddering.'[23] His definition of it as lawless, arbitrary power was grounded in a long-established French tradition, but by calling it a form of government in itself, rather than a mere corruption of monarchy, Montesquieu emphasized all the restraints that true monarchy ought to observe. Controversy over this classification made despotism a commonplace of political discussion for the next forty years. Nearly all writing on politics between 1748 and the onset of the French Revolution took Montesquieu as its starting-point. Most of it was little more than a commentary on his ideas.

Whether or not Montesquieu's successors agreed with him about the nature of despotism, they followed him almost unanimously in thinking it thoroughly bad. '*Despotism*', wrote Jaucourt in the *Encyclopedia* in 1754, 'is equally harmful to princes and to peoples at all times and in all places, because it is everywhere the same in its principle and its effects. . .human nature always rises against a government of this sort.'[24] Rousseau, who thought monarchy itself quite bad enough, thought that despotism was a corruption of it, and so even worse. Rousseau's concern in the *Social Contract* was to elaborate a theory of legitimate sovereignty. But a despot, on his definition, was one who usurped sovereignty. This was the ultimate political crime, the temptation to which kings were always prone. Not that these opinions were in any way central to his argument; they were simply among the comments all writers felt bound to make on Montesquieu's formulations. Many others Rousseau accepted, but the *Social Contract*'s main concern was not with such matters. It was a return to the previous century's preoccupation with the origins of political authority, taking up problems not pursued since Locke. Accordingly, it occupied a rather isolated position in the development of political thought. Like most of what Rousseau wrote, it was outside the mainstream. Rousseau differed from all his predecessors in placing sovereignty permanently and inalienably in the hands of the people as a whole. He differed from his contemporaries (though not from Hobbes) in declaring that sovereign power could not be divided or separated between a number of institutions. Such principles, along with Rousseau's hostility to monarchy, appealed to the constitution-makers of the Convention of 1792. In adopting these principles, however, they ignored or overlooked Rousseau's condemnation of representation, and his assertion that his ideas could only truly apply in small states. The *Social Contract* was an extremely ambiguous work, certain ideas in it suited them, and they applauded Rousseau for propounding them. It was the ambiguity that impressed the previous generation, however, exasperated by a

[23] *Esprit des lois*, Bk. III, ch. X.
[24] *Encyclopédie*, art. *Despotisme*.

book which was so difficult, abstract, and obscure. They much preferred to consider practical contemporary problems and tangible abuses which could be remedied.

Hate it though they did, most writers agreed that despotism was a very effective form of government. Subject to no restraint, despots got things done. And by the 1760s the programmes of reform being urged upon governments were ever more vast. The economic theories of the physiocrats in particular, advocating a return to the 'natural order' in the economy by sweeping away a whole range of artificial restraints, were so ambitious that few existing governments could be confident of the power to carry them through. Certainly none was so rash as to try; it would, it seemed, require nothing less than a despot to bring in the natural order. In 1767 Le Mercier de la Rivière suggested this in *The Natural and Essential Order of Political Societies*. He was not, he explained, advocating one of those terrible *arbitrary* despots described by Montesquieu. What was needed was *legal* despotism, the unrestrained rule of one man, but one who ruled only according to law—the law of nature. These ideas were echoed in the writings of other physiocrats, but the paradox was too much for most contemporaries to stomach. 'Give me no more talk', wrote Rousseau, 'of your *legal despotism*. I have no taste for it, nor could I even understand it; I only see in it two contradictory words which, brought together, mean nothing to me.'[25] This was a typical reaction to the physiocratic proposal—bad means could never safely be relied upon to achieve good ends. Even those kings who heard about 'legal despotism', such as Gustavus III, dismissed the idea as utopian. Had they come across it, they would have given a similar reception to the term 'enlightened despotism'; but it was invented, like 'absolutism', by nineteenth-century historians looking back on the preceding age and dazzled by the prospect of restless, reforming monarchs, apparently modernizing all they touched. This was to overlook the profound alarm which these activities aroused among the monarchs' subjects, to whom no degree of enlightenment or benevolence justified despotism. Yet the very activity thrust upon later eighteenth-century governments by the cost of international competition looked, to a generation reared on Montesquieu, like the beginning of the dreaded slide into that worst of all governments. Maupeou's *coup d'état* in 1771, brushing aside the intermediary power of the *parlements*, showed Frenchmen how illusory were the restraints on governmental power. Not surprisingly, the first calls for the resurrection of the estates-general were heard in that year; and the restoration of the old *parlements* three and a half years later did nothing to silence advocates of representative institutions of one sort or another. The success of the thirteen American colonies in throwing off British authority seemed to show, at precisely this moment, the strength of elective assemblies. When in 1787 and 1788 the French government attempted to remedy the disastrous results of its own financial incompetence with a series of radical reforms, it was confronted with the united opposition of the whole political nation.

[25] Rousseau to Mirabeau, 26 July 1767, quoted in Derathé, loc. cit. 75.

It was not the substance of the reforms that offended, but the authority by which they were introduced. The government found that nothing but the estates-general could command public acceptance, for the experience of the preceding twenty years had taught that only a national representative assembly was likely to be strong enough to banish the spectre of despotism from French political life once and for all.

The Business of Government

By 1789 opposition to despotism had become a rallying cry attracting mass support. But whether many of those who loudly denounced despots were thinking of Montesquieu's careful definitions seems doubtful. The meaning of the term evolved with frequent usage, and by the late 1780s probably meant little more to most people than government which exceeded its legitimate authority. The problem which most threatened the stability of pre-modern constitutions lay in what *did* constitute the legitimate authority and business of government.

Some matters were traditionally agreed to be pre-eminently a government's concern--for instance religion, an issue so explosive and contentious that only an agreed supreme authority could maintain the peace. Few considered religion a safe subject to be left to individual conscience; and only when rulers, such as James II of England, deliberately set out to change the established religion of the state, was their sovereignty over such matters challenged. Opponents of Louis XIV might denounce, as cruel and unjust, his abrogation of the toleration which Protestants had enjoyed under the Edict of Nantes, but none denied his right to do it.

From the governmental viewpoint, control of religion was an essential element in the control of public order—another of its accepted prerogatives. It was generally agreed that however governments had come into being one of their most important objects was to maintain public tranquillity, so that every man might go about his business secure and unmolested. In the armed forces, governments disposed of the ultimate weapon to quell civil disturbances; but they also used their powers to prevent or anticipate such disturbances. Most believed it essential to control the grain trade in order to keep the populace adequately fed. The populace thoroughly approved of this, and when governments began to experiment with freeing the market from the 1760s onwards, they encountered profound popular hostility on account of the rising prices which followed. Similarly, most governments believed that the interests of public order required a policy on poverty, so that beggars and sturdy vagabonds should not disturb the peace. The prison-like poor houses evident almost everywhere, designed to shut away such dangerous and alarming elements, were all government-authorized and often government-supported. On the other hand police forces in the modern sense were practically unknown, and everyday responsibility for public order was usually in the hands of local men of property who in normal times saw no need for—and resented —the intervention of the central government. Localities were largely self-governing; landlords expected to have public authority delegated to them in addition to the private power they wielded over their tenants or vassals. Any moves by central governments to diminish or deprive them of such authority were likely to meet with fierce resistance.

In the maintenance of public order no power was more important than justice, another traditional sphere of government. A king was nothing if not a supreme judge, the fount of justice, the final authority to whom his subjects could appeal. All governments provided a system of courts to administer the law. Few were centralized; on the principle that justice ought to be readily accessible and within every reach, it was felt undesirable that they should be. The travelling judges of the English assize circuits were exceptions; higher courts in most countries, the most striking examples being the French provincial *parlements*, sat permanently in provincial centres and were staffed by local notables. Inevitably they tended to apply the law in their own interests. Such partiality was still more obvious in lower courts, which throughout much of the continental countryside were not the king's courts at all, but private jurisdictions belonging to lords. Even in England the justices of the peace were the most prominent local landowners. There, indeed, the likelihood of clashes with government was small, since government was in the last analysis subject to a parliament which represented primarily these same landowners. But one reason for the success of the 1688 revolution, which inaugurated the era of parliamentary supremacy, was that James II had alienated large segments of the ruling orders through his replacement of local justices by Catholic or pro-Catholic upstarts. Obviously a king's control of justice was acceptable only so long as it did not run contrary to the interests of his leading subjects.

When contemporaries spoke of 'matters of state', however, they normally meant foreign affairs, the business of the state *par excellence*. Protecting the members of a community against foreign enemies was considered far more important than protecting them against one another, and any glance at a government's balance sheet shows that the greatest part by far of its resources was spent on the essential instruments of international relations—the armed forces. It is true that by the later eighteenth century states such as Great Britain and France were spending even more of their income on servicing huge levels of debt, but these in turn had been incurred to finance earlier wars. Kings and parliaments might quarrel over the authority each was entitled to exercise over foreign and defence policy, but nobody ever claimed, as they sometimes did in the case of public order or justice, that any part of these matters could be left in private hands.

The requirements of foreign policy could be construed very widely indeed. Many believed that economic life was merely an extension of international competition. 'Commerce', said Colbert, 'is a perpetual and peaceable war of wit and energy among all nations.'[26] By the late eighteenth century this view was under attack in the countries of its first triumph, but it had won acceptance throughout the rest of Europe. Its corollary was that governments

[26] Quoted in C. Wilson, *Mercantilism* (1958), 23.

had a duty to manage and direct economic life—to promote the state's wealth was to promote its power. In England this largely took the form of protecting native merchants and manufacturers against foreign competitiors by discriminatory legislation. In France and elsewhere positive government action was enlisted to encourage and subsidize various industries in order to eliminate dependence on foreign imports. Even physiocrats who did not believe in government interference in economic life, believed that the state should attack customs and institutions which impeded economic freedom. Only in the Dutch republic was the state expected to have no economic policy beyond protecting the freedom of its citizens to do as they liked.

The needs of defence largely dictated the weight and pattern of taxation. Nobody challenged the principle that governments needed to levy taxes, but equally, nobody believed that the right of governments to levy taxes was limitless. The most dangerous political disputes arose when governments attempted to extend taxes, for deep in the political consciousness of most Europeans lay a feeling that new direct taxes at least should not be imposed without the consent of those who were to pay them. Where estates and parliaments were still strong, this principle was enshrined in regular constitutional practice, and it was rash to flout it. But even where the apparatus of consent had disappeared the principle was not forgotten; it took the determination and prestige of a Louis XIV to create a new and permanent direct tax, the capitation, in 1695, and subsequent new French impositions were always for a strictly limited period. When it became clear later in the eighteenth century that they would require perpetual renewal, the *parlements* who registered them began to call for the revival of representative assemblies to make these renewals legitimate. The trouble with new taxes was that they almost invariably involved changes in traditional exemptions and privileges; they would presumably not have been necessary if merely increasing traditional burdens had sufficed. When Joseph II sought in 1789 to increase the tax revenue from peasants, he felt obliged to diminish the dues they owed their lords. He was accused (not unjustly) of threatening the whole established structure of society. Similar, though less obviously true, charges were brought against most new taxes introduced in this period, for changes in taxation were a major element promoting social change—something that those who were satisfied with society as it was, were determined to resist.

11. The Machinery of State

In the later eighteenth century most people who thought about public affairs were convinced that the power of governments had increased, was increasing, and ought to be diminished. They were right in believing that states now wielded more power than they had a century beforehand. Yet governments were largely staffed by men who shared completely the attitudes and outlook of the governing groups who formed the political nation in each state. They had seldom sought to accumulate power for its own sake. They simply had no alternative if they were to continue to do adequately what was traditionally expected of them—something that was not possible without trespassing increasingly in fields traditionally felt to be beyond a government's competence.

The measure of a government's power is its ability to enforce its policies. The sign of a growth in this power, therefore, was the increasing size and sophistication of the machinery through which it was exercised—above all the armed forces and the administration.

Armies

The size of armies showed a steady increase which was not necessarily reflected by the size of forces actually in combat. No eighteenth-century war saw as many troops engaged as those of the 1690s and 1700s; the French Marshal Saxe estimated in 1746 that the maximum size for a manageable army in battle was 46,000, half the number regularly deployed in the battles of the Spanish Succession war. But in 1660 few states had anything resembling a standing army; while in 1800 standing armies were found everywhere.

This was the result of the 'military revolution' of the century before 1660, a change in basic battle tactics first evolved by the Dutch and the Swedes, and proved with spectacular effect in the Thirty Years War. These tactics relied upon armies of small, versatile, highly trained, and highly manoeuvrable units rather than on the large and cumbersome masses of former years. But such sophisticiation, requiring elaborate training and drilling, was inevitably more costly; and the cost was only increased if at the end of wars forces which had been so laboriously built up were disbanded, only to be reassembled and retrained when new hostilities broke out. To be effective, training and drilling had to be constant and armies had to be kept constantly in being. Numbers always fell when wars ended, the discharge of surplus soldiers and sailors often creating serious social problems. But increasingly states retained a substantial kernel of troops as a professional basis for re-expansion.

The crucial development was France's adoption of a standing army between 1640 and 1680. Louis XIV's domination of Europe was largely based on the fact that a country with over twice the population of its nearest rival could maintain a standing army of commensurate size, better armed, better disciplined, and better trained than any its rivals could produce. Planned at 30,000 men in 1659, it had already expanded to over 97,000 by 1666. In 1710, at the height of the Spanish Succession war, there were 360,000 troops in Louis XIV's service out of a population of 21 million. Such enormous wartime expansion was in turn a response to the fact that, from the 1680s onwards, France's rivals had come to realize that the only way to combat her power was to organize on a comparable scale. By 1693 the Dutch had an army of 93,000 and the insular British, whose hostility to standing armies was enshrined in their Common Law, authorized one in 1690. Within six years Britain had 90,000 soldiers, peacetime numbers never falling subsequently below about 20,000. Even those not directly involved against Louis XIV could see the logic. Early defeats at the hands of the Swedes convinced Peter I of Russia of the need for a reliable and up-to-date standing army. Most of his massive reforms were designed to this end and by 1731 Russia had a permanent force of over 132,000. Even a small state like Piedmont, by herculean efforts, had built up a standing force of 43,000 by 1734. Nowhere, however, was a standing army given more priority than in Brandenburg-Prussia. It began modestly enough, as a force of 12,000 men retained after the Northern War of 1655–60 to meet any threat from Sweden. It proved its value in 1675 when it defeated the hitherto invincible Swedes at Fehrbellin. In the 1680s it stood at between 25,000 and 30,000 men. Between 1713 and 1740 Frederick William I never fought a war, but he built up a standing force of 83,000, the basis of an army which dazzled Europe with its exploits under his son. When Frederick II died in 1786 the Prussian army had hardly fired a shot in anger for twenty-three years, but it stood at over 190,000—only 46,000 less than that of France for a population far less than half the size. And its organization, drill, and even style of uniform were imitated throughout Europe as French ways had been a century before.

Mercenaries—troops not legally the subjects of the state employing them—were a major element in professional standing armies. Rulers preferred foreign soldiers when they could get them, either because they were afraid to arm their own subjects, or because they believed their own nationals could contribute more to the country's wealth and power as civilians. 'A German', wrote Saxe, 'serves us for three men, he saves one for the kingdom, takes one from our enemies, and serves us as a man.'[1] In the early eighteenth century the peacetime strength of the French army included 20,000 foreign troops, among them regiments of Germans, Swiss, and Irish. In the Prussian army foreigners never numbered less than half the strength, and often far more. In 1751 they accounted for 83,000 out of a total of 133,000. The recruitment of mercenaries was easiest in poor or mountainous areas or in the overpopulated small states of Germany. The main activity of a principality such as Hesse-Cassel throughout the eighteenth century was the hiring out of its citizens as soldiers to foreign states, notably Great Britain.

[1] Quoted in A. Corvisier, *L'Armée française de la fin du XVIIe siècle au ministère de Choiseul: le Soldat* (1964), i. 260.

Armies were now too big to be entirely made up of mercenaries. They needed to be supplemented from a state's native population. Pressing criminals or vagrants was one way of doing this; British magistrates were empowered to press the unemployed into service as the need arose. The unemployed were already however the main source of volunteers, turning to the armies when other means of securing food, shelter, and clothing were exhausted. And none of these methods produced a committed soldiery. Political writers reared on the classics were always extolling the virtues of citizen armies such as that of republican Rome, but the nearest contemporary approximation to this ideal was a series of haphazard systems of conscription. In France a militia, created in 1688, was reorganized in 1726, to provide 60,000 men between the ages of sixteen and forty every six years, selected by drawing lots. Lots were also drawn for military service in Spain. In Russia from the time of Peter I every household belonged to a group obliged to furnish a recruit regularly for twenty-five-year service in the army. Frederick William I divided his domains into cantons, each of which was allotted to a particular regiment or regiments as a recruiting zone; all able-bodied men were liable to be conscripted at need for terms of indefinite service. Conscripts seldom spent all their time with the colours; in peacetime they might be called up only once or twice a year for short periods of training. That way they were less of a financial burden, yet remained at the state's disposal. But far from embodying the patriotic fervour dreamed of by the theorists, conscripts were among the most reluctant of warriors. The burden fell only on those too poor or weak to evade it; anybody who could be construed as useful to society enjoyed exemption. In France all townsmen escaped the militia draw; the rich could always buy themselves substitutes. Even in Prussia one-fifth of the population was exempt. Most armies, therefore, were a blend of rootless mercenaries, jobless volunteers, pressed vagrants and criminals, and defenceless conscripts. Their commitment and morale was vividly reflected in astronomical rates of desertion. The French army lost one man in every four or five between 1716 and 1763, a rate which rose in time of war. Between 1713 and 1740 the Prussian army had over 30,000 deserters, and almost three times as many during the Seven Years War alone. The only antidote considered by military authorities to this, their most serious problem, was rigorous and savage discipline; but arguably this did more to exacerbate the problem than to solve it.

If the rank and file of armies was made up of society's dregs, they were commanded and led by its cream. Noblemen considered themselves uniquely fitted by birth and heredity for leading troops into battle, and many believed that governments had an obligation to provide them with this opportunity. Most army officers were members of the ruling aristocracies, who, considering themselves well qualified by nature, were often reluctant to undergo the training and discipline that military professionalism increasingly demanded. The undoubted courage of such officers seldom made up for their incompetence. The British and French governments found it lucrative to sell commissions—a system which favoured the richest rather than the most capable. The best officers in the field tended to be petty nobles whose lack of other resources bound them most strictly to a military career. Such men abounded in Brandenburg, a poor country of small estates, and they contributed much to the efficiency of the Prussian army. In France and Great Britain they could never afford to rise beyond the lower ranks. Nor was it a coincidence that the branches with the least social prestige, such as the artillery and the engineers, were the ones demanding the most expertise and training and largely officered by non-nobles. As governments increasingly realized the advantages of training for officers in all branches, military cadet schools began to be established. The first one of importance was set up in Piedmont in 1677. Frederick William I established the Berlin cadet corps in 1717, and a similar institution was founded in Russia in 1731. A French military school was set up in 1751, an Austrian school a year later. Specialist schools of artillery and military engineering began to appear. These institutions never succeeded in channelling all future officers. Even in Prussia only about one-third of the officer corps under Frederick II had passed through the cadets. But they did succeed in improving the proficiency of the poor military careerist and they also served as centres of military thinking. The tactics of Napoleon, himself the product of a pre-revolutionary French military academy, were rooted in the theory evolved in such institutions since 1750.

The main purpose of armies was of course defence and attack against foreign enemies, but in an age without substantial police forces they were also the ultimate guarantee of public order. No peasant uprising was able to resist for long once professional troops were sent in. Sustained rebellions, such as that of the Languedoc Camisards, or Pugachev's, owed much of their success to the fact that foreign wars absorbed most of the government's forces. Troops were extensively used to prevent violence in times of famine, policing markets and protecting grain convoys; an extra argument in favour of employing foreign mercenaries was that they would be less easily moved by the sight of distress if they were not compatriots of the sufferers. Recalcitrant subjects could also be coerced by billeting, for troops who were well disciplined on duty were notoriously brutal and unruly at other times. The most famous example of this was the French *dragonnades* of the 1670s and 1680s, when Louis XIV battered thousands of Huguenot families into abandoning their faith by billeting the roughest troops of the French army on them.

In such ways the evolution of professional standing armies directly increased the power of governments. No wonder Englishmen regarded them as the greatest potential threat to their liberties. Less obvious, but just as important, were the indirect ways in which they increased state power. They needed to be supplied, for instance, with munitions, clothing, and equipment. The standardization of uniforms and equipment, which was the logical corollary of the standardization of tactics, demanded a level of mass production never before seen. These requirements made immense fortunes for the private contractors who undertook to supply them—men like the Vienna Jews Oppenheimer and Wertheimer under Leopold I, or the Berlin partners

Splitgerber and Daum, who dominated army contracting and armaments manufacture in Prussia in the first half of the eighteenth century. But in their turn such enterprises tended to become dependent on continuing government orders, since no private customer bought on such a scale. Great manufacturers therefore acquired an interest in supporting the established order. British governments traded military supply contracts for parliamentary votes, making the relationship quite explicit. Where private contractors could find neither the capital nor the manpower to supply a state's military needs, the state was forced to provide them on its own account. The earliest factories were established not by private enterprise, but by states, to manufacture military supplies. The most spectacular example is the 200 or so factories founded in Russia under Peter I, all of them primarily designed to supply the tsar's war machine. Forty-three per cent were state owned, with lavish state subsidies and privileges helping to establish the rest. But state mines, foundries, powder mills, and woollen manufactories were set up even in commercially advanced countries, through which hundreds of thousands of workers became directly dependent on the state for their livelihood.

Large standing armies required civilian administrators to manage them. Perhaps the basic achievement of Louis XIV's war minister Louvois, a prerequisite of all the others, was to subject all French soldiers, however high-ranking, to civilian control, exercised by a numerous war-office staff at the centre and by intendants, each with their own staff in turn, assigned to each major military unit and responsible for all aspects of supply and logistics. Even as late as 1797, there was no such centralized system of control in Great Britain, but the number of civilians administering military affairs was still almost 600. Piedmont's enormous army could be maintained only at the cost of sacrificing everything else in the poor and sparsely populated state to it; and the same was true of Prussia, where from almost the first days of the standing army the war office (*Generalkriegskommissariat*) became the basic organ of the government. This principle did not change after 1723, when Frederick William I submerged the office into a General Directory. The whole aim was to place the state's resources even more completely at the disposal of military needs. To this extent the whole administrative apparatus of the Prussian state can be viewed as an adjunct of military administration. Indeed, it is difficult to see how the nobility could have been brought to regard administration as an acceptable alternative career if it had not been.

Navies

Navies expanded in the same way as armies. Powers that had both land and sea frontiers pursued fluctuating naval policies, depending on changing views of their relative importance. Only Great Britain, secure in island isolation, consistently regarded the navy as more important than the army. 'The first Article of an Englishman's political creed', wrote Halifax, 'must be that he believeth in the sea.'[2]

In 1660 standing navies—unlike armies—were nothing new, but since they

[2] Quoted by J. S. Bromley in *New Cambridge Modern History, VI, The Rise of Great Britain and Russia 1688–1715/21* (1970), 796.

were very expensive to equip and maintain, they had never been very large. Nor could they be expanded quickly in an emergency, except by the conversion of unsuitable merchant ships. In an age when the winning and protection of overseas trade was increasingly regarded as a major objective in the policy of states, this seemed to make little economic sense. It was better to keep a substantial, professional fleet in being, whatever the cost. Since most admirals at this early date were trained as soldiers, they believed that the lessons of the military revolution applied equally at sea. Maximizing the firepower of fleets required the same intensive and constant training, and standardizing of equipment, as armies were now undergoing. Consequently, by 1680 no major navy was still using converted merchantmen, not even temporarily. Fleets were increasingly made of a few standard classes of purpose-built ships, which sought to triumph by disciplined firepower, rigid tactics, and weight of numbers.

In the 1660s the largest European fleet was that of the Dutch, with about 100 ships, 4,800 guns, and 21,000 men. By the end of their third war with the Dutch, in the mid-1670s, the English had surpassed them; from then on the Dutch navy went into a steady decline from which it never substantially rallied. English naval predominance was not finally achieved until after the mid-1690s, for up to that time the French had pursued a vigorous policy of naval construction. In 1688 the French fleet was over twice the size of the Dutch, and even outnumbered the English, though not in capital ships. It was not until after the defeat of La Hogue (1692), that France turned away from large-scale naval construction and put most of her maritime effort into cheaper privateering. This policy was later reversed, and in the late 1770s France took control of the Atlantic from the British with a fleet of around eighty ships of the line. But by then the British had over twice that number (174 in 1783) and won back supremacy at the battle of The Saints (1782). The French, though the second naval power in Europe, could not have achieved their success without British mismanagement and the alliance of a substantial Spanish fleet of almost sixty ships of the line, built up since mid-century. The only other significant fleet was that of Russia, created from scratch by Peter I, and lifted out of a mid-eighteenth century decline by Catherine II. Its power was largely confined to the Baltic and the Black Sea, but in these areas it was the dominant force with 37 ships of the line in the Baltic in 1785, and 12 in the Black Sea.

Ships, not manpower, were the true gauge of naval strength. Nevertheless, with each ship of the line requiring a crew of between 400 and 800, substantial numbers were needed. The British navy had between 40,000 and 50,000 sailors in the 1690s, rising to well over 80,000 a century later. In 1789 the French navy had 75,000 men. Unlike armies, only a very small proportion of navies was made up of mercenaries. Peter I had no alternative but to officer the new-born Russian navy with foreigners, but this was an expedient designed to last only until native Russians could be trained. The ordinary seamen were conscripted peasants just like Russian soldiers. Elsewhere, officers and men alike tended to be the state's own subjects. In

France, Colbert sought to underpin his rapid naval expansion by the introduction, between 1668 and 1673, of a system of 'classes' which made all subjects of seagoing experience liable to conscription into the navy at need. In 1737 a similar system was established in Spain. In both cases, however, there was widespread resistance to the registration that was the basis of such a system, and like militia recruitment it fell mostly on those unable to find pretexts for evading it. No such experiment was tried in Great Britain, where it has been estimated that at the end of the eighteenth century the average ship's crew included 15 per cent volunteers, 15 per cent conscripted from debtors, criminals, and unemployed, and over 50 per cent pressed into service by violence. Pay did not change over the whole eighteenth century and was often in arrears. Food was poor, discipline as harsh as in the Prussian army. Mutiny was surprisingly rare, but the moment ships reached port desertion became a major problem. Between 1776 and 1783 alone it was estimated that 42,000 men deserted from the British navy.

Naval officers tended to be recruited from a wider social range than those of armies, since even the lowliest seagoing officer required a level of expertise and technical knowledge that only prolonged training or experience could impart. When Louis XIV declared in 1683 that his aim was to officer his new navy entirely with noblemen, not enough nobles could be induced to undergo the rigours of naval training for the achievement of this ideal. Instead the ranks of French naval officers remained rigidly divided between a privileged, socially exclusive 'grand corps', and a majority of commoners who had learned their seamanship in trade. In 1733 a Naval Academy was founded at Portsmouth for 'the sons of the Nobility and Gentry', but it had difficulty in recruiting such people and never supplied more than a tiny minority of British naval officers. Most officers entered the service because they had connections with ship's captains. This meant that they were mostly recruited from the lower fringes of the gentry. The absence of purchase, in striking contrast with army practice, kept out rich amateurs, but promotion remained a matter more of cultivating and manipulating connections than recognition of ability.

Navies created even more civilian employment than armies. Besides requiring just as much supply in the form of provisions, clothing, and ordnance, they also needed to build and maintain their ships. This was why they were so much more expensive. By the end of the seventeenth century, the British navy was already the largest industry in the country: the largest employer, the largest importer of raw material, the largest shipbuilder, and one of the largest buyers of agricultural produce. Naval dockyards were the greatest and most versatile industrial concentrations of the age. At the height of war in the 1690s, British naval dockyards had a total workforce of over 4,200 men, with Chatham and Portsmouth employing well over 1,200 each. A century later expenditure on the navy accounted for just less than one-sixth of national expenditure (in peacetime) and was only surpassed in size for a single item by debt service. In France at the same time, naval expenditure was less than a twelfth, less than half that of the army, and was also exceeded by debt service and tax-recovery; but it was still a major recurring commitment.

Prodigious sums were being spent in the 1780s on a new naval harbour at Cherbourg, whose construction required a work force numbering 3,000. No private enterprise ever attained anything on this scale; nothing boosted the internal power of states as much as these efforts to maintain their external strength.

Justice and Police

The judiciary was perhaps the only branch of the state that did not expand significantly in this period, for many states were already over-endowed with courts of law even in 1660, littered with layer upon layer of jurisdictions, both general and specialized, each answerable to its own court, with its panel of judges, its bar and its clerks. This complex pattern survived in many places throughout the eighteenth century. The French town of Angers, with a population late in the century of 34,000, boasted no less than fifty-three different courts of law—an extreme example, but symptomatic of a general principle. In France the excessive number of courts was compounded by over-staffing. The chief feature of the enormous seventeenth-century expansion in venality of office had been to make the whole judiciary venal. And since the government had an interest in creating as many offices as it could sell, the staff of many French courts was expanded far beyond the needs of the business they had to conduct.

Indeed, their business had a positive tendency to shrink. The growth, common to most states, of a corps of professional administrators exercising wide powers by direct delegation from central authority trespassed increasingly on the traditional administrative powers of courts. The French (and sub-sequently, the Spanish) intendants, for instance, had specific competence over justice and police. Not surprisingly they were continually denounced by lawcourts and often found their orders countermanded by them. Such resistance was made more formidable by the magistrates' independence of tenure. French venal offices were pieces of real property of which their owners could not be deprived without the refund of the original purchasing price. The constant diatribes of the French *parlements* against the intendants were made with the confidence born of assured independence. There was no venality in England, but after 1701 judges could not be removed except by joint petition of both houses of parliament—a response to repeated royal attempts to purge the bench of unco-operative members. At the lowest level justice was often in unpaid private hands; so courts of law, though essential to the functioning of the state, did not necessarily increase its power. In fact they were the main obstacle to that increase, though not an insuperable one. Once Louis XIV was dead, the *parlements* clamoured loudly against growing executive power, scoring some notable provincial triumphs. They were how-ever unable to reverse the over-all trend; their resistance only made the government more determined to override them. The 1760s, when resistance reached its peak, ended with the reforms of Maupeou which attempted to abolish their venal offices. In states without a long tradition of judicial independence, such as Prussia or Russia, judges did not see resistance as part of their business; justice was a branch of administration, courts were staffed by obedient dependents, and were strictly limited to a judicial role. Only in Great Britain did judicial independence survive unchecked, for there no centralized administrative structure appeared. Parliament, representing the very groups that formed the backbone of the judiciary, could see no need of one; and what was now done on the continent by centrally directed intendants or presidents of provincial chambers continued to be the concern of local JPs meeting in quarter sessions.

Between the private power of men of property on the one hand, and the organized strength of armies on the other, public authorities had only the slenderest of forces to maintain everyday public order. Nor were such forces usually under central control. Towns usually employed a handful of guards or watchmen. Rural parishes would each have one or two officers chosen by election or lot, and always part-time, in charge of public order. The most sophisticated, centralized, police force was the French *maréchaussée*, which became steadily more numerous and well organized over the period, but which, even in the 1780s, numbered less than 4,000 for a population of over 28 millions. A French town of 5,000 inhabitants might have four police-men to maintain law and order within its precincts and a radius of perhaps 30 miles. Big cities had their own, supplementary forces. The Lyons city guard numbered eighty-five; that of Mainz was thirty-two strong. A great capital such as London had police forces totalling perhaps 3,000, but two-thirds of these were only part-timers with competence over limited localities, none armed, and none under government control. To English (though not Scottish) ears, the very word 'police' evoked ideas of France, public informers, and tyranny. And Paris was certainly better policed than London. A lieutenant of police, responsible directly to the government, was created in 1667. In addition to an office staff of twenty-seven, administering everything from roadsweeping to food supplies, he employed about 1,500 full-time police officers. He could also summon up as many reserves, mostly part-time, before resorting to troops, not to mention a huge number of part-time informers or police spies, impossible to enumerate but reputedly ubiquitous—a feature which greatly interested Joseph II when he inquired about the Parisian police in 1776. In 1782, inspired by the French example, he created a police force in Vienna largely made up of anonymous spies and informers—a secret police in fact. Its business was described in 1790 as 'to discover all persons who are or might be dangerous to the state. . .to discover any discontent arising among the people, all dangerous thoughts and especially any incipient rebellion, and to nip these in the bud. . .secretly and unnoticeably to influence public opinion in favour of any government measure.'[3] Such comprehensive functions would have been quite beyond any of Europe's motley police only a generation before.

The growth in the ambitions and efficiency of police forces was paralleled in the sphere of prisons. When the English penal reformer John Howard

---

[3] Quoted in E. Wangermann, *From Joseph II to the Jacobin Trials* (2nd edn., 1969), 37.

toured Europe in the 1770s and 1780s inspecting penal arrangements, he repeatedly noted that new institutions had been purpose-built in recent years. Few prisons were large, not having been designed as places of punishment. Most were designed to house those awaiting trial or punishment, or debtors held at the request, and usually at the expense, of their creditors. Political prisoners, or aristocratic profligates shut up at the request of their families, tended to be held in great fortresses like the Tower of London, the Peter-Paul fortress in St. Petersburg, or the Bastille in Paris. Most convicted criminals were not imprisoned, but sentenced to capital or corporal punishments, sent to penal colonies, or made to serve in the galleys of Mediterranean naval powers. The nearest equivalents to the modern prison were the enormous poor houses and hospitals designed to sweep vagrants from the streets and set them to public employment, which often numbered their inmates in hundreds. Howard drew no clear distinction between them and prisons proper. Yet workhouses regimented those they housed, clothed them, fed them, and kept them occupied. Prisons simply shut them away pending further decisions, providing only the barest necessities for survival. They were often overcrowded, insanitary, disease-ridden, and violent. They were also very insecure, and savage punishment did not deter escape attempts. Older prisons were equally vulnerable to attack from outside, and as symbols of authority they were obvious targets when order broke down. In the Gordon riots of 1780 most of London's major prisons were opened and set on fire. The crowds which stormed the Bastille on 14 July 1789 were looking for arms rather than wronged prisoners; but it was natural that they should go on to demolish the prison, to show that the authority it represented was no more.

Financial Institutions

Taxes rose as larger and more sophisticated armed forces cost more money. Governments had to establish more effective machines for gathering in these extra resources. In 1660 much direct tax collection was in the hands of local landlords who alone had enough coercive power to ensure regular returns, and who worked unpaid. This system lasted throughout the period in places such as Russia, the Austrian dominions, and Great Britain; but usually only at the cost of those in charge according themselves favoured treatment and taking frequent official or unofficial rake-offs. To eliminate this corrupt practice the French government attempted to collect new direct taxes intro- duced after 1695 through its own officers; but it never employed enough, and was compelled to rely at all levels on private contractors intent on profiteering.

Direct taxes, however, seldom accounted for the bulk of a government's revenue. Indirect levies normally made up far more. They were easier to assess, and being accumulated largely from small payments, easier to extract. On the other hand they required more complex machinery to administer, and above all abundant manpower. In Spain the preponderance of indirect over direct taxes was overwhelming. At the beginning of the eighteenth century it was estimated (with some exaggeration) that over 80,000 men were involved in collecting them. To maintain such an apparatus had been beyond the resources or ambitions of early modern states, and most had preferred to put the collection in the hands of tax-farmers, who paid the state for the right to collect and in return were allowed to run the system at a profit. Most of France's indirect revenues were leased from 1681, for periods which stabilized themselves from 1726 at six years, to a company of financiers known as the farmers-general. This body controlled the largest group of employees in France, apart from the armed forces. In the late 1770s they numbered 30,000 or more, scattered throughout the country wherever there was a customs post or tax-office. Technically employees of the state, they took their orders from the farmers-general and remitted the funds they collected to them. Increasingly however, governments found such arrangements unsatisfactory. The profits made by tax-farmers and the private control they exercised over public revenues were coming to be seen as losses to the state. Accordingly, tax-farming was abandoned in England between the 1670s and 1690s and revenue officers came under the direct control of the state. By the 1790s the customs, excise, and various other fiscal branches of the British government employed nearly 14,000 officers, a body of men notorious as political appointees who were expected to use all their influence in supporting the government at election times. In 1770 tax-farming was likewise abandoned in the Austrian-ruled duchy of Milan. In Prussia, excise revenues were never farmed out, but were levied by local authorities until 1766. In that year Frederick II put them in the hands of a centrally directed *régie*, modelled in organization on the French general farms and staffed largely by Frenchmen. They soon became notorious for their rapacity, but their efficiency was reflected in a rapid rise in public revenues and a striking decline in smuggling. Of the 14,000 public officials in Prussia in 1789, most were revenue officers. This number may seem small, and has often been praised as a sign of efficiency in comparison with other European states.[4] But when Prussia's small population is taken into account, the numbers appear proportionately greater than in many states.

Revenue officers were the teeth of government—the only agents of the state with whom most people came into regular contact. It was through the ever-increasing demands they made that most people came to appreciate the growth in governmental power. And it was towards them in the first instance that they tended to demonstrate resentment. Riots in Berlin marked the inauguration of the *régie* in 1766. The popular uproar caused by Walpole's proposal to extend the British excise in 1733 nearly brought his government down. Everywhere it was normal for the populace to protect smugglers against revenue officers, and if the latter attempted to act alone they risked serious injury or even death. A report to the British parliament in 1733 noted that 'the number of custom-house officers who have been beaten, abused and wounded since Christmas 1723 [was] no less than 250, besides six others

---

[4] See, e.g. W. L. Dorn, 'The Prussian bureaucracy in the eighteenth century', *Political Science Quarterly* (1932), 261.

who have been actually murdered in the execution of their duty. . .'[5]

Governments, however, are never wholly dependent on income from taxation. They also constantly borrow. And just as the cost of war brought higher taxation, it also brought unprecedentedly heavy borrowing, which led to a search for new institutions of credit. The Dutch republic was much envied for raising most of its loans on the credit of the estates of the various provinces, themselves largely representing the burghers who lent most of the money. The existence of the Bank of Amsterdam maintained a high level of financial confidence, which produced low interest rates. Public debts were cheap to raise: in 1672 the government was paying $3\frac{1}{2}$ per cent, half or less than the interest paid by most other governments. The result was that the republic could raise larger loans and sustain greater military efforts than its rivals. Bankruptcies in France in 1648 and England in 1672, by contrast, showed the fragility of the credit arrangements upon which these states relied. As a remedy, the Bank of England was established in 1694, with parliamentary backing. From the start, its prime function, unlike the Bank of Amsterdam, was to channel most of the money lent to the British government in long-term loans. After some initial uncertainties, its success was spectacular. Interest on British government loans had dropped to 3 per cent by the mid-eighteenth century, and during the American war no less than 40 per cent of the British war effort was paid for out of borrowing. In 1674 the French attempted to create a state bank, which Louis XIV closed down after Colbert's death in 1683. A second attempt was made in 1720 by John Law, but his Royal Bank collapsed in the Europe-wide financial crash of that year, creating a profound suspicion of all organs of public credit in France. Consequently the French government continued to depend on loans at high interest rates from such bodies as the farmers-general or individual Dutch or Swiss financiers, or it obtained cheaper loans through institutions enjoying better credit, such as the corporation of Paris, the clergy, provincial estates, or corporations of venal office-holders. This reliance limited the government's ability to reform these bodies or diminish their considerable privileges in matters of taxation. In all these ways its freedom of action was far less than of its British or Dutch rivals.

With the examples of the Dutch, and later the British, before them politicians were dazzled by the possibilities of expanded credit. Central banks such as that established in Vienna in 1705, proliferated, but they failed more often than they succeeded because governments were too precipitate or greedy in tapping their resources. There were failures in Sweden in 1664 and again in 1745, in Denmark in 1757, and in Spain in 1796. Even the cheap and easy credit enjoyed by the Dutch republic had long-term dangers. It saddled the state with an enormous burden of debt service which could not be repudiated, but could only be met by a crippling level of taxation, raised mainly through excises. This produced an economy of high wages and high prices which reduced Dutch competitiveness in the long run and so speeded

[5] Quoted in N. Williams, *Contraband Cargoes: seven centuries of smuggling* (1959), 111.

the republic's eighteenth-century decline. The great wars up to 1713 had been fought, observed the conservative statesman Van de Spiegel in 1782, not 'at the charge of the present generation, but at the charge of posterity'.[6] Paradoxically this situation had many similarities to that of France in the 1780s. Only Great Britain seemed endlessly able to contract new loans without overwhelming herself; and even there politicians could always command widespread support when they set up sinking funds to diminish the over-all level of the national debt. With almost half of its stock in the hands of Dutch financiers, the debt appeared to hold the country hostage to the caprices of foreigners. The establishment of the income tax in 1799 showed that even the credit of the 'modern Carthage' could no longer subsidize a major war effort without the addition of more tax-revenue.

Administrative Centralization

The traditional pattern of authority and administration was decentralized. Medieval rulers had extended their authority by confirming local powers and customs rather than attacking them. But as the ambitions of states grew, the traditional autonomy of localities came to seem more of an obstacle than an aid to governmental purposes. Accordingly, rulers began to seek ways, not of destroying the traditional machinery, but of by-passing it. The key to efficiency seemed to be centralization, the most celebrated example being that of France, where this period saw the triumph of the intendants. Originally commissioners sent into the provinces on specific missions connected with taxation or public order, they gradually evolved into permanent provincial agents of the central government. By the 1680s the whole country was divided into administrative units called generalities, themselves subdivided into subdelegations. Each generality was headed by an intendant, presiding over a number of subdelegates. Recruited largely from the narrow world of the Parisian judicial nobility, the intendants' loyalties were to the king rather than to the provinces where they were posted. Nor did they own their offices, unlike most members of the judiciary. Their powers, defined as relating to 'justice, police, and finances' were wide and open-ended; but their establishment came only after many years of obstruction, denunciation, and hostility on the part of *parlements*, local estates where they existed, and governors. They knew that smooth administration depended upon co-operation with these powers rather than on overriding or ignoring them. An intendant was an administrative factotum: in order to gather taxes or regulate public works or public order, he had to be in almost constant negotiation with a myriad of older local authorities with a say in such matters. Otherwise there were spectacular breakdowns; provincial government could be immobilized, as in Brittany in the 1760s or Guyenne in the 1780s. Later in the eighteenth century intendants even began to be accused by ministers of being too concerned to protect their generalities and not zealous enough for royal interests. This was not the popular view, however.

[6] Quoted in C. Wilson, *Economic History and the Historian: Collected Essays* (1969), 124.

The most important decisions, observed the physiocrat Gournay in the 1750s, were increasingly being made by administrators in their offices (*bureaux*). Gournay coined a new word to describe this form of government—bureaucracy. The term was pejorative from the start, for Gournay, who also coined the term *laissez-faire*, believed on economic grounds that a state's interference in the lives of its citizens should be minimal. This was the natural view of society's traditional governors, whose powers the growth of bureaucracy could only curtail. By 1789 hostility to bureaucratic centralization was widespread throughout French society.

Around 1700, however, it seemed one of the keys to the efficiency of Louis XIV's state. So when his grandson succeeded to the throne of Spain, and went to Madrid surrounded by French advisers, it was natural that the system should be introduced there too. The first Spanish intendants were created in 1711, to co-ordinate military supplies, and in 1718 a network of civilian intendants was created for the whole of Spain. After initial hostility from established local authorities, the experiment was suspended in 1721. Only in 1749 was it re-established, but from then on it worked so successfully that from 1764 it was progressively extended to the American colonies. Even so, conflicts with the powerful municipal councils of the Spanish kingdoms, and old-established district officers, were constant on both sides of the Atlantic. Kings supported the new officers because of, as Charles III put it in 1764, 'the advantages which the establishment of the intendancies. . .has brought to my royal exchequer in the better administration of its revenues, and to my army in the secure provision of supplies',[7] but it was only at the cost of outraging those groups that still conducted the bulk of everyday local administration.

Neither French nor Spanish intendants underwent any formal training in administration. They learned while on the job. Their German counterparts, by contrast, benefited from a long tradition of administrative or 'cameralistic' studies in German universities. These bodies were almost all controlled by the states in which they were established. They were regarded by rulers primarily as training establishments for state servants, whether clerics or administrators; their faculties of law were really schools of administration. This emphasis increased in the eighteenth century, as many universities were influenced by the example of Halle. Cameralist writers, many of them products of, or professors at, German universities, also produced a substantial body of administrative theory far more influential on the policies of German states than the more abstract speculations of French philosophers. Most members of the Prussian administrative machine in the eighteenth century were graduates of Halle, soaked in cameralistic doctrines; in addition, from 1770 onwards, they were subjected to examinations of competence. By this time Prussian bureaucracy had acquired the reputation of the most efficient in Europe.

Prussian administration bore the mark of cameralism in that, unlike the

---

[7] Quoted in J. Lynch, *Spanish Colonial Administration 1782–1810; the Intendant System in the Viceroyalty of the Rio de la Plata* (1958), 50.

system of intendants, it comprised no officials acting alone. At every level they were grouped into chambers or boards of officials, who kept a check on one another. Around 1700 the fashion for such 'colleges' swept northern Europe. 'There cannot be good administration except with colleges,' wrote Leibniz to Peter I; 'their mechanism is like that of watches, whose wheels mutually keep each other in movement.'[8] Each Prussian provincial chamber was made up of a president and two directors, and between fifteen and twenty other councillors. Each also had a numerous staff, and all were well paid by the standards of most of Europe. Officials, never employed in their native provinces, were often (and increasingly) retired army officers, bringing to their tasks all the qualities, advantageous or otherwise, of Europe's most prestigious army. At every level administrative institutions were subject to the surveillance of a *fiscal*, who reported independently on the conduct of their members to the government. The power of provincial chambers was far more complete and just as far-reaching as that of intendants. The power of estates had largely been destroyed by the early eighteenth century; the nobles whose independent spirit normally gave such institutions their importance looked upon administration not so much as a threat, as a potential livelihood, especially after Frederick II abandoned his father's policy of recruiting bourgeois administrators. Yet the aims of administration were more narrowly conceived than in France. Prussian bureaucrats existed to maximize the revenues, and for little else. They won promotion or otherwise largely on a basis of the increase in the tax-yield of their departments. The ubiquitous system of checks ruled out initiative, and therefore discouraged those who might be inclined to employ their powers for other purposes, however benevolent.

Centralization had far less success and less impact in Russia, where Peter I sought, with characteristic clear-sightedness, to create a uniform, centralized governmental structure. By his death the old amorphous, military provinces of Russia had been replaced by fifty smaller 'governments', which, however, hardly survived him. Until the 1770s the only effective units of centrally controlled local authority were regions of military recruitment, although the local taxation machinery was subject to the surveillance of *fiscals* or procurators on the Prussian model. In 1775, as a direct result of the inadequacies revealed by Pugachev's rebellion, a new law on provincial administration was introduced. Although it appeared to limit rather than to extend central power by providing for certain functions to be performed by elected nobles, in practice these duties were always subordinate and of little importance. After 1775 Russia was once again divided into a number of 'governments', numbering fifty by the 1790s, each ruled by panels of centrally appointed administrators with wide but carefully compartmentalized powers—an obvious parallel with the Prussian system. The Russian bureaucracy numbered 16,000 before this law, which was not large for the most populous state in Europe. But the new order introduced a multiplicity of new institutions, all of which

[8] Quoted in B. H. Sumner, *Peter the Great and the Emergence of Russia* (1951), 126.

needed to be staffed, to begin a bureaucratic expansion which went on un-checked throughout the nineteenth century.

The main obstacles to centralization in Russia were the immense size of the country, its poor communications, and the scarcity of capable personnel. The great problem in the Habsburg domains was the strength and variety of well-established local governmental institutions, all manned by officers who regarded themselves as perfectly competent, with no need for any extension of central control. Nor was there any such extension in Hungary or the southern Netherlands. In Hungary the county assemblies of nobles, and in the Netherlands the municipal oligarchies, continued to be the sole agents of authority, implementing orders from the centre only in ways they found convenient. Most of the other Habsburg domains had royal governors and staffs, known as *gubernia*, alongside the administrative and fiscal apparatus maintained by the provincial estates. After the reforms of the late 1740s had reduced meetings of estates to an annual formality, the power of the *gubernia* began to grow rapidly. Joseph II accelerated this process by abandon-ing the traditional provinces as units of administration altogether and dividing his domains into thirteen uniform governments, themselves subdivided into circles, each headed by a *Kreishauptmann*. He also decreed the use of German as the universal language of administration. Not all of these reforms survived Joseph's brief reign, but they had two important results. In the long term they laid the foundations (as in Russia) of a modern bureaucracy, loyal to the state rather than to the locality or province. More immediately they outraged, by their suddenness, all the local susceptibilities that Maria Theresa's slower but equally relentless policies had already rubbed raw. Joseph's resolute and uncompromising use of state power was aimed at the complete reorganization of his domains; but the reaction to it came close to overthrowing authority itself.

Only two major states avoided some degree of bureaucratic centralization, nor was it a coincidence that both were governed by representative institutions. In the Dutch republic the mainsprings of power were municipal oligarchies. There was no effective central government independent of the states-general, a body which itself had no freedom to act independently of its provincial mandatories. The Dutch local authorities therefore controlled such central authority as there was, without any conflict of interests. A similar situation obtained in Great Britain. For a brief period during the interregnum Cromwell had governed England through major-generals, a sort of intendant system, which left unhappy memories among a landed class accustomed to admini-stration on the crown's behalf as justices in quarter-sessions. The Restoration brought back the authority at county level of local landowners, and the eighteenth-century parliament firmly upheld the autonomy of the counties. The land tax was collected, the militia commanded, the poor law administered, and criminal justice dispensed by local gentlemen, for the most part unpaid. This same class controlled the state through its virtual monopoly of parlia-mentary representation. Again, therefore, there was no conflict of interests. When Englishmen complained of the proliferation of government officers, they were not worried about centralization. Their concern was about the way offices were distributed to those who promised to support the government in elections or in votes in parliament itself—the 'power of patronage' or 'the influence of the crown'. It was ironical that this practice, denounced as an abuse by countless sponsors of 'place bills' from 1689 onwards, and by the 'economical reformers' of the 1770s and 1780s, was the very foundation of stable parliamentary government, upon which the local autonomy of the British counties ultimately depended.

Central Authority

To match the concentration of power at provincial and local level, central authority was becoming more unified and streamlined. In the later seventeenth century the most diffuse central authority was that of Spain, where every branch of the state was presided over by a council responsible only to the king. There were councils for each province—for Castile, for Aragon, for the Indies—and for each department of state—war, finances, the Inquisition. This machinery reflected the growth in the state's activities over the years: the standard solution to an administrative problem was to set up a council. Similarly in the Austrian domains, where each territory, such as Hungary, Bohemia, or Transylvania, was ruled from its own court chancellery in Vienna, while all military affairs were supervised by the *Hofkriegsrat* and the revenues of the royal domains by the *Hofkammer*. The scattered domains of the elector of Brandenburg, in contrast, were ruled by 1660 as one unit, but the military ambitions of the great elector allowed the general war commissariat to usurp, or at least duplicate, the authority of other financial and administrative institutions in the state from 1679 onwards. In such states, the complexity of central government led to cumbersome, slow, and inefficient administration. Authority was scattered, uncertain, and often self-contradictory. These were drawbacks which, it was increasingly argued, modern states could not afford.

As in provincial administration, France offered an impressive alternative model. The French administration was run by individual ministers: the chancellor or keeper of the seals (justice), the comptroller-general (finances), and the secretaries of state for war, the navy, foreign affairs, and the king's household. In addition each secretary had a general responsibility for a number of provinces. Policies were made by councils; the Privy Council was a supreme administrative tribunal from the ranks of whose officers most intendants were recruited. The secretaries of state, however, had the executive authority in implementing policies. The efficiency of this system seemed to prove itself under Louis XIV and was introduced into Spain when Philip V ascended the throne there; but the competence of the Spanish secretaries was wider, the system superimposed on the old conciliar structure rather than completely replacing it. By this time, moreover, the general disillusion which characterized Louis XIV's last years had produced much criticism of the system within France itself. When Louis died, a new and more Spanish-looking system, called *Polysynodie*, was introduced, in which each of the major branches of state was given an executive council superior to the secretary of state. Each council was composed mainly not of career administrators but the sort of great lords whom Louis XIV had largely excluded from power. Their inexperience rapidly told; the councils became scenes of undignified squabbling, and by 1718 the experiment had been abandoned. The power of the secretaries re-emerged, and was never threatened again until 1789. The complaints of 'ministerial despotism' so common during the crisis which culminated in that year, showed how dangerously effective many Frenchmen believed this power to be.

The French system had had few imitators outside Spain. More influential was the Swedish system—the main branches of administration run by the fashionable institution of colleges, but also under the constant scrutiny and direction of a Council of the Realm or Senate, (*Råd*) made up largely of great magnates (and not to be confused with the diet). Theoretically it held the constitutional balance between crown and diet. After 1680 Charles XI succeeded in reducing the senate to a branch of royal government, and during the 'age of freedom' between 1720 and 1772 it was equally subordinate to the diet, functioning as a central administrative clearing house rather than the independent constitutional watchdog it had claimed to be in the 1660s and 70s. The idea of a senate was copied by Peter I when he reorganized Russian central administration after 1711. When Peter came to the throne, the central administration of Russia was divided between thirty and forty departments with little to co-ordinate their work. By 1711, under the un-precedented strain of Peter's wars, chaos reigned. The senate, conceived originally as a sort of regency council during the tsar's absence on campaign, soon acquired a co-ordinating role—part clearing house, part administrative tribunal similar to the French privy council. The *fiscals* who spied upon the administration at all levels reported to it, and it was in itself subject to the supervision, from 1722, of a procurator-general, the personal representative of the tsar. Beneath the Senate, meanwhile, administrative departments were reorganized into colleges. Unlike its Swedish model, the Russian senate grew more powerful over the mid-eighteenth century. During that confused period it was the most stable element in the government. When Peter III seemed determined to by-pass it in 1762 it threw its support behind his wife Catherine in overthrowing him. Nevertheless, in 1768 she set up an imperial council, which rapidly deprived it of much administrative initiative, to the advantage of a handful of state secretaries reminiscent of those of France.

The most celebrated consolidation of central authority in this period was that operated by Frederick William I of Prussia. Increasingly infuriated by the constant jurisdictional quarrels between the civilian administration and the general war commissariat, this blunt monarch in 1723 decreed that they should all be brought under the co-ordinating control of a single General Directory. The king himself presided over this body, which included the heads of all the more important administrative chambers or colleges. It never extended its control to matters of justice, education, or foreign affairs, and in subsequent years certain departments periodically escaped from submission to it. But its general control over the Prussian bureaucracy was maintained until 1806, and it put an end to most of the confusion and inter-departmental friction which had done so much to slow down governmental procedures before the 1720s. It also proved an inspiration to Austrian reformers seeking to regenerate their ramshackle state after the loss of Silesia. In 1749 a central feature of Haugwitz's reform plans was the creation of a *Directorium* to co-ordinate the whole of the state's administrative activities in the Austrian and Bohemian lands. This unified control lasted only until 1761, when under a plan of Kaunitz the *Hofkammer* recovered its independent financial authority and the *Directorium* became known by the old name of court chancellery. But Austrian and Bohemian administration were not again separated, all non-Hungarian provincial authorities took their orders from, and sent their reports to, the chancellery alone; policy was now co-ordinated by a new council of state. Without such a preliminary unification of central authority. Joseph II could hardly have considered his own even more radical reforms.

The growth of bureaucracy is one of the keys to the much debated question of 'enlightened despotism'. Many late-eighteenth-century states implemented reforms that philosophers and their followers applauded, and even took credit for. Sometimes, as in the case of the easing of restrictions on the grain trade, governments were obviously influenced by the writings of reformers. Perhaps more often, reforms were a matter of practical common sense, owing little to theorists. In either case, monarchs were seldom the driving force. Much historiographical energy has been expended in trying to discover which works of Enlightenment the so-called 'despots' had read to impel them into action. In practice this probably mattered little. The ideas for reform, whether derived from reading or from necessity, emanated mostly from the growing bodies of professional administrators by whom monarchs were surrounded— the men who had to solve government's everyday problems. All most monarchs did was to authorize courses of action which often they only imperfectly understood. The real innovators of the eighteenth century, whether self-consciously men of Enlightenment or not, were not the kings but their bureau-cratic advisers. The conventional polite distinction which opponents of government usually drew, between well-intentioned kings and their wicked advisers, contained, in this regard, more than a grain of truth.

Nor is it any coincidence that Great Britain and the Dutch republic are normally deemed to have escaped 'enlightened despotism', for these two states were the great exceptions in the trend towards consolidation of central authority. Decisions of the Dutch states-general required unanimity, reflecting the fact that sovereign power resided in the provinces, which administered their own affairs separately. Even the stadtholder, who dominated govern-ment in time of war when decisive action was imperative, had to work through the provinces rather than through any central administrative organs. In the British state, Ireland and (before 1707) Scotland, not to mention the American colonies, were separately administered, without any attempt to treat them uniformly. When tentative steps in this direction were taken, in the 1760s and 1770s, they brought the British empire crashing down. Centralization may have been an essential step in the modernization of states; but for those who attempted it, it often proved more trouble than it was worth.

Policy-Making and Opposition

Policy-making, deciding how, and to what ends, the state's resources should be deployed, was a matter for kings alone. Their personal authorization was required for all acts of state, from declarations of war down to the granting of pensions; and once their decision was made, in theory nobody had the right to oppose it. As Louis XIV warned an over-importunate Colbert in 1671: 'After I have heard your arguments and those of your colleagues, and have given my opinion on all of your claims, I do not ever wish to hear further talk about it . . . after a decision that I give you I wish no word of reply.'[9]

In practice kings never made policy without taking advice, nor was it generally considered right that they should. How they sought this advice varied considerably. The most remote style of government was that of Frederick II of Prussia. Frederick believed councils, and even regular meetings with individual ministers, to be a dangerous waste of time. He reviewed his ministers and their departments once a year; their contact with him was almost entirely in writing and they never met together to concert policy. The king made all important (and many unimportant) decisions himself, alone, on the basis of streams of short memoranda which flowed constantly in to him from all departments of state. Yet Frederick's habits were undeniably against the trend of the age, which was towards policy-making by councils. 'It is of the essence of all well-regulated monarchies', wrote a French councillor of state in 1777, 'to be governed by counsel. Our kings have never departed from this principle; they have had around them from time immemorial a Council composed of men wise, enlightened, worthy of esteem and public confidence and they have made it a law to do nothing important without taking their Council's advice.'[10] Austrian monarchs never acted without ministerial advice, but they took it haphazardly and individually. The influence of members of their secretarial or personal staffs was as great as that of major officers of state. The result, Kaunitz believed, was near-disaster for the Austrian state in the mid-eighteenth century, and on his advice a council of state, made up of all the principal ministers, was set up in 1761. Seven years later an imperial council along the same lines was set up in Russia. That frenetic reformer, Peter I, had certainly not been afraid to seek advice from any quarter that seemed useful, but he had never met regularly with his ministers to discuss and concert policy. After the need to co-ordinate a war effort against the Turks impelled Catherine II to inaugurate such meetings in 1768, the institution proved so effective that it became the government's permanent nerve-centre.

Councils were nothing new to Spain, but regular meetings of the king's principal advisers were. Each of the administrative councils which proliferated

---

[9]   Quoted in C.W. Cole, *Colbert and a Century of French Mercantilism* (1939) i. 290.

[10]   Quoted in M. Antoine, *Le Conseil du Roi sous le règne de Louis XV* (1970), 26.

under the Spanish system was supposed to prepare a *consulta*, or written opinion, which the king might accept or reject in the privacy of his closet. Ministers met regularly and individually with the king, but not until 1787 was a council of ministers created. Even that did not survive beyond 1792.

There were obvious defects in conciliar government, described very well by Frederick in his *Political Testament* of 1752.

It is not from big assemblages that wise advice comes [he wrote], for Ministers are mutually divided by intrigues, private hatreds and passions intrude into the affairs of State, the system of debating questions by dispute is often too lively, casting shadows instead of bringing light, and, finally, secrecy, which is the soul of business, is never well kept by so many people.[11]

As an example of these drawbacks, he cited France. Yet France had not suffered from them under Louis XIV. Louis had made internal policy in the Council of Dispatches (on which all the secretaries of state, the comptroller-general, and the chancellor sat); and foreign policy in the *conseil d'en haut*, made up of three or four trusted advisers dignified with the title of minister of state, but attending solely at the monarch's pleasure and not *ex officio*. Rivalries there certainly were, notably between the Colbert and Le Tellier families, but Louis never allowed such antagonisms to hold up decisions, making it quite clear that his own word was final and immutable. Catherine II professed to follow the same approach.

I have given myself principles, a plan of government and conduct from which I never depart [she told the French ambassador].[12] My will once stated never varies. Here everything is constant; every day resembles that which has preceded it. As it is known what can be depended upon, nobody is worried. As soon as I have given somebody a place, he is certain, unless he commits a crime, to keep it. In this way, I remove all sustenance for troubles, rumours, quarrels, and rivalries; and so you see no intrigues around me; as the end of intriguers can only be to drive out men in office in order to put themselves in their place, under my government these troubles would be pointless.

Whether Catherine entirely lived up to these professions remains disputable; but it is certain that neither Louis XV nor Louis XVI had their predecessor's firmness. Louis XV protected his own authority by positively encouraging faction among his counsellors. The result was fluctuating policy and the inter-ministerial intrigue so despised by Frederick. Far from never changing his mind, Louis XV changed it repeatedly, and changed his minsters just as often. Louis XVI governed largely by majority vote, which again put a premium on scheming among ministers to alter the balance of the council. These disorders reached their height during minorities such as that of Louis XV himself between 1715 and 1723, or of Charles XI of Sweden between 1660 and 1672, when the absence of an undisputed final authority made councils a byword for factionalism and rudderless politics. Regents did little to restrain such passions, for they were not kings, their term of power was

[11] Quoted in C. A. Macartney (ed.), *The Habsburg and Hohenzollern Dynasties in the seventeenth and eighteenth centuries* (1970), 335.

[12] Quoted in L. P. Ségur, *Souvenirs et anecdotes sur le règne de Louis XVI* (1909 edn.), 156.

limited, and politicians jostled for the most advantageous position when the monarch came into his own.

A further spur to conciliar intrigue was the desire to become first minister. Under an absolute monarchy the sole qualification necessary was the confidence of the monarch. There was no difference in principle between a well-qualified minister and a favourite. The period offers plenty of examples of favourites with no obvious governmental capacities, or adventurers who shook states to their foundations on the strength of personal relationships with rulers—men like Law in France, Alberoni, Squillace, or Godoy in Spain, Potemkin in Russia, Struensee in Denmark, or Bute in Great Britain. Yet with the expanding number of professional administrators providing a pool of trained talent upon which rulers could increasingly draw, favouritism was on the decline. Dominant ministers such as Tanucci in Naples, Pombal in Portugal, Floridablanca in Spain, and Fleury, Choiseul, Maupeou, or Maurepas in France were all very experienced in public affairs when they achieved primacy. Kings such as Louis XIV and Frederick II none the less resolutely set their faces against the idea of a first minister, believing that royal authority was too important and too precious to be delegated. They both regarded themselves as the first servant of the state. Few monarchs however had their consistency, or the singleness of mind necessary to make their personal authority constantly effective. Even the rigid self-discipline of these two was not enough to cope efficiently with all the business that flowed in to them.

Ministerial life under absolute monarchs was precarious. Ministers or councillors were subject to dismissal at a whim, and though fallen ministers were seldom now executed, they were often disgraced, imprisoned, or exiled, and seldom returned to power. The great exceptions were the parliamentary states such as Venice, the Dutch republic, Sweden, and above all Great Britain. In these countries there was either no monarch, or the position of ministers did not depend entirely upon the royal favour. Here, ministers were unlikely to succeed unless they could command the confidence of members of the legislature too. In Great Britain policy was made by a small cabinet consisting of the monarch and the holders of the major offices of state. From the 1690s onwards it was tacitly understood that the latter should also be members of parliament, so as to promote liaison between the major institutions of the state. When, after 1714, Hanoverian monarchs ceased to attend cabinet meetings, the way was open for the emergence of a minister such as Walpole, who based his power on channelling all contact between the king on the one hand, and the cabinet and the House of Commons on the other. The king could dismiss a minister, certainly, but unless he could find a replacement who could handle parliament, the fallen minister could 'storm the closet' and force himself back into power. 'Ministers are the Kings in this Country', George II once ruefully observed,[13] and many of George III's early troubles stemmed from his refusal to recognize the facts of political life in

---

[13] Quoted in W. C. Costin and J. S. Watson, *The Law and Working of the Constitution: Documents 1660–1914* (1952), i. 376.

appointing Bute to head a ministry, when the latter was quite without parliamentary prestige or experience.

Another of George III's problems was his reluctance to recognize the legitimacy of opposition to royal policies. It was a common delusion of the age that there can be only one correct course of action. It appears in Rousseau's argument that the General Will can never be wrong because it always wills the public advantage,[14] and again in calls for British politicians to unite behind a 'patriotic line of conduct'. No monarch as self-righteous as George III could help resenting attacks on his government's policies in such an atmosphere. Yet he was not alone in believing that the government had a right to be supported. Most people in British public life professed to abhor 'systematic opposition' as the work of ambitious factions rather than of men of true public spirit. To avoid the stigma of disloyalty, parliamentary opponents of the government tended to congregate around the heir to the throne, forming a 'reversionary interest' and hoping for power when the king died; or they laid claim to a 'patriotism' which alleged that the king's or the country's best interests were being betrayed by the incumbent ministry. Even these subterfuges were widely regarded as shabby. Patriotism, said that great defender of conservative attitudes, Samuel Johnson, was the last refuge of a scoundrel.

However disreputable, parliamentary opposition was at least tolerated. By the end of the eighteenth century it was well on the way to becoming institutionalized, but under absolute monarchy it had no acknowledged place. The whole ideology supporting such government condemned resistance to the royal will, and those whose opposition to royal policies was too overt were likely to be accused of republicanism (a favourite term of abuse among kings), rebellion, or even treason. Opposition to an absolute monarch was more than disreputable, it was dangerous. Yet 'reversionary interests' tended to congregate, as in Great Britain, around the heir to the throne. Those who, from the 1690s onwards, regarded Louis XIV's policies as disastrous for France pinned their hopes on the ultimate succession of his grandson, the duke of Burgundy. They sought to influence his education to their way of thinking. Similarly, those who felt the pace of reform too slow in Austria under Maria Theresa looked forward to the succession of Joseph II to sole power, while opponents of Catherine II planned for the ultimate succession of the Grand Duke Paul. The most effective opponents of governments in such states, however, were not those who sought power in the future, but those who already possessed it—office-holders who disapproved of current policies. At local or provincial levels, established authorities were notorious for their ability and willingness to sabotage the execution of government policies. One reason for the growth of centralized bureaucracies was to circumvent this sort of obstruction. But it occurred at the very centre too: royal councils were more often bitterly divided than at one, and ministers who were overruled seldom saw it as any part of their business to defend

[14] *Social Contract*, Bk. II, ch. 3.

their rivals' policies. Collective responsibility was unknown; many royal councillors deliberately obstructed their colleagues' policies.

The perpetual and unintermittent envy, ill-feeling, and calumnies among the Ministers [recalled Maria Theresa of the political system she inherited in 1740] led to the most injurious animosities and consequently gave rise to incurable prejudices whereby the most salutary measures were thwarted, or when advice was given, it was usually coloured by innumerable arbitrary prejudices, so that the Prince was often placed in a situation of extreme embarrassment. And while many of my forebears have been accused of dilatoriness and indecision in the governance of their Provinces and State, the sole true reason for this was the constant disharmony between the Ministers and the obstinate insistence of each on his own opinion, which naturally could not fail to make the Monarch the more undecided, because he might suppose his own opinion to be mistaken.[15]

When a minister opposed a policy, she noted, he made it his business to incite the estates of provinces in which he was influential to obstruct or denounce it. Similar tactics were employed by rival ministers of Louis XV; they encouraged the *parlements* to block or remonstrate against policies they disliked, so as to sap the monarch's confidence in the measures adopted and the men who had proposed them. To oppose governments, was, of course, part of the function of local estates and *parlements*. This was why estates had the power to grant taxes, and *parlements* to remonstrate against new laws. But they were at their most effective, paradoxically, only when they received support and encouragement from members of the very governments they were denouncing.

[15] Quoted in Macartney, *The Habsburg and Hohenzollern Dynasties*, 110.

12. International Relations

The power of governments did not grow for its own sake. Most rulers accepted that governments existed to uphold and not disturb the established order of things, and that to attempt to extend their power was a hazardous process. But they had to defend themselves, and to maintain or improve their position against foreign competitors—the most fundamental obligation of all. States which neglected their own security laid themselves open to incalculable dangers in an age when new powers of unprecedented strength and predatory appetite were increasingly active in international affairs. So international competition and war were the main spur to domestic innovation. Eventually, these innovations provoked severe crises within several of the greater states, to shake their fabric even more seriously than foreign enemies could. But it is hard to see how they could have been avoided without taking international risks that most governments would have regarded as irresponsible.

Diplomacy: the Ends

By 1660 the wars of religion were over. As Louis XIV declared when the emperor and the pope appealed to him for help in driving the Turks from the gates of Vienna in 1683, crusades were no longer in fashion. This is not to say that religion had lost all importance. Louis himself promised Charles II French help in catholicizing England in 1670. The revocation of the Edict of Nantes played an important role in uniting outraged Protestant states against Louis in the late 1680s. Pious sentiments about the desirability of alliances with co-religionists continued to be expressed well into the eighteenth century, and as late as 1768 the Russians intervened in Poland to protect an Orthodox minority against persecution. But in such cases religion was never the only and seldom even the paramount consideration. Other principles concerned statesmen far more.

Dynasticism was one such principle. The main object of Habsburg policy was to maintain both the Spanish and Austrian thrones in the family by intermarriage between the branches or by renunciations on the part of those who married outside. Louis XIV's refusal to recognize the renunciations of his Spanish Habsburg mother and wife provided his main justification for attacking the Spanish Netherlands in 1666 and involving France in the Spanish Succession war in 1702. Spanish attempts to recover Italian possessions lost in 1713 for the sons of Queen Elizabeth Farnese disrupted international affairs throughout the early eighteenth century; and Joseph II's attempts to engross the Bavarian succession in the 1770s kept Germany tense. Nothing occasioned more wars than disputed successions in the 130 years before 1789, yet domains built up by dynasticism were often geographically messy and difficult to defend. It became a major object of diplomacy to rationalize and consolidate such territories whenever possible. Louis XIV's real objectives in the southern Netherlands or along the Rhine were to seize fortified towns which would make his frontier more easily defensible. Frederick II was eager to partition Poland in order to absorb the corridor of Polish territory which separated Prussia from Brandenburg.

The motives of kings were not always so rational. When Louis attacked the Spanish Netherlands, or when Frederick seized Silesia, they were both new in power, young, and anxious to achieve glory. On his deathbed Joseph II was unrepentant about the way his restlessness had disturbed Europe. 'I have always considered the military profession as my vocation,' he proclaimed, almost in the same breath as he expressed regret for making so few happy, 'and the development of the strength, the courage and the prestige of the army as the principal object of my life.'[1] Clearly certain monarchs went to war for the adventure and glory of it, with very little thought for the misery they might cause, or the troubles they might create within their own domains.

Sudden extensions of territory seldom occurred without war, because they upset the balance of power, a nebulous principle which commanded the lip-service of most statesmen throughout the period. It required that no state should be allowed to grow so powerful that it could dominate the rest; if it did, its power must be offset by an alliance or coalition. The obvious example was the grand alliance drawn together by William III in the late 1680s and early 1690s to oppose the pretensions of Louis XIV. Too strong an alliance, such as that which united France, Austria, and Russia against Prussia in the Seven Years War could also be construed as disturbing the balance. Although the object of a balance of power was the peaceful maintenance of the *status quo*, in practice it led to frequent wars, and was often invoked as meaninglessly as religion, dynastic right, or any other principle to justify states in doing what they had decided to do. In the mouths of British eighteenth-century statesmen it often seemed to mean anything detrimental to the interests of France.

Republics did not always follow the same principles as monarchies. They were without dynastic ambitions, nor were they greatly attracted by glory for its own sake. The only territorial ambition of the Dutch was for barrier fortresses in the southern Netherlands to protect them from French on-slaughts such as that of 1672. With a prosperity based largely upon trade, the Dutch republic's slogan in international affairs in the seventeenth century was 'free ships, free goods'. Rival states did not find this notion at all appealing, and England and France set up tariff barriers against Dutch traders.

The promotion of trade became increasingly important as a diplomatic objective. 'Commerce', wrote Colbert, 'causes a perpetual combat in peace and war among the nations of Europe, as to who shall win the most of it.'[2] He enthusiastically supported Louis XIV's invasion of the Dutch republic in 1672 because he believed it would ruin Dutch trade. The Swedes spent much

---

[1] Quoted by B. Behrens in *Historical Journal* (1975), 407.
[2] Quoted in Cole, *Colbert and a Century of French Mercantilism*, i. 343.

of the seventeenth century in attempting to make the Baltic a 'Swedish lake', so as to profit from a monopoly of its valuable trade. The spectacular prosperity produced by overseas colonies made economic competition between maritime states a world-wide business. With the Protestant succession secure, the promotion of overseas trade became the main objective of British policy throughout the eighteenth century. Even the northern powers, fearful that the British aim was nothing less than the monopoly of Europe's trade with the rest of the world, formed themselves in 1780 into an 'armed neutrality' to resist the interference of the British navy with their shipping.

What was absent from the conduct of international relations was the idealism and devotion to high causes which had been the driving force behind the wars of religion. Prudent statesmen had learned to fear and mistrust such transports. In their place they elevated the rational calculation of their states' interests—*raison d'état*. 'One must disabuse oneself', wrote the Prussian diplomat Bielfeld in 1760, 'of the speculative ideas held by ordinary men about justice, equity, moderation, candour, and the other virtues of nations and their rulers. *In the end everything depends on power*'.[3]

Diplomacy: the Means

As in internal affairs, so in international relations this period saw an increasing professionalism and sophistication in the machinery at the disposal of governments. The practice of maintaining permanent ambassadors or envoys in the main capitals of Europe was already well established. By 1661, France already had twenty-two permanent representatives abroad; by 1715, thirty-two. Six years later, Russia had twenty-one. Even a minor German state such as Hanover had sixteen permanent representatives in 1714. The selection and training of such representatives was a haphazard business. Most had no thought of a career in diplomacy, for no career structure had emerged anywhere until near the end of the eighteenth century. They generally looked upon service abroad as a form of exile, only undertaken in the hope of eventual preferment at home. Service abroad was expensive; representatives in major capitals were usually great noblemen prepared to supplement their meagre stipends generously from their own private means. Subordinates were normally their friends or dependents. Consular posts were usually occupied by natives of the countries or towns to which they were accredited. Schemes which were floated in the eighteenth century in France, Prussia, and Russia for systematic training of future diplomats never lasted long. In a world governed by noblemen who owed their positions to worldly experience rather than formal training, only foreign envoys of similar background could expect to be taken seriously.

Foreign representatives were the formal means of communication between governments, but they also sent home private reports on public affairs in general. The dispatches of efficient ambassadors are among the most useful historical sources. Envoys also co-ordinated less public activities, managing

---

[3] Quoted in A. Sorel, *L'Europe et la Révolution française* (5th edn. 1905), i. 26.

spy-rings, intercepting each other's dispatches, and distributing propaganda. Ambassadors of rich states paid secret subsidies to those they found useful, and took endless pains to assure their country's prestige in struggles for precedence over other ambassadors. 'Ratisbon', a newly appointed British minister to the seat of the imperial diet was warned in the 1760s, 'is full of ceremony. You cannot spit out of the window without offending the head or paraphernalia of an *Excellence*. . .Ceremonial there is looked on as essential and subject to contests.'[4] The most famous contests were those in which Louis XIV first revealed his pretensions to European supremacy in 1661. After a pitched battle in the streets of London between the retinues of the French and Spanish ambassadors, Louis threatened war and had his precedence recognized.

In 1660 foreign ministries were practically non-existent or formed part of agencies with other duties. This was because foreign relations were the supreme affair of kings—a mystery, a secret, a prerogative which only they could or should control and understand. Such attitudes persisted far into the eighteenth century, often long after regular bureaucratic procedures had emerged. The French department of foreign affairs was large and well organized under a secretary of state by the time Louis XIV died. But this did not prevent Louis XV from conducting a secret diplomacy of his own from 1745 until his death, alongside, and not always in entire harmony with, official policy. By this time Prussia, Sweden, Russia, Spain, and the Austrian empire all had separate foreign offices. In 1782 the British finally divided the general duties of the two secretaries of state into home and foreign, with one of the secretaries in complete control of each; but they still remained far behind their continental rivals in the scale of their organization. In 1797 the whole staff of the foreign office was still only twenty-four, when as long before as 1705 the Russian foreign service had employed over forty translators alone. The prestige, efficiency, and professionalism of Louis XIV's foreign office was an inspiration to his rivals, but apart from its diplomatic successes perhaps its most lasting achievement was the triumph of French as the language of diplomacy. In 1660 Latin or Italian had been more favoured; by 1713, the peace of Utrecht, French had no serious challengers. Henceforth diplomatic personnel were not necessarily expected to speak the language of the country to which they were posted, but they were expected to know French.

Such agreed conventions were rare. Attempts had indeed been made to elaborate universal rules of conduct, a system on international law. The most celebrated and influential was that of the Dutch statesman Grotius, elaborated in *Of the Law of War and Peace* in 1625. Grotius was concerned with whether war can be just, and whether its conduct is bound by any rules. He implied that there were laws which determined such issues, an amalgam of customs and the natural law promulgated by God, which was that men naturally sought to coexist with one another in peace. This law recognized

---

[4]   Quoted in D. B. Horn, *The British Diplomatic Service, 1689—1789* (1961), 24.

that states had certain common rights and common duties; it also gave them the right to punish violators of these conventions. Richard Zouche, an Oxford professor who died in 1661, emphasized that custom was the true basis of the law of nations. Pufendorf, on the other hand, in *Of the Law of Nature and of Peoples* (1672), recognized no binding obligations but those of the law of nature; but all believed that certain international acts can be unjust. This principle was so contrary to the spirit of eighteenth-century diplomacy that it is no surprise that it was challenged. In *The Law of Peoples*, published in 1758, the Swiss diplomat Vattel argued that nations were in a sort of Hobbesian state of nature in their relations with one another—all free, all equal, and all the sole judges of justice and injustice. There could be no unjust wars; for law between nations was purely voluntary. When a state's actions appeared on the face of it unjust, the only possible presumption was that its true motivation was its own view of justice; in any case, there was no redress.

Practical men realized that no international rules were enforceable without international consensus. The Peace of Westphalia set an important precedent in this direction, resulting from a congress of diplomats rather than from negotiations between individual states. Most states were represented, and most subsequent wars were concluded at similar gatherings. In this way peace was renewed with a semblance of general assent, but since no machinery was ever set up to perpetuate the work of congresses, consensus rapidly broke down. The period abounded in suggestions for the establishment of supra-national institutions for preserving the peace. Such were Penn's *Essay towards the Present and Future Peace of Europe* (1693) and Saint-Pierre's *Project for Settling an Everlasting Peace in Europe* (1712). The number of editions of these works shows the level of interest in their ideas, natural perhaps after the carnage of Louis XIV's last two wars. But statesmen took no notice; indeed, it is arguable that in pursuit of their interests they were growing ever more ruthless.

Louis XIV

Louis XIV's ambitions and achievements dominated the international history of the first half of this period; the memory of them haunted the whole of it. Louis had no grand design. He desired glory—renown, reputation, and honour, not only among contemporaries, but in the view of posterity. The struggles for diplomatic precedence which marked the beginning of his personal rule arose from this, in default of better opportunities. 'Everything was calm everywhere' he reminisced with evident regret; 'peace was established with my neighbours, probably for as long as I myself might wish. . .my age and the pleasure of being at the head of my armies, might have made me desire rather more external activity.'[5] He also wanted to restrain and thwart the ambitions and influence of the Habsburg powers Spain and Austria, which he regarded as France's natural enemies. Because of his opposition to the Habsburgs, Louis sought to strengthen his eastern frontier. What was new and alarming

[5] *Oeuvres de Louis XIV* (1806 edn.), i. 14–18.

about these very traditional preoccupations was the scale, organization, and efficiency of the forces Louis deployed in pursuit of them. For at least twenty years other states had nothing comparable to pit against him.

Accordingly, the period of Louis's greatest success lay before the mid-1680s. In 1662 he bought Dunkirk from the English and negotiated the succession to Lorraine. When Philip IV of Spain died in 1665, Louis laid claim to various territories in the southern Netherlands, on the grounds that his wife's dowry, agreed at the Peace of the Pyrenees in 1659, had not been paid. In the War of Devolution (1667–8) he invaded these territories and Franche Comté. The Spaniards offered no serious resistance, but the Dutch and English, at war with each other when Louis invaded, rapidly concluded peace, to form an alliance and prevent Louis from engrossing the entire southern Netherlands. Shaken, but reassured by a secret agreement with the Emperor Leopold to partition the Spanish empire between them should its sickly child-king Charles II die without heirs, Louis decided to settle for limited gains. At Aix-la-Chapelle in 1668 he gave up Franche Comté, but kept a number of fortified cities in Flanders. He undoubtedly regarded this settlement as an interim one.

Louis's immediate objective now, however, was to revenge himself on the Dutch. They had been his allies before 1667, but they had gone on to betray him and thwart his designs. He resented their republicanism and their Protestantism, his hatred only fanned by Colbert's constant emphasis on their economic power and the necessity for curbing it. 'There [is] in France', noted the Dutch envoy in 1668, 'profound dissatisfaction with this State, without any concealing of the king's intention to take revenge without fail for what has been done.'[6] Louis spent the next four years planning an invasion of the Republic. To discriminatory tariffs imposed in 1667 on imports by Dutch ships, Colbert added even heavier impositions in 1671. French diplomacy detached first England (in the secret treaty of Dover, 1670) and then Sweden from Dutch alliances. Thus prepared, in 1672 Louis launched a massive invasion while the English fleet engaged the Dutch at sea.

The Dutch never defeated Louis in the field, but they prevented him from overrunning their country by opening the dykes and flooding his access to Holland. Moreover the invasion brought to power the intransigent stadtholder William III. Spain was encouraged to join the Dutch in 1673; and the next year a number of German states joined the alliance under the leadership of the emperor. 1674 also saw the English parliament force Charles II to withdraw from the war, and three years later a defensive alliance with the Dutch was cemented by William III's marriage to the daughter of Charles's brother and heir. Louis's revenge expedition against the 'herring merchants' had become a general war, which lasted six years.

Louis was not unduly deterred. He simply abandoned his Dutch objectives and concentrated once more on the vulnerable Spanish territories along his border. Undefeated militarily, at the Peace of Nijmegen in 1678 he won

[6] Quoted in H. H. Rowen, *The Ambassador prepares for War: the Dutch Embassy of Arnauld de Pomponne* (1957), 31.

Franche Comté and further gains in the southern Netherlands and Alsace. The Dutch had survived, but the strengthening of the frontiers more than made up for this in French eyes. Along them Louis now proceeded to set up a so-called 'iron barrier' of fortifications. Where gaps still existed he filled them by a policy of 'reunions', a staggeringly arrogant process in which territories once dependent upon new French acquisitions were themselves annexed. This policy did nothing to soothe the German and imperial susceptibilities first offended in the 1670s, but the Empire was leaderless as the Turks drove Leopold's forces back to the gates of Vienna itself in 1683. Only the Spaniards offered any resistance to Louis, which resulted for them in the loss of Luxemburg, also in 1683. The truce of Ratisbon the next year, intended to last twenty years, confirmed Louis in all his gains since 1678. It was the high point of his reign in terms of diplomatic and territorial success.

From then on the tide began to flow against France. Vienna had not fallen to the Turks and the Austrians now began to drive them back into the Balkans. The revocation of the Edict of Nantes outraged Protestant opinion throughout Europe and notably the elector of Brandenburg, who forsook Louis to join a defensive federation of German states known as the League of Augsburg (1686); the news of his adherence brought in the emperor too. In England the revocation coincided with the accession of the Catholicising James II and alerted his subjects to the dangers of Catholic rule. By three years of precipitate and insensitive Romanising, James provoked leading Englishmen into inviting William III, his son-in-law, to depose him. William was Louis XIV's most inveterate opponent, whose whole life was devoted to constructing barriers against French aggression. If, as in previous wars, Louis had struck at the southern Netherlands, William would probably not have risked sailing for England. Instead, Louis chose to invade Germany, where he was convinced his real enemies lay. In devastating the Rhineland he inaugurated a nine-years war with an act that completed the unity of the major German princes against him, and allowed William to sail without qualms to England, where he took over without serious opposition. The result of these enormous miscalculations was to confront Louis with a coalition of unprecedented strength and unity, resolutely led by William and Leopold, and financed by the combined wealth of the two great maritime powers. This time he was stopped dead in his tracks.

The War of the League of Augsburg (1688–97) was the greatest international conflict since the Thirty Years War. Louis was facing armies which were for the first time a match for his own. His fleet was crippled at La Hogue in 1692 and thereafter run down. Economic disasters enervated the population and diminished its capacity to bear the new taxes and heavier recruitment brought by the war. His armies continued to win battles and sieges, but none of these victories brought decisive advantages. By 1693 exhaustion had set in, and Louis began to negotiate. It was not however until 1697 that the Peace of Ryswick was finally concluded. Louis surrendered many of the gains of the previous twenty years, such as Lorraine and Luxemburg. He also recognized William III as king of England and agreed to the

Dutch garrisoning a number of barrier fortresses in the southern Nether-lands. Though France retained some of her earlier conquests, such as Franche Comté, Ryswick was a defeat. Much of what Louis had striven for since 1661 had come to nothing.

The Spanish Succession

The main victim of Louis XIV's aggressions was Spain, who lost many of her central-European possessions. Louis believed he had a right to them through the claims of his wife in the Spanish Succession. When he married her in 1659 she renounced these claims, but it was uncertain whether she could do this under Spanish law, and in any case French recognition of the renunciation was conditional upon payment of the bride's dowry, which had still not been made when Philip IV died in 1665. This was Louis's pretext for starting the War of Devolution, by which he made clear to the Austrian Habsburgs that should the Spanish branch fail they could not expect to succeed without a French challenge. This prospect induced Leopold I to make the secret partition agreement of 1668.

But Charles II did not die. In fact he spent much of his reign at war with Louis. The result was that by 1697 France had already acquired by conquest many of the territories assigned to her under the 1668 agreement. Since Charles was childless, the succession question remained open. Only two points were clear. One was that the Spaniards were determined to avoid any par-tition of their empire. The other was that the maritime powers were not prepared to see either Louis or Leopold become king of Spain. For the power of Spain to be united with that of the Empire or France would totally upset the balance of power created at Ryswick. Both Louis and Leopold recognized this; each vested his claim in a descendant with no near prospect of succeeding to his own throne—Louis in his grandson Anjou, and Leopold in his younger son the Archduke Charles.

After the sobering experience of the previous nine years, Louis was anxious to avoid war on this issue. He negotiated with the ruler who held the Euro-pean balance after Ryswick—William III. Eventually they agreed (1698) that Spanish possessions in Italy should be divided between the French and Austrian claimants, but that the rest of the empire should go to the electoral prince of Bavaria, a child descended from Leopold by his first marriage. Neither Leopold nor the Spaniards were consulted, and when the electoral prince died the next year, negotiations had to begin afresh. It was now agreed (1700) that the Austrian claimant Archduke Charles should receive the whole empire with the exception of the Italian territories, which should go to Anjou. But Italy, the essential link between Austria and Spain, was the one area where the Austrians could make no concessions, and they refused to accept the treaty. Louis was preparing to fight to enforce it as the Spanish king's health waned, but when Charles finally died on 1 November 1700, it was found that his will left the whole Spanish empire, undivided, to Anjou.

Louis could not have been expected to refuse this windfall. Leopold, equally, could never accept the spurning of all his family's claims and pretensions. This did not make a general war inevitable. Anjou was recognized as Philip V of Spain by the maritime powers, without whose support the Austrians were no match for Louis. But Louis now overplayed his hand: he declared that Anjou could not renounce his rights in the French succession. Spain was flooded with French advisers and French troops occupied the Spanish Netherlands, expelling the Dutch from their barrier fortresses. The balance of power was being upset, the Ryswick settlement overthrown. Louis recognized James II's son as James III when the old exile died. Commercial advantages in the Spanish empire were transferred from England to France. It was this string of provocations that eventually forced the Dutch and the English back into an alliance with the emperor.

So began the war of the Spanish Succession (1702–13). France was fighting the same enemies as in the previous war. This time she had the alliance of Spain; but this time too she had to commit extensive forces to Spain and to Italy as well as to the Rhine and the Netherlands. Now Louis's enemies had trained and seasoned armies which easily matched his own; enemy commanders such as Marlborough and Eugene outshone the French generals. Until 1711, therefore, the war was a series of terrible disasters for France. Enormous battles were fought—Blenheim, Ramillies, Oudenarde—in which there were thousands of casualties and the French were beaten. France itself was invaded, and in the catastrophic winter of 1708–9 Louis sued for terms. He agreed to the most extreme demands of the triumphant allies, but when they demanded that he should send French troops to help the Archduke Charles to drive Philip V, his own grandson, from the peninsula, Louis refused. The war went on and French prospects even began to improve. Nothing helped them so much, however, as the death in 1711 of Leopold's successor, the childless Emperor Joseph I, for this made the Archduke Charles emperor. The prospect now, should he make good his claim to Spain, was of an enormous shift in the balance of power towards the Austrians. The war-weary Dutch and English felt disinclined to continue fighting for such an objective. When Louis agreed that the French and Spanish crowns should never be united, the maritime powers were prepared to accept the obvious preference of the Spaniards for Philip V. Only the Austrians—understandably—wished to continue the fight, but deserted by their allies they were unable to carry on long.

Under the treaties of Utrecht (1713) and Rastadt (1714) the Spanish empire was at last divided. Philip V was recognized as heir to Spain and the overseas possessions, but the Austrians took the Netherlands and (with the exception of Sicily, which went to Savoy), the Italian territories. It was agreed that the French and Spanish crowns should never be united. The Dutch were guaranteed a strengthened barrier in the Netherlands, and the Protestant succession to the British throne was generally recognized. The British also gained various colonial territories and commercial concessions in the Spanish empire. With the death of Louis XIV in 1715, a whole chapter in international relations was closed. Louis had made good his family's claim to the throne of Spain, but only at the cost of pushing France's resources to the point of exhaustion. The Dutch had their barrier against

French aggression, but they had also stretched their own resources to the limit. The Austrians too were exhausted; acquisitions such as the Netherlands were arguably a source of weakness rather than strength. French pretensions to European hegemony had been decisively thwarted, but this threat had given place to another—the preponderance of the only power to emerge from the settlement with substantial gains and energies to spare—Great Britain.

The Rise of Great Britain

The sixteenth and early seventeenth centuries had seen the international power and prestige of England shrinking. The larger and better-organized continental states overtook her. Internal conflicts and disorders in the 1630s and 1640s seemed only to confirm this long decline. Yet, properly marshalled, English strength could be considerable, as Cromwell's adventurous foreign policy demonstrated in the 1650s. This decade saw the first of the Dutch wars (1652–4), which were to be the main feature of English foreign policy for the next twenty years: the second (1665–7) was not as successful for the English as the first, and the third (1672–4) in alliance with the French, brought no gains at all. But in the course of these wars Dutch commerce had been seriously damaged and British merchants began to accumulate a growing proportion of the carrying trade. By the eighteenth century they had secured the greater part of it.

This was not foreseen in the 1660s and 1670s, when the internal quarrels and weaknesses that had bedevilled the pre-Cromwellian decades seemed to have returned, ensuring that England could be kept either neutral or ineffectual in its policies by shrewd diplomacy. Louis XIV exploited this situation to the full, bribing first Charles II and then his opponents. The change came with the revolution of 1688–9, which brought to power a king, William III, determined to throw England's weight into the coalition against Louis XIV, and a parliament which had no alternative but to acquiesce in his policy if it wished to keep him on the throne. William's policy required an unprecedented marshalling of resources. A growing navy and a huge new army were paid for by doubling the rate of taxation and organizing the state's credit more effectively than ever before. Naturally the suddenness of these developments imposed strains, but generations of peace had given the British economy a spare capacity to absorb them that other states did not enjoy. So British power was exerted, but not exhausted, against Louis XIV, and by 1713 Great Britain (into which Scotland was now fully integrated) was recognized as a European power the equal of France and the emperor, and far ahead of the Dutch republic.

Tied though it was after 1714 to the electorate of Hanover through its new ruling dynasty, Great Britain did not seek territorial gains on the continent or feel threatened by weak borders. It was widely agreed that the main objective of policy should be commercial. 'It is this nation's interest', Queen Anne declared from the throne in 1714, 'to aggrandise itself by trade.'[7] How

---

[7] Quoted in G. Holmes and W. A. Speck, *The Divided Society: parties and politics in England 1694–1716* (1967), 96.

this was best done was, however, a matter for bitter disagreement. Whigs maintained that the struggle against Louis XIV, as well as serving the balance of power, also helped to enervate Britain's potentially greatest trade rival. Tories tended to believe that isolation and a strong fleet would be more effective, and cheaper too. But whoever was in control of it, British policy was marked by the single-minded pursuit of commercial advantages. The prospect of breaking into the trade of the Spanish empire sustained enthusiasm for the Succession war. Nothing did more to push the country into that war than the grant of the *asiento*, the right to import a quota of black slaves into the Spanish empire, to a French company. In 1713 the British won this right. Nothing did more than the war to strengthen the already close economic links between Great Britain and Portugal, confirmed in the Methuen treaty of 1703, which enabled the British to siphon off much of the newly dis-covered gold of Brazil. Most striking of all, perhaps, the peace of Utrecht left Britain with a colonial empire second only to that of Spain. Control of the Mediterranean was acquired through Minorca and Gibraltar. In North America the French ceded Nova Scotia and Newfoundland to add to the twelve British mainland colonies already established.

Colbert was dead, but many Frenchmen saw that the arguments he had used about Dutch commercial predominance in the 1660s now applied to the British. Already in the 1690s the strategist Vauban was arguing that the most effective way of curbing William III's power was to unleash privateers against British shipping. They wrought such havoc that in 1696−7 and 1711−13 mercantile interests in England were almost as loud as the highly taxed landed interest in clamouring for peace. Inevitably, however, as the strength of the maritime powers frustrated Louis XIV's ambitions, the French began to think (as Colbert had) of rivalling them overseas as well as attacking them. After Louis XIV had given his support to exploration south and west from Quebec, a new colony was set up (1699) in Louisiana. The British gains at Utrecht were a setback to these policies; but the world-wide colonial rivalry that was to dominate Franco-British relations throughout the eighteenth century had clearly begun with the century itself.

The Decline of the Dutch Republic and Sweden

As Great Britain rose, so the Dutch republic declined. In 1660 she was the greatest commercial and naval power in Europe; by 1713 she was still formidable, but had been overtaken in both these spheres by Great Britain. The desire for security against French aggression from the south made her, for at least another generation, practically a British satellite, long after real danger from this quarter had disappeared.

Yet the decline was largely relative. Dutch money and credit remained a mainstay of both grand alliances. Dutch troops outnumbered English or imperial troops on the Spanish Succession battlefields. At Utrecht they achieved the barrier for which they had striven for forty years. Nor did commerce begin to decline noticeably until about 1730. So there was no contraction, but there was no expansion either, so that long before they actually declined the Dutch were outpaced by states whose resources were much larger, once they chose to marshal them. French and British merchants began to take increasingly large slices of trade where the Dutch had hitherto held a virtual monopoly. The aggressive designs of France from the 1660s turned the Republic's attention from promoting trade to protection of the homeland. In the hurried peace of Breda in 1667 they gave up New York to England and afterwards concentrated on keeping the overseas colonies they had rather than acquiring new ones. And the efforts required to counter the French threat burdened the state with a debt which could only be serviced by one of the highest rates of taxation in Europe. This in its turn could only be borne by high wages, which led to Dutch goods and services being slowly undercut by those of other countries. By the early eighteenth century the profitability of Dutch industry was down: better returns on capital could be obtained from foreign investments such as the British national debt.

The decline in Dutch importance was compounded by a policy of neutrality in most major wars up to 1780. Their only intervention, at the behest of their English allies in the Austrian Succession war between 1744 and 1748, gained them nothing that could not have been secured by neutrality, for the French had no more territorial designs in the Netherlands. As the French threat receded, and trade became once more the Republic's main concern, neutrality was generally agreed to be the best policy. Inevitably, however, this produced a gradual estrangement from Great Britain, who regarded neutral shipping in time of war as potentially hostile. This policy almost pushed the Republic into war with Great Britain in 1758−9. Hostilities finally broke out in 1780. They proved disastrous. Britain, isolated in Europe, was still able to disrupt Dutch trade completely. It was a vivid demonstration of the changed relative power of the two states over a century.

Another sign of the relative decline of the Dutch republic was its falling share of the Baltic trade. In the seventeenth century Dutch prosperity was largely based upon their acting as an entrepôt between the Baltic and the rest of Europe. In 1661, three-quarters of the ships passing the Sound flew the Dutch flag. One of their main concerns was that no power should gain complete control of the sea's shoreline, threatening their commercial monopoly with a political one.

This, however, was Sweden's aim. The years since 1621 had seen a steady expansion of Swedish territory on the eastern shore of the Baltic. The Peace of Oliva in 1660 brought Sweden as near to her monopolistic ambitions as she ever got, expelling the Danes from the eastern shore of the Sound and winning territory and ports in Pomerania. The next thirty-seven years, under the minority and then the personal rule of Charles XI, saw no further advances. Sweden's only major intervention in international affairs, the invasion of Brandenburg as the auxiliary of Louis XIV, ended in disaster. The Brandenburg elector's new professional army defeated the hitherto invincible Sweden at Fehrbellin (1675).

Like the Dutch republic, Sweden was powerful mainly because other states were weak, but her basic strength was far flimsier. Her Baltic empire was built up by bold kings leading well-disciplined armies which lived off enemy territories. Sweden, with a tiny population, was too poor to maintain a standing army or navy of any size from her own resources. Port tolls were disappointing in their yield and pitched at levels which positively discouraged traffic, so they were of little help. Accordingly, Sweden found it far easier to conquer territories than to hold them down. She was a great power only when actually at war, and even then only so long as her armies remained undefeated. Defeats in the field left her possessions on the southern and eastern Baltic shores untenable.

All this was demonstrated by the meteoric career of Charles XII, who came to the throne in 1697, and spent most of his twenty-one-year reign at war. Increasingly discontented with Sweden's still-dominant position in the Baltic, a coalition of powers including Russia, Denmark, and Poland set out to exploit the accession of a boy by dismembering the more exposed outposts of his empire. In 1700 they inaugurated the Great Northern War, but they had not bargained for the military vigour of the new Swedish king, who knocked Denmark out of the war and smashed a Russian army at Narva in Estonia in the first year. Campaigns in Poland led to her eventual withdrawal from the coalition and the deposition of her king in 1707, leaving Russia to fight on alone. The Swedish hegemony in the Baltic seemed stronger than ever, and the maritime powers, who were engaged in their own struggle over the Spanish succession, feared that Charles might move against the emperor, defeat him, and so ensure the triumph of Louis XIV.

These nightmares were dispelled in 1709, when a Swedish army under Charles invaded Russia, to be totally destroyed at Pultava in the Ukraine. Charles escaped with a few followers to Turkish territory, where he remained until 1714. The old northern coalition re-formed and proceeded to deprive Sweden of most of her territories on the eastern and southern Baltic shores. Charles's return to Sweden renewed some of the country's military vigour, but his earlier success was not repeated. After his death in action in 1718 the war-weary country thought of little but concluding a swift peace, which eventually came with the treaty of Nystad in 1721.

This treaty marked the end of Sweden as a major international power. Russia restored conquests made in Finland, but took control of Ingria, Estonia, and Livonia. Prussia, which had joined the coalition late, took the port of Stettin; Hanover, whose elector as George I of Great Britain had used the world's greatest fleet to further his ambitions, obtained Bremen. Thus the Swedish empire was partitioned out of existence, and the country which had been the terror of northern Europe for a century withdrew to the sidelines, under a parliamentary regime under which domestic party advantage assumed more importance than international ambitions. Foreign adventures were not totally renounced; there was a brief war against Russia in 1740–1 and an invasion of Prussian Pomerania in the Seven Years War. Both proved ignominious failures, confirming that the collapse of Swedish power was permanent. Gustavus III, though he controlled the Swedish state as no king had since Charles, was not able to emulate the latter's early successes when he invaded Russia in 1788. When the Danes invaded the Swedish mainland, only a British threat to send a fleet against them saved Gustavus. Sweden came out of this brief war, as she had out of every one since 1707, empty-handed, with western powers to thank that the result had not been far worse.

The Emergence of Russia

With hindsight we can see that Swedish power was always flimsily based and in over-all decline from the Peace of Oliva onwards. But this was not at all clear to contemporaries. Charles XII wielded well-established power which northern Europe had learned to fear. This made his defeat at Pultava all the more shocking. It also directed the attention of the whole of Europe towards the power that had so unexpectedly triumphed in this clash.

In 1660 Russia had not been a European power. She was isolated from western Europe by Turkish power in the south, the great shapeless mass of Poland to the west, and by a blanket of Swedish territory around the Baltic. No western power maintained permanent representation in Moscow, while Russian missions to the west were sporadic. Nor was it immediately clear that Peter I would change any of this when he assumed full power in 1695. His visits to Holland and England in 1698 made him an object of curiosity rather than respect. His defeat at Narva surprised nobody. What the whole of Europe underestimated was his persistence. Peter was determined to make Russia a first rate power, with an army and navy the equal of any. By founding his new capital of St. Petersburg on the gulf of Finland in 1703, he showed that he meant his Baltic presence to be permanent, and the victory at Pultava ensured that it would be. The main significance of the treaty of Nystad was that Russia replaced Sweden as the dominant power in the Baltic. All the maritime powers of the west, whose interests in the region were vital, now had to deal with her and for the first time take her seriously.

Even then it was not clear how permanent the growth in Russian power and importance would be. Many expected or hoped that it would disappear with Peter, and after his death there were long periods when internal power struggles left Russia without firm direction. But Peter had begun processes which could not easily be stopped. 'The power of Muscovy', Charles XII remarked, '. . .has risen so high thanks to the introduction of foreign military discipline.'[8] The habits Peter had inculcated perpetuated themselves: there was no going back once a modern army and navy had been created, however much they periodically fell into neglect. Pultava created the idea that Russian infantry were invincible; it did not require this reputation to be put to the test for Russia to become a feared potential enemy and a sought-after ally. And now that she had her Baltic 'window to the west', she was inexorably drawn into the west's diplomatic network. Anti-western reactions under weak mid-century monarchs could not disengage her, and when resolute intervention in the west became state policy again, as under Elizabeth and Catherine II, her impact was all the greater. Russia was not rich, but she had

---

[8]   Quoted in Sumner, *Peter the Great and the Emergence of Russia*, 64.

enormous reserves of manpower, without the legal traditions or institutions of resistance to obstruct monarchs determined to organize these reserves. The limitless power of the tsar enabled Peter to reorganize the whole state as a war machine, and while we should not overestimate the permanency of his reforms or their efficiency, the very scale of Russian resources, however inefficiently deployed, made them formidable. Never again would Russia relapse into the semi-oriental isolation of former years.

The western powers were quick to recognize the new realities. British fleets were sent to the Baltic no less than ten times between 1714 and 1727 to protect Sweden from Russian attack; and when they proved relatively ineffective Peter was able to boast that the power of his newly created navy rivalled that of the world's greatest. In 1726 the Austrians concluded a Russian alliance, which was to last, with vicissitudes, until 1762. France alone had nothing to gain from Russia's emergence, for it complicated her traditional policy of maintaining allies—Sweden, Poland the Ottoman empire —in Austria's rear. Russia now outflanked and overshadowed these weak states, so it was no wonder the Austrians sought her friendship and supported the Russian candidate when the throne of Poland fell vacant in 1733.

When Charles XII had defeated the Poles in 1707, he had deposed King Augustus II (who was also elector of Saxony) and established Stanislas Leszczynski, a French protégé, in his place. When Charles was defeated himself, two years later, the Russians deposed Leszczynski and restored Augustus. Poland became a virtual Russian protectorate—another sign of growing power. The Poles however resented this subservience, and when Augustus died in 1733 Leszczynski, now Louis XV's father-in-law, was elected to succeed him. The Russians refused to accept him, and imposed Augustus III, son of the previous king, by force of arms; when the Austrians supported them, France declared war.

Yet there was little that France could effectively do about a country so far away. The main battlefields of the War of the Polish Succession (1733–8) were along the Rhine and in Italy. France promised the maritime powers that she would keep out of the southern Netherlands, which kept them neutral. The grand alliance that had confronted Louis XIV did not therefore re-form, and France, though she was unable to reinstate Stanislas, had him installed at the peace as duke of Lorraine. When he finally died in 1768 he was succeeded by his daughter the queen of France, and so the ambition of Louis XIV to incorporate the duchy into the French kingdom was at last fulfilled—but only at the expense of implicitly recognizing the new and unwelcome Russian hegemony in the east.

The Struggle for Italy and the Retreat of Austrian Power

The main result of the Polish Succession war could be seen in Italy, the flashpoint of international relations in the west for thirty-five years after the Peace of Utrecht. In 1713 Austria received most of the Spanish possessions in Europe. Many Spaniards bitterly resented this; although they might happily concede the loss of the southern Netherlands, which had brought Spain nothing but trouble, they still dreamed of their former power in Italy. These regrets found expression in the policies of Queen Elizabeth Farnese, herself an Italian. Elizabeth, Philip V's second wife, had no hope of seeing either of her sons by Philip succeed to a throne—unless one could be won in Italy. After 1713, therefore, Spain was western Europe's most dissatisfied state and her Italian ambitions the greatest threat to the newly established balance of power. In 1717, on a flimsy pretext, she invaded and occupied Austrian Sardinia almost without a struggle, and the next year, emboldened by success, she turned to Sicily.

These ambitions were only checked by a new and unprecedented coalition, the triple alliance of The Hague (1717). The basis of this alliance was the determination of Great Britain and France to keep the peace in Europe: together they could hold the balance. The Dutch, anxious to avoid war at all costs, joined in this endeavour. The alliance became quadruple with the adherence of the Emperor, against whose new-found Italian hegemony Spanish ambitions were mainly directed. Results came quickly. In 1718 at Cape Passaro a British fleet cut off the Spanish forces in Sicily. The next year a French force invaded northern Spain. Under these pressures Spain rapidly collapsed; she was forced to renounce her Italian ambitions, while Austria consolidated her position by exchanging Sardinia for Sicily.

The final details were left to be settled by a congress, but by the time it met continued Spanish restlessness had made an amicable outcome impossible. Moreover, the legacy of a generation's warfare against Great Britain and Austria had left many Frenchmen uneasy about the new alliance with these powers, especially when it was directed against a Bourbon monarch who ought to be France's natural ally. Accordingly, secret negotiations were opened in the early 1720s for a Franco-Spanish alliance cemented by the marriage of Louis XV to a Spanish infanta. France would support the claims of Elizabeth Farnese's son Don Carlos to the succession of the Italian duchies of Parma and Tuscany. It was another ten years, however, before this axis was finally established, for in 1724 a new French government, anxious lest Louis XV should die before the promised infanta was old enough to marry and give him an heir, abruptly renounced the bargain. The Spaniards were so offended that they made overtures to the Emperor, with whom they signed the treaty of Vienna in 1725. This inaugurated a period of intense diplomatic confusion. Spain and Austria were still basically opposed over Italy and by 1729 Spain was once more making overtures to France, in search of a guarantee of Don Carlos's succession to the Italian duchies. France, anxious above all to keep the peace, was reluctant to commit herself without Britain, but when Parma finally fell vacant in 1730, and the Austrians marched in troops, Walpole refused to become involved in action to expel the invaders. This was the end of the Anglo-French understanding. French diplomats at the time, and many French historians since, saw the peace-keeping professions of this collaboration as merely a cloak for 'English preponderance'. Walpole's refusal to act to preserve the power balance, followed by a new Anglo-Austrian agreement in 1731, seemed to confirm the essentially selfish mainsprings of

British policy. From then on Britain and France slowly drifted back into their old rivalry.

The Austrians did evacuate Parma for Don Carlos—by negotiation and not by force. They made this concession in return for Spanish confirmation of the Pragmatic Sanction. The Pragmatic Sanction was a self-imposed diplomatic liability, which placed Austria at a major disadvantage in all her international dealings between 1714 and 1740. The reign of Leopold I had seen a considerable advance in Austrian power and territory. Having reached the gates of Vienna in 1683, the Turks had subsequently been rolled back into the Balkans. At the Peace of Passarowitz (1718) Leopold's son Charles VI gained territory as far south as Belgrade to add to his recent acquisitions in the Netherlands and Italy. His Italian gains were consolidated in the next few years and Spanish ambitions against them were thwarted. Only Great Britain and Russia had been so successful within living memory. But in Charles's eyes all this was for nothing if it was to be divided up at his death owing to the fact that his sole surviving heir was a daughter. In the event of male heirs failing in the Habsburg family, the succession was regulated by a complicated set of family agreements. The Pragmatic Sanction, promulgated in 1719, was designed to replace these agreements by guaranteeing the succession of all the hereditary lands, undivided, to Maria Theresa. Within a few years it had been accepted by the various Habsburg domains, but Charles would not feel satisfied until it had won full international recognition. His policy until the end of his reign was dominated by this aim. Thus it was fundamental to the 1725 and 1731 agreements with Spain, the 1726 alliance with Russia, and the renewed pact of 1731 with Great Britain. Extending the ranks of confirming powers was also a major war aim pursued by Charles in the Polish Succession war.

This war, however, proved disastrous for him. Great Britain refused to become involved, despite the alliance of 1731. The Dutch remained neutral, while the Russians confined their exertions to Poland. Spain meanwhile concluded the long-sought alliance with France (1733) to make a combined attack upon the Austrian territories in Italy. Charles, unable to withstand their onslaughts, opened negotiations within two years. The negotiations were unhurried, however, until 1737, when Charles committed himself to a new eastern war begun by his Russian allies. The Turks, urged on by French diplomacy, showed unexpected vigour and rolled back the Austrian forces. Thus pressed, Charles hastened to conclude a final peace in the west, under yet another treaty of Vienna, in 1738.

For Charles it was a qualified disaster. He secured French recognition of the Pragmatic Sanction, Parma passed back from Spanish to Austrian control, and Tuscany (whose ruling dynasty had also at last failed in 1737) went to Maria Theresa's husband, Francis Stephen of Lorraine. But Lorraine was lost to Stanislas Leczynski, and Naples and Sicily were abandoned to Don Carlos. On top of all this came losses in the east: at the peace of Belgrade in 1739 most of the gains of Passarowitz, including Belgrade itself, were returned to the Turks. When Charles died in 1740, his dominions had shrunk and the state was militarily and financially exhausted. The Pragmatic Sanction had won general acceptance, but many of the important states had hedged their recognition. Spain was still unsatisfied in Italy, coveting the duchy of Parma that Don Carlos had given up in return for Naples; while in the north the new king of Prussia was about to make the most audacious move of the century against the rich but exposed province of Silesia.

The Emergence of Prussia

At the accession of Frederick II, Prussia was a second-rank power with a large but untried army. This had been her situation since the days of the great elector, who had laid down the pattern of the Prussian state by subordinating all its resources to building up military power. The first success of this policy came when the new army defeated the dreaded Swedes at Fehrbellin in 1675. Yet Brandenburg did not play a role of any importance in the subsequent wars. When the Elector Frederick allied himself with the Austrians against France, he was rewarded by imperial recognition as king of Prussia, but he did not pursue his father's policy of ruthlessly subordinating the state to military needs. It was not resumed until the reign of his son Frederick William I. By the latter's death in 1740 Prussia had a highly efficient bureaucracy, plenty of financial reserves, and the fourth-largest army in Europe, but even Frederick William put this strength to little use. His sole international successes were the acquisition of a slice of Swedish Pomerania (1719), and recognition by the emperor of his claims to the ultimate succession of the duchy of Berg, in return for confirmation of the Pragmatic Sanction (1728).

It took his son Frederick to show what Prussian military power was capable of achieving. Succeeding to the throne several months before the Emperor Charles VI died, he used the uncertainty surrounding Maria Theresa's succession to resurrect an old and tenuous Prussian claim to Silesia. Without any warning, he simply invaded the province, overran it, and routed an opposing Austrian army. The effect was similar to that of Pultava. Most of Europe saw at once that a new power had emerged and concluded that an old one was about to collapse. In the rush to dismember the Austrian empire everyone forgot the Pragmatic Sanction. When France and Spain encouraged the elector of Bavaria to press his claims to the Austrian succession, Frederick joined them in the league of Nymphenburg. In this way the first Silesian War escalated into a general conflict—the War of the Austrian Succession (1741–8).

No power had any interest in the complete disappearance of the Habsburgs from the diplomatic stage. But France desired to see them weakened, while Prussia, Spain, and Bavaria wished to gain important territories at their expense. Although the Hungarians rallied to Maria Theresa, and she never lost control of the Austrian lands, most of these predators achieved their aims at the final peace. Yet owing to divisions among them, it was a long war. In return for the cession of Silesia, Frederick abandoned his allies and withdrew from the war no less than three times between 1742 and 1745. The French soon achieved their only specific war aim, the election of Charles Albert of Bavaria as Emperor (1742), but when he died in 1745 they were unable to prevent the election of Maria Theresa's husband, Francis-Stephen. After that French efforts were largely devoted to supporting Spanish ambitions in Italy, where Elizabeth Farnese now coveted Parma.

Nothing prolonged the war as much as the entry of Great Britain in 1744. Britain had been at war with Spain (the notorious 'War of Jenkin's Ear') over trading rights in South America since 1739. She had financed a so-called German 'Pragmatic Army' in 1743 to support Maria Theresa, and also subsidized the Austrians on a generous scale. Not until France and Spain renewed their ten-year-old alliance in 1743, however, were Britain and France drawn into direct confrontation. The powers lined up as they had under Louis XIV; the new force of Prussia stayed on the sidelines, husbanding her gains, after 1745. The battlefields were the old ones too, in Italy and the southern Netherlands. But the conflict between Britain and France was soon carried all over the world, with the two powers beginning to see that they were involved in a contest over something far greater than the Austrian succession or the balance of power in Italy. Both sides realized that the Peace of Aix-la-Chapelle in 1748 was merely a truce, enabling each to prepare for the more crucial contest ahead.

The most permanent result of this peace was the settlement of the Italian problem. The death of Philip V in 1745 had removed the ambitious influence of his queen from Spanish policy-making, but in 1748 her son Don Philip gained the long-coveted Parma. Compensated by Tuscany ten years before, the Austrians soon resigned themselves to this loss. The 1748 settlement accordingly left all parties satisfied in Italy, whose affairs played no further important role in international relations until the French invasion of 1796.

The peace also brought the ultimate triumph of the Pragmatic Sanction. Maria Theresa made good her claim to the undivided succession of the Habsburg lands and the election of her husband as Emperor brought the imperial crown back into the family. Nothing else was permanently settled, however. The Austrians remained unreconciled to the loss of Silesia and to the emergence of Prussia as an equal in north Germany that this loss symbolized. European diplomatic history down to the French Revolution was to be dominated by Austria's desire for revenge or compensation for the losses of the war of 1740–8.

The Diplomatic Revolution

No power emerged from the Austrian Succession war with much faith in traditional alliances. The rise of Prussia provided alternatives. The appearance of this new great power both provoked and facilitated a major realignment in European diplomacy.

The initiative came from the Austrians. In 1749 a new voice in Maria Theresa's counsels, Kaunitz, convinced the empress that Austria's main enemy and rival was no longer France, but Prussia. The aim should be to recover Silesia. And since she would never accomplish this single-handed, he suggested that it should be done in alliance, not with Austria's traditional British and Dutch friends, but with France. These ideas created a good deal of scepticism among the empress's counsellors. Most were ready to agree that Great Britain had treated Austria shabbily in the recent war, but they could not believe that France would be prepared to abandon her new-found Prussian ally, much less join in an attack on him. Kaunitz was sent to Paris to explore the possibilities, but when he returned in 1753 nobody was surprised to learn that he had made no apparent progress. The French found their Prussian alliance altogether too convenient: it balanced the Habsburg power in Germany; it kept the Germans divided and George II worried by the threat to Hanover. Against these obvious interests Kaunitz could only argue that Frederick was unreliable. But French diplomats felt confident that, since Frederick had no alternative alliances, he would not betray them.

Nor did Frederick have any such intention. He knew that he was too formidable both to the Austrians and to Hanover for the French to do without him. Ultimately, however, the Hanoverian question was to alter his position. The British knew that Hanover was their weak spot. No amount of colonial gains in wartime would be of use if the French or their allies overran Hanover and used it to win all their losses back in peace negotiations. A strong party on Louis XV's council did favour precisely this policy of 'conquering America in Germany'. The aim of British diplomacy was to neutralize Germany in any future conflict by appealing to the other new power of the century, Russia. Under the convention of St. Petersburg (1755) Russia undertook, in return for a subsidy, to attack Prussia if she threatened Hanover. Frederick had always regarded Russia as potentially his most formidable enemy, and, thoroughly alarmed, he hastened to assure the British that he had no designs on Hanover. He supported this by offering to underwrite the neutrality of Germany in any future Anglo-French war, an undertaking embodied in the Convention of Westminster in January 1756.

It was this agreement that precipitated the diplomatic revolution, for the news of it drove Louis XV into the arms of the Austrians. Now he suddenly found, as Kaunitz had always predicted, that Frederick was making agreement with his main enemies, with whom France was already in a state of undeclared war. In May 1756 France and Austria concluded the treaty of Versailles, a formal defensive alliance guaranteeing mutual help should either side be attacked by any power other than Great Britain. It was not all that Kaunitz (now in control of Austrian foreign policy) wanted. He now planned a triple assault on Prussia by the forces of Austria, Russia, and France. The French were well aware of this, but refused any hint of an offensive alliance, since the convention of Westminster was far from an Anglo-Prussian alliance. These agreements simply enabled the British and the French to pursue their duel on the seas of the world without distractions and diversion of resources in Europe.

Such calculations however reckoned without the reactions of other powers. The Franco-Austrian agreement neutralized the southern Netherlands and led the Dutch to abandon their traditional British alliance and proclaim neutrality. The Anglo-Prussian agreement enraged the Russians, who reacted by signing an offensive agreement with the Austrians against Prussia and opening negotiations for an alliance with France. Thus Britain found herself increasingly isolated, with the friendship only of the slippery Frederick. Frederick himself meanwhile saw his own position rapidly deteriorating in the face of encirclement by hostile powers. Resolved to strike first, at a moment convenient to himself rather than to Kaunitz, in August 1756 he invaded his most vulnerable neighbour, the kingdom of the Russian-protected king of Poland, Saxony.

So began the Seven Years War on the continent of Europe. Anglo-French relations had drifted into all-out war the previous year. It was everything that Kaunitz had been working for for seven years. Within a year of Frederick's march into Saxony both Russia and France had committed themselves to sending armies against him. He had no help to rely on beyond annual subsidies from Great Britain and an Anglo-Hanoverian army of uncertain value on his west flank. It nearly cost the survival of Prussia. Frederick and his generals won a number of spectacular battles and the Anglo-Hanoverian army, after surrendering to the French in 1757, took the field again and tied them down far from the Prussian heartland for much of the war. But the combined resources of Frederick's enemies were so great that the destruction of his power would only have been a matter of time if they had co-operated more closely. In the summer of 1759 the British swept the French fleet from the seas, but Frederick's forces were completely defeated by an Austro-Russian force at Kunersdorf; he was saved only by quarrels between the victors which prevented them from following up their success. Even then his resources diminished each year. By 1762 he was once again on the point of defeat, when the Russian empress, a bitter personal enemy, died, and was replaced by Peter III, an equally fervent admirer. At once the new tsar withdrew Russia from the coalition and began to offer Frederick an alliance, which was his salvation. With the French already putting out peace feelers towards Britain, the Austrians were left alone in the field. In these circumstances the two German states concluded peace at Hubertusburg in 1763.

This peace enshrined no great changes; it merely confirmed the situation that had existed since 1745. Frederick kept Silesia and Maria Theresa came out of the war empty-handed. Prussia's place in the ranks of the great powers was confirmed, even though her economy and state organization were shattered by the effort, taking at least a decade to recover. Austria now gave up all hope of recovering Silesia, but not of achieving compensation elsewhere. Her restlessness, demonstrated in her designs on Bavaria and on the Balkans, were to bedevil international peace in the second half of the century as Spanish ambitions in Italy had in the first. Kaunitz's calculation that Austria was not strong enough to act alone was confirmed at Hubertusburg. The alliance with France therefore continued, cemented by the marriage in 1770 between the Archduchess Marie-Antoinette and the heir to the French throne, to become one of the cornerstones of Austrian policy down to 1792. It brought a generation of peace to western Europe and an end to battles and manoeuvrings in the Netherlands and along the Rhine. It left France free, for the first time in the century, to concentrate all her resources on the naval contest with Great Britain.

Anglo-French Rivalry

The idea that Britain and France were each other's natural trading and colonial rivals had taken root at the beginning of the eighteenth century. Until the 1740s their basic rivalry was obscured by co-operation to maintain the peace of Europe, but this co-operation was completely destroyed in the scramble for Austria. France's colonial trade meanwhile was beginning to expand at a far faster rate, alarming British merchants and ministers, and inspiring the French to greater boldness. A year after the renewal of the family compact in 1743, open war broke out between Britain and France, which had immediate repercussions both at sea and in overseas posts and settlements. The British took Louisbourg, the key to French Canada, the French laid siege to Madras. There were no major naval battles, but by 1748 French overseas trade had been brought to a virtual standstill by a British blockade. On the other hand, the French had thrown the British government into a momentary panic in 1745 by helping a rebellion led by the son of the Stuart pretender; they had overrun the southern Netherlands, and in 1748 it looked as though they were likely to improve on Louis XIV and overrun the Dutch republic too. It was this that induced the British finally to make peace and give up Louisbourg.

The war had been only a preliminary round. Its main importance had been to force both sides into thinking about how the next encounter could be more decisive. By her power on land, France had forced Britain to give up the fruits of supremacy at sea, leading some Frenchmen to argue that America could be conquered in Germany, by overrunning George II's beloved Hanover with French troops. Others argued that most Englishmen thought Hanover merely a nuisance and that the issue could be decided only on the seas. France should accordingly avoid any involvements on the continent and devote her resources to building up a strong navy. This conflict was unresolved when hostilities were resumed in 1755. The result was that France entered the war with the worst of both worlds: a heavy continental commitment to the Austrian alliance and a navy not yet strong enough to outmatch the British. A similar debate had meanwhile gone on in England. Parliamentary opponents of successive governments denounced involvement on the continent, and particularly policies designed to protect the 'despicable electorate' of Hanover. But George II's successive ministers were obliged to defer to their master's concern for his native land; and in the Seven Years War even Pitt, among the loudest in his denunciations of Hanover since the 1730s, began to see that America could be conquered on the banks of the Elbe by tying down French resources.

The Seven Years War proved this. Along the Ohio and in India hostilities had never really ceased after the 1748 peace, as colonists and traders sought to establish advantageous positions. By 1754, these clashes had become so serious that home governments felt obliged to send troops. In 1755 there was all-out war in North America, with regular forces engaged on both sides and the British beginning to harass French shipping in European waters. War was formally declared only in 1756, as the two sides found themselves drawn into European confrontations. Initially it went extremely badly for the British, but gradually the distraction of the French in Germany, the disarray of their ministers, and Britain's superior reserves of seamen and naval facilities, began to tell. In Pitt the British had a minister with devastating strategic vision and fixity of purpose. He would subsidize Prussia and keep French resources tied down in Europe while British fleets cut France off from all her overseas contacts, which would then be captured one by one. 1759 saw the triumph of this policy, as the French navy was swept from the seas in spectacular victories and most of the main French overseas posts were captured. The blockade reduced French trade to nothing, while in 1762 Spain's trade too came under attack as war was declared and Havana captured. But by now Pitt had fallen and George III was on the throne, determined on a policy of peace. War weariness, resentment of high wartime taxes, and fears that the total victory aimed at by Pitt would bring the whole continent together in an anti-British coalition—all this won his policy support. At the Peace of Paris in 1763, therefore, concessions were made. France regained her West Indian islands; Great Britain took Canada and received Florida from Spain. With all its concessions, the peace was a British triumph. The acquisition of Canada left the thirteen colonies secure against French encirclement. But as Pitt complained, to give back so much stored up trouble for the future. 'The ministers', he argued, 'seem to have lost sight of the great fundamental principle that France is chiefly, if not solely, to be dreaded by us in the light of a maritime and commercial power...we have given her the means of recovering her prodigious losses and becoming once more formidable to us at sea.'[9]

Such was certainly Choiseul's aim in the years that followed. He pursued a policy of naval expansion and when he fell in 1770 he was preparing to come to the aid of the Spaniards in a dispute with the British over the Falkland Islands. The British, overconfident in their island security, had meanwhile isolated themselves in Europe. By unilaterally abandoning Frederick II in 1762, before he had made peace with the Austrians, they deprived themselves of their only continental ally. Frederick's alliance with Russia, and the Austro-French alliance, left no opportunities for agreement with any other great powers, and a major objective of French diplomacy was to perpetuate this isolation. Diplomatically, the two decades after 1763 were as triumphant for France as the preceding seven years had been disastrous.

The seal was set on French successes by the revolt of the British North American colonies. The French had nothing to do with fomenting it, but they welcomed the breakdown of the British empire. They believed, like the British themselves, that the independence of America would ruin British prosperity. So when the colonists, having declared their independence, put out feelers towards France, they were not discouraged. When their victory at Saratoga in 1777 showed that they were capable of defeating the British, France concluded a formal alliance with the United States, 'not,' as Louis

---

[9]   Quoted in J. H. Plumb, *Chatham* (1953), 90.

XVI put it, 'with any idea of territorial aggrandizement for us, but solely as an attempt to ruin [England's] commerce and to sap her strength, by supporting the revolt and the separation of the colonies.'[10] War actually broke out in 1778. In 1779 the French were joined by the Spaniards, in 1780 by the Dutch, to create a combination of naval power that even the British could not match. For crucial periods they lost control of the sea—for the first time since 1692—during which the French were able to ship supplies and 7,000 troops to the rebels. The decisive American victory of Yorktown in 1781 was the work of an army that was half French and a French fleet which prevented the British from being relieved. The British also lost a number of West Indian islands and found themselves opposed from 1780 by an Armed Neutrality of northern powers, resentful of the traditional British claim to search neutral shipping for warlike goods. The war was a complete disaster for Great Britain. Late British victories hardly altered matters, and in the Peace of Paris, 1783, Britain recognized the loss of the thirteen colonies, Tobago, Minorca, Florida, and Senegal. France took modest gains—Tobago and trading posts in Senegal and India—but felt amply rewarded by Britain's discomfiture.

Britain's pride was indeed humbled. Subsequent years witnessed belated but strenuous efforts to end her diplomatic isolation in Europe. In 1786 she even concluded a commercial treaty with France; although in 1788, as French power began to collapse, there was again tension between the two powers over political instability in Holland. But British trade and prosperity did not suffer the expected setback: and Louis XVI found his government having to count the crippling cost of a war from which few material gains had accrued, and in which the adversary, despite his defeat, had not been seriously weakened.

Poland and the Eastern Question

Just as the Austro-French alliance kept western Europe at peace for a generation after 1763, so the alliance made between Russia and Prussia in 1762 kept the east tranquil. Their successful co-operation, however, depended upon tacit recognition of Russian hegemony in Poland. The Russians' setting themselves up as the guardians of Poland's anarchic constitution suited the Prussians too. Frederick II had no interest in a strong Poland, but was very concerned to keep the Russians at arm's length. It was better to let them dominate the buffer state, rather than annex it. When Augustus III, who had reigned since the succession war, died in 1763, Frederick II lent his support to the Russian nominee for the succession—not Augustus's son but Catherine II's former lover and a known reformer, Stanlislas Poniatowski.

The Polish diet had no alternative but to elect Poniatowski. Nevertheless resentment at Russian domination was widespread and grew when it became clear how powerless the new king was in the face of his original sponsors. Matters came to a head over Russian attempts to secure representation in the

---

[10]   Quoted in B. Faÿ, *Louis XVI ou la fin d'un monde* (1955), 148.

Polish diet for the Orthodox minority in Catholic Poland. When the diet proved hostile, the Russians fomented a confederation which, with the help of Russian troops, forced it to make the required concessions. No sooner was this done, however, than anti-Russian nobles formed a new confederation and the country was plunged into civil war (1768). It was clear that only Russian troops could finally pacify Poland, but this naturally alarmed all other surrounding states who regarded Poland as a buffer. The Turks, who were the first to take alarm, declared war in 1768. With this distraction of Russian energies, the chaos in Poland continued for several years. It was clear nevertheless that once the Turkish war was over, Russian troops would swamp Poland, threatening a general war which might engulf Germany as well as the whole of eastern Europe. In anticipation of this, the Austrians in 1769 moved into the Polish county of Zips, a former dependency of the Hungarian crown, ostensibly to protect a weak sector of their frontier. In 1771 they proclaimed its formal annexation.

Their example was decisive. Suddenly Poland's neighbours began to see that, without sacrificing the buffer state, they could all make substantial and useful gains while at the same time avoiding conflict. Accordingly, Prussia and Russia agreed in May 1771 to partition Poland. Maria Theresa, despite having given the others the idea, was hard to convince that she too should participate, but Kaunitz felt no such scruples. By deliberately delaying Austrian acquiescence, he emerged with the largest and most valuable slice in the tripartite partition of 1772. Under this agreement Poland lost 29·5 per cent of her territory and 35·2 per cent of her population. The largest proportion of each went to the Austrians in the south. In the east, the Russians closed up a huge salient in their frontier. Frederick II, who gained least in ostensible terms, fulfilled a dream he had long cherished but believed impossible—he took west Prussia, which closed the territorial gap between Pomerania and east Prussia along the Baltic coast.

The Russo-Turkish war, begun in 1768, went on until 1774. Since their victories over the Austrians in the 1730s, which had caused universal surprise, the Turks had done little to consolidate their position in the Balkans or along the Black Sea coast and nothing to update their military technology or organization. By going to war in 1768 completely unprepared, they suffered a staggering series of defeats. Within a year the Russians had penetrated as far south as Bucharest; and in 1770, in one of the most spectacular naval feats of the century, the Russian Baltic fleet sailed round Europe and smashed a Turkish fleet at Chesmé, off the coast of Asia Minor. In 1774, after another successful campaign in the Balkans, the Russians forced the Turks to conclude the peace of Kütchük Kainardji, under which the Turks received back their Balkan provinces, but lost their monopoly of the north shore of the Black Sea. The Crimea was made an independent state and the Russians won access to the sea around Azov and Kherson.

These Russian successes alarmed the Austrians, who had disturbing visions of the Russians overrunning all the Balkans and perhaps even taking Constantinople. For the next few years however they were distracted from this theatre by the prospect of acquiring Bavaria as compensation for Silesia. When, after the Bavarian elector's sudden death without direct heirs late in 1777, Joseph II made an agreement to allow Austria to take over Bavaria, Frederick II denounced the move as disruptive of the power balance in Germany. Armies were mobilized and there was fighting for several months in 1778. Joseph was forced to desist, however, when the French made it clear that they were not prepared to help him win Bavaria; they wanted a peaceful Germany so that they might concentrate all their resources against Great Britain. By the Peace of Teschen in 1779 Austria acquired simply a strip of former Bavarian territory along the Inn, while the elector-palatine took over Bavaria. Yet Joseph remained unsatisfied, and in 1784–5 he attempted to negotiate an exchange of Bavaria for the Austrian Netherlands. Again Frederick objected and launched a league of German princes (*Fürstenbund*), to block the proposal. This, and the continued refusal of France to support Austrian designs on Bavaria, finally laid the issue to rest.

Only now did Joseph II turn his full attention to the Balkans. In 1783 he had concluded an alliance with Catherine II to partition the Turkish empire in the same way as Poland. In 1783 Russia annexed the Crimea, as most diplomats had been predicting since Kütchük Kainardji, and in 1787 she finally provoked the Turks into declaring a new war. The Austrians honoured the 1783 treaty by joining in the next year. The part they played proved ignominious and ended when Joseph died in 1790. The Russians too made less progress than they hoped, their gains provoking Prussian and British hostility, not to mention an invasion by Gustavus III of Sweden (1788–90). The treaty of Jassy (1792) was an acknowledgement that the plan to partition the Turkish empire had failed; but, in extending the Russian frontier to the Dniester and by confirming the annexation of the Crimea, it spelt the end of the Black Sea as a Turkish lake and the arrival of Russia as the dominant power—Peter I's dream realized at last.

The French Collapse

The growing power of Russia had been obvious for the best part of the century, and her domination of the Black Sea long predicted. But few had foreseen the sudden collapse of France brought about by the Revolution. In 1786 she was still the arbiter of Europe, without whom the Austrians or the Spaniards dared not make a move, and whose friendship was being simultaneously sought by Great Britain and Russia.

By this time the strains caused by participation in the American war had plunged the Dutch republic into a profound domestic crisis, in which popular forces confronted the traditional monarchical and authoritarian claims of the House of Orange.[11] The Prussians, backed by the British who wished to see strong government in the Republic, supported the monarchical side. France supported the co-called 'patriots'; but when the Prussians, with British support, invaded the country and proscribed the patriots in 1787, the French

[11] See below, p. 311–13.

were too weak to do anything but protest. This was a sign of things to come. Totally absorbed in their internal problems, the French abandoned foreign affairs. When in 1790 the Spaniards invoked the family compact to secure French naval help against Britain in a dispute over Nootka Sound, on the Pacific coast of North America, they were spurned by the National Assembly. Many participants in the debate denounced war as an instrument of national policy. So France was a cipher in international affairs for almost five years after the invasion of Holland. When Louis XVI fled and was recaptured in the summer of 1791 the Prussians and Austrians felt free to make threatening pronouncements, but they hardly expected to have to act on them. France was manifestly defenceless, her army's morale eaten away by pernicious revolutionary ideas and habits. In British eyes, a weak France was the best guarantee of European security. 'Unquestionably', declared Pitt in February 1792,[12] 'there never was a time in the history of this country, when, from the situation of Europe, we might more reasonably expect fifteen years of peace than at the present moment.' It was perhaps the most celebrated miscalculation in all diplomatic history.

[12] Quoted in J. H. Rose, *William Pitt and the Great War* (1911), 32.

THE CRISIS OF THE OLD ORDER

13. The Crisis

During the last thirty or so years of the eighteenth century Europe was convulsed by an enormous crisis which would be remembered as the Age of Revolutions. Its consequences would be momentous for the whole world, and ever since historians have debated the nature of the crisis, its causes, and its results.

Contemporaries too were baffled by the scale of the upheavals through which they were living, especially when they contemplated the unprecedented scenes of the French Revolution. Adherents of the revolution, who could be found all over the European world in the 1790s, liked to see themselves as part of a single movement, for long dedicated to the overthrow of all previously established authorities, attitudes, and habits. But the revolutions of the 1790s were not brought about by revolutionaries, nor were they the product of a revolutionary movement. They were situations resulting from the collapse of the previous order; the situations produced the revolutionaries, not the revolutionaries the situations. The collapse of the old order resulted, in general, not from attacks by those excluded from its rewards, but from conflicts between its main beneficiaries—rulers and their ruling orders.

The main cause of these conflicts was the burden of international competition in an age of inflation. Governments believed that the main threats to their power were external. They seldom foresaw that the measures they took to meet these external dangers might eventually provoke far more serious internal problems. By the time this became clear it was sometimes too late. There was nothing fundamentally new about the problem. Antagonisms between governments and their principal subjects over the limits of governmental power and the state's financial demands were as old as history. It was the scale of the problem that was new. Military preparedness in an age of ever-increasing technical sophistication and an ever-widening range of conflict made government more costly than ever before. This created a financial problem, which was only compounded by rising prices. In the search for new sources of revenue and better ways of organizing the state to support the military machine, the problem became organizational. Because the necessary innovations could only occur through radical changes in laws and habits, it was also constitutional.

This was the level at which the crisis broke: when ruling groups upon whose acquiescence and co-operation governments normally depended refused to accept the reforms which the latter considered essential. Their refusal immobilized the state, for it was incapable of functioning without them. In these circumstances constitutional life broke down and governments had to withdraw or fight. But they could fight only if they could call upon elements of support hitherto excluded from public life by the entrenched position of the groups they had now antagonized. This was to challenge the very basis upon which society and politics functioned, and most public men shrank from such a leap in the dark. Those who did not, succeeded only in unleashing uncontrollable forces which brought both the government and the social order crashing down.

Untouched Areas

The crisis of the Old Order did not affect all countries, although sooner or later its consequences spread to most of them. Smaller states, particularly in Italy and Germany, were largely unaffected by the military competition which lay at the root of the problem. They knew that they were no match for any of the great powers and did not strain their resources in vain attempts. States such as Denmark, Tuscany, Baden, or Mainz witnessed often far-reaching reforms, but reforms inspired more by the abstract political and economic discussions of the age than by harsh military necessity. Monarchs such as Archduke Peter-Leopold of Tuscany (later Emperor Leopold II) or Margrave Carl-Friedrich of Baden, immune from the international ambitions which were the real motivation of the more famous so-called 'enlightened despots', had read 'enlightened' writers, corresponded with them, and were advised by their disciples. Their experiments in law, economics, education, and admini- stration were inspired by a genuine desire to improve their realms. Struensee, a German doctor whose liaison with the Danish queen gave him complete power in Denmark between 1770 and 1772, attempted in this brief period to turn the state into an Enlightenment paradise. The creed of such rulers was well expressed in the mid-1770s by the education minister to the elector of Mainz: 'It is the duty of every honest sovereign to protect his people against beggary and to bring wealth and prosperity to his country by good admini- stration, encouragement of agriculture, trade, the mechanical arts, the building of factories, etc. He is prince for this reason, to make his people happy.'[1] In that they lacked the ulterior motives of the better-known rulers of the greater states, yet persisted in reforms, these minor rulers alone truly deserve the description 'enlightened'. But equally, because their policies were inspired by no inexorable necessity, they never felt obliged to go to extremes in order to win them acceptance. Neither the policies, nor their attempts to impose them, were fundamental threats to the existing order—with the possible exception of Struensee's short-lived plans for Denmark. Consequently these minor states, though sometimes shaken by conservative reactions, especially after the disappearance of reforming rulers, were never brought anywhere near collapse by conflicts over reform.

Some of the largest realms in Europe were also relatively untouched by the crisis. Spain was fortunate in never being involved in a prolonged war

[1] Quoted in T. C. W. Blanning, *Reform and Revolution in Mainz 1743–1803* (1974), 165. This book is perhaps the best description of reform and its fate in a small state.

effort after mid-century. She avoided direct involvement in wars as long as she could, and when involvement came, it was marginal and relatively short-lived. France bore most of the burden of the Family Compacts. In consequence, Charles III was never impelled to seek new sources of revenue regardless of the consequences and established groups were thus never seriously antagonized. Significant reforms were introduced by Charles, and did not pass unopposed. But they were inspired by similar considerations to those that moved the rulers of smaller states; and although Charles III and his advisers undoubtedly believed that to improve the efficiency and the benevolence of Spanish government would promote the country's international strength, this was never their overriding and immediate motive. No element of the reform pro-gramme was considered so urgent to national security that it must be pushed through at all costs. The moment opposition looked serious, the government desisted. So there was no important agrarian reform, though much talk of it. Centralization progressed, but the privileges and autonomy of the powerful municipalities were not seriously infringed. The Jesuits were expelled and the political independence of the church curbed, but its entrenched wealth and privileges left largely untouched. Above all, no new taxes were introduced, and no major extensions of existing ones. Changes were piecemeal, occurring slowly. Only in the South American empire was there a rapid increase in the Madrid government's power, constituting a challenge to established local groups and habits and, predictably, sowing the seeds of the independence movement which was to fragment the empire in the early nineteenth century.

Another example is Prussia, although here the reasons for escaping the crisis are very different. Far from avoiding the international race, from 1740 onwards Prussia was one of its pacemakers. The burden on her economy and society was enormous, yet at no point was there any important collision between the government and the governed over the state's insatiable demands. At first sight this is very surprising. Unlike most other European states, however, Prussia had been organized solely for war since the mid-seventeenth century. The nobility, poor and territorially weak, had no institutional voice and no remembered tradition of one, except in outlying areas. So there was no rallying point for resistance. Above all, the nobility had a vested interest in a state organized for war, for military and administrative service offered them an income and a livelihood which their small and impoverished lands could never provide. They had not always appreciated this; earlier traditions of independence lingered into the early eighteenth century, long after the great elector had set the state on its new course of militarism; and throughout his life, Frederick William I regarded the nobility as the greatest enemy of royal authority. His son, on the contrary, chose to identify himself totally with his nobles, preferring them for all positions of power and authority, avoiding any attack on their social and economic position, and ensuring that their fiscal privileges remained untouched. The weight of Prussia's war expenditure, and the cost of reconstruction after 1763, was borne by the towns and the peasantry, elements unable to defend themselves against the warrior state and its noble supporters. The nobility responded to Frederick's protection by promoting all his exactions and never giving him a moment's worry about their loyalty.[2]

In 1773–4 Russia passed through an enormous crisis in the form of the Pugachev rebellion. It was the most extensive and spectacular popular movement of the century, provoked by the ever-increasing demands, both fiscal and organizational, of a state with boundless international ambitions. But Pugachev and his followers were defeated precisely because a clash between the government and the governing class did not occur. The forces of order saw their fundamental community of interest in the face of the popular challenge and survived it more convinced than ever that they must stick together. Since the time of Peter I Russia had been organized for war just as deliberately as was Prussia. The nobility, lacking any tradition of common action or collective self defence, was unable to think of itself in terms divorced from serving the state. Their emancipation from this obligation in 1762 left many nobles confused and uncertain about their role. With no attachment to the soil, and no significant regional loyalties, with personal tax exemption, yet almost limitless powers over their sullen serfs, Russian nobles regarded the state as a benefactor, provider, and ally quite as much as an exacting master. And if the emancipation of 1762 began a process of questioning established institutions which was ultimately to lead many nobles to denounce the tsarist state, the Pugachev explosion retarded such developments for a generation. In the reorganization of provincial government of 1775, and above all by the Charter of the Nobility ten years later, the government made strenuous efforts to please the nobility and provide it with a satisfying role outside military service. But whether attempting to redirect noble energies or to woo noble loyalties, the Russian government was always careful to do nothing to alienate its most important subjects. It took care that the populace alone should bear the burden of its international adventures; in Catherine II's eyes, the outburst of protest released by Pugachev showed that the populace should be more firmly managed, not less. This could be achieved only with the whole-hearted co-operation of a pampered and contented nobility. 'As for me,' Catherine told the French ambassador in 1789,[3] 'I shall remain an aristocrat. It is my job.'

The British Empire

The British empire was not the first political system to be affected by the crisis, but it came to a head there first, with the declaration by which the thirteen American colonies asserted their independence on 4 July 1776. The example set by the colonists, an example of aggrieved subjects successfully defying the demands of their government, encouraged rebellion and resistance everywhere.

---

[2]   It has been argued that Prussia did undergo a crisis in the late eighteenth century: see H. Brunschwig, *Enlightenment and Romanticism in Eighteenth Century Prussia*. But it is not the crisis suggested here; it came after the outbreak of the French Revolution, and was rather economic and psychological in character.

[3]   Quoted in F. Fox, 'Negotiating with the Russians: Ambassador Ségur's Mission to Saint-Petersburg, 1784–9', *French Historical Studies* (1971), 71.

The mid-century overseas struggle with France had been fought to establish a self-sufficient commercial empire. The peace of Paris in 1763 brought success, but it also brought the problems of organizing and defending the empire so as to depend as little as possible upon outsiders. This was the spirit behind the various acts of trade to which the thirteen colonies were subject. In 1763 it was clear however, that these acts were being flouted wholesale in North America. Even during the recent war the colonists of New England had insisted on supplying the blockaded French West Indies in return for their sugar, which was cheaper and of higher quality than that of the exhausted British Antilles. Attempts to stop this trade had done much to stir up hostility to the imperial power in New England. The advent of peace made the government all the more determined to make British dependencies use British sugar. Accordingly, American customs officers, most of whom were absentees, were ordered to return to their posts and enforce new tariffs rigorously. The effect was to confirm the hostility of colonial merchants already alienated by rough handling during the war.

But the British government had far more extensive plans. As a result of the peace of Paris, the French had been expelled from Canada, but few believed this was the end of their North American ambitions. So British North America needed to be defended, if not against the French then against the restless Indian tribes of the interior with whom they had often allied. The rising of Pontiac in 1763, terrorizing the middle colonies for months on end, vividly demonstrated the need. It was therefore proposed to keep a standing army in America, at an estimated cost of £350,000 a year. With the national debt standing at almost £130 million, and interest at almost £5 million, British tax payers were reluctant to shoulder the new burden alone. A new cider tax introduced in 1763 had already caused widespread unrest in south-western England. So in 1765 stamp-duty was imposed on all public papers in the colonies. It seemed only just that the colonies, hitherto exempt from all taxes except their own local levies, should contribute towards the extremely modest cost of their own defence. Nobody foresaw the violence of the colonial reaction.

In British North America, perhaps the most literate society in the world, a tax on paper affected far more people than it would have in Europe. Above all, it affected the mercantile, legal, and landowning groups, the men of property, the American equivalent of European nobilities. Besides, in colonial eyes the expulsion of French power from Canada made a garrison less, not more, necessary. It was true that the amount demanded was hardly crippling, but it would have been a precedent for further violations of the colonies' traditional fiscal autonomy. The mouthpieces of the propertied groups in America, the colonial assemblies, denounced the act with the cry, 'no taxation without representation'. Rejecting British constitutional pieties which claimed that all British subjects were 'virtually' represented at Westminster, they would concede to parliament no powers in America except perhaps that of regulating the trade of the empire as a whole. In October 1765 representatives of nine of them met together in New York to condemn the British action—an ominous step towards united action later. Meanwhile, colonial merchants, already bitter at almost ten years of commercial harassment by the British authorities, banded themselves into associations pledged not to import British goods until the repeal of the Stamp Act. In the growing towns of the seaboard, following the example of Boston, outraged lawyers and notables organized the populace into bands of vigilantes calling themselves Sons of Liberty, dedicated to opposing the act by threats or violence against stamp importers and distributors, and indeed all those who symbolized or embodied British authority.

Had Grenville's government remained in power, force might have been met with force. But in July 1765, for reasons that had nothing to do with America, Grenville fell. The Whigs who replaced him had always opposed the Stamp Act and now repealed it (1766). At the same time they passed a Declaratory Act asserting the British parliament's right to make laws binding America in all cases whatsoever—deliberately making no mention of whether this included the right to tax. North America was swept by jubilant demonstrations. The colonists thought that they had brought down the ministry and forced repeal; and, although it was untrue, the conviction was to guide their actions later.

Certain British politicians were still determined to tax America. The very next year Townshend, on behalf of yet another British ministry, introduced a range of duties on British goods imported into America. Such duties were trade regulations, he claimed, and so not the sort of internal taxes the colonies were thought to object to. But their avowed aim was far from regulating trade; it was to raise a revenue for maintaining colonial governors and judges independently of grants from the local legislatures on which they had hitherto depended. As such it was a direct attack on the power of these assemblies. The result was a new explosion of protest in America, renewed non-importation agreements and wholesale defiance of the customs. It now became clear that the colonists denied the Westminster parliament any right to levy revenue in America—a position nobody in British public life would accept. Most of the Townshend duties were abandoned in 1770, but not before the conflict over them had destroyed all remaining trust between the colonies and the metropolis. By the time they disappeared, most colonists were convinced that any policy initiative by the home government must be a plot against their liberties; whilst the British parliament was almost unanimous in believing that the colonists were determined on an independence which would ruin the empire.

The government's plans in 1767 were not limited to America. It was felt that Ireland too should now be brought more closely under central control. Ever since the late 1720s Ireland had been managed with a view to not antagonizing the Anglican landlord 'Ascendancy' which held power there. All government patronage had been placed in the hands of a group of parliamentary managers called 'undertakers', who undertook to secure majorities in the Irish parliament. The king's representative, the lord-lieutenant, made only rare visits. In these circumstances the fury of the handful of self-styled

Irish 'patriots' who disliked the tutelage in which the parliament of West-minster kept that of Dublin, was directed against these Irish agents of British domination rather than against domination itself. From the early 1750s, the undertakers had increasingly played the two sides off against one another, and in 1767 the British government decided to reassert its authority. It wished to increase the Irish revenue with the object of raising the Irish military establishment from 12,000 to 15,000 men; the new soldiers would be for imperial defence. This measure was to be pushed through, with the help of the undertakers if possible, but without it if necessary. When a new lord-lieutenant, Townshend (brother of the author of the notorious American duties) ran into predictable opposition from them, it was decided that he should reside permanently in Ireland, where he would deprive them of all their patronage and redistribute it to his own supporters. This plan, unlike American ones, worked. By 1770 the lord-lieutenant was in complete control of the Irish parliament and the military augmentation had gone through. But it had been achieved only by the removal of the buffer between the Ascendancy and the British government, and by the reduction of the Dublin parliament, supposedly the Ascendancy's representative body, to an obedient tool of the Crown.

By 1770, therefore, many people in America and Ireland were coming to believe that George III's governments were bent on subverting the liberties which all British subjects thought had been vouchsafed to them by the 'glorious' revolution of 1688. The persecution of Wilkes, the government's most outrageous critic, by imprisoning him in 1763, expelling him from parliament in 1765, and refusing to accept his repeated re-elections in 1768, seemed to show a similar determination even in England. George III personally was much blamed by opposition Whigs, but his undeniably vigorous views were only important because they commanded the sympathy of a substantial parliamentary majority, and one which (contrary to Whig mythology) gave this support freely. Most members of parliament believed that, in difficult times, the king's government had a right to their support in resolute policies. North, who became prime minister in 1770, promised just this sort of firm administration and for the next twelve years had the backing of both king and commons in a course which brought Great Britain to the brink of disaster.

America was lost. After two years in which tensions with the colonies seemed to relax somewhat, 1772 saw new provocations from both sides. In America, the defiance of the customs service culminated in the burning of a customs schooner. North's government, meanwhile, launched a new scheme to provide the governor of the most turbulent colony, Massachussetts, with an independent income. Above all, North approved a proposal to help the crisis-ridden East India Company by allowing it to import tea surpluses into America at prices which undercut both legitimate merchants and smugglers. The result, in 1773, was the Boston Tea Party, when colonists disguised as Indians threw the first consignment of tea into Boston harbour. Meanwhile the Boston town meeting had inaugurated a network of correspondence between the main colonial cities, in order to co-ordinate resistance to further

British moves. These, when they came, were drastic, for the government was convinced that firm action must be taken now or never. 'The question', observed the secretary for American affairs, '. . .is whether these laws are to be submitted to? If the people of America say no, they say in effect that they will no longer be a part of the British empire.'[3] Accordingly, under a series of acts which the colonists dubbed 'intolerable', the port of Boston was closed, the seat of Massachussetts government transferred, the colonial charter suspended, and a military governor installed. The colonists found they were dealing, for the first time since 1763, with a British government sure of its aims and secure in its parliamentary support. In resisting it they were pushed to greater extremes. Convinced now that the moves against Boston were an ominous warning to them all, they met in the first continental congress in September 1774 to co-ordinate their action. Parliament, they now claimed, had no legislative, much less fiscal, rights over the colonies, which were in effect independent states under the king. But George III was an orthodox man: he never questioned that the British domains were governed by the king in parliament, or that the two were inseparable. Hopes for a last minute reconciliation were dashed when, early in 1775, British troops and Massachussetts militia opened fire on one another at Lexington and Concord. When a second continental congress met in May it found itself organizing a war and named Washington commander-in-chief. The British too began to build up an army, including many German mercenaries. An 'Olive Branch Petition' to George III from a congress still reluctant to make the final break was brushed aside, creating a receptive colonial audience in the spring of 1776 for Paine's pamphlet *Common Sense*, denouncing monarchy in general and George III in particular. Most of the Declaration of Independence, when it came that summer, was a recital of acts of tyranny committed against the colonies in the king's name.

The crisis lasted until the outcome of the War of Independence was clear, five years later. By that time, France had joined the struggle on the colonial side and French diplomacy had brought Spain and the Dutch republic into the war against Great Britain. Opposed abroad by the whole of Europe and America, the British parliament soon found itself in trouble at home too. The gentlemen of England, convinced that the survival of British wealth and power was at stake in the war, could not understand why they were not winning it. By 1778, many were beginning to turn against a government which was so signally failing to protect British interests and some were beginning to question the very system by which it held power. Since 1766 Whigs excluded from power had been claiming that royal patronage was maintaining a venal majority in parliament indifferent to the true wishes of the country. It was nonsense, but persuasive nonsense, which spread as failure piled on failure. Parliament should be reformed, many began to think, in order to diminish the government's influence and make MPs more responsive to the views of those who elected them. In 1779, a series of county 'associations'

[3] Quoted in M. Jensen, *The Founding of a Nation: a history of the American Revolution 1763–1776* (1968), 459–60.

were set up to petition parliament for reform—'economical' reform in the sense of the elimination of wasteful sinecures to curb patronage, and parliamentary reform in the sense of the elimination of pocket and rotten boroughs and the redistribution of their seats to the counties. In the spring of 1780 a national assembly of the movement was held and forty-one reform petitions reached parliament. The commons was induced to resolve that the crown's influence had increased, was increasing, and ought to be diminished, but it could not be persuaded to agree to any positive changes. Meanwhile only seventeen out of the original forty-one reform associations sent deputies to their national assembly. So support for reforms, born of a wave of frustration rather than deep conviction in the first place, was already on the wane when the Gordon riots broke out in London. The riots drove any further ideas of tampering with the established order from the minds of a frightened gentry.

Meanwhile Ireland seemed to be going the same way as America. The parallel between the constitutional position of Ireland and that of the thirteen colonies was too close to escape notice, and American resistance evoked widespread enthusiasm in the 'Protestant nation' of the Ascendancy. 'We are all Americans here,' wrote an Irish peer from Cork in 1775, 'except such as are attached securely to the Castle or papists.'[4] The Catholic majority, cautiously hoping for some measures of relief sponsored from London, was more guarded; but the enthusiasm was shared by the nonconformist Protestants of Ulster, with many links in America from decades of emigration. Discontent was fanned by economic depressions in the 1770s resulting from the disruption of trade with America and many listened with renewed interest to the traditional complaints of 'patriots' against Ireland's subjection to England. The cry went up for 'free trade', to allow Ireland control of her own economic destiny; but these calls made no headway in the Dublin parliament, locked in the tutelage established by Townshend. The war with France changed the situation, however, for Ireland, drained of troops for American service, seemed wide open to invasion from the traditional Catholic enemy. To meet this threat, Protestants began to band themselves spontaneously into corps of uniformed Volunteers, which by the middle of 1779 no self-respecting Protestant had failed to join. By then, too, the danger had passed, but the Volunteers did not disband. Instead, they turned to political agitation, backing the call for free trade. They won vocal support from the Whig opposition in England, and, dragging cannon labelled 'Free trade or else', they finally intimidated the Dublin parliament into backing their demand. Faced with a unanimous call from the Irish political nation, backed by organized force of arms, North had little alternative but to abrogate the laws of trade binding Ireland (December 1779–January 1780). Yet now this only cleared the way for more radical claims. Under the leadership of the parliamentary 'patriot' Grattan, the Volunteers raised their demands to the abrogation of the laws that subjected the Dublin parliament to overriding from London. They now claimed legislative independence.

[4] Quoted in R. B. McDowell, *Irish Public Opinion 1750–1800* (1944), 41. 'The Castle' was Dublin Castle, the seat of the lord-lieutenant.

In 1782 independence was theirs, for by then the Whigs had taken power in London. North's government, which did not long survive the news of defeat at Yorktown, was replaced by the only group which had consistently stood out against his discredited policies. The main achievement of the Whigs' brief tenure of power (1782–3) was to clear up the mess he had left. Irish legislative independence was conceded, and for ten years the Ascendancy was left to squabble over what to do with it.[5] Measures of 'economical reform' were passed, with uncertain effect. Most important of all, by the Peace of Paris of 1783 the loss of America and the independent existence of the United States were acknowledged, though the government was defeated when it attempted to make generous trading terms with the new nation. Having rejected the benefits of British rule, thought most MPs, the Americans could not seriously expect any commercial privileges from the mother country. Grimly, they braced themselves for commercial decline amid the ashes of an empire.

But there was no decline. Within a few years British trade with America had surpassed its pre-war volume, while French merchants were bitterly complaining that American interlopers were ruining their trade with their own Caribbean colonies. Great Britain gained politically, too, by shedding the burden of an issue which had sown deep and bitter divisions within the political nation. After 1783, under the unadventurous but firmly based leadership of Pitt the younger, the wounds were allowed to heal. Pitt had the instincts of a reformer, but he knew that he owed his power to a consensus, chastened by the upheavals of the late 1770s, of social conservatism. He never staked this power on pushing reforms through—he would sooner abandon them than create divisions. The result was that, when Great Britain faced the challenge of the French Revolution a decade later, government and governing class were united in their opposition to its influence.

In Great Britain the impact of American independence scarcely outlasted the war. Elsewhere in Europe it was much more enduring. The colonists began their struggle in order to defend their rights as Englishmen. By the time they declared independence, they were invoking the Rights of Man. They proclaimed it self-evident that men were created equal, that they had an inalienable right to liberty, that legitimate governments required the consent of the governed, and that peoples had a right to alter governments which ignored these principles. There was nothing strange or unfamiliar about these ideas in 1776, but it was breathtakingly new to see them acted upon. Republics existed, but not for over a century had a serious attempt been made to establish a new one. Events in America showed that governments could be called to account and established authority successfully resisted; political theory was not just a game for wrangling pedants, but a matter of immediate practical importance. Events in America widened the horizons of political possibility; they inspired and encouraged all those who opposed established authority—whether their aim was to promote change or to prevent it.

[5]   See below, p. 328.

The Habsburg Empire

In 1740 the most ramshackle of the major powers of Europe was the hetero-geneous collection of territories ruled from Vienna. The war that began in that year proved it, and the survival of the Habsburg state owed more to conflicts of interest among other powers than to its own strength. Even so, at the peace of Dresden (1745) Maria Theresa had to reconcile herself to losing almost all of the rich province of Silesia to Prussia.

When I saw [she later wrote][6] that I must put my hand to the Peace . . . my state of mind suddenly changed, and I directed my whole attention to in-ternal problems and to devising how the German Hereditary Lands could still be preserved and protected. . .The high policy of this House changed com-pletely; formerly it was directed toward holding the balance of power against France. Now there was no more thought of that, only of internal consolidation . . .My one endeavour was to inform myself of the situation and resources of each Province, and then to acquire a thorough understanding and picture of the abuses which had crept into them and their administrative services, resulting in the utmost confusion and distressfulness.

She instructed Haugwitz, who had made a reputation for ruthless admini-stration in the corner of Silesia that was retained, to draw up a comprehensive plan of reform, which he produced in 1748.

The aim was to establish a standing army of 108,000 men. The problem was to pay for it. Haugwitz's proposal was to raise the money by taxing hitherto exempt noble lands in the Austrian and Bohemian territories, and to remove the maintenance of the new army from the control of the estates of the various provinces. To facilitate long-term planning the estates were to grant taxes for ten-year periods. The new revenues should be raised and administered in each province, not as previously by agents of the estates, but by appointees of the central government, responsible directly to it.

It was one of the most radical plans for political reform of the century. At one blow it attempted to tax the nobility, to silence their main organs of power and expression, the estates, for a decade, and to deprive them of most of their administrative powers. Predictably, it encountered impassioned opposition, both from most of the empress's senior advisers before it was promulgated, and from the estates when they were asked to accept it. In several provinces it was approved only after major concessions from the government, while in Carinthia there was a flat refusal. This the empress ignored; she imposed the plan by what she called 'royal right'. Resistance was never pushed to extremes; the boldness of the reforms took the nobility's breath away and they felt compensated in some degree for their losses by being guaranteed exclusive access to the host of new administrative posts created by the plan. Besides, the Seven Years War soon absorbed their energies and emphasized the importance of more efficient state organization. But they were now alerted to the dangers of increasing government power and the problems it was bound to confront them with.

---

[6] Quoted in Macartney (ed.), *The Habsburg and Hohenzollern Dynasties in the seventeenth and eighteenth centuries*, 115–16.

Also alerted were the Hungarian nobility, whose tax-exemptions and constitutional privileges had been confirmed by the empress as recently as 1740, in return for their promise of support against Frederick II. There was no thought of extending the Haugwitz plan to Hungary, but every intention of making the kingdom pay for some share of the increased military burden. At a convocation of the diet in 1751 a 50 per cent tax-increase was requested; most of it was eventually granted, but only in return for substantial concessions. The assembly broke up in an atmosphere of ill will and mistrust. It next met in 1764, only to be confronted with further tax-demands, proposals to end noble exemptions, and a plan to limit the obligations of serfs towards their lords,[7] all of which were bluntly rejected. Maria Theresa reacted by dissolving the diet and promulgating new serfdom regulations regardless, this time by 'right of majesty'. She never convoked a Hungarian diet again.

The chief activity of the remaining thirteen years of Maria Theresa's reign was the extension of laws, designed to protect the serfs, to the various heredi-tary lands. These measures inevitably diminished the powers of nobles over their peasants, but they had very little opportunity for effective protest. The estates never recovered the rights they abandoned in 1748, and though most continued to meet, it was to consent to imperial proposals, not to discuss them. So by 1780, in the space of just over thirty years, Austrian and Bohemian nobles had seen the government reduce their consitutional role to nothing, destroy their tax exemption, and significantly restrict their powers over their peasants. Their Hungarian brethren knew that it would dearly like to do the same to them. And then the old empress died, leaving her impulsive and unpredictable son Joseph II in sole command of the state.

Ever since his earliest manhood Joseph had dreamed of the day when he could use the plenitude of his authority to attack the social structure of his hereditary dominions. Only when entrenched vested interests had been destroyed, he believed, could the state be run in a more enlightened way, and fullest military efficiency be achieved. He believed that the reform efforts begun in 1748 could and should be carried much further. Austria would be a match for Prussia militarily only when she was organized with similar thoroughness. He embarked almost immediately on a headlong programme of pushing the trends of the previous thirty years to their logical conclusions.

Joseph further diminished the power of landlords over their peasants and announced his intention of raising taxation in order to support a standing army of almost 300,000 men. He launched a cadastral survey of all the land of the monarchy in order to provide an accurate basis for tax assessments independent of the declarations of landholders. The so-called 'physiocratic urbarium' of 1789, based on this survey, abolished all forced-labour services and tried to commute them.[8] This was the most revolutionary of all Joseph's measures, for it would have destroyed the economic position of the great

---

[7]   See above, p. 99.
[8]   See above, p. 101–2.

landowners. They would have been forced to sell most of their lands, the great estates would have been broken up, a class of peasant proprietors created, and the power of the nobility ruined. The opposition of Joseph's principal noble counsellors was almost unanimous. There were loud and threatening protests from provincial estates for the first time since 1748. But the protests heard in the Austrian provinces were nothing to those which came in from the more outlying dominions of the empire, especially from Hungary and the Netherlands.

In all the reforms of Maria Theresa's reign, the distinctive character of each territory had always been respected. When reform was attempted, it was always within the framework of local customs and conditions. Joseph had no respect for such matters. He was determined to convert the empire into a unitary state, governed everywhere according to uniform principles, and everywhere subject to the same laws. On his mother's death, he refused to submit to separate coronations in Hungary and Bohemia and had all the crowns, hats, swords, and other symbols of sovereignty in the various Habsburg dominions brought to Vienna. In 1784 he decreed that German should be the universal official language of the empire, and in the next few years an attempt was made to abandon all its historic administrative and judicial divisions and replace them with thirteen uniform districts. The deep particularism of every part of the empire was outraged, even in German-speaking provinces. 'What does it concern the people of the Tyrol', wrote a nobleman of that province,[9] 'what happens in Bohemia, Moravia, and other countries? The Tyrolese have their own sovereign, their own laws, their own constitution, and their own country. It is a matter of pure accident that their prince also happens to rule over other countries.'

The Hungarian nobles were even more bitter. In addition to all the affronts he delivered to the separate character of Hungary, Joseph was particularly concerned to destroy the nobles' most treasured attribute—their tax-exemption. His method was to blackmail them into surrendering this privilege in return for the abrogation of a series of prohibitive tariffs which kept most foreign imports out of Hungary but which at the same time virtually excluded Hungarian agricultural products from their most convenient market, Austria. Since agriculture was the main source of income for the nobles, they were the immediate sufferers. The preparation of the land-survey from 1785 onwards nourished noble suspicions that Joseph was preparing to subject them to taxation. They blamed the widespread peasant unrest of the mid-1780s on the excitement bred by Joseph's restless style of government. It was unfortunate for Joseph that at this moment he was forced to put himself at their mercy. Called upon by the Russians to honour an alliance made against the Turks, he needed the co-operation of the local authorities in Hungary in order to recruit troops and build up supplies. Rather than face a full diet (which he had never done) in 1788 he convoked the county assemblies, a lower level of representation. Far from being more docile than the estates, however, these assemblies were the very embodiment of noble power and

---

[9] Quoted in Blanning, *Joseph II and Enlightened Despotism*, 73.

refused to agree to his requests. Only a full diet was competent to handle these matters, they claimed, and once the cry was raised most members of the royal administration in Hungary began to echo it. Some nobles went so far as to solicit Prussian help in finding a new, non-Habsburg king for Hungary. By the end of 1789, Hungary was completely beyond Joseph's control, in the grip of a national noble revolt against rule from Vienna. In January 1790, recognizing that he had no choice but to surrender, Joseph returned the crown of St. Stephen to Hungary and revoked all his reforming edicts except those granting religious toleration and personal freedom to the serfs. He even hinted at the convocation of a diet. But by now such retreats could only fan the agitation, as did Joseph's death a month later. The jubilant Hungarian nobles were resolved to make the accession of Leopold II the occasion for reversing what they saw as forty years of constitutional usurpation.

The Netherlands, meanwhile had completely renounced Habsburg authority. Hungary had a long history of turbulence and resistance to authority, but the southern Netherlands were notoriously docile. Maria Theresa's government appreciating this, had done nothing to disturb the situation. 'The peoples of those provinces', the empress wrote to Joseph just before she died,[10] 'hold to their traditional prejudices—perhaps ridiculous; but since they are obedient and faithful and pay more taxes than our exhausted and discontented German provinces, what more can we ask of them?' In Joseph's eyes, however, these distant and idiosyncratic domains were a liability—his attempts to exchange them for Bavaria show that. If he could not get rid of them, he could at least assert greater central control over them and perhaps thereby make them more directly useful. So the full range of reforms which historians call 'Josephism' was applied willy-nilly to the provinces of the southern Netherlands. It was applied without regard to the traditional customs of the region, embodied in hallowed constitutional documents normally confirmed by each new ruler, Joseph included. The most famous of these, the *Joyeuse Entrée* of Brabant, stipulated that all important reforms and all new taxes should be introduced with the consent of the estates, which had the right to present remonstrances on subjects of discontent. There was great variety in the composition of the estates of the various Netherlands provinces, but most contained representatives of the nobility and the municipal oligarchies of this highly urbanized region. All contained a substantial body of clergy.

Since the eradication of Louvain-based Jansenism earlier in the century, the southern Netherlands had been a bastion of Catholic orthodoxy and subservience to the Pope. Joseph's church policies were therefore ill received. In 1781 religious toleration was introduced, contrary to the *Joyeuse Entrée*. Between 1783 and 1786 most direct links with Rome were severed, the number of religious holidays was halved, 163 houses of contemplative orders were dissolved, and the education of intending priests reorganized into government-controlled seminaries. Demonstrations by the inmates of these

[10] Quoted in W. W. Davis, *Joseph II — an Imperial Reformer for the Austrian Netherlands* (1974), 114.

seminaries against the spirit of innovation they represented inaugurated open resistance to Joseph's rule in the last weeks of 1786.

Unfortunately this example of unrest came at a time when every other important element in the Austrian Netherlands was disaffected and ripe for resistance. An economic depression which began in 1786 created urban discontent, aggravated by Joseph's attempts to restrict the powers of guilds. The introduction, at the beginning of 1787, of a series of radical administrative and judicial reforms alienated nearly everybody who occupied an established position of public authority. Under these measures, the ancient and complex structure of government in the Netherlands was swept away, to be replaced by nine administrative units, each governed by an intendant responsible to a supreme council in Brussels. None of the reforms had been discussed by the estates, for in Joseph's view, as he told them in 1789, 'I do not need your consent to do good.'[11] They, on the contrary, believed that under the *Joyeuse Entrée* and other charters like it, he needed their consent to do anything at all. Encouraged by the example of the seminarians, in the spring of 1787 the various estates put themselves at the head of a protest movement which swept all ranks of society, demanding the complete abolition of all Joseph's reforms. So shaken were the Brussels authorities by the strength of the movement that without consulting Joseph, they agreed to all these demands.

Joseph was disgusted; but, faced with a *fait accompli*, he could only temporize and give a gracious reception to a deputation from the estates. His military commitments in the east prevented him from dispatching enough troops to settle matters at once, by force. This was his long-term aim, however, and by the autumn a reinforced provincial government was once more initiating reforms, notably in the church. Renewed protests from the estates were overridden, and popular demonstrations dispersed with bloodshed. Resistance was encouraged by the example of France. The estates began to refuse to vote the funds which Joseph so desperately needed to keep his ill-starred war against the Turks going. The emperor's patience broke, and in June 1789, at the very moment when the eyes of all Europe were upon the first meeting of a national representative body in France for 175 years, a body expected to set permanent limits to 'despotism', Joseph abrogated the *Joyeuse Entrée*. At that moment, the cause of the French and the Belgians (as some were beginning to call themselves) seemed one. To evade arrest, the two most prominent leaders of the opposition, the lawyers Van der Noot and Vonck, had already fled abroad; the former formed a volunteer 'patriot' army in Holland, the latter, from the territory of the prince-bishop of Liège, itself shaken by revolution in August, concentrated on organizing a secret revolutionary society called 'For Altar and Hearth' (*Pro Aris et Focis*). Violent resistance met the attempts of Joseph's agents to levy taxes unapproved by the estates, and more demonstrators were shot down. But the garrison was badly deployed, and in October Van der Noot's forces crossed the frontier

[11] Quoted in Davis, op. cit. 112.

to defeat an Austrian force. Failure to reverse this defeat by means of reinforcements sparked off a new wave of patriotic risings in the cities. The
authorities tried to avoid a final débâcle by restoring the *Joyeuse Entrée*
and abandoning all the reforms wholesale, as Joseph had by now already
done in Hungary, but here also it was too late. With Van der Noot's triumphal
entry into Brussels, Austrian power evaporated. The various provinces proclaimed themselves sovereign states, and Joseph lived just long enough to
hear that, on 7 January 1790, in an autonomously convoked estates-general,
they had renounced his authority and proclaimed themselves the United
States of Belgium.

Northern Europe

Among lesser European rulers, none was closer in character to Joseph II
than Gustavus III of Sweden. His acquaintance with the writings of the
Enlightenment was far deeper than Joseph's and he was far less impetuous,
but they were at one in their taste for military glory. Having spent the 1770s
assuring the stable functioning of the new constitution he had promulgated
in 1772, by 1780 he was beginning to dream of expeditions against Danish
Norway, or against Russia. But wars required money, which only diets could
grant; their consent was also necessary for the very declaration of war.
Gustavus was no enemy of diets, or of the nobility who dominated them,
but he resented opposition. Economic difficulties provoked plenty of this in
the diet of 1786, especially from the house of nobles, and therefore he did
not reveal to it the advanced state of his plans for war. By the time the next
one met, in February 1789, he had invaded Russia and needed funds to sustain
the campaign. But since he had not sought the diet's consent before declaring
war, the noble house, deeply suspicious of his motives, refused to co-operate.
A group of Finnish nobles had already condemned the war and sabotaged the
campaign in their country. Gustavus began to see himself as the victim of a
noble plot, which he sought to defeat by appealing openly to the anti-noble
prejudices of commoners. His Act of Union and Security of 1789 which
sweepingly increased the crown's independence of the diet, was overwhelmingly
passed by the three non-noble houses because it abrogated a whole range
of noble privileges. Gustavus went on to force the nobles to vote unlimited
funds by intimidating their sessions with a royalist mob. These steps were
so radical that he could hardly retrace them when the war emergency ended
the next year. Everybody knew that the king was pondering further reforms,
and many nobles feared that they could only be the victims once more. This
was the atmosphere in which noble plotters assassinated the king in March
1792.

Kings [declared the nobleman who wielded the pistol][12] . . .only have authority
through the confidence of the nation, and this confidence is only theirs so
long as they remain worthy of it through their respect for the law and for
liberty. . .Can he remain our king, the man who has violated his oath to the

---

[12] Quoted in C. Nordmann, *Grandeur et liberté de la Suède (1660–1792)* (1971),
446–7.

people to maintain the Constitution of 1772, drawn up by him and accepted without amendment by the Swedish nation? My conviction is that this perjurer has ceased to be king. Between the nation and him, the pact is broken. . .Since there is no legal remedy, it is permitted to oppose violence with violence.

So near had social conservatism come to the language of revolution.

The death of Gustavus was the last of a long line of defeats suffered by innovating governments. Only in one state did authority seem to emerge the victor—the untypical case of the Dutch republic. Here, the very title of the triumphant authority had always been uncertain before, and its final victory was only assured by foreign arms.

In the 1770s the alignments of Dutch politics were much what they had been a century earlier—Prince William V of Orange was emerging from a long minority during which the republican party which dominated the states-general had largely controlled the destinies of the state. The Orangists, with popular and noble support, favoured a British alliance, whilst the republicans, representing the commercial urban oligarchies and especially that of Amsterdam, preferred a more independent if not positively pro-French stand. Thus when war broke out between Britain and France in 1778 it posed an acute problem which went to the heart of Dutch domestic politics. For the republicans, who called themselves 'patriots', the humbling of Great Britain seemed to be a way of recovering some of the commercial prosperity that had so obviously been lost over the century. Besides, the republicanism of the American rebels struck a favourable chord in Dutch traditions; not to mention the enormous and expanding colonial market which would be opened by the end of British power in North America and possibly in India too. The Orangists, disorganized after the powerlessness of the minority years, were unable to resist the drift towards war, and in 1780 the Dutch became the allies of France and the United States. In time of war, the prince of Orange traditionally commanded the armed forces, but William V, no man of energy, had no stomach for a war against Great Britain. When the war proved disastrous, he and his party were held responsible by the 'patriots' who had done so much to bring it about. Patriotism was now coming to mean more than the traditional political stance of the urban oligarchies. It meant sympathy for the Americans and all they stood for, independently of hostility to Great Britain. Its ideals were most clearly expressed in *An Address to the Netherlands People*, an inflammatory pamphlet distributed in 1781 by the radical nobleman Van der Capellen. He urged the people (whom he did not closely define) to resist the power of the prince and resume control of the state for themselves. The Netherlands, he declared, was like a joint-stock company, whose directors were ultimately only the servants of the shareholders. And since the prince controlled the army, with which he might suppress any reforming movement, Van der Capellen urged the formation of armed and uniformed 'Free Corps', not unlike the Irish Volunteers. With continued reverses in the war giving these ideas wide currency, Free Corps began to appear. By 1784 they numbered 28,000 volunteers and were holding their first national convention. At the same time there was a mounting attack on princely power. Many municipal councils abolished the right of the prince to nominate certain of their members. The court was expelled from The Hague, and the prince relieved of the stadtholdership and command of the armed forces of certain provinces, notably Holland itself. His Hohenzollern wife chafed impatiently at these humiliations, but William V himself seemed supine under them.

Although the patriot movement had some support from the Regent class, the urban oligarchs who were the traditional bulwark of republicanism, its main strength came from the lesser bourgeoisie who had hitherto enjoyed no share in the exercise of power. This did not make an authentic popular movement, but it did make it, by contemporary standards, democratic. The main patriot concern was to introduce a greater elective element into politics, and in 1786 patriots imposed what they hoped would be the first of many popularly elected town councils on Utrecht. Such developments, however, threatened not only princely power, but also the traditional oligarchic authority of the Regents. Some of the latter, alarmed, began belatedly to see advantages in princely power as a focus of stability.

It took foreign intervention to resolve matters. Even after the war both the British and the French worked hard to sustain their respective supporters in the republic. The British encouraged and subsidized the Orangists, while the French supported the 'patriots'. Neither side intervened actively: patriot success made French action unnecessary, and the British had no continental forces and no allies willing to act with them. But in 1786 the death of Frederick II brought to the Prussian throne a king without his predecessor's anti-British prejudices, an enemy of democratic ideas, and the brother of the princess of Orange. Frederick William II believed that the time had come to restore order in the Netherlands. In 1787, with British support, he used the pretext of an armed confrontation between his sister and a detachment of Free Corps to issue an ultimatum to the Republic. The princess must have satisfaction. Without leaving time for discussion, the king sent 20,000 Prussian troops into the Netherlands, where they met no resistance. The Free Corps melted away. Many 'patriots' fled abroad, to France, or to the now-chaotic southern Netherlands. Advised by the British ambassador and backed by the Prussian army, the Orange party began a purge of its former opponents. The old order was restored in the towns and the constitutional authority of the prince refurbished with a two-power guarantee.

As so often in the history of the Republic, Dutch internal problems had been settled by outside circumstances. The 'patriots' were unlucky that Frederick II died and that the Austrians and Russians were distracted by Turkish problems in the Balkans, giving Prussia the freedom she needed. Above all, they were unlucky that, at this very moment, their French protectors were prevented from intervening by the collapse of their own state from within.

France: the Collapse of the Old Order

France was lucky that no crisis struck her down as early as the last years of

Louis XIV. The unprecedented scale of Louis's war efforts, especially after 1689, had already pushed his government into a wide range of innovatory policies. Administration was centralized and the power of its agents increased to a degree never before seen. The tax-exemption of the nobility was ended by the introduction of the capitation in 1695 and by the *dixième* of 1710 a crude attempt was made, for the war's duration, to tax income. A series of poor harvests added to the discontents produced by such measures, and there was a peasant uprising in the Cevennes. Above all, a truly colossal debt was built up. Such was the chaos of French accounting that a clear estimate of its exact size is almost impossible; but between 2,300 and 2,400 million *livres* does not seem excessive, costing about 100 million *livres* a year or five-sixths of the king's annual revenue, to service.

On this occasion the situation was saved by bankruptcy. Not one, enormous, cataclysmic bankruptcy—though the collapse of Law's 'system' in 1721 was almost that—but a whole series of renunciations, consolidations, and interest reductions which lasted from 1713 to 1726. By the time the value of the *livre* was stabilized in 1726, and the frenetic financial experiments of a decade had been abandoned, the level of the debt was down to 1,700 million *livres* and the annual cost of its service to 47 million. But the chaos of those years, if it saved the situation for the moment, bequeathed two fatal legacies to the future. One was a mistrust of public banks and paper money—too many people had been ruined by them and had passed the lessons of experience on to their children. This was unfortunate, because a public bank was the most obvious way of obtaining advantageous credit for a government, as the English and Dutch experience showed. The other legacy was a horror of bankruptcy itself—the ultimate breach of public faith, by which a government renounced its obligations and robbed its creditors of their money. These twin prejudices deprived future governments of cheap, easy loans and of the possibility of shedding the burden of expensive and difficult ones.

The years between 1726 and 1741 were the golden age of France's old financial system. The debt remained moderate and the Polish Succession war was largely paid for by reintroducing the *dixième* tax of 1710. But when fighting resumed against Great Britain in 1744 not even a renewed *dixième* could match the expenses of war on a world scale. In 1749, therefore, as soon as the war was over and at the very moment that Haugwitz was introducing his own reform plan in the Habsburg empire, the comptroller-general Machault introduced a new peacetime tax of a twentieth of annual income, the *vingtième*. Although the *parlements* registered the new tax with little demur, it created immediate controversy. New taxes in time of war were understandable, but new peacetime taxes were unprecedented; so was a tax which admitted of no exemptions. Particularly outraged were the clergy and the greater provinces with estates, who were able to use their leverage as engines of governmental credit to win exemption (in the clergy's case) or lighter treatment. When in 1756, after the outbreak of a new war, a second *vingtième* was imposed for its duration, the *parlements* themselves raised an outcry. Inspectors making assessments for the new tax were passionately denounced. 'This type of inquisition,' declared the Toulouse *parlement*,[13] 'as unworthy of Your Majesty as of the warlike people subject to him, is not unlike a census of slaves. Everything is uncovered, discussed, tested and assessed like goods whose use was allowed us by grace and whose ownership belonged to the revenue.' But the government's demands did not stop there. In 1760 a third *vingtième* was introduced, along with various surcharges, for the war's duration. By 1763 the French king was laying claim to well over 25 per cent of the income of all his non-clerical subjects—a higher tax burden than in any state except the Dutch republic. Even then the cost of the war was only borne with the aid of constant new loans.

Machault's blunt and brutal manner had antagonized all major interests—the clergy, the provincial estates, the *parlements*, and the financiers upon whom the government depended for continued credit. Choiseul's post-war policy was to rebuild French strength by conciliation. Above all, he sought to work with the *parlements*, encouraging them in their attacks on the Jesuits, seeking their advice on the state's financial problems, and appointing magistrates to the ministry. By abandoning the third *vingtième* the moment the war ended, and promising that nothing would be done to revise assessments, he induced them to agree to a prolongation of the second *vingtième* to 1770. Even so, the governments of the 1760s had no easy time with the *parlements*, whose influence and power reached their height, especially in the provinces. There were confrontations with the courts of Besançon, Grenoble, and Toulouse. Those of Pau and Rennes had to be dissolved and remodelled, so violent were their clashes with the crown's local agents. Seeing such moves as a threat to all *parlements* and their right to remonstrate against new laws, some magistrates formulated the idea that the various courts were only 'classes' of a single, indivisible *parlement*. All the courts began to make much use of the vocabulary of national rights, for which they claimed to be the spokesmen; their remonstrances, nominally secret, were openly printed and widely circulated, an influential vehicle of political education. By this time they had absorbed the thought of Montesquieu, who had assigned a fundamental role in all true monarchies to 'intermediary powers' such as themselves. When the king was moved to reassert his position by replying to their strictures, the authority to which he laid claim sounded suspiciously like the despotism that Montesquieu had so roundly condemned.

All this helps to explain the outcry against the work of Maupeou, who became chancellor in 1768. He had no real quarrel with the *parlements*, but, determined to overthrow Choiseul, he chose to provoke the Paris *parlement* in order to accuse Choiseul of supporting its defiance. Louis XV was growing old and, never a friend of the *parlements*, he wanted to silence them once and for all. Choiseul was dismissed; but the *parlement* could not be induced to end the judicial strike with which it had responded to Maupeou's attack.

---

[13] Quoted in M. Marion, *Histoire financière de la France depuis 1715* (1914), i. 181.

The chancellor reacted early in 1771 by the dismissal and exile of its members and their replacement by more amenable magistrates. At the same time he sought to court public opinion by the creation of a whole network of lower jurisdictions easy of access, the abolition of judicial fees and venality of office in the new courts, and the promise of a new law code. When the provincial *parlements* protested, they too were remodelled. The powers of the new *parlements* were unchanged; some of them continued to remonstrate. But their strength had been broken. The way was clear for the introduction of reforming policies without opposition.

Little use was made of this opportunity. Maupeou's colleague Terray, in charge of the finances, did profit from it to extend the second *vingtième* to 1781 and to authorize a revision of assessments. Terray's most important achievements, however, did not need the magistrates' consent—the first steps towards diminishing the role of private enterprise in government finance, and a partial bankruptcy in 1770. Maupeou's promised law code never materialized and his vaunted 'free justice' was paid for by heavier taxes. The remodelling of the *parlements* was a political expedient, not a plan of reform, and the ministry had no programme for profiting from it. Louis XV wanted to end his days in peace, not to launch radical changes.

Nevertheless the upheaval of the early 1770s was the turning-point for the old regime, for these years brought to the surface a crisis of confidence in French public life. Some publicists, notably Voltaire, applauded Maupeou's firmness, naïvely taking his talk of judicial reform at its face value. But most of the French political nation, thoroughly steeped in Montesquieu, saw nothing but an unpardonable attack on the intermediary powers. 'We are on the verge of a crisis,' wrote Diderot in April 1771, 'which will end in slavery or liberty; if it is slavery, it will be a slavery like that which exists in Morocco or Constantinople. If all the parlements and dissolved ... farewell to every privilege of the various estates constituting a corrective principle which prevents the monarchy from degenerating into despotism.'[14] The *parlements* themselves, convinced now of their own powerlessness, went to their downfall calling for a convocation of the ultimate intermediary power, the representative assembly of the whole nation, the half-forgotten estates-general.

Isolated calls of this sort had been heard in times of crisis before, notably during Louis XIV's last dismal years. Some provincial *parlements* in the 1760s had called for the revival of defunct provincial estates. But never since the mid-seventeenth century had the demand been so consistent or widespread as in 1771. Terray's financial operations made it all the more urgent. In 1770 he had broken the taboo on bankruptcy, making this a crisis of financial confidence too. Maupeou's despotic behaviour hardly reassured potential lenders; and the way Terray went on to push through a whole range of tax-increases, against no serious opposition, convinced more and more people, at a time of sudden economic hardship, that new constitutional machinery was

---

[14] Quoted in J. Lough, *An Introduction to eighteenth century France* (1960), 192.

required. By the time of Louis XVI's accession in 1774, many Frenchmen were coming to believe, with the aggrieved British colonists in America, that there should be no taxation without representation. Certainly every one of Louis's major ministers took this view. Turgot hoped eventually to introduce representative assemblies at all levels of government. Necker introduced two experimental provincial assemblies and projected a third. Provincial assemblies were also a major element in the reform proposals of Calonne and Brienne in 1787. Several *parlements*, despite fears of erecting a rival power, petitioned for representative systems of administration in their own provinces. The problem was a lack of unanimity about the form and functions of these bodies; so deep did suspicion of the government's motives now run, that proposals emanating from ministers were viewed as mere devices to give the semblance of consent without any real power of prevention. This was why the *parlements* disliked Necker's assemblies and called instead for the revival of provincial estates whose ancient constitutions were beyond ministerial tampering.

The accession of Louis XVI was universally hailed as an opportunity for a new start. A clean sweep was made of the ministry and the old *parlements* were restored. Often characterized as a step of craven weakness which destroyed the regime's last hope of survival, this restoration was in fact advised by most of the new ministers and widely welcomed by the public. Nor did the *parlements* return unrepentant. Though they achieved victories at a local level in clashes with intendants in the next decade, they returned weakened and disunited, their membership torn apart by recriminations over the Maupeou years. Between 1774 and 1787 they never prevented the government from implementing any policy or raising any tax on which it was really determined. The real problem of these years was to persuade the irresolute young king to give determined support to any policy at all.

Louis XVI's governments pursued only two objectives with any consistency. The first was to support the American rebels in their conflict with Great Britain. This war brought long-sought revenge for the humiliation of 1763, but the price was high. America and all that it stood for became wildly fashionable in France, with eager discussion of the political ideas and representative institutions of the new nation, which contrasted very favourably with those of France. 'I was singularly struck', reminisced the comte de Ségur in 1824,[15] 'to see such a unanimous outbreak of lively and general interest in the revolt of a people against a king. . .I was far from being the only one whose heart then throbbed at the news of newborn liberty reawakening to shake off the yoke of arbitrary power.' At the same time the cost of the war, which ran to over 1,300 millions, dealt a ruinous blow to the already overburdened finances of the state. Financed largely by huge loans negotiated by Necker at crippling rates of interest, the war bequeathed a debt whose service was absorbing half the revenue in 1786.

Moreover the easiest and most obvious remedy was ruled out. The second

[15] *Souvenirs et anecdotes sur le règne de Louis XVI*, 61.

policy upon which Louis XVI's ministries were unanimous was the avoidance of bankruptcy. Turgot, the former intendant and physiocratic theorist, made it the keystone of his programme when he took charge of the finances in 1774; but within two years he had fallen, having antagonized everybody by a doctrinaire insistence on reforming guilds, abolishing the *corvée*, and removing restrictions on the wine and grain trades, all in the space of eighteen months. Louis XVI, his confidence in Turgot shaken by the scale of the outcry, dismissed him without the opportunity to attempt further reforms. To retain the confidence of the financial world, Louis was next persuaded to entrust the finances to Necker, a Swiss banker with an anti-physiocratic record. Necker was vain, and revelled in the reputation of a financial miracle worker. More than anything he loved applause. He had little sympathy with the way the regime worked, and sought to reform its budgetary procedures entirely. He despised the *parlements* and advocated provincial assemblies in order to eclipse them. But by his ability to raise loans he financed the American war without introducing new taxation, which made him a popular favourite. In 1781 he published the *Compte Rendu*, the first public balance sheet of the French state's finances ever, which purported to show a modest surplus. But when, the same year, he tried to use his popularity to force the king to give him over-all control of policy, he was refused, and resigned. His two fleeting successors did not command the same credit, and had to bear the odium of raising taxes: in 1783 a third *vingtième* was introduced, to last until three years after the peace. Finally, that same year, the king appointed another former intendant, Calonne, who saw that, with taxes at their highest level within memory and bankruptcy politically impossible, further loans were essential. To generate the necessary confidence in the financial community, he launched an expensive and extravagant programme of public works, while privately conducting a comprehensive survey of the whole structure of government to see how it might best be reformed.

By 1786 Calonne's conclusions were ready. The imminent lapse of the third *vingtième* and the poor performance of recently floated loans made it not a minute too soon. By the end of the year the king was convinced by his minister's argument that 'the sole means of managing finally to put the finances truly in order, must consist in revivifying the whole state by recasting everything that is vicious in its constitution.'[16] The plan had three main points. The tax structure was to be reformed by abandoning the *vingtièmes* and substituting a universal land tax levied in kind, the 'territorial subvention'; there would also be a new stamp tax. Secondly, the principal taxpayers were to be associated with the process of assessing and levying the new taxes in provincial assemblies elected by landowners. Thirdly, the mark of Calonne's physiocratic advisers was evident in proposals to boost production (and therefore ultimately the tax-yield) by such steps as the abolition of internal customs barriers and the freeing of the grain trade. Since all these measures

---

[16] Quoted in A. Goodwin, 'Calonne, the Assembly of French Notables of 1787 and the origins of the Révolte Nobiliaire', *English Historical Review* (1946), 209.

would take time to be effective, the state would need more loans. To create the confidence essential for yet more credit, Calonne believed that his plans needed an unprecedented show of national consensus. After all the discussion since 1771, he considered convoking the estates-general, but decided that they would be too unpredictable. Instead he proposed to lay his plan before an Assembly of Notables, whose members would be the most prominent figures in the kingdom, but nominated by the king, not elected. The Notables assembled in February 1787.

From the start everything went wrong. The clergy in the assembly were determined to resist all reforms which undermined the church's privileges. Most of the nobles were willing to agree to the new taxes but were suspicious of the proposed provincial assemblies, where they were guaranteed no representation, and which they feared would have no real restraining power. Nobody at all accepted Calonne's diagnosis of the problem. He announced a probable deficit of 160 million *livres* for 1788—what then had happened to the surplus disclosed by Necker in 1781? Necker himself, who had never ceased to defend his administration's record in copious writings, asked the same question. Either Necker must have been wrong, or Calonne himself must be responsible for the problems he was now proposing to remedy. Either way, what really seemed to be wrong was that the taxpayers had no effective way of controlling the government's financial policies. The new plan contained none. There was only one body competent to undertake reforms and enjoying the authority it would need, announced Lafayette, a notable and the most celebrated veteran of the American war: that was the estates-general.

In the face of this unexpected criticism, while the king's ministers fell to squabbling among themselves, Louis, disgusted, dismissed Calonne and entrusted the government to Brienne, an archbishop who had led the clerical opposition in the Notables. To everyone's astonishment, Brienne took up his predecessor's plan almost unchanged, but not surprisingly he was no more successful with it. With the call for the estates-general now growing Brienne had the assembly dissolved and prepared to implement the plan in the more traditional way, by having its various elements registered by the *parlements*. But these bodies, whose principal magistrates had been prominent among the Notables, were determined not to sanction proposals that the Notables had felt unable to agree to. The only body with that right, declared the Paris *parlement* in August 1787, was the estates-general. When the king, ignoring this call, conducted a forced registration of the new fiscal edicts, the Paris *parlement* denounced it as illegal. The king retorted by exiling the magistrates. It was a summer of deadlock; and even in September, when a compromise was reached, it backfired. Against a background of vague talk about convoking the estates in 1792, the government offered to abandon the proposed tax reforms in return for the registration of new loans and a further prolongation of the two existing *vingtièmes*. A special 'royal session' of the *parlement* was held on 19 November to register the proposals, in which the king, unprecedentedly, invited discussion. But he refused to take a vote, and when the opportunist duc d'Orleans protested (somewhat dubiously) that this was illegal, the flustered king replied, 'I don't care. . .it is legal because I wish it.'[17]

Despotism could not have been more succinctly defined. Here was a government which, despite all its talk of representative assemblies and consultation, seemed determined to impose its will subject to no restraints. Public discussion and denunciation of the government, which had been growing ever since the Notables had met, now reached a climax. The Paris *parlement*, calling still for the estates-general in 1789 at the latest, turned its denunciations against arbitrary imprisonments, the provincial courts joining in the chorus. After further months of noisy stalemate, the government concluded that the only way forward was to sweep away the opposition of the *parlements* altogether in the manner of Maupeou—only more thoroughly. The reforms of keeper of the seals Lamoignon, introduced simultaneously throughout France in May 1788, were intended to do this. The *parlements* were not abolished, but their competence was restricted from below by the elevation of a number of lower courts into the new status of *grand bailliage*. Above all, they lost the rights of registration and remonstrance—the twin keys to their power—to a new single, central 'Plenary Court'.

These reforms brought fifteen months of growing crisis to their climax. There was an explosion of public fury at this ultimate act of despotism against the only obstacle to governmental power. The spearhead of the movement was an almost universal 'noble revolt'. Everywhere groups of nobles assembled spontaneously to concert plans of resistance. Many resigned from public positions. Officers refused to order their troops to fire on anti-government demonstrators. The assembly of the clergy refused to vote the government funds. In Dauphiné a group of notables took it upon themselves to convoke the long-defunct provincial estates, which demanded a liberal constitution for a quasi-independent 'Dauphin nation'. Most petty magistrates, lawyers, and other prominent non-nobles joined the resistance. In Rennes, Pau, and Grenoble there were violent popular demonstrations against the government. Far from expediting the reform plans, the *coup* of May 1788 brought business to a standstill.

Whether the furore might nevertheless have died away like that of 1771 cannot be known. Brienne thought it might. But to ride it out he needed an assured income, and at this moment the financial system suddenly collapsed. The financiers who normally advanced the government short-term credits refused to lend. Brienne had made no secret of his plans to dispense with their services when he could, so they had no interest in sustaining him. Besides, the future revenues against which their advances were normally made looked uncertain after 13 July, when a freak storm destroyed much of the harvest. And so the credit that fourteen years of desperate innovations had failed to shore up finally ran out. The suspension of payments by the treasury on 16 August was tantamount to a bankruptcy. A week before, Brienne had desperately sought to boost confidence by announcing the convocation of

[17] See J. Egret, *La Pré-Révolution française 1787–1788* (1962), 191.

the estates-general for 1 May 1789. A week later, his policies in ruins, he was dismissed. The recall of Necker, the financial miracle-worker, to replace him, showed that the government was as bankrupt of ideas as it was of funds. It was the end of the old regime.

Yet apart from the estates-general there was no obvious replacement. Even Brienne had admitted his own lack of ideas when, on 5 July 1788, he had invited public debate on the form and functions of the forthcoming assembly. Arthur Young's observations of October 1787[18] still held good ten months later:

One opinion pervaded the whole company, that they are on the eve of some great revolution in the government; that everything points to it;. . .with a *deficit* impossible to provide for without the Estates General of the kingdom, yet no ideas formed on what would be the consequence of their meeting. . .All agree, that the States of the kingdom cannot assemble without more liberty being the consequence; but I meet with so few men that have any just ideas of freedom, that I question much the species of this new liberty that is to arise.

[18]   *Travels in France*, 16 Oct. 1787.

14. Europe in Revolution

Few people foresaw the upheavals of the 1790s, and even fewer worked consciously to bring them about. The constitutional struggles which gave birth to these unforeseen events were the results of attempts by leading subjects to resist innovating governments. But the victory of the forces of resistance, whether in America in 1776, in Ireland in 1782, in Belgium and Hungary in 1790, or in France in 1788, itself brought innovations. Governments had been successfully defied, power had fallen from their hands. What now was to be done with this power, and who was to decide?

The defeat of the governments had been brought about by coalitions. Noblemen and churchmen had led the forces of resistance which covered a far broader social range. Without the enthusiastic support of many bourgeois outside the social élite, the leaders of what in France was called the 'third estate', the resistance to despotism would have been far less formidable. These forces, hitherto excluded from participation in public life, now demanded their reward—a permanent place in that life. Until now, claimed Abbé Sieyès in the most famous pamphlet of 1789, the third estate in the political order had been nothing. Now what it wanted was *to be Something.*[1]

The French bourgeoisie, emancipated and exhilarated by its own role in the collapse of monarchical authority, was not the first to claim a place in the sun. In the 1760s the politics of the city-state of Geneva had revolved around the efforts of the freemen of the city, who alone might call themselves citizens, to break the oligarchy of a narrow patriciate. These conflicts, and the issues involved, were trumpeted throughout Europe by the intervention of d'Alembert, Rousseau, and Voltaire. In 1768 the citizens secured the greater role to which they aspired, but in 1781 an attempt by non-citizen residents of the city (the vast majority of the population) to improve their own access to citizenship led to the intervention the next year of French troops, who restored the pre-1768 situation.[2] The Dutch 'patriot' movement of the early 1780s, also suppressed with the aid of foreign troops, was another bourgeois movement against oligarchy. Because these movements occurred in small, weak states they were defeated. France however, was neither small nor weak; no foreign power in 1789 felt strong enough, or involved enough, to intervene in order to restore the authority of a king who only three years before had appeared as Europe's arbiter. So events in France were allowed to take their chaotic course, and by the time the powers began to think seriously of intervention, in 1791, it was too late. By then, the old order in France had

[1] E. J. Sieyès, *What is the Third Estate?*, ed. S. E. Finer (1963), 51–2.
[2] The fullest account of the upheavals in Geneva and their significance is in Palmer, *Age of the Democratic Revolution*, i. 111–39, 358–61.

gone for ever, and few Frenchmen had a vested interest in its being restored. The invasion of politics by the bourgeoisie had created a nation of revolutionaries. It had also inspired all those who opposed the existing order elsewhere in Europe to imitate what had been done.

1789: the Transfer of Power

One of the most important manifestations of opposition to Maupeou's *coup d'état* in 1771 had been a series of protest strikes by advocates. Ever since that time it had been clear that bourgeois might play an important role in politics. Necker appealed to them as part of literate public opinion with his *Compte Rendu* of 1781. When Calonne encountered opposition from the Notables, he too launched a pamphlet appeal to the general public. By 1788 the *parlements* had succeeded in mobilizing this force against 'despotism', and when Brienne finally conceded the convocation of the estates-general for 1789, he did so in a deliberate attempt to outbid his opponents for bourgeois support. 'Since the Nobility and the Clergy are abandoning the King, who is their natural protector,' he remarked, 'he must throw himself into the arms of the Commons in order to crush both.'[3] This campaign was inaugurated by the royal declaration of 5 July 1788 which invited a public debate on the composition and powers of the estates general. The implication was that the ancient division of the estates into three equal orders (clergy, nobility, and the third estate) deliberating separately and voting by order, was not sacrosanct and might be changed in order to benefit the third estate.

Brienne's fall did not alter this policy. Necker abandoned all Brienne's reform proposals, recalled the *parlements*, and reconvened the Notables to deliberate on the composition of the forthcoming estates. The Paris *parlement* suspected that the constitutional battle was not yet won. Believing that the government still hoped to tamper with the composition of the estates for despotic purposes and that in these circumstances precedent was the only sure guide, the *parlement* announced on 25 September 1788 that the estates should be convened according to the forms of their last meeting, in 1614. This was the first time that any of the major protagonists in the previous seventeen months of quarrelling had taken a clear position about the future. It repolarized opinion: to many bourgeois, the forms of 1614 seemed designed to condemn them to perpetual political impotence, always outvoted by the other two orders; a number of liberal nobles also thought that the traditional arrangements would constitute a block to all progress. Through the agency of a still mysterious co-ordinating body, the 'committee of 30', they now used the occasion of the *parlement*'s pronouncement to launch a campaign in favour of changing the composition of the estates to the disadvantage of what now began to be called the 'privileged orders'. Pamphlets called for the doubling of the third estate's numbers, and for voting by head. When the second Assembly of Notables followed the *parlement*'s example

---

[3] Quoted in Egret, *La Pré-Révolution*, 306.

and pronounced for the forms of 1614, the clamour only increased, and Necker, fearing for his popularity, conceded in December that the third estate should have double representation. But he said nothing about vote by head, without which double representation was meaningless. So as 1789 began there had been a major realignment of forces in France. 'The controversy', observed the Swiss journalist Mallet du Pan in January,[4] 'has completely changed. King, despotism and constitution are now minor questions. The war is between the Third Estate and the other two orders.'

The first four months of 1789 were dominated by elections to the estates, a process which involved more Frenchmen in politics than at any time in the century, before or after. In each electoral district the three orders met in separate assemblies to choose their deputies, and, having chosen them, to draw up grievance lists (*cahiers*) upon which they expected action once the estates met. The elections took place against a background of intense economic hardship, the worst winter since 1709 following the poor harvest in 1788. Some economic difficulties, such as a glut in wine production, went back to the 1770s, when the economic expansion of Louis XV's reign had lost momentum, but the harvest failure made everything worse, pushing up the price of food and depressing demand for manufactures, on which so many households, rural as well as urban, depended to make ends meet. No wonder that many peasants that spring ceased to pay taxes, and found the dues to their lords an intolerable burden. No wonder too that there were riots in Brittany and Paris. In these circumstances the relative moderation of the *cahiers* is all the more surprising. Noble and clerical *cahiers* were still largely preoccupied with the struggle against despotism, many of them seeing provincial liberties and the revival of local estates as the best barriers to it. Third-estate grievances were more varied, but many peasant discontents were strained out of the final *cahiers* by the urban lawyers who drew them up. They suggested moderate reforms, to secure equality before taxes and the law, the correction of specific political abuses, decentralization of power, and showed a limitless faith in the ability of the estates to put everything right. There was little sign of any disenchantment with the monarchy, with the hierarchy of wealth and property, or with the established religion. Nobody foresaw, even now, the extent of the changes the next few years would bring. Nobody even seemed to want change on that scale.

Despite profound turbulence and schisms in electoral assemblies most of the scheduled 1200 deputies were in Versailles when the estates convened on 4 May 1789–300 each from the nobility and clergy, 600 from the third estate. The vast majority of the nobles were predictable conservatives, bound by their electors not to agree to any deliberation or voting in common with the other estates. The third estate contained not a single peasant or artisan, and only a handful of representatives of commercial interests. What it represented overwhelmingly was the 'professional' bourgeoisie of lawyers (over

---

[4] Quoted in G. Lefebvre, *The Coming of the French Revolution* (1947), 45.

half the deputies were legally trained) and public officials. These were the groups who had conducted the elections. They had made good use of this fact to promote their own demands in the *cahiers* and to take most of the representation for themselves. The most interesting delegation however was that of the clergy, where, in contrast with the quinquennial assemblies of the clergy under the old order, representation was not dominated by the bishops. Only forty-six secured election, whereas there were over 200 parish clergy, full of grievances against what they called 'episcopal despotism', and natural allies of the third estate into which they had been born. We should not exaggerate the unanimity of any of the orders. The nobles had an important minority of supporters of the third's pretensions and the third had its determined conservatives. But in June 1789 it was to be the divisions within the clergy that proved decisive.

The estates assembled in an atmosphere of boundless hope and optimism, but these sentiments soon turned sour. In opening speeches the king denounced the spirit of innovation and Necker confined himself to financial technicalities. No mention was made of the central question in political debate since the previous December, common voting by head. When a third-estate suggestion that these matters should be discussed after a common verification of credentials was spurned by the other two orders, the third refused to transact any business. Finally, after six weeks of stalemate in which much good feeling evaporated, the third voted to proceed with verification of powers after inviting the other two orders to join them. Once more the nobility refused, but the clergy split, and a number of parish priests broke ranks to join the third. Long imbued with the argument of Sieyès's *What is the Third Estate?* that only those who bore common burdens constituted a nation, and that privileged orders were outside it, the third now declared itself the National Assembly and provisionally authorized tax collection. This finally shook the king out of his torpor. On 23 June he held a 'royal session' in which he announced the sort of programme of reforms that had been expected six weeks before. But he coupled it with a repudiation of the previous week's events and an order that the three estates should remain separate; so the over-all effect was to antagonize a third estate which had already sworn, as a self-styled National Assembly, never to disperse until it had given France a constitution (20 June). The clergy who had broken ranks refused to obey the new order and common verification of powers continued. Certain nobles even drifted over. On 27 June the king capitulated and ordered the three estates to unite into one body.

Several ministers and courtiers were now thoroughly alarmed. No sooner had the order to unite been given than plans were set on foot to reverse the collapse of royal authority. Thirty thousand troops began to converge on Versailles, and on 12 July a *coup* appeared imminent when Necker was dismissed. Despite his dismal performance at the opening of the estates, Necker's popularity was undiminished. His one positive act since returning to power had been to reimpose controls on the grain trade, which reassured the populace during that grim winter. His dismissal now constituted a challenge. It came at a time of frustrated hopes after weeks of deadlock, mounting suspicion of governmental duplicity, and at the very moment when the price of bread in Paris reached its highest level of the year. Paris exploded at the news. Troops were known to be approaching and a frantic search for arms began at all the city's strong points. Customs barriers were sacked and monasteries violated. The regiment of French Guards, the capital's permanent garrison, joined the insurgents, to play a decisive role in the overthrow on 14 July of the most formidable strongpoint of all—the Bastille. No arms were found, and only a handful of insignificant prisoners, but the fall of the Bastille became a symbol of the overthrow of monarchical power—even though the king had really lost control of the situation eleven months before. And it did prevent the king from regaining the initiative. The capital had exploded in his face, his principal agents there were lynched, and the army had proved unreliable. Once again, Louis found himself with little choice but to surrender. Necker was recalled; on 17 July the king journeyed to Paris to confirm the new regime which had been established there. As the populace went out of control and began sacking customs posts on 12 July, the body of third-estate electors, who had chosen the Parisian delegates to the estates, reconvened and seized control of the resistance movement. To support their authority they set up a bourgeois militia, which they called the National Guard and placed under the command of the most famous revolutionary veteran in France, Lafayette.

All this Louis now confirmed. If there had been plans to dissolve or coerce the National Assembly they were quietly abandoned. The king's brother and other protagonists of firm action fled the country. The jubilant deputies renounced all binding mandates and declared themselves a constituent assembly whose main function would be to give France a permanent written constitution. They set about drafting a preamble setting out the fundamental rights they were seeking to establish. But the turbulence was far from over. Up and down the country, municipal authorities were deposed and superseded by groups of bourgeois notables imitating the Paris electors. Units of the National Guard were thrown together everywhere, and deployed to prevent further outbreaks of the very popular violence which had thwarted royal duplicity. But this force was only effective in the towns, whereas the most spectacular upheavals of the second half of July 1789 occurred in the countryside, where the atmosphere of expectation created by the *cahiers*, coupled with the breakdown of law and order and the presence (owing to the economic crisis) of larger than usual numbers of unemployed vagabonds, had created a mood of dangerous paranoia. The prolonged inactivity of the estates, along with wild talk of aristocratic plots, alarmed a peasantry already nervous about the safety of ripening crops after two lean years. Consequently, these weeks witnessed a 'great fear' sweeping many parts of rural France, with rumours of brigands in the pay of vengeful noblemen let loose to terrorize the rural populace into submission. The peasants reacted by attacking their presumed enemies, their landlords. Manor houses were burned, agents attacked, and the payment of seignorial dues, which had begun to flag along with taxes earlier in the spring, now ceased altogether. The members of the National

Assembly who now governed France (if anybody did) were faced by a dilemma. Whatever divided them, they were all men of property, scandalized at the attacks on the rights of landlords. Yet they were powerless to prevent them. The bourgeois majority had no real idea what to do; it took nobles to make the imaginative leap of launching a wholesale renunciation of feudal rights on the heady night of 4 August. In a session of theatrical enthusiasm, the whole complex of seignorial rights and dues, private tolls, even tithes, was abolished. The news calmed the peasantry, and once the harvest began relative peace returned to the countryside. When, on 11 August, the torrent of renunciations of 4th emerged as a formal decree, it was stipulated that the owners of the former dues were to receive compensation for their loss; but the peasantry never noticed this proviso, or, if they did, they ignored it.

The National Assembly had to meet yet another challenge in 1789 before its triumph was assured. Having finally promulgated its Declaration of the Rights of Man and the Citizen[5] on 26 August, it spent much of September discussing the powers of the king under the future constitution. This was done in the full knowledge that Louis had not yet given his assent to the August decrees. Instead of yielding now to pressure, Louis, encouraged by incipient splits between radical and conservative bourgeois deputies, began once more to move up troops. Having learnt from events in July, however, how to counteract such manoeuvres, radical deputies called upon their contacts in Paris to organize further popular demonstrations. Since the municipal revolution of July this was easier, for political assemblies now met daily in every district of the capital and a well-organized 'patriotic' press had emerged, sensitive to any danger to the Assembly. Economic conditions were propitious: grain remained scarce and bread dear, since the harvest had not yet been processed and rural unrest had led to hoarding of stocks. So when rumours reached Paris on 5 October of a banquet in which soldiers trampled the red white and blue cockade which since July had been the national symbol, an angry crowd of Parisian women set off for Versailles to demand retribution and an improvement in food supplies. They also called, following the lead given by the 'patriotic' press, for the king's removal to Paris, where he would be under the eye of the populace. Lafayette and the National Guard were unable to prevent a massacre of royal bodyguards. Nothing, it soon appeared, would appease the crowd but the king's abandonment of Versailles, to which Louis was forced to agree. Ten days after his arrival in the capital escorted by the crowds, the assembly transferred its sessions there too.

Louis now sanctioned the August decrees—he had little alternative. By invoking its popular allies, the National Assembly had finally defeated the crown's hopes of reasserting itself. The king was Paris's prisoner. The Assembly was determined not to be, and before it proceeded with its constitution making, it passed a 'martial law against tumults' designed to prevent any further popular disturbances. But the Assembly's power was moral rather

---

⁵   See below, p. 330–1.

than physical, and in the conflicts which lay ahead, no party was long able to resist the temptation to invoke the populace once again in order to secure its own ends—this time against the elected representatives themselves.

Revolutions Averted and Aborted, 1782–92

The events of 1789 in France created a surge of enthusiasm elsewhere in Europe which quite dwarfed that which had followed the American revolution. Here was a struggle for liberty and national regeneration taking place in the very heart of Europe, not half a world away. In Great Britain it came immediately after a year of celebrations marking the centenary of the 'glorious' revolution of 1688; and many Englishmen rather patronizingly applauded the efforts of the French to catch up with English liberty. They were not pleased when veterans of the reform movements of the 1760s and 1770s suggested, as did Richard Price in his famous *Discourse on the Love of our Country* of 1789, that the French had now overtaken the English. Price rhapsodized at the sight of

THIRTY MILLIONS of people, indignant and resolute, spurning at slavery, demanding liberty with an irresistible voice; their king led in triumph, and surrendering himself to his subjects. . .Behold kingdoms. . .starting from sleep, breaking their fetters, and claiming justice from their oppressors! Behold, the light. . .after setting AMERICA free, reflected to FRANCE, and there kindled into a blaze that lays despotism in ashes, and warms and illuminates EUROPE![6]

In Geneva and the Dutch republic, defeated patriots saw in France the triumph of their own principles, their hopes rekindled. Belgian rebels saw themselves, initially at least, as involved in an identical struggle. In the small states of Germany the ground had already been well prepared by a furious debate over the sale of Hessian and Brunswick soldiers to Great Britain for use against the Americans, during which the vices of despotism had been thoroughly exposed. Everybody recognized them as the same now denounced by the French. German literary men were almost unanimous in the rapturous welcome that they gave to the news from France and customers fought in bookshops for accounts of events in Paris. Even in Russia there were scenes of enthusiasm; Russian nobles who happened to be in Paris in 1789 were completely carried away. 'The cry of freedom rings in my ears,' wrote the young Count Stroganov, 'and the best day of my life will be that when I see Russia regenerated by such a revolution.'[7]

But revolutions are not caused by enthusiasm; indeed, the extravagant language of enthusiasts, in alerting governments to danger, is often counterproductive. It certainly was in and after 1789. Even before that, the challenge to the existing order had been decisively thrown back everywhere except in

[6] Quoted in A. Cobban, *The Debate on the French Revolution 1789–1800* (1960), 64.

[7] Quoted in P. Dukes, 'Russia and the Eighteenth Century Revolution' *History* (1971), 380.

France. Foreign troops had smashed the Genevan and Dutch reform movements. In Ireland the Volunteer movement, which had pressed so unanimously for legislative independence before 1782, split apart almost immediately after attaining it. As in France seven years later, 'patriots' divided into those who wished to concentrate on limiting governmental power, and those who wished to admit hitherto unprivileged groups to participation in public life. The former party, led by Flood, saw that legislative independence meant nothing if the lord-lieutenant could still control a servile parliamentary majority in English interests. They therefore sought parliamentary reform to diminish the power of patronage. But generations of suspicion led them to oppose the proposals of Grattan for Catholic emancipation. For Flood, and perhaps the majority of Irish Protestants, access to parliament for Catholics undermined the very principle on which the Ascendancy was based. For ten years Pitt's government played so skilfully on such divisions that English control of Irish affairs in essentials was scarcely less than before 1782. The divided Volunteers became little more than veterans' associations, and a servile parliamentary majority was once more built up. When in the early 1790s the Catholics began to agitate for emancipation on their own behalf, a government alarmed by events in France used its parliamentary control to make them a series of concessions. By 1793 the Catholic position had so much improved that only the crucial right to parliamentary representation was left to concede. But this alarmed many members of the Ascendancy even more. The revolutionary example of France threw an explosive element into an Irish situation which was already full of dangerous tension.

A similar split proved the undoing of the Belgian revolutionaries in 1790. The differences between the followers of Van der Noot and Vonck were already clear before the collapse of Austrian power. Van der Noot stood for the restoration of the old order disturbed by Joseph II. Vonck on the other hand, deeply influenced first by the aspirations of the neighbouring Dutch patriots, and then by the principles of 1789 emanating from France, wished to profit from the end of the old order to admit hitherto powerless elements to a share in government and do away with the oligarchical character of the old institutions. Both sought the end of Austrian power, but once this was achieved, the split appeared. Van der Noot, in charge of the revolutionary government, began to persecute and imprison 'Vonckists' who declared that the new regime was more aristocratic than the old and dedicated to perpetuating the sort of institutions already swept away in France. With the suppression of Vonckist mutiny among the troops in April 1790, Van der Noot's followers, who called themselves 'statists', spread the rumour that the Vonckists were working for the restoration of Austrian power. Nor was this altogether untrue, for by now Joseph II had been succeeded by his brother Leopold, who though he shared many of Joseph's aims, deplored his autocratic methods. Thinking that Leopold might prove a sympathetic ruler, Vonck and his followers sent out feelers from their exile in France. It was clear however, that they commanded no popular support in Belgium. Rumours of a plot to assassinate Van der Noot and the statist leadership, in the wake of Austrian triumphs over the new state's army, brought thousands of armed peasants flocking into Brussels in May and June 1790, led by their priests. They had come to defend their traditional habits and religion against the twin assaults of autocrats and democrats. As the Austrians advanced in September, many of these peasant enthusiasts were conscripted, but they proved ineffective against the emperor's professionals. In December 1790 Brussels was reoccupied by Leopold's armies, and leading statists fleeing to Holland. Vonckists mean-while were allowed to return home, but not to the triumph they had hoped for. Leopold was too prudent to follow up his victory with new provocations. Although he permitted open political discussion, he refused to go beyond restoring the situation that had existed under Maria Theresa. Only now did the disappointed Vonckists begin to look towards the French example as Belgium's best hope of a more democratic regime.

The Austrian recovery was favoured by new diplomatic circumstances. Leopold abandoned his brother's adventurous foreign policy, unilaterally concluded an armistice with the Turks (September 1790), and made an accord with Prussia (Convention of Reichenbach, July 1790). Not only did these moves release troops to restore internal order; they ended Prussian support for rebellious elements in both the Netherlands and Hungary. With Prussia standing aside, France incapacitated, and the British and Dutch positively welcoming the return of order to the southern Netherlands, Leopold had a free hand. It was more difficult in Hungary, where Joseph's death had fanned, not stilled, agitation. A passion for Hungarian dress and Magyar speech swept the nobility. The talk of national rights and liberties now emanating from France echoed and encouraged traditional Hungarian rhetoric. The records of Joseph's hated cadastral survey were destroyed, and imperial officials threatened or expelled. There were even mutinous signs among the emperor's Hungarian regiments. When elections for a new diet were held, candidates of the petty nobility, resentful of the great magnates who were the main props of Habsburg authority, swept the board. They arrived in Buda calling for the virtual separation of Hungary from the rest of the Habsburg domains. Among their more extreme demands were for the king to submit himself once more to election, for the restoration of the right to rebel (as in Poland), for annual diets, and for a separate Hungarian army and foreign policy. But Leopold played skilfully on their numerous divisions—between magnates and lesser nobility, Catholics and Protestants, Magyars and peri-pheral groups such as Serbs, Croats, and Rumanians—as well as their fear of the peasantry, who had welcomed many of Joseph's reforms and were in a restive and unpredictable state throughout 1790. Leopold ostentatiously poured thousands of imperial troops into the country as the diet sat. The result was the same thing as in the Netherlands—the restoration of the 1780 situation.

Leopold II was not a reactionary. He believed in many of his brother's policies and did not abandon them all. Religious toleration and the personal freedom of serfs remained in force throughout his dominions. He seems to have planned to reintroduce later, more contentious aspects of Joseph's programme, such as his tax reforms. But Leopold was a constitutionalist. He believed that the emperor must work through the established representative bodies and promote reform by consent. So not only the Hungarian diet and the various Netherlands estates, but also the estates of the various Austrian and Bohemian provinces, were restored to active life. Through them he hoped to lead the nobility towards acquiescence in necessary reforms. But his constitutionalism had two sides. Kings as well as constituted bodies must be respected. He had begun by admiring the attempts of the French to give themselves a constitution; but when, in the summer of 1791, the monarchy itself came under open attack, he joined the king of Prussia in issuing the declaration of Pillnitz (27 August) to warn the French that the fate of Louis XVI was not a matter of indifference to Europe. It was a cautious threat, for Leopold had no real wish to become involved in the turbulent affairs of France. The effect in France, however, was to propel the country ever faster along the road to involving herself once more in the affairs of the rest of Europe.

France: the Revolutionary Consensus and its Collapse

By the end of October 1789 most Frenchmen hoped or believed that the Revolution was over. Two royal *coups* had been averted and power transferred to the Nation's representatives, who, having loudly proclaimed the principles by which they were guided, were now embarking upon the task of devising a constitution. The conflict between the orders, which had dominated most political discussion between September 1788 and June 1789, seemed a thing of the past, as did all the trappings of what was now contemptuously termed 'feudalism', abandoned on 4 August. Certain elements in the clergy and nobility however, remained unreconciled to their losses. Ever since the departure of the king's brother and a handful of courtiers in the aftermath of the Bastille's fall, a trickle of outraged nobles had followed them into emigration. But most striking about the year between October 1789 and October 1790 was the broad agreement of all parties, best symbolized at the Feast of the Federation on 14 July 1790, the first anniversary of the fall of the Bastille, when Louis XVI, king of the French, restorer of liberty, swore to observe the constitution on the 'altar of the fatherland' in the presence of almost 400,000 citizens, his former subjects. What was the consensus which this event was supposed to symbolize?

First it was an agreement about the principles contained in the Declaration of the Rights of Man and the Citizen. Despotism, aristocracy, privilege, feudalism,—all were gone. Sovereignty now resided in the Nation alone, a body of free and equal citizens bound only by the law, the expression of their general will as interpreted by their elected representatives. The end of political life was to conserve the natural and imprescriptible rights of man—liberty, property, security, and resistance to oppression. Thought was free, expression was free, and the law was the same for everybody, especially in matters of taxation and access to public office. Those who held public office were accountable to the Nation, rigorously bound by a constitution designed to prevent abuse of power.

The Assembly's main purpose was to draft a constitution, whereby France would be regenerated and given new life according to better principles. The constitution was not completed until 1791, but already early in October 1789 the Assembly had sketched its main outlines. The country was to be governed by an executive branch consisting of the king, and a legislative branch of a single chamber. Their powers were to be quite separate, and no minister might sit in the legislature. The king might veto new laws, but not if they were passed again by two subsequent legislatures. The judiciary, also separate according to orthodox Montesquieuan principles, would have its independence assured by the election of judges.

Justly famous as the first liberal constitution in European history, the constitution of 1791 never came fully into operation. The administrative reorganization of France by the assembly proved more permanent. Everybody accepted that no corner of French life should be left untouched, and that all manner of abuses and pointless habits would be destroyed. There was a sense that this was a unique opportunity to clear away the debris of centuries and build the foundations for a better future, an opportunity that might never recur. 'Let us make haste', declared the noble deputy Duport,[8] 'while we are still in our political youth, while the fire of liberty still burns within us and our holy and generous enthusiasm still endures.' The deputies agreed that the system to be introduced should be rational, representative, and uniform. Administration must be decentralized, and controlled by elected representatives. The old provinces and generalities, along with their governors and intendants, were abandoned. They were replaced by eighty-three departments, each governed by an elected general council, and each made up in its turn of a number of districts and communes, whose officers were also elected. The judicial system was reorganized similarly. The *parlements* and their subordinate courts disappeared, and so did the venal offices occupied by their judges. Trial by jury was introduced, and a start was made on the long-postponed task of reforming the labyrinth of old laws and customs and replacing it by a uniform code applicable everywhere in France. Only in two fields could the deputies be accused of being less than true to their own avowed principles. One was the question of slavery, which they were forced to admit as economically necessary to the colonies, however free and equal men might theoretically be. The other was the franchise, which, the deputies rapidly decided, could not possibly be extended to all citizens, especially those without property. So only 'active' citizens, who paid the equivalent of at least three days' labour in taxes, might vote. Even higher qualifications were demanded of those hoping to be elected. Most deputies who, only a few days before these provisions were passed in October 1789, had approved the martial law against tumults, saw such restrictions as essential in order to restrain popular excesses. But the effect was to disenfranchise many citizens who had had a say in the elections for the estates-general, the very populace who had twice that year already saved the Revolution from royal counter-attack. The

8 Quoted in N. Hampson, *A Social History of the French Revolution* (1963), 118.

franchise restrictions were denounced in the press and in the many popular revolutionary societies which had sprung up in Paris and other major towns. They did much to direct popular suspicions at the Assembly as well as at the king, and so to undermine the revolutionary consensus.

The franchise was not, however, one of the three great issues that really destroyed the consensus. The first of these was the religious question, which went right back to the night of 4 August when tithes were abolished, and with them, the source of the lower clergy's income. Some new provision had to be made for paying the clergy—the obvious one would have been to utilize the revenues of that tenth of France that was owned by great ecclesiastical dignitaries or corporations. But in November 1789 the Assembly made this impossible when it nationalized the church lands, in order to sell them off as a way of dealing with the national debt. The Assembly thus assumed the burden of financing the church, and it seemed natural that, at the same time, it should reorganize and regenerate it along the same lines as the state. Few objected when in February 1790 monasteries and convents were suppressed as useless, but problems arose when the ecclesiastical committee of the Assembly produced a comprehensive plan for the church, the Civil Constitution of the Clergy. This document attempted to redress many of the lower clergy's grievances: they were now assured of decent salaries and the power of bishops was drastically restricted. The ecclesiastical map was redrawn on more rational principles and a number of superfluous bishoprics were abolished. The Jansenistic sentiments of some members of the committee were apparent in all this, but thus far many clergy had no objections. Much more controversial was the principle that all clergy were now to be elected by active citizens among the laity, a radical break with Catholic tradition. Even more alarming, no provision was made for consulting the pope over the proposals. In the eyes of the Assembly the pope was a foreign prince, entitled to respect as the international figurehead of Christianity, but not to any say in how a sovereign nation chose to organize its religious life.

Even these aspects of the civil constitution might have caused fewer problems if the church had been consulted before it became law. But the Assembly refused to countenance a national council of the church, for in its dogma the clergy as a separate order had disappeared in June 1789 and could not be revived. In these circumstances many deeply disturbed clerics, who wished only to do what the church ordained, were left at a loss. They looked instinctively for guidance to the one authority whose rights the Assembly denied—the pope. As long as he refused to give a public opinion (and his silence lasted until the spring of 1791) many clergy did not feel justified in accepting the new ecclesiastical order. The Assembly was not anti-religious, much less anti-Catholic. Most of its members were conventionally devout men who had merely sought to extend to the religious life of the nation the principles which were being introduced in other areas. But their authority had never been so openly defied since they came to power. They were affronted by the clergy's apparent indifference to the general will of the Nation and decided, in a fateful moment, to root out those who defied them. In November

1790 an oath to the constitution was imposed on all beneficed clergy. Those who refused it were to be deprived.

The result left the Assembly astonished and scandalized. Only seven out of 160 bishops took the oath, and just over half of the rest of the clergy. When the pope finally spoke out against the civil constitution, many who had taken the oath withdrew it. The clergy had been forced to declare themselves for or against, not only the civil constitution, but the whole of the Revolution itself. The oath created two churches, a 'constitutional' one obedient to the Revolution, but rejected by Rome, and a non-juring one approved by the pope, but which from now on patriots increasingly regarded as suspect. The first sings of a turning against the Revolution by the Catholic church had already appeared early in 1790 in Montauban and Nîmes, where a largely Protestant bourgeoisie had antagonized local Catholic majorities by seizing power in July 1789. The oath of the clergy now generalized the antagonism. Non-juring priests constituted a network of potential counter-revolutionaries and objects of suspicion to patriots throughout France. Hitherto counter-revolution had been the preserve of a few impractical royalist plotters and of *émigrés*. Now whole populations were exposed every Sunday to the views of clerics who had spurned the National Assembly's authority. God was recruited onto the side of counter-revolution. He divided Frenchmen as they had not been divided since the spring of 1789.

No sooner was this apparent than a further complication arose—the question of the king. Louis XVI and his family did not like what had happened since 1789, but they were apparently resigned to it. Confined to Paris, they dreamed of restoring the old order, and even secretly paid for dubious advice on counter-revolution. But not until the religious schism were they moved to any positive action. Ironically, by this time some of the deputies who had been most radical in 1789 were beginning to feel a need to rally round the king in order to give the new order stability. They hoped to win his support by introducing conservative amendments to the constitution before its final promulgation. These manoeuvres took place against a background of more popular unrest than had been seen since 1789 in Paris; unemployment was widespread, largely owing to the disappearance of lavish noble consumption in these anti-aristocratic times. Popular discontents showed themselves in demonstrations against suspected counter-revolutionary elements, such as non-juring priests; and when it was learned that the king preferred the latter, hostility turned to him. After being prevented by crowds from spending Easter 1791 in the country, he continued for two months to negotiate with the conservative deputies, while secretly planning an escape. On 20 June the royal family set out at night for the Austrian Netherlands. They nearly reached safety, but were stopped at Varennes and brought back to Paris.

The flight to Varennes and its aftermath brought the Revolution to a new crisis. Royalists and counter-revolutionaries were outraged, and so were foreign monarchs. The declaration of Pillnitz was a direct result of it. Conservative revolutionaries in France—now the vast majority of the National

Assembly—were horrified that the main symbol of stability at the hub of the constitution should try to abandon the Revolution. They soon rallied behind the story that Louis had been kidnapped or abducted, and although he was temporarily suspended, it was clearly intended to restore his full authority as soon as possible. For the Parisian populace and the radical journalists of the capital, however, Louis's flight merely confirmed what they had long suspected—that the king was a counter-revolutionary in league with non-juring priests, *émigrés*, and reactionary foreign monarchs. There was an out-burst of popular republicanism. The political clubs of the capital, which ever since 1789 had set the tone of debate on public issues, led demands for the king's deposition and the declaration of a republic. A mass demonstration to sign a republican petition was dispersed on 17 July by Lafayette and the National Guard at a cost of fifty lives—the Revolution's first republican martyrs. 'They shot down workers like chickens' observed one bitter par-ticipant.[9] In the aftermath of the 'massacre of the Champ de Mars' the support of most deputies for it was shown when hundreds of them seceded from the Jacobin club, which had given hesitant support to the petition, to form a rival association of distinctly conservative views, the Feuillant club. For the two months which remained to the Assembly, the Feuillants worked frantically to make last-minute changes to the constitution which would restrain its democratic elements and make it more acceptable to Louis. Their only major success, in the event, was to exclude the Civil Constitution of the Clergy, thus making it susceptible of easy amendment by subsequent legislatures. And owing to their failure to secure repeal of a self-denying ordinance (passed in May before the flight to Varennes) which excluded constituent Assembly members from subsequent legislatures, they enjoyed little influence over the Legislative Assembly which met, after the formal promulgation of the constitution, on 1 October 1791.

It was clear to the new deputies, most of whom had had two years of sobering political experience at local level, that Frenchmen were now bitterly divided. Over religion, the monarchy, and the political rights of the populace, the constituent Assembly had failed to establish a consensus; yet without one, the constitution could hardly be expected to work smoothly. This was clearly shown by the fate of the first steps taken to improve security. Counter-revolution apparently derived its driving force from two elements, the non-juring clergy and the *émigrés* assembling in arms across the frontier. Since Varennes the numbers of *émigrés* had swelled enormously. The Assembly therefore passed two laws: one which declared non-juring priests to be 'suspects', liable to summary treatment in disturbed areas, the other declaring that all *émigrés* who did not return to France by 1792 would forfeit their property and be treated as traitors. The king's veto of both laws—his undoubted right—branded him as the protector of traitors and suspects. In these cir-cumstances the leaders of radical opinion in the new assembly, called Brissotins after their most prominent member, or Girondins from the geographical

    [9] Quoted in G. Rudé, *The Crowd in the French Revolution* (1959), 89.

origin of some of their most eloquent spokesmen, began to look for a policy that would force every citizen to take sides openly for or against the Revolution. They found it in war.

The idealists of the Constituent Assembly had leaned heavily towards pacifism, refusing to honour treaties made by the monarchy and periodically denouncing war as an instrument of policy. Intensely suspicious of the army as a potential instrument of royal counter-revolution, they had encouraged political activity in the ranks and the breakdown of traditional military discipline. A massive defection of noble officers after Varennes had completed the process. So France was quite unprepared for war. But war would require a massive national effort which only enemies of the Nation would shirk. It would galvanize true patriots and turn counter-revolution into treason. Ironically, counter-revolutionaries also supported a warlike policy. Either they thought, like the royal family, that foreign troops would simply walk in and rescue them and restore the old order; or they thought, with Lafayette and certain other conservative generals, that it would revitalize the army and pave the way for a military dictatorship. Only advocates of compromise, such as the Feuillant leaders, or frightened radicals, such as Robespierre, opposed the warlike drift, and they were ignored. The policy had several false starts: Leopold II deftly sidestepped a number of attempts to trap him into hostile acts. But after Leopold's death in March 1792, his son Francis II was attracted by the drama of making a stand against revolutionary upstarts. An agreement to co-operate with Prussia in the event of hostilities with France was concluded: and on 20 April 1792 France declared war. This was perhaps the most decisive turning-point in the whole French Revolution. It finally destroyed the consensus of 1789; within months, the monarchy would fall, and within a year France would be collapsing into civil war. The war, in a famous phrase, revolutionized the Revolution.

Europe at War, 1792–7

If Prussia and Austria had combined to act decisively the moment war was declared, Louis XVI's wildest dreams and Robespierre's blackest fears might have been realized. But their contempt for the demoralized French army was confirmed by the lamentable behaviour of French troops in the first skirmishes. Besides, they were far more worried about the situation in eastern Europe.

The problem lay in Poland, where the partition of 1772 had inaugurated a period of national reappraisal and self-questioning. Polish territory had been carved up without consultation of the Poles themselves, who could only look on helplessly. Nor was there anything to prevent the repetition of such an event, unless Poland could acquire an inner strength she had not possessed for centuries. This, however, King Stanislas Poniatowski and a group of noble reformers were determined to create. They began by reforming the system of education in the vacuum left by the dissolution of the Jesuits; and by the mid-1780s they were sponsoring widespread discussion of constitutional reform. The culmination of this movement was the Four Years' Diet (1788–92), which met at a moment when Russia, guarantor of the ancient constitution since 1773, was embroiled with the Turks. When the diet called for the withdrawal of troops stationed in Poland since the partition, the hard-pressed Russians agreed, and Poland began to build up her own army. In 1791 the diet agreed to a new constitution, under which the monarchy became hereditary. The *liberum veto*, by which a single deputy could block any legislation, was abolished. The power of the great magnates was diminished by the exclusion of landless nobles, who were usually their retainers, from political assemblies; and for the first time towns were given a limited legislative voice. All these changes were for the moment uncontested by the Prussians, if only because they diminished Russian power in Poland. The Russians were naturally alarmed, as were a number of Polish magnates, and the two naturally turned to each other for help after the Russians concluded peace with the Turks in February 1792. They now moved 60,000 troops up to the Polish frontier and Catherine, who did not differentiate between the events in Paris and those in Warsaw, declared 'I shall fight Jacobinism, and beat it in Poland.'[10] Pro-Russian magnates were now easily induced to form a confederation. They appealed to the Russians for support in defending the ancient constitution and Polish 'liberties', and Catherine's forces invaded. By the end of July King Stanislas's forces had capitulated and the constitution of the previous year was rescinded. Many of the leading reformers fled abroad, and the country was subjected to renewed Russian occupation. With the two other partitioning powers of 1772 preoccupied with France in the west, Catherine might have been content with this, but she felt it wiser to divide them. She offered the less involved, Prussia, a new partition, which was eventually agreed on in January 1793. Under it, Poland lost half its population and almost half of its territory. Russia took the Polish Ukraine and 3,000,000 inhabitants, Prussia increased her population by 1,000,000, absorbed a huge salient of Polish territory which pointed like an arrow at Berlin, and took the long-coveted ports of Danzig and Thorn. Austria merely looked on helplessly, her forces tied down in the Netherlands and along the Rhine.

For the war in the west had not provoked the military promenade they had expected. In July 1792, in the wake of some easy initial victories, the allied commander Brunswick had issued a confident manifesto in which he threatened to sack Paris if Louis XVI were harmed. It only served to accelerate the overthrow of the monarchy. On 19 August allied forces invaded France, but a month later they were stopped in a skirmish at Valmy (20 September)—the first victory of the armies of the French Revolution. The Prussians thereupon withdrew to concentrate on Poland, leaving the Austrians to face France alone. Their forces proved no match for the revolutionaries, and the frightened small states along the French frontier which had joined the alliance fared no better. Between September and November French troops invaded and occupied Savoy and the electorate of Mainz. Within four weeks of defeating an Austrian army at Jemappes, on 6 November 1792, they had also overrun the southern

---

[10] Quoted in Palmer, *Age of the Democratic Revolution*, i. 434.

Netherlands. The revolutionary expansion of France had begun; on 19 November the Convention declared that it would 'accord fraternity and help to all peoples who wish to recover their liberty.' A month later it proclaimed that in every territory occupied by French armies existing taxes would be abolished, along with tithes, seignorial dues, serfdom, nobility, and all privileges. Elections would be organized, and the French would withdraw as soon as the inhabitants had set up a 'free and popular' form of government. The revolutionaries had often proclaimed that their principles were of universal application. Now they were prepared to impose them everywhere by force of arms. The execution of Louis XVI in January 1793 was a gage thrown down to the monarchies of Europe, with whom the new republicans spurned all compromise. Beyond compromise too was another new doctrine, first implemented in November 1792 when the Convention voted to annex Savoy. This was that France was entitled to 'natural' frontiers—the Rhine, the Alps, and the Pyrenees. Under this doctrine any Belgian rebels against Austria would certainly get fraternity and assistance, but only in order to become French citizens, whether they liked it or not.

These gradiloquent programmes depended on military success, but the spring of 1793 saw the tide ebb once more. The occupation of the Netherlands alarmed the British, who hitherto had been quite happy not to involve themselves on the continent. They began to mobilize their forces, and relations with France rapidly deteriorated. The Convention declared war on 1 February 1793, and Pitt began to pour money into organizing a coalition. By the end of the summer it included Spain and the Dutch republic as well as the German powers, and had the goodwill of Russia. Resistance to the French stiffened and their most successful general of the previous autumn, Dumouriez, defected to the Austrians. Along the whole eastern frontier French forces were rolled back. The Austrians recovered Belgium, the Spaniards invaded Roussillon. In March 1793 attempts to impose conscription sparked off a major internal rebellion against the Revolution in the Vendée. This turbulent region was to sap the strength of the republic for years. Then early in the summer came the 'Federalist revolt', when many of the major provincial cities of France renounced the authority of Paris. It took six months of bitter and bloody civil war and terror to repress the movement, in the course of which the Convention was moved to sanction methods whose savagery shocked Europe. Ultimately they were successful: by the spring of 1794 France had the strongest government since the old regime and had begun to score new victories. But in the summer of 1793 she was only saved from total disaster by the slowness and disunity of the coalition's efforts against her.

Neither of the major German powers had any real interest in invading France. Austria merely wished to regain the Netherlands and Prussia wished to expel French troops from German soil. Otherwise, both were far more concerned with events in Poland than in France, for the Poles had not proved as compliant under the second partition as under the first. Even those who had called in the Russians in 1792 had expected a restoration of the situation before the Four Years' Diet, not a new partition. Throughout the subsequent winter, anti-foreign feeling built up in Poland to such an extent that inner divisions, so fatal previously, were forgotten. A rising was planned, with a Polish veteran of the American war, Kosciuszko, as its leader and figurehead. It broke out prematurely, in March 1794, when the Russians arrested several of the conspirators, but at first Kosciuszko's military skill achieved some successes. Riotous crowds drove the Russian garrisons from Warsaw and Cracow, and Kosciuszko managed to recruit peasant support with a guarded promise of serf emancipation. France refused to support the movement, despite appeals, on the grounds that its true aims were aristocratic; but to Russia and Prussia the rising was plainly Jacobinical, and Austria rejected Kosciuszko's overtures because she was more interested in a share of any further partition than in a war to sustain Polish independence. Another partition was the only solution. All the powers could see the advantage of a buffer state like Poland to keep them apart, but if Polish turbulence was to endanger the peace of the region every few years, that advantage was perhaps more trouble than it was worth. By the end of 1794 the rebellion was over, put down with great ruthlessness by the most battle-seasoned general in Europe, Suvurov. Over ten thousand were massacred to induce Warsaw to surrender. In the aftermath, Poland was simply partitioned out of existence. This time the Austrians had their share; Catherine had found the Turks more formidable than she had expected after Austria had abandoned her in 1790, and she now believed that Austrian support was essential for future Balkan enterprises. She was prepared to buy it with a slice of Poland. The Prussians were reluctant to admit Austria to a deal from which she had been excluded in 1793, but to oppose it would have risked war with Russia, whose troops, by occupying Poland, held the whip hand. So in October 1795 the third partition of Poland was tripartite. Poland disappeared from the map and although in later years the partitioning powers were to find that the Polish people were not so easily absorbed, and that common frontiers exacerbated mutual tensions, in 1795 they congratulated themselves on solving a problem which had distracted them too long from the danger in the west.

For in the autumn of 1793 the French had begun to recover. As the Committee of Public Safety regained control at home, its armies began to do more than simply hold the frontier. Foreign invaders were confined to the enclaves they had established in Flanders, in Roussillon, and in Toulon, which the British had occupied from the sea. In the spring of 1794 the French were able to take the offensive; in June the Austrians were defeated at Fleurus and Belgium was once more overrun. French troops poured into the Rhineland, and crossed the Alps and the Pyrenees. In January 1795, perhaps the harshest winter since 1709, they were able to drag their artillery across the frozen mouths of the Rhine and invade the hitherto untouched Dutch republic. There was no resistance. William V fled, and the 'patriots', defeated in 1787, re-emerged to welcome the French as liberators. What made the French triumph certain was the withdrawal from the coalition of Prussia. Worried about the uncertain situation in Poland, and deprived of subsidies by a suspicious Great Britain, Prussia had opened talks with the French in November

1794. In April and May 1795 peace was concluded, on a basis of French recognition of a Prussian hegemony over north Germany, while Prussia undertook to leave France a free hand on the Rhine's left bank and to abandon her protectorate over the Dutch.

After this the coalition rapidly fell apart. The resurgent Dutch patriots, having set up a 'Batavian republic', agreed in a peace of May 1795 to cede various southern districts to France, to pay an indemnity of 100 million florins, and to maintain an army of occupation. In July the Spaniards also made peace by ceding their half of Hispaniola in the West Indies to France. Even the British sent out peace feelers, and a general peace in 1795 seemed a real possibility. All hope of that, however, was destroyed when in October the Convention formally annexed Belgium. This was perfectly consistent with the doctrine of 'natural frontiers' proclaimed in 1792, but it made any agreement with either Austria or Great Britain impossible. The Netherlands were Austrian territory, and it was the lynchpin of British continental policy to keep France out of the low countries.

So the struggle continued into 1796. Against Great Britain, France was powerless, apart from harassing her trade by unleashing privateers. Against Austria, however, she could now throw all her military strength. For the summer of 1796 a great pincer movement was planned against the Austrian heartland, moving through Bavaria in the north, and Lombardy in the south. In Germany progress was slow, but in Italy an unknown young general, appointed at the last minute, conducted a brilliant campaign which by the spring of 1797 had driven the Austrian armies back up the Alpine passes. One by one General Bonaparte also knocked out the small states of the peninsula. The Italian theatre had originally been viewed as secondary, but Bonaparte's startling successes made it the centre of operations. The plunder of Italy kept his army well paid and bolstered the Republic's finances. The Directors who were now the government of France were increasingly forced to confirm anything that Bonaparte chose to do. Their war aims were to reach the 'natural frontiers' and to use gains in Italy as bargaining counters to secure them in peace negotiations. Bonaparte however dissolved the states of northern Italy and set up 'sister republics' under French protection. In April 1797, within 100 miles of Vienna, he even took it upon himself to end hostilities by concluding the Preliminaries of Leoben. The Emperor acknowledged the loss of Belgium in return for French recognition of gains along the Dalmatian coast and in Venetia, but nothing was said about restoring the old order in northern Italy, or about the left bank of the Rhine. These terms were broadly repeated in the definitive treaty of Campo Formio, which ended the war the following October. The Rhine question was left for resolution, as if this was still the old regime, to a later congress to be held at Rastadt.

After five years of enormous upheavals, peace had been restored to the continent. Only Great Britain was left in the field against France, and even she, wracked by financial instability, popular unrest, naval mutinies, and incipient civil war in Ireland, had opened peace negotiations in 1797. The price demanded by the French—restoration of all British colonial gains—was too high. But the republicans were confident that, isolated in Europe, Britain could soon be brought to her knees.

Republicanism and Terror

The first casualty of the war launched so recklessly by the Legislative Assembly in 1792 was the monarchy. To this extent the war did all that the Brissotins expected of it—it simplified issues and clarified problems; it also hastened their resolution.

The catastrophic early defeats in the summer created an atmosphere of crisis in Paris. Robespierre's warnings now seemed justified, the enemy was at the gates, and the counter-revolution seemed about to triumph. So when Louis XVI vetoed yet another decree against non-juring priests and a new one convoking 20,000 *fédérés* (provincial national guards) to Paris in order to permit the garrison of the capital to leave for the front, there was an outburst of popular fury. Ever since Varennes popular republicanism had been a growing force in Parisian politics. Popular anxieties were exacerbated in the spring of 1792 by a decline in the value of the *assignat*, the revolutionary paper-money launched in 1789, and by shortages of colonial products such as sugar. There were outbursts of popular price-fixing, and retailers were threatened. It was natural that anti-royalists should try to tap this effervescence for political purposes, and on 20 June, in response to a royal attempt to dismiss Girondin ministers and replace them with Feuillants, a crowd of 8,000 invaded the Tuileries palace and subjected the royal family to threats and insults. 'Tremble, tyrants,' they shouted, 'the *sansculottes* are here!'[11]

Polite circles throughout Europe were appalled to see the French king at bay before a bloodthirsty mob. But although the *sansculottes* were not in general rich, neither were they poor or unemployed. Although the term was more political, moral, and stylistic than social or economic, most *sansculottes* were artisans or wage-earners[12] who believed that the Revolution should bring them a say in power and guarantee them a livelihood. They knew that the king was a symbol of order and a rallying point for men of property—especially since the Champ de Mars massacre the year before. They resented their own exclusion from the political life of active citizens. As they saw it, only they had the strength and the unswerving faith in the Revolution's ideals now required to save it from its enemies at home and abroad. The populace of Paris had already played a crucial role in the Revolution—notably in 1789. But at that time their action had been spontaneous and disorganized. 1792 saw the beginning of something different—an organized and self-consciously political popular movement, constantly active and vigilant against any attempts to undermine the work and achievements of the Revolution.

The demonstration of 20 July was merely a foretaste of what was to come. On the one hand, it encouraged Louis to equivocate further until

---

[11] Rudé, *The Crowd in the French Revolution*, 100.

[12] They therefore did not wear the expensive knee-breeches—*culottes*—of the rich and the leisured. Hence the name.

foreign help arrived; on the other, it showed what organized popular forces could do. Throughout July, as the news from the frontiers worsened, both sides prepared for a final showdown; while the Girondins, like the Feuillants before them, desperately sought an impossible compromise. On 11 July the Assembly declared that the Fatherland was in danger and conscripted all those owning pikes into national service. This gave the populace a legitimate excuse for arming themselves. By this time too, the assemblies of the forty-eight 'sections' into which the capital was divided were in permanent session, admitting passive as well as active citizens. The *fédérés* were arriving from the provinces and were rapidly recruited to the anti-royal forces. Brunswick's threats, which became known on 29 July, were the last straw. Convinced now that only the removal of the king could destroy internal treason, the leaders of the sections began to plan an insurrection, which finally took place on 10 August. On that day, the Commune of Paris declared itself 'insurrectional'; *sansculottes* and *fédérés*, numbering perhaps 20,000, stormed the Tuileries palace from which the king had already fled. Nearly 400 of the besiegers fell in the assault, and 600 Swiss guards who had defended the palace. The most important casualties were however the Legislative Assembly and the throne itself. Power in France had in effect been seized by the insurrectional Commune. The terms it now dictated were the abolition of the monarchy and the election of a national Convention to draft a new, more democratic, republican constitution.

The Convention met on 20 September and the next day it formally abolished the monarchy. Before then other ominous precedents had been set. The removal of royal obstructionism opened the way for new penal laws against non-jurors and *émigrés* and for widespread arrests of suspects. The prisons of Paris were full to overflowing throughout August, and this became a source of anxiety to *sansculottes* now enlisting to fight the invading powers. Rumours were rife of a 'prison plot', a mass breakout by counter-revolutionaries bent on murdering defenceless wives and children of patriots while their menfolk were away at the front. In this hysterical atmosphere, on 2 September mobs began to attack the prisons and massacre their inmates. When the frenzy died down a week later, half the prison population of Paris, many of them very improbable counter-revolutionaries, had been slaughtered—between 1,100 and 1,400 people. There was only one word for such methods of dealing with internal enemies—Terror. In September 1792 all the bourgeois politicians of Paris professed to abhor it, but within a year the exigencies of war would induce the Convention to agree to institutionalize Terror as an instrument of government. 'No one had dreamt of establishing a system of terror', one deputy later recalled,[13] 'It established itself by force of circumstances; no one's will organized it but everyone's will contributed to its creation.'

Before these extremes were reached there was another period of calm. On the very day the Convention met, the allied advance was stopped at

---

[13] Quoted in N. Hampson, *The French Revolution: a concise history* (1975), 139.

Valmy, and the victories of the ensuing months eased the tensions in Paris. Two questions dominated the Convention's early months—what to do with the king and what to do about Paris. On both the deputies were divided. The Girondins, who had launched the crisis that destroyed the monarchy, had sought at the last minute to save it. They now hoped to save Louis's life too, though they dared not deny, once he was brought to trial, that he had·been guilty of treason toward the Nation. What worried them most was the new power of the popular movement. Paris, in their view, held the National Convention prisoner and inhibited its freedom of action; their main concern until May 1793 was to break the Commune's power at all costs. In this they appealed for support to the provinces, whom, they alleged, the popular movement was depriving of all say in the government of the Republic. The Girondins were opposed by a large body[14] of deputies headed by an eloquent group who normally sat on the high benches to the left of the tribune in the Convention—the Mountain or 'Montagnards'. The Montagnards were unequivocal about the king—he should be put on trial, found guilty, and executed. His crimes against the Nation were unpardonable, and in any case it would be madness to let such a symbol of reaction live after deposing him. Most Montagnards were no more enthusiastic about the *sansculottes* than the Girondins. But they recognized that without them the monarchy could not have been overthrown, and that they harnessed undreamed-of energies behind the war· effort. Above all, they saw that for the moment the power of Paris was a fact of political life that must be lived with. Any overt quarrel between the capital and the Convention, if sustained over a long period, seemed likely to lead only to internal chaos and defeat in the war, with unimaginable counter-revolutionary consequences.

These attitudes explain much about the politics of the first half of 1793. Louis was put on trial before the Convention. It was a foregone conclusion that he would be found guilty—if he were innocent, then the very legitimacy of the Convention would be dubious. The only serious disputes were over whether the sentence (of death) should be submitted to a popular vote of the nation as a whole, and whether Louis, after sentence, should be reprieved. In both cases Girondins said yes and Montagnards said no, but the Montagnards triumphed and on 21 January 1973 Louis XVI was guillotined. No sooner had this fateful step been taken than a period of renewed difficulties began. The British joined the allies and there were defeats for the French forces in the Netherlands. With the value of the *assignat* plummeting throughout the spring, to reach only 36 per cent of its face value by June, there were popular demonstrations over shortages. Some *sansculottes* began to call for price controls—a 'maximum'—and they loudly blamed all these troubles on the machinations of aristocrats, priests, and traitors. This was the moment of the outbreak of the Vendée rebellion—a bitter peasant revolt against the Revolution and all it had stood for since 1789, against the power of

---

[14] The traditional view that the Girondins formed a majority in the Convention has been convincingly challenged by Alison Patrick, *The Men of the First French Republic* (1972), a fundamental reappraisal of the politics of the Convention.

townsmen, against economic depression, against the attack on the church, and against outside intrusions symbolized by military conscription. In *sansculotte* eyes, this rising only confirmed long-nourished suspicions that treason was everywhere, especially in the countryside, where reactionary peasants were withholding essential food supplies from the true patriots in the towns. Agitation began for the formation of 'revolutionary armies' of patriotic citizens to forage for food and to terrorize the Revolution's rural enemies into submission. Much of the machinery of the Terror, and the 'revolutionary government' under whose auspices it was to occur, was set up in March 1793. A revolutionary tribunal was established, vigilance committees were set up everywhere, 'representatives on mission' were sent out from the Convention to centralize authority in the provinces, the death penalty was decreed for armed rebels, a Committee of Public Safety was formed.

One problem continued to impede the efficiency of such measures—the hostility between the Girondins and the Paris Commune. The Girondins constantly denounced the 'blood drinkers' of the capital, and launched repeated attempts to curb their power. The sections, encouraged by a vocal popular press dominated by the bloodthirsty nostrums of such writers as Marat and Hébert, talked ominously of a new insurrection to purge the Convention. A first attempt at this was narrowly averted on 10 March. The Montagnards deplored such talk, but eventually many of them concluded that this was perhaps the only way to end the suicidal vendetta. They lent tacit support, in May, to a plan to coerce the Convention. On 2 June, after a false start two days before, the Convention was surrounded by units of the Parisian National Guard, which since 10 August had been a popular rather than a bourgeois organization, controlled by the sections. They demanded, and got, a purge of the deputies. Twenty-nine leading Girondins were put under house arrest. When seventy-four more signed a protest against these events, they too were arrested. The Montagnards were now in control of the Republic—nominally, at least.

In practice the purge of the Girondins marked the beginning of a period in which the Convention nearly lost control of France. Throughout the provinces during the spring, especially in the great cities of the south, the local authorities had watched events in Paris with disquiet. They formed a ready audience for Girondin accusations against Paris, resentful over the apparent helplessness of their deputies in the face of the popular movement. 'It is evident', wrote one of the Bordeaux deputies who gave the Girondins their name '. . .that the Commune, that the sections of Paris, vilify national representation as much as possible. It is evident that the national representation cannot deliberate, cannot discuss the matters that appear to be put before it. It is always amid tumults, catcalls, all sorts of shouting that terror extracts decrees."[15] Even before 2 June conservative elements had seized power in

---

[15] Quoted in A. Forrest, *Society and Politics in Revolutionary Bordeaux* (1975), 102–3.

Lyons and Marseilles and denounced events in Paris. Now, after the purge of the Girondins, half France rose in revolt against what was regarded as a captive Convention. The centralization of power, so contrary to the principles of 1789, had made government the tool of the Paris Commune, the rebels declared. Their aim was to restore the authority of the localities. Montagnards called this 'Federalism' and alleged that it was a royalist-inspired plot to fragment the republic. It did not in reality have even that degree of co-ordination. Beyond the exchange of fraternal delegates there was little co-operation between the centres of revolt. Each was preoccupied with its local problems and indifferent to events beyond the horizon. This lack of co-ordination and co-operation helped the government to pick off the centres of 'Federalism' during the autumn. But the danger before it did so should not be underestimated. It took until the end of the year to reduce Marseilles, Toulon, and Lyons; and the Vendée rebels, first in the field, continued to resist for years. The defeat of the combination of external and internal enemies which assailed the republic throughout 1793 demanded unprecedented energies and completely novel methods.

First the Convention made a number of bold gestures to capture popular support. It declared the final abolition of feudal dues without compensation. It approved the principle of the 'revolutionary armies'. It cobbled together a hasty democratic constitution which it promulgated and promptly suspended until the return of more tranquil times. In August it issued the decree of the *levée en masse*—an attempt to mobilize every citizen in every corner of national life behind the war effort. All this however did not satisfy the *sansculottes*, who wanted price controls and positive measures to organize the 'revolutionary armies'. On 4 and 5 September, in the wake of renewed bread shortages, the sections mobbed the Convention yet again and forced the reluctant deputies to concede these demands. A 'general maximum' on all food prices was now introduced, a forced loan on the rich, and a conveniently vague law against suspects. The effect of these measures was finally to institutionalize Terror as an instrument of government. They unleashed the energies of the *sansculottes* in a campaign of unlimited vengeance against all suspect elements.

There was not in fact one Terror, but several. There was an anarchic, spontaneous, popular terror whose victims are impossible to enumerate. Perhaps they came to 10,000 or 12,000. Its main instruments were the 'revolutionary armies', in many cases little more than mobile, patriotic lynch-gangs, preying upon peasants, the rich, anybody who in their view behaved suspiciously, 'everybody who had the air of an aristocrat'.[16] Their heyday was the autumn of 1793; one of their favourite policies was 'dechristianization', which involved closing churches, obliterating Christian symbols, and persecuting priests. In these paranoid times even the 'constitutional' church,

---

[16] Quoted in the standard treatment of this phenomenon, R. C. Cobb, *Les Armées révolutionnaires* (1961–3), ii. 559.

its clergy, and their adherents were suspected of the same sympathies as non-jurors. Then there was the Terror unleashed against the centres of the 'Federalist revolt' as government forces resumed control in Lyons, Marseilles, Nantes, or Toulon. Here, amid some semblance of judicial process, the incidence of repression has been calculated: 84 per cent of death sentences in the Terror were passed in the provinces, 21 per cent alone in Nantes and the Vendée region. The areas around Marseilles, Lyons, Toulon, and Bordeaux contributed 22 per cent more. Only regions along active war fronts, where forcible changes of allegiance were frequent, saw comparable levels of repression. Seven thousand, almost half of the 16,594 calculated victims[17] of the Terror, perished during December and January 1793–4, when the central authorities were re-establishing their control of the Federalist centres and punishing rebels. Finally there was the centralized, mechanical Terror of the spring of 1794, conducted increasingly by the revolutionary tribunal in Paris. The more spectacular repressions in the provinces, such as the mass drownings of Nantes, or the mass shootings of Toulon and Lyons, were authorized by representatives on mission whose responsibility to the Convention was only nominal. The Committee of Public Safety, which effectually governed France throughout this period, deplored such rough and ready methods, and steadily worked to bring repression under central control. Increasingly cases were reserved for judgement in Paris, where, during June and July 1794, the total of executions began to rise again as the law of 22 Prairial (10 June) stripped defendants of most of their judicial protection. Disgust in the Convention at the growing bloodthirstiness of the government did much to bring the rule of the Committee of Public Safety to an end on 9 Thermidor (27 July). By that time not only had perhaps 30,000 people been executed; nearly half a million had passed through the prisons as 'suspects' and perhaps 10,000 had died from the conditions in which they were confined. The supreme irony was that most of these unfortunate victims were not the 'aristos', former nobles or priests so beloved of legend, but ordinary people who had been forced to make lethal choices in emergencies over which they had little or no control.

The gradual assertion of central control over the Terror was part of a larger process of centralizing all authority which went on throughout what a new republican calendar now called 'the Year II of Liberty'.[18] With the formal suspension of the new constitution on 10 October 1793, it was decreed that the government of France was to be 'revolutionary until the peace' and on 4 December (14 Frimaire) a detailed decree set out the principles and functions of 'revolutionary government'. Revolutionary government suspended all the principles of 1789 until the war was won. Both the revolutionary constitutions (of 1791 and 1793) had enshrined the virtues of decentralization, separation of powers, elections, and non-political justice.

[17] All these figures are from D. Greer, *The Incidence of the Terror during the French Revolution* (1935).
[18] The new year, of twelve months of thirty days, each of three ten-day weeks, began on 21 September, anniversary of the monarchy's abolition. The revolutionary calendar remained in use for about twelve years.

Revolutionary government actually reversed these principles, restoring in effect many of the characteristics of the old regime. But the emergency justified everything. 'We must', declared Robespierre, 'organize the despotism of liberty to crush the despotism of kings.'[19] The rule of the Committee of Public Safety was more ambitious than that of any preceding regime. Not only did it organize an unprecedentedly comprehensive war effort, which put 750,000 fully armed and equipped men in the field by the summer of 1794; it also made every commune in France directly responsible to the central government; it curbed the inflation rate, controlled food supplies and prices closely, and was even looking in its last months at the control of wages. But to attain this degree of authority, it had to sweep away all rivals, including the very popular movement that had imposed the Terror. The demonstrations of September 1793 were the *sansculottes*' last triumph. By accepting so much of their programme, the government gained control of it, and by the spring the sectional assemblies and vigilance committees which had been the sinews of popular power had been bureaucratized and robbed of initiative. The *sansculottes* had meanwhile enervated themselves with frenzied dechristianization and foraging in the revolutionary armies, so that when in March 1794 the Committee of Public Safety turned the machinery of the Terror against the popular leaders of the Commune, the latter were unable to organize a new insurrection to save themselves. Nor were the *sansculottes* able to prevent the dissolution of the revolutionary armies a few days later.

There were ghoulish people who enjoyed the Terror, but they were never particularly numerous. Most of its supporters saw it as a regrettable temporary necessity, dictated by the emergency. And as soon as order was restored in the provinces and the war began to go better, calls began to be heard for an end to the killing. Throughout the spring a policy of clemency was advocated by Danton, an unscrupulous but eloquent demagogue. But the shady circles in which he moved cast well-justified suspicion on his motives, and, having dispatched the popular leaders, the government in April also liquidated Danton's 'indulgents'. Increasingly dominated by Robespierre, the Committee of Public Safety seemed more and more inclined to view any criticism of its conduct as treason. The law of 22 Prairial seemed designed against just such critics; and the increasing pace of executions after it, at a moment when the armies were now winning battles again, seemed particularly pointless. Robespierre appeared out of control. Ever since the autumn he had been alarmed by dechristianization. Some sort of Supreme Being, he felt, was the basis of morality, the Revolution was a moral event, and atheism was aristocratic. On 8 June he organized a 'Festival of the Supreme Being' to rededicate the state to religion, at which he presided like some patriotic pope. He seemed bent on political and moral dictatorship, established by purge. By July many deputies felt themselves threatened; even various members of the Committee fell out with Robespierre, and their quarrels were carried to the floor of the Convention. This was the opportunity for moderate opinion: the

---

[19] Quoted in J. Godechot, *Les Institutions de la France sous la Révolution et l'Empire* (1951), 257.

Committee's unity was broken, with both factions appealing for the support of the deputies at large. Robespierre failed to win it. Desperately he turned to the Commune, which he had packed with his own nominees, but they were unable to mobilize the *sansculottes* in his favour. The Parisian populace resented the Committee's attempts to impose wage restraint, not to mention the earlier purge of their leaders. And so Robespierre and his closest collaborators were executed. The events of 9 Thermidor did not put an end to the Terror overnight, but within a matter of days the process of dismantling it, and the system of government that had sustained it, was begun.

Reaction and Terror

The most appalling feature of the Terror to contemporaries and later generations, was the contrast with the original benevolent and humanitarian ideals of the Revolution. How could Robespierre, who conducted a lonely crusade against capital punishment in the Constituent Assembly, become the advocate of wholesale executions three years later? The history of the Revolution was full of such paradoxes, explained by hostile observers in terms of plots and hypocrisy. Few were prepared to recognize that the Terror was unpremeditated, a product of wartime emergency. And they often failed to notice that war was pushing the other states of Europe in similar directions. The war against the 'tyrants' of the old regime only made them more tyrannical.

From the start, even before war, many rulers, alarmed by the collapse of authority in France, moved to suppress signs of sympathy with the Revolution among their own subjects. First in the field was Catherine II, who regarded Radischev's tract against serfdom of 1790, the *Journey from St. Petersburg to Moscow*, as an incitement to rebellion, and condemned its author first to death and then to exile. In subsequent years many other writers were arrested or persecuted. In 1792 20,000 books were burned by the authorities in Moscow alone. Paul I, who succeeded Catherine in 1796, was even more vehement, persecuting 'Jacobinism' with an army of police spies. 'Whoever reads the newspapers is dangerous,' reported a French observer of Paul's regime. 'Whoever discusses them—Jacobin.'[20] In Austria Leopold II hoped despite everything to continue the reforms inaugurated by his brother and actually dismantled the secret police apparatus built up in Joseph's last years. But Leopold's death practically coincided with the outbreak of war, which gave ministers already worried by his policies the perfect excuse to urge repressive policies upon his impressionable successor. Those whose ascendancy had been challenged by Joseph now rallied behind the government to form a united front against the popular unrest which greeted the outbreak of war and the total abandonment of all ideas of social or fiscal reform. The initial defeats in the Netherlands and Austria's exclusion from the second Polish partition brought a new and even more reactionary set of ministers to power and the reconstitution of the secret police. The rising of Kosciuscko in the rump of Poland, and the renewed defeats of the summer of 1794 brought yet

[20] Quoted in Dukes, *History* (1971), 385.

another crisis in which mere suppression of newspapers and eavesdropping on coffee-house conversation seemed scarcely enough. 'Jacobinism' had to be broken before it took serious hold. A series of 'conspiracies' were conveniently uncovered by *agents provocateurs* in the circles still devoted to the reforms launched by Joseph in Bohemia, Hungary, and Vienna itself. These revelations were made an excuse for arresting the empire's few genuine subversives, but also many more former 'Josephinians' who had noticed with approval the similarity between many of the achievements of the Revolution of 1789 and the aims of the former emperor. In Hungary in 1795 eighteen suspects were condemned to death (although only seven were actually executed) and another sixteen were given prison sentences. In Vienna the criminal court actually acquitted six of the accused, but fifteen more were sent to prison. The trials were followed by new laws which made public criticism of the government a criminal offence, placed censorship under the control of the police ministry, and dissolved suspicious organizations such as masonic lodges. By 1801 the police ministry considered that these measures had been a total success. 'The Welfare of the State', it reported, '. . .inexorably demanded ruthless measures to prevent the spread of the pernicious disease, the firm application of these measures has had the desired effect—so much so that since then no more revolutionary movement was to be perceived in any part of the Monarchy . . .'[21]

If 1794 saw the climax of the revolutionary crisis in France, beyond her frontiers, 1795 was a more important turning-point. This was the year the French armies went over to the offensive, overran Belgium, Holland, and the Rhine's left bank, and placed revolutionaries in positions of authority— former Vonckists in Belgium, former patriots in the Dutch Republic. These republican successes encouraged sympathizers everywhere, after years of dashed hopes. The winter of 1795, the longest and coldest in living memory, also created widespread popular unrest below the level of articulate political discussion. But these perils only made governments the more resolute against the danger. In addition to the repression in Austria, 1795 witnessed governmental attacks on the only revolutionary cell in Spain, which resulted in five death sentences (later commuted), and in Naples, where ever since a visit by the French fleet in 1792 secret revolutionary clubs had flourished. These societies were wracked by internal divisions, which eventually, in 1794, brought them to the government's horrified attention: the queen of Naples was, after all, the sister of the unfortunate Marie-Antoinette, whom the French had guillotined the previous autumn. Again there were rumours of a plot. Of fifty-three Jacobinical suspects arrested and tried by a special court, three were executed, while a riot at the place of execution left six dead and thirty-five wounded. It is not clear that the riot arose from sympathy with the Jacobins; indeed, in the panicky atmosphere after the first arrests something like the great fear of 1789 had swept the Neapolitan countryside and brought thousands of armed peasants pouring into the

[21] Quoted in Wangermann, *From Joseph II to the Jacobin Trials*, 190.

capital to protect their monarch against French plots and sympathizers. And this underlines an important fact: 'Jacobins', or those so-called, were seldom men of the people outside France. Mostly they were bourgeois—teachers, students, lawyers, religious unfrocked by half a century of anti-monastic governments, occasional soldiers. They represented social groups far less numerous in their own countries than in France, but not unnaturally inspired by their French counterparts' successes to pursue similar goals. But because of their fatal weakness in the face of determined governments and their lack of popular support, the terror campaigns launched against them were mild compared to the Terror in France. It is true that, despite everything, they or their heirs often had their hour of triumph, after French armies marched in and sought local collaborators. But the price of this collaboration was that they cut themselves off even further from the rest of their compatriots. The aristocrats whom the invaders had ejected bitterly resented these upstarts who had replaced them, and the xenophobic populace despised them as lackeys of arrogant and extortionate foreigners.

The major exception was Great Britain. In England, revolutionary sympathies never spread very far, least of all among the bourgeoisie. They, like the rest of their compatriots, believed that England had already secured her liberty by revolution a century earlier. This was not to say that the British constitution was so perfect that it was beyond reform. A tradition, at least twenty years old in 1789, of agitation for parliamentary reform showed that; and the example of constitution-making in France over the next two years lent fresh vigour to the movement. Protestant dissenters now renewed their calls for full civil equality with Anglicans, pointing to and applauding French examples. In 1792, as the *sansculottes* emerged as a permanent force in French politics, many English artisans took up the call for political rights. Corresponding societies were founded to co-ordinate this campaign in London and other important towns. Taking sides in the great debate over the revolution launched in 1790 by Burke's impassioned *Reflexions on the Revolution in France*, they adopted Paine's great rejoinder, *The Rights of Man*, as their Bible. Scarcely had this English popular movement taken shape, however, than news arrived of the September massacres, Louis XVI's execution, and the declaration of war. There was an enormous conservative backlash. Even before this, not all the populace had favoured parliamentary reform, as the 'church and king' riots in Birmingham in 1791 had shown. Now traditional hatred of the French, encouraged by 'loyalist associations' of propertied roughs, and a government-subsidized 'anti-Jacobin' press, left the democrats isolated. The government, like that of France, labelled all criticism of the prevailing order in time of war as treason. In 1794 a series of prosecutions was launched against leading members of the corresponding societies. In Scotland ferocious judges browbeat juries and the accused were condemned. London juries however refused to convict, with the acquittal of the leading democrats giving renewed impetus to their calls for manhood suffrage and annual parliaments. The harsh winter and astronomical bread prices of 1795 heightened popular sympathy for the movement. The life of the king was even threatened by a mob, giving the government an excuse for more decisive action. By this time parliamentary wellwishers of France had dwindled to a handful, so Pitt had no trouble in passing a series of acts which gave him extraordinary powers against subversives. Habeas Corpus was suspended, newspapers and public assemblies subjected to licensing by local magistrates, criticism of the constitution or the established order became an offence. It was the English version of 'revolutionary government'—suspension of normal civil liberties for the duration of the emergency, backed by the almost unanimous sympathy of the propertied orders who identified popular participation in politics with the massacres and bloodshed in France. Ferociously applied by the magistrates, these emergency powers stifled the popular movement or drove it underground. And although there was talk of insurrection here and there in the late 1790s, there was never any serious danger. When the fleet mutinied in 1797 against its appalling conditions, the influence of some 'Jacobin' propaganda was detected; but much more significant were the continued professions of loyalty by the mutineers. As the crew of the *Montagu* declared 'there is no doubt if ever we do fall in with an enemy to our loving King and Country there is no doubt but we will let them know that we are Englishmen and men which are true to our Country.'[22]

So in England there was a sort of 'revolutionary government', much legalized intimidation, but no need for a terror. It was different in Ireland, where the first effect of the French Revolution was to revive agitation, as in England, for parliamentary reform. Most sympathetic to French aspirations were the Protestant dissenters of Ulster; it was in Belfast, in 1791, that the 'Society of United Irishmen' was founded, its aim to secure equal political rights for all Irishmen irrespective of religion. Although founded by Protestants, the most numerous beneficiaries of its programme would be the long-disadvantaged Catholics. The British government saw this, but also, seeing that the French Revolution and the Catholic church had fallen out, it made a bold effort to outbid the United Irishmen for Catholic support by conceding voting rights for Catholics (1793). All that was now left to concede was the right to sit in parliament, but that final concession was deemed too dangerous in the panicky atmosphere of 1795. The effect was to push many politically active Catholics into the United Irishmen who, under the stress of government harassment since the outbreak of war, had adopted a frankly republican and nationalist stance. Ireland's only salvation, they now believed, lay in a democratic republic totally separated from England. Had the United Irishmen been able to attain their original aim of sinking religious differences and uniting all the inhabitants of Ireland behind a common national programme, they might have succeeded. But in the Ulster countryside sectarian fighting had broken out between Protestant peasants and Catholics who were threatening their hold on the land by offering higher rents to landlords. The Protestants sought to deter them by the traditional Irish method of rural terrorism, with organized gangs which struck at dawn, calling themselves Peep o'Day

[22] Quoted in B. Dobrée and G. E. Manwaring, *The Floating Republic* (1937 edn.), 223.

boys. The Catholic rival gangs were named Defenders, and 1795 saw a number of pitched battles between the two sides. These clashes repolarized sectarian differences. Ulster Protestants came to feel a renewed identity of interests with the Anglican landlords of the Ascendancy, who in their turn sought to organize Protestant opinion in the semi-masonic Orange Lodges. Defenderism meanwhile spread to the other provinces and became identified with the United Irishmen. The Dublin authorities, thoughly alarmed by the narrow failure of a French landing in 1796, flooded the countryside with regular and irregular troops who were encouraged in a terrorism of their own against the Catholic peasantry. By 1798 the United Irishmen had concluded that the only course left was an armed rising coinciding with a French invasion. But before their plan matured the government arrested the leaders, the rising which followed was uncoordinated, and the French expendition was too small to have much success. Nevertheless by the middle of 1798 half of Ireland was in open armed rebellion which took a full-scale army the rest of the year to put down. By the time they had finished at least 30,000 people had lost their lives. This was the British Terror, as destructive of human life as that of France.

Towards Dictatorship

Those who had plotted Robespierre's downfall had few immediate aims beyond killing him before he could kill them; but they launched a new phase. With his remarkable knack for summarizing the general mood in France, Mallet du Pan observed in the summer of 1794 that 'the most ardent and general passion is to reach some end to the Revolution and to be delivered from the war.'[23] The two were inseparable. To end the Revolution was not to reverse it, but rather to create a new stability in which its fruits might be enjoyed. Only military victory could assure this, in a war where the enemy protected and sponsored *émigrés* and counter-revolutionaries. And military victory brought its own dangers from ambitious generals. Everybody knew about Cromwell, and Burke had predicted as early as 1790 that sooner or later France would become a military dictatorship. For five years successive post-Thermidorian regimes struggled to avoid this fate, but their inability to control events in France without military help made them more and more the prisoners of generals such as Bonaparte. Nobody except a few deluded politicians was surprised when he took power in 1799: what was quite unforeseen was the speed and efficiency with which he brought a decade's turmoil to an end, when a whole succession of previous regimes had failed so ignominiously.

The Thermidorian regime, which ran from July 1794 to October 1795, was too obsessed by the ghost of Robespierre. Its main concern was to dismantle the Terror, revolutionary government, and everything associated with the bloody memory of the Year II. The Committee of Public Safety was gradually shorn of its powers. The number of executions, after a final purge of Robespierrists in the days following his fall, fell off rapidly, the law of

---

[23] Quoted in A. Fugier, *La Révolution française et l'empire napoléonien* (1954), 92.

22 Prairial was repealed and the revolutionary tribunal reorganized. Thousands of 'suspects' were released from prison; in the autumn the powers of the vigilance committees, the main instruments of the Terror at local level, were tightly restricted. This did not end the killings: the Terror had created many scores now to be settled in a counter–or 'White'–terror, which gathered force late in 1794 and reached its height the following summer. Hundreds of former officials and terrorists, especially in the south-east where repression had been at its most ferocious, were now picked off by terror gangs calling themselves 'companies of Jesus' or 'companies of the sun'. In the towns, *sansculottes* were harassed by well-dressed, well-off bands of bourgeois bullies, *muscadins*, or 'gilded youth'. Jacobin clubs, the ideological nerve-centres of the Montagnard dictatorship, were closed. As if to renounce both the de-christianization of late 1793, and Robespierre's cult of the Supreme Being, not to mention what remained of the utterly discredited 'constitutional' church of 1790, in September 1794 the Convention declared that the republic had no established religion. This was hardly calculated to reassure the Catholic church or woo it from its alliance with the counter-revolution.

By the end of 1794 public opinion was turning not only against the Terror, but against the Convention itself. The misery of the winter of 1795 was largely beyond its control, but the abandonment of the maximum on grain prices in the depths of the coldest December of the century seemed to make matters worse than ever; and so did the final collapse of the *assignat*, the revolutionary paper currency, which entered its final and most spectacular phase over the following spring. It was a winter of rising prices, chronic shortages of all necessities, epidemic disease, and malnutrition. In desperation, the *sansculottes* made two last attempts to coerce the Convention into more decisive action. To the slogan of 'Bread and the Constitution of 1793!', *sansculottes* invaded the Convention hall on 12 Germinal Year III (1 April 1795), demanding action on food supplies. They were dispersed by promises, but nothing was done, and after a month's apparent inactivity they came again in greater force (1–2 Prairal/20–21 May). Once again the Convention made conciliatory noises, but the next day the army was called in to lay siege to the eastern districts of Paris from which the insurgents had come. They had little choice but to surrender. Over the next few weeks the whole area was disarmed, thousands were arrested, and nineteen ringleaders were executed. It was the end of the popular movement. It was also the first time in the Revolution that the regular army had played a decisive part in determining its course.

With the populace cowed and defeated, the Convention at last felt it safe to restore France to constitutional life, but not under the constitution of 1793. A new constitution of the Year III was now worked out, comprising a two-'council' legislature and an executive of five 'Directors' chosen by the councils but independent of them. The councils' members were to be chosen by a complex system of indirect election, but only substantial property-owners were to be allowed to vote at all. Thus the spirit of the 1791 constitution (minus the king) was restored, and machinery of state remaining the monopoly of men of property. Within these limits, the Directory made an honest attempt to make a representative regime work against formidable odds, and sometimes the persistence of those who made the experiment has not been given the credit it deserves among historians agonizing over the lost promise of the Year II or dazzled by the glittering successes of Napoleon. What vitiated the experiment was that, with the French people still bitterly divided, the men who ran the directorial regime did not trust the instrument of their own choice—elections. Even before the experiment began, scared by the royalist sentiments which flared up when the British landed a party of *émigrés* at Quiberon Bay in June 1795, the Convention voted that two-thirds of the members of the first new legislature were to be members of the Convention. The aim was to assure continuity and a smooth beginning for constitutional life, in contrast to 1791. But the 'decree of the two-thirds' so enraged the royalists who had hoped to do well in the elections that in the Convention's last days, they staged an uprising in Paris itself (10−14 Vendémiaire Year IV/2−6 October 1795). They were defeated by expedients which were to become classic under the Directory. The natural enemies of the insurgents were unleashed against them—in this case the Jacobins, *sansculottes*, and former terrorists who had been disarmed after Prairial, who were now released from prison and rearmed. The army was once again called in, and the commander of the troops who routed the rebels (with rather more force than the legendary 'whiff of grape-shot') was Bonaparte. From this time onwards, troops were stationed permanently in the capital, and whoever could command their loyalty was sure of the last word in political conflicts.

We should not underestimate the achievements of the directorial regime which now took power. Above all, it grasped the financial nettle which had deterred every successive regime since 1787. The years 1795 and 1796 saw the *assignats* fall to their lowest point. At the end of 1795 they stood at 0·8 per cent of their face value and by the beginning of 1796 were worth literally less than the paper they were printed on. Their suspension in February was followed by a new land-backed paper currency, the 'territorial mandate'. But its rate of exchange with the *assignat* was fixed at such an unrealistic level that it too went into a rapid decline which left it scarcely more valuable than the *assignat* by mid-summer. In February 1797 both types of paper ceased to be legal tender. This inaugurated a deflation almost as rapid and spectacular as the inflation that had preceded it; the government now had to pay its debts, for the first time since 1789, at real rather than depreciated values. But paper money had driven out specie, which was slow to reappear and even harder to recover in the form of taxes, now seriously in arrears. By September 1797, the crisis had become so serious that the unthinkable was at last faced. The government renounced two-thirds of its debts, the first bankruptcy since 1771. The public debt was the only legacy of the old order that all revolutionary regimes had regarded as sacrosanct—even if the inflation of the *assignats* had made it easy to do so. Now that too was largely dispensed with. It was the last great revolutionary act, shedding the incubus that had destroyed the old order. But it was accompanied, symbolically, by a return to former ways. Few things in 1789 had united Frenchmen more than their hatred of indirect taxes. By sweeping them all away, however, the Constituent Assembly had abandoned the easiest and most effective means of levying revenue. The tax-arrears that had built up by 1797 were largely the result of the difficulties of recovering direct levies. The Directory now reintroduced indirect taxes in the form of stamp-duties and tolls—not without opposition. Toll barriers, burnt down by mobs in 1789 and now rebuilt, were the scene of frequent disturbances, but no subsequent regime was able to do without indirect taxes.

Despite these solid achievements, the Directory proved unable to establish any lasting political stability. Its politics were a perpetual seesaw between Jacobinism, which sought a return to the severe policies of the Year II, and royalism, which saw elections as a strategy to bring about the restoration of Louis XVI's brother.[24] It began in a pro-Jacobin mood, following the defeat of the royalist rising in Vendémiarie. But when, in the spring of 1796, the Jacobins seemed ready to use popular discontent over scarcity and high prices as a springboard for taking over the government, their club was closed. Their more extreme members, led by the communistic Babeuf, joined together in a 'conspiracy of Equals' in the hope of effecting a *coup* and restoring the Year II. The conspiracy was betrayed, but in the aftermath the government's policies swung markedly to the right, persecution of former Vendémiairists and royalists was relaxed, negotiations opened with the pope, and there was a revival of re-ligious practice in the countryside. The result was reflected in the elections of the spring of 1797, when half the members of the former Convention who had stayed on in 1795 retired. Only a handful were re-elected; most of the vacant seats were taken by an assortment of royalists and conservatives held together by their hostility to Jacobinism and to most of the Directors. Later in the sum-mer, a crisis arose, when the majority in the councils made clear its rift with the executive by passing laws favourable to priests and *émigrés*. The three Directors at odds with the councils determined to cut through it with a *coup d'état*. In answer to an appeal for help, Bonaparte, fretting in Italy at delay in confirming his preliminaries of Leoben, sent his deputy Augereau. With his support the three Directors, in the *coup* of 19 Fructidor Year V (4 Sept. 1797) replaced their two colleagues and quashed the spring election results in half the departments. The peace of Campo Formio and the breaking off of negotiations with Pitt, who had hoped that the new majority might restore the monarchy, rapidly followed. The forces of the left were once more unmuzzled, and the 'second Directory' began.

If peace could have been maintained, for all the illegality of its base the second Directory might have survived. Having done so once, the Directors had little compunction about tampering with elections. When the elections of spring 1798 replaced the last of the former Convention's members with predominantly Jacobin sympathizers, they were purged in an attempt to make the legislature more amenable (22 Floreal Year VI/11 May 1798). Such

[24] The dauphin, Louis XVII, had died in captivity in mysterious circumstances in 1795.

measures showed the Directors' strength but when they relied on this same strength to influence the internal affairs of the Batavian and Cisalpine 'sister republics', to promote the power of those local 'patriots' most willing to serve French purposes, the rest of Europe was alarmed. Despite the virtual achievement of the 'natural' frontiers, French ambition seemed to be not at an end. The successes of 1795–7 had revived the Girondin arrogance of 1792, a view that the Republic was not subject to the normal rules of international relations. It was 'the Great Nation', fated to dictate terms of its own choosing to Europe. In this spirit French troops occupied Switzerland in January 1798 at the invitation of 'patriotic' rebels, and in March proclaimed a new Helvetic sister republic. At the same time, the murder of a French general in Rome provoked an invasion of the papal states and a Roman republic was proclaimed in their place. But the most extraordinary example of French arrogance was the Egyptian expedition of 1798. For much of the century Frenchmen had believed that there must be a way of defeating Great Britain more easily than by launching an invasion across the Channel. The most favoured idea was to strike at her trade and colonies; and although the American War had shown the pitfalls of such thinking, its attraction persisted. The idea now was to strike at Indian trade by commandeering the Isthmus of Suez and redirecting non-British eastern trade along routes far shorter than that round the Cape. The restless Bonaparte favoured this idea, which led the Directors to favour it too. They felt safer with the Republic's most successful general away in Egypt, and so in May 1798 an expedition set sail under Bonaparte's command. On arrival it rapidly conquered Egypt.

It was one thing to be at war with Great Britain; it was quite another to wage war by invading the territories of third parties. Egypt was Turkish territory; the eastern Mediterranean was also a Russian area of interest. These two powers now sank their traditional differences for the Turks to allow Russian ships through the Bosphorous. When Nelson severed Bonaparte's communications with Europe by destroying the French fleet at the battle of the Nile (1 August 1798) the Turks formally declared war on France and the Russians began to negotiate an alliance with the British. A fourth member of this new coalition was Naples, who at British instigation opened a new continental war by invading the Roman republic. The operation misfired, French troops rapidly occupied the Neapolitan kingdom, and their general, following the precedent of Bonaparte, ignored his orders and proclaimed a 'Parthenopean' republic. France now seemed to control the whole of Italy. The Austrians, alarmed, agreed to allow Russian troops to cross their territory in order to help the king of Naples. On hearing this, France declared war on the Emperor (12 March 1799).

The war of the second coalition was disastrous in its early months. With Bonaparte lost in Egypt and a seasoned Russian army under Suvorov active in Italy and Switzerland, the Republic underwent a long series of crushing defeats. At the same time there was a revival of royalist rural terrorism in the west of the country, while Belgian peasants had revolted against French authority in November 1798. It began to look like another 1793 crisis, and it was natural that the Jacobinical policies that had saved the Republic then should win renewed popularity. The summer of 1799 accordingly witnessed the regime's last great leftward swing. Political clubs flourished, conscription was rigorously enforced, and there was talk of resurrecting the Terror. New severe steps were taken against the relatives of *émigrés* and a forced loan was decreed against the rich. Such severities provoked royalist uprisings in the south-west, but more seriously, they alarmed all moderates, who had no wish to return to the bloody and uncertain days of 1793. Desperately they looked around for somebody to save them.

Bonaparte chose this moment to abandon his army in Egypt and make a dash for France. He knew what was happening there, and although he was lucky to get across the Mediterranean without interception, there was nothing accidental about his appearance. He knew his moment had come. Sieyès, who had emerged from years of prudent obscurity to become a Director, believed that it was time to abandon the constitution of the Year III and impose another which gave the executive greater power. He naturally turned to Bonaparte, the undefeated general, the peacemaker of 1797, untainted by the quarrels of the previous eighteen months. He thought he could handle the general once the *coup* was over. And so on 18 Brumaire, Year VIII (9 November 1799) Bonaparte and his soldiers dismissed the Directors and the legislative councils, and he and Sieyès embarked on drafting yet another constitution. It was the end of the Directory, and it finally brought to power the long-dreaded soldier who was to end the Revolution.

15. The Revolutionary Impact

The age of revolutions saw the origins of many of the forces that were to shape the modern world. It saw the beginnings of most of the institutions and habits which we still recognize and practise. Equally, it heralded the end of an older order of things. The French Revolution gave the Old Order the name by which we still know it. In doing so it emphasized the scale of its break with the past. But historians have been disputing about the question ever since. Were the changes brought by the revolutionary age as rapid, or as decisive, or as profound as contemporaries liked to believe? Did the decade of revolution destroy the old Europe in one short but epic struggle? Or did it merely mark the opening shot in a battle which was to rage on into the twentieth century? To answer these questions fully would involve us in investigations that go far beyond the range of this book. Here, we can do no more than try to assess how much of the pre-revolutionary world had already gone for ever by 1800.

New Ideologies

The French Revolution produced a comprehensive programme for change which appealed to reformers throughout Europe. Though compounded of elements largely drawn from the thought of the Enlightenment, before 1789 this programme hardly existed as a single entity. Certain axioms which were later absorbed into it were widely accepted, particularly those of Montesquieu. Most people agreed that despotism was wholly bad and that in good governments powers were balanced and separated in order to prevent abuses. Rulers themselves, even when they rejected representative institutions, were prepared to acknowledge that they ought to use their power responsibly. Frederick II was not the only monarch to view himself as the first servant of the state, who owed his people wise administration and, where necessary, benevolent reforms. But such rulers did not believe that the ruled had any legitimate recourse if this trust was betrayed. It is true that in the English-speaking world ideas were further advanced. There, the prevailing order had been founded by a revolution, justified by Locke in terms of the rights of peoples to change rulers who threatened their liberties. But the heroic days of 1688 were already far off. Parliament was now established to express the nation's will and to enact such changes as it might think necessary. Revolution was not treated as either a serious possibility or a legitimate option, even in the British dominions.

It was the revolt of the American colonies that first shook this complacency. It showed that a successful revolt against established authority was possible and could be justified in terms of generalized human rights. When Jefferson wrote, in the Declaration of Independence, that governments derived their

just powers from the consent of the governed, and 'that whenever any Form
of Government becomes destructive of these ends, it is the Right of the
People to alter or to abolish it', he threw down a challenge to most of the
governments in Europe. American independence provoked a debate, all
through the 1780s, over the issues of the revolution and the principles upon
which the new United States were organizing themselves. Ideas of representative government and republicanism got a thorough airing, and so did certain
social doctrines which were to reappear later. The first frontal attack on the
idea of aristocracy came in Mirabeau's pamphlet *Considerations on the
order of Cincinnatus* of 1784. Here the young noble adventurer attacked the
formation in America of a hereditary association of independence war veterans.
It was an attempt he said, to create an aristocracy, incompatible with the life
of a republic. Similarly, the idea of a national convention to draft a constitution derived from the American convention of 1787. Nevertheless,
America provided no comprehensive revolutionary ideology. Events there
filled Europeans with vague—and often ludicrously ill-informed—enthusiasms
and fuelled many a debate. But more than anything the colonial revolt lent
force to trends already in existence, such as the denunciation of despotism
and the spreading conviction that representation ought to be introduced or
extended. The American revolution may have inspired a revolutionary atmosphere in Europe; but it was left to the French to provide a detailed and
positive programme.

The programme did not emerge fully grown. It developed between 1789 and
1794, largely reflecting the issues that arose in French politics during that
time. First to emerge was a new form of hostility to despotism: only a
national assembly could legitimately organize a nation and make its laws. The
agitation for the estates-general produced this idea, and Rousseau's notion
of the General Will was widely invoked to justify it: only in such an assembly
could the general will of the nation, the ultimate sovereign authority, express
itself. The second point was the product of the struggle over the representation
of the third estate and of arguments like those of Sieyès in *What is the Third
Estate?*: there should be no separate privileged orders within a nation. Anybody who advocated special status for nobles or clergymen was an aristocrat;
and it was no coincidence that 'aristocratic' became a revolutionary's favourite
term of abuse. The night of 4 August gave birth to a further principle—
hostility to what was called 'feudalism'. The whole apparatus of seignorial
rights and dues, venal offices, and prescriptive customs by which the everyday life of the old order had been conducted should be swept away. Late in
August 1789 the Declaration of the Rights of Man and the Citizen, conceived
as the preamble to a constitution, codified these principles into a single document, adding a number of others, such as freedom of thought and expression,
careers open to the talents, equality before the law, and the inviolability
of property.

The declaration has often been described as the old order's 'death certificate', in that nearly all the rights it proclaimed were implicit condemnations
of aspects of that order. It was also a manifesto for change, along rational

lines carried out by elected bodies representing a nation of politically free and equal citizens. Until 1792 it summarized what the French Revolution was all about, its catechism of political faith. Events were to add to it still further, however. The fall of the monarchy, brought about to protect the Revolution's achievements, made the programme synonymous with republicanism. The war launched in the spring of 1792 became a struggle against kings; and tyranny, in the eyes of revolutionaries, had become a fundamental feature of the old order. Finally, the ever deepening rift between revolutionary France and the Catholic church lent the ideology a distinct anti-religious quality. With the split over the civil constitution and papal condemnations of the Revolution, the rift became open. The dechristianization of 1793 widened it, and the Convention's final disestablishment of even the 'constitutional' church in September 1794 did nothing to close it. This is not to say that the Revolution paid no homage to saints: but they were secular ones, historic revolutionaries such as Brutus or the Gracchi, or writers who shared its distaste for the old order, such as Rousseau. Jean-Jacques had been dead eleven years when the estates-general met, but his influence was everywhere. The fact that his ideas were widely misunderstood, that men attributed their own notions to him, does not diminish his importance. Here was the one pre-revolutionary writer to declare that men had been corrupted by society, and who in his own life had rejected this corrupt world. The men of 1789 were out to destroy the same world he had rejected; it was natural that they should invoke his name in doing so, and natural too that, when the new church of Sainte-Geneviève was converted into a 'pantheon', or tomb for the nation's greatest men, Rousseau's remains should be transferred to it.

The ideology of revolutionary Europe in the 1790s was something completely new, an international programme for the destruction of the old order. Wherever the French armies went they took it with them. Wherever they went monarchs were deposed, republics created, aristocracies abolished, church lands confiscated, administration rationalized, and representative government established by conventions. Even where they did not penetrate, reformers called for many of the same things. 'Patriots' who had been active before 1789, for instance Dutch, Genevan, or Irish reformers, now adopted the French programme as the epitome of what they themselves, with less clarity of vision, had been striving for. Even the English 'Jacobins', whose calls for more frequent parliaments and franchise extension were deeply rooted in native traditions, accepted French ideas when they were presented in plain English by Thomas Paine. His *Rights of Man* denounced kings, aristocrats, and established churches. It upheld the right of peoples to control their own destinies, bound by no restraints that were not self-imposed. It ridiculed hereditary powers and privileges and scorned any idea that Great Britain had a constitution. Much of the book was concerned with correcting specifically British abuses in British ways—but Paine's opponents saw well enough that it was the French revolutionary gospel that he was preaching, and so did the French electors who made him a member of the Convention in 1792.

The Rights of Man was however not merely an echo of French principles. It was primarily a reply to Burke's *Reflexions on the Revolution in France*, which appeared in 1790. At that time the revolutionary ideology was still developing, but Burke had already seen enough of it to know that it was hateful. Not the least of the reasons for the continuing success of his denunciations was that many of his direst predictions—the increasing bloodshed, and the inevitability of a military dictatorship to end the chaos—came true. With the publication of his attack, a counter-revolutionary ideology, a defence of the old order, began to develop. Burke was concerned to show that the revolution of 1688 had nothing in common with the events now occuring in France. He was appalled by the 'ignorance, rashness, presumption and lust of plunder',[1] which he blamed on the inexperience and attachment to abstract principles of the National Assembly. The old order had had its abuses, but nothing that could not have been easily remedied if the estates-general had followed the example of the British parliament. Its virtues far outweighed its vices, and Burke waxed romantic and lyrical about the generosity of the privileged orders and the beauty of Marie Antoinette. He defended the institutions destroyed by the revolutionaries and poured scorn on the state of affairs that had replaced them. Revolutions like that of France, he implied, created far more and far worse evils than they destroyed. 'When ancient opinions and rules of life are taken away, the loss cannot possibly be estimated. From that moment we have no compass to govern us; nor can we know distinctly to what port we steer.'[2] Exalting (in a strikingly Rousseau-like way) the importance of feelings and prejudices born of long habit, Burke proclaimed the superiority of the wisdom of the centuries over that of any particular generation. Men had no right to dispense with the heritage they received from their ancestors. They had a duty to pass it on for posterity. None of Burke's arguments more infuriated Paine. 'Every age and generation', he riposted,[3] 'must be as free to act for itself, *in all cases*, as the age and generation which preceded it. The vanity and presumption of governing beyond the grave, is the most ridiculous and insolent of all tyrannies.' Perhaps the most influential part of Burke's argument was his explanation of why the Revolution in France had occurred at all. If the old order had been as sound and viable as he claimed, he was unable to attribute its downfall to its own weakness. So he blamed outside forces. One was the spirit of envy and greed animating the moneyed interest, the other a philosophic plot. 'Men of letters, fond of distinguishing themselves, are rarely averse to innovation,' he sourly observed.[4] Respect and faith in established values had been systematically undermined in the preceding generations by a 'literary cabal' of philosophers intolerant of all disagreement and anxious for the political power to impose their destructive views.

In other words, the Enlightenment had caused the Revolution. This was

[1] *Reflexions* (Everyman edn. 1910), 44.
[2] Ibid. 75.
[3] *Rights of Man* (Everyman edn. 1915), 12.
[4] *Reflexions*, 107.

an idea with a long historiographical future, containing sufficient truth to make us still take it seriously. It is impossible to imagine the French Revolution without the Enlightenment, without the spirit of rationality and utility preached by 'philosophy'. But this is a long way from attributing the Revolution to a long-meditated and carefully planned plot by philosophers to destroy the established order, as those threatened by French principles now increasingly began to do. Plots are an easy explanation of events whose complexity defies ready understanding; to the French Catholics of the south, for example, the Revolution was nothing more than a conspiracy by long-persecuted Protestants to seize power for themselves and wreak revenge on their persecutors. All the pre-revolutionary critics of the Enlightenment now came into their own, for here was the catastrophe they had long been predicting. The most successful of these veterans was Barruel, who in 1797 wove all the plot theories into a single great synthesis in his *Memoirs to serve for the History of Jacobinism*. He argued that the Enlightenment had been determined from the start to destroy the old order—its chosen instrument was Freemasonry. The case of the Illuminati showed this conspiracy in action, and athough it had failed in Bavaria, it had manifestly worked in France. The evidence was the network of Jacobin clubs throughout France, which kept the Revolution going and were merely, in reality, masonic lodges come out into the open. Even defenders of Freemasonry, like the Scotsman Robison who wrote in the same year as Barruel, blamed much of the recent troubles on the perversion of the cult by Illuminati. For several years already a conservative German periodical, *Eudämonia*, had been propagating the masonic plot myth east of the Rhine. The chief contributor of these articles was probably the former mason J. A. Starck. Breaking with masonry in 1780, he had already written voluminous denunciations of it. The climax of his campaign came in 1803 with the publication of his *Triumph of Philosophy in the Eighteenth Century* in which he claimed, like Robison, that the Illuminati had subverted the whole masonic movement to an extent unrevealed in Bavaria, that the lodges were tools of the philosophic sect and this sect the true author of Europe's disorder.

Such reasoning naturally appealed to frightened monarchs. It reassured them that the established order, basically sound, could only be subverted by alien forces—forces which could be destroyed if kings remained vigilant. The Jacobin plots uncovered in the Habsburg domains, in Spain, and in Naples in 1794 convinced them that they were on the right track. Plot-detection and suppression became a leading feature of counter-revolutionary ideology. So did the persecution of writers, book burning, and the suppression of Freemasonry. The poison which had destroyed France must not be allowed to gain a hold in countries as yet untouched. This suspicion of intellectual activity even reached into the realms of education. There was no point in over-educating the masses. Typical of this complex of attitudes was the outlook of Frederick William II of Prussia, who in 1794 denounced writings which

shake the foundations of practical religion, without which no civil society can stand. It is. . .necessary to crack down with vigour and persistence against all writings which attack the principles of the existing government and social structure, or describe the measures of the government from a misguided and spiteful point of view, or defend disobedience or refractoriness against either laws or legitimate authority; or encourage ordinary men to engage in useless meditation about topics which far transcend their understanding and judgement.[5]

By 1800 Europe stood ideologically divided in a way quite unknown before 1789. Everywhere there were now advocates of comprehensive reform along lines which were rational and representative. Although this programme derived its inspiration from a revolution, in theory at least it could have been introduced without one. In practice there was no chance of this, for events in France had so terrified established authorities elsewhere that they were unable mentally to separate the two. Thus the Revolution also gave birth to an ideology of Conservatism, in which all change was regarded as equally dangerous. When it had flourished, before 1789, the old order had felt little need to protect itself from change. It had often actively promoted it. Now that it was dying and only change could save it, the old order completely rejected this remedy lest it hasten the fatal moment.

Economic Disruption

The French Revolution broke out at a moment of acute economic crisis. The long expansion of French prosperity in the mid-eighteenth century had begun to falter around 1770. A series of bad harvests inaugurated thirty years of difficulties and recession, which reached their climax in 1788–9. Already in 1788 the wine trade was facing a crisis of over-production, manufacturing industry was beginning to suffer from English competition introduced by the commercial treaty of 1786, and even the booming colonial trade of the western ports was beginning to waver uncertainly. On top of all this came a catastrophic harvest and a severe winter. National food prices rose by a half and in some regions they doubled or trebled. Industrial production fell by half, unemployment rose proportionally. Such circumstances were bound to affect the development of the political crisis, and go far towards explaining the fall in revenue, the difficulties of credit, the urban riots, and the rural unrest which all played such a crucial role in the events of 1789. What is often forgotten is that the political crisis, far from ending the economic difficulties, prolonged and aggravated them. Economically, the Revolution was a disaster for France.

The men who ruled France between 1789 and 1799 did not believe in controlling the economy. They had learned the lesson taught by the economists of the previous generation; that the best way to enrich a country was to abstain from all interference with the 'natural' course of its economic life. Between 1793 and 1795 they were forced to abandon their principles by pressure from Paris. Price-controls were introduced and then subsidies for the price of key commodities. But as soon as the *sansculottes* were

---

[5] Quoted in Epstein, *Genesis of German Conservatism*, 460.

defeated, controls were once more abandoned. In theory this economic liberalism should have acted as a stimulant. The abandonment of grain price controls should have promoted production, especially since the population continued to expand throughout the decade. The abolition of seignorial dues should also have encouraged agricultural production by leaving the producer a greater surplus for investment. The abolition of trade guilds and corporations in 1791 freed industry from the restrictions of a medieval code of values and opened the way for cheap mass production. The ending of all internal dues, tolls, and customs barriers should have encouraged a more rapid circulation of trade. No doubt in the long run these changes did operate in this way. For the generation that lived through the Revolution, however, they were cancelled out by new obstacles to expansion.

The decision to confiscate and sell church lands was of major economic importance for two reasons. First it flooded the market with new land hitherto immobilized in mortmain. When this flow began to dry up it was supplemented by the properties of those who had emigrated or been condemned to death. In this way perhaps a quarter of the land of France was 'unnaturally' thrown onto the market during the revolutionary decade. Despite the land-hunger of the peasantry, they did not benefit much from this massive transfer of property. Most of it was sold in lots too big for them to afford. The main beneficiaries were the richer bourgeoisie, who thus at a crucial moment were induced to invest their surplus capital in land rather than in industry. There was nothing new about this preference; but for the economic development of France it was unfortunate that, at a moment when the temptation to squander capital on office had disappeared with the abolition of venality, and when the removal of traditional obstacles to free trade and production created unprecedented commercial opportunities, the rich bourgeoisie preferred to immobilize its resources in landed property to an even greater extent than before.

In the inflationary conditions of the mid-1790s, however, they could hardly be blamed. The main cause of inflation was the depreciation of the *assignats*, whose introduction was the second consequence of the nationalization of church property. The aim was to issue a paper currency backed by the proceeds of the sale of the national lands. At first it seemed to work. Not until 1792 did the *assignats* begin to depreciate seriously, and even at the beginning of 1793 they still stood at 75 per cent. The disasters of the next six months pulled them down more rapidly, so that by August they stood at 40 per cent. The period of Terror and revolutionary government arrested the decline for a time by the controls it imposed on all aspects of economic life. But the Thermidorian regime, by abandoning these controls, opened the way to the final spectacular depreciation of 1795 and the eventual abandonment of the paper-money experiment in 1797. The only real beneficiaries had been debtors, who had been able to discharge their burdens in depreciated paper, especially after the *assignats* had become legal tender in April 1793. For the government, itself the biggest debtor of all, it was fatally easy to meet new obligations by printing yet more *assignats*. But when taxes were also being paid in the same depreciating paper, it was a vicious circle. The economic cost of taking the line of least resistance was high: a debtors' paradise is no place to encourage productive investment, and as the Director Larevellière-Lépeaux later recalled, by the end of 1795 'All public credit was dead and all confidence shattered; cash sales alone were made in private transactions, or with interest charges that rendered every transaction impossible or ruinous.'[6] Precious metals were driven out of circulation, and even in 1799, as confidence began to recover, specie had still not reappeared in the quantities of a decade earlier. Many wages were paid in kind; over much of France in 1795–6 a natural economy of exchange and barter had come into existence. Prices and wages rose phenomenally—for example the salaries of civil servants under the directory were 3,000 per cent higher than in 1790. When, after 1797, a return was finally made to metal currency, the high wages conceded under inflation conditions made labour ruinously expensive, prolonging unemployment and industrial torpor.

It was not the inflation of the *assignats* alone that had created the industrial depression. It was there before 1789, and the Revolution merely aggravated it. The destruction of the ecclesiastical corporations, the emigration of many lavish-spending noblemen, the obvious dangers to those who stayed of living too ostentatiously, and a new-found preference among the rich for rural obscurity—all created a serious crisis in the luxury and service industries which had been the economic backbone of many pre-revolutionary towns. Urban unemployment and bankruptcy soared, while urban populations declined spectacularly. The population fell in Nancy by a twelfth, in Bordeaux by a tenth, in Rheims by a third, in Lyons by a quarter. Lyons, as the silk weaving capital, was perhaps the most luxury-dependent city of all; of the 8,000 workshops it had supported in 1789, only 3,500 were still there in 1800. Perhaps the most striking collapse was that of overseas trade, the economic sector that had been expanding most spectacularly before the Revolution on the basis of trade with the West Indies. But the Revolution plunged the West Indies into chaos; in August 1791 a massive slave rising broke out in Saint-Domingue, the richest island. As a result, by 1792 the trade of Bordeaux had shrunk by a third. On top of this, in 1793, came the war with Great Britain, in which the enemy resorted to blockade. Even the British navy could not cut off French overseas trade altogether, but whereas in 1789 it had accounted for a quarter of French economic activity, in 1796 the proportion had fallen to a mere 9 per cent. Although there was a certain recovery after the general peace of 1797, which opened the frontiers of several previously hostile states to French trade, the British had captured the bulk of the colonial empire, and so the basis of the pre-revolutionary boom was permanently destroyed.

Ironically, the war, which did so much to aggravate economic difficulties, also provided the only positive stimulus. The unprecedented mobilization of resources associated with the *levée en masse* and the revolutionary government of the Year II gave a sharp boost to production of all goods for military

[6]   Quoted in S. E. Harris, *The Assignats* (1930), 208.

purposes. Mining, metallurgy, and woollen production (for uniforms) did not undergo the depression of other industries—although even they suffered falls in production for a time. Large-scale mining was blighted for a decade when reforms in property law transferred ownership of the subsoil to surface proprietors. But government founded new munitions factories and subsidized production of essential war goods where they would normally have collapsed for lack of capital. The French cotton industry was actually saved by the war. In 1789 it seemed on the verge of annihilation in the face of British competition. War with Great Britain, along with French conquests beyond the frontiers, closed much of the continent to cheaper British cottons and left French producers with a virtual monopoly.

Even so, the Revolution did more damage than good to the French economy. It reinforced the preference of the rich for investing in land rather than industry without doing anything to improve the quality of agriculture. Indeed, by making laws of inheritance more egalitarian, it encouraged the morcellation of property which had always been one of the main obstacles to an agricultural revolution. Its over-all effect was to reinforce rather than destroy traditional patterns of economic behaviour; and that was the real disaster, for up to the 1780s the prospects for change had been quite promising. The expansion of the economy had not been catastrophically behind that of Great Britain. And although by 1790 the British had begun to pull markedly ahead as the industrial revolution gathered pace, it is possible that France would have followed the same course within a few years. The Revolution ensured that she did not, postponing her industrial 'take-off' for at least another generation.

Disruption was not confined to France. In the southern Netherlands, which the Republic finally annexed, 'feudalism' was abolished, church lands sold, and the *assignats* introduced, with results similar to those in France. But this region had better coal and metallurgical resources than France, and its incorporation into so large a country opened a far wider market than they had hitherto enjoyed. The stimulus to Belgian industry perhaps outweighed the disruption of economic life in other spheres. Other countries in the French orbit, lacking the industries to benefit in this way, had few gains to offset against the losses caused by the arrival of the French. In the Batavian republic and in Italy traditional cloth manufactures were annihilated by larger-scale and more advanced French competition. They were deprived at the same time of access to rival British goods. The blockade, with which the British responded to their exclusion, destroyed the sea-borne trade of these countries as it did that of France. And meanwhile the arrival of French armies brought ruthless requisitioning, penal taxation, and in the Dutch case heavy reparations. Even in countries not subjected to French occupation, the strain of war against the republic took its economic toll. Spain had already financed a large part of her participation in the American war by issuing paper money. After an initial depreciation these notes recovered their value and continued to circulate, an important element in Spanich currency. But when Spain declared war against France in the 1790s more notes were issued than the economy could absorb, and a rapid depreciation set in. It never matched that of the *assignats*, but by 1799 the notes had lost almost half their value, and prices had soared ahead of wages. When in 1796 Spain switched alliances from Great Britain to France, her trade with her South American colonies was at once savagely cut by British sea power.

Much work remains to be done before we can draw firmer conclusions about the economic impact of the Revolution outside France. But one thing is clear—the one area which did not suffer substantially was England. By 1789, the British economy had already entered upon the rapid expansion that marked its take-off into the industrial revolution, and the years 1788–92 saw a trading boom. Entry into the war, which involved a massive switch to military production, an area drastically run down since 1783, posed serious problems of readjustment; and the mid-1790s, coinciding with the notorious winter and poor harvest of 1795, were a period of constant difficulties. In 1797 a run on the Bank of England forced it to suspend gold payments. Thomas Paine expected this to bring about the collapse of British power, but he was disappointed. The bank's investors agreed to accept paper, and as a result the British financial system was strengthened rather than weakened because the possibility of future runs was eliminated. Meanwhile, as in France, the demands of the military machine stimulated shipbuilding, iron-founding, and woollens, and since these industries were already more sophisticated and better developed than those of France, Great Britain was pushed even further ahead. Above all, the collapse of the French navy and the chaos brought by the Revolution to the French West Indies enabled the British to destroy their rival's colonial empire and most of the trade it sustained. Thanks to the French Revolution, Great Britain obtained what continentals had feared and resisted for the best part of a century—the virtual monopoly of Europe's links with the rest of the world. She also completed, practically unopposed, the construction of a new overseas commercial empire to replace that shattered by the loss of the American colonies. It is true that, if once the continent could be closed to British exports and re-exports, the British economy might still be seriously damaged. The Directory saw this and sketched the outlines of such a system. Later Napoleon was to apply it thoroughly. But it needed time to make it work properly, and time was on the side of the rich, united, and seagoing island state.

Gains and Losses: The Populace

The French Revolution could not have happened without popular intervention in politics at crucial moments. In July and October 1789, in August 1792, and in June and September 1793 it was the Parisian populace who determined the course of the Revolution, which they regarded as a beneficial force, something to be defended and fought for. In order to do this they organized themselves in Paris in 1792 into the first self-consciously political popular movement in history, that of the *sansculottes*. At the same time, English working men were launching a popular movement of their own, that of the corresponding societies. In 1792, it has been said, 'the people' enter politics.[7] It was all the more tragic and ironic that at the end of the day the Revolution did so little for them.

There were admittedly two important ways in which 'the people' benefited from the Revolution. In the first place, French peasant proprietors and those who lived wherever French armies went, were relieved of the burden of 'feudalism'. Serfs in France and western Germany were emancipated, dues in cash or kind were eliminated, seignorial prerogatives over game disappeared. A man now owned what he owned, without obligations to any outside authority except the state. Secondly, during the brief heyday of the *sans-culottes*, working men (and women) experienced political life for the first time. In France they even exercised a voice in national political decisions; and the English 'Jacobins', though deprived of that, nevertheless learned to organize themselves rather than riot spasmodically and ineffectively in the old way. These heady events created precedents and founded traditions of popular political action in both countries from which future generations derived inspiration and instruction. But by 1800 the leading participants in the heroic days of 1792–5 were persecuted, silent, or dead. Their Revolution had failed.

Revolutionary gains had to be exacted by shows of force at moments when the constituted authorities were too weak to offer resistance. The majority of the National Assembly in 1789 had no desire to destroy 'feudalism' until rural disorder forced its hand. They tried to stipulate payment of compensation for the loss until peasant resistance showed that it could not be enforced. Even the final abolition of seignorial dues without compensation in 1793 was a ploy by a government facing civil war to win peasant support. The triumph of the *sansculottes* in 1793–4 was made possible only because the Convention was divided against itself, one side turning to the people of Paris for allies. But even the Montagnards did this with reluctance, and as soon as they could they threw off the restraints of popular power, just as their predecessors had done in October 1789 when, saved from counter-revolution by the October days, they immediately passed the martial law against tumults. The assemblies were prepared to accept popular help in an emergency, but had no intention of sharing power with the lower orders on a permanent basis. The Revolution may have made all men citizens, but most of them were not active citizens, and had no significant rights. Political rights went with property, and when the populace showed signs of disputing this they were shot down or cowed into submission. In his newspaper *The People's Friend*, Marat summarized the situation vividly in July 1792.

The people lack everything against the upper classes who oppress them [he wrote].[8] If they have stopped oppressing us by their rank, it was to put us down by their riches; it is by this title above all that they have managed to deprive us of all means of defence. . .The poor lack everything and nobody comes to their aid, the rich lack nothing and everybody is eager to serve them.

---

[7] G.A. Williams, *Artisans and Sansculottes: popular movements in France and Britain during the French Revolution* (1968), 4.

[8] Quoted in M. Vovelle (ed.), *Marat: textes choisis* (1963), 220.

In addition to the end of seignorial exactions, French peasants hoped that the Revolution would give them land. Many were already landowners, but few had enough even for self-sufficiency. Yet not many could afford the expensive lots in which 'national lands' were sold off, and rural communities were forbidden to form syndicates to buy them. And when, after 1793, common lands began to be divided up, the biggest shares went to those who owned most land already. Only the richest peasants derived much benefit. The laws of 8 and 13 Ventôse Year II (26 February and 3 March 1794) which authorized distribution of small parcels of 'suspects'' land to the poor, never had time to take effect, even if their intention was serious, which many historians doubt. The death penalty was authorized for anybody who advocated an 'agrarian law', that is, a redistribution of property in favour of the poor. So most peasants remained as land hungry at the end of the Revolution as at the beginning, and their only success was in resolute defence of collective rights against repeated attempts by successive revolutionary assemblies to abolish them. Besides, only proprietors benefited from the end of 'feudalism'. Renters of land (which most peasants were) derived no advantage, and when tithes were abolished their landlords were authorized to raise rents in proportion, thus negating yet another supposed gain. Meanwhile the rural industries on which they depended to supplement their incomes had been depressed. Law and order had broken down over large tracts of the countryside, especially after 1795, with brigands and bandits (this time not imaginary as in 1789) swarming everywhere. Military conscription took a far heavier toll of able-bodied farm hands than the old order's militia; and in 1793 rural areas were terrorized by the 'revolutionary armies' of *sansculottes*. In the Vendée and many other western departments it proved too much; the burden of 'feudalism' in these areas had been so light before 1789 that there was no compensation in its abolition. It was little wonder that they spent much of the decade in revolt or in sporadic guerilla warfare against the new order, fighting for the restoration of Church and King.

The Belgian peasant revolt in 1798 shows that the innovations brought by the French to the rural life of other countries were not always welcomed. Yet it remains true that rumours of the upheavals in France caused unrest in regions that did not experience French principles at first hand. Kosciuscko tried to enlist the support of Polish serfs against the partitioning powers by offering them emancipation. In Russia the years 1796–8 saw more peasant unrest than at any time since the Pugachev revolt, with 278 outbreaks occurring in thirty-two provinces. 'All the peasants', wrote a landlord in 1797,[9] 'have. . .the thought that there should be no nobles. . .This is the self-same. . . spirit of insubordination and independence, which has spread through all Europe.' In Ireland in 1798 there was a full-scale peasant war, in which the rebels espoused the revolutionary principles of the United Irishmen. Had it not been for several years of brutal pre-emptive terrorism by government troops they might never have gone to such lengths. Yet neither in Ireland, Poland, nor Russia, did the peasantry derive any benefit from their revolutionary

    [9] Quoted in Dukes, 'Russia and the Eighteenth Century Revolution', 383.

action. The aftermath was a repression even more severe and determined than before.

For the populace of French towns the first tangible result of the Revolution was a rise in unemployment, as the old employers of servants, and consumers of luxury goods, deserted the turbulent centres of disorder. Those who were thrown out of work were unable to turn for help, as they had previously, to their guilds, for in March 1791 guilds were abolished, as vehicles of 'exclusive privileges'. Nor were those still lucky enough to be employed allowed to combine to improve their own position: strikes were denounced as the work of counter-revolutionaries. 'Liberty must exist for everybody,' the Paris municipality announced to carpenters striking for higher wages in April 1791, 'even for masters.'[10] When such announcements failed to prevent a wave of strikes, the National Assembly passed the Le Chapelier law (14 June 1791) which made all fraternities and unions of working men illegal. Meanwhile, in Great Britain, strikes were being interpreted as part of the same subversive pattern represented by the corresponding societies. From 1796 acts of parliament began to be passed forbidding combinations of workers in specific industries. They culminated in the general Combination Acts of 1799 and 1801, which imposed similar restrictions to those of the Le Chapelier law on the activities of British workers. Meanwhile, the break with the church and dechristianization reduced the number of holidays for saints' festivals observed in France, and the working week was further increased by the introduction in 1793 of the revolutionary calendar, which allowed a day of rest every tenth day instead of every seventh. Nor did the Revolution do anything to end perhaps the most hated innovation of the last years of the old order, the *livret*, without which a worker was unable to change jobs, and which put him at the mercy of any employer who refused to sign him off.

All wage-earners suffered severely from the inflation of the *assignats* and shortages of essential supplies. The old order, in its last decades, had been moving hesitantly towards the abandonment of its traditional controls on the price of grain and bread. The populace expected the Revolution to reverse this trend—one reason for their adulation of Necker in 1789, for he was no free-trader. The bourgeois deputies had little sympathy with the popular view, but in 1793–4 the Montagnards accepted it for political reasons and applied controls with rigour. The result was stable bread prices, steady supplies, and a respite from the depreciation of the *assignats*. The abandonment of controls by the Thermidorian regime, coinciding with poor harvests and a severe winter, brought an awful contrast. It was little wonder that the *sansculottes* always looked back to the Year II as the climax of the Revolution. 'We were better off', people were saying in 1795, 'under the reign of Robespierre; then we were not in need.' It was now, too, that the first signs appeared of popular disgust with the whole Revolution: 'We shall have a king in a fortnight; then we shall not be without bread.'[11] Only with the good harvests of 1796–8, and a rise in real wages

[10] Quoted in Godechot, *Les Institutions de la France sous la Révolution et sous l'Empire*, 183.
[11] Quoted in Rudé, *The Crowd in the French Revolution*, 150 and 164.

associated with the deflation after the bankruptcy of 1797, did the condition of urban workers begin to improve again, but even then the slow recovery from general economic depression still left unemployment high.

Those without work, the poor and the indigent, suffered more from the Revolution than anybody. In abolishing feudal dues and confiscating ecclesiastical lands, the Revolution destroyed most of the revenue of hospitals and charitable institutions, all branches of the church. The campaign against the aristocracy also dried up many of the most generous sources of private charity. Despite much talk, copious legislation, and grandiose planning, no national system of poor relief was provided to replace this old structure. Measures taken were soon rendered ineffective by lack of funds and the sudden collapse of poor relief came at a time when the ranks of the poor were swollen by the new unemployed. The extremes of unreality were reached by the Convention which, authorizing public assistance to the deserving poor, forbade alms-giving and begging on the grounds that they encouraged the undeserving. To reinforce this prohibition, all private charitable institutions were also banned. Thus the poor were less well prepared than at any time in the century to face the classic subsistence crisis of 1795, when a bad harvest was followed by a rigorous winter. Many of the social problems of the Directory—brigandage, rampant prostitution, the massive abandonment of new-born children—merely reflect the poor responding in the traditional way to their problems, but in unprecedented numbers. Many simply failed to survive at all. In Rouen, the mortality rate doubled in 1795—6, and trebled the year after. These years also saw a spectacular rise in suicide rates, as people at their wits' end opted for a quick death rather than a slow one. Able-bodied men, it is true, could join the Republic's armies, more numerous now than at any time in French history, and be assured of a certain minimum of food and clothing. If they went with General Bonaparte to Italy, they might find rich plunder and be paid in gold and silver, which were unobtainable in France. Yet desertion rates, and the astonishing resistance to conscription which was perhaps the most extensive popular movement of the decade, suggest that few found the army attractive. And besides women could not become soldiers, nor could children, the old, the sick. Their lot had always been hard, but all the evidence suggests that the effect of the Revolution was to make it far harder.

Only by realizing this can we fully understand the Revolution, for much of its history was dominated and directed by fear of counter-revolution. Counter-revolution was not a figment of popular imagination, even if those whose intention was to go back beyond 1789 in every particular were never very numerous. What made them dangerous was the appeal they made to the much vaguer anti-revolutionary sentiments of ordinary people who had made few gains from all the upheaval, and wanted it to stop. This was what fuelled both the peasant revolts of the west and the urban defiance of the so-called 'Federalist' revolt, not to mention much individual resistance. Only 16¾ per cent of those who emigrated from revolutionary France were nobles. One-third of *émigrés* were ordinary peasants or artisans. Only 14¾ per cent of the unknown victims of the Terror were nobles or clergy, whereas almost 60 per cent were from the populace. These groups, over 41,000 in all, were ordinary people who had incautiously allowed their disillusionment with the Revolution to show. Millions more suffered in oppressive silence.

Gains and Losses: The 'Privileged Orders'

Everybody knows that the French Revolution was anti-aristocratic, that it abolished privileges, titles, and even the nobility itself. Everybody knows that many nobles emigrated, that many lost their lands, and that many died on the guillotine. But what was the precise extent of these changes?

With the abolition of fiscal and other privileges, with the end of venality and the introduction of careers open to the talents, former nobles lost many of their financial and social advantages. With the abolition of nobility itself and all its outward signs in February 1790, nobles ceased to enjoy the prestige and precedence formerly accorded them. But for the state to cease to recognize nobility did not mean that nobles disappeared. They remained convinced of their apartness, they continued to intermarry with one another and to prefer each other's company. In fact they became far more exclusive than before, since the legal disappearance of nobility entailed the disappearance of all the recognized ways of ennoblement, so new nobles were no longer recruited. Thanks to the Revolution, for the first time ever the myth that nobility was only of the blood began to approximate to reality.

The Revolution destroyed the old, glittering centre of noble life and aspirations, the court of Versailles. It is no coincidence that it was the court nobility led by the king's spectacularly stupid brother the count d'Artois, who began the emigration in the aftermath of 14 July. But the emigration did not drain France of her nobility. Only 16,431 were officially classed as *émigrés*, and three out of four noble families were probably unaffected by the emigration. Moreover the Terror added only 1,158 nobles to the list of revolutionary casualties. They catch the eye because they were spectacular, bearers of famous names, former men of power, rather than because they were numerous. Only during the last phase of the Terror, in June and July 1794, was it turned against former nobles as such, when 20 per cent of its noble victims perished. Most nobles simply went to ground, retired to the country, and behaved modestly. As a result they emerged from a decade's turmoil with some at least of their former social prestige intact. The Revolution brought about the end of noble absenteeism and the return to the land that publicists had called for in vain throughout the foregoing century. Those who followed this course were far less likely to be killed or reduced to poverty than their *émigré* cousins, who, when they were not fighting recklessly alongside the armies of the coalitions, passed most of their lives in frustrated and penurious boredom.

After 1792 those who had emigrated forfeited their lands. For a brief period in the Year II, so did their relatives. These confiscated properties, joined to the pool of 'national lands', were eventually sold off. No reliable figures are available even now for noble land losses in France as a whole and amounts varied substantially from region to region. One estimate suggests that at least 12,500 noble families suffered some loss of lands. But much was secretly bought back by relatives when it came on the market, so that perhaps not more than a fifth of noble land passed finally into other hands. In many regions it was at least another century before nobles ceased to be the largest landowners. It is true that the nobility's losses cannot be measured only in terms of lands. They lost their income from feudal dues, from venal office, and from government securities after the bankruptcy of 1797. Borrowing to repurchase confiscated lands imposed additional strains on income. But the nobility was not wiped out. Under the Directory, with the resurgence of royalism, nobles began cautiously to re-emerge. The defeat of the Quiberon Bay landing in 1795, in the aftermath of which 748 *émigrés*, most of them noble, were executed, showed that the king was unlikely to be restored by force. It also deprived the emigration of much of its glamour. So that by 1800 most nobles were prepared to cut their losses and accept much of the work of the Revolution. Their main concern was now identical with that of all men of property, noble or not. They would support any regime which could guarantee a return to stability and a period of secure calm after so many years of upheaval.

In France, then, the Revolution heralded the decline of nobility and began the process, but it came nowhere near to completing it. The Empire and the Restoration were to bring the nobility an Indian summer. Outside France, the effect of the Revolution was to give nobilities a new lease of life, as monarchical governments and their greater subjects closed ranks against the menace of revolutionary principles. Joseph II's fiscal reforms were abandoned, Gustavus III's openly anti-noble policies ended with his assassination, and in Prussia, where the nobles and the government had not clashed since before 1740, 1791 saw the promulgation of a long-awaited general code of laws. Its most distinctive feature was a comprehensive statement of noble rights and privileges. 'The noble', it declared, 'has an especial right to places of honour in the state.'[12] It went on to catalogue a series of prerogatives at total variance with all that the French Revolution now stood for. Nobles everywhere could say Amen. The lesson of France had awakened them to the dangers of division among themselves and clashes with monarchs. In 1780 their powers had been under attack from rulers in many parts of Europe. By 1800 the only danger to their position seemed to come from the French government, not their own.

Nor did the Catholic church suffer as much damage as might be thought from its feud with the French Revolution. Arguably, it was much stronger in 1800 than a decade beforehand, despite the loss of its institutional position in France. The old Gallican church, with its lands, its liberties, its regular assemblies and its fiscal privileges, was gone for good. The clergy would never again form a separate order in the state. Their monopoly of education was shattered. Cruel persecution was unleashed against them after 1792, cul-

---

[12]   Quoted in Palmer, *Age of the Democratic Revolution*, i. 511.

minating in the dechristianization of 1793. Nearly 25,000 of the *émigrés*, a quarter of the total, were clergy; 920 clerics, or $6\frac{1}{2}$ per cent of the total number of victims, perished officially in the Terror; many more must have died in quasi-religious upheavals like that of the Vendée. The total of clerical casualties may even have been as high as 5,000. During this time, too, between 3,000 and 4,000 people of both sexes who had taken vows of clerical celibacy yielded to the pressure of 'patriotic' public opinion, and renounced their vocation by marrying. When, in February 1795, the free exercise of religion (though without any outward display) was allowed, many churches had fallen into ruins or been converted to other uses, and regular religious observance took some time to reorganize itself.

But religion had survived, and so had the Catholic church; and now it had the assurance that those who braved the periodic Directorial anti-religious reactions to come to church really believed in what they were doing. Gone was the old problem of sorting out the faithful from the mere conformists. Although this change had involved a drastic fall in the number of practising Catholics, it was not as drastic as might be expected. The closing years of the eighteenth century saw a religious revival in France which owed something to the counter-revolutionary interpretation of the Revolution as the consequence of a philosophic plot. 'Natural religion', that philosophic bromide, was now rejected, and God's purposes were once more portrayed as mysterious and awe-inspiring. The same false prophets who had derided the church had plotted the chaos of the Revolution. The revival also owed something to the example of martyrdom set by the clergy who perished for their faith under the Terror. Against such inspiration, deistic cults such as 'Theophilanthropy', launched in 1796 and briefly encouraged by the Directory, won few adherents. It is true that the church, emerging hesitantly from persecution, remained split between the 'constitutionals' who had taken the oath of 1790, and those who had refused it. But even this experience had important lessons. When the Convention declared that the state patronized no religion, Catholics found that they had a faith which existed independently of the political order. The whole sad history of the civil constitution of the clergy illustrated the dangers of trying to link politics and religion too closely. By 1800, therefore, many French Catholics were within sight of accepting, like the former nobles, that the restoration of the king was not necessarily the best thing for their interests. What was now most needed was a regime which, whatever its character, provided conditions in which the faithful could worship God in peace and security.

Outside France the Revolution saved the Catholic church and the papacy from dissolution. Ever since the disbanding of the Jesuits in 1773, papal authority had received a series of blows which seemed calculated to destroy every vestige of central authority in the church. In France and the Habsburg lands monasteries had been dissolved without reference to Rome. In Germany and Tuscany bishops had proclaimed that, in effect, the bishop of Rome had no more authority than they themselves. In France, Spain, Portugal, Naples, and all the lands ruled by Joseph II the pope was unable to communicate with the faithful without the secular ruler's consent. Jansenism and Febronianism seemed about to triumph, and the French Civil Constitution of the Clergy would mark their apotheosis. In fact, it proved a turning-point. The refusal of the National Assembly to allow a national council of the French church forced the French clergy to look to Rome for a ruling on the new order. Papal authority was once more thrown into relief. When, as a result of Roman intransigence, the French state began to turn against the church, the rulers of Catholic Europe realized once more what strength they derived from organized religion. Their attacks on Rome ceased. Papal authority revived. The promulgation of the bull *Auctorem Fidei* in 1794, by which the pope condemned Ricci's recent experiments in Tuscany and by implication all that Jansenism now stood for, demonstrated the confidence of this revival. The pope could still be attacked physically by the revolutionary armies—in 1798 his states could even be turned into a 'sister republic' —but his spiritual authority remained intact. As a papal representative told Bonaparte in 1796,[13] 'You might, out of vengeance, sack, burn and destroy Rome, St. Peter's, etc., but religion will remain standing in spite of your attacks. If you only want the pope to issue general exhortations to peace, to obedience towards legitimate power, he will willingly do it.' The general appeared much taken with this argument, but said it would never convince the Directory. He saw, as they did not, that there could be no end to the Revolution until France and the Catholic church were at peace.

The Bourgeoisie Triumphant?

Historians love to disagree about everything, but they have always been unanimous that the French Revolution was a triumph for the bourgeoisie. The third estate, which won control of the National Assembly in June 1789 by securing common voting by head, was a body of bourgeois. The policies pursued by successive governing assemblies, both anti-aristocratic and anti-popular, could only be designed to benefit the bourgeoisie. And wherever the French Revolution was exported, the invaders relied overwhelmingly on bourgeois sympathizers in the conquered countries to set up new regimes. This period saw the emergence of bourgeois class-consciousness, and the emergence, too, of a myth to legitimize it. It was perhaps expressed most clearly by Barnave, the Feuillant leader, in writings unpublished until half a century after he was guillotined in 1793.

The reign of the aristocracy [he wrote][14] lasts as long as. . .landed property continues to be the only wealth. . .As soon as arts and trade begin to spread among the people and create a new means of wealth and help for the labouring class, a revolution is in preparation in political laws; a new distribution of wealth prepares a new distribution of power.

In other words, the bourgeoisie (which is what Barnave really meant by the people), had taken political power, and had the right to do so, because it

---

[13] Quoted in Latreille, *L'Église catholique et la Révolution Française*, i. 229.
[14] F. Rude (ed.), *Barnave: Introduction à la Révolution Française* (1960), 9.

already controlled the greatest economic power in the form of industrial and liquid wealth.

Marxist historians have found this interpretation very congenial. For them, the arrival of the bourgeoisie in power in 1789 represented the throwing off by the forces of capitalism of the constraints of feudalism, the relics of an archaic and obsolete economic order. The evidence they point to is the destruction of feudalism on the night of 4 August 1789, the onslaught on all vestiges of the old aristocratic order, the elevation of individual rights by revolutionary legislation, and the persistent attachment of all the successive revolutionary assemblies to economic freedom, subject to no outside controls either from government, from corporate organizations or from the workforce.

Yet is is clear that the bourgeoisie had not captured the greatest economic power in pre-revolutionary France. Nobody would deny that they held most of the commercial riches, although most industrial wealth was probably noble-owned. But neither of these sectors were predominant in the French economy—growing though they were. Land remained far more important than both of them put together until well into the nineteenth century. If we are to assign the bourgeoisie any significant share at all of French wealth before 1789, we can do so only by including its holdings of traditional, essentially landed, forms. It was in this area that the bourgeoisie gained most from the Revolution. Thanks to the purchase of nationalized church lands, the bourgeoisie's share of landed property increased dramatically. In the Toulouse region, for example, 93 per cent of national lands were bought by the bourgeoisie. So by the end of the Revolution the economic power of the bourgeoisie had undoubtedly increased—its members now owned between 30 and 40 per cent of French landed wealth, which, with their holdings of liquid assets, made them the most powerful economic and social group in the country. But this situation was a result of the Revolution rather than a cause of it. Moreover the nature of this power was traditional rather than new. Land remained the essential element, the Revolution positively accelerating the bourgeois' traditional preference for investing in proprietary wealth rather than reinvesting in trade. If we add to this the dramatic collapse of French overseas trade brought by the Revolution, it seems probable that the character of the French bourgeoisie was less commercial in 1799 than a decade earlier, and that capitalism, far from triumphing, had suffered a serious setback.

Nor should this surprise us, if we look closely at the composition of the assemblies which ruled France during the revolutionary decade. Out of 648 deputies of the third estate who sat in the Constituent Assembly, only eighty-five came from the world of trade, finance, or industry. Out of 891 members of the Convention, only eighty-three came from these sectors. The surprising thing is that bodies in which commercial interests had so little representation should do anything at all for the development of capitalism. In the short run the economic results of their rule were largely disastrous, but in the longer term, we cannot deny that the abolition of feudal dues, internal customs·barriers, price controls, and the prohibition of workers' organizations, would favour the development. of capitalism in agriculture, trade, and industry. The removal of all these restraints, however, was only superficially a coherent programme. In reality it came about piece-meal and haphazardly. No deputies proposed the abolition of feudal dues until the peasant unrest of July 1789 left the Assembly with little alternative. The idea of abolishing internal customs barriers went back at least to Colbert, and had been familiar to all well-educated men of every economic viewpoint for years. So had the abandonment of price-controls, which the old order itself had been sporadically experimenting with since the 1760s. The Le Chapelier law, passed to combat a strike wave in 1791, merely reinforced the hostility of the old order to strikes. In other words, most of the new economic principles introduced by the Revolution had been familiar to the old order, and the one aspect which had not—the abolition of feudal dues—had come about against the better judgement of most men of property, whatever their social background.

In the long term, then, the Revolution did favour the men of liquid wealth, the capitalists, but the immediate picture was more confused. In the larger cities, men of trade and commerce took over local power from the old élites, at least until the advent of the bureaucratic empire of Napoleon. But at regional and above all national level the leadership of the Revolution was drawn overwhelmingly from the legal profession and from landowners. Not surprisingly, the most immediate gains went to precisely these groups. It was they who profited most from the abolition of noble privileges and from the introduction of careers open to the talents. It is true that the Revolution abolished the venality whereby public officials had purchased office, and that it did so at unrealistically low rates of compensation. But the rapid expansion of the state apparatus seen in the 1790s created plenty of new opportunities for the educated. By 1794 the civil service had expanded fivefold, the central administration eightfold. Bourgeois had always monopolized the lower and middle ranks of justice and administration. Now, through election, they gained access to the highest offices and to the political power which directed the state machine. Hitherto, political power had been virtually a noble monopoly. Between 1789 and 1799, however, France was governed and reformed by overwhelmingly bourgeois assemblies, largely elected by bourgeois voters. No subsequent regime was ever able substantially to reverse these advances.

Nor is it surprising that a lawyers' revolution should be so preoccupied with property. The French Revolution was above all a triumph for the (very legalistic) view that property is the measure of all things. The Declaration of the Rights of Man and the Citizen declared property one of the natural and imprescriptible rights that it was the aim of all political associations to preserve. The distinction between active and other citizens was a matter of property qualifications. The reluctance of each successive revolutionary assembly to face bankruptcy was born of a reverence for invested property. Perhaps the bluntest expression of the principle came from Boissy d'Anglas, as he introduced that property-owners' charter, the constitution of the Year III, in 1795.

We ought to be governed [he declared] [15] by the best elements among us. The best are the most educated and those most interested in the maintenance of the laws. Now, with very few exceptions, you only find such men among those possessing property, who are attached to the country containing it, the laws which protect it, and the peace which preserves it...A country governed by property-owners belongs to the social order, one governed by those without property is in a state of nature.

Nobody had ever believed, even before 1789, that those who had no property should have any say in public affairs. But before 1789 property was not the sole, or even perhaps the most important qualification. There was also nobility, birth, privilege—qualities which (at least in theory) had nothing to do with property but which gave those who possessed them certain intangible but nevertheless real advantages over those who did not. It is true that by the 1780s these advantages perhaps meant less than they once had; and that, as in England, a community of property-owners was beginning to emerge among whom distinctions of birth were secondary. But the convocation of the estates-general resurrected the old, moribund distinctions for electoral purposes, invidiously imposing political disadvantages on all those, men of property or not, who were not nobles. It was this insistence on distinguishing between men whose possessions made them equal that turned the bourgeoisie so vehemently against the 'privileged orders' and against 'aristocracy'. Even so, they attacked nobility, not noble property. The attack on 'feudalism' was not their doing, but the work of the peasants. The bourgeoisie tried to ensure that the losers should be compensated, even though most of the latter were nobles. And the only nobles who forfeited their lands in subsequent years were those who proved themselves traitors by emigrating or otherwise breaking the law. The property of the rest went unmolested. In fact, under the constitutions of 1791 and 1795, as property-owners former nobles were guaranteed a say in the future government of the country. The Revolution had replaced a society dominated by nobles, with one dominated by landed notables, most of whom were bourgeois and no longer ashamed to be so.

It is true that not all bourgeois who lived through the Revolution gained from it. The merchants of the western ports were badly hit by the collapse of overseas trade. Manufacturers of luxury goods saw their markets shrink with the disappearance of noble ostentation. *Rentiers* suffered from the payment of their annuities in depreciating *assignats* and the eventual loss of most of their investments in the bankruptcy of 1797. Nevertheless, since most bourgeois had gained far more than they had lost, they had a huge vested interest in the survival of the Revolution's main work. It also left them increasingly worried by the inability of successive regimes to restore stability on this basis. In setting their face against a return to 1793 (with its price-controls, taxes on the rich, and popular power) and a restoration of church and king (with its threat to restore the old autocracy and the confiscated ecclesiastical lands), the Directors had widespread bourgeois support. But

---

[15] Quoted in A. Mathiez, *After Robespierre: the Thermidorian Reaction* (1931), 237.

their failure to make these policies work gradually produced disillusionment. By 1799 the notables were prepared to sacrifice the blessings of constitutional life, if that was what was required to guarantee them the secure enjoyment of the previous decade's gains.

The triumph of the French bourgeoisie served as an example and an inspiration to fellow bourgeois in other countries throughout the next century. But contemporaries felt less sure about its lessons. What most non-French bourgeois noticed, in the 1790s, were the excesses of popular power, the terror and apparent anarchy. Most of them shrank from the risk of similar disorders which might be provoked by too reckless agitation for political rights. In England, by the mid-1790s, calls among the Protestant dissenters for extension of the franchise and repeal of civil disabilities had much diminished. Parliamentary reform had lost most of its friends outside the corresponding societies, and had been postponed by at least a generation. Similarly, the Catholic bourgeoisie of Ireland placed its hopes of obtaining full civil rights in co-operation with, rather than by agitation against, the British government. The United Irish revolutionaries had to look for most of their support among the peasantry. Only in countries where the French armies penetrated did local bourgeois spring to prominence and find themselves for the first time possessed of political power; and these gains were often made at the cost of branding themselves as traitors by co-operating with foreign invaders. Only where a strong and coherent bourgeois political movement had already existed before the French arrived did a puppet bourgeois regime win any widespread recognition of legitimacy from its subjects—and so the only continental bourgeoisie outside France to reap permanent political benefits from the Revolution was the Dutch. And even these were acquired at the cost of endangering bourgeois fortunes in the commercial catastrophe of war against England.

*   *   *

The triumph of the Revolution, partial though it was, meant the end of the old order. Even those who dreamed of bringing that order back, no longer thought in ways that it would have recognized. New ideologies had emerged; old orthodoxies had been thrown off. Politics had been transformed; over much of Europe the old prescriptive, irrational, haphazard thicket of liberties, privileges, and endlessly overlapping jurisdictions had been swept away, the soil on which it had grown permanently eroded. But the Revolution had done nothing to arrest some of the deeper trends present long before 1789—the growth in state power, the accelerating pace of economic change, the growing strength of the British and Russian empires. The crisis which brought the downfall of the old European order had resulted from attempts to resist such developments and their implications. It broke under the strain. But when the paroxysm which resulted from this breakdown was over, the underlying trends re-emerged more strongly than ever. The Revolution had merely destroyed most of what still stood in their way.

Bibliography

General

General surveys of parts of this period abound, although studies of the whole of it are rare. Most tend to end either at 1715 or at 1789. The most detailed in English is contained in volumes v–viii of the *New Cambridge Modern History* (1957–70), though some of the volumes are rather patchy both in quality and coverage. For the political history of certain obscure areas the old *Cambridge Modern History* continues to be useful. The six relevant volumes in the American *Rise of Modern Europe* series (ed. W. L. Langer) are now very dated, though full of detail. Curiously lacking in lustre are the revised volumes of the French *Peuples et Civilisations* series: R. Mandrou, *Louis XIV en son temps 1661–1715* (1973) and A. Soboul, G. Lemarchand, and M. Fogel, *Le Siècle des Lumières, I l'Essor 1715–1750*, 2 vols. (1977). The same might be said of Mandrou's *La Raison du Prince: L'Europe Absolutiste 1649–1775* (1980). Since the war the French have been happier approaching their history thematically, concentrating on the structure of human society rather than the train of events. This approach is brilliantly exemplified by P. Chaunu, *La Civilisation de l'Europe classique* (1966), and *La Civilisation de l'Europe des lumières* (1971). The nearest things to such analyses in English are G. N. Clark's old but still impressive *The Seventeenth Century* (1929), R. M. Hatton, *Europe in the Age of Louis XIV* (1969), or the lavishly illustrated collection by a group of distinguished scholars, edited by Alfred Cobban, *The Eighteenth Century* (1969).

Good concise surveys in English of the more traditional sort are in the Longmans' *General History of Europe* series: D. H. Pennington, *Seventeenth Century Europe* (1970), M. S. Anderson, *Europe in the Eighteenth Century* (3rd edn., 1987), and F. L. Ford, *Europe: 1780–1830* (1970). E. N. Williams, *The Ancien Regime in Europe: government and society in the major states 1648–1789* (1970), is a competent review, though limited in scope and very conventional in approach. G. R. R. Treasure, *The Making of Modern Europe, 1648–1780* (1985) sets out more imaginatively, but also ends up in a conventional mould. Shorter, and illustrated, is the American survey by I. Woloch, *Eighteenth Century Europe: Tradition and Progress 1715–1789* (1980), but the most valuable recent one-volume works, packed with unusual information, are T. Munck, *Seventeenth Century Europe 1598–1700* (1990) and J. Black, *Eighteenth Century Europe 1700–1789* (1990). Important segments of the period are covered in J. W. Stoye's thoughtful *Europe Unfolding 1648–1688* (1969) and its companion volumes in the Fontana *History of Europe* series, O. Hufton, *Europe: Privilege and Protest 1730–1789* (1980), and G. Rudé, *Revolutionary Europe 1783–1815* (1964).

The *economic history* of this period is increasingly treated separately. The most exciting approach here covers a wide chronological range, but is consistently relevant: F. Braudel, *Civilisation and Capitalism, 15th–18th Centuries*, 3 vols. (1981–4). Its third volume owes a lot to I. Wallerstein, *The*

Modern World-System, 3 vols. (1974–90). More concise, less ambitious, but less tendentious treatments are R. Davis, *The Rise of the Atlantic Economies* (1973), and J. de Vries, *The Economy of Europe in an age of Crisis 1600–1750* (1976). Volumes 2, 3 and 4 of *The Fontana Economic History of Europe*, edited by C. M. Cipolla (1973–6) are also extremely valuable.

National Histories vary in quality. For seventeenth-century *England* a reliable guide is B. Coward, *The Stuart Age: A History of England 1603–1714* (1980), while for the succeeding century the most exciting and readable introduction is R. Porter, *English Society in the Eighteenth Century* (1982). The middle years are also covered in the first volume of the *New Oxford History of England*: P. Langford, *A Polite and Commercial People: England 1727–1783* (1989). *Scotland* is covered in T. C. Smout's model *History of the Scottish People 1560–1830* (1969) and *Ireland* by volume 4 of the *New History of Ireland*, edited by T. W. Moody and W. E. Vaughan (1986) or, more concisely, D. Dickson, *New Foundations: Ireland 1660–1800* (1987).

General books on *French history* are surprisingly rare, and for this period volumes VII–IX of E. Lavisse (ed.), *Histoire de France* (1906–10) have yet to be replaced. A concise set of little books by H. Méthivier, *Le Siècle de Louis XIV* (1950), *Le Siècle de Louis XV* (1966), and *La Fin de l'ancien régime* (1970) give the political outlines, but are marred by insular reading and perverse interpretations. They were republished as a single volume, *L'Ancien Régime en France*, in 1981. Economic and social history are covered in F. Braudel and E. Labrousse, *Histoire économique et sociale de la France*, ii, *1660–1789* (1970), but the work is maddeningly arranged and often written in a foggy style. A much crisper interpretation is P. Goubert's two-volume *l'Ancien Régime* (1969–73), the first volume of which is available in English translation (1973). An interesting interpretative essay in English is C. B. A. Behrens, *The Ancien Régime* (1967). A. Cobban's *A History of Modern France,* i, *Old Regime and Revolution 1715–1799* (1957), badly needs to be replaced; until it is J. Lough, *An Introduction to Eighteenth Century France* (1960), is probably a better first approach. For the revolutionary period, however, there is the excellent and up-to-date D. M. G. Sutherland, *France 1789–1815: Revolution and Counter-Revolution* (1985).

On *Spain* J. Lynch, *Spain under the Habsburgs*, vol. ii (1969), is a first-rate textbook on the seventeenth century, and it now has a sequel in *Bourbon Spain, 1700–1808* (1989). For more detail, a lifetime's study is distilled into R. Herr, *Rural Change and Royal Finances in Spain at the End of the Old Regime* (1991). Much remains to be said about *Portugal* but the outlines can be got from H. Livermore, *A New History of Portugal* (1966), and there is a surprising amount on domestic matters in C. R. Boxer, *The Portuguese Seaborne Empire 1415–1825* (1969). A more limited chronological range is covered in depth by C. A. Hanson, *Economy and Society in Baroque Portugal 1668–1708* (1981).

Settecento Riformatore, with six volumes out so far (1969–87) is F. Venturi's monumental survey of Enlightenment Italy. A more concise view by his pupils is D. Caparnetto and G. Ricuperati, *Italy in the Age of Reason 1685–1789* (1987). A French approach is J. Delumeau, *L'Italie de Botticelli à Bonaparte* (1974). Vols. ii and iii of D. Mack Smith, *A History of Sicily* (1968–9), are packed with useful information.

The standard history of *Germany* in English is that by Hajo Holborn. Vol. ii (1964) covers this period. So does R. Vierhaus, *Germany in the Age of*

Absolutism (1988). A deep and thought-provoking introduction to seventeenth-century *Austria* is R. J. W. Evans, *The Making of the Habsburg Monarchy 1550–1700* (1979). Much lighter for the eighteenth century is E. Wangermann, *The Austrian Achievement 1700–1800* (1973), but it was written before the magisterial P. G. M. Dickson, *Finance and Government under Maria Theresia*, 2 vols. (1987) and v. 1 of D. E. D. Beales, *Joseph II* (1987). For *Hungary* the detail in H. Marczali, *Hungary in the Eighteenth Century* (1910), is still unmatched, although E. Palmenji (ed.), *A History of Hungary* (1975), shows the results of more modern research. The history of *Prussia* continues to be written largely in terms of monarchs. F. L. Carsten, *The Origins of Prussia* (1954), has useful late chapters on the great elector, and F. Schevill (1947) has written a critical biography of him. Of the endless (and for the most part astonishingly useless) series of books on Frederick II, one of the most sensible is the biography by W. Hubatsch (1976). H. Brunschwig, *Enlightenment and Romanticism in Prussia* (Eng. trans. 1975), has an unconvincing argument, but is very informative.

Modern work on *northern Europe* is brought together in P. Jeannin, *L'Europe du nord-ouest et du nord aux XVIIe et XVIIIe siècles* (1969). The *Dutch republic* in the seventeenth century is well covered by works like P. Geyl, *The Netherlands in the Seventeenth Century*, ii *(1648–1715)* (1964), and K. D. H. Haley, *The Dutch in the Seventeenth Century* (1972). The following century is much less well served. One must go back to P. J. Blok, *History of the People of the Netherlands* v. 5 (1912), or glean information from C. R. Boxer's *The Dutch Seaborne Empire 1600–1800* (1965). *Sweden* is now served by a fine general history, C. Nordmann, *Grandeur et liberté de la Suède 1660–1792* (1971) and it is treated alongside other nordic countries in D. Kirby, *Northern Europe in the Early Modern Period: The Baltic World 1492–1772* (1990) and H. A. Barton, *Scandinavia in the Revolutionary Era 1760–1815* (1986).

N. Davis, *God's Playground* v. 1 (1981) is now the standard introduction in English to early modern Poland down to 1795; it may be supplemented by J. T. Lukowski, *Liberty's Folly: The Polish-Lithuanian Commonwealth in the Eighteenth Century* (1991). There is a wide choice on *Russia*. M. T. Florinsky, *Russia: a history and an interpretation* (1953), is valuable and full, while more detail can be found in M. S. Anderson, *Peter the Great* (1978) and I. de Madariaga, *Russia in the Age of Catherine the Great* (1981).

Introductory

The literature on the 'seventeenth-century crisis' is already immense, although it only emerged as a concept in the early 1950s. The major articles in English are collected in T. H. Aston (ed.), *Crisis in Europe 1560–1660* (1965). Attempts continue to be made to fit it into general surveys of the period. One of the most successful and thought-provoking is H. Kamen, *European Society 1500–1700* (1980); another is C. Wilson, *The Transformation of Europe 1558–1648* (1975). The most concise assault on the problem is T. K. Rabb, *The Struggle for Stability in Early Modern Europe* (1975). For arguments that nothing specially critical has been proved about seventeenth-century events, see J. P. Cooper's introduction to the *New Cambridge Modern History*, vol. iv (1970), and J. H. Elliott, 'Revolution and Continuity in Early Modern Europe', *Past and Present* 42 (1969). That would not, however, be the view of the recent, brilliant, J. A. Goldstone, *Revolution and Rebellion in the Early Modern World* (1991).

Chapter 1

Historical demography is making such rapid strides that no bibliography could hope to be useful for long. The major achievements of the 1950s and early 1960s are collected in D. V. Glass and D. E. C. Eversley (eds.), *Population in History* (1965). New developments are periodically incorporated into reissues of sound French manuals such as M. Reinhard and A. Armengaud, *Histoire générale de la population mondiale* (1961), or P. Guillaume and J. P. Poussou, *Démographie historique* (1970). English population has now been definitively mapped by E. A. Wrigley and R. Schofield, *The Population History of England 1541–1871* (1989), as has that of France by J. Dupâquier and his collaborators in *Histoire de la Population Française, II De la Renaissance à 1789* (1988). Both have relevance beyond the countries they examine. A wide-ranging treatment of plague is J. N. Biraben, *Les Hommes et la peste en France et dans les pays européens et méditerranéens*, 2 vols. (1976).

Prices are dealt with in a general way in ch. VII of the *Cambridge Economic History of Europe*, vol. IV. More specific studies of fundamental importance are E. J. Hamilton, *War and Prices in Spain 1651–1800* (1947), J. Thorold Rogers, *History of Agriculture and Prices in England*, 7 vols. (1866–1902), N. W. Posthumus, *Inquiry into the History of Prices in Holland*, 2 vols. (1946–64) and Ernest Labrousse, *Esquisse du mouvement des prix et des revenus en France au XVIIIᵉ siècle*, 2 vols. (1933). These classic accounts are all now subject to reservations, but they still form the basis of all serious study. A vitally important contribution to their assessment is M. Morineau, 'De quelle réalité l'histoire des prix est-elle le miroir?', *Annales E.S.C.* (1968).

The standard introduction to *agricultural questions* is still B. H. Slicher van Bath, *The Agrarian History of Western Europe A.D. 500–1850* (1962), a remarkable work of synthesis with a useful bibliography. Useful too, especially for the east, is W. Abel, *Agricultural Fluctuations in Europe from the Thirteenth to the Twentieth Centuries* (1970). Russia is generally covered by J. Blum, *Lord and Peasant in Russia from the ninth to the nineteenth century* (1961), and in more detail by M. Confino, *Domaines et seigneuries en Russie* (1966). Blum casts his net more widely in *The End of the Old Order in Rural Europe* (1978), although not all that he trawls up is entirely acceptable. On *Austria* E. M. Link, *The Emancipation of the Austrian Peasant 1740–1798* (1949), is sketchy, but there is useful detail in B. M. Kiraly, *Hungary in the later eighteenth century* (1969). *Poland* is covered by W. Kula, *An Economic Theory of the Feudal System* (English trans. 1976), and J. Topolski, 'La régression économique en Pologne du XVIᵉ au XVIIIᵉ siècle', *Acta Poloniae Historica*, vii (1962), while 'feudalism' in general is dealt with in a very useful series of articles in *Annales historiques de la Révolution Française* (1969), 155–371. *Swedish* agriculture is fully treated in E. F. Heckscher's *Economic History of Sweden* (1954) and *Spanish* in J. Vicens Vives, *Economic History of Spain* (1969). R. Forster, 'Obstacles to agricultural growth in eighteenth century France', *American Historical Review* (1970) and P. M. Jones, *The Peasantry and the French Revolution* (1989), are useful discussions on *France*, while M. Morineau, *Les Faux-Semblants d'un démarrage économique: agriculture et démographie en France au XVIIIᵉ siècle* (1971), conclusively resolves a central controversy. P. Goubert, *Cent mille provinciaux au XVIIᵉ siècle* (1968), and E. Le Roy Ladurie, *Paysans de Languedoc* (1969), are convenient distillations of their authors' monumental theses. *Dutch* agriculture figures prominently in Slicher van Bath, op. cit., but see too his 'The rise of intensive husbandry in the Netherlands' in J. S. Bromley and E. H. Kossman (eds.), *Britain and the Netherlands*, i (1960). On *Catalonia* P. Vilar, *La Catalogne dans l'Espagne moderne*, 3 vols. (1962), will yield, with some burrowing, all that anyone might wish to know. Fundamental finally on *England* are E. Kerridge, *The Agricultural Revolution* (1967), who convincingly challenges the traditional view that it was mainly an eighteenth-century phenomenon, a view outlined in J. D. Chambers and G. E. Mingay, *The Agricultural Revolution 1750–1880* (1966). The latest state of the question is summarized in J. V. Beckett, *The Agricultural Revolution* (1990). Useful compilations of articles are W. E. Minchinton (ed.), *Essays in Agrarian History*, 2 vols. (1968), and E. L. Jones, *Agriculture and Economic Growth, 1650–1815* (1967). Jones' 'Agricultural origins of industry', *Past and Present* 40 (1968), is also very stimulating.

Chapter 2

Many works on towns are covered in the bibliography to Chapter 6 (below). On their economic role the pioneering work is R. Mols, *Introduction à la démographie historique des villes d'Europe du XIVe au XVIIIe siècle*, 3 vols. (1954–6). A further generation's work was synthesized in 1984 by J. de Vries, *European Urbanisation 1500–1800*, building on such landmarks as E. A. Wrigley, 'A simple model of London's importance in changing English society and economy, 1650–1750', *Past and Present* 37 (1967). An important two-volume collection of essays is J. P. Poussou, J. Meyer, *et al.*, *Études sur les Villes en Europe Occidentale* (Paris, 1983). G. Roupnel, *La Ville et la campagne au XVIIe siècle: étude sur les populations du pays Dijonnais* (1936), is a beautifully written classic. The standard work on guilds in France is E. Coornaert, *Les Corporations en France avant 1789* (1941) but it has now been largely superseded by M. Sonenscher, *Work and Wages: Natural Law, Politics and the Eighteenth Century French trades* (1989). On the structure of wealth, and attitudes to investment, G. V. Taylor, 'Noncapitalist wealth and the origins of the French Revolution', *American Historical Review* (1967), is of wider relevance than its title suggests. Monetary history in this period is surveyed by P. Vilar, *A History of Gold and Money 1450–1920* (Eng. trans. 1976); the finest study of European banking is H. Lüthy, *La Banque Protestante en France de la révocation de l'Edit de Nantes à la Révolution*, 2 vols. (1956–61), but the work of J. F. Bosher (cited in the footnotes, p. 38) has added significantly to our knowledge. The same could be said, in the case of England, for P. G. M. Dickson, *The Financial Revolution in England* (1967). There is more available on the industrial revolution than on the economic organization it replaced, but most works begin by surveying the old order. The most important treatments of the problem of 'take-off' are W. W. Rostow, *The Stages of Economic Growth* (1960)—which coined the term—and D. S. Landes, *The Unbound Prometheus: technological change in Europe since 1750* (1969). A fine economic history of England on the eve of industrialization is C. Wilson, *England's Apprenticeship 1603–1767* (1965). The early chapters of W. L. Blackwell, *The Beginnings of Russian Industrialisation 1800–1860* (1968) look at Europe's other major industrial region, and W. O. Henderson, *Studies in the Economic Policy of Frederick the Great* (1963), deals with Prussia. P. Deane, *The First Industrial Revolution* (1965), is by now a much reissued classic. Useful too for England are the early chapters of P. Mathias, *The First Industrial Nation* (1969). *The Causes* *of the Industrial Revolution in England* edited by R. M. Hartwell (1967), is a convenient collection of key articles, including a brilliant comparison of French and English growth by F. Crouzet. The early chapters of A. S. Milward and S. B. Saul, *The Economic Development of Continental Europe 1780–1880* (1973), give a picture of the industrial situation on the mainland at the end of this period, as does C. Trebilcock, *The Industrialisation of the Continental Powers 1780–1914* (1981), and no booklist would be complete without mentioning E. Labrousse's monumental (but sadly unfinished) work *La Crise de l'économie française à la fin de l'ancien régime et au début de la Révolution* (1944).

Chapter 3

There are a number of good general works on European activity overseas in this period. An outstanding synthesis on the earlier part is K. G. Davies, *The North Atlantic World in the Seventeenth Century* (1975), while activity further east is studied in N. Steensgard, *The Asian Trade Revolution of the Seventeenth Century* (1975). A sound survey of the later period is G. Williams, *The Expansion of Europe in the Eighteenth Century* (1966); J. H. Parry, *Trade and Dominion: the European Overseas Empires in the Eighteenth Century* (1971), is a more interpretative treatment. M. Devèze, *L'Europe et le monde à la fin du XVIIIe siècle* (1970), is much broader in chronological scope than it sounds, and its geographical sweep is impressive. M. Savelle, *Empires to Nations: Expansion in America 1713–1824* (1975), is a comparative treatment of all the transatlantic colonies, while their integration with Europe is the subject of P. K. Liss, *Atlantic Empires: The Network of Trade and Revolution 1713–1826* (1983). Histories of individual empires are also useful, notably J. H. Parry, *The Spanish Seaborne Empire* (1966), and C. R. Boxer's studies of the Dutch and Portuguese empires (cited above, pp. 380 and 381). Boxer's *The Golden Age of Brazil 1695–1750* (1962) is a fine individual study as is J. Israel, *Dutch Primacy in World Trade, 1585–1740* (1989). A major contribution to French colonial history is J. Tarrade, *Le Commerce colonial de la France à la fin de l'ancien régime; l'évolution du régime de l'Exclusif de 1763 à 1789* (1972); the growth of France's most spectacular port is analysed in P. Butel, *Les Négociants bordelais: l'Europe et les Îles au XVIIIe siècle* (1974), and one of the fastest-growing sectors of trade in this century is surveyed in L. Dermigny, *La Chine et l'occident. Le Commerce à Canton au XVIIIe siècle (1719–1833)* (1964). V. T. Harlow, *The Founding of the Second British Empire 1763–93*, 2 vols. (1952–64), is now a classic. R. Davis, *A Commercial Revolution. English Overseas Trade in the Seventeenth and Eighteenth Centuries* (1967), briefly synthesizes a lifetime's work in the field. The major modern study of *Mercantilism* is E. F. Heckscher's work of that title (Eng. trans. 1931). Developments in historiography since that time can be followed in D. C. Coleman, *Revisions in Mercantilism* (1969), and P. Deyon, *Le Mercantilisme* (1969). R. L. Meek critically analyses extracts from the French economists in *The Economics of Physiocracy* (1962), and in *Precursors of Adam Smith 1750–1775* (1973) he casts a wider net. The standard work of Physiocracy is still G. Weulersse, *Le Mouvement physiocratique en France de 1756 à 1770*, 2 vols. (1910). Three successor volumes take the story down to the Revolution. Smith's *Wealth of Nations* is easily available in several good editions and still reads wonderfully well.

There has been an explosion of writing on slavery in the last twenty years.

Most works feel obliged to survey the previous literature. D. B. Davis, *The Problem of Slavery in the Age of Revolution 1770–1823* (1975) is a fine exploration of the question's subtleties, while R. Anstey, *The Atlantic Slave Trade and British Abolition 1760–1810* (1975), briskly and convincingly resolves a number of controversial issues. A lively and polemical overview is R. Blackburn, *The Overthrow of Colonial Slavery 1776–1848* (1988), while a more sober analysis comes from D. Eltis, *Economic Growth and the Ending of the Transatlantic Slave Trade* (1987).

Chapter 4

A comprehensive catalogue of the main features of Europe's ruling orders can be found in M. L. Bush, *Noble Privilege* (1983) and *Rich Noble, Poor Noble* (1988), while J. K. Powis, *Aristocracy* (1984) reflects pithily on problems of interpretation. Very old now, but still useful, are the essays in A. Goodwin (ed.), *The European Nobility in the Eighteenth Century* (1953). A more recent survey in French is J. Meyer, *Noblesses et pouvoirs dans l'Europe d'Ancien Régime* (1973), which makes a real attempt to view the problems of nobilities as a whole. Their military involvement is examined in A. Corvisier, *Armies and Societies in Europe, 1494–1789* (Eng. trans. 1979). A sound and readable survey of the English ruling orders is J. V. Beckett, *The Aristocracy in England 1660–1914* (1986), while M. L. Bush, *The English Aristocracy: A Comparative Synthesis* (1984) puts them in a continental context. English-language contributions to discussions of the French nobility can be found in D. Johnson (ed.), *French Society and the Revolution* (1976), a collection of articles from *Past and Present*. The most provocative recent French treatment is G. Chaussinand-Nogaret, *The French Nobility in the Eighteenth Century* (1976, Eng. trans. 1985). In *Origins of the Russian Intelligentsia* (1966), M. Raeff provides a convenient survey of the question in Russia, and R. E. Jones, *The Emancipation of the Russian Nobility 1762–1785* (1973), is even better. The most convenient work on Prussia, H. Rosenberg's *Bureaucracy, Aristocracy and Autocracy: the Prussian Experience 1660–1815* (1958) is very schematic and not as helpful as one might hope. For other areas, material has often to be gleaned from more general works, such as B. K. Kiraly's *Hungary in the later Eighteenth Century* (1969). Much material on landownership can be found in the French collection *L'Abolition de la féodalité dans le monde occidental*, 2 vols. (1971); while J. P. Cooper, 'Patterns of inheritance and settlement by great landowners from the fifteenth to the eighteenth centuries' in J. Goody, J. Thirsk, and E. P. Thompson (eds.), *Family and Inheritance: Rural Society in Western Europe 1200–1800* (1976), is a dense and difficult survey, but brings together a wide range of very disparate material.

Chapter 5

The study of peasant life was brilliantly renewed in the last generation by a number of outstanding theses on the French peasantry. The most influential, were P. Goubert, *Beauvais et le Beauvaisis de 1600 à 1730* (1960) and E. Le Roy Ladurie, *Les Paysans de Languedoc*, 2 vols. (1966). The study of the peasantry is consequently much further advanced for France than for most other countries. On the psychology of rural life G. Lefebvre, *The Great Fear of 1789* (1973), first published in 1932, remains an influential classic. A convenient synthesis for the earlier period is P. Goubert, *The French Peasantry in the Seventeenth Century* (Eng. trans. 1986), while P. M. Jones, *The Peasantry in the French Revolution* (1989) does the same for the later. The study of poverty in France has been renewed for English-speaking readers by O. H. Hufton, *The Poor of Eighteenth Century France, 1750–1789* (1975), which draws heavily upon, and points the way to, all the latest French work; the same author provides a useful introductory sketch of Europe as a whole, 'Life and death among the very poor' in A. Cobban (ed.), *The Eighteenth Century* (1969). J. Blum, *The End of the Old Order in Rural Europe* (1978) chronicles the abolition of the various forms of servitude, building upon his earlier *Lord and Peasant in Russia from the Ninth to the Nineteenth Century* (1961), which concentrates heavily, despite its title, on this period. There is no work on the Habsburg lands as a whole, but in addition to the study by E. M. Link (cited in the footnotes), W. E. Wright, *Serf, Seigneur and Sovereign: agrarian reform in eighteenth century Bohemia* (1966), provides a useful case study. Arthur Young's *Tour in Ireland* (1780) is the most vivid account of conditions there, although he should be read in the corrective light of L. M. Cullen, *Economic History of Ireland since 1660* (1972) and the essays in C. H. F. Philpin (ed.), *Nationalism and Popular Protest in Ireland* (1987). The classic account of the English peasantry faced by enclosure, J. L. and B. Hammond, *The Village Labourer* (1911), is beautifully written and powerful to read, but largely rejected for its dramatic exaggerations by later historians. The more sober view is reflected in J. D. Chambers and G. E. Mingay, *The Agricultural Revolution* (1966). Passion however still guides some of the most stimulating work on English rural disturbances. See, for example, E. P. Thompson, 'The moral economy of the English crowd in the eighteenth century', *Past and Present* 50 (1971), and his study of game legislation, *Whigs and Hunters* (1975). Rural unrest is authoritatively discussed in Y. M. Bercé, *Revolt and Revolution in Early Modern Europe* (1987), while P. Burke offers a stimulating and wide-ranging account of *Popular Culture in Early Modern Europe* (1978). A standard treatment of crime and its influence is J. M. Beattie, *Crime and the Courts in England 1660–1800* (1986).

Chapter 6

Urban history had undergone a striking rebirth, and this period has been one of the most notable beneficiaries. Here again, the French have taken the lead, with impressive theses on particular towns such as that of Garden on Lyons (cited in the footnotes), P. Deyon, *Amiens, capitale provinciale* (1967), J. C. Perrot, *Genèse d'une ville moderne: Caen au XVIIIe siècle* (1975), or J. P. Bardet, *Rouen aux XVIIe et XVIIIe siècles*, 2 vols. (1983). Paris itself has not been studied on such a scale, but J. Kaplow, *The Names of Kings: Parisian labouring poor in the eighteenth century* (1972), is a passionate and extremely useful survey of one group analysed from a different angle by D. Roche, *The People of Paris* (Eng. trans. 1987). For Russia are interesting approach is J. T. Alexander, 'Catherine II, bubonic plague and the problem of industry in Moscow', *American H. R.* (1974). Among German towns, Mainz has been particularly well covered by two outstanding works written from different yet complementary angles: F. G. Dreyfus, *Sociétés et mentalités à Mayence dans la seconde moitié du XVIIIe siècle* (1968), and T. C. W. Blanning, *Reform and Revolution in Mainz 1743–1803* (1974). Exemplary works on Italy are J. Georgelin, *Venise au siècle des Lumières* (1978) and H. Gross, *Rome in the Age of Enlightenment* (1990). In

England only London has so far received attention on this scale—see M. D. George's classic *London Life in the Eighteenth Century* (1925). For a more recent selection of work, see P. A. Clark, *Urban History: a reader* (1976) and P. Borsay, *The English Urban Renaissance: Culture and Society in the Provincial Town 1660–1770* (1989). The problems of the urban poor are treated by O. H. Hufton for France (cited above, p. 386), D. Marshall, *The English Poor in the Eighteenth Century* (1926), for England, and more generally by J. P. Gutton, *La Société et les pauvres en Europe XVIᵉ–XVIIIᵉ siècles* (1974). G. Rudé, *The Crowd in History 1730–1848* (1964), compares popular disturbances in England and France. For servants there is S. Maza, *Servants and Masters in Eighteenth Century France* (1983) and J. J. Hecht, *The Domestic Servant Class in Eighteenth Century England* (1956), both very useful studies—but not all servants were domestic; see P. Laslett and R. Wall (eds.), *Household and Family in Past Time* (1972). On the vexed question of the bourgeoisie the essential modern starting-point is chs. 3 and 6 of A. Cobban, *The Social Interpretation of the French Revolution* (1964). Where the debate has led from there can best be followed in G. V. Taylor, 'Non-capitalist wealth and the origins of the French Revolution', *American Historical Review* (1967), and C. Lucas, 'Nobles, bourgeois and the origins of the French Revolution', *Past and Present* 60 (1973), the latter reprinted in D. Johnson (ed.), *French Society and the Revolution* (1976).

Chapter 7

A convenient and general introduction to religious history is G. R. Cragg, *The Church in the Age of Reason (1648–1789)* (1960). For the Catholic church, a brilliant survey of the problems, and an extensive bibliography, is to be found in the work of J. Delumeau, cited in the chapter footnotes. Volume 19 of Fliche and Martin's *Histoire de l'Église* by E. Préclin and E. Jarry (1955–6) is full of useful information not easily accessible elsewhere; and there are important insights in volume one of A. Latreille, *l'Église catholique et la Révolution Française* (1946). More recent research is represented by the essays in W. J. Callahan and D. Higgs (eds.), *Church and Society in Catholic Europe of the Eighteenth Century* (1979). On the decline of witchcraft, the later chapters of K. V. Thomas's impressive *Religion and the Decline of Magic* (1973) are essential reading, as is R. Mandrou, *Magistrats et sorciers en France au XVIIᵉ siècle* (1968). H. Kamen, *The Spanish Inquisition* (1965), is a useful history of that peculiar institution, while the Papacy's fortunes can be studied in vols. 31–7 of L. von Pastor's *History of the Popes* (1940–50) or O. Chadwick, *The Popes and European Revolution* (1981). For Orthodoxy and Old Belief P. Pascal, *Avvakum et les débuts du Rascol: la crise religieuse au XVIIᵉ siècle en Russie* (1938), is an important study in detail, but R. O. Crummey, *The Old Believers and the World of Antichrist* (1970) is more wide ranging. The religious history of England should be approached through the various works of Norman Sykes, notably *Church and State in England in the Eighteenth Century* (1934) and *From Sheldon to Secker* (1959). The history of nonconformity is introduced by the essays in G. F. Nuttall and O. Chadwick (eds.), *From Uniformity to Unity 1662–1962* (1962), while D. Hempton, *Methodism and Politics in British Society 1750–1850* (1984), supplements that fundamental—and surprisingly readable—source for Methodism, John Wesley's *Journal*. K. S. Pinson, *Pietism as a Factor in the Rise of German Nationalism* (1934), is misleadingly titled, for its treatment of

Pietism as a whole is full. Students of this period are fortunate in having the best book in English on Jansenism to cover one of its key episodes—D. Van Kley, *The Jansenists and the Expulsion of the Jesuits from France 1757–1765* (1975). The best concise French survey is L. Cognet, *Le Jansénisme* (1961). Religious controversy in France is covered in R. R. Palmer, *Catholics and Unbelievers in Eighteenth Century France* (1939); and J. McManners's study of Angers in the eighteenth century, *French Ecclesiastical Society under the Ancien Régime* (1960), is the most brilliant and charming single study in English of any aspect of pre-Revolutionary France.

Chapter 8

Good general works on the Enlightenment are not uncommon. The most engaging and readable are perhaps the twin volumes of P. Hazard, *The European Mind 1680–1715* (1935, Eng. trans. 1953), and *European Thought in the Eighteenth Century* (1946, Eng. trans. 1954). A more up-to-date treatment is now N. Hampson, *The Enlightenment* (1968). The fullest modern synthesis, widely acclaimed, is Peter Gay, *The Enlightenment: an Interpretation*, 2 vols. (1966–9). Its impact in individual countries emerges from R. Porter and M. Teich (eds.), *The Enlightenment in National Context* (1981). Locke's works are easily available in many editions, there is a careful biography of him by M. Cranston (1957), and an older and more comprehensive study by R. I. Aaron (1937). F. Manuel, *A Portrait of Isaac Newton* (1968) analyses the life and opinions of the other great English Enlightenment hero. A. R. Hall, *The Scientific Revolution 1500–1800* (1954), is a clear and comprehensive account of that movement, as is the same author's *From Galileo to Newton 1630–1730* (1963). A brilliant analysis of the role of religion is H. R. Trevor-Roper, 'Religious origins of the Enlightenment' in *Religion, the Reformation and Social Change* (1968). On Montesquieu, the authoritative biography is R. Shackleton, *Montesquieu: a critical biography* (1960); and E. Labrousse, *Pierre Bayle* (1963–4), 2 vols., has similar standing for its own subject. The controversy over Bayle can be approached through P. Dibon (ed.), *Pierre Bayle* (1959). On academies M. Ornstein, *The Role of the Scientific Societies in the Seventeenth Century* (1913), is still useful, while E. Cochrane, *Tradition and Enlightenment in the Tuscan Academies 1690–1800* (1961), is a good case study. French academies are exhaustively analysed in D. Roche, *Le Siècle des Lumières en Province*, 2 vols. (1978) and R. Hahn, *The Anatomy of a Scientific Institution. The Paris Academy of Sciences 1666–1803* (1971). J. Lough, *The Encyclopédie* (1971), embodies a lifetime's work on the subject, as does A. M. Wilson, *Diderot* (1972). The marketing of his great work, and its successors, is chronicled in R. Darnton, *The Business of Enlightenment: A Publishing History of the Encyclopédie 1775–1800* (1979). T. Besterman, *Voltaire* (1969), is disappointingly idiosyncratic and has not replaced either R. Pomeau, *La Religion de Voltaire* (1956) or I. O. Wade, *The Intellectual Development of Voltaire* (1970). H. T. Mason, *Voltaire: A Biography* (1981) is the best point of entry to knowledge of this massively researched figure.

Chapter 9

On Natural Religion, R. N. Stromberg's *Religious Liberalism in Eighteenth Century England* (1954) is a clear and concise discussion of English controversies.

So is R. W. Harris, *Reason and Nature in 18th Century Thought* (1968). Butler's *Analogy* and Hume's *Dialogues* are easily available in many editions; so are Paine's *Age of Reason* and Rousseau's *Emile*. The best account of Meslier is M. Dommanget, *Le Curé Meslier* (1965); T. D. Kendrick's *The Lisbon Earthquake* (1956) is an admirable study of that event. On the revocation of the Edict of Nantes W. C. Scoville, *The Persecution of the Huguenots and French Economic Development 1680–1720* (1960), remains standard and B. C. Poland, *French Protestantism and the French Revolution* (1957), is also excellent and wider in scope than its title suggests. The tercentenary in 1985 produced some notable studies, such as R. Gwynn, *Huguenot Heritage* and J. Garrisson, *L'Edit de Nantes et sa Révocation*. D. D. Bien, *The Calas Affair* (1960), is a brilliant analysis of this famous case. There is no adequate survey of the role of the Jesuits in education. On French educational theory, however, G. Snyders, *La Pédagogie en France aux XVIIe et XVIIIe siècles* (1965), is useful and stimulating, as is the massive L. W. B. Brockliss, *French Higher Education in the Seventeenth and Eighteenth Centuries: A Cultural History* (1987); very idiosyncratic on England is K. Hans, *New Trends in Education in the Eighteenth Century* (1951). P. Chevallier, *Loménie de Brienne et l'ordre monastique 1766– 1789*, 2 vols. (1959–60), describes the attack on monasticism in France, although neither this nor the fall of the Jesuits has yet been adequately studied on a European scale. The easiest introduction to Helvétius is in the volume of selections from *De l'esprit* by G. Besse (1969). For developments in the law an extremely useful volume of extracts from major theorists is James Heath, *Eighteenth Century Penal Theory* (1963). The best book on opposition to the *philosophes* is R. R. Palmer's *Catholics and Unbelievers in Eighteenth Century France* (1939). Boswell's *Life of Johnson* is a massive commentary on English intellectual life from the viewpoint of a vigorous conservative. No biographer of Rousseau has excelled his own *Confessions* but M. Cranston's two-volume *Jean-Jacques* (1983–90) offers a clear portrait. Those frustrated in the belief that enlightenment had not gone far enough are brilliantly studied in Robert Darnton, *Mesmerism and the End of the Enlightenment in France* (1967), and *The Literary Underground of the Old Regime* (1982). On Freemasonry and kindred groups J. M. Roberts, *The Mythology of the Secret Societies* (1972), is now standard.

Chapter 10

A good general introduction to states and their business remains, despite its age and arguable premisses, M. Beloff, *The Age of Absolutism 1660–1815* (1954). Important too is G. Durand, *Etats et institutions, XVIe–XVIIIe siècles* (1969). F. Durand has produced a particularly valuable survey of republican states, *Les Républiques au temps des monarchies* (1973); and there are some stimulating if not always convincing ideas in F. Venturi, *Utopia and Reform in the Enlightenment* (1971). P. Goubert, *l'Ancien Régime ii—les pouvoirs* (1973) is a valuable survey of French government, and E. Carcassonne, *Montesquieu et le problème de la constitution française au XVIIIe siècle* (1926), explores the theoretical background. *Princes and Parliaments in Germany from the fifteenth to the eighteenth century*, by F. L. Carsten (1959), gives access to some obscure but fascinating constitutional struggles. Useful material can also be found in contributions to the debate on 'Enlightened Despotism'—notably F. Bluche, *Le Despotisme éclairé* (1968) and most recently, the indispensable H. M. Scott (ed.), *Enlightened Absolutism* (1990). In a class by itself here is the brief discussion by T. C. W. Blanning, *Joseph II and Enlightened Despotism* (1970). The works of Locke, Montesquieu, and Rousseau are all easily available and do not make difficult reading. Voltaire's political attitudes are explored in P. Gay, *Voltaire's Politics: the poet as realist* (1959). Essential reading are a number of essays in P. Francastel (ed.), *Utopie et institutions au XVIIIᵉ siècle* (1963) and notably the excellent contribution by Derathé, cited in the footnotes. Derathé's *Jean-Jacques Rousseau et la science politique de son temps* (1950) also remains the best treatment of its subject. The most stimulating Marxist approach to the idea of the state in this period and beyond is P. Anderson, *Lineages of the Absolutist State* (1974). A. R. Myers, *Parliaments and Estates in Europe to 1789* (1975), brings together an immense amount of useful information, much of it covering this period, while some of the paradoxes of the way states developed are thoughtfully discussed in J. H. Shennan, *Liberty and Order in Early Modern Europe* (1986). A brilliant comparative discussion of why and how states broke down is J. A. Goldstone, *Revolution and Rebellion in the Early Modern World* (1991).

Chapter 11

Many books recommended as further reading for other chapters would also be useful here, such as A. Corvisier's *Armies and Societies in Europe 1494–1789* (1979). Authoritative too are M. S. Anderson, *War and Society in Europe of the Old Regime 1618–1789* (1988) and G. Parker, *The Military Revolution: Military Innovation and the Rise of the West (1500–1800)* (1988). D. Chandler, *The Art of Warfare in the Age of Marlborough* (1975), is a comprehensive study of one important phase of military development. Incomparably the best-documented navy is the British. Start with M. Lewis, *The Navy of Britain* (1948), and go on to the same author's *Social History of the Navy (1793–1815)* (1960), J. Ehrman, *The Navy in the War of William III 1689–97* (1953) is a superb study in detail. Important works, such as those of Dorn and Dorwart on Prussian administration, and M. Antoine's superlative account of the council of Louis XV, are cited in the chapter's footnotes. They may be supplemented by such studies as G. Pagès, *La Monarchie d'ancien régime en France* (1928)—old, but still full of stimulating ideas—or the more recent studies by H. C. Johnson, *Frederick the Great and his Officials* (1976), W. Hubatsch, *Frederick the Great: absolutism and administration* (1976) or J. P. Le Donne, *Ruling Russia: Politics and Administration in the Age of Absolutism 1762–1796* (1984). The chaos of the French financial system has been expertly and thought-provokingly disentangled by Bosher's *French Finances*; while the Austrian administration in action is exemplified in H. E. Strakosch, *State Absolutism and the Rule of Law* (1967) or P. G. M. Dickson, *Finance and Government under Maria Theresia*, 2 vols. (1987). J. T. Alexander, *Autocratic Politics in a National Crisis* (1969), studies policy-making in Russia during the Pugachev emergency, and B. Kemp, *King and Commons 1660–1832* (1957), examines how English central government worked and evolved throughout the period. J. H. Plumb, *The Growth of Political Stability in England 1675–1725* (1967), has thrown important light on this problem. The strength of the English state is the subject of J. Brewer, *The Sinews of Power: War, Money and the English State, 1688–1783* (1989), while opposition is analysed (from different angles) in A. S. Foord, *His Majesty's Opposition* (1964), and J. A. W. Gunn, *Factions No More* (1972). For France, the best treatment of the *parlements* is J. Egret, *Louis XV et l'opposition parlementaire 1715–1774* (1970), while most aspects of French political life receive coverage in K. M. Baker (ed.), *The French Revolution and the Creation of Modern Political Culture, I The Political Culture of the Old Regime* (1987).

Chapter 12

All older textbooks give very detailed attention to diplomatic history, but there is now an outstanding diplomatic history of the period in D. McKay and H. M. Scott, *The Rise of the Great Powers 1648–1815* (1983). The ideals of diplomacy are analysed with still-unsurpassed skill by the first volume of Albert Sorel's *L'Europe et la Révolution Française* (1885), published in an English translation by A. Cobban and J. W. Hunt (1969). Diplomatic institutions may be studied in A. Picavet, *La Diplomatie française au temps de Louis XIV* (1930), and D. B. Horn, *The British Diplomatic Service 1689–1789* (1961). R. M. Hatton (ed.), *Louis XIV and Europe* (1976), is a valuable collection of articles, but readers should beware of the editor's tendency to find all that Louis did justified. From this point of view J. B. Wolf, *Louis XIV* (1968), provides a more credible portrait. Hatton's *Charles XII of Sweden* (1968) is however a masterly biography and essential for any understanding of the great northern war. D. B. Horn's *Great Britain and Europe in the Eighteenth Century* (1967) surveys British relations with each major state, and his chapter on the Diplomatic Revolution in the *New Cambridge Modern History*, vii, is a superb distillation of a lifetime's study. Authoritative too is H. M. Scott, *British Foreign Policy in the Age of the American Revolution* (1990). L. J. Oliva, *Misalliance: French Policy in Russia during the Seven Years' War* (1964), is also important on this war. Dutch foreign policy and the problems confronting it are succinctly outlined in A. C. Carter, *Neutrality or Commitment: the evolution of Dutch Foreign Policy 1667–1795* (1975). B. H. Sumner, *Peter the Great and the Emergence of Russia* (1951), remains the best introduction to Russia's rise, but the early chapters of M. S. Anderson, *The Eastern Question* (1966), analyse the problems posed by this rise very clearly. The Polish dimension of this question is explained convincingly in H. H. Kaplan, *The First Partition of Poland* (1962), while Austrian ambitions can be studied in P. P. Bernard, *Joseph II and Bavaria* (1965) and D. E. D. Beales, *Joseph II* (1987).

Chapter 13

The outstanding modern approach to the crisis is volume i of R. R. Palmer, *The Age of the Democratic Revolution*, subtitled *The Challenge* (1961). It does not entirely follow the lines suggested here, but it is a brilliant and thought-provoking interpretation. A French version of the Palmer thesis was published by J. Godechot, in 1965, and has been translated as *France and the Atlantic Revolution of the Eighteenth Century* (1965). Yet another crisis is discerned by F. Venturi, *The First Crisis of the Old Regime 1768–1776* (Eng. trans. 1990), while many of the ideas to be found in Goldstone's *Revolution and Rebellion in the Early Modern World* have relevance here. The literature on the crisis in the British empire is immense. Perhaps the best introduction is I. R. Christie, *Crisis of Empire* (1966), while from an American standpoint the best approach remains Merill Jensen, *The Founding of a Nation* (1968). These works have bibliographies which cover the more detailed problems involved. The Irish crisis is covered, somewhat idiosyncratically, by R. B. McDowell, *Ireland in the Age of Imperialism and Revolution 1760–1801* (1979). Dickson's *Finance and Government under Maria Theresia* and Beales's *Joseph II* are now definitive on Austria. W. W. Davis, *Joseph II: an imperial reformer for the Austrian Netherlands* (1974), is very full, but like all other works on Joseph should be read in the light of Beales's researches. S. Schama, *Patriots and Liberators: Revolution in the Netherlands 1780–1813* (1977), replaces all previous accounts of the crisis in the northern Netherlands. On France, like America, the literature is endless. It is surveyed, and an interpretation offered, in W. Doyle, *Origins of the French Revolution* (2nd edn., 1988). Fatal turning points are suggested by J. C. Riley, *The Seven Years War and the Old Regime in France: The Economic and Financial Toll* (1986) and D. Echeverria, *The Maupeou Revolution: A Study in the History of Libertarianism: France 1770–1774* (1985). The emergence of a powerful public opinion is discussed in J. R. Censer and J. Popkin (eds.), *Press and Politics in Prerevolutionary France* (1987). J. Egret, *The French Pre-Revolution, 1787–88* (1962, Eng. trans. 1977) is the classic treatment of the regime's death throes. Out-dated in many respects thanks to more recent research, G. Lefebvre, *The Coming of the French Revolution* (Eng. trans. 1947), is still useful reading and a fine example of historical writing.

Chapter 14

No justice can be done, in a short bibliographical note, to the enormous range of writing available on the French Revolution and the decade in which it took place. The most convenient introduction is W. Doyle, *The Oxford History of the French Revolution* (1989) which takes in events outside France, as does v. 2 of Palmer's *Age of the Democratic Revolution: The Struggle* (1964). A convenient work of reference is C. Jones, *The Longman Companion to the French Revolution* (1989) while an up-to-date French perspective on Europe as a whole is J. Bérenger *et al.*, *L'Europe à la fin du XVIIIe siècle (vers 1780–1802)* (1985). J. Godechot, *The Taking of the Bastille* (1965, Eng. trans. 1970) is an excellent analysis of that event. J. McManners provides an elegant and perceptive survey of religious questions in *The French Revolution and the Church* (1969), while Parisian upheavals are best approached through G. Rudé, *The Crowd in the French Revolution* (1959). A convenient distillation of abundant recent work on Counter-Revolution is J. Roberts, *The Counter-Revolution in France 1787–1830* (1990). The Convention can no longer be understood without reference to Alison Patrick's analysis which is mentioned on p. 342. N. Hampson, *The Life and Opinions of Maximilien Robespierre* (1974), presents a dazzling and original picture of the problem of interpreting this controversial figure. The later history of Revolutionary France is well covered in M. J. Sydenham, *The First French Republic 1792–1804* (1974).

The most convenient survey of international relations is A. Fugier, *La Révolution française et l'empire napoléonien* (1954) while T. C. W. Blanning sharply analyses *The Origins of the French Revolutionary Wars* (1986). J. Godechot, *La Grande Nation* (1956), 2 vols., chronicles French expansion and Blanning, *The French Revolution in Germany* (1983) exposes its depredations with his customary verve. The situation in Russia is boldly encapsulated in the article by P. Dukes cited on p. 327, and that in Austria by Wangermann's *From Joseph II to the Jacobin Trials* (1969, 2nd edn.). There are useful chapters too in C. A. Macartney, *The Habsburg Empire in 1790–1918* (1968). The

English popular movement has had its history revolutionized by Part I of E. P. Thompson, *The Making of the English Working Class* (1963), and is compared to its French counterpart in G. A. Williams's superb brief survey *Artisans and Sansculottes* (1968), but the fullest history is now A. Goodwin, *The Friends of Liberty* (1979). Standard on the Irish situation is M. Elliott, *Partners in Revolution: The United Irishmen and France* (1982). The later chapters of R. Herr, *The Eighteenth Century Revolution in Spain* (1958) demonstrate how the crisis struck the Iberian peninsula. The middle ones of S. J. Woolf, *A History of Italy 1700–1860* (1979) do the same for that peninsula; while K. Epstein, *The Genesis of German Conservatism* (1966), explores the impact east of the Rhine.

Chapter 15

Many of the works mentioned in connection with Chapter 14 are of value here too. Fundamental reading on the impact of the Revolution as a whole is A. Cobban, *The Social Interpretation of the French Revolution* (1964), which started a series of debates which are only just over. The large questions on a European scale are raised by F. L. Ford, 'The revolutionary and Napoleonic era: how much of a watershed?', *American Historical Review* (1963), and a bleak balance sheet is drawn up for France in R. Sédillot, *Le Coût de la Révolution Française* (1987). A symposium in *French Historical Studies* (1990) shows where all the scholarly debates had reached in the year of the Revolution's bi-centenary. The path by which they reached that point is concisely charted by T. C. W. Blanning, *The French Revolution: Aristocrats Versus Bourgeois?* (1987), and there are some interesting and detached reflections in L. Hunt, *Politics, Culture and Class in the French Revolution* (1984). On the clash of ideologies J. Godechot, *The Counter-Revolution: doctrine and action 1789–1804* (Eng. trans. 1971), is illuminating; so is J. M. Roberts, *The Mythology of the Secret Societies* (1972). Much remains to be done on the Revolution's economic impact, but F. Crouzet, 'Wars, blockade and economic change in Europe, 1792–1815', *Journal of Economic History* (1964), points in a promising direction, while G. Best, *War and Society in Revolutionary Europe 1770–1870* attempts to take stock of the physical upheaval. The memory of the Revolution is evoked by E. J. Hobsbawm, *Echoes of the Marseillaise* (1990), but how much was really changed? A. J. Mayer, *The Persistence of the Old Regime* (1981) thinks that much of the Old European Order survived until 1914.

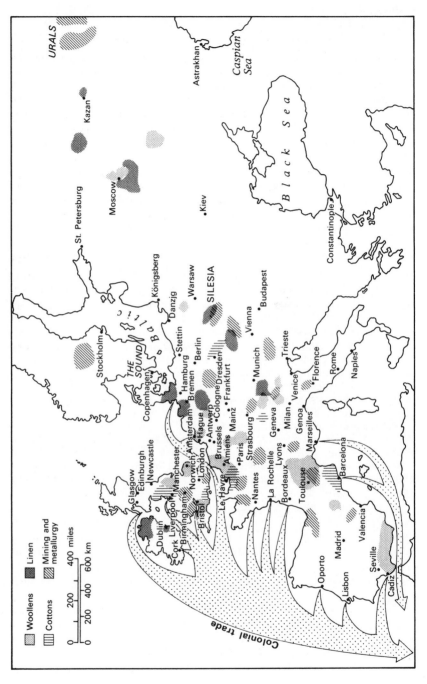

MAP I. Towns and Economic Life 1660–1800

Woollens

Cottons

Linen

Mining and metallurgy

0   200   400 miles

0   200   400   600 km

URALS

Kazan

St. Petersburg

Moscow

Kiev

Astrakhan

Caspian Sea

Black Sea

Constantinople

Königsberg

Danzig

Warsaw

SILESIA

Budapest

Vienna

Stockholm

THE SOUND

Baltic

Copenhagen

Stettin

Hamburg

Bremen

Berlin

Dresden

Cologne

Frankfurt

Mainz

Munich

Trieste

Florence

Rome

Naples

Venice

Milan

Genoa

Geneva

Strasbourg

Amiens

Paris

Lyons

Marseilles

Toulouse

Bordeaux

La Rochelle

Nantes

Le Havre

Amsterdam

Hague

Antwerp

Brussels

London

Norwich

Bristol

Birmingham

Manchester

Liverpool

Newcastle

Edinburgh

Glasgow

Dublin

Cork

Barcelona

Valencia

Madrid

Seville

Cadiz

Lisbon

Oporto

Colonial trade

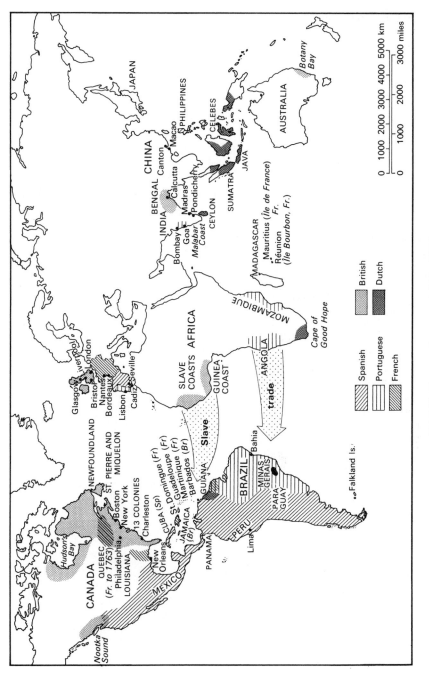

MAP II. Europe Overseas 1660–1800

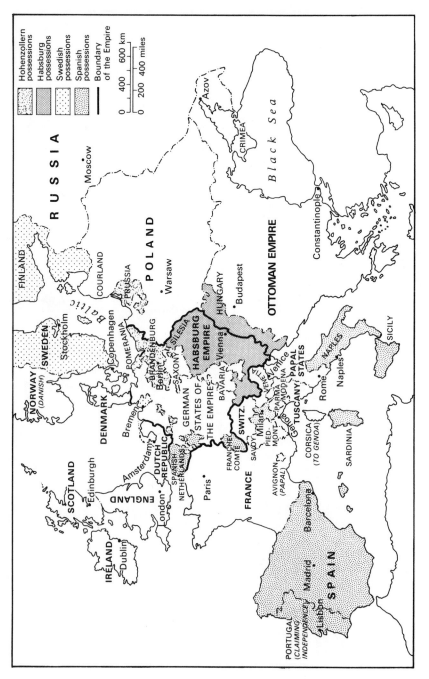

MAP III. European States in 1660

Hohenzollern
possessions

Habsburg
possessions

Swedish
possessions

Spanish
possessions

Boundary
of the Empire

0   400   600 km
0   200   400 miles

RUSSIA

Moscow

FINLAND

COURLAND

PRUSSIA

POLAND

Warsaw

CRIMEA

Azov

Black Sea

Constantinople

OTTOMAN EMPIRE

Budapest

HUNGARY

Baltic

SWEDEN

Stockholm

NORWAY
(DANISH)

DENMARK

Copenhagen

POMERANIA

BRANDENBURG

Berlin

SILESIA

SAXONY

GERMAN
STATES OF
THE EMPIRE

HABSBURG
EMPIRE

Vienna

BAVARIA

SWITZ.

VENICE
Venice

MODENA

PARMA

Milan

PIED.
MONT.

SAVOY

PAPAL
STATES

TUSCANY

Rome

Naples

NAPLES

SICILY

SARDINIA

CORSICA
(TO GENOA)

GENOA

AVIGNON
(PAPAL)

FRANCHE
COMTE

Bremen

SCOTLAND

Edinburgh

IRELAND

Dublin

ENGLAND

London

Amsterdam

DUTCH
REPUBLIC

SPANISH
NETHERLANDS

Paris

FRANCE

SPAIN

Madrid

Barcelona

Lisbon

PORTUGAL
(CLAIMING
INDEPENDENCE)

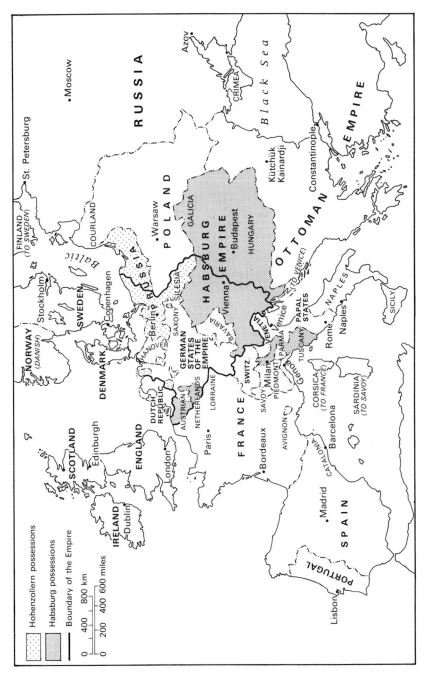

MAP IV. European States in 1789

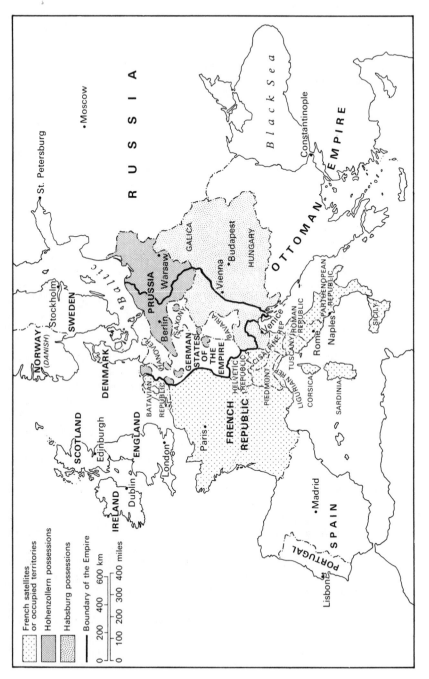

MAP V. European States c. 1800

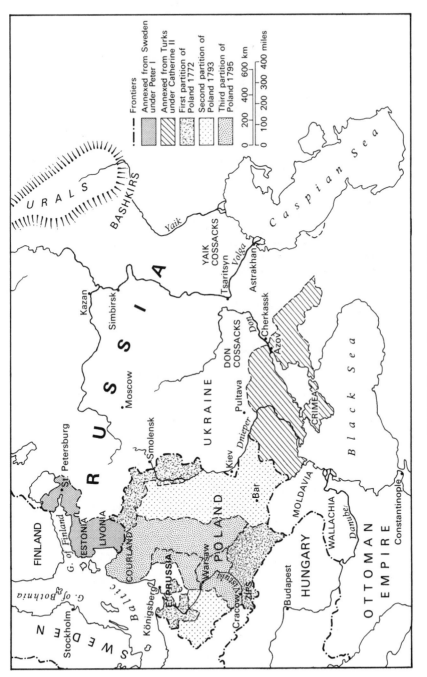

Frontiers

Annexed from Sweden
under Peter I

Annexed from Turks
under Catherine II

First partition of
Poland 1772

Second partition of
Poland 1793

Third partition of
Poland 1795

0   200   400   600 km

0   100   200   300   400 miles

URALS

BASHKIRS

Yaik

YAIK
COSSACKS

Tsaritsyn

Volga

Astrakhan

Caspian Sea

Kazan

Simbirsk

R U S S I A

Moscow

St. Petersburg

Smolensk

FINLAND

G. of Finland

ESTONIA

LIVONIA

COURLAND

G. of Bothnia

Baltic

Stockholm

S W E D E N

Königsberg

E. PRUSSIA

Warsaw

P O L A N D

ZIPS

Cracow

Budapest

HUNGARY

MOLDAVIA

WALLACHIA

Danube

Bar

Kiev

Dnieper

UKRAINE

Pultava

DON
COSSACKS

Don

Cherkassk

Azov

CRIMEA

Black Sea

OTTOMAN

EMPIRE

Constantinople

MAP VI. Eastern Europe 1660–1800

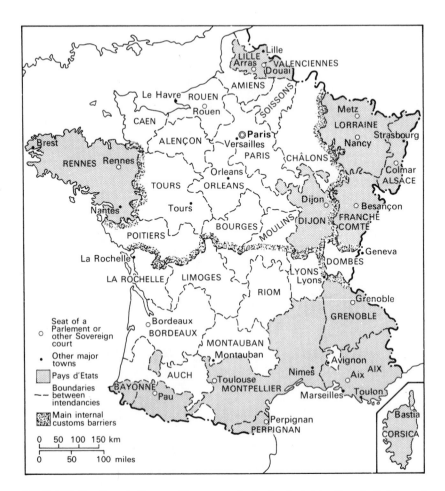

MAP VII. Pre-Revolutionary France: principal administrative, judicial, and fiscal subdivisions

TABLE

Spain (cont'd)

Ferdinand VI	1746–59
Charles III	1759–88
Charles IV	1788–1808

Sweden

Charles XI	1660–97
Charles XII	1697–1718
Ulrica Leonora	1718–20
Frederick I	1720–51
Adolphus-Frederick	1751–71
Gustavus III	1771–92
Gustavus IV	1792–1809

Russia

Alexis	1645–76
Fedor III	1676–82
Ivan V	1682–96
Peter I	1682–1725
(co-ruler 1682–96)	
Catherine I	1725–7
Peter II	1727–30
Anna	1730–40
Elizabeth	1741–62
Peter III	1762
Catherine II	1762–96
Paul	1796–1801

Brandenburg–Prussia

Frederick William (the Great Elector)	1640–88
Frederick I (of Prussia)	1688–1713
Frederick William I	1713–40
Frederick II	1740–86
Frederick William II	1786–97
Frederick William III	1797–1840

Poland

John II Casimir	1648–68
Michael Wisniowiecki	1669–73
John III Sobieski	1674–96
Augustus II (also of Saxony)	1697–1704
Stanislas Leczinski	1704–9
Augustus II	1709–33
Augustus III	1733–63
Stanislas Poniatowski	1764–95

Table 403

Dutch Republic (Stadtholders)

(Stadtholderless Republic)	1649−72
William III	1672−1702
(Stadtholderless Republic)	1702−47
William IV	1747−51
William V	1751−95
Batavian Republic	1795−1806

Popes

Alexander VII	1655−67
Clement IX	1667−9
Clement X	1670−6
Innocent XI	1676−89
Alexander VIII	1689−91
Innocent XII	1691−1700
Clement XI	1700−21
Innocent XIII	1721−4
Benedict XIII	1724−30
Clement XII	1730−40
Benedict XIV	1740−58
Clement XIII	1758−69
Clement XIV	1769−74
Pius VI	1775−99
Pius VII	1800−23

INDEX

Aachen, 42, 270, 283

Abbeville, 42

'Absolutism', 81, 224, 233, 237, 262, 263

Academies, 178, 188, 189–91, 192, 205, 208, 210, 212, 215, 216, 217

Adriatic, 223

Africa, 48, 53, 55, 56, 57

Agriculture, 11–27, 28, 33, 34, 35, 43, 44, 62, 66, 67, 68, 86, 87, 96, 104–5, 106, 113, 114, 115, 120, 122, 127, 148, 210, 247, 308, 363, 365, 376

Aix-la-Chapelle (*see* Aachen)

Alaska, 61

Alberoni, Cardinal Giulio (1664–1752), 262

Alembert, Jean Le Rond d' (1717–83), 190, 191, 192, 193, 194, 196, 204, 205, 212, 214, 217, 321

Alexei, Tsar (1629–76), 162, 163

Algarotti, Francesco (1712–64), 180

Alps, 114, 223, 337, 338, 339

Alsace, 271

America (*see* colonies, thirteen colonies, United States), 25, 38, 43, 47, 48, 49, 50, 51, 54, 55, 56, 58, 59, 60, 62, 63, 64, 65, 114, 155, 165, 206, 254, 275, 283, 284, 286, 287, 291, 297, 316, 321, 366

American Revolution (*see* thirteen colonies), 9, 35, 287–8, 290, 299–305, 311, 317, 319, 321, 327, 338, 355, 357–8, 365

Amiens, 42

Amsterdam, 28, 37, 38, 39, 146, 187, 223, 251, 311

Angers, 248

Anglican Church, 108, 119, 151, 156, 157 158, 159, 160, 161, 163–5, 171, 182, 201, 204, 232, 301, 349

Anne, Queen of Great Britain (1665–1714), 274

Anzin, 36

Aragon, 229, 257

Arc, Chevalier d' (1721–1795), 93, 94

Armed Neutrality (1780), 267, 288

Aristotle, 174, 175, 178, 179, 180

Arkwright, Richard (1732–92), 45, 46

Armies, 7, 29, 41, 80–1, 89, 93–4, 110–111, 114, 120, 124, 125, 129, 134, 145, 226, 229, 238, 239, 241–5, 246, 247, 249, 254, 255, 271, 274, 276, 277, 278, 282, 291, 296, 298, 301, 305, 307, 320, 324, 325, 335, 346, 352, 370, 374

Arminianism (*see* Latitudinarianism), 164–5, 166, 197

Arnauld, family, 168, 169
    Antoine (1612–94), 168, 169, 188

Artois, Comte d' (1757–1836), 371

Asia, 47, 58

Asia Minor, 289

Asiento, 51, 275

Assignats, 340, 342, 352, 353, 363, 366, 369, 377

Astrakhan, 123

Asturias, 105

Atheism, 194–5, 199, 200

Atlantic, 55, 61, 246, 254, 295

Augereau, Pierre François (1757–1816), 354

Augsburg, League of, 271–2

Augustus II of Saxony, king of Poland (1670–1733), 279

Augustus III of Saxony, king of Poland (1696–1763), 279, 288

Aulic Council, 227

Aurangzeb, Mughal Emperor (1658–1707), 59

Australia, 61

Austria, 6, 37, 62, 82, 97, 98, 101, 109, 157, 158, 159, 172, 202, 207, 212, 218, 221, 227, 229, 244, 250, 251, 257, 259, 260, 263, 265, 266, 268, 269, 272, 273, 279, 280, 282, 283, 284, 285, 286, 287, 288, 289, 290, 291, 305, 306, 307, 308, 310, 313, 328, 329, 330, 333, 335, 336, 337, 338, 339, 347, 348, 355

Austrian Succession, war of, 276, 282–3, 286

Avignon, 221

Avvakum, archpriest (*c.* 1620–81), 162–3

Azov, 289